T0296715

SECURITY CONTROLS EVALUATION, TESTING, AND ASSESSMENT HANDBOOK

SECURITY CONTROLS EVALUATION, TESTING, AND ASSESSMENT HANDBOOK

LEIGHTON JOHNSON

AMSTERDAM • BOSTON • HEIDELBERG • LONDON
NEW YORK • OXFORD • PARIS • SAN DIEGO
SAN FRANCISCO • SINGAPORE • SYDNEY • TOKYO

Syngress is an imprint of Elsevier

Acquiring Editor: Chris Katsaropoulos
Editorial Project Manager: Anna Valutkevich
Production Project Manager: Mohana Natarajan
Cover Designer: Mark Rogers

Syngress is an imprint of Elsevier
225 Wyman Street, Waltham, MA 02451, USA

Notices
Knowledge and best practice in this field are constantly changing. As new research and experience
broaden our understanding, changes in research methods, professional practices, or medical
treatment may become necessary.

Practitioners and researchers must always rely on their own experience and knowledge in evaluating
and using any information, methods, compounds, or experiments described herein. In using such
information or methods they should be mindful of their own safety and the safety of others, including
parties for whom they have a professional responsibility.

To the fullest extent of the law, neither the Publisher nor the authors, contributors, or editors, assume
any liability for any injury and/or damage to persons or property as a matter of products liability,
negligence or otherwise, or from any use or operation of any methods, products, instructions, or
ideas contained in the material herein.

British Library Cataloguing-in-Publication Data
A catalogue record for this book is available from the British Library

Library of Congress Cataloging-in-Publication Data
A catalog record for this book is available from the Library of Congress

ISBN: 978-0-12-802324-2

For information on all Syngress publications
visit our website at http://store.elsevier.com/Syngress

Typeset by Thomson Digital

Dedication

I dedicate this book to Marie, my secretary, for her continued support, initial editing of the text, and constant efforts to complete this project. I appreciate the full support of the crew at the BARCROFT SBUKS, especially Quanah, Dante, Jackie, Mars, Raynel, Ellen, and Lee, as I wrote of this while there over the past few months. Further, RKS has provided support and guidance during the research and writing efforts.

Contents

Online Contents

Introduction

The approach of this book is to take FISMA, NIST guidance, and DOD policy guidance and provide a detailed hands-on guide to performing assessment events in the federal space since, as of March 2014, all agencies are following the same guidelines under the NIST-based Risk Management Framework as found in Special Publication (SP) 800-37, rev. 1. This book will provide assessment guidance for federal civilian agencies, DOD and IC-type authorization efforts following the CNSS 4015, DIACAP/RMF-DOD validator, and NIST-based SCA requirements and documentation along with my practical experience of performing and overseeing these efforts for 12 different federal agencies on 31 different types of systems over the past 4.5 years.

We will use the NIST SP 800-53A, NIST SP 800-115, DOD's RMF Knowledge Service, and the NIST control families assessment guides for our exploration of the needs, requirements, and actual test and evaluation efforts for all of the security controls. Each of the controls has a unique way it can and should be evaluated through test, examination, and key personnel interviews and each of these will be explained and discussed. We will supplement this process with detailed technical, operational, and administrative knowledge for each control, as needed, with data from the various best practices Special Publications from NIST, technical support data available from various security vendors, best business practices gathered from industry, and in-depth knowledge of controls and their assessment gleaned from hands-on utilization and evaluation efforts.

SECTION 1

1

Introduction to Assessments

Within the US government's requirements for operating and maintaining federal information systems safely and securely is the built-in need to validate and verify the operational, technical, and managerial security for each system, office, data component, and individual bit of information that is used, exchanged, stored, acted upon, and utilized by the governmental agency. Each governmental agency is required by law (both Federal Information Security Management Act (FISMA) and *Privacy Act*) to ensure the data and information it retains during the normal course of its activities be confidential (if it is *not* public information), accurate, and retrievable when needed. This process for ensuring the security of the systems and information is known in the federal community as "assessment" and is usually conducted by relatively independent organizations and individuals called "assessors." This handbook is developed to provide assessors and other interested personnel the guides, techniques, tools, and knowledge to conduct these assessments for most all federal information systems. We will examine the needs and requirements for assessments, look at the methodologies for providing the assessments in three distinct formats (*basic, focused,* and *comprehensive*), and go in depth on the actual assessment techniques of examinations, interviews, and testing for and of each of the security controls as defined in the National Institute of Standards and Technology (NIST) Special Publication (SP) 800-53. SP 800-53 defines the security controls needed, required, or recommended for each federal information system. This security control "catalog" is extremely extensive and contains a vast number and types of security controls throughout the managerial, operational, and technical domains.

Generally speaking these three security control arenas cover:

1. *Management*: Actions taken to manage the development, maintenance, and use of the system
   a. Examples are policies, procedures, and rules of behavior.

2. *Operational*: Day-to-day mechanisms and procedures used to protect operational systems and environment
   a. Examples are awareness training, configuration management, and incident response.

3. *Technical*: Hardware/software controls used to provide protection of the IT system and the information it stores, processes, and/or transmits
   a. Examples are access controls, authentication mechanisms, and encryption.

Now, an assessment is required by the federal organization to ensure and document that the system under review has the basic security components and requirements to meet the federal standards for operating on a federal network. These requirements are defined in several locations, starting with Public Law 107-347, Title III of the E-Government Act of 2002, otherwise known as the FISMA. The Office of Management and Budget (OMB) also has security requirements for systems to meet when deploying them onto federal networks in its Circular A-130, Appendix 3. Additional requirements are found throughout the federal statutory and regulatory environment in the various laws (i.e., Health Insurance Portability and Accountability Act (HIPAA)/Health Information Technology for Economic and Clinical Health Act (HITECH)/Computer Fraud and Abuse Act (CFAA), etc.), Presidential Directives (E.O. 13236, etc.), and agency regulations (Department of Health and Human Services (HHS) HIPAA Security and Privacy Rules, DODI 8510.01M, US Army AR 25-2, etc.).

By definition in NIST SP 800-53A, an assessment is: "The testing and/or evaluation of the managerial, operational, and technical security controls to determine the extent to which the controls are implemented correctly, operating as intended and producing the desired outcome with respect to meeting the security requirements for an information system or organization." As we begin to explore the processes, procedures, techniques, and means of testing and evaluating the various security components and controls used throughout the security industry, we will keep in mind the applicability and effectiveness needs for each control reviewed, each technique employed, and each policy or procedure recommended. Assessments require a large amount of skills, knowledge, and testing techniques, as well as automated and manual toolsets in order to accomplish the goal of providing assurance to the management and executives that the risks they are about to take are acceptable and reasonable for the level of security they desire within their systems. We will discuss the available tools and their usage when conducting the testing phase of each assessment. So, let us begin with the first area to be covered, the background for the security and risk process and what is at stake, the confidentiality, integrity, and availability of our systems.

2

Risk, Security, and Assurance

The US government has long maintained the need and the requirement to evaluate and ascertain the IT systems operating on its networks and backbones were as secure as possible. Over the past 25 years, various organizations within the federal government have developed and operated under multiple different methodologies to provide the assurance to managers and executives that the IT systems were safe, secure, and trustworthy. This process began back in the 1970s and 1980s in the US government Intelligence Community (IC) with the original directives for ensuring confidentiality of the systems and the data retained in these systems.

The current security practices and processes all focus on managing and mitigating risks associated with the confidentiality, integrity, and availability of the information associated with the operation and maintenance of each federal IT system. The risk review, tolerance criteria, and management activities all are associated with the actual data stored on the IT system, the downstream liabilities of others using those same data, and the legal and regulatory requirements for the use and storage of those same data and information. The National Institutes of Standards and Technology (NIST) has produced a series of documents and publications which are designed to provide federal agencies guidance and best practices for these agency actions and activities with the relevant data and information. These publications are mostly found on their specific security website at http://csrc.nist.gov and are openly available to all who are interested.

There are many frameworks and guidelines available for organizational-level and corporate-level risk management. The available guides include COBIT 5, COSO, FAIR, ISO 31000, ISO 27000, and others. Many of these risk frameworks are industry-specific and further research for your industry should reveal which risk approach and framework are appropriate for your organization. Our goal here is to let you know there are many ways to address risk in an organization, with NIST providing the primary way within the US government. To evaluate, examine, and assess risk, the assessor will need to know the organizational approach to risk and how these risks are mitigated, transferred, or otherwise treated.

The NIST approach to risk management is found in Special Publication (SP) 800-37, rev. 1 entitled *Guide for Applying the Risk Management Framework to Federal Information Systems: A Security Life Cycle Approach*. This guide was published in February 2010 and recently was updated (June 2014) to include the federal requirements for continuous monitoring and ongoing system authorizations. As defined by NIST, risk management is the process that provides for IT managers and executives to make risk-based decisions on the security and assurance of the

IT systems under their control. These decisions are the result of balancing the operational and economic costs of the protective components and achieve the resultant gains in the organization's mission capability by protecting and defending these various IT systems and the associated information which support the organization's missions. Risk is defined in SP 800-37, rev. 1 as a measure of the extent to which an entity is threatened by a potential circumstance or event, and a function of:

1. The adverse impacts that would arise if the circumstance or event occurs
2. The likelihood of occurrence

RISK MANAGEMENT

NIST opens up SP 800-37 with the following: "Organizations depend on information technology and the information systems that are developed from that technology to successfully carry out their missions and business functions. Information systems can include as constituent components, a range of diverse computing platforms from high-end supercomputers to personal digital assistants and cellular telephones. Information systems can also include very specialized systems and devices (e.g., telecommunications systems, industrial/process control systems, testing and calibration devices, weapons systems, command and control systems, and environmental control systems). Federal information and information systems are subject to serious threats that can have adverse impacts on organizational operations (including mission, functions, image, and reputation), organizational assets, individuals, other organizations, and the Nation by compromising the confidentiality, integrity, or availability of information being processed, stored, or transmitted by those systems. Threats to information and information systems include environmental disruptions, human or machine errors, and purposeful attacks. Cyber-attacks on information systems today are often aggressive, disciplined, well-organized, well-funded, and in a growing number of documented cases, very sophisticated. Successful attacks on public and private sector information systems can result in serious or grave damage to the national and economic security interests of the United States. Given the significant and growing danger of these threats, it is imperative that leaders at all levels of an organization understand their responsibilities for achieving adequate information security and for managing information system-related security risks."[1]

When NIST published SP 800-37, rev. 1 in early 2010, it changed the entire government's approach to risk and risk management. Prior to that point, certification and accreditation (C&A) had focused most efforts on a "snapshot" view of security as sufficient to ensure the security of IT systems as referenced in the FISMA and OMB guidance documents in use during the previous 8 years (FISMA) and 25 years (OMB A-130). This shift in the approach to security moved the viewpoint to focus now on risks in an operating environment that is ever changing, ever evolving, fluid, and full of emerging threats.

The goal of this risk management approach is to provide for mission accomplishment by:

1. Better securing the IT systems which store, process, or transmit organizational information

---

[1]SP 800-37, rev. 1, updated version June 2014, p. 1.

2. Enabling management to make well-informed risk-based decisions to justify the expenditures that are part of an IT budget
3. Assisting management in authorizing the IT systems on the basis of the supporting documentation resulting from the performance of risk management

As part of the risk management process, each organization is recommended to review all risks at an organizational level, a business unit/department level, and the IT system level. Managing these IT-related risks is a detailed, complex, multifaceted activity which requires senior management support for the strategic and organizational goals for tolerating and treating risks, midlevel managers to plan for and conduct the projects, and then operating the systems that are core to the organization. NIST SP 800-39 *Managing Information Security Risk* defines these three levels as the Tier 1 (organizational level), Tier 2 (mission and business process level), and Tier 3 (information system level of risk management).

SP 800-39 goes further to define these three tiers as follows:

1. "Tier 1 addresses risk from an *organizational* perspective by establishing and implementing *governance* structures that are consistent with the strategic goals and objectives of organizations and the requirements defined by federal laws, directives, policies, regulations, standards, and missions/business functions. Governance structures provide oversight for the risk management activities conducted by organizations and include: (i) the establishment and implementation of a *risk executive (function)*; (ii) the establishment of the organization's risk management strategy including the determination of *risk tolerance*; and (iii) the development and execution of organization-wide *investment strategies* for information resources and information security."[2]

2. "Tier 2 addresses risk from a *mission/business process* perspective by designing, developing, and implementing mission/business processes that support the missions/business functions defined at Tier 1. Organizational mission/business processes guide and inform the development of an enterprise architecture that provides a disciplined and structured methodology for managing the complexity of the organization's information technology infrastructure. A key component of the enterprise architecture is the embedded information security architecture that provides a roadmap to ensure that mission/business process-driven information security requirements and protection needs are defined and allocated to appropriate organizational information systems and the environments in which those systems operate."[3]

3. "All information systems, including operational systems, systems under development, and systems undergoing modification, are in some phase of the system development life cycle. In addition to the risk management activities carried out at Tier 1 and Tier 2 (e.g., reflecting the organization's risk management strategy within the enterprise architecture and embedded information security architecture), risk management activities are also integrated into the system development life cycle of organizational information systems at Tier 3. The risk management activities at Tier 3 reflect the organization's risk management strategy and any risk related to the cost, schedule, and performance requirements for individual information systems supporting the mission/business

[2]SP 800-39, March 2011, p. 11.
[3]SP 800-39, March 2011, p. 17.

functions of organizations. Risk management activities take place at every phase in the system development life cycle with the outputs at each phase having an effect on subsequent phases."[4]

So for assessing risk and the security controls used to control risk, an understanding of risk management within the organization is paramount to provide the right kind of assessment along with recommendations for risk mitigation.

RISK ASSESSMENTS

Within the risk construct that has been produced by the NIST, there are major criteria for risk assessments at every point within the life cycle of the information system under review. NIST SP 800-39 states this as follows: "The second component of risk management addresses how organizations *assess* risk within the context of the organizational risk frame. The purpose of the risk assessment component is to identify:

1. threats to organizations (i.e., operations, assets, or individuals) or threats directed through organizations against other organizations or the Nation;
2. vulnerabilities internal and external to organizations;
3. the harm (i.e., consequences/impact) to organizations that may occur given the potential for threats exploiting vulnerabilities; and
4. the likelihood that harm will occur. The end result is a determination of risk (i.e., the degree of harm and likelihood of harm occurring).

To support the risk assessment component, organizations identify:

1. the tools, techniques, and methodologies that are used to assess risk;
2. the assumptions related to risk assessments;
3. the constraints that may affect risk assessments;
4. roles and responsibilities;
5. how risk assessment information is collected, processed, and communicated throughout organizations;
6. how risk assessments are conducted within organizations;
7. the frequency of risk assessments; and
8. how threat information is obtained (i.e., sources and methods)."[5]

There are many different ways to conduct risk assessments. The publisher of this book has several different books currently available on risk assessments and the methods for conducting them, so I will not attempt to add to those data. NIST has produced a guide to conducting risk assessments too under the NIST SP 800-30, rev. 1 publication.

---

[4]SP 800-39, March 2011, p. 21.
[5]SP 800-39, March 2011, p. 7.

SECURITY CONTROLS

CNSSI 4009, the US government's authoritative source of definitions within the security arena, defines security controls as: "The management, operational, and technical controls (i.e., safeguards or countermeasures) prescribed for an information system to protect the confidentiality, integrity, and availability of the system and its information" and defines the assessment of these controls as: "The testing and/or evaluation of the management, operational, and technical security controls to determine the extent to which the controls are implemented correctly, operating as intended, and producing the desired outcome with respect to meeting the security requirements for an information system or organization."[6]

So understanding the controls and their functions is of utmost value to both the assessor and the organization. Within the risk community, there are several catalogs of security controls available. We will be examining the controls in this book from the NIST SP 800-53 Control Catalog with its 18 areas of controls and from the ISO 27001 International Security Management Catalog with its 11 areas of controls. Chapters 8 and 9 delineate the controls, their requirements, and methods of assessment. Next we look at the legal and regulatory frameworks for security and the assessment requirements for security controls.

[6]CNSSI-4009, April 2010, p. 65.

Statutory and Regulatory GRC

Today's security world includes a major change from the past. All security and corporate managers now need to be concerned with compliance and governance of risks, security, and the information usage in their systems. These processes have evolved over the past 10 years into an area known as GRC. GRC is an acronym for governance, risk, and compliance and includes corporate considerations of risks, methods, and techniques for the gathering and evaluations of risks, and then reporting those identified risks to regulators, outside entities, and corporate Boards of Directors.

The standard statutory and regulatory order of precedence for US laws and regulations is not always easy to follow and understand. There are many levels of legal requirements throughout the security community. With the separation of national and state levels of laws, there are often conflicting legal and regulatory needs and reporting actions which need to be addressed and accounted for by the security and legal staff of an organization. All of these areas of the law lead to the GRC oversight and compliance reporting activities with which an organization must comply with or potentially face penalties, fines, or even incarceration of its corporate officers.

Generally, the US order of precedence for legal statutes and regulations is as follows:

1. Constitution
2. Public Law
3. Executive Orders (EOs) – Presidential Directives
4. Agency regulations
5. Industry best practices

There are, of course, deviations to these layers based on legal rulings and court findings. Each level of the precedence requires legal review and consultation, so always include your legal and compliance staff as you develop and produce your reports and conduct your security business events.

STATUTORY REQUIREMENTS

As part of our review of the compliance and governance requirements before, during, and after security assessments, we will now explore the statutory laws which are currently in place for these efforts. Additionally, we will discuss the laws that were passed and since superceded which form the foundation of our current legal framework for assessments and auditing of security and components.

Privacy Act – 1974

We start with the first major piece of legislation passed in the United States that covered security and privacy, the Privacy Act of 1974, *Public Law 95-579, 88 Statute 1896*. The Privacy Act was designed to balance the US government's need to maintain information about individuals with the rights of the individuals themselves. It focuses on four basic policy objectives:

- Restrict disclosure of individual's personal data.
- Increase rights of access to agency records.
- Grant individuals the right to seek amendment to the records retained on them.
- Establish a code of fair information practices.

As the Privacy Act has been amended over the years since its original passage it now covers Personal Identifiable Information (PII).

CFAA – 1986

The Computer Fraud and Abuse Act (CFAA) – *Title 18 U.S.C., Statute 1030* – is a law designed to address legal and illegal access to federal and financial IT systems. It was intended to reduce cracking of computer systems and to address federal computer-related offenses. The CFAA is the actual federal law which makes it illegal to hack/crack a governmental computing system. It deals with:

- Cases with a compelling federal interest
- Cases in which computers of the federal government or certain financial institutions are involved
- Cases in which the crime itself is interstate in nature
- Cases in which computers are used in interstate and foreign commerce

ECPA – 1986

The Electronic Communications Privacy Act (ECPA) was passed in 1986 – *Public Law 99-508, Statute 1848* – and extends the government restrictions on wiretaps from telephone calls to include transmissions of electronic data by computer. The ECPA updated the Federal Wiretap Act of 1968, which addressed interception of conversations using "hard" telephone lines, but did not apply to interception of computer and other digital and electronic communications. Several subsequent pieces of legislation, including the USA PATRIOT Act, clarify and update the ECPA to keep pace with the evolution of new communications technologies and methods, including easing restrictions on law enforcement access to stored communications in some cases. The ECPA provisions are as follows:

- Title I of the ECPA, which is often referred to as the Wiretap Act, prohibits the intentional actual or attempted interception, use, disclosure, or "procure[ment] [of] any other person to intercept or endeavor to intercept any wire, oral, or electronic communication." Title I also prohibits the use of illegally obtained communications as evidence.

- Title II of the ECPA, which is called the Stored Communications Act (SCA), protects the privacy of the contents of files stored by service providers and of records held about the subscriber by service providers, such as subscriber name, billing records, or IP addresses.
- Title III of the ECPA, which addresses pen register and trap and trace devices, requires government entities to obtain a court order authorizing the installation and use of a pen register (a device that captures the dialed numbers and related information to which outgoing calls or communications are made by the subject) and/or a trap and trace (a device that captures the numbers and related information from which incoming calls and communications coming to the subject have originated). No actual communications are intercepted by a pen register or trap and trace. The authorization order can be issued on the basis of certification by the applicant that the information likely to be obtained is relevant to an ongoing criminal investigation being conducted by the applicant's agency. [1]

CSA – 1987

The *Computer Security Act (CSA), Public Law 100-235, Title 101, Statute 1724*, was designed to improve security and privacy of sensitive information in federal information system. Other provisions of the CSA included:

- Requires federal agencies to establish standards and guidelines under National Institute of Standards and Technology (NIST) direction and guidance
- Requires that any federal computer system that processes sensitive information have a customized security plan (System Security Authorization Agreement (SSAA))
- Requires that users of those systems undergo security training
- Requires NIST responsible, National Security Agency (NSA) to advise:
  - Assessing the vulnerability of federal computer systems
  - Developing standards
  - Providing technical assistance with NSA support
  - Developing training guidelines for federal personnel

CCA – 1996

The Information Technology Management Reform Act of 1996 – *Public Law 104-106, Statute 186* – has played a critical role in the development and evolution of federal security actions, activities, and statutes. This law, better known as the Clinger–Cohen Act (CCA), provided or included the following:

- Implemented the Capital Planning Investment Control (CPIC) IT budget planning process.
- Granted to the Director, Office of Management and Budget (OMB), authority to oversee the acquisition, use, and disposal of IT by the federal government.
- Established Chief Information Officer (CIO) positions in every department and agency in the federal government.
- Established the CIO council with 28 major agencies and OMB.
- Under this Act, *OMB grades IT projects and funds accordingly* – with an "at risk" category. The risk is not receiving initial or continuation funding for the project.
- Defines National Security Systems (NSS) as a system that:
  - Involves intelligence activities
  - Involves cryptologic activities related to national security

  - Involves command and control of military forces
  - Involves equipment that is an integral part of a weapon or weapon system
  - Is critical to the direct fulfillment of military or intelligence missions
- Annual IT reporting to Congress.

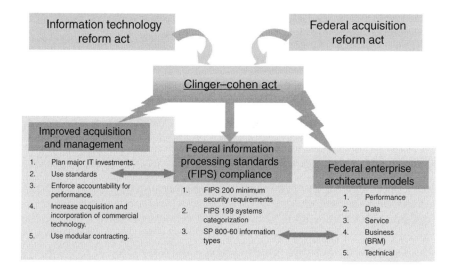

- The CCA established the process within the federal government of creation and development of the standards and architectural requirements for security through the use of Federal Enterprise Architecture (FEA) Reference Models and the attendant Information Types as currently found in SP 800-60. Defined an IT architecture (ITA) for evolving and acquiring IT through the use of Enterprise Architecture:
  - FEA
  - US Department of Defense (DOD) Architecture Framework (DODAF)

HIPAA – 1996

Health Insurance Portability and Accountability Act (HIPAA) – *Public Law 104-191, 10 Statute 1936* – enacted August 21, 1996, originally had Title I protecting health insurance coverage for workers and their families when they change or lose their jobs and Title II, known as the Administrative Simplification (AS) provisions, requiring the establishment of national standards for electronic health care transactions and national identifiers for providers, health insurance plans, and employers.

The effective compliance date of the updated HIPAA Privacy Rule was April 14, 2003, with a 1-year extension for certain "small plans." The HIPAA Privacy Rule regulates the use and disclosure of protected health information (PHI) held by "covered entities."

The regulatory part of the HIPAA Privacy Rule is explained later in this chapter; however, suffice to say that the Department of Health and Human Services (HHS) has extended the HIPAA Privacy Rule to independent contractors of covered entities who fit within the definition of "business associates." This has led to the concept of "downstream liability": for PHI and users of the extended PHI in the "covered entities" area. Now, PHI is any information held by a covered entity which concerns health status, provision of health care, or payment for health care that can be linked to an individual.

Cover entities can disclose PHI without a patient's written authorization only to facilitate treatment, payment, or health care operations. Any other disclosures of PHI require the covered entity to obtain written authorization from the individual for the disclosure.

EEA – 1996

The Economic Espionage Act (EEA) of 1996 (*Public Law 104-294, 110 Stat. 3488*, enacted October 11, 1996) dealt with industrial espionage (e.g., the theft or misappropriation of a trade secret and the National Information Infrastructure Protection Act), and four other areas of action that Congress deemed appropriate and the US Sentencing Commission reports regarding encryption or scrambling technology, and other technical and minor amendments:

- Covers trade secrets and economic espionage.
- Most uses have been in trade secret area.
- First criminal prosecution under espionage part performed in 2010.
- *Economic espionage*: Criminalizes the misappropriation of trade secrets (including conspiracy to misappropriate trade secrets and the subsequent acquisition of such misappropriated trade secrets) with the knowledge or intent that the theft will benefit a foreign power. Penalties for violation are fines of up to US$500,000 per offense and imprisonment of up to 15 years for individuals, and fines of up to US$10 million for organizations.
- *Theft of trade secrets*: Criminalizes the misappropriation of trade secrets related to or included in a product that is produced for or placed in interstate (including international) commerce, with the knowledge or intent that the misappropriation will injure the owner of the trade secret. Penalties for violation of section 1832 are imprisonment for up to 10 years for individuals (no fines) and fines of up to US$5 million for organizations.
- The term "trade secret" means all forms and types of financial, business, scientific, technical, economic, or engineering information, including patterns, plans, compilations, program devices, formulas, designs, prototypes, methods, techniques, processes, procedures, programs, or codes, whether tangible or intangible, and whether or how stored, compiled, or memorialized physically, electronically, graphically, photographically, or in writing if:
  - The owner thereof has taken reasonable measures to keep such information secret.
  - The information derives independent economic value, actual or potential, from not being generally known to, and not being readily ascertainable through proper means by, the public.
- The Act can be employed to accomplish several purposes:
  - It can be used to protect a company's valuable intellectual property by prosecuting dishonest competitors who steal a company's trade secrets.
  - It can also be used against a company that finds itself with trade secrets belonging to a competitor.

GISRA – 1998

Government Information Security Reform Act (GISRA) – Floyd D. Spence National Defense Authorization Act for Fiscal Year 2001. Title X, Subtitle G – *Government Information Security Reform Act (GISRA)*, Public Law 106-398, passed October 30, 2000. This Act:

- Established roles and responsibilities for information security, risk management, testing, and training
- Authorized NIST and NSA to provide guidance for security planning:
  - This resulted in several DOD Directives and the Federal Information Processing Standards (FIPS) 102 process which has now been replaced with the Federal Information Security Management Act (FISMA) process described in NIST SP 800-37.
- Had a 2-year sunset clause
- Required agencies to perform periodic threat-based risk assessments for systems and data
- Required agencies to develop and implement risk-based, cost-effective policies and procedures to provide security protection for information collected or maintained either by the agency or for it by another agency or contractor
- Required that agencies develop a process for ensuring that remedial action is taken to address significant deficiencies
- Required agencies to report annually to the OMB on the security of their information systems and to make information system security part of their regular process of doing business (e.g., in budget requests)

Except for the new annual program reviews, the role of the agency Inspector General, and the annual reporting requirement, the Act essentially codifies the existing requirements of OMB Circular No. A-130, App. III, "Security of Federal Automated Information Resources."

USA PATRIOT Act – 2001

Uniting and Strengthening America by Providing Appropriate Tools Required to Intercept and Obstruct Terrorism Act – *Public Law 107-56, 115 Statute 252*. Passed as a result of the 9-11 terrorist acts on the United States, the USA PATROIT Act provided for the following security-related activities:

- Amended the definition of "electronic surveillance" to exclude the interception of communications done through or from a protected computer where the owner allows the interception, or is lawfully involved in an investigation.
- Secret Service jurisdiction was extended to investigate computer fraud, access device frauds, false identification documents or devices, or any fraudulent activities against US financial institutions.
- Specified the development and support of cybersecurity forensic capabilities:
  - Directs the Attorney General to establish regional computer forensic laboratories that have the capability of performing forensic examinations of intercepted computer evidence relating to criminal activity and cyberterrorism, and that have the capability

of training and educating federal, state, and local law enforcement personnel and prosecutors in computer crime, and to "facilitate and promote the sharing of Federal law enforcement expertise and information"

- National Security Letter (NSL):
  - It is a demand letter issued to a particular entity or organization to turn over various records and data pertaining to individuals. They require no probable cause or judicial oversight and also contain a gag order, preventing the recipient of the letter from disclosing that the letter was ever issued.
  - Can order "requiring the production of any tangible things (including books, records, papers, documents, and other items) for an investigation to protect against international terrorism or clandestine intelligence activities, provided that such investigation of a United States person is not conducted solely upon the basis of activities protected by the first amendment to the Constitution"
- Redefined money laundering to:
  - Include making a financial transaction in the United States in order to commit a violent crime
  - The bribery of public officials and fraudulent dealing with public funds
  - The smuggling or illegal export of controlled munition and the importation or bringing in of any firearm or ammunition not authorized by the US Attorney General
  - The smuggling of any item controlled under the Export Administration Regulations
- Roving wiretaps are wiretap orders that do not need to specify all common carriers and third parties in a surveillance court order.
- Information sharing for critical infrastructure protection:
  - Increase the ability of US law enforcement to counter terrorist activity that crosses jurisdictional boundaries

FISMA – 2002

The FISMA – Title III of E-Government Act of 2002 (Public Law 107-347) – passed in February 2002 provides the following:

- OMB has oversight over E-government:
  - Federal government (organizations and IGs) must report Information Assurance (IA) status to OMB annually and quarterly.
  - OMB provides reports to Congress annually.
  - Congressional Security Grade (originally known as the FISMA score, this is now known as the Cybersecurity Grade).
- NIST publishes standards and guidelines; NSA serves as Technical Advisor.
- Requires all federal agencies, besides DOD and the IC, to conduct reviews and accreditations for their information systems on a periodic basis (every 3 years) and a select subset of security controls to be reviewed annually. All of the federal government must follow the NIST-defined C&A processes, with the exception of defense and intelligence organizations.

Sarbanes–Oxley – 2002

The Sarbanes–Oxley Act (SOX) – *Public Law 107-204, 116 Statute 745* – was passed in July 2002. This Act set in place the revised standards for risk, operations, accounting and reporting, compliance, and governance for all US public company boards of directors, management, and public accounting firms. The SOX was enacted as a result of several major corporate scandals during the late 1990s including Enron, Tyco, and WorldCom. As a result of SOX, top management must now individually certify the accuracy of financial information. Additionally, penalties for fraudulent financial activity are much more severe and there is now a requirement for increased oversight by the corporate boards of directors and the independence of the outside auditors who review the accuracy of corporate financial statements.

The SOX contains 11 titles, or sections, ranging from additional corporate board responsibilities to criminal penalties, and requires the Securities and Exchange Commission (SEC) to implement rulings on requirements to comply with the law. The SOX also created a new, quasi-public agency, the Public Company Accounting Oversight Board (PCAOB), which is charged with overseeing, regulating, inspecting, and disciplining accounting firms in their roles as auditors of public companies. The SOX also covers issues such as auditor independence, corporate governance, internal control assessment, and enhanced financial disclosure as follows:

- Addressed specific areas such as:
  - Top management must individually certify the accuracy of financial information.
  - Provided for penalties for fraudulent financial activity which are much more severe than previously listed and legalized.
  - Increased the independence of the outside auditors who review the accuracy of corporate financial statements.
  - Increased the oversight role of boards of directors.
- SOX reporting criteria:
  - Assess both the design and the operating effectiveness of selected internal controls related to significant accounts and relevant assertions, in the context of material misstatement risks.
  - Understand the flow of transactions, including IT aspects, in sufficient detail to identify points at which a misstatement could arise.
  - Evaluate company-level (entity-level) controls, which correspond to the components of the Committee of Sponsoring Organizations of the Treadway Commission (COSO) framework.
  - Perform a fraud risk assessment.
  - Evaluate controls designed to prevent or detect fraud, including management override of controls.
  - Evaluate controls over the period-end financial reporting process.
  - Scale the assessment based on the size and complexity of the company.
  - Rely on management's work based on factors such as competency, objectivity, and risk.
  - Conclude on the adequacy of internal control over financial reporting.

Health Information Technology for Economic and Clinical Health Act – 2009

The *Health Information Technology for Economic and Clinical Health (HITECH) Act* is Title XIII of the American Recovery and Reinvestment Act of 2009 (Public Law 111-5). The HITECH Act set meaningful use of interoperable electronic health record (EHR) adoption in the health care system as a critical national goal and incentivized EHR adoption. HITECH introduced a refinement of the Meaningful Use concept to health care in the United States. The main components of Meaningful Use are as follows:

- The use of a certified EHR in a meaningful manner, such as e-prescribing
- The use of certified EHR technology for electronic exchange of health information to improve quality of health care
- The use of certified EHR technology to submit clinical quality and other measures

The Meaningful Use of EHRs intended by the US government incentives is categorized as follows:

- Improve care coordination.
- Reduce health care disparities.
- Engage patients and their families.
- Improve population and public health.
- *Ensure adequate privacy and security.*

The HITECH Act requires HIPAA-covered entities to report data breaches affecting 500 or more individuals to HHS and the media, in addition to notifying the affected individuals. This Act extends the complete privacy and security provisions of HIPAA to business associates of covered entities. This includes the extension of newly updated civil and criminal penalties to business associates. As explained in the section "HIPAA – 1996," this introduced the "downstream liability" legal concept to health care and medical providers. These changes are also required to be included in any business associate agreements with covered entities.

Another significant change brought about in Subtitle D of the HITECH Act is the new breach notification requirements. This imposes new notification requirements on covered entities, business associates, vendors of personal health records (PHRs), and related entities if a breach of unsecured PHI occurs. Both HHS and the Federal Trade Commission (FTC) were required under the HITECH Act to issue regulations associated with the new breach notification requirements and they did so with the HHS rule published in the *Federal Register* on August 24, 2009, and the FTC rule published on August 25, 2009.

EXECUTIVE ORDERS/PRESIDENTIAL DIRECTIVES

The Executive Office of the President derives its authority from the Constitution. It has issued several EOs and directives (Presidential Policy Directive (PPD)/Homeland Security Presidential Directive (HSPD)/National Security Presidential Directive (NSPD)) to order protection of critical national assets. There are three current types of these documents:

- PPD
- HSPD

- NSPD
  There are multiple documents of relevance to security testing. These include:
- *EO 12958: Classified National Security Information (1995)* – Created new standards for the process of identifying and protecting classified information, and led to an unprecedented effort to declassify millions of pages from the US diplomatic and national security history. When issued in 1995, set the National Archives and Records Agency director (otherwise known as the Chief Archivist of the US government) as the definitive authority to declassify data outside of DOD.
- *EO 13228: Establishing the Office of Homeland Security and the HS Council (2001)* – Initiates a comprehensive strategy to secure the United States from terrorist attacks.
- *EO 13231: Critical Infrastructure Protection (CIP) in the Information Age (October 2001)* – States policy to protect critical infrastructure against compromise. Established the following:
  - Committee on National Security Systems (*CNSS*), combination of two previous national security committees:
    - National Security Telecommunications and Information Systems Security Committee (*NSTISSC*)
    - National Computer Security Committee (*NCSC*)
- *Chaired* by DOD CIO:
  - *Issues* policies, directives, instructions, and advisory memorandums related to NSS
- *EO 13526: Classified National Security Information – 2009:*
  - Sets a uniform system for classifying, safeguarding, and declassifying national security information, including information relating to defense against transnational terrorism.
  - Added fourth unclassified data type – Controlled Unclassified Information (CUI).
  - It revokes and replaces the previous EOs in effect for this, which were EO 12958 and EO 13292.
- *EO 13636: Improving Critical Infrastructure Cybersecurity – 2013:*
  - Designed to assist critical infrastructure companies improve cybersecurity practices through the NIST Cybersecurity Framework development
  - Increases volume, timeliness, and quality of cyber-threat information sharing
- *HSPD-7: Homeland Security Directive 7 (2003)* – Directs the identification and prioritization of Critical Infrastructure (CI) assets and key resources to protect them from terrorist attacks. *Supersedes PDD-63.*
- *HSPD-12: Homeland Security Directive 12 (2004)* – Directs a common identification standard that is "secure and reliable" to verify employee identity. It further specified secure and reliable identification that:
  - Is issued based on sound criteria for verifying an individual employee's identity
  - Is strongly resistant to identity fraud, tampering, counterfeiting, and terrorist exploitation
  - Can be rapidly authenticated electronically
  - Is issued only by providers whose reliability has been established by an official accreditation
    - This directive is primary document for all US government efforts for Personal Identity Verification (PIV) cards and the DOD Common Access Card (CAC) usage.

- *HSPD-20/NSPD-51*: National Continuity Policy which sets the United States Government (USG) policy for Continuity of Operations (COOP) and Continuity of Government (COG):
  - "COG" means a coordinated effort within the federal government's executive branch to ensure that National Essential Functions continue to be performed during a catastrophic emergency.
  - "COOP" means an effort within individual executive departments and agencies to ensure that Primary Mission Essential Functions continue to be performed during a wide range of emergencies, including localized acts of nature, accidents, and technological or attack-related emergencies.
  - Defines the eight National Essential Functions of the USG:
    - Ensuring the continued functioning of our form of government under the Constitution, including the functioning of the three separate branches of government
    - Providing leadership visible to the nation and the world and maintaining the trust and confidence of the American people
    - Defending the Constitution of the United States against all enemies, foreign and domestic, and preventing or interdicting attacks against the United States or its people, property, or interests
    - Maintaining and fostering effective relationships with foreign nations
    - Protecting against threats to the homeland and bringing to justice perpetrators of crimes or attacks against the United States or its people, property, or interests
    - Providing rapid and effective response to and recovery from the domestic consequences of an attack or other incident
    - Protecting and stabilizing the nation's economy and ensuring public confidence in its financial systems
    - Providing for critical federal government services that address the national health, safety, and welfare needs of the United States
- *PPD 21: Critical Infrastructure Security and Resilience (March 2013)* – Replaces HSPD-7:
  - Executive branch will:
    - Develop a situational awareness capability that addresses both physical and cyber aspects of how infrastructure is functioning in near-real time
    - Understand the cascading consequences of infrastructure failures
    - Evaluate and mature the public–private partnership
    - Update the National Infrastructure Protection Plan
      Develop a comprehensive research and development plan

FEDERAL PROCESSING STANDARDS

Under the Information Technology Management Reform Act (Public Law 104-106), the Secretary of Commerce approves standards and guidelines that are developed by the NIST for federal computer systems. These standards and guidelines are issued by NIST as FIPS for use government-wide. NIST develops FIPS when there are compelling federal government requirements such as for security and interoperability and there are no acceptable industry standards or solutions. Under Section 5131 of the Information

Technology Management Reform Act of 1996 and the FISMA of 2002 (Public Law 107-347), NIST develops standards, guidelines, and associated methods and techniques for federal computer systems:

- Including those needed to assure the cost-effective security and privacy of sensitive information in federal computer systems
- When there are compelling federal requirements and there are no existing voluntary industry standards

The FISMA does not include a statutory provision allowing agencies to waive the provisions of mandatory FIPS. Waivers approved by the head of agencies had been allowed under the CSA, which was superseded by FISMA. Therefore, the waiver procedures included in many FIPS are no longer in effect. The applicability sections of each FIPS should be reviewed to determine if the FIPS is mandatory for agency use. FIPS do not apply to NSS (as defined in Title III, Information Security, of FISMA).

FIPS-140 – Security Requirements for Cryptographic Modules

This standard specifies the security requirements that will be satisfied by a cryptographic module utilized within a security system protecting sensitive but unclassified information (hereafter referred to as sensitive information). The standard provides four increasing, qualitative levels of security: Level 1, Level 2, Level 3, and Level 4.

These levels are intended to cover the wide range of potential applications and environments in which cryptographic modules may be employed. The security requirements cover areas related to the secure design and implementation of a cryptographic module. These areas include cryptographic module specification, cryptographic module ports and interfaces; roles, services, and authentication; finite state model; physical security; operational environment; cryptographic key management; electromagnetic interference/electromagnetic compatibility (EMI/EMC); self-tests; design assurance; and mitigation of other attacks.[1]

FIPS-186 – Digital Signature Standard (DSS)

This Standard specifies algorithms for applications requiring a digital signature, rather than a written signature. A digital signature is represented in a computer as a string of bits. A digital signature is computed using a set of rules and a set of parameters that allow the identity of the signatory and the integrity of the data to be verified. Digital signatures may be generated on both stored and transmitted data.

Signature generation uses a private key to generate a digital signature; signature verification uses a public key that corresponds to, but is not the same as, the private key. Each signatory possesses a private and public key pair. Public keys may be known by the public; private keys are kept secret. Anyone can verify the signature by employing the signatory's public key. Only the user that possesses the private key can perform signature generation.

A hash function is used in the signature generation process to obtain a condensed version of the data to be signed; the condensed version of the data is often called a message digest. The message digest is input to the digital signature algorithm to generate the digital signature. The hash functions to be used are specified in the Secure Hash Standard (SHS), FIPS 180. FIPS **approved** digital signature algorithms **shall** be used with an appropriate hash function that is specified in the SHS.

---

[1]FIPS-140-2, p. iii.

The digital signature is provided to the intended verifier along with the signed data. The verifying entity verifies the signature by using the claimed signatory's public key and the same hash function that was used to generate the signature. Similar procedures may be used to generate and verify signatures for both stored and transmitted data.[2]

A digital signature algorithm allows an entity to authenticate the integrity of signed data and the identity of the signatory. The recipient of a signed message can use a digital signature as evidence in demonstrating to a third party that the signature was, in fact, generated by the claimed signatory. This is known as nonrepudiation, since the signatory cannot easily repudiate the signature at a later time. A digital signature algorithm is intended for use in electronic mail, electronic funds transfer, electronic data interchange, software distribution, data storage, and other applications that require data integrity assurance and data origin authentication.

FIPS-190 – Guideline for the Use of Advanced Authentication Technology Alternatives

This guideline describes the primary alternative methods for verifying the identities of computer system users, and provides recommendations to federal agencies and departments for the acquisition and use of technology which supports these methods. Although the traditional approach to authentication relies primarily on passwords, it is clear that password-only authentication often fails to provide an adequate level of protection. Stronger authentication techniques become increasingly more important as information processing evolves toward an open system environment. Modern technology has produced authentication tokens and biometric devices which are reliable, practical, and cost-effective. Passwords, tokens, and biometrics can be used in various combinations to provide far greater assurance in the authentication process than can be attained with passwords alone.

FIPS-191 – Guideline for the Analysis Local Area Network Security

This FIPS standard covers the security objectives of confidentiality, integrity, availability, and nonrepudiation.

The following goals should be considered to implement effective LAN security.

- Maintain the confidentiality of data as it is stored, processed or transmitted on a LAN;
- Maintain the integrity of data as it is stored, processed or transmitted on a LAN;
- Maintain the availability of data stored on a LAN, as well as the ability to process and transmit the data in a timely fashion;
- Ensure the identity of the sender and receiver of a message;

Adequate LAN security requires the proper combination of security policies and procedures, technical controls, user training and awareness, and contingency planning. While all of these areas are critical to provide adequate protection, the focus of this document is on the technical controls that can be utilized.[3]

---

[2]FIPS-186-4, p. 1.
[3]FIPS-191, p. 9.

FIPS-199 – Standards for Security Categorization of Federal Information and Information Systems

FIPS-199 addresses the task defined in FISMA for all federal agencies to develop standards for categorizing information and information systems. It defines three levels of *potential impact* on organizations or individuals should there be a breach of security (i.e., a loss of confidentiality, integrity, or availability). The application of these definitions must take place within the context of each organization and the overall national interest.

> Security categorization standards for information and information systems provide a common framework and understanding for expressing security that, for the federal government, promotes:
>
> (i) Effective management and oversight of information security programs, including the coordination of information security efforts throughout the civilian, national security, emergency preparedness, homeland security, and law enforcement communities; and
>
> (ii) Consistent reporting to the Office of Management and Budget (OMB) and Congress on the adequacy and effectiveness of information security policies, procedures, and practices.
>
> This publication establishes security categories for both information1 and information systems. The security categories are based on the potential impact on an organization should certain events occur which jeopardize the information and information systems needed by the organization to accomplish its assigned mission, protect its assets, fulfill its legal responsibilities, maintain its day-to-day functions, and protect individuals. Security categories are to be used in conjunction with vulnerability and threat information in assessing the risk to an organization.[4]

Determining the security category of an information system requires slightly more analysis and must consider the security categories of all information types resident on the information system. For an information system, the potential impact values assigned to the respective security objectives (confidentiality, integrity, availability) shall be the highest values (i.e., high water mark (HWM)) from among those security categories that have been determined for each type of information resident on the information system.

FIPS-200 – Minimum Security Requirements for Federal Information and Information Systems

> FIPS-200 specifies minimum security requirements for information and information systems supporting the executive agencies of the federal government and a risk-based process for selecting the security controls necessary to satisfy the minimum security requirements. This standard will promote the development, implementation, and operation of more secure information systems within the federal government by establishing minimum levels of due diligence for information security and facilitating a more consistent, comparable, and repeatable approach for selecting and specifying security controls for information systems that meet minimum security requirements.[5]

The minimum security requirements cover various security-related areas with regard to protecting the confidentiality, integrity, and availability of federal information systems

---

[4]FIPS-199, p. 1.
[5]FIPS-200, p. 1.

and the information processed, stored, and transmitted by those systems. The 17 areas represent a broad-based, balanced information security program that addresses the management, operational, and technical aspects of protecting federal information and information systems.

Policies and procedures play an important role in the effective implementation of enterprise-wide information security programs within the federal government and the success of the resulting security measures employed to protect federal information and information systems. Thus, organizations must develop and promulgate formal, documented policies and procedures governing the minimum security requirements set forth in this standard and must ensure their effective implementation.

FIPS-200 continues with listing the standard security control families as defined in SP 800-53 for use in the minimum security baselines, which we will discuss in Chapter 9.

FIPS-201 – Personal Identity Verification of Federal Employees and Contractors

FIPS-201 specifies the architecture and technical requirements for a common identification standard for Federal employees and contractors. The overall goal is to achieve appropriate security assurance for multiple applications by efficiently verifying the claimed identity of individuals seeking physical access to federally controlled government facilities and logical access to government information systems.

The Standard contains the minimum requirements for a Federal personal identity verification system that meets the control and security objectives of Homeland Security Presidential Directive-12 [HSPD-12], including identity proofing, registration, and issuance. The Standard also provides detailed specifications that will support technical interoperability among PIV systems of Federal departments and agencies. It describes the card elements, system interfaces, and security controls required to securely store, process, and retrieve identity credentials from the card.[6]

The FIPS-201 continues with listing all of the NIST Special Publications which are related to the standard including:

1. SP 800-73
2. SP 800-76
3. SP 800-78
4. SP 800-79
5. SP 800-87
6. SP 800-96
7. SP 800-156
8. SP 800-157

FIPS-201 stipulates a PIV card must be personalized with identity information for the individual to whom the card is issued, in order to perform identity verification by both humans and automated systems. Humans can use the physical card for visual comparisons, whereas automated systems can use the electronically stored data on the card to conduct automated identity verification.

---

[6]FIPS-201, p. iii.

REGULATORY REQUIREMENTS

Each agency of the US government which has oversight authority for industry activities provides regulatory guidance to those organizations, either public or private, in various forms and methods. We will briefly discuss the applicable regulations here which are relevant to security controls and testing.

DOD

The DOD has a long and detailed history of providing guidance and regulatory direction for security of its systems and methods. It started this process in the 1970s and 1980s with the initial issuance of DOD 5200 series of publications. These documents initially focused on providing guidance on the security objective of confidentiality on large-scale, mainframe-based systems. Various DOD agencies have provided these documents and regulations including the NSA, Defense Information Assurance Program (DIAP) Office, Defense Information Systems Agency (DISA), and the DOD CIO Office and, for the most part, are available at the Defense Technical Information Center (DTIC) (http://www.dtic.mil/dtic/) site. Recently (March 2014), DOD has moved all assessment and authorization criteria over to the NIST-based Risk Management Framework (RMF) with some defense-related modifications. Current DOD regulations now reflect the same requirements as the NIST-based documentation and standards for all assessment actions. The primary regulatory guidance currently in use at DOD under the cybersecurity series are the 8500 series of instructions and manuals.

DOD Instruction (DODI) 8500.01 – Cybersecurity:

> DOD will implement a multi-tiered cybersecurity risk management process to protect U.S. interests, DOD operational capabilities, and DOD individuals, organizations, and assets from the DOD Information Enterprise level, through the DOD Component level, down to the Information Security (IS) level as described in National Institute of Standards and Technology (NIST) Special Publication (SP) 800-39 and Committee on National Security Systems (CNSS) Policy (CNSSP) 22.[7]

This regulatory policy provides guidance to DOD agencies and entities in the following areas:

1. Risk management
2. Operational resilience
3. Integration and interoperability
4. Cyberspace defense
5. Performance
6. DOD information
7. Identity assurance
8. Information technology
9. Cybersecurity workforce
10. Mission partners

---

[7]DODI 8500.01, March 14, 2014, p. 2.

DODI 8510.01 – Risk Management Framework (RMF) for DOD Information Technology (IT):

This instruction policy document implements the NIST-developed RMF by establishing the RMF for DOD IT, establishing associated cybersecurity policy, and assigning responsibilities for executing and maintaining the RMF. The RMF replaces the DOD Information Assurance Certification and Accreditation Process (DIACAP) and manages the life-cycle cybersecurity risk to DOD IT.

This document is the singular one which resets all of DOD over to the RMF from the previous methods of certification and accreditation known as DIACAP and DOD Information Technology Security Certification and Accreditation Process (DITSCAP). All activities for assessments and authorizations of DOD IT systems are now to be performed utilizing the NIST approach as defined in SP 800-37, rev. 1 and in accordance with DOD supplemental guidance and the CNSS Instruction (CNSSI)-1253.

CNSS

The CNSS sets US government–level information assurance policies, directives, instructions, operational procedures, guidance, and advisories for US government departments and agencies for the security of NSS. It consists of representation from 21 US government executive branch departments and agencies. In addition to the 21 Members, there are representatives serving as Observers from 14 additional organizations. The CNSS provides a forum for the discussion of policy issues; sets national policy; and promulgates direction, operational procedures, and guidance for the security of NSS. The CNSS stated mission is: "The CNSS is directed to assure the security of NSS against technical exploitation by providing: reliable and continuing assessments of threats and vulnerabilities and implementation of effective countermeasures; a technical base within the USG to achieve this security; and support from the private sector to enhance that technical base assuring that information systems security products are available to secure NSS" [2].

NSS are information systems operated by the US government, its contractors, or agents that contain classified information or that:

- Involve intelligence activities
- Involve cryptographic activities related to national security
- Involve command and control of military forces
- Involve equipment that is an integral part of a weapon or weapon system(s)
- Are critical to the direct fulfillment of military or intelligence missions (not including routine administrative and business applications)

The primary documents of interest to assessors and testers from CNSS are the following:

CNSSI 1253 – Security Categorization and Control Selection for National Security Systems:

This instruction provides all federal government departments, agencies, bureaus, and offices with guidance on the first two steps of the RMF, categorize and select, for NSS. Additionally, this instruction provides NSS guidance in the following four areas:
- This instruction does not adopt the HWM concept from FIPS-200 for categorizing information systems.

- The definitions for moderate and high impact are refined from those provided in FIPS-199.
- The associations of confidentiality, integrity, and/or availability to security controls are explicitly defined in this instruction.
- The use of security control overlays is refined in this instruction for the national security community.

This instruction has been explicitly specified by DOD under DODI 8510.01 as the definite guide for categorization of all DOD IT systems, NSS and non-NSS.

CNSSP 22 – Policy on Information Assurance Risk Management for National Security Systems:

This policy document requires the implementation of an integrated organization-wide program for managing IA risk to organizational operations (i.e., mission, functions, and reputation), organizational assets, individuals, other organizations, and the nation resulting from the operation and use of NSS. On adoption of this CNSSP No. 22 in January 2012, CNSS Policy No. 6, "National Policy on Certification and Accreditation of National Security Systems," dated October 2005, and National Security Telecommunications and Information Systems Security Instruction (NSTISSI) 1000, "National Information Assurance Certification and Accreditation Process (NIACAP)," dated April 2000, were cancelled.

This policy states the following:

It is the CNSS policy that all organizations that own, operate, or maintain NSS ensure organizational operations by establishing and implementing an IA risk management program for their NSS that will:

a. Establish a risk executive (function) to ensure the program is consistent with the provisions of NIST Special Publication (SP) 800-39; provide guidance to and oversight of the organization's risk management program and development of the risk management strategy; communicate organization-wide threat, vulnerability, and risk-related information; and provide a strategic view for managing IA risk throughout the organization.
b. Establish processes to identify IA risks from an organization-wide perspective; determine which risks are acceptable; achieve operational effectiveness by selecting, implementing, and assessing safeguards and countermeasures to adequately mitigate unacceptable risks; and take any additional corrective actions as necessary.
c. Establish processes to deploy security controls throughout the organization consistent with its enterprise architecture, taking advantage of the common control concept as described in NIST SP 800-37 to cost-effectively implement IA security controls within the organization.
d. Establish processes to develop and maintain existing organizational policies and procedures to integrate IA risk management throughout the information system lifecycle (e.g., acquisition, design, development, integration, distribution, operation, maintenance, and retirement).[8]

HHS

The US HHS, Center for Medicare and Medicaid Services, the Office for Civil Rights enforces the HIPAA Privacy Rule, which protects the privacy of individually identifiable health information; the HIPAA Security Rule, which sets national standards for the security of

---

[8]CNSSP 22, p. 4.

electronic PHI; the HIPAA Breach Notification Rule, which requires covered entities and business associates to provide notification following a breach of unsecured PHI; and the confidentiality provisions of the Patient Safety Rule, which protect identifiable information being used to analyze patient safety events and improve patient safety.

HIPAA Security Rule

The Security Rule requires covered entities to maintain reasonable and appropriate administrative, technical, and physical safeguards for protecting e-PHI.

Specifically, covered entities must:

- Ensure the confidentiality, integrity, and availability of all e-PHI they create, receive, maintain or transmit;
- Identify and protect against reasonably anticipated threats to the security or integrity of the information;
- Protect against reasonably anticipated, impermissible uses or disclosures; and
- Ensure compliance by their workforce.

The Security Rule defines "confidentiality" to mean that e-PHI is not available or disclosed to unauthorized persons. The Security Rule's confidentiality requirements support the Privacy Rule's prohibitions against improper uses and disclosures of PHI. The Security rule also promotes the two additional goals of maintaining the integrity and availability of e-PHI. Under the Security Rule, "integrity" means that e-PHI is not altered or destroyed in an unauthorized manner. "Availability" means that e-PHI is accessible and usable on demand by an authorized person.

HHS recognizes that covered entities range from the smallest provider to the largest, multi-state health plan. Therefore the Security Rule is flexible and scalable to allow covered entities to analyze their own needs and implement solutions appropriate for their specific environments. What is appropriate for a particular covered entity will depend on the nature of the covered entity's business, as well as the covered entity's size and resources.

Therefore, when a covered entity is deciding which security measures to use, the Rule does not dictate those measures but requires the covered entity to consider:

- Its size, complexity, and capabilities,
- Its technical, hardware, and software infrastructure,
- The costs of security measures, and
- The likelihood and possible impact of potential risks to e-PHI.

Covered entities must review and modify their security measures to continue protecting e-PHI in a changing environment. [3]

HIPAA Privacy Rule

The Privacy Rule protects all "individually identifiable health information" held or transmitted by a covered entity or its business associate, in any form or media, whether electronic, paper, or oral. The Privacy Rule calls this information "protected health information (PHI)."

"Individually identifiable health information" is information, including demographic data, that relates to:

- The individual's past, present or future physical or mental health or condition,
- The provision of health care to the individual, or
- The past, present, or future payment for the provision of health care to the individual, and that identifies the individual or for which there is a reasonable basis to believe can be used to identify the individual.

Individually identifiable health information includes many common identifiers (e.g., name, address, birth date, Social Security Number).

The Privacy Rule excludes from protected health information employment records that a covered entity maintains in its capacity as an employer and education and certain other records subject to, or defined in, the Family Educational Rights and Privacy Act. [4]

HITECH Breach Reporting

The HIPAA Breach Notification Rule, 45 CFR §§ 164.400-414, requires HIPAA covered entities and their business associates to provide notification following a breach of unsecured protected health information. Similar breach notification provisions implemented and enforced by the Federal Trade Commission (FTC), apply to vendors of personal health records and their third party service providers, pursuant to section 13407 of the HITECH Act.

Protected health information (PHI) is rendered unusable, unreadable, or indecipherable to unauthorized individuals if one or more of the following applies:

1. Electronic PHI has been encrypted as specified in the HIPAA Security Rule by "the use of an algorithmic process to transform data into a form in which there is a low probability of assigning meaning without use of a confidential process or key" (45 CFR 164.304 definition of encryption) and such confidential process or key that might enable decryption has not been breached. To avoid a breach of the confidential process or key, these decryption tools should be stored on a device or at a location separate from the data they are used to encrypt or decrypt. The encryption processes identified below have been tested by the National Institute of Standards and Technology (NIST) and judged to meet this standard.
   (i) Valid encryption processes for data at rest are consistent with NIST Special Publication 800-111, Guide to Storage Encryption Technologies for End User Devices
   (ii) Valid encryption processes for data in motion are those which comply, as appropriate, with NIST Special Publications 800-52, Guidelines for the Selection and Use of Transport Layer Security (TLS) Implementations; 800-77, Guide to IPsec VPNs; or 800-113, Guide to SSL VPNs, or others which are Federal Information Processing Standards (FIPS) 140-2 validated
2. The media on which the PHI is stored or recorded has been destroyed in one of the following ways:
   (i) Paper, film, or other hard copy media have been shredded or destroyed such that the PHI cannot be read or otherwise cannot be reconstructed. Redaction is specifically excluded as a means of data destruction.
   (ii) Electronic media have been cleared, purged, or destroyed consistent with NIST Special Publication 800-88, Guidelines for Media Sanitization such that the PHI cannot be retrieved. [5]

OMB REQUIREMENTS FOR EACH AGENCY

OMB evaluates expenditure effectiveness, and provides oversight of administration procurement, fiscal management, information management, and regulatory policy. It issues two types of relevant documents:

1. Circulars
2. Memorandums

Over the past 15 years, OMB has often provided guidance and direction to federal agencies for security activities through these two types of issuances. I will highlight some of the more prevalent ones here, but always review all issuances for applicability before starting your assessment.

Circulars:

1. *A-130*, Appendix III:
   a. Security for Federal Information Systems.
   b. Requires executive branch agencies:
      - Plan for security.
      - Ensure appropriate officials are assigned with security responsibility.
      - Review security controls for systems.

- Authorized system processing prior to operations and periodically thereafter – defines this as every 3 years.
c. Defines "adequate security" as:
  - "Security commensurate with the risk and magnitude of the harm resulting from the loss, misuse, or unauthorized access to or modification of information … provide appropriate confidentiality, integrity, and availability, through the use of cost-effective management, personnel, operational, and technical controls."
d. Requires accreditation of federal IS to operate based on an assessment on management, operational, and technical controls.
e. Defines two types of federal systems:
  - Major Application (MA):
    (i) An application that requires special attention to security due to the risk and magnitude of the harm resulting from the loss, misuse, or unauthorized access to or modification of the information in the application.
    (ii) All federal applications require some level of protection. Certain applications, because of the information in them, however, require special management oversight and should be treated as major. Adequate security for other applications should be provided by security of the systems in which they operate.
  - General Support System (GSS):
    (i) An interconnected set of information resources under the same direct management control which shares common functionality. A system normally includes hardware, software, information, data, applications, communications, and people.
    (ii) A system can be, for example, a local area network (LAN) including smart terminals that supports a branch office, an agency-wide backbone, a communications network, a departmental data processing center including its operating system and utilities, a tactical radio network, or a shared information processing service organization (IPSO), such as a service provider.
f. Remains a crucial component of the overall cybersecurity body of regulations. Last updated in 2000, it requires or specifies:
  - Risk-based approach to assess and react to threat and vulnerabilities
  - Security plans and identification and correction of deficiencies
  - Incident Response capabilities
  - Interruption planning and continuity support
  - Technical controls consistent with NIST guidance
  - Periodic review of status and controls
  - Information sharing (MA only) and public access controls
  - Responsibility assignment
  - Periodic reporting of operational and security status

Memorandums:
1. *M-02-01 – Guidance for Preparing and Submitting Security Plans of Action and Milestones* (October 2001): OMB has always viewed POAMs as a budget document because of

the resource allocations associated with fixes and repairs. Therefore, OMB tracks all POAMs and requires agencies to report the status of these periodically.

    a. POAMs contain:
- Weaknesses
- Point Of Contact (POC)
- Resources required
- Scheduled completion date
- Milestones with completion dates
- Changes to milestones
- How weakness was identified
- Current status

    b. POAM is living document – nothing deleted, just updated. The POAM register stays with the system as long as the system is active.

2. *M04-04 – e-Authentication Guidance for Federal Agencies*:

    a. Requires "e-Authentication" Risk assessments for all electronic transactions

    b. Defines criteria for access to federal services online

    c. Especially relevant to assessors since there are specific levels of authentication required for systems and agencies which need to be verified and assessed

3. *M06-15 – Safeguarding PII*:

    a. Requires privacy policies for each agency and the public release of these policies

4. *M06-19 – PII Reporting*:

    a. Requires reporting of potential PII data breach events to federal CERT within 1 h of discovery of breach

5. *M07-16 – Safeguarding Against and Responding to the Breach of Personally Identifiable Information*:

    a. Requires a public Breach Notification Policy for each agency

    b. Requires an agency-based Incident Handling Policy

6. *M10-15 – FY 2010 Reporting Instructions for the Federal Information Security Management Act and Agency Privacy Management*:

    a. This memorandum set in place the continuous monitoring criteria for all agencies which has resulted in the NIST SP 800-137 and various continuous monitoring programs across the US governmental agencies.

7. *M10-28 – Clarifying Cybersecurity Responsibilities and Activities of the Executive Office of the President and the Department of Homeland Security (DHS)*:

    a. Sets OMB as reporting agency and DHS as gathering agency for cybersecurity data and events

8. *M14-03 and M14-04*:

    a. Both cover security of federal agencies and current reporting requirements.

    b. M14-03 establishes requirement for Information Security Continuous Monitoring (ISCM) under DHS control.

    c. M14-04 establishes change in FISMA reauthorization if ISCM program is active.

I have highlighted the initial list of documents, instructions, regulations, and laws which have bearing on assessments and testing of security controls on systems. There are many other federal documents which have relevance to operating and maintaining security for systems. However, they are varied and other sector-specific so each area has its own criteria which are added to what has been described here. There are also industry-specific security requirements available, such as the Payment Card Industry Data Security Specifications (PCI-DSS), so always check when beginning to assess a system for what regulations, laws, and industry criteria are applicable prior to commencing with your assessment.

References

[1] US Justice Department website, https://it.ojp.gov/default.aspx?area=privacy&page=1285.
[2] CNSS website, https://www.cnss.gov/CNSS/about/about.cfm [retrieved 9/12/2014].
[3] OCR website, http://www.hhs.gov/ocr/privacy/hipaa/understanding/srsummary.html [retrieved 9/12/2014].
[4] OCR website, http://www.hhs.gov/ocr/privacy/hipaa/understanding/summary/index.html [retrieved 9/12/2014].
[5] HHS OCR website, http://www.hhs.gov/ocr/privacy/hipaa/administrative/breachnotificationrule/index.html [retrieved 9/12/2014].

4

Federal RMF Requirements

Over the past 10–15 years there have been multiple efforts to provide testers, evaluators, auditors, and validators the guidance and techniques to ensure the systems they were reviewing meet the federal criteria for accreditation and security. As described in Chapters 1 and 2, these activities have culminated in the NIST developing Risk Management Framework (RMF) as defined in SP 800-37, rev. 1. Laura Taylor, in her Syngress Press book *FISMA Compliance Guide*, has a good and detailed explanation (Chapter 3) of the various C&A processes as used, previously implemented, and developed by the various components of the US government; so I won't go into great detail here about those varied procedures and implementations. However, there are some points with respect to the security testing conducted under each of these techniques which do have bearing on this book, so I will discuss these throughout this handbook.

FEDERAL CIVILIAN AGENCIES

NIST produced the RMF in 2010 and OMB issued a memorandum subsequently which requires all federal civilian agencies to follow this guidance for all IT systems under their control. In accordance with FISMA, DOD and Intelligence Community (IC) were exempt from following this guidance, but both organizations have agreed to follow RMF since FISMA was approved and became law in 2002.

FISMA had originally required each agency certify and accredit all IT systems and report on their security status to Congress annually. NIST then developed the SP 800-34 Certification and Accreditation Guide in 2004 to provide guidance to the federal agencies on how this process was to be completed and what steps were required to successfully fulfill each of the agency's needs. This process provided the major inputs to the annual FISMA reporting statistics for each agency over the next several years. I performed many C&A efforts for various federal civilian agencies following this process and it was somewhat long and detailed, but not nearly as arduous as the DOD and IC processes as explained below.

Along with the effort for the C&A activities, NIST produced the Security Controls Catalog, SP 800-53, which delineated the various types, kind, and families of security controls that are available for the IT systems. NIST did this in conjunction with various security vendors, product producers, and the security professionals throughout the industry. This resulted in a detailed, very rich catalog of security controls within the operational, technical, and management arenas to allow selection of controls based on location, operating environment, data categorization, and mission/business objectives for each system as it was developed, implemented, and operated in the governmental space. Along with SP 800-53, the testing guide for each control was produced in SP 800-53A which was, and still is, aligned with each control as found in SP 800-53. SP 800-53A defines the methods, concepts, and techniques to be used to evaluate each control. Further discussion on SP 800-53 will be found in Chapters 8 and 9.

DOD – DIACAP – RMF FOR DOD IT

DOD started their approach to C&A with the advent of DITSCAP in the late 1980s. DITSCAP stands for DOD Information Technology Security Certification and Accreditation Process and was designed and predicated on an infrastructure approach to security. As it began to be practiced, I experienced an overwhelming proliferation of paperwork associated with the DITSCAP. Literally everything needed to be documented, including facilities components: the Heating, Ventilation, & Air Conditioning (HVAC) systems and their controls, the physical security of the structures and surrounding environment, the fire suppression and detection systems employed in the building (s), etc. These review and evaluation processes led to vast amounts of paperwork, documentation for each C&A effort. Along with this, there were no reciprocity agreements so the efforts were reduplicated for each system, even if they were housed in the same room in the same building. All of this led to massive amounts of documents to be reviewed for each accreditation and whole companies were formed based on their abilities and expertise in developing all of these "accreditation" documents. These various efforts led to a standardization of the methods of assessment which became known as the Validator Requirements and the Security Test and Evaluation (ST&E) report. Observing the actions of a system was determined to be an acceptable method of assessment, based on the notes and observances of the validator. Document reviews of system documentation became an important part of the assessment process. These are two types of the Validator Requirements as practiced during the DITSCAP era of DOD C&A actions.

When FISMA and the Paperwork Reduction Acts were passed in 2002, there was great hope that these governmental laws would influence the DOD leaders into implementing some means and methods for reducing this volume of paperwork associated with DITSCAP packages. And, to some degree, it did. When the DOD CIO signed the Interim Guidance document to implement FISMA in DOD in June 2004, Department of Defense (DOD) Information Assurance Certification and Accreditation Process (DIACAP) was created. DIACAP stands for DOD Information Assurance Certification and Accreditation Program and created a new process for C&A in DOD. Gone were the volumes of data required for accreditation and born were four new documents: System Identification Profile (SIP), DIACAP Implementation Plan (DIP), Scorecard, and Plan of Action and Milestones (POAM). The SIP was the document in which the system description and all of its parameters were defined and described. The DIP was the document in which the DOD-defined security controls assigned to the system were documented with their implementation status. The Scorecard was the DIACAP validator's document to describe the results of the ST&E efforts and the resulting residual risks associated with the system. The POAM was the document which identifies any residual risks which required further fixing or remediation. This DIACAP process was finalized in late November 2007 with the final issuance of DODI 8510.01 regulatory instruction from DOD to all of its component organizations. Each test effort required all four documents plus additional documents, known as artifacts, to prove the security and assurance to the Designated Accreditation Authority (DAA) who would then approve the use of the system within DOD. The development of the Scorecard process and the DODI 8510–designated certifying authority led to detailed organizational efforts for testing, evaluation, and assessments of the thousands of systems within DOD for each component and agency. Testing then rose to a relatively independent status and, as such, agents for the Certifying Authority, validators, and assessors all became more important to the process than ever before.

During the past 7 years of use, however, the DOD mission focus after FISMA was made law caused security to take a less than optimal role in the command leadership. This led to actual testing of systems being conducted quickly, but not always thoroughly. It was the general "hurry up and get it over with" mentality on the part of commanders, especially in the field in overseas locations. There were, naturally, several incidents which propelled senior leadership to change their perspective and begin to see the value of the testing and evaluation portion of the DIACAP process. These events have led the services to allow full examination and testing of systems in recent times.

IC – ICD 503

The IC within the US government is made up of various agencies and organizations which support the intelligence missions of the government. There has been a long-standing practice within the IC to evaluate and extensively test security controls, components, and devices. This process was first developed in the late 1960s and early 1970s in the access control area with mainframes. As systems were developed, the critical area of confidentiality was addressed by various IC organizations which led to the development of the testing and evaluation criteria found in the Rainbow Series of documents produced by the National Security Agency (NSA). These documents provided the initial examination and evaluation requirements for various computer components and equipment. There were, and still are, a series of different colored cover books (hence the "Rainbow" title) each of which focused on a select area of equipment and each volume provided testing criteria for examiners and validators to verify the security of the equipment under test.

This process gradually evolved over time to become the Director of Central Intelligence Directive (DCID) 6/3 certification process under the control and oversight of the Office of the Director of Central Intelligence (the DCI of DCID). This process focused on the physical side of security to ensure the classified data in the systems were safe and the levels and types of encryption at which the data were stored for the same reason.

This process developed a two-stage evaluation methodology. The primary focus points for testing and evaluation of systems in the first stage included:

- *System architecture analysis*: This step verifies that the system architecture complies with the architecture description in the security plan. The interfaces between the system under test and other systems must be identified and evaluated to assess their effectiveness in maintaining the security posture of the infrastructure.

- *Software, hardware, and firmware design analysis*: This step evaluates how well the software, hardware, and firmware reflect the security requirements of the security plan and the security architecture of the system.
- *Network connection rule compliance analysis*: This step evaluates the intended connections to other systems and networks to ensure the system design will enforce specific network security policies and protect the IS from adverse confidentiality, integrity, availability, and accountability impacts.
- *Integrity analysis of integrated products*: This step evaluates the integration of Commercial-Off-The-Shelf (COTS) or Government Off-The-Shelf (GOTS) software, hardware, and firmware to ensure that their integration into the system design complies with the system security architecture. The product security functionality should be verified by the certification team to confirm that the needed security functions are present and properly integrated into the system.
- *Life cycle management analysis*: This step verifies that change control and configuration management practices are in place, or will be, and are sufficient to preserve the integrity of the security-relevant software and hardware.
- *Security requirements validation procedure preparation*: This step defines the procedures to be used to verify compliance with all the defined security requirements. The security requirements document must identify the type of review required to validate each requirement. If test procedures are prepared, they should be added to the security plan.
- *Vulnerability assessment*: The initial evaluation analysis steps conclude with a vulnerability assessment to identify the residual risk. A vulnerability assessment evaluates security vulnerabilities with regard to confidentiality, integrity, availability, and accountability and recommends applicable countermeasures. It uses techniques such as static penetration, flaw hypothesis, and threat–vulnerability pairing to determine the ability to exploit the vulnerabilities.

The second stage of testing and evaluation was usually conducted subsequent to the analysis from the first stage and included:

- *ST&E*: This step validates the correct implementation of identification and authentication, audit capabilities, access controls, object reuse, trusted recovery, and network connection rule compliance. It assesses the technical implementation of the security design, and ascertains that security software, hardware, and firmware features have been implemented as documented in the Security Agreement.
- *Penetration testing*: This step assesses the system's ability to withstand intentional attempts to circumvent system security features by exploiting technical security vulnerabilities. It may include internal and external penetration attempts based on common vulnerabilities for the technology being used.
- *TEMPEST and RED-BLACK verification*: This step may be required to validate that the equipment and site meet TEMPEST and RED-BLACK verification security requirements.
- *Validation of Communication Security (COMSEC) compliance*: This step validates that NSA-approved COMSEC is in use and that approved COMSEC key management procedures are used. It evaluates how well the COMSEC materials and procedures meet the requirements defined in the Security Agreement.

- *System management analysis*: This step examines the system management infrastructure to determine whether it adequately supports the maintenance of the environment, mission, and architecture described in the Security Agreement. It also provides an indication of the effectiveness of the security personnel.
- *Site evaluation*: This step validates that the site operation of the information system is accomplished as documented in the Security Agreement. It analyzes the operational procedures for the IS, environment, personnel security, and physical security to determine whether they pose any unacceptable risks to the information being processed.
- *Contingency plan evaluation*: This step analyzes the contingency, backup, and continuity of service plans to ensure the plans are consistent with the requirements identified in the Security Agreement. The plans should consider natural disasters, enemy actions, or malicious actions.
- *Risk management review*: This step assesses the operation of the system to determine whether the risk to confidentiality, integrity, availability, and accountability is being maintained at an acceptable level. This is the final review before developing the recommendation to the Designated Accrediting Authority.

In 2008, the IC changed the criteria for assessments and testing with the publication of Intelligence Community Directive (ICD) 503, which is more aligned with the NIST guidance than the independent guidance as used before under DCID 6/3. This process focuses on reciprocity, the concept that if one organization approves and authorizes a system, another federal organization can use this approval without minimal additional work and testing by accepting the originating organization's authorization. The second area of change under ICD 503 is the concept that security includes all areas of concern, not just confidentiality; so more emphasis is placed on integrity and availability in addition to the previous focus points.

FEDRAMP

The US government placed an emphasis on "Cloud First" for IT support in 2010. The resultant program to guide the various agencies is Federal Risk and Authorization Management Program (FedRAMP). The FedRAMP is a US government agency (General Services Administration (GSA) is led with NIST providing security guidance)-developed risk management program focused on security for cloud-based systems. It provides a standard approach for conducting security assessments of cloud systems based on an accepted set of baseline security controls and consistent processes that have been vetted and agreed upon by agencies across the federal government. Agencies can leverage security assessments for cloud services that have already received provisional authorization under FedRAMP.

FedRAMP is a government-wide program that provides a standardized approach to security assessment, authorization, and continuous monitoring for cloud-based services. FedRAMP uses a "do once, use many times" framework that intends to saves costs, time, and staff required to conduct redundant agency security assessments and process monitoring reports. The purpose of FedRAMP is to:

- Ensure that cloud based services have adequate information security;
- Eliminate duplication of effort and reduce risk management costs; and

- Enable rapid and cost-effective procurement of information systems/services for Federal agencies.

Conformity assessment is a key part of FedRAMP. Conformity assessment is a "demonstration that specified requirements relating to a product, process, system, person or body are fulfilled."[1] Conformity assessment is built on a set of internationally recognized standards that help ensure that the program consistently supports the appropriate level of rigor and independence required.

FedRAMP uses a conformity assessment process to ensure that cloud computing services and systems offered by Cloud Service Providers (CSP) meet specified security requirements. CSPs will be required to use qualified, accredited Third Party Assessment Organizations to perform independent assessments on their service and systems. Third Party Assessment Organizations (3PAO) perform initial and periodic assessment of CSP systems per FedRAMP requirements, provide evidence of compliance, and play an ongoing role in ensuring that CSPs meet requirements. FedRAMP provisional authorizations must include an assessment by an accredited 3PAO to ensure a consistent assessment process.

Under FedRAMP, CSP authorization packages must include an assessment by an accredited 3PAO to ensure a consistent assessment process. Accredited 3PAOs perform initial and periodic assessment of CSP systems per FedRAMP requirements, provide evidence of compliance, and play an on-going role in ensuring that CSPs meet requirements. [1]

NIST CYBERSECURITY FRAMEWORK

Recognizing that the national and economic security of the United States depends on the reliable functioning of critical infrastructure, the President issued Executive Order 13636, Improving Critical Infrastructure Cybersecurity, in February 2013. It directed NIST to work with stakeholders to develop a voluntary framework – based on existing standards, guidelines, and practices – for reducing cyber risks to critical infrastructure. This Executive Order calls for the development of a voluntary Cybersecurity Framework ("Framework") that provides a "prioritized, flexible, repeatable, performance-based, and cost-effective approach" to manage cybersecurity risk for those processes, information, and systems directly involved in the delivery of critical infrastructure services. The Framework, developed in collaboration with industry, provides guidance to an organization on managing cybersecurity risk.

The Framework focuses on using business drivers to guide cybersecurity activities and considering cybersecurity risks as part of the organization's risk management processes. The Framework consists of three parts: the Framework Core, the Framework Profile, and the Framework Implementation Tiers. The Framework Core is a set of cybersecurity activities, outcomes, and informative references that are common across critical infrastructure sectors, providing the detailed guidance for developing individual organizational Profiles. Through

---

[1]ISO/IEC 17000.

use of the Profiles, the Framework will help the organization align its cybersecurity activities with its business requirements, risk tolerances, and resources. The Tiers provide a mechanism for organizations to view and understand the characteristics of their approach to managing cybersecurity risk. [2]

References

[1] From the FedRAMP website at: http://cloud.cio.gov/fedramp.
[2] http://www.nist.gov/cyberframework/upload/cybersecurity-framework-021214.pdf.

Risk Management Framework

The basic framework for security controls and their evaluation throughout the US government has been, and currently is, the Risk Management Framework as defined in SP 800-37, rev. 1. This chapter is providing a brief overview of that process as defined by NIST and some of the background on the expected methods and techniques for treatment of the various risks that an assessor will need to be cognizant of when testing and examining systems and controls. Figure 5.1 is from SP 800-37, rev. 1 and shows the basic flow of the risk management process for reviewing, implementing, and assessing the security controls for a federal system. This process is now utilized as the standard for all federal systems.

Each step of the Risk Management Framework requires detailed knowledge components, understanding the scope and mission of the system under review and external data about the organization, personnel, and activities. The six steps of the Risk Management Framework cover the full picture of the system and its intended use in the federal space. All US governmental agencies now use this defined process to assess and authorize their IT systems for use on a federal network, including DOD and the IC. The following is another representation of the Risk Management Framework with the NIST Special Publications used for guidance on each step added for further clarification:

Risk Management Framework

Starting point

FIPS-199/SP 800-60

Categorize information system
Define criticality/sensitivity of information system according to potential worst case, adverse impact to mission/business.

FIPS-200/SP 800-30/SP 800 53
Select security controls
Select baseline security controls; apply tailoring guidance and supplement controls as needed based on risk assessment.

SP 800-18/SP 800-34/SP 800-70
Implement security controls
Implement security controls within enterprise architecture using sound systems engineering practices; apply security configuration settings, document security controls.

SP 800-53A
Assess security controls
Determine security control effectiveness (i.e., controls implemented correctly, operating as intended, meeting security requirements for information system).

SP 800-37
Authorize information system
Determine risk to organizational operations and assets, individuals, other organizations, and the nation; if acceptable, authorize operation.

SP 800-37/SP 800-53A
Monitor security state
Continuously track changes to the information system that may affect security controls and reassess control effectiveness.

Security life cycle

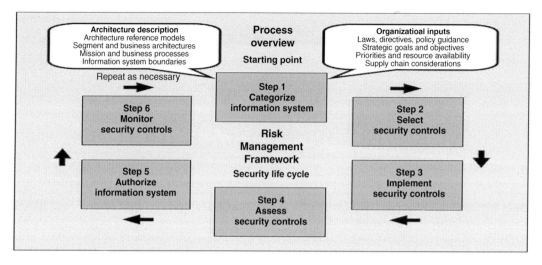

FIGURE 5.1   Risk Management Framework.

Each step of the Risk Management Framework has delineated steps for accomplishment of the specific requirements within each step. Tasking parameters are defined by required events to be completed, primary and secondary roles and responsibilities for each task, and final results for each task and, subsequently, each step of the framework.

STEP 1 – CATEGORIZATION

The primary goal of this step is to categorize the information system and the information processed, stored, and transmitted by that system based on an impact analysis. The objectives of this step are as follows:

- Produce the FIPS-199 Categorization Document for the system.
- Document is utilized in multiple locations and on multiple efforts:
  - Storage Service Provider (SSP)
  - Budgets and CPIC activities
  - System of Records Notice (SORN)
  - Program Objective Memorandum (POM) and Program of Requirements (POR) actions for DOD and the military services

Categorization of the information system is based on an impact analysis.
It is performed to determine:
  - The types of information included within the security authorization boundary
  - The security requirements for the information types
  - The potential impact on the organization resulting from a security compromise

The result is used as the basis for developing the security plan, selecting security controls, and determining the risk inherent in operating the system.

The identified tasks for step 1 are as follows:

1. Categorize the information system and document the results of the security categorization in the security plan.
2. Describe the information system (including system boundary) and document the description in the security plan.
3. Register the information system with appropriate organizational program/management offices.

The guidance from the SP 800-37, rev. 1 gives additional insight to categorization: "The security categorization process is carried out by the information system owner and information owner/steward in cooperation and collaboration with appropriate organizational officials (i.e., senior leaders with mission/business function and/or risk management responsibilities). The security categorization process is conducted as an organization-wide activity taking into consideration the enterprise architecture and the information security architecture. This helps to ensure that individual information systems are categorized based on the mission and business objectives of the organization. The information system owner and information owner/steward consider results from the initial risk assessment as a part of the security categorization decision. The security categorization decision is consistent with the organization's *risk management strategy* to identify potential impact to mission/business functions resulting from the loss of confidentiality, integrity, and/or availability. The risk management strategy provides guidance and relevant information to authorizing officials (e.g., risk assessment methodologies employed by the organization, evaluation of risks determined, risk mitigation approaches, organizational risk tolerance, approaches for monitoring risk over time, known existing aggregated risks from current information systems, and other sources of risk).

The results of the security categorization process influence the selection of appropriate security controls for the information system and also, where applicable, the minimum assurance requirements for that system. Security categorization determinations consider potential adverse impacts to organizational operations, organizational assets, individuals, other organizations, and the Nation. The organization may consider decomposing the information system into multiple subsystems to more efficiently and effectively allocate security controls to the system. One approach is to categorize each identified subsystem (including dynamic subsystems). Separately categorizing each subsystem does not change the overall categorization of the information system. Rather, it allows the constituent subsystems to receive a separate allocation of security controls from NIST Special Publication 800-53 instead of deploying higher-impact controls across every subsystem. Another approach is to bundle smaller subsystems into larger subsystems within the information system, categorize each of the aggregated subsystems, and allocate security controls to the subsystems, as appropriate. Security categorization information is documented in the system identification section of the security plan or included as an attachment to the plan."[1]

---

[1]SP 800-37, rev. 1, June 2014 edition, p. 21.

STEP 2 – SELECTION

The primary goal of this step is to select an initial set of baseline security controls for the information system based on the security categorization, tailoring and supplementing the security control baseline as needed based on an organizational assessment of risk and local conditions. The objectives of this step are as follows:

- Identify security controls needed.
- Select minimum security control baseline.
- Build monitoring strategy for identified controls.

The security control baseline is established by determining specific controls required to protect the system based on the security categorization of the system. The baseline is tailored and supplemented in accordance with an organizational assessment of risk and local parameters. The security control baseline, as well as the plan for monitoring it, is documented in the security plan.

The identified tasks for step 2 are as follows:

1. Identify the security controls that are provided by the organization as common controls for organizational information systems and document the controls in a security plan (or equivalent document).
2. Select the security controls for the information system and document the controls in the security plan.
3. Develop a strategy for the continuous monitoring of security control effectiveness and any proposed or actual changes to the information system and its environment of operation.
4. Review and approve the security plan.

The guidance from the SP 800-37, rev. 1 gives additional insight to control selection:

The security controls are selected based on the security categorization of the information system. After selecting the applicable security control baseline, organizations apply the tailoring process to align the controls more closely with the specific conditions within the organization (i.e., conditions related to organizational risk tolerance, missions/business functions, information systems, or environments of operation). The tailoring process includes:

(i)   identifying and designating common controls in initial security control baselines;
(ii) applying scoping considerations to the remaining baseline security controls;
(iii) selecting compensating security controls, if needed;
(iv) assigning specific values to organization-defined security control parameters via explicit assignment and selection statements;
(v)   supplementing baselines with additional security controls and control enhancements, if needed; and
(vi) providing additional specification information for control implementation, if needed.

Organizations use risk assessments to inform and guide the tailoring process for organizational information systems and environments of operation. Threat data from risk assessments provide critical information on adversary capabilities, intent, and targeting that may affect organizational decisions regarding the selection of additional security controls, including the associated costs and benefits. Risk assessment results are also leveraged when identifying common controls to help determine if such controls available for inheritance meet the security requirements for the system and its environment of operation (including analyses for potential single points of failure). The security plan contains an overview of the security requirements for the information system in sufficient detail to determine that the security controls selected would meet those requirements. The security plan, in addition to the list of security controls to be implemented, describes the intended application of each control in the context of the information system with sufficient detail to enable a compliant implementation of the control. During the security control selection process organizations may begin planning for the continuous monitoring process by developing a monitoring strategy. The strategy can include, for example, monitoring criteria such as the volatility of specific security controls and the appropriate frequency of monitoring specific controls. Organizations may choose to address security control volatility and frequency of monitoring during control selection as inputs to the continuous monitoring process. The monitoring strategy can be included in the security plan to support the concept of near real-time risk management and ongoing authorization. Information system owners *inheriting* common controls can either document the implementation of the controls in their respective security plans or reference the controls contained in the security plans of the common control providers. Information system owners can refer to the security authorization packages prepared by common control providers when making determinations regarding the adequacy of common controls inherited by their respective systems.

For net-centric architectures where subsystems may be added or removed from an information system dynamically, the organization includes in the security plan for the system:

(i) descriptions of the functions of the dynamic subsystems;
(ii) the security controls employed in the subsystems;
(iii) constraints/assumptions regarding the functions of the dynamic subsystems and the associated security controls in the subsystems;
(iv) dependencies of other subsystems on the proper functioning of the security controls of the dynamic subsystems;
(v) procedures for determining that the dynamic subsystems conform to the security plan, assumptions, and constraints; and
(vi) the impact of the dynamic subsystems and associated security controls on existing security controls in the information system. While inclusion of a dynamic subsystem may impact the information system or some of the currently identified subsystems, it does not necessarily mean the subsystem will impact the *security* of the system or other subsystems. That is, not all subsystems are security relevant.

Changes in the net-centric architectures that exceed the anticipated limits of the security plan may not be allowed or may require reassessment prior to being approved. When security controls are designated as common controls, the organization ensures that sufficient information is available to information system owners and authorizing officials to support the risk management process. When security services are provided by external providers (e.g., through contracts, interagency agreements, lines of business arrangements, licensing agreements, and/or supply chain arrangements), the organization:

(i) defines the external services provided to the organization;
(ii) describes how the external services are protected in accordance with the security requirements of the organization; and
(iii) obtains the necessary assurances that the risk to organizational operations and assets, individuals, other organizations, and the Nation arising from the use of the external services is acceptable.

The organization also considers that replicated subsystems within a complex information system may exhibit common vulnerabilities that can be exploited by a common threat source, thereby negating the redundancy that might be relied upon as a risk mitigation measure. The impact due to a security incident against one constituent subsystem might cascade and impact many subsystems at the same time.[2]

---

[2] SP 800-37, rev. 1, June 2014 edition, p. 25.

STEP 3 – IMPLEMENTATION

The primary goal of this step is to implement the security controls and describe how the controls are employed within the information system and its environment of operation. The objectives of this step are as follows:

- Install security controls into system.
- Document controls as installed.

The security controls specified in the security plan are implemented by taking into account the minimum organizational assurance requirements. The security plan describes how the controls are employed within the information system and its operational environment. The security assessment plan documents the methods for testing these controls and the expected results throughout the system life cycle.

The identified tasks for step 3 are as follows:

1. Implement the security controls specified in the security plan.
2. Document the security control implementation, as appropriate, in the security plan, providing a functional description of the control implementation (including planned inputs, expected behavior, and expected outputs).

The guidance from the SP 800-37, rev. 1 gives additional insight to implementation of controls: "Security control implementation is consistent with the organization's enterprise architecture and information security architecture. The information security architecture serves as a resource to allocate security controls (including, for example, security mechanisms and services) to an information system and any organization-defined subsystems. Early integration of information security requirements into the system development life cycle is the most cost-effective method for implementing the organizational risk management strategy at Tier 3. Security controls targeted for deployment within the information system (including subsystems) are allocated to specific system components responsible for providing a particular security capability. Not all security controls need to be allocated to every subsystem. Categorization of subsystems, information security architecture, and allocation of security controls work together to help achieve a suitable balance. Allocating some security controls as common controls or hybrid controls is part of this architectural process. Organizations use best practices when implementing the security controls within the information system including system and software engineering methodologies, security engineering principles, and secure coding techniques. Risk assessment may help inform decisions regarding the cost, benefit, and risk trade-offs in using one type of technology versus another for control implementation. In addition, organizations ensure that mandatory configuration settings are established and implemented on information technology products in accordance with federal and organizational policies (e.g., Federal Desktop Core Configuration). Information system security engineers with support from information system security officers employ a sound security engineering process that captures and refines information security requirements and ensures the integration of those requirements into information technology products and systems through purposeful security design or configuration. When available, organizations consider the use of information technology products that have been tested, evaluated, or validated by approved, independent, third-party assessment facilities. In addition, organizations satisfy, where applicable, minimum assurance requirements when implementing security controls. Assurance requirements are directed at the activities and actions that security control developers and implementers define and apply to increase the level of confidence that the controls are implemented correctly, operating as intended, and producing the desired outcome with respect to meeting the security requirements for the information system. Assurance requirements address the quality of the design, development, and implementation of the security functions in the information system. For higher-impact systems (i.e., potential high-value targets) in situations where specific and credible threat information indicates the likelihood of advanced cyber-attacks, additional assurance measures are considered. Organizations consider any implementation-related issues associated with the integration and/or interfaces among common controls and system-specific controls.

For the identified common controls inherited by the information system, information system security engineers with support from information system security officers coordinate with the common control provider to determine the most appropriate way to apply the common controls to the organizational information systems. For certain management and operational controls, formal integration into information technology products, services, and systems may not be required. For certain types of operational and/or technical controls, implementation may require additional components, products, or services to enable the information system to utilize the previously selected common controls to the fullest extent. If selection of common controls previously had been deferred, identification of common controls inherited by the information system is revisited to determine if better determinations can be made at this point in the system development life cycle. Information system owners can refer to the authorization packages prepared by common control providers when making determinations regarding the adequacy of the implementations of common controls for their respective systems. For common controls that do not meet the protection needs of the information systems inheriting the controls or that have unacceptable weaknesses or deficiencies, the system owners identify compensating or supplementary controls to be implemented. Risk assessment may help determine how gaps in protection needs between systems and common controls affect the overall risk associated with the system, and how to prioritize the need for compensating or supplementary controls to mitigate specific risks. To the maximum extent and consistent with the flexibility allowed in applying the tasks in the RMF, organizations and their contractors conduct initial security control assessments (also referred to as developmental testing and evaluation) during information system development and implementation. Conducting security control assessments in parallel with the development and implementation phases of the system development life cycle facilitates the early identification of weaknesses and deficiencies and provides the most cost-effective method for initiating corrective actions. Issues found during these assessments can be referred to authorizing officials for early resolution, as appropriate. The results of the initial security control assessments can also be used during the security authorization process to avoid delays or costly repetition of assessments. Assessment results that are subsequently reused in other phases of the system development life cycle meet the reuse requirements (including independence) established by the organization."[3]

---

[3]SP 800-37, rev. 1, June 2014 edition, p. 28.

STEP 4 – ASSESSMENT

The primary goal of this step is to assess and evaluate the security controls using appropriate assessment procedures to determine the extent to which the controls are implemented correctly, operating as intended, and producing the desired outcome with respect to meeting the security objectives of the system. The objective of this step is as follows:

- Conduct evaluation of system security with the following questions answered:
  - Are the controls:
    - Implemented correctly?
    - Operating as intended?
    - Producing the desired outcome?

The security control assessment follows the approved plan, including defined procedures, to determine the effectiveness of the controls in meeting security requirements of the information system. The results are documented in the security assessment report.

The identified tasks for step 4 are as follows:

1. Develop, review, and approve a plan to assess the security controls.
2. Assess the security controls in accordance with the assessment procedures defined in the security assessment plan.
3. Prepare the security assessment report documenting the issues, findings, and recommendations from the security control assessment.
4. Conduct initial remediation actions on security controls based on the findings and recommendations of the security assessment report and reassess remediated control(s), as appropriate.

The guidance from the SP 800-37, rev. 1 gives additional insight to assessment: "Security control assessments determine the extent to which the controls are implemented correctly, operating as intended, and producing the desired outcome with respect to meeting the security requirements for the information system. Security control assessments occur as early as practicable in the system development life cycle, preferably during the development phase of the information system. These types of assessments are referred to as *developmental testing and evaluation* and are intended to validate that the required security controls are implemented correctly and consistent with the established information security architecture. Developmental testing and evaluation activities include, for example, design and code reviews, application scanning, and regression testing. Security weaknesses and deficiencies identified early in the system development life cycle can be resolved more quickly and in a much more cost-effective manner before proceeding to subsequent phases in the life cycle. The objective is to identify the information security architecture and security controls up front and to ensure that the system design and testing validate the implementation of these controls.

The information system owner relies on the technical expertise and judgment of assessors to:

(i) assess the security controls employed within or inherited by the information system using assessment procedures specified in the security assessment plan; and
(ii) provide specific recommendations on how to correct weaknesses or deficiencies in the controls and reduce or eliminate identified vulnerabilities. The assessor findings are an

unbiased, factual reporting of the weaknesses and deficiencies discovered during the security control assessment.

Organizations are encouraged to maximize the use of automation to conduct security control assessments to help:

(i) increase the speed and overall effectiveness and efficiency of the assessments; and
(ii) support the concept of ongoing monitoring of the security state of organizational information systems.

When iterative development processes such as agile development are employed, this typically results in an iterative assessment as each cycle is conducted. A similar process is used for assessing security controls in COTS information technology products employed within the information system. Even when iterative development is not employed, organizations may choose to begin assessing security controls prior to the complete implementation of all security controls listed in the security plan. This type of *incremental assessment* is appropriate if it is more efficient or cost-effective to do so. For example, policy, procedures, and plans may be assessed prior to the assessment of the technical security controls in the hardware and software. In many cases, common controls (i.e., security controls inherited by the information system) may be assessed prior to the security controls employed within the system.

The organization ensures that assessors have access to:

(i) the information system and environment of operation where the security controls are employed; and
(ii) the appropriate documentation, records, artifacts, test results, and other materials needed to assess the security controls.

In addition, assessors have the required degree of independence as determined by the authorizing official. Security control assessments in support of initial and subsequent security authorizations are conducted by independent assessors. Assessor independence during continuous monitoring, although not mandated, facilitates reuse of assessment results when reauthorization is required. When security controls are provided to an organization by an external provider (e.g., through contracts, interagency agreements, lines of business arrangements, licensing agreements, and/or supply chain arrangements), the organization ensures that assessors have access to the information system/environment of operation where the controls are employed as well as appropriate information needed to carry out the assessment. The organization also obtains any information related to existing assessments that may have been conducted by the external provider and reuses such assessment information whenever possible in accordance with the reuse criteria established by the organization. Descriptive information about the information system is typically documented in the system identification section of the security plan or included by reference or as attachments to the plan. Supporting materials such as procedures, reports, logs, and records showing evidence of security control implementation are identified as well. In order to make the risk management process as timely and cost-effective as possible, the reuse of previous assessment results, when reasonable and appropriate, is strongly recommended. For example, a recent audit of an information system may have produced information about the effectiveness of selected security controls. Another opportunity to reuse previous assessment results comes from programs that test and evaluate the security features of commercial information technology products. Additionally, if prior assessment results from the system developer are available, the security control assessor, under appropriate circumstances, may incorporate those results into the assessment. And finally, assessment results are reused to support reciprocity where possible."[4]

STEP 5 – AUTHORIZATION

The primary goal of this step is to authorize information system operation based on a determination of the risk to organizational operations and assets, individuals, other organizations, and the nation resulting from the operation of the information system and the decision that this risk is acceptable. The objective of this step is as follows:

- Obtain authority to operate approval for system.

The residual risks identified during the security control assessment are evaluated and the decision is made to authorize the system to operate, deny its operation, or remediate the deficiencies. Associated documentation is prepared and/or updated depending on the authorization decision.

The identified tasks for step 5 are as follows:

1. Prepare the plan of action and milestones based on the findings and recommendations of the security assessment report excluding any remediation actions taken.
2. Assemble the security authorization package and submit the package to the authorizing official for adjudication.
3. Determine the risk to organizational operations (including mission, functions, image, or reputation), organizational assets, individuals, other organizations, or the nation.
4. Determine if the risk to organizational operations, organizational assets, individuals, other organizations, or the nation is acceptable.

The guidance from the SP 800-37, rev. 1 gives additional insight to authorization: "The explicit acceptance of *risk* is the responsibility of the authorizing official and cannot be delegated to other officials within the organization. The authorizing official considers many factors when deciding if the risk to organizational operations (including mission, function, image, or reputation), organizational assets, individuals, other organizations, and the Nation, is acceptable. Balancing security considerations with mission and operational needs is paramount to achieving an acceptable authorization decision. The authorizing official issues an authorization decision for the information system and the common controls inherited by the system after reviewing all of the relevant information and, where appropriate, consulting with other organizational officials, including the organization's risk executive (function). Security authorization decisions are based on the content of the security authorization package and, where appropriate, any inputs received from key organizational officials, including the risk executive (function). The authorization package provides relevant information on the security state of the information system including the ongoing effectiveness of the security controls employed within or inherited by the system. Inputs from the risk executive (function), including

---

[4]SP 800-37, rev. 1, June 2014 edition, p. 31.

previously established overarching risk guidance to authorizing officials, provide additional organization-wide information to the authorizing official that may be relevant and affect the authorization decision (e.g., organizational risk tolerance, specific mission and business requirements, dependencies among information systems, and other types of risks not directly associated with the information system). Risk executive (function) inputs are documented and become part of the security authorization decision. Security authorization decisions, including inputs from the risk executive (function), are conveyed to information system owners and common control providers and made available to interested parties within the organization (e.g., information system owners and authorizing officials for interconnected systems, chief information officers, information owners/stewards, senior managers).

The *authorization decision document* conveys the final security authorization decision from the authorizing official to the information system owner or common control provider, and other organizational officials, as appropriate. The authorization decision document contains the following information:

(i) authorization decision;
(ii) terms and conditions for the authorization; and
(iii) authorization termination date.

The security *authorization decision* indicates to the information system owner whether the system is:

(i) authorized to operate; or
(ii) not authorized to operate.

The *terms and conditions* for the authorization provide a description of any specific limitations or restrictions placed on the operation of the information system or inherited controls that must be followed by the system owner or common control provider. The *authorization termination date*, established by the authorizing official, indicates when the security authorization expires. Authorization termination dates are influenced by federal and/or organizational policies which may establish maximum authorization periods. Organizations may choose to eliminate the authorization termination date if the continuous monitoring program is sufficiently robust to provide the authorizing official with the needed information to conduct ongoing risk determination and risk acceptance activities with regard to the security state of the information system and the ongoing effectiveness of security controls employed within and inherited by the system.

If the security control assessments are conducted by qualified assessors with the required degree of *independence* based on federal/organizational policies, appropriate security standards and guidelines, and the needs of the authorizing official, the assessment results can be cumulatively applied to the reauthorization, thus supporting the concept of ongoing authorization. Organizational policies regarding ongoing authorization and formal reauthorization, if/when required, are consistent with federal directives, regulations, and/or policies.

The authorization decision document is attached to the original security authorization package containing the supporting documentation and transmitted to the information system owner or common control provider. Upon receipt of the authorization decision document and original authorization package, the information system owner or common control provider acknowledges and implements the terms and conditions of the authorization and notifies the authorizing official. The organization ensures that authorization documents for both information systems and for common controls are made available to appropriate organizational officials (e.g., information system owners inheriting common controls, risk executive (function), chief information officers, senior information security officers, information system security officers). Authorization documents, especially information dealing with information system vulnerabilities, are:

(i)   marked and appropriately protected in accordance with federal and organizational policies; and
(ii) retained in accordance with the organization's record retention policy.

The authorizing official verifies, on an ongoing basis, that the terms and conditions established as part of the authorization are being followed by the information system owner or common control provider."[5]

STEP 6 – MONITORING

The primary goal of this step is to monitor the security controls in the information system on an ongoing basis including assessing control effectiveness, documenting changes to the system or its environment of operation, conducting security impact analyses of the associated changes, and reporting the security state of the system to designated organizational officials.

The objectives of this step are as follows:

• Operate and maintain system security within acceptable risk tolerance.
• Update system securely and safely.
• Conduct mission successfully.

After an Authorization to Operate (ATO) is granted, ongoing continuous monitoring is performed on all identified security controls as well as the political, legal, and physical environment in which the system operates. Changes to the system or its operational environment are documented and analyzed. The security state of the system is reported to designated officials. Significant changes will cause the system to reenter the security authorization process. Otherwise, the system will continue to be monitored on an ongoing basis in accordance with the organization's monitoring strategy.

The identified tasks for step 6 are as follows:

1. Determine the security impact of proposed or actual changes to the information system and its environment of operation.
2. Assess the technical, management, and operational security controls employed within and inherited by the information system in accordance with the organization-defined monitoring strategy.
3. Conduct remediation actions based on the results of ongoing monitoring activities, assessment of risk, and outstanding items in the plan of action and milestones.

---

[5]SP 800-37, rev. 1, June 2014 edition, p. 36.

4. Update the security plan, security assessment report, and plan of action and milestones based on the results of the continuous monitoring process.

5. Report the security status of the information system (including the effectiveness of security controls employed within and inherited by the system) to the authorizing official and other appropriate organizational officials on an ongoing basis in accordance with the monitoring strategy.

6. Review the reported security status of the information system (including the effectiveness of security controls employed within and inherited by the system) on an ongoing basis in accordance with the monitoring strategy to determine whether the risk to organizational operations, organizational assets, individuals, other organizations, or the nation remains acceptable.

7. Implement an information system disposal strategy, when needed, which executes required actions when a system is removed from service.

The guidance from the SP 800-37, rev. 1 gives additional insight to ongoing monitoring: "The authorizing official or designated representative reviews the reported security status of the information system (including the effectiveness of deployed security controls) on an ongoing basis, to determine the current risk to organizational operations and assets, individuals, other organizations, or the Nation. The authorizing official determines, with inputs as appropriate from the authorizing official designated representative, senior information security officer, and the risk executive (function), whether the current risk is acceptable and forwards appropriate direction to the information system owner or common control provider. The use of automated support tools to capture, organize, quantify, visually display, and maintain security status information promotes the concept of *near real-time risk management* regarding the overall risk posture of the organization. The use of metrics and dashboards increases an organization's ability to make risk-based decisions by consolidating data from automated tools and providing it to decision makers at different levels within the organization in an easy-to-understand format. The risks being incurred may change over time based on the information provided in the security status reports. Determining how the changing conditions affect the mission or business risks associated with the information system is essential for maintaining *adequate security*. By carrying out ongoing *risk determination* and *risk acceptance*, authorizing officials can maintain the security authorization over time. Formal reauthorization actions, if required, occur only in accordance with federal or organizational policies. The authorizing official conveys updated risk determination and acceptance results to the risk executive (function)."[6]

The Risk Management Framework Authorization Package, as referenced above, has three required documents produced during the assessment and authorization process which are required to obtain an ATO for federal systems. These three documents are the System Security Plan (as defined in SP 800-18), Security Assessment Report (as defined in SP 800-37 and SP 800-53A), and the POAM (as defined in OMB Memorandum M02-01). The following diagram

---

[6]SP 800-37, rev. 1, June 2014 edition, p. 41.

shows the RMF steps with the approximate steps where each of these documents are generated during the process:

SSP	**Categorize**	Identify system and security objectives
	Select	Identify controls
	Implement	Integrate
SAR		
POAM	**Assess**	Test and verify
Authorization decision	**Authorize**	Approval
	Monitor	Maintain

Continuous Monitoring for Current Systems

The objective of a continuous monitoring program is to determine if the complete set of planned, required, and deployed security controls within an information system or inherited by the system continues to be effective over time in light of the inevitable changes that occur. In 2010, OMB issued guidance to US governmental agencies that continuous monitoring of security controls would now be required for all systems. This began the developmental process for the ongoing efforts to create, develop, and maintain a continuous monitoring program for each agency. NIST provided some guidance when they issued SP 800-137, "Information Security Continuous Monitoring (ISCM) for Federal Information Systems and Organizations," in September 2011.

There are several different ISCM programs currently in deployment in various governmental agencies including the Continuous Diagnostic and Mitigation (CDM) effort from DHS and Continuous Monitoring Risk System (CMRS) from DISA in DOD. These efforts will continue to evolve over the next several years. As part of this effort, OMB and NIST are providing guidance and directions on moving to an event-driven authorization process known as Ongoing Authorization (OA) within agencies that have an active ISCM. Recent supplemental guidance to SP 800-37, rev. 1 provides this guidance and it is worth the effort to obtain this document and review it for your area of interest.

Roles and Responsibilities

The Risk Management Framework acknowledges that organizations have widely varying missions and organizational structures, so there may be differences in naming conventions for risk management-related roles and how specific responsibilities are allocated among organizational personnel (e.g., multiple individuals filling a single role or one individual filling multiple roles). However, the basic functions remain the same. The application of the Risk Management Framework is flexible, allowing organizations to effectively accomplish the intent of the specific tasks within their respective organizational structures to best manage information system-related security risks.

Many risk management roles have counterpart roles defined in the routine system development life cycle processes carried out by organizations. Whenever possible, organizations should align the risk management roles with similar (or complementary) roles defined for the system development life cycle.

ORGANIZATIONAL ROLES

White House

This is the US government executive office given statutory authority to issue Executive Orders, proclamations, Presidential Decision Directive (PDD)/HSPD/Nation Safe Drivers (NSD), and similar documents that initiate action, stop action, or require general notice be given (Fig. 6.1). These directives and orders drive the creation and promulgation of executive policy throughout the Executive Branch and agencies.

Congress

This is the US government legislative body responsible for the US Code and the general, permanent laws of the nation that it contains. Congress's power to authorize the appropriation of federal spending to carry out government activities drives a lot of the laws and their implementation efforts across the government.

OMB

The Office of Management and Budget is the Executive Branch agency which evaluates expenditure effectiveness, and provides oversight of administration procurement, fiscal

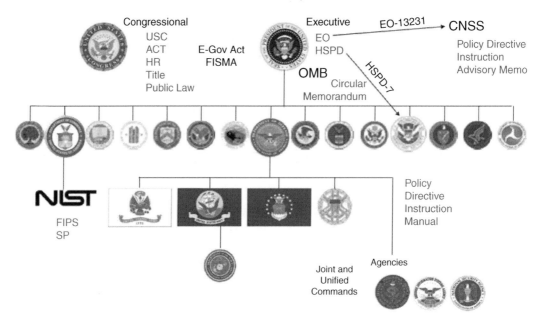

FIGURE 6.1   General statutory and regulatory agency structure.

management, information management, and regulatory policy, to include management of information systems and their security.

NIST

National Institute of Standards and Technology (NIST), an agency of the US Department of Commerce, has statutory responsibility to ensure that standards and measures are developed to improve performance, and is *charged by law* with responsibility for information security standards, metrics, tests, and various other means to support Executive Branch agencies' missions. NIST issues Special Publications (SP), Federal Information Processing Standards (FIPS), Information Technology Laboratory (ITL) Bulletins, NIST Interagency Reports (NISTIR), and other guidance.

CNSS

Formerly known as NSTISSC, the Committee on National Security Systems (CNSS) provides a participative forum to examine national policy and promulgates direction, operational procedures and instructions (CNSSI), and other forms of authoritative guidance for national security systems. The CNSS is composed of 21 agencies with the US government with NSS systems and is chaired by the Department of Defense (DOD) CIO.

NSA

1. The National Security Agency (NSA) is the US government's formal cryptological organization and is part of the US DOD.

2. The NSA has responsibility for ensuring that all cryptographic methods and systems used to protect US federal government (USFG) information and systems are sufficiently strong, for penetrating adversary systems and codes, and to ensure that all national security information is protected appropriately whether in transit or at rest.

NIAP

National Information Assurance Partnership (NIAP) is an initiative partnership between the NIST (Commerce) and the NSA (DOD) to evaluate and attempt to meet the needs and requirements of IT/IA product producers and consumers to evaluate functionality and pedigree.

DHS

The US Department of Homeland Security is responsible for overseeing the protection of the .gov domain and for providing assistance and expertise to private sector owners and operators. The US Computer Emergency Response Team (US-CERT) is an agency within DHS. The DHS agency's work benefits the information technology community and the public at large. DHS plays a key role in securing the federal government's civilian cyber networks and helping to secure the broader cyber ecosystem through:

- Partnerships with owners and operators of critical infrastructure such as financial systems, chemical plants, and water and electric utilities
- The release of actionable cyber alerts
- Investigations and arrests of cybercriminals
- Education about how the public can stay safe online

DOD

The DOD is the US governmental agency responsible for the security of the nation and its allies. It has a long history of developing and providing security to the United States, its citizens, and the general public in the United States and overseas. IT security has always maintained a high profile within DOD and continues so today with many security programs, processes, procedures, and guidance documents. NSA, Defense Intelligence Agency (DIA), and all of the military services are all part of DOD and follow these directives, instructions, and regulations.

INDIVIDUAL ROLES

The primary individual roles, as defined in SP 800-37, rev. 1, are as follows:

- Authorizing official/DAA
- Authorizing official designated representative
- Chief information officer
- Senior agency information security officer

- Information system owner
- Information system security officer
- Program manager (PM)
- Security control assessor
- User representative

System Owner

The *information system owner* is an organizational official responsible for the procurement, development, integration, modification, operation, maintenance, and disposal of an information system. The system owner is the singular primary role within the RMF. This role has primary responsibilities for 4.5 of the 6 steps within the RMF and is the lead role for the entire process. DOD has defined this role in DODI 8510.01 at the PM or systems manager (SM) level within the DOD acquisition process.

The primary objectives of the system owner are to:

- Procure, develop, integrate, modify, operate, or maintain an information system
- Prepare the system security plan and conduct risk assessment
- Inform agency officials of the need for certification and accreditation
- Ensure appropriate resources are available
- Provide necessary system-related documentation
- Prepare plan of action and milestones to reduce or eliminate vulnerabilities in the information system
- Assemble final accreditation package and submit to authorizing official
- Also act as user representative – in RMF arena

The information system owner is responsible for addressing the operational interests of the user community (i.e., users who require access to the information system to satisfy mission, business, or operational requirements) and for ensuring compliance with information security requirements.

In coordination with the information system security officer, the information system owner is responsible for the development and maintenance of the security plan and ensures that the system is deployed and operated in accordance with the agreed-upon security controls.

In coordination with the information owner/steward, the information system owner is also responsible for deciding who has access to the system (and with what types of privileges or access rights) and ensures that system users and support personnel receive the requisite security training (e.g., instruction in rules of behavior).

Based on guidance from the authorizing official, the information system owner informs appropriate organizational officials of the need to conduct the security authorization, ensures that the necessary resources are available for the effort, and provides the required information system access, information, and documentation to the security control assessor. The information system owner receives the security assessment results from the security control assessor. After taking appropriate steps to reduce or eliminate vulnerabilities, the information system owner assembles the authorization package and submits the package to the authorizing official or the authorizing official designated representative for adjudication.

Authorizing Official

The *authorizing official* is a senior official or executive with the authority to formally assume responsibility for operating an information system at an acceptable level of risk to organizational operations and assets, individuals, other organizations, and the nation.

Authorizing officials typically have budgetary oversight for an information system *or* are responsible for the mission and/or business operations supported by the system.

Through the security authorization process, authorizing officials are *accountable* for the security risks associated with information system operations.

The primary objectives of the authorizing official are to:

- Executive with authority and ability to evaluate the security risks
- Has either IT business oversight or budgetary responsibility
- Balance cost/benefit
- Must be government employee
- Make accreditation decisions
- Review security status reports from continuous monitoring operations
- Probably initiate reaccreditation actions based on status reports

Accordingly, authorizing officials are in management positions with a level of authority commensurate with understanding and accepting such information system-related security risks. Authorizing officials also approve security plans, memorandums of agreement or understanding, and plans of action and milestones and determine whether significant changes in the information systems or environments of operation require reauthorization. They can deny authorization to operate an information system or if the system is operational, halt operations, if unacceptable risks exist.

Authorizing officials coordinate their activities with the risk executive (function), chief information officer, senior information security officer, common control providers, information system owners, information system security officers, security control assessors, and other interested parties during the security authorization process. With the increasing complexity of missions/ business processes, partnership arrangements, and the use of external/shared services, it is possible that a particular information system may involve multiple authorizing officials. If so, agreements are established among the authorizing officials and documented in the security plan.

Authorizing officials are responsible for ensuring that all activities and functions associated with security authorization that are delegated to authorizing official designated representatives are carried out. The role of authorizing official has inherent US government authority and is assigned to government personnel only.

Information System Security Officer

The *information system security officer* is an individual responsible for ensuring that the appropriate operational security posture is maintained for an information system and as such works in close collaboration with the information system owner.

The primary objectives of the information system security officer are to:

- Be primary advisor to the system owner on security matters
- Manage the security aspects of the information system

- Assist the system owner:
  - Develop and enforce security policies for the information system.
  - Manage and control changes to the information system and assess the security impacts of those changes.

The information system security officer also serves as a principal advisor on all matters, technical and otherwise, involving the security of an information system.

The information system security officer should have the detailed knowledge and expertise required to manage the security aspects of an information system and, in many organizations, is assigned responsibility for the day-to-day security operations of a system. This responsibility may also include, but is not limited to, physical and environmental protection, personnel security, incident handling, and security training and awareness.

The information system security officer may be called upon to assist in the development of the security policies and procedures and to ensure compliance with those policies and procedures.

In close coordination with the information system owner, the information system security officer often plays an active role in the monitoring of a system and its environment of operation to include developing and updating the security plan, managing and controlling changes to the system, and assessing the security impact of those changes.

Information System Security Engineer

The *information system security engineer* is an *individual, group, or organization* responsible for conducting information system security engineering activities.

Information system security engineering is a process that captures and refines information security requirements and ensures that the requirements are effectively integrated into information technology component products and information systems through purposeful security architecting, design, development, and configuration.

The primary objectives of the information system security engineer are to:

- Work as part of the development team
- Employ and install security control best practices
- Coordinate security-related activities:
  - Equivalent to DIACAP Information Assurance Office (IAO)

Information system security engineers are an integral part of the development team (e.g., integrated project team), designing and developing organizational information systems or upgrading legacy systems. They employ best practices when implementing security controls within an information system including software engineering methodologies, system/security engineering principles, secure design, secure architecture, and secure coding techniques.

System security engineers coordinate their security-related activities with information security architects, senior information security officers, information system owners, common control providers, and information system security officers.

Security Architect

The *information security architect* is an *individual, group, or organization* responsible for ensuring that the information security requirements necessary to protect the organization's core missions and business processes are adequately addressed in all aspects of enterprise architecture including reference models, segment and solution architectures, and the resulting information systems supporting those missions and business processes.

The primary objectives of the information security architect are to:

- Adequately addresses security requirements in enterprise architecture:
  - Reference models
  - Segment and solution architectures
  - Resulting information systems
- Act as a liaison between the enterprise architect and information system security engineer
- Act as an advisor to senior officials on following topics:
  - System boundaries
  - Assessing severity of deficiencies
  - POAMs
  - Risk mitigation approaches
  - Security alerts

The information security architect serves as the liaison between the enterprise architect and the information system security engineer and also coordinates with information system owners, common control providers, and information system security officers on the allocation of security controls as system-specific, hybrid, or common controls.

In addition, information security architects, in close coordination with information system security officers, advise authorizing officials, chief information officers, senior information security officers, and the risk executive (function), on a range of security-related issues including, for example, establishing information system boundaries, assessing the severity of weaknesses and deficiencies in the information system, plans of action and milestones, risk mitigation approaches, security alerts, and potential adverse effects of identified vulnerabilities.

Common Control Provider

The *common control provider* is an individual, group, or organization responsible for the development, implementation, assessment, and monitoring of common controls (i.e., security controls inherited by information systems)

Common control providers are responsible for:

- Documenting the organization-identified common controls in a *security plan* (or equivalent document prescribed by the organization)
- Ensuring that required assessments of common controls are carried out by qualified assessors with an appropriate level of independence defined by the organization
- Documenting assessment findings in a *security assessment report*
- Appending a *plan of action and milestones* for any controls having weaknesses or deficiencies
- Ensuring that common controls within and across systems are properly documented and that documentation and communication are continuous

Security plans, security assessment reports, and plans of action and milestones for common controls (or a summary of such information) are made available to information system owners *inheriting* those controls after the information is reviewed and approved by the senior official or executive with oversight responsibility for those controls.

Authorizing Official Designated Representative

The *authorizing official designated representative* is an organizational official that acts on behalf of an authorizing official to coordinate and conduct the required day-to-day activities associated with the security authorization process.

The primary objectives of the authorizing official designated representative are to:

- Selected by the authorizing official
- Make certain decisions:
  - Planning and sourcing of the security certification and accreditation activities
  - Acceptance of the system security plan
  - Determination of risk to agency operations, assets, and individuals
- Prepare accreditation decision letter
- Obtain authorizing official's signature on appropriate documents

Authorizing official designated representatives can be empowered by authorizing officials to make certain decisions with regard to the planning and resourcing of the security authorization process, approval of the security plan, approval and monitoring of the implementation of plans of action and milestones, and the assessment and/or determination of risk.

The designated representative may also be called upon to prepare the final authorization package, obtain the authorizing official's signature on the authorization decision document, and transmit the authorization package to appropriate organizational officials.

The only activity that cannot be delegated to the designated representative by the authorizing official is the authorization decision and signing of the associated authorization decision document (i.e., the acceptance of risk to organizational operations and assets, individuals, other organizations, and the nation).

Information Owner/Steward

The *information owner/steward* is an organizational official with statutory, management, or operational authority for specified information and the responsibility for establishing the policies and procedures governing its generation, collection, processing, dissemination, and disposal.

The information owner:

- Is an agency official with statutory or operational authority
- Is responsible for establishing rules for appropriate use of the information
- May, or may not, be the information system owner
- Can also be known as the data owner in the IC arena

In information-sharing environments, the information owner/steward is responsible for establishing the rules for appropriate use and protection of the subject information (e.g., rules of behavior) and retains that responsibility even when the information is shared with or provided to other organizations. The owner/steward of the information processed, stored, or transmitted by an information system may or may not be the same as the system owner. A single information system may contain information from multiple information owners/stewards. Information owners/stewards provide input to information system owners regarding the security requirements and security controls for the systems where the information is processed, stored, or transmitted.

Risk Executive (Function)

The risk executive (function) is an individual or group within an organization that helps to ensure that:

- Risk-related considerations for individual information systems, to include authorization decisions, are viewed from an organization-wide perspective with regard to the overall strategic goals and objectives of the organization in carrying out its core missions and business functions.
- Managing information system-related security risks is consistent across the organization, reflects organizational risk tolerance, and is considered along with other types of risks in order to ensure mission/business success. The risk executive (function) coordinates with the senior leadership of an organization to:
  - Provide a comprehensive, organization-wide, holistic approach for addressing risk – an approach that provides a greater understanding of the integrated operations of the organization
  - Develop a risk management strategy for the organization providing a strategic view of information security-related risks with regard to the organization as a whole
  - Facilitate the sharing of risk-related information among authorizing officials and other senior leaders within the organization
  - Provide oversight for all risk management-related activities across the organization (e.g., security categorizations) to help ensure consistent and effective risk acceptance decisions
  - Ensure that authorization decisions consider all factors necessary for mission and business success
  - Provide an organization-wide forum to consider all sources of risk (including aggregated risk) to organizational operations and assets, individuals, other organizations, and the nation
  - Promote cooperation and collaboration among authorizing officials to include authorization actions requiring shared responsibility
  - Ensure that the shared responsibility for supporting organizational mission/business functions using external providers of information and services receives the needed visibility and is elevated to the appropriate decision-making authorities
  - Identify the organizational risk posture based on the aggregated risk to information from the operation and use of the information systems for which the organization is responsible

The risk executive (function) presumes neither a specific organizational structure nor formal responsibility assigned to any one individual or group within the organization. The head of the agency/organization may choose to retain the risk executive (function) or to delegate the function to another official or group (e.g., an executive leadership council). The risk executive (function) has inherent US government authority and is assigned to *government personnel only*.

User Representative

User representatives:

- Represent the operational interests of the user community
- Identify mission and operational requirements:
  - Serve as liaisons for the user community
  - Assist in the security certification and accreditation
- Comply with the security requirements and security controls
- Are identified in DOD, CNSS, and original 800-37 documents, but not in 800-37, rev. 1

Agency Head

The *head of agency* (or chief executive officer) is the highest-level senior official or executive within an organization with the overall responsibility to provide information security protections commensurate with the risk and magnitude of harm (i.e., impact) to organizational operations and assets, individuals, other organizations, and the nation resulting from unauthorized access, use, disclosure, disruption, modification, or destruction of:

1. Information collected or maintained by or on behalf of the agency
2. Information systems used or operated by an agency or by a contractor of an agency or other organization on behalf of an agency

Agency heads are also responsible for ensuring that:

1. Information security management processes are integrated with strategic and operational planning processes.
2. Senior officials within the organization provide information security for the information and information systems that support the operations and assets under their control.
3. The organization has trained personnel sufficient to assist in complying with the information security requirements in related legislation, policies, directives, instructions, standards, and guidelines.

Through the development and implementation of strong policies, the head of agency establishes the organizational commitment to information security and the actions required to effectively manage risk and protect the core missions and business functions being carried out by the organization. The head of agency establishes appropriate accountability for information security and provides active support and oversight of monitoring and improvement for the information security program. Senior leadership commitment to information security establishes a level of due diligence within the organization that promotes a climate for mission and business success.

Agency head requirements from A-130 and FISMA are as follows:

- Plan for adequate security.
- Assign responsibilities.
- Review security controls.
- Authorize processing.

Security Control Assessor

The *security control assessor* is an *individual, group, or organization* responsible for conducting a comprehensive assessment of the management, operational, and technical security controls employed within or inherited by an information system to determine the overall effectiveness of the controls (i.e., the extent to which the controls are implemented correctly, operating as intended, and producing the desired outcome with respect to meeting the security requirements for the system).

The primary objectives of the security control assessor are to:

- Provide an independent assessment
- Assess the security controls:
  - Implemented correctly
  - Operating as intended
  - Producing the desired outcome
- Provide recommended corrective actions

Security control assessors also provide an assessment of the severity of weaknesses or deficiencies discovered in the information system and its environment of operation and recommend corrective actions to address identified vulnerabilities.

In addition to these responsibilities, security control assessors prepare the final security assessment report containing the results and findings from the assessment.

Prior to initiating the security control assessment, an assessor conducts an assessment of the security plan to help ensure that the plan provides a set of security controls for the information system that meet the stated security requirements.

The required level of assessor independence is determined by the specific conditions of the security control assessment. For example, when the assessment is conducted in support of an authorization decision or ongoing authorization, the authorizing official makes an explicit determination of the degree of independence required in accordance with federal policies, directives, standards, and guidelines.

Assessor independence is an important factor in:

- Preserving the impartial and unbiased nature of the assessment process
- Determining the credibility of the security assessment results
- Ensuring that the authorizing official receives the most objective information possible in order to make an informed, risk-based authorization decision

The information system owner and common control provider rely on the security expertise and the technical judgment of the assessor to:

- Assess the security controls employed within and inherited by the information system using assessment procedures specified in the security assessment plan

- Provide specific recommendations on how to correct weaknesses or deficiencies in the controls and address identified vulnerabilities

This role has been named many different titles such as:

1. DIACAP Validator
2. Certifying Agent
3. Certifying Authority
4. System Certifier

Senior Information Security Officer

The *senior information security officer* is an organizational official responsible for:

- Carrying out the chief information officer security responsibilities under FISMA
- Serving as the primary liaison for the chief information officer to the organization's authorizing officials, information system owners, common control providers, and information system security officers

The senior information security officer:

- Possesses professional qualifications, including training and experience, required to administer the information security program functions
- Maintains information security duties as a primary responsibility
- Heads an office with the mission and resources to assist the organization in achieving more secure information and information systems in accordance with the requirements in FISMA

The senior information security officer (or supporting staff members) may also serve as authorizing official designated representatives or security control assessors. The role of senior information security officer has inherent US government authority and is assigned to government personnel only.

Chief Information Officer

The *chief information officer* is an organizational official responsible for:

- Designating a senior information security officer
- Developing and maintaining information security policies, procedures, and control techniques to address all applicable requirements
- Overseeing personnel with significant responsibilities for information security and ensuring that the personnel are adequately trained
- Assisting senior organizational officials concerning their security responsibilities, and, in coordination with other senior officials, reporting annually to the head of the federal agency on the overall effectiveness of the organization's information security program, including progress of remedial actions

The chief information officer, with the support of the risk executive (function) and the senior information security officer, works closely with authorizing officials and their designated representatives to help ensure that:

- An organization-wide information security program is effectively implemented resulting in adequate security for all organizational information systems and environments of operation for those systems.
- Information security considerations are integrated into programming/planning/ budgeting cycles, enterprise architectures, and acquisition/system development life cycles.
- Information systems are covered by approved security plans and are authorized to operate.
- Information security-related activities required across the organization are accomplished in an efficient, cost-effective, and timely manner.
- There is centralized reporting of appropriate information security-related activities.

The chief information officer and authorizing officials also determine, based on organizational priorities, the appropriate allocation of resources dedicated to the protection of the information systems supporting the organization's missions and business functions. For selected information systems, the chief information officer may be designated as an authorizing official or a coauthorizing official with other senior organizational officials. The role of chief information officer has inherent US government authority and is assigned to government personnel only.

DOD ROLES

There are some differences in the roles and responsibilities between the NIST-defined roles and the DOD-implemented roles under SP 800-37 and the DODI 8510 regulation. These differences include the DOD-defined roles of Principal Accrediting Authority (PAA), Information Assurance Manager (IAM), and IAO as reflected in Fig. 6.2 from 8510.01.

DoDI 8510.01 DIACAP	NIST SP 800-37, revision 1, security authorization
Heads of the DoD components	Head of agency (CEO)
Principal Accrediting Authority (PAA)	Risk executive (function)
Chief Information Officer (CIO)	CIO
No equivalent	Information owner/steward
Senior information assurance officer (SIAO)	Senior information security officer (SISO)
Principal Accrediting Authority (PAA)	Authorizing official (AO)
Designated accrediting authority (DAA)	
No equivalent	Authorizing official designated representative
PM/SM	Common control provider
PM/SM	Information system owner (ISO)
Information Assurance Manager (IAM)	Information system security officer (ISSO)
IAO	
No equivalent	Information security architect
IAO	Information system security engineer (ISSE)
Certifying Authority (CA)	Security control assessor (SCA)
Validator	
User representative (UR)	No equivalent
Certification and accreditation (C&A)	Assess and authorize (A&A)

FIGURE 6.2 DODI 8510.01 roles and acronyms compared with NIST SP 800-37.

SECTION II

Introduction

WHAT IS AN ASSESSMENT?

An assessment of a system or application is the process of reviewing, testing, and evaluating the components, documentation, and all parameters of this system or application for the purpose of ensuring it is as secure as possible, within an organization's risk tolerance, while it is operational and being utilized for its intended purpose.

As SP 800-53A on page 9 says, "An assessment procedure consists of a set of assessment *objectives*, each with an associated set of potential assessment *methods* and assessment *objects*. An assessment objective includes a set of *determination statements* related to the particular security or privacy control under assessment. The determination statements are linked to the content of the security or privacy control (i.e., the security/privacy control functionality) to ensure traceability of assessment results back to the fundamental control requirements. The application of an assessment procedure to a security or privacy control produces assessment *findings*. These findings reflect, or are subsequently used, to help determine the overall effectiveness of the security or privacy control." This results in determining if the control is, as SP 800-53A points out:

1. Implemented correctly
2. Operating as intended
3. Producing the desired outcome in relation to the security requirements of the system or application under review

Assessment *objects* identify the specific *items being assessed* and include *specifications, mecha-nisms, activities,* and *individuals.*

1. *Specifications* are the document-based *artifacts* (e.g., policies, procedures, plans, system security and privacy requirements, functional specifications, architectural designs) associated with an information system, in other words – the documentation.
2. *Mechanisms* are the specific hardware, software, or firmware *safeguards and countermeasures* employed within an information system, in other words – the technical controls.
3. *Activities* are the specific protection-related *actions* supporting an information system that involve people (e.g., conducting system backup operations, monitoring network traffic, exercising a contingency plan), in other words – the processes.
4. *Individuals,* or groups of individuals, are *people* applying the specifications, mechanisms, or activities described above, in other words – the people.

The entire point of these various assessment areas and their coverage of the system and network under review is to provide assessment evidence that the decision makers can use to make their operational decisions from a viewpoint of trustworthiness as found in the following figure from SP 800-53A:

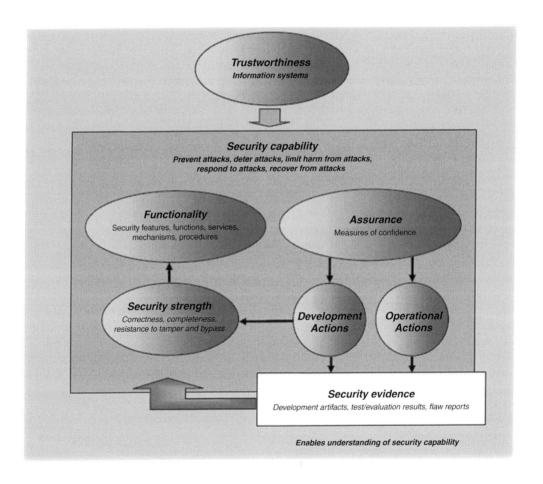

EXPERIENCES AND THE PROCESS

I have conducted and overseen over 30 assessment efforts for 11 different agencies and 4 commercial corporations during the past 4 years. There are always areas for improvement for each system. I view this as my job to determine if the system is really as secure as it can get, to make sure all users are reasonably safe and secure, and to make an analysis of the organizational and management policies and procedures to secure the national assets for the governmental agency that has requested our services. My assessment team and I have reviewed large-scale data centers with many highly sensitive government systems installed, small systems for federal microagencies with less than 100 employees, a single server web-based system with public access information, and just about every type of system in between.

Assessment Process

The process I have developed over the years of conducting assessments, validations, and audits in support of authorization efforts has produced multiple ATOs for each and every effort I have been engaged for both contractually as an independent validator and governmentally while working for federal agencies. The typical steps which I follow for an assessment when I conduct a review cover all of the areas defined in this handbook, defined by the SP 800-37, rev. 1, process and usually produce SARs with defined areas of improvement for the organization to mitigate and repair, along with efforts of remediation which were performed and successfully completed during the assessment process. The standard steps are as follows:

1. *Gather documents about system*: The initial area for review I always start with is the already existing documentation for the system or application under test. These documents should provide the core areas for scrutiny and evaluation.
2. *Review statutory and regulatory requirements*: In the US governmental process, every system must conform to various statutory (law) and regulatory (policies and regulations) requirements, usually based on the information types used, processed, or held by the system and the system's mission. Therefore, I look for areas of both compliance conformance and substantive agreement between the system, its documents, and the external requirements.
3. *Conduct "GAP" analysis (15 steps)*: As discussed and defined in Chapter 8, I conduct the "GAP" analysis for all relevant system documents and supporting documentation. The steps are defined in that chapter.
4. *Conduct risk assessment per SP 800-30*: NIST put out the basic guide for risk assessments, SP 800-30, many years ago and I have adopted the use of that process in all of our endeavors and it has proven to be a trustworthy and successful methodology for conducting risk assessments under all circumstances where I have applied it.
5. *Visit site – conduct preassessment*: The first visit to the system location is usually conducted as part of the standard governmental project "kickoff" meeting event. We gather the documents during this process if they have not already been delivered to us beforehand.
   a. *Status*: System status, project status, and mission status are all areas for discussion during this initial visit. Equipment status is a primary focus during this step so we can be prepared for any potential area of concern or suspicion.

b. *Expectations*: During this visit, we conduct some expectation management with both the staff and the on-site management about our process, work efforts during the actual assessment visit, and our interchanges with the on-site personnel.

6. *Build SAP and ROE*: As part of the standard preparation for conducting an assessment, I will develop the Security Assessment Plan (SAP) which defines what actual steps are to be conducted during the assessment, what tools will be used, and what review techniques with what rigor to be applied will be utilized during the conduct of the actual on-site assessment.

There will be developed as part of this effort a document known as the Rules of Engagement (ROE) which defines the actual steps to be performed for the entire assessment, including any outside testing, interview conduct, and inspections as required by the organization. This ROE is a legal-type document which needs approval at the highest level possible above the AO since it can include penetration testing parameters and outside engagement events. I have often gotten this ROE signed by the organizational CIO or Chief Information Security Officer (CISO), whereas the SAP often needs only the AO signature for final approval.

7. *Submit SAP and ROE for approval and acceptance*: Once these two documents are finalized, I submit them to the contracting officer, if on contract to perform these activities, and they then route them for approval and signatures. I do *not* start the actual assessment visit until I have received the signed approved documents back through official means. Since these are legal documents for liability purposes I will not start the on-site engagement until I have these signed documents literally in hand.

8. *Conduct assessment*: Once the SAP and ROE are approved, I schedule the on-site visit to conduct the actual assessment activities. During this time I and my assessment team prepare for the visit by refamiliarizing ourselves with the tools of the trade, as well as reviewing the documentation for the system under review in order to properly conduct the interviews and examinations.

a. *On-site visit*: The on-site visit usually will start with an "in-briefing" meeting with the management of the location wherein we discuss expectations for the visit, reconfirm the interview scheduling, and introduce the team to the site staff.

  - *Interview key personnel*: The interviews are conducted with key operational personnel for the system under review, the facilities manager for the location, the security personnel for both the location and the system under review, the system owner, if on-site, the system administration staff members for the location and the system under review, as well as any developers associated with the system under review.

  - *Examine system – get demo if possible*: I will obtain a demonstration of the system from the staff in order to observe the processing, security controls in action as well as the input and output activities for the system. I will have the system run through its normal processing activities while watching it perform each action step. This allows me to see the security controls for Access Control, identification and authentication, system integrity, and system and communications protection in operation to verify their activities.

  - *Conduct a "security walk-through" inspection*: Invariably I get the site facility manager to escort me and I will conduct a security "walk-through" inspection of the facility the system is housed in to include observing the physical security controls, checking out the fire suppression and detection controls in the facility, the HVAC system and its controls, and the utilities connected to the facility and their physical access. I will also observe the backup power capability of the location employed within the system. All of these inspections will verify physical and environmental, maintenance, media protection, and contingency planning controls for the system.

- *Test system with tools as defined in SAP*: The actual automated testing is conducted on the system with various tools and techniques to obtain evidence of compliance and security control configurations. Most, if not all, of the vulnerability scanners available produce results showing compliance with operating system configurations and patches loaded on the system. We will utilize various scan tools for the components of the system as defined in the SAP, such as database scanners, network mappers, vulnerability scanners, website scanning tools, and other specialized tools if necessary. Other automated tools will also be used for various tests to include file integrity checkers, wireless detection tools, if needed, and, if defined in the SAP and ROE, penetration testing tools to check the various security controls sets including Access Control, identification and authentication, system and communications protection, audit and accounting, and system integrity controls.

9. *Initial analysis of results*: On completion of the tool(s) running through their operations, I review the results with our assessment team for identification of high- or medium-impact deficiencies or weaknesses. Additionally, we review the outputs from the test to ensure successful completion of the testing.

10. *Provide customer/client with Remediation Report for action*: Each automated tool used provides a method for immediate identification of problems and issues discovered during the tool operation and we take this data and provide it to the system administration staff either during the testing or right after completion in what I term a "Remediation Report" to allow the on-site staff to correct any deficiency or weakness of significant impact as soon as possible. Often the automated tool will produce results which need interpretation and evaluation since the tool often does not know which areas are externally mitigated. This results in what are known as "false-positive" results which require explanation and then removal from the final report.

11. *Receive proof of remediation effort artifact evidence*: On remediation, the on-site staff for the system under review provides the assessment team either the opportunity to rerun the automated tools to verify repair or the proof of remediation through the use of "screen shots" or output reports from the devices or machines in question. These documents and artifacts then get attached to or included in the SAR.

12. *Build SAR*: We start the development of the SAR during the testing phase by reviewing the examination and interview results and building the results from those parts of the evaluation. Once the testing phase is completed and our initial Remediation Report is delivered, we include the results of the scans and other tests in the SAR.
Following the template we have developed for the SAR, all areas are included, along with a full control-by-control results table in the SAR.

13. *Review SAR with customer for additional action items*: When the initial SAR is completed, we conduct a review of the preliminary results with the client to point out any additional areas or items which can be fixed, repaired, or remediated before the final delivery. The client often then addresses some or all of these areas and provides additional supporting documentation or proof of remediation and we include that in the final SAR.

14. *Develop final SAR*: Once all the reviews and discussions are completed, I complete the SAR in its final version and prepare the briefing for the AO to go with the report.

15. *Develop Certification Letter*: On full completion of the SAR and revisions to the SSP as the result of the assessment, I often am asked to complete a Certification Letter to the AO stating the results of the assessment and my opinion on the risks of the system and my recommendation for authorization.

16. *Deliver SAR and Certification Letter to system owner and client*: This is the final step of the process where I deliver the final SAR, final version of the SSP, and the Recommendation Letter to the AO and to the system owner for action.

Assessment Process

FOCUS

In order to conduct an assessment evaluation for a system or application, the focus initially needs to be on what areas are of highest impact, highest value, and highest volatility. Once that has been determined, the focus shifts to the rest of the system or application in order to cover all possible areas of impact since in the security arena, any method of attack or ingress into the system is possible today. As SP 800-115 tells us, some assessments focus on verifying that a particular security control (or set of controls) meets requirements, while other assessments are intended to identify, validate, and assess a system's exploitable security weaknesses. Assessments are also performed to increase an organization's ability to maintain a proactive computer network defense. Assessments are not meant to take the place of implementing security controls and maintaining system security. SP 800-53A gives some more guidance on the focus and process as follows:

Building an effective assurance case (An assurance case is a body of evidence organized into an argument demonstrating that some claim about an information system holds (i.e., is assured). An assurance case is needed when it is important to show that a system exhibits some complex property such as safety, security, or reliability.) for security and privacy control effectiveness is a process that involves:

(i) Compiling evidence from a variety of activities conducted during the system development life cycle that the controls employed in the information system are implemented correctly, operating as intended, and producing the desired outcome with respect to meeting the security and privacy requirements of the system and the organization; and

(ii) Presenting this evidence in a manner that decision makers are able to use effectively in making risk-based decisions about the operation or use of the system.

The evidence described above comes from the implementation of the security and privacy controls in the information system and inherited by the system (i.e., common controls) and from the assessments of that implementation. Ideally, the assessor is building on previously developed materials that started with the specification of the organization's information security and privacy needs and was further developed during the design, development, and implementation of the information system. These materials, developed while implementing security and privacy throughout the life cycle of the information system, provide the initial evidence for an assurance case.

Assessors obtain the required evidence during the assessment process to allow the appropriate organizational officials to make objective determinations about the effectiveness of the security and privacy controls and the overall security and privacy state of the information system. The assessment evidence needed to make such determinations can be obtained from a variety of sources including, for example, information technology product and system assessments and, in the case of privacy assessments, privacy compliance documentation such as Privacy Impact Assessments and Privacy Act System of Record Notices. Product assessments (also known as product testing, evaluation, and validation) are typically conducted by independent, third-party testing organizations. These assessments examine the security and privacy functions of products and established configuration settings. Assessments can be conducted to demonstrate compliance to industry, national, or international information security standards, privacy standards embodied in applicable laws and policies, and developer/vendor claims. Since many information technology products are assessed by commercial testing organizations and then subsequently deployed in millions of information systems, these types of assessments can be carried out at a greater level of depth and provide deeper insights into the security and privacy capabilities of the particular products."[1]

The specialized focus from an assessor is needed when the system under test or the application in question is in a high volatile environment, has just remediated security issues which have repaired, or requires an independent verification and validation review for further operations on a federal network.

The SP 800-115 guide for technical assessments provides some focus for all testing events, too. "To accomplish technical security assessments and ensure that technical security testing and examinations provide maximum value, NIST recommends that organizations:

- **Establish an information security assessment policy**. This identifies the organization's requirements for executing assessments, and provides accountability for the appropriate individuals to ensure assessments are conducted in accordance with these requirements. Topics that an assessment policy should address include the organizational requirements with which assessments must comply, roles and responsibilities, adherence to an established assessment methodology, assessment frequency, and documentation requirements.
- **Implement a repeatable and documented assessment methodology**. This provides consistency and structure to assessments, expedites the transition of new assessment staff, and addresses resource constraints associated with assessments. Using such a methodology enables organizations to maximize the value of assessments while minimizing possible risks introduced by certain technical assessment techniques. These risks can range from not gathering sufficient information on the organization's security posture for fear of impacting system functionality to affecting the system or network availability by executing techniques without the proper safeguards in place. Processes that minimize risk caused by certain assessment techniques include using skilled assessors, developing comprehensive assessment plans, logging assessor activities, performing testing off-hours, and conducting tests on duplicates of production systems (e.g., development systems). Organizations need to determine the level of risk they are willing to accept for each assessment, and tailor their approaches accordingly.
- **Determine the objectives of each security assessment, and tailor the approach accordingly**. Security assessments have specific objectives, acceptable levels of risk, and available resources. Because no individual technique provides a comprehensive picture of an organization's security when executed alone, organizations should use a combination of techniques. This also helps organizations to limit risk and resource usage.
- **Analyze findings, and develop risk mitigation techniques to address weaknesses**. To ensure that security assessments provide their ultimate value, organizations

[1]SP 800-53A, rev. 4, IPD, p. 8.

should conduct root cause analysis upon completion of an assessment to enable the translation of findings into actionable mitigation techniques. These results may indicate that organizations should address not only technical weaknesses, but weaknesses in organizational processes and procedures as well."[2]

As we begin the process of developing our assessment plans and procedures, it is now appropriate to seek guidance on methods, techniques, process flows, and objectives for our security testing, evaluations, and assessments.

GUIDANCE

Within the framework of the RMF process, SP 800-53A provides the specialized guidance and process flow for conducting the actual test and assessment events on each security control implemented in the system or application under evaluation. RMF step 4 – assessment – is the directed step within the RMF (SP 800-37, rev. 1) that provides the general guidance for conducting this step. Specialized assessment methodologies and techniques for testing and examining network-based processes and nonspecific security requirements are defined and explained in SP 800-115. The listing of the tasks for this assessment phase given in the next subsections is from SP 800-53A with some additional areas of focus and detail provided as we start the assessment activities.

SP 800-53A

See Fig. 7.1.

An assessment procedure consists of a set of assessment *objectives*, each with an associated set of potential assessment *methods* and assessment *objects*. An assessment objective includes a set of *determination statements* related to the particular security or privacy control under assessment. The determination statements are linked to the content of the security or privacy control (i.e., the security/privacy control functionality) to ensure traceability of assessment results back to the fundamental control requirements. The application of an assessment procedure to a security or privacy control produces assessment *findings*. These findings reflect, or are subsequently used, to help determine the overall effectiveness of the security or privacy control.

Assessment objects identify the specific items being assessed and include *specifications, mechanisms, activities,* and *individuals*. Specifications are the document-based artifacts (e.g., policies, procedures, plans, system security and privacy requirements, functional specifications, architectural designs) associated with an information system. Mechanisms are the specific hardware, software, or firmware safeguards and countermeasures employed within an information system. Activities are the specific protection-related actions supporting an information system that involve people (e.g., conducting system backup operations, monitoring network traffic, exercising a contingency plan). Individuals, or groups of individuals, are people applying the specifications, mechanisms, or activities described above.

Assessment methods define the nature of the assessor actions and include *examine, interview,* and *test*. The *examine* method is the process of reviewing, inspecting, observing, studying, or analyzing one or more assessment objects (i.e., specifications, mechanisms, or activities). The purpose of the examine method is to facilitate assessor understanding, achieve clarification, or obtain evidence. The *interview* method is the process of holding discussions with individuals or groups of individuals within an organization to once again, facilitate assessor understanding, achieve clarification, or obtain evidence. The *test* method is the process of

---

[2]SP 800-115, p. ES-1, ES-2.

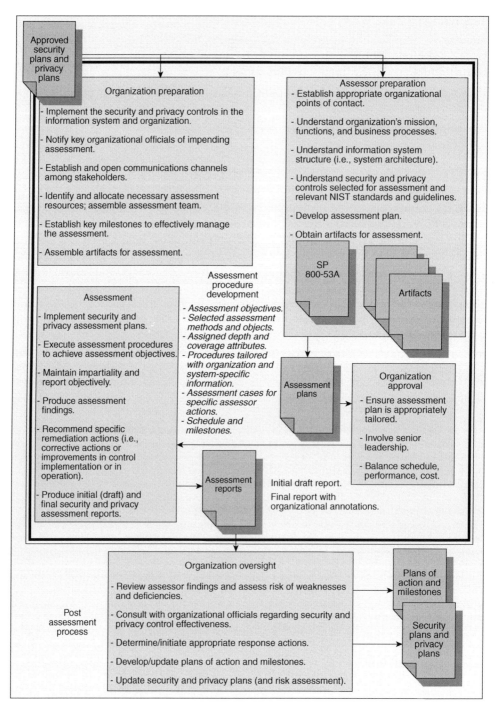

Approved security plans and privacy plans

Organization preparation

- Implement the security and privacy controls in the information system and organization.
- Notify key organizational officials of impending assessment.
- Establish and open communications channels among stakeholders.
- Identify and allocate necessary assessment resources; assemble assessment team.
- Establish key milestones to effectively manage the assessment.
- Assemble artifacts for assessment.

Assessor preparation
- Establish appropriate organizational points of contact.
- Understand organization's mission, functions, and business processes.
- Understand information system structure (i.e., system architecture).
- Understand security and privacy controls selected for assessment and relevant NIST standards and guidelines.
- Develop assessment plan.
- Obtain artifacts for assessment.

SP 800-53A

Artifacts

Assessment procedure development
- *Assessment objectives.*
- *Selected assessment methods and objects.*
- *Assigned depth and coverage attributes.*
- *Procedures tailored with organization and system-specific information.*
- *Assessment cases for specific assessor actions.*
- *Schedule and milestones.*

Assessment

- Implement security and privacy assessment plans.
- Execute assessment procedures to achieve assessment objectives.
- Maintain impartiality and report objectively.
- Produce assessment findings.
- Recommend specific remediation actions (i.e., corrective actions or improvements in control implementation or in operation).
- Produce initial (draft) and final security and privacy assessment reports.

Assessment plans

Organization approval
- Ensure assessment plan is appropriately tailored.
- Involve senior leadership.
- Balance schedule, performance, cost.

Assessment reports

Initial draft report.

Final report with organizational annotations.

Organization oversight
- Review assessor findings and assess risk of weaknesses and deficiencies.
- Consult with organizational officials regarding security and privacy control effectiveness.
- Determine/initiate appropriate response actions.
- Develop/update plans of action and milestones.
- Update security and privacy plans (and risk assessment).

Post assessment process

Plans of action and milestones

Security plans and privacy plans

FIGURE 7.1   SP 800-53A assessment case flow.

exercising one or more assessment objects (i.e., activities or mechanisms) under specified conditions to compare actual with expected behavior. In all three assessment methods, the results are used in making specific determinations called for in the determination statements and thereby achieving the objectives for the assessment procedure.

Assessment methods have a set of associated attributes, *depth* and *coverage*, which help define the level of effort for the assessment. These attributes are hierarchical in nature, providing the means to define the rigor and scope of the assessment for the increased assurances that may be needed for some information systems. The depth attribute addresses the rigor of and level of detail in the examination, interview, and testing processes. Values for the depth attribute include *basic*, *focused*, and *comprehensive*. The coverage attribute addresses the scope or breadth of the examination, interview, and testing processes including the number and type of specifications, mechanisms, and activities to be examined or tested, and the number and types of individuals to be interviewed. Similar to the depth attribute, values for the coverage attribute include *basic*, *focused*, and *comprehensive*. The appropriate depth and coverage attribute values for a particular assessment method are based on the assurance requirements specified by the organization. As assurance requirements increase with regard to the development, implementation, and operation of security and privacy controls within or inherited by the information system, the rigor and scope of the assessment activities (as reflected in the selection of assessment methods and objects and the assignment of depth and coverage attribute values) tend to increase as well.[3]

In addition to selecting appropriate assessment methods and objects, each assessment method (i.e., examine, interview, and test) is associated with depth and coverage attributes that are described in (SP 800-53A), Appendix D. The attribute values identify the rigor and scope of the assessment procedures executed by the assessor. The values selected by the organization are based on the characteristics of the information system being assessed (including assurance requirements) and the specific determinations to be made. The depth and coverage attribute values are associated with the assurance requirements specified by the organization (i.e., the rigor and scope of the assessment increases in direct relationship to the assurance requirements).[4]

RMF Step 4 – Assess Security Controls

As part of the Risk Management Framework, SP 800-37, rev. 1 provides the following tasks and guidance for each task during the prosecution of the assessment phase:

Task 1: assessment preparation – Develop, review, and approve a plan to assess the security controls.
Primary role of responsibility: Security Control Assessor.

The *security assessment plan* provides the objectives for the security control assessment, a detailed roadmap of how to conduct such an assessment, and assessment procedures. The assessment plan reflects the type of assessment the organization is conducting (e.g., developmental testing and evaluation, independent verification and validation, assessments supporting security authorizations or reauthorizations, audits, continuous monitoring, assessments subsequent to remediation actions). Conducting security control assessments in parallel with the development/acquisition and implementation phases of the life cycle permits the identification of weaknesses and deficiencies early and provides the most cost-effective method for initiating corrective actions. Issues found during these assessments can be referred to authorizing officials for early resolution, as appropriate. The results of security control assessments carried out during system development and implementation can also be used (consistent with reuse criteria) during the security authorization process to avoid system fielding delays or costly repetition of assessments. The security assessment plan is reviewed and approved by appropriate organizational officials to ensure that the plan is consistent with the security objectives of the organization, employs state-of-the practice tools, techniques, procedures, and automation to support

---

[3]SP 800-53A, rev. 4, IPD, p. 9–10.
[4]*Ibid.*, p. 18.

the concept of continuous monitoring and near real-time risk management, and is cost-effective with regard to the resources allocated for the assessment. The purpose of the security assessment plan approval is two-fold:

(i) to establish the appropriate expectations for the security control assessment; and
(ii) to bound the level of effort for the security control assessment.

An approved security assessment plan helps to ensure that an appropriate level of resources is applied toward determining security control effectiveness. When security controls are provided to an organization by an external provider (e.g., through contracts, interagency agreements, lines of business arrangements, licensing agreements, and/or supply chain arrangements), the organization obtains a security assessment plan from the provider.

Organizations consider both the *technical expertise* and level of *independence* required in selecting security control assessors. Organizations also ensure that security control assessors possess the required skills and technical expertise to successfully carry out assessments of system-specific, hybrid, and common controls. This includes knowledge of and experience with the specific hardware, software, and firmware components employed by the organization. An independent assessor is any individual or group capable of conducting an impartial assessment of security controls employed within or inherited by an information system. Impartiality implies that assessors are free from any perceived or actual conflicts of interest with respect to the development, operation, and/or management of the information system or the determination of security control effectiveness. Independent security control assessment services can be obtained from other elements within the organization or can be contracted to a public or private sector entity outside of the organization. Contracted assessment services are considered independent if the information system owner is not directly involved in the contracting process or cannot unduly influence the independence of the assessor(s) conducting the assessment of the security controls. The authorizing official or designated representative determines the required level of independence for security control assessors based on the results of the security categorization process for the information system and the ultimate risk to organizational operations and assets, individuals, other organizations, and the Nation. The authorizing official determines if the level of assessor independence is sufficient to provide confidence that the assessment results produced are sound and can be used to support a risk-based decision on whether to place the information system into operation or continue its operation. In special situations, for example when the organization that owns the information system is small or the organizational structure requires that the security control assessment be accomplished by individuals that are in the developmental, operational, and/or management chain of the system owner, independence in the assessment process can be achieved by ensuring that the assessment results are carefully reviewed and analyzed by an independent team of experts to validate the completeness, consistency, and veracity of the results. The authorizing official consults with the Office of the Inspector General, the senior information security officer, and the chief information officer to discuss the implications of any decisions on assessor independence in the types of special circumstances described above. This discussion may occur prior to each security assessment or only once if an organization is establishing an organizational policy and approach for specific special circumstances that will be applied to all information systems meeting the specific special circumstance criteria. Security control assessments in support of initial and subsequent security authorizations are conducted by independent assessors.[5]

Task 2: security control assessment – Assess the security controls in accordance with the assessment procedures defined in the security assessment plan.
Primary role of responsibility: Security Control Assessor.

Security control assessments determine the extent to which the controls are implemented correctly, operating as intended, and producing the desired outcome with respect to meeting the security requirements for the information system. Security control assessments occur as early as practicable in the system development life cycle, preferably during the development phase of the information system. These types of assessments

---

[5]SP 800-37, rev. 1, updated June 2014, p. 30.

are referred to as *developmental testing and evaluation* and are intended to validate that the required security controls are implemented correctly and consistent with the established information security architecture. Developmental testing and evaluation activities include, for example, design and code reviews, application scanning, and regression testing. Security weaknesses and deficiencies identified early in the system development life cycle can be resolved more quickly and in a much more cost-effective manner before proceeding to subsequent phases in the life cycle. The objective is to identify the information security architecture and security controls up front and to ensure that the system design and testing validate the implementation of these controls.

The information system owner relies on the technical expertise and judgment of assessors to:

(i) assess the security controls employed within or inherited by the information system using assessment procedures specified in the security assessment plan; and
(ii) provide specific recommendations on how to correct weaknesses or deficiencies in the controls and reduce or eliminate identified vulnerabilities.

The assessor findings are an unbiased, factual reporting of the weaknesses and deficiencies discovered during the security control assessment. Organizations are encouraged to maximize the use of automation to conduct security control assessments to help:

(i) increase the speed and overall effectiveness and efficiency of the assessments; and
(ii) support the concept of ongoing monitoring of the security state of organizational information systems.

When iterative development processes such as agile development are employed, this typically results in an iterative assessment as each cycle is conducted. A similar process is used for assessing security controls in COTS information technology products employed within the information system. Even when iterative development is not employed, organizations may choose to begin assessing security controls prior to the complete implementation of all security controls listed in the security plan. This type of *incremental assessment* is appropriate if it is more efficient or cost-effective to do so. For example, policy, procedures, and plans may be assessed prior to the assessment of the technical security controls in the hardware and software. In many cases, common controls (i.e., security controls inherited by the information system) may be assessed prior to the security controls employed within the system.

The organization ensures that assessors have access to:

(i) the information system and environment of operation where the security controls are employed; and
(ii) the appropriate documentation, records, artifacts, test results, and other materials needed to assess the security controls.

In addition, assessors have the required degree of independence as determined by the authorizing official (see SP 800-53A, Appendix D.13 and Appendix F.4). Security control assessments in support of initial and subsequent security authorizations are conducted by independent assessors. Assessor independence during continuous monitoring, although not mandated, facilitates reuse of assessment results when reauthorization is required. When security controls are provided to an organization by an external provider (e.g., through contracts, interagency agreements, lines of business arrangements, licensing agreements, and/or supply chain arrangements), the organization ensures that assessors have access to the information system/environment of operation where the controls are employed as well as appropriate information needed to carry out the assessment. The organization also obtains any information related to existing assessments that may have been conducted by the external provider and reuses such assessment information whenever possible in accordance with the reuse criteria established by the organization. Descriptive information about the information system is typically documented in the system identification section of the security plan or included by reference or as attachments to the plan. Supporting materials such as procedures, reports, logs, and records showing evidence of security control implementation are identified as well. In order to make the risk management process as timely and cost-effective as possible, the reuse of previous assessment results, when reasonable and appropriate, is strongly recommended. For example, a recent audit of an information system may have produced information about the effectiveness of selected security controls. Another opportunity to reuse previous assessment results comes from programs that test and evaluate the security features of commercial information technology products. Additionally, if prior assessment results from the system developer are available, the security control assessor, under appropriate circumstances, may incorporate those results into the assessment. And finally, assessment results are reused to support reciprocity where possible.[6]

Task 3: security assessment report – Prepare the security assessment report documenting the issues, findings, and recommendations from the security control assessment.
Primary role of responsibility: Security Control Assessor.

The results of the security control assessment, including recommendations for correcting any weaknesses or deficiencies in the controls, are documented in the *security assessment report*. The security assessment report is one of three key documents in the security authorization package developed for authorizing officials. The assessment report includes information from the assessor necessary to determine the effectiveness of the security controls employed within or inherited by the information system based upon the assessor's findings. The security assessment report is an important factor in an authorizing official's determination of risk to organizational operations and assets, individuals, other organizations, and the Nation. Security control assessment results are documented at a level of detail appropriate for the assessment in accordance with the reporting format prescribed by organizational and/or federal policies. The reporting format is also appropriate for the type of security control assessment conducted (e.g., developmental testing and evaluation, self-assessments, independent verification and validation, independent assessments supporting the security authorization process or subsequent reauthorizations, assessments during continuous monitoring, assessments subsequent to remediation actions, independent audits/evaluations).

Security control assessment results obtained during system development are brought forward in an interim report and included in the final security assessment report. This supports the concept that the security assessment report is an evolving document that includes assessment results from all relevant phases of the system development life cycle including the results generated during continuous monitoring. Organizations may choose to develop an *executive summary* from the detailed findings that are generated during a security control assessment. An executive summary provides an authorizing official with an abbreviated version of the assessment report focusing on the highlights of the assessment, synopsis of key findings, and/or recommendations for addressing weaknesses and deficiencies in the security controls.[7]

Task 4: remediation actions – Conduct initial remediation actions on security controls based on the findings and recommendations of the security assessment report and reassess remediated control(s), as appropriate.
Primary roles of responsibility: Information system owner or common control provider; Security Control Assessor.

The security assessment report provides visibility into specific weaknesses and deficiencies in the security controls employed within or inherited by the information system that could not reasonably be resolved during system development or that are discovered post-development. Such weaknesses and deficiencies are potential vulnerabilities if exploitable by a threat source. The findings generated during the security control assessment provide important information that facilitates a disciplined and structured approach to mitigating risks in accordance with organizational priorities. An updated assessment of risk (either formal or informal) based on the results of the findings produced during the security control assessment and any inputs from the risk executive (function), helps to determine the initial remediation actions and the prioritization of such actions. Information system owners and common control providers, in collaboration with selected organizational officials (e.g., information system security engineer, authorizing official designated representative, chief information officer, senior information security officer, information owner/steward), may decide, based on an initial or updated assessment of risk, that certain findings are inconsequential and present no significant risk to the organization. Alternatively, the organizational officials may decide that certain findings are in fact, significant, requiring immediate remediation actions. In all cases, organizations review assessor findings and determine the severity or seriousness of the findings (i.e., the potential adverse impact on organizational operations and assets, individuals, other organizations, or the Nation) and whether the findings are

---

[6]SP 800-37, rev. 1, updated June 2014, p. 31.

sufficiently significant to be worthy of further investigation or remediation. Senior leadership involvement in the mitigation process may be necessary in order to ensure that the organization's resources are effectively allocated in accordance with organizational priorities, providing resources first to the information systems that are supporting the most critical and sensitive missions and business functions for the organization or correcting the deficiencies that pose the greatest degree of risk. If weaknesses or deficiencies in security controls are corrected, the security control assessor reassesses the remediated controls for effectiveness. Security control reassessments determine the extent to which the remediated controls are implemented correctly, operating as intended, and producing the desired outcome with respect to meeting the security requirements for the information system. Exercising caution not to change the original assessment results, assessors update the security assessment report with the findings from the reassessment. The security plan is updated based on the findings of the security control assessment and any remediation actions taken. The updated security plan reflects the actual state of the security controls after the initial assessment and any modifications by the information system owner or common control provider in addressing recommendations for corrective actions. At the completion of the assessment, the security plan contains an accurate list and description of the security controls implemented (including compensating controls) and a list of residual vulnerabilities.

Organizations can prepare an optional addendum to the security assessment report that is transmitted to the authorizing official. The optional addendum provides information system owners and common control providers an opportunity to respond to the initial findings of assessors. The addendum may include, for example, information regarding initial remediation actions taken by information system owners or common control providers in response to assessor findings, or provide an owner's perspective on the findings (e.g., including additional explanatory material, rebutting certain findings, and correcting the record). The addendum to the security assessment report does not change or influence in any manner, the initial assessor findings provided in the original report. Information provided in the addendum is considered by authorizing officials in their risk-based authorization decisions. Organizations may choose to employ an *issue resolution process* to help determine the appropriate actions to take with regard to the security control weaknesses and deficiencies identified during the assessment. Issue resolution can help address vulnerabilities and associated risk, false positives, and other factors that may provide useful information to authorizing officials regarding the security state of the information system including the ongoing effectiveness of system-specific, hybrid, and common controls. The issue resolution process can also help to ensure that only substantive items are identified and transferred to the plan of actions and milestones.[7]

SP 800-115

The SP 800-115, "Technical Guide to Information Security Testing and Assessment," provides the basic NIST-directed technical aspects of conducting information security assessments for federal systems, networks, and applications. This guide presents technical testing and examination methods and techniques that an organization might use as part of an assessment, and offers insights to assessors on these methods, their execution, and the potential impact they may have on systems and networks.

SP 800-115 provides assessment guidance for conducting technical reviews of systems. The document focuses the reviews thusly:

Dozens of technical security testing and examination techniques exist that can be used to assess the security posture of systems and networks. The most commonly used techniques from the standpoint of this document will be discussed in more depth later in this guide, and are grouped into the following three categories:

a. **Review Techniques**. These are examination techniques used to evaluate systems, applications, networks, policies, and procedures to discover vulnerabilities, and are generally conducted manually. They include documentation, log, rule-set, and system configuration review; network sniffing; and file integrity checking. Section 3 provides additional information on review techniques.

[7]SP 800-37, rev. 1, updated June 2014, p. 32–33.

b. **Target Identification and Analysis Techniques**. These testing techniques can identify systems, ports, services, and potential vulnerabilities, and may be performed manually but are generally performed using automated tools. They include network discovery, network port and service identification, vulnerability scanning, wireless scanning, and application security examination.

c. **Target Vulnerability Validation Techniques**. These testing techniques corroborate the existence of vulnerabilities, and may be performed manually or by using automatic tools, depending on the specific technique used and the skill of the test team. Target vulnerability validation techniques include password cracking, penetration testing, social engineering, and application security testing.

Since no one technique can provide a complete picture of the security of a system or network, organizations should combine appropriate techniques to ensure robust security assessments. For example, penetration testing usually relies on performing both network port/service identification and vulnerability scanning to identify hosts and services that may be targets for future penetration. Also, multiple technical ways exist to meet an assessment requirement, such as determining whether patches have been applied properly.[8]

SP 800-115 goes on further with some strong cautionary warnings about testing:

Testing involves hands-on work with systems and networks to identify security vulnerabilities, and can be executed across an entire enterprise or on selected systems. The use of scanning and penetration techniques can provide valuable information on potential vulnerabilities and predict the likelihood that an adversary or intruder will be able to exploit them. Testing also allows organizations to measure levels of compliance in areas such as patch management, password policy, and configuration management.

Although testing can provide a more accurate picture of an organization's security posture than what is gained through examinations, it is more intrusive and can impact systems or networks in the target environment. The level of potential impact depends on the specific types of testing techniques used, which can interact with the target systems and networks in various ways—such as sending normal network packets to determine open and closed ports, or sending specially crafted packets to test for vulnerabilities. Any time that a test or tester directly interacts with a system or network, the potential exists for unexpected system halts and other denial of service conditions. Organizations should determine their acceptable levels of intrusiveness when deciding which techniques to use. Excluding tests known to create denial of service conditions and other disruptions can help reduce these negative impacts.[9]

So always be aware of the test environment, the operational mission and business environment, and the potential effects of the test methods and techniques the assessor is planning on using during the test activities on these important areas.

RMF Knowledge Service

Recently, DOD has adopted the NIST-based RMF as their guiding process for conducting assessments and authorizations of DOD unclassified and classified systems. With this effort underway, DOD has provided an online resource within the DOD network known as the RMF Knowledge Service at http://rmfks.osd.mil. This resource, available to only those personnel who have access and clearance to the DOD network, provides the DOD-specific criteria, testing methods, and validation procedures for all SP 800-53-based controls as they are installed and implemented in DOD systems. The RMF Knowledge Service is formatted after and based on the previously implemented DIACAP Knowledge Service which has provided guidance and procedures for conducting testing and evaluations in the DOD operating

---

[8]SP 800-115, p. 2-2, 2-3.
[9]SP 800-115, p. 2–4.

space for the past 7 years. Since the transition timeline for moving to RMF in DOD is several years long, I expect both Knowledge Service sites to be available to authorized users for quite some time to come.

ISO 27001/27002

The international standard for Information Security Management Systems is the ISO standard of documents in the ISO 27000 series. Within the initial 2 documents, ISO 27001 and ISO 27002, there are defined 14 security control classes of controls. Control Class 12.7 in the ISO 27001/27002 provides the basic guidance for auditing and reviewing the ISO control classes. It is entitled *12.7 Information Systems Audit Considerations* and provides that IT audits should be planned and controlled to minimize adverse effects on production systems, or inappropriate data access. It ties into the subsequent ISO documents in the 27000 series ISO 27007 and 27008 referenced as follows:

ISO/IEC 27007:2011 Information Technology – Security Techniques – Guidelines for Information Security Management Systems Auditing

ISO/IEC 27007 provides guidance for accredited certification bodies, internal auditors, external/third party auditors and others auditing ISMSs against ISO/IEC 27001 (*i.e.* auditing the *management system* for compliance with the standard).

ISO/IEC 27007 reflects and largely refers to ISO 19011, the ISO standard for auditing quality and environmental management systems - "management systems" of course being the common factor linking it to the ISO27k standards. It provides additional ISMS-specific guidance.[10]

ISO/IEC TR 27008:2011 Information Technology – Security Techniques – Guidelines for Auditors on Information Security Management Systems Controls

ISO TR 27008: This standard (actually a "technical report") on "technical auditing" complements ISO/IEC 27007. It concentrates on auditing the information security controls, whereas '27007 concentrates on auditing the management system elements of the ISMS.

This standard provides guidance for all auditors regarding "information security management systems controls" selected through a risk-based approach (*e.g.* as presented in a statement of applicability) for information security management. It supports the information security risk management process and internal, external and third-party audits of an ISMS by explaining the relationship between the ISMS and its supporting controls. It provides guidance on how to verify the extent to which required "ISMS controls" are implemented. Furthermore, it supports any organization using ISO/IEC 27001 and ISO/IEC 27002 to satisfy assurance requirements, and as a strategic platform for information security governance.

Most of the testing guidance and methods referenced within the ISO arena are formulated around international audit mechanisms, techniques, and practices, such as Control Objectives for Information and Related Technology (COBIT), COSO, and others. As such, we will discuss the individual methods in Chapter 9 when we examine the control-specific testing techniques.

[10]Retrieved from http://www.iso27001security.com/index.html on 9/19/2014.

Assessment Methods

Now we reach the actual assessment actions part of this book. This chapter opens the window on the process of assessing, testing, and evaluating the system or application. The NIST guidance provides a path through the evaluation process utilizing test objectives with one or more of the associated defined test methods to be applied toward the test objects under review. It has been my experience in performing these RMF-based assessments that the clients often want at least two methods of evaluation per control to be conducted and reported on during the process. Depending on the rigor to be applied to the assessment, this level of review can significantly increase the amount of effort and schedule for each test, and therefore extend the schedule for the entire evaluation.

The purpose of NIST Special Publication 800-53A (as amended) is to establish common assessment procedures to assess the effectiveness of security controls in federal information systems, specifically those controls listed in *NIST Special Publication 800-53 (as amended), Recommended Security Controls for Federal Information Systems and Organizations*. The assessment methods and procedures are used to determine if the security controls are implemented correctly, operating as intended, and producing the desired outcome with respect to meeting the security requirements of the organization. Organizations and other entities, such as commercial corporations, use the recommended assessment procedures from SP 800-53A as the starting point for developing more specific assessment procedures, which may, in certain cases, be needed because of platform dependencies or other implementation-related considerations. The assessment procedures in SP 800-53A can be supplemented by the organization, if needed, based on an organizational assessment of risk. Organizations must create additional assessment procedures for those security controls that are not contained in SP 800-53. The employment of standardized assessment procedures promotes more consistent, comparable, and repeatable security assessments of federal information systems. SP 800-53A does provide a lot of guidance in the forefront of the document about setting up this process. It starts with the following:

> An assessment procedure consists of a set of assessment *objectives*, each with an associated set of potential assessment *methods* and assessment *objects*. An assessment objective includes a set of *determination statements* related to the particular security or privacy control under assessment. The determination statements are linked to the content of the security or privacy control (i.e., the security/privacy control functionality) to ensure traceability of assessment results back to the fundamental control requirements. The application of an assessment procedure to a security or privacy control produces assessment *findings*. These findings reflect, or are subsequently used, to help determine the overall effectiveness of the security or privacy control.

Assessment objects identify the specific items being assessed and include *specifications*, *mechanisms*, *activities*, and *individuals*.

a.) Specifications are the document-based artifacts (e.g., policies, procedures, plans, system security and privacy requirements, functional specifications, architectural designs) associated with an information system.
b.) Mechanisms are the specific hardware, software, or firmware safeguards and countermeasures employed within an information system.
c.) Activities are the specific protection-related actions supporting an information system that involve people (e.g., conducting system backup operations, monitoring network traffic, exercising a contingency plan).
d.) Individuals, or groups of individuals, are people applying the specifications, mechanisms, or activities described above.

Assessment methods define the nature of the assessor actions and include *examine*, *interview*, and *test*. The *examine* method is the process of reviewing, inspecting, observing, studying, or analyzing one or more assessment objects (i.e., specifications, mechanisms, or activities). The purpose of the examine method is to facilitate assessor understanding, achieve clarification, or obtain evidence. The *interview* method is the process of holding discussions with individuals or groups of individuals within an organization to once again, facilitate assessor understanding, achieve clarification, or obtain evidence. The *test* method is the process of exercising one or more assessment objects (i.e., activities or mechanisms) under specified conditions to compare actual with expected behavior. In all three assessment methods, the results are used in making specific determinations called for in the determination statements and thereby achieving the objectives for the assessment procedure.[1]

EVALUATION METHODS AND THEIR ATTRIBUTES

Both of the primary testing documents from NIST, SP 800-53A and SP 800-115, address various methods and techniques for different kinds of testing activities. SP 800-53A states it as follows:

Assessment methods have a set of associated attributes, *depth* and *coverage*, which help define the level of effort for the assessment. These attributes are hierarchical in nature, providing the means to define the rigor and scope of the assessment for the increased assurances that may be needed for some information systems.

a.) The depth attribute addresses the rigor of and level of detail in the examination, interview, and testing processes. Values for the depth attribute include *basic*, *focused*, and *comprehensive*. The coverage attribute addresses the scope or breadth of the examination, interview, and testing processes including the number and type of specifications, mechanisms, and activities to be examined or tested, and the number and types of individuals to be interviewed.
b.) Similar to the depth attribute, values for the coverage attribute include *basic*, *focused*, and *comprehensive*. The appropriate depth and coverage attribute values for a particular assessment method are based on the assurance requirements specified by the organization.

These attributes are further explained in the supplemental NIST guidance for assessments for each family of controls found on the NIST site. The supplemental guidance is provided to assist the assessment activity for each family of controls as they are reviewed. The action statements provided in the assessment test plans are written using the basic (i.e., foundation) level of assessment depth and coverage attribute values. An increased rigor and/or scope of the action statement can be expressed by replacing the basic level of assessment depth and

[1]SP 800-53A, rev. 4, IPD, p. 9.

coverage attribute value with other defined values. The potential attribute values for varying depth and coverage for the assessment methods (examine, interview, and test) in the action statements are as follows:

Coverage Attribute Values:

Basic Sample attribute value is used to indicate a 'basic' level of scope or breath of coverage; that is, a representative sample of assessment objects (by type and number within type) to provide a level of coverage necessary for determining if the control meets the 'basic' criteria listed below.

Focused Sample attribute value is available for use to indicate a 'focused' level of scope or breadth coverage; that is, an extended *basic sample* to include other specific assessment objects important to achieving the assessment objective to provide a level of coverage necessary for determining if the control meets the 'focused' coverage criteria listed below.

Sufficiently Large Sample attribute value is available for use to indicate a 'comprehensive' level of scope or breadth of coverage; that is, an extended *focused sample* to include more assessment objects to provide a level of coverage necessary for determining if the control meets the 'comprehensive' coverage criteria listed below.

Depth Attribute Values:

Specific action verbs identified in SP 800-53A, Appendix D, in the definition of the examine method are employed in the application of the Action Steps of the Assessment Cases to indicate level of rigor for examining the different types of assessment objects (i.e., documentation, activities and mechanisms) as follows:

Examine documentation rigor – 'reading':

Review attribute value for reading documentation is used for the 'basic' level of rigor and level of detail; that is, a high-level examination of documentation looking for required content and for any obvious errors, omissions, or inconsistencies.

Study attribute value for reading documentation is available for use for the 'focused' level of rigor and level of detail; that is, an examination of documentation that includes the intent of 'review' and adds a more in-depth examination for greater evidence to support a determination of whether the document has the required content and is free of obvious errors, omissions, and inconsistencies.

Analyze attribute value for reading documentation is available for use for the 'comprehensive' level of rigor and level of detail; that is, an examination of documentation that includes the intent of both 'review' and 'study'; adding a thorough and detailed analysis for significant grounds for confidence in the determination of whether the required content is present and the document is correct, complete, and consistent.

Examine activities and mechanisms rigor – 'watching':

Observe attribute value for watching activities and mechanisms is used for the 'basic' level of rigor and level of detail; that is, watching the execution of an activity or process or looking directly at a mechanism (as opposed to reading documentation produced by someone other than the assessor about that mechanism) for the purpose of seeing whether the activity or mechanism appears to operate as intended (or in the case of a mechanism, perhaps is configured as intended) and whether there are any obvious errors, omissions, or inconsistencies in the operation or configuration.

Inspect attribute value for watching activities and mechanisms is available for use for the 'focused' level of rigor and level of detail; that is, adding to the watching associated with 'observe' an active investigation to gain further grounds for confidence in the determination of whether that the activity or mechanism is operating as intended and is free of errors, omissions, or inconsistencies in the operation or configuration.

Analyze attribute value for watching activities and mechanisms is available for use for the 'comprehensive' level of rigor and level of detail; that is, adding to the watching and investigation of 'observe' and 'inspect' a thorough and detailed analysis of the information to develop significant grounds for confidence in the determination as to whether the activity or mechanism is operating as intended and is free of errors, omissions, or inconsistencies in the operation or configuration. Analysis achieves this by both leading to further observations and inspections and by a greater understanding of the information obtained from the examination.

Interview individual or group rigor:

Basic attribute value for interviewing individuals and groups is used for the 'basic' level of rigor and level of detail; that is, a high-level interview looking for evidence to support a determination of whether the control meets the 'basic' interview criteria listed below.

Focused attribute value for interviewing individuals and groups is available for use for the 'focused' level of rigor and level of detail; that is, an interview that includes the intent of 'basic' and adds a more in-depth interview for greater evidence to support a determination of whether the control meets the 'focused' interview criteria listed below.

Comprehensive attribute value for interviewing individuals and groups is available for use for the 'comprehensive' level of rigor and level of detail; that is, an interview that includes the intent of both 'basic' and 'focused'; adding a thorough and detailed analysis for significant grounds for confidence in the determination of whether the control meets the 'comprehensive' interview criteria listed below.

Test Mechanisms and Activities rigor:

Basic attribute value for mechanisms and activities is used for the 'basic' level of rigor and level of detail; that is, a basic level of testing looking for evidence to support a determination of whether the control meets the 'basic' test criteria listed below.

Focused attribute value for mechanisms and activities is available for use for the 'focused' level of rigor and level of detail; that is, a focused level of testing that includes the intent of 'basic' and adds a more in-depth testing for greater evidence to support a determination of whether the control meets the 'focused' test criteria listed below.

Comprehensive attribute value for mechanisms and activities is available for use for the 'comprehensive' level of rigor and level of detail; that is, a comprehensive level of testing that includes the intent of both 'basic' and 'focused'; adding a thorough and detailed analysis for significant grounds for confidence in the determination of whether the control meets the 'comprehensive' test criteria listed below.

The depth and coverage attributes do not alter the logical sequencing, totality, or selection of evidence gathering actions; rather these attributes served as providing/supporting degrees of assessment rigor.[2]

These detailed explanations provide a good basis for understanding the different levels of assessment as well as defining how each attribute is uniquely identified and assessed during the differing levels of assessment: basic, focused, and comprehensive. To the assessor, the method for evaluating a control is often flexible based on organizational requests and assessor experience. Hence, assessor-defined parameters are often identified within the action statement for selecting an appropriate depth (i.e., level of detail required) and coverage (i.e., scope) of application of the assessment method for assessing the security control.

As assurance requirements increase with regard to the development, implementation, and operation of security and privacy controls within or inherited by the information system, the rigor and scope of the assessment activities (as reflected in the selection of assessment methods and objects and the assignment of depth and coverage attribute values) tend to increase as well.

I am going to put together the various criteria for evaluation and the methods interweaving the guidance to give a picture of how the methods, specifications, objects, and the activities

---

[2]Assessment cases (initial public draft) for special publication 800-53a, revision 1, *Guide for Assessing the Security Controls in Federal Information Systems and Organizations*, June 2010, retrieved from csrc.nist.gov on 9/20/2014.

work together to build a complete assurance case that is usable, presentable, and, as best as possible, comprehensive enough for use in a Security Assessment Report to the organization's executives and authorizing officials.

PROCESSES

SP 800-115 gives the following explanation of what we are endeavoring to accomplish with the testing, evaluations and assessments. "An information security *assessment* is the process of determining how effectively an entity being assessed (e.g., host, system, network, procedure, person—known as the assessment *object*) meets specific security objectives. Three types of assessment methods can be used to accomplish this—testing, examination, and interviewing. *Testing* is the process of exercising one or more assessment objects under specified conditions to compare actual and expected behaviors. *Examination* is the process of checking, inspecting, reviewing, observing, studying, or analyzing one or more assessment objects to facilitate understanding, achieve clarification, or obtain evidence. *Interviewing* is the process of conducting discussions with individuals or groups within an organization to facilitate understanding, achieve clarification, or identify the location of evidence. Assessment results are used to support the determination of security control effectiveness over time."[3]

For each of the methods below, I will first provide the NIST guidance, and then supplement the process flows with additional suggested techniques and procedures that I have used during assessments over the years.

Please note: The "bold" attribute used in each of these three method descriptions is directly from the NIST documents.

Interviews

Interviewing is the process of conducting discussions with individuals or groups within an organization to facilitate understanding, achieve clarification, or identify the location of evidence. This process for the assessment is often the initial step accomplished once the assessment team is on-site and ready to start the actual evaluation.

Method: Interview.

Assessment objects: Individuals or groups of individuals.

Definition: The process of conducting discussions with individuals or groups within an organization to facilitate understanding, achieve clarification, or lead to the location of evidence, the results of which are used to support the determination of security and privacy control existence, functionality, correctness, completeness, and potential for improvement over time.

Guidance: Typical assessor actions may include, for example, interviewing agency heads, chief information officers, senior agency information security officers, authorizing officials, information owners, information system and mission owners, information system security officers, information system security managers, personnel officers, human resource managers,

---

[3]SP 800-115, p. ES-1.

facilities managers, training officers, information system operators, network and system administrators, site managers, physical security officers, and users.

Security Content Automation Protocol (SCAP)-validated tools that support the Open Checklist Interactive Language (OCIL) component specification may be used to automate the interview process for specific individuals or groups of individuals. The resulting information can then be examined by assessors during the security and privacy control assessments.

Attributes: Depth and coverage:

- The *depth* attribute addresses the rigor of and level of detail in the interview process. There are three possible values for the depth attribute:
  - *Basic*:
    - *Basic interview*: Interview that consists of broad-based, high-level discussions with individuals or groups of individuals. This type of interview is conducted using a set of generalized, high-level questions. Basic interviews provide a level of understanding of the security and privacy controls necessary for determining whether the controls are implemented and free of obvious errors.
  - *Focused*:
    - *Focused interview*: Interview that consists of broad-based, high-level discussions **and more in-depth discussions in specific areas** with individuals or groups of individuals. This type of interview is conducted using a set of generalized, high-level questions **and more in-depth questions in specific areas where responses indicate a need for more in-depth investigation**. **Focused** interviews provide a level of understanding of the security and privacy controls necessary for determining whether the controls are implemented and free of obvious errors **and whether there are increased grounds for confidence that the controls are implemented correctly and operating as intended**.
  - *Comprehensive*:
    - *Comprehensive interview*: Interview that consists of broad-based, high-level discussions and more in-depth, **probing** discussions in specific areas with individuals or groups of individuals. This type of interview is conducted using a set of generalized, high-level questions and more in-depth, **probing** questions in specific areas where responses indicate a need for more in-depth investigation. **Comprehensive** interviews provide a level of understanding of the security and privacy controls necessary for determining whether the controls are implemented and free of obvious errors and whether there are **further** increased grounds for confidence that the controls are implemented correctly and operating as intended **on an ongoing and consistent basis, and that there is support for continuous improvement in the effectiveness of the controls**.
- The *coverage* attribute addresses the scope or breadth of the interview process and includes the types of individuals to be interviewed (by organizational role and associated responsibility), the number of individuals to be interviewed (by type), and specific individuals to be interviewed. (The organization, considering a variety of factors (e.g., available resources, importance of the assessment, the organization's overall assessment goals and objectives), confers with assessors and provides direction on the type, number, and specific individuals to be interviewed for the particular attribute value described.) There are three possible values for the coverage attribute:

- *Basic*:
  - *Basic interview*: Interview that uses a representative sample of individuals in key organizational roles to provide a level of coverage necessary for determining whether the security and privacy controls are implemented and free of obvious errors.
- *Focused*:
  - *Focused interview*: Interview that uses a representative sample of individuals in key organizational roles **and other specific individuals deemed particularly important to achieving the assessment objective** to provide a level of coverage necessary for determining whether the security and privacy controls are implemented and free of obvious errors **and whether there are increased grounds for confidence that the controls are implemented correctly and operating as intended**.
- *Comprehensive*:
  - *Comprehensive interview*: Interview that uses a **sufficiently large** sample of individuals in key organizational roles and other specific individuals deemed particularly important to achieving the assessment objective to provide a level of coverage necessary for determining whether the security and privacy controls are implemented and free of obvious errors and whether there are **further** increased grounds for confidence that the controls are implemented correctly and operating as intended **on an ongoing and consistent basis, and that there is support for continuous improvement in the effectiveness of the controls**.[4]

Examinations

Examinations primarily involve the review of documents such as policies, procedures, security plans, security requirements, standard operating procedures, architecture diagrams, engineering documentation, asset inventories, system configurations, rule-sets, and system logs. They are conducted to determine whether a system is properly documented, and to gain insight on aspects of security that are only available through documentation. This documentation identifies the intended design, installation, configuration, operation, and maintenance of the systems and network, and its review and cross-referencing ensures conformance and consistency. For example, an environment's security requirements should drive documentation such as system security plans and standard operating procedures—so assessors should ensure that all plans, procedures, architectures, and configurations are compliant with stated security requirements and applicable policies. Another example is reviewing a firewall's rule-set to ensure its compliance with the organization's security policies regarding Internet usage, such as the use of instant messaging, peer-to-peer (P2P) file sharing, and other prohibited activities.

Examinations typically have no impact on the actual systems or networks in the target environment aside from accessing necessary documentation, logs, or rule-sets. One passive testing technique that can potentially impact networks is network sniffing, which involves connecting a sniffer to a hub, tap, or span port on the network. In some cases, the connection process requires reconfiguring a network device, which could disrupt operations. However, if system configuration files or logs are to be retrieved from a given system such as a router or firewall, only system administrators and similarly trained individuals should undertake this work to ensure that settings are not inadvertently modified or deleted.[5]

---

[4]SP 800-53A, rev. 4, IPD, p. D-4.
[5]SP 800-115, p. 2-3, 2-4.

Method: Examine.

Assessment objects: Specifications (e.g., policies, plans, procedures, system requirements, designs), mechanisms (e.g., functionality implemented in hardware, software, firmware), and activities (e.g., system operations, administration, management, exercises).

Definition: The process of checking, inspecting, reviewing, observing, studying, or analyzing one or more assessment objects to facilitate understanding, achieve clarification, or obtain evidence, the results of which are used to support the determination of security and privacy control existence, functionality, correctness, completeness, and potential for improvement over time.

Supplemental guidance: Typical assessor actions may include, for example, reviewing information security policies, plans, and procedures; analyzing system design documentation and interface specifications; observing system backup operations; reviewing the results of contingency plan exercises; observing incident response activities; studying technical manuals and user/administrator guides; checking, studying, or observing the operation of an information technology mechanism in the information system hardware/software; or checking, studying, or observing physical security measures related to the operation of an information system.

SCAP-validated tools that support the OCIL component specification may be used to automate the collection of assessment objects from specific, responsible individuals within an organization. The resulting information can then be examined by assessors during the security and privacy control assessments.

Attributes: Depth and coverage:

- The *depth* attribute addresses the rigor of and level of detail in the examination process. There are three possible values for the depth attribute:
  - *Basic*:
    - *Basic examination*: Examination that consists of high-level reviews, checks, observations, or inspections of the assessment object. This type of examination is conducted using a limited body of evidence or documentation (e.g., functional-level descriptions for mechanisms; high-level process descriptions for activities; actual documents for specifications). Basic examinations provide a level of understanding of the security and privacy controls necessary for determining whether the controls are implemented and free of obvious errors.
  - *Focused*:
    - *Focused examination*: Examination that consists of high-level reviews, checks, observations, or inspections **and more in-depth studies/analyses** of the assessment object. This type of examination is conducted using a **substantial** body of evidence or documentation (e.g., functional-level descriptions **and, where appropriate and available, high-level design information** for mechanisms; high-level process descriptions **and implementation procedures** for activities; the actual documents **and related documents** for specifications). **Focused** examinations provide a level of understanding of the security and privacy controls necessary for determining whether the controls are implemented and free of obvious errors **and whether there are increased grounds for confidence that the controls are implemented correctly and operating as intended**.

- *Comprehensive*:
  - *Comprehensive examination*: Examination that consists of high-level reviews, checks, observations, or inspections and more in-depth, **detailed, and thorough** studies/analyses of the assessment object. This type of examination is conducted using an **extensive** body of evidence or documentation (e.g., functional-level descriptions and, where appropriate and available, high-level design information, **low-level design information, and implementation information** for mechanisms; high-level process descriptions and **detailed** implementation procedures for activities; the actual documents and related documents for specifications (while additional documentation is likely for mechanisms when moving from basic to focused to comprehensive examinations, the documentation associated with specifications and activities may be the same or similar for focused and comprehensive examinations, with the rigor of the examinations of these documents being increased at the comprehensive level)). **Comprehensive** examinations provide a level of understanding of the security and privacy controls necessary for determining whether the controls are implemented and free of obvious errors and whether there are **further** increased grounds for confidence that the controls are implemented correctly and operating as intended **on an ongoing and consistent basis, and that there is support for continuous improvement in the effectiveness of the controls**.
- The *coverage* attribute addresses the scope or breadth of the examination process and includes the types of assessment objects to be examined, the number of objects to be examined (by type), and specific objects to be examined. (The organization, considering a variety of factors (e.g., available resources, importance of the assessment, the organization's overall assessment goals and objectives), confers with assessors and provides direction on the type, number, and specific objects to be examined for the particular attribute value described).

There are three possible values for the coverage attribute:

(i) *Basic*
  - Basic examination: Examination that uses a representative sample of assessment objects (by type and number within type) to provide a level of coverage necessary for determining whether the security and privacy controls are implemented and free of obvious errors.

(ii) *Focused*
  - Focused examination: Examination that uses a representative sample of assessment objects (by type and number within type) **and other specific assessment objects deemed particularly important to achieving the assessment objective** to provide a level of coverage necessary for determining whether the security and privacy controls are implemented and free of obvious errors **and whether there are increased grounds for confidence that the controls are implemented correctly and operating as intended**.

(iii) *Comprehensive*
  - Comprehensive examination: Examination that uses a **sufficiently large** sample of assessment objects (by type and number within type) and other specific assessment objects deemed particularly important to achieving the assessment objective to provide a level of coverage necessary for determining whether the security and privacy controls are implemented and free of obvious errors and whether there are **further** increased grounds for confidence that the controls are implemented correctly and operating as intended **on an ongoing and consistent basis, and that there is support for continuous improvement in the effectiveness of the controls**.[6]

[6]SP 800-53A, rev. 4, IPD, p. D-2.

Observations

It is a fact that considerable data can be collected by just observing. Direct observation is an underused and valuable method for collecting evaluation information. "Seeing" and "listening" are key to observation. Observation provides the opportunity to document activities, behavior, and physical aspects without having to depend on peoples' willingness and ability to respond to interview questions or isolate the exact document which is relevant to a particular control or risk. As described above from the examination phase of testing, observing practices and implementation of procedures is often a good evaluation method for review of control implementation, especially in the operational control families. Often we are observing system backup operations, observing incident response activities, observing the operation of an information technology mechanism in the information system hardware/software, or observing physical security measures related to the operation of an information system.

The two primary methods of observation which I employ are the use of system-level demonstrations and what I term "security walk-throughs." System demonstrations are a great way to observe the actions of the system under review, especially for systems which are new or recently modified. The demonstration should include log-in actions, standard system processing, and system-level interactions and reporting. There are a lot of areas of security control implementations which can be observed during demonstrations. Access controls and identification and authorization actions to log into a system, password protection, and methods of system and communications protection are all areas of significance and focus during an observation of system demonstration of functionality and processing.

A "security walk-through inspection" consists of my observer walking throughout a facility and looking for the methods of physical security employed within the facility. Identification of physical access controls for sections of the facility, methods of intrusion detection, deployed fire detection and suppression components, and HVAC controls which are used in the facility are all "observed" and accounted for during the walk-through and recorded in the assessment report as examined through observation. I have employed this technique to conduct focused examinations.

Document Reviews

Documentation review determines if the technical aspects of policies and procedures are current and comprehensive. These documents provide the foundation for an organization's security posture, but are often overlooked during technical assessments. Security groups within the organization should provide assessors with appropriate documentation to ensure a comprehensive review. Documents are reviewed for technical accuracy and completeness will include security policies, architectures, and requirements; standard operating procedures; system security plans and authorization agreements; memoranda of understanding and agreement for system interconnections; and incident response plans.

Documentation review can discover gaps and weaknesses that could lead to missing or improperly implemented security controls. Assessors typically verify that the organization's documentation is compliant with standards and regulations such as FISMA, and look for policies that are deficient or outdated. Common documentation weaknesses include OS security procedures or protocols that are no longer used, and failure to include a new OS and its protocols. Documentation review does not ensure that security controls are implemented properly – only that the direction and guidance exist to support security infrastructure.

Results of documentation review can be used to fine-tune other testing and examination techniques. For example, if a password management policy has specific requirements for minimum password length and complexity, this information can be used to configure password-cracking tools for more efficient performance.

1. *"Gap" analysis process*: The initial document reviews which start off the assessment process often provide data to the assessor and the assessment team to use in providing focus and pinpoint areas of potential concern to review, examine, evaluate, and test the system or application under review. These document reviews allow the assessment team to identify recently repaired controls, areas of volatility in controls and protection, and potentially areas overlooked or reduced in strength of control protection. This leads to a "gap analysis" which can determine what requirements, operational criteria, security objectives, and compliance needs are and are not being met by the system under review. This "gap analysis" process often has been used to discover areas of weakness in policies, procedures, and reporting for systems and applications. The "gap analysis" process which I often used is described as follows:

   (a) Review each authorization package using the 15-step methodology outlined below. Using this defined process for review promotes consistency and quality of package analysis.
   - Review current documents for completeness and accuracy, based on the established security baseline.
   - Review current documents for System Security Classification and level determination.
   - Catalog current documents into security areas.
   - Develop mapping for current documents to FISMA, DOD IA regulations (if applicable), NIST guidance, US governmental agency regulations (if applicable), and FIPS standards (DODI 8510.01, SP 800-37, SP 800-53, SP 800-53A, FIPS-199, etc.).
   - Review current documents for mapping status.
   - Identify preliminary documents, policies, plans, or procedures with questionable mapping status.
   - Research any missing or unclear policies, procedures, plans, or guidelines in support documentation.
   - Develop questions and issue report for customer remediation, answers, and identification.
   - Identify agency standards and guidelines for document creation and development.
   - Develop missing and required policies, plans, or procedures, as required such as:
     (i) System of Record Notice (SORN) to register the system
     (ii) Residual risk assessment
     (iii) Plan of Action and Milestone (POAM)
     (iv) Any additional Assessment and Authorization (A&A)-related artifacts as part of the submission package, such as:
       • Security Concept of Operations (CONOPS)
       • Security policies
       • Security architecture drawings and documents
       • Security User Security Manual and Standing Operating Procedures (USM/SOP)
       • Continuity of Operations (COOP)

- Incident Response Plan
- Contingency Plan
- Configuration Management Plan
  - Submit these developed documents for review, comment, revision, and approval.
  - Once all documents and questions are answered, review vulnerability scans for actual technical controls implemented versus controls documented.
  - Develop report on controls assessment.
  - Complete required RMF certification and accreditation worksheets, documents, and forms.
  - Develop SCA ATO Recommendation and Risk Assessment Reports, IAW the agency requirements.
  - The completed review is then submitted to the quality assurance review for the internal consistency, completeness, and correctness (3C) review.
    - (i) The consistency, completeness, and correctness of the documentation are determined, and if quality standards are met, the documentation is then passed on to final submittal phase.

Testing

Testing involves hands-on work with systems and networks to identify security vulnerabilities, and can be executed across an entire enterprise or on selected systems. The use of scanning and penetration techniques can provide valuable information on potential vulnerabilities and predict the likelihood that an adversary or intruder will be able to exploit them. Testing also allows organizations to measure levels of compliance in areas such as patch management, password policy, and configuration management.

Although testing can provide a more accurate picture of an organization's security posture than what is gained through examinations, it is more intrusive and can impact systems or networks in the target environment. The level of potential impact depends on the specific types of testing techniques used, which can interact with the target systems and networks in various ways—such as sending normal network packets to determine open and closed ports, or sending specially crafted packets to test for vulnerabilities. Any time that a test or tester directly interacts with a system or network, the potential exists for unexpected system halts and other denial of service conditions. Organizations should determine their acceptable levels of intrusiveness when deciding which techniques to use. Excluding tests known to create denial of service conditions and other disruptions can help reduce these negative impacts.

Testing does not provide a comprehensive evaluation of the security posture of an organization, and often has a narrow scope because of resource limitations—particularly in the area of time. Malicious attackers, on the other hand, can take whatever time they need to exploit and penetrate a system or network. Also, while organizations tend to avoid using testing techniques that impact systems or networks, attackers are not bound by this constraint and use whatever techniques they feel necessary. As a result, testing is less likely than examinations to identify weaknesses related to security policy and configuration. In many cases, combining testing and examination techniques can provide a more accurate view of security.[7]

Method: Test.

Assessment objects: Mechanisms (e.g., hardware, software, and firmware) and activities (e.g., system operations, administration, management; exercises).

---

[7]SP 800-115, p. 2–4.

Definition: The process of exercising one or more assessment objects under specified conditions to compare actual with expected behavior, the results of which are used to support the determination of security and privacy control existence, functionality, correctness, completeness, and potential for improvement over time. (Testing is typically used to determine if mechanisms or activities meet a set of predefined specifications. It can also be performed to determine characteristics of a security or privacy control that are not commonly associated with predefined specifications, with an example of such testing being penetration testing.)

Supplemental guidance: Typical assessor actions may include, for example, testing access control, identification and authentication, and audit mechanisms; testing security configuration settings; testing physical access control devices; conducting penetration testing of key information system components; testing information system backup operations; testing incident response capability; and exercising contingency planning capability.

SCAP-validated tools can be used to automate the collection of assessment objects and evaluate these objects against expected behavior. The use of SCAP is specifically relevant to the testing of mechanisms that involve assessment of actual machine state. The National Checklist Program catalogs a number of SCAP-enabled checklists that are suitable for assessing the configuration posture of specific operating systems and applications. SCAP-validated tools can use these checklists to determine the aggregate compliance of a system against all of the configuration settings in the checklist (e.g., CM-6) or specific configurations that are relevant to a security or privacy control that pertains to one or more configuration settings. SCAP-validated tools can also determine the absence of a patch or the presence of a vulnerable condition. The results produced by the SCAP tools can then be examined by assessors as part of the security and privacy control assessments.

Attributes: Depth and coverage:

- The *depth* attribute addresses the types of testing to be conducted. There are three possible values for the depth attribute:
  - *Basic* testing:
    - *Basic testing*: Test methodology (also known as *black box* testing) that assumes no knowledge of the internal structure and implementation detail of the assessment object. This type of testing is conducted using a functional specification for mechanisms and a high-level process description for activities. Basic testing provides a level of understanding of the security and privacy controls necessary for determining whether the controls are implemented and free of obvious errors.
  - *Focused* testing:
    - *Focused testing*: Test methodology (also known as *gray box* testing) that assumes **some** knowledge of the internal structure and implementation detail of the assessment object. This type of testing is conducted using a functional specification **and limited system architectural information (e.g., high-level design)** for mechanisms and a high-level process description **and high-level description of integration into the operational environment** for activities. Focused testing provides a level of understanding of the security and privacy controls necessary for determining whether the controls are implemented and free of obvious errors **and whether there are increased grounds for confidence that the controls are implemented correctly and operating as intended**.

- *Comprehensive* testing:
  - *Comprehensive testing*: Test methodology (also known as *white box* testing) that assumes **explicit and substantial** knowledge of the internal structure and implementation detail of the assessment object. This type of testing is conducted using a functional specification, **extensive** system architectural information (e.g., high-level design, **low-level design) and implementation representation (e.g., source code, schematics)** for mechanisms, and a high-level process description and **detailed** description of integration into the operational environment for activities. Comprehensive testing provides a level of understanding of the security and privacy controls necessary for determining whether the controls are implemented and free of obvious errors and whether there are **further** increased grounds for confidence that the controls are implemented correctly and operating as intended **on an ongoing and consistent basis, and that there is support for continuous improvement in the effectiveness of the controls**.
- The *coverage* attribute addresses the scope or breadth of the testing process and includes the types of assessment objects to be tested, the number of objects to be tested (by type), and specific objects to be tested. (The organization, considering a variety of factors (e.g., available resources, importance of the assessment, the organization's overall assessment goals and objectives), confers with assessors and provides direction on the type, number, and specific objects to be tested for the particular attribute value described. For mechanism-related testing, the coverage attribute also addresses the extent of the testing conducted (e.g., for software, the number of test cases and modules tested; for hardware, the range of inputs, number of components tested, and range of environmental factors over which the testing is conducted.)
  There are three possible values for the coverage attribute:
  - *Basic*:
    - *Basic testing*: Testing that uses a representative sample of assessment objects (by type and number within type) to provide a level of coverage necessary for determining whether the security and privacy controls are implemented and free of obvious errors.
  - *Focused*:
    - *Focused testing*: Testing that uses a representative sample of assessment objects (by type and number within type) **and other specific assessment objects deemed particularly important to achieving the assessment objective** to provide a level of coverage necessary for determining whether the security and privacy controls are implemented and free of obvious errors **and whether there are increased grounds for confidence that the controls are implemented correctly and operating as intended**.
  - *Comprehensive*:
    - *Comprehensive testing*: Testing that uses a **sufficiently large** sample of assessment objects (by type and number within type) and other specific assessment objects deemed particularly important to achieving the assessment objective to provide a level of coverage necessary for determining whether the security and privacy controls are implemented and free of obvious errors and whether there are **further** increased grounds for confidence that the controls are implemented correctly

and operating as intended **on an ongoing and consistent basis, and that there is support for continuous improvement in the effectiveness of the controls.**[8]

Automated

NIST SP 800-115 has a large discussion on automated testing techniques and tools available to run against systems to verify their compliance and programmatic actions against known baselines. These test mechanisms include vulnerability scanning, file and directory integrity checking, penetration testing, and others. We will discuss these tools and techniques in Chapter 10.

Manual

Manual testing is often used by assessors to provide a method of processing review and output business rule confirmation by applying known test data inputs and manually either walking through the process a step at a time or allowing the system to run with the manually developed test "scripts" and reading the results. Once the results are produced, a comparison is performed to ensure there are no anomalies between the expected results and the actual results. These manual processes have a long history within the auditing community wherein the auditors would apply test data to a system, run Computer-Aided Audit Tools (CAAT) or manually generated code snippets known as "scripts" against the system with the test data loaded, and compare the output with the expected results to verify processing, business rules, and coded logic patterns within the system under test.

---

[8]SP 800-53A, rev. 4, IPD, p. D-6.

CHAPTER

9

Assessment Techniques for Each Kind of Control

Once we determine, which controls are to be assessed and our proposed methods and techniques for evaluation, we begin development of the security assessment plan (SAP) as per SP 800-37, rev. 1 defined requirements. In both SP 800-53A and SP 800-115, there are defined areas for test considerations to be included in various sections of the SAP. The SAP is the current version of what had been previously known as the ST&E plan. The security test and evaluation (ST&E) plan was the primary document that the validator, the assessor, and the certifying agent used to guide the actual performance of the review throughout the course of the activity. The SAP defines methods and procedures for testing, evaluating, and assessing the various security controls in the system. Included in the SAP developmental process is an additional document, the rules of engagement (ROE) document, which is designed for oversight and approval for assessment and internal and external testing, including penetration testing and network scanning.

SECURITY ASSESSMENT PLAN DEVELOPMENTAL PROCESS

1. *Develop security assessment policy*: Organizations should develop an information security assessment policy to provide direction and guidance for their security assessments. This policy should identify security assessment requirements and hold accountable those individuals, who are responsible for ensuring that assessments comply with the requirements. The approved policy should be disseminated to the appropriate staff, as well as third parties, who are to conduct assessments for the organization. The policy should be reviewed at least annually and whenever there are new assessment-related requirements.
2. *Prioritize and schedule assessment*: Organizations should decide which systems should undergo assessments and how often these assessments should be done. This prioritization is based on system categorization, expected benefits, scheduling requirements, applicable regulations where assessment is a requirement, and resource availability. Technical considerations can also help determine assessment frequency, such as waiting until known weaknesses are corrected or a planned upgrade to the system is performed before conducting testing.

3. *Select and customize testing techniques*: There are many factors for organizations to consider when determining, which techniques should be used for a particular assessment. Factors include the assessment objectives, the classes of techniques that can obtain information to support those objectives, and the appropriate techniques within each class. Some techniques also require the organization to determine the assessors' viewpoint (e.g., internal versus external) so that the corresponding techniques can be selected.

4. *Determine logistics of assessment*: This includes identifying all required resources, including the assessment team; selecting environments and locations from where to perform the assessment; and acquiring and configuring all necessary technical tools.

5. *Develop the assessment plan*: The assessment plan documents the activities planned for an assessment and other related information. A plan should be developed for every assessment to provide the rules and boundaries to which assessors must adhere. The plan should identify the systems and networks to be assessed, the type and level of testing permitted, logistical details of the assessment, data handling requirements, and guidance for incident handling.

6. *Address legal considerations*: Organizations should evaluate potential legal concerns before commencing an assessment, particularly, if the assessment involves intrusive tests (e.g., penetration testing) or if the assessment is to be performed by an external entity. Legal departments may review the assessment plan, address privacy concerns, and perform other functions in support of assessment planning.

SECURITY ASSESSMENT ACTIONS

Now that we have defined the plan for the assessment, along with the objectives, testing methods, and expected actions, let us discuss the actual and specific control assessment process and mechanisms. I have retrieved data from the federal standards (FIPS-200) and the testing guide from NIST (SP 800-53A) to compile this list as well as my own experience testing and evaluating controls for each area and family of controls that is referenced as follows:

1. NIST SP 800-53, rev. 4 controls
   There are 205 base controls in 18 families. The base XX[1]-1 control for each family is the policy control used to ensure that there is a core organizational policy for this family of security controls. So, AC-1 is the policy control for access control and IR-1 is the policy control for incident response and so on, through each of the 18 families of controls. Additionally, most of the rest of the security controls in each family has enhancements of the control designated by the number of the enhancement inside a parenthesis. So AC-2 control has XX enhancements designated as AC-2 (1) (2) and so on. "The security control enhancements section provides statements of security capability to:
   (i)   Add functionality/specificity to a control; and/or
   (ii) Increase the strength of a control. In both cases, control enhancements are used in the information systems and environments of operation, which require greater protection than provided by the base control due to the potential adverse

---

[1]XX refers to the 2 character family identifier – such as AC for Access Control and IR for Incident Response.

organizational impacts, or when organizations seek additions to the base control functionality/specificity based on organizational assessments of risk.

Security control enhancements are numbered sequentially within each control so that the enhancements can be easily identified, when selected to supplement the base control. Each security control enhancement has a short subtitle to indicate the intended security capability provided by the control enhancement. The numerical designation of a control enhancement is used only to identify the particular enhancement within the control. The designation is not indicative of either the strength of the control enhancement or any hierarchical relationship among the enhancements. Control enhancements are not intended to be selected independently (i.e., if a control enhancement is selected, then the corresponding base security control must also be selected)."[2]

Controls are defined in many ways throughout the various catalogs of security controls (SP 800-53, ISO 27002, DHS EBK, etc.), but mostly all the security controls are found to be within certain types, based upon their use and make-up. Typically, I find the following definitions for the types of security controls used:

- *Preventive*: This control set is the primary control set needed for any system. The preventive control is designed to stop some negative event from happening, inhibit attempts to violate security policies, or provide the ability to stop potentially an adverse incident from occurring.
- *Detective:* This class of controls is designed to indicate that some adverse activity or condition is currently happening. These controls are intended to identify and characterize an incident in progress or an incident that is considered active.
- *Corrective*: The corrective control set is designed to limit the extent of any adverse event and usually, it is used and deployed in conjunction with detective controls. These controls are intended to limit the extent of any damage caused by an incident.
- *Directive*: This control set mandates the behavior of an entity by specifying what actions are, or are not, permitted. These controls are primarily security policies and regulatory guidance.
- *Deterrent*: Deterrent controls are intended to discourage individuals from intentionally violating information security policies or procedures. These controls are placed into effect to "keep the good people good." These usually take the form of constraints that make it difficult or undesirable to perform unauthorized activities and mention the consequences of these activities in order to influence a potential intruder not to violate the security.
- *Supplemental*: The special use or specialized focus of various types of security controls as needed or required by some special event, incident, or activity from an internal or external source is the control set known as supplemental controls.
- *Recovery*: This control set provides the capability to restore lost computing resources or capabilities and help recover monetary losses caused by a security incident. Recovery controls are neither preventive nor detective, but often are included as disaster recovery or contingency plans.

[2]SP 800-53, rev. 4, p.e 12.

SECURITY CONTROLS BY FAMILY

The breakouts for testing of each individual control follow this area. I have included the NIST SP800-53A, rev. 4 guidance for each control in the testing sections.

A. *Access control (AC) family*

FIPS-200 provides the following criteria for this family of controls: "Organizations must limit information system access to authorized users, processes acting on behalf of authorized users, or devices (including other information systems) and to the types of transactions and functions that authorized users are permitted to exercise."

The primary assessment areas for these controls include:

a. Audit system components that enable the limitation of information system access to authorized users

b. Review security elements in a system so that they limit access to processes acting on behalf of authorized users

c. Assess controls on a system that facilitate the limitation of information system access to the devices (including other information systems)

d. Inspect system controls that govern the types of transactions and functions that authorized users are permitted to exercise

Control number	Control name	Assessment methods	Notes and guidance	SP 800-53A Guidance
AC-1	Access control policy and procedures	Review the organizational access control policy. Interview about and discuss policy implementation with Security Officer and System Owner.	SP 800-12, SP 800-100	*Examine:* Access control policy and procedures; other relevant documents or records. *Interview:* Organizational personnel with access control responsibilities; organizational personnel with information security responsibilities.
AC-2	Account management	Review the organizational access control procedures. Review account management documents and request forms. Interview about and discuss procedural actions and implementation efforts with Security Officer and System Owner.		*Examine:* Access control policy; procedures addressing account management; security plan; information system design documentation; information system configuration settings and associated documentation; list of active system accounts along with the name of the individual associated with each account; list of conditions for group and role membership; notifications or records of recently transferred, separated, or terminated employees; list of recently disabled information system accounts along with the name of the individual associated with each account; access authorization records; account management compliance reviews; information system monitoring records; information system audit records; other relevant documents or records. *Interview:* Organizational personnel with account management responsibilities; system/network administrators; organizational personnel with information security responsibilities. *Test:* Organizational processes account management on the information system; automated mechanisms for implementing account management.
AC-2(1)	Account management: Automated system account management	Review the organizational access control policy and procedures. Test the access control system via scanners and compliance checkers.		*Examine:* Access control policy; procedures addressing account management; information system design documentation; information system configuration settings and associated documentation; information system audit records; other relevant documents or records. *Interview:* Organizational personnel with account management responsibilities; system/network administrators; organizational

Control number	Control name	Assessment methods	Notes and guidance	SP 800-53A Guidance
				personnel with information security responsibilities; system developers. *Test*: Automated mechanisms implementing account management functions.
AC-2(2)	Account management: Removal of temporary/emergency accounts	Review the organizational access control procedures. Review account management documents and request forms. Interview about and discuss procedural actions and implementation efforts with Security Officer and System Owner. Test the access control system via scanners and compliance checkers.		*Examine*: Access control policy; procedures addressing account management; security plan; information system design documentation; information system configuration settings and associated documentation; information system-generated list of temporary accounts removed and/or disabled; information system-generated list of emergency accounts removed and/or disabled; information system audit records; other relevant documents or records. *Interview*: Organizational personnel with account management responsibilities; system/network administrators; organizational personnel with information security responsibilities; system developers. *Test*: Automated mechanisms implementing account management functions.
AC-2(3)	Account management: Disable inactive accounts	Review the organizational access control procedures. Review account management documents and request forms. Interview about and discuss procedural actions and implementation efforts with Security Officer and System Owner. Test the access control system via scanners and compliance checkers.		*Examine*: Access control policy; procedures addressing account management; security plan; information system design documentation; information system configuration settings and associated documentation; information system-generated list of temporary accounts removed and/or disabled; information system-generated list of emergency accounts removed and/or disabled; information system audit records; other relevant documents or records. *Interview*: Organizational personnel with account management responsibilities; system/network administrators; organizational personnel with information security responsibilities; system developers. *Test*: Automated mechanisms implementing account management functions.
AC-2(4)	Account management: Automated audit actions	Review the organizational access control procedures. Review account management documents and request forms.		*Examine*: Access control policy; procedures addressing account management; information system design documentation; information system configuration settings and associated documentation;

		Interview about and discuss procedural actions and implementation efforts with Security Officer and System Owner. Test the access control system via scanners and compliance checkers.	notifications/alerts of account creation, modification, enabling, disabling, and removal actions; information system audit records; other relevant documents or records. *Interview:* Organizational personnel with account management responsibilities; organizational personnel with information security responsibilities. *Test:* Automated mechanisms implementing account management functions.
AC-2(5)	Account management: Inactivity logout	Review the organizational access control procedures. Review account management documents and request forms. Interview about and discuss procedural actions and implementation efforts with Security Officer and System Owner. Test the access control system via scanners and compliance checkers.	*Examine:* Access control policy; procedures addressing account management; security plan; information system design documentation; information system configuration settings and associated documentation; security violation reports; information system audit records; other relevant documents or records. *Interview:* Organizational personnel with account management responsibilities; system/network administrators; organizational personnel with information security responsibilities; users that must comply with inactivity logout policy.
AC-2(6)	Account management: Dynamic privilege management	Review the organizational access control procedures. Review account management documents and request forms. Interview about and discuss procedural actions and implementation efforts with Security Officer and System Owner. Test the access control system via scanners and compliance checkers.	*Examine:* Access control policy; procedures addressing account management; information system design documentation; information system configuration settings and associated documentation; system-generated list of dynamic privilege management capabilities; information system audit records; other relevant documents or records. *Interview:* Organizational personnel with account management responsibilities; system/network administrators; organizational personnel with information security responsibilities; system developers. *Test:* Information system implementing dynamic privilege management capabilities.
AC-2(7)	Account management: Role-based schemes	Review the organizational access control procedures. Review account management documents and request forms. Interview about and discuss	*Examine:* Access control policy; procedures addressing account management; information system design documentation; information system configuration settings and associated documentation; information system-generated list of privileged user accounts and

(Continued)

Control number	Control name	Assessment methods	Notes and guidance	SP 800-53A Guidance
		procedural actions and implementation efforts with Security Officer and System Owner. Test the access control system via scanners and compliance checkers.		associated role; records of actions taken when privileged role assignments are no longer appropriate; information system audit records; audit tracking and monitoring reports; information system monitoring records; other relevant documents or records. *Interview:* Organizational personnel with account management responsibilities; system/network administrators; organizational personnel with information security responsibilities. *Test:* Automated mechanisms implementing account management functions; automated mechanisms monitoring privileged role assignments.
AC-2(8)	Account management: Dynamic account creation	Review the organizational access control procedures. Review account management documents and request forms. Interview about and discuss procedural actions and implementation efforts with Security Officer and System Owner. Test the access control system via scanners and compliance checkers.		*Examine:* Access control policy; procedures addressing account management; information system design documentation; information system configuration settings and associated documentation; system-generated list of information system accounts; information system audit records; other relevant documents or records. *Interview:* Organizational personnel with account management responsibilities; system/network administrators; organizational personnel with information security responsibilities; system developers. *Test:* Automated mechanisms implementing account management functions.
AC-2(9)	Account management: Restrictions on use of shared/group accounts	Review the organizational access control procedures. Review account management documents and request forms. Interview about and discuss procedural actions and implementation efforts with Security Officer and System Owner. Test the access control system via scanners and compliance checkers.		*Examine:* Access control policy; procedures addressing account management; information system design documentation; information system configuration settings and associated documentation; system-generated list of shared/group accounts and associated role; information system audit records; other relevant documents or records. *Interview:* Organizational personnel with account management responsibilities; system/network administrators; organizational personnel with information security responsibilities. *Test:* Automated mechanisms implementing management of shared/group accounts.

AC-2(10)	Account management: Shared/group account credential termination	Review the organizational access control procedures. Review account management documents and request forms. Interview about and discuss procedural actions and implementation efforts with Security Officer and System Owner. Test the access control system via scanners and compliance checkers.	*Examine:* Access control policy; procedures addressing account management; information system design documentation; information system configuration settings and associated documentation; account access termination records; information system audit records; other relevant documents or records. *Interview:* Organizational personnel with account management responsibilities; system/network administrators; organizational personnel with information security responsibilities; system developers. *Test:* Automated mechanisms implementing account management functions.
AC-2(11)	Account management: Usage conditions	Review the organizational access control procedures. Review account management documents and request forms. Interview about and discuss procedural actions and implementation efforts with Security Officer and System Owner. Test the access control system via scanners and compliance checkers.	*Examine:* Access control policy; procedures addressing account management; information system design documentation; information system configuration settings and associated documentation; system-generated list of information system accounts and associated assignments of usage circumstances and/or usage conditions; information system audit records; other relevant documents or records. *Interview:* Organizational personnel with account management responsibilities; system/network administrators; organizational personnel with information security responsibilities; system developers. *Test:* Automated mechanisms implementing account management functions.
AC-2(12)	Account management: Account monitoring/A typical usage	Review the organizational access control procedures. Review account management documents and request forms. Interview about and discuss procedural actions and implementation efforts with Security Officer and System Owner. Test the access control system via scanners and compliance checkers.	*Examine:* Access control policy; procedures addressing account management; information system design documentation; information system configuration settings and associated documentation; information system monitoring records; information system audit records; audit tracking and monitoring reports; other relevant documents or records. *Interview:* Organizational personnel with account management responsibilities; system/network administrators; organizational personnel with information security responsibilities. *Test:* Automated mechanisms implementing account management functions.

(Continued)

Control number	Control name	Assessment methods	Notes and guidance	SP 800-53A Guidance
AC-2(13)	Account management: Disable accounts for high-risk individuals	Review the organizational access control procedures. Review account management documents and request forms. Interview about and discuss procedural actions and implementation efforts with Security Officer and System Owner. Test the access control system via scanners and compliance checkers.		*Examine:* Access control policy; procedures addressing account management; information system design documentation; information system configuration settings and associated documentation; system-generated list of disabled accounts; list of user activities posing significant organizational risk; information system audit records; other relevant documents or records. *Interview:* Organizational personnel with account management responsibilities; system/network administrators; organizational personnel with information security responsibilities. *Test:* Automated mechanisms implementing account management functions.
AC-3	Access enforcement	Review the organizational access control procedures. Review account management documents and request forms. Interview about and discuss procedural actions and implementation efforts with Security Officer and System Owner. Test the access control system via scanners and compliance checkers.		*Examine:* Access control policy; procedures addressing access enforcement; information system design documentation; information system configuration settings and associated documentation; list of approved authorizations (user privileges); information system audit records; other relevant documents or records. *Interview:* Organizational personnel with access enforcement responsibilities; system/network administrators; organizational personnel with information security responsibilities; system developers. *Test:* Automated mechanisms implementing access control policy.
AC-3(1)	Access enforcement: Restricted access to privileged functions		Withdrawn: Incorporated into AC-6	
AC-3(2)	Access enforcement: Dual authorization	Review access control documentation to ensure organization implements dual authorization control for specified actions and activities. Test system with scripts or automated mechanisms for dual control		*Examine:* Access control policy; procedures addressing access enforcement and dual authorization; security plan; information system design documentation; information system configuration settings and associated documentation; list of privileged commands requiring dual authorization; list of actions requiring dual authorization; list of approved authorizations (user privileges); other relevant

		documents or records. *Interview:* Organizational personnel with access enforcement responsibilities; system/network administrators; organizational personnel with information security responsibilities; system developers. *Test:* Dual authorization mechanisms implementing access control policy.	requirements. Discuss with System Owner, Operations staff, and Security Officer.
AC-3(3)	Access enforcement: Mandatory access control	*Examine:* Access control policy; mandatory access control policies; procedures addressing access enforcement; security plan; information system design documentation; information system configuration settings and associated documentation; list of subjects and objects (i.e., users and resources) requiring enforcement of mandatory access control policies; information system audit records; other relevant documents or records. *Interview:* Organizational personnel with access enforcement responsibilities; system/network administrators; organizational personnel with information security responsibilities; system developers. *Test:* Automated mechanisms implementing mandatory access control.	Review the organizational access control procedures. Review account management documents and request forms. Interview about and discuss procedural actions and implementation efforts with Security Officer and System Owner. Test the access control system via scanners and compliance checkers.
AC-3(4)	Access enforcement: Discretionary access control	*Examine:* Access control policy; discretionary access control policies; procedures addressing access enforcement; security plan; information system design documentation; information system configuration settings and associated documentation; list of subjects and objects (i.e., users and resources) requiring enforcement of discretionary access control policies; information system audit records; other relevant documents or records. *Interview:* Organizational personnel with access enforcement responsibilities; system/network administrators; organizational personnel with information security responsibilities; system developers. *Test:* Automated mechanisms implementing discretionary access control policy.	Review the organizational access control procedures. Review account management documents and request forms. Interview about and discuss procedural actions and implementation efforts with Security Officer and System Owner. Test the access control system via scanners and compliance checkers.
AC-3(5)	Access enforcement: Security-relevant information	*Examine:* Access control policy; procedures addressing access enforcement; security plan; information system design documentation; information system configuration settings and associated documentation;	Review the organizational access control procedures. Review account management documents and request forms.

(Continued)

Control number	Control name	Assessment methods	Notes and guidance	SP 800-53A Guidance
		Interview about and discuss procedural actions and implementation efforts with Security Officer and System Owner. Test the access control system via scanners and compliance checkers.		information system audit records; other relevant documents or records. *Interview:* Organizational personnel with access enforcement responsibilities; system/network administrators; organizational personnel with information security responsibilities; system developers. *Test:* Automated mechanisms preventing access to security-relevant information within the information system.
AC-3(6)	Access enforcement: Protection of user and system information		Withdrawn: Incorporated into MP-4 and SC-28	
AC-3(7)	Access enforcement: Role-based access control	If assessing a Microsoft deployment, review active directory roles and groups. Check to ensure that group policy objects (GPOs) are implemented and active.		*Examine:* Access control policy; role-based access control policies; procedures addressing access enforcement; security plan, information system design documentation; information system configuration settings and associated documentation; list of roles, users, and associated privileges required to control information system access; information system audit records; other relevant documents or records. *Interview:* Organizational personnel with access enforcement responsibilities; system/network administrators; organizational personnel with information security responsibilities; system developers. *Test:* Automated mechanisms implementing role-based access control policy.
AC-3(8)	Access enforcement: Revocation of access authorizations	Review the organizational access control procedures. Review account management documents and request forms. Interview about and discuss procedural actions and implementation efforts with Security Officer and System Owner. Test the access control system via scanners and compliance checkers.		*Examine:* Access control policy; procedures addressing access enforcement; information system design documentation; information system configuration settings and associated documentation; rules governing revocation of access authorizations, information system audit records; other relevant documents or records. *Interview:* Organizational personnel with access enforcement responsibilities; system/network administrators; organizational personnel with information security responsibilities; system developers. *Test:* Automated mechanisms implementing access enforcement functions.

AC-3(9)	Access enforcement: Controlled release	Review the organizational access control procedures for external release of information and access. Review account management documents to ensure that appropriate access requirements are documented for any informational release outside system boundaries. Interview about and discuss procedural actions and implementation efforts with Security Officer and System Owner.	*Examine:* Access control policy; procedures addressing access enforcement; information system design documentation; information system configuration settings and associated documentation; list of security safeguards provided by receiving information system or system components; list of security safeguards validating appropriateness of information designated for release; information system audit records; other relevant documents or records. *Interview:* Organizational personnel with access enforcement responsibilities; system/network administrators; organizational personnel with information security responsibilities; system developers. *Test:* Automated mechanisms implementing access enforcement functions.
AC-3(10)	Access enforcement: Audited override of access control mechanisms	Review the organizational access control procedures. Review account management documents and request forms. Interview about and discuss procedural actions and implementation efforts with Security Officer and System Owner. Test the access control system via scanners and compliance checkers.	*Examine:* Access control policy; procedures addressing access enforcement; information system design documentation; information system configuration settings and associated documentation; conditions for employing audited override of automated access control mechanisms; information system audit records; other relevant documents or records. *Interview:* Organizational personnel with access enforcement responsibilities; system/network administrators; organizational personnel with information security responsibilities. *Test:* Automated mechanisms implementing access enforcement functions.
AC-4	Information flow enforcement	Review documentation for system to ensure that information flow control is installed and active. Flow control regulates where information is allowed to travel within an information system and between information systems (as opposed to who is allowed to access the information) and without explicit regard	*Examine:* Access control policy; information flow control policies; procedures addressing information flow enforcement; information system design documentation; information system configuration settings and associated documentation; information system baseline configuration; list of information flow authorizations; information system audit records; other relevant documents or records. *Interview:* System/network administrators; organizational personnel with information security

(Continued)

Control number	Control name	Notes and guidance	Assessment methods	SP 800-53A Guidance
			to subsequent accesses to that information. Ensure all automated mechanisms for information flow are active and functioning correctly by testing flow control components with test data and scripts. Discuss with System Owner, Security Officer, and operations staff.	responsibilities; system developers. *Test:* Automated mechanisms implementing information flow enforcement policy.
AC-4(1)	Information flow enforcement: Object security attributes		Review access control documentation to ensure that security-labeling attributes are utilized for proper information flow enforcement. This process compares security attributes associated with information (data content and data structure) and source/destination objects, and respond appropriately (e.g., block, quarantine, alert administrator), when flows are not explicitly allowed by policies. Test with scripted test data to ensure that labeling efforts are applied and functioning correctly. Discuss with Security Officer, System Owner, and security staff.	*Examine:* Access control policy; information flow control policies; procedures addressing information flow enforcement; information system design documentation; information system configuration settings and associated documentation; list of security attributes and associated information, source, and destination objects enforcing information flow control policies; information system audit records; other relevant documents or records. *Interview:* System/network administrators; organizational personnel with information security responsibilities; system developers. *Test:* Automated mechanisms implementing information flow enforcement policy.
AC-4(2)	Information flow enforcement: Processing domains		Review system documentation to ensure processing domains are implemented successfully. The protected processing domains are processing spaces that have controlled interactions with other processing spaces, thus enabling control of information flows between	*Examine:* Access control policy; information flow control policies; procedures addressing information flow enforcement; information system design documentation; information system security architecture and associated documentation; information system configuration settings and associated documentation; information system audit records; other relevant documents or records. *Interview:* System/network administrators; organizational personnel with information security

		these spaces and to/from data/information objects. Evaluate the implementation of processing domain structures to ensure that full and complete structures are installed correctly. Discuss with security architect, security engineer, Security Officer, System Owner, and development staff	responsibilities. *Test:* Automated mechanisms implementing information flow enforcement policy.
AC-4(3)	Information flow enforcement: Dynamic information flow control	Review flow control documentation to ensure dynamic conditions and events will trigger changes in the information flow enforcement processes. Test with scripted test data to simulate changing conditions and review results with Security Officer, System Owner, and security staff.	*Examine:* Access control policy; information flow control policies; procedures addressing information flow enforcement; information system design documentation; information system security architecture and associated documentation; information system configuration settings and associated documentation; information system audit records; other relevant documents or records. *Interview:* System/network administrators; organizational personnel with information security responsibilities; system developers. *Test:* Automated mechanisms implementing information flow enforcement policy.
AC-4(4)	Information flow enforcement: Content check encrypted information	Review flow control documentation to ensure that all encrypted information and traffic is reviewed via decryption or isolated due to inability to decrypt for security purposes. Discuss with System Owner, Security Officer, and security staff.	*Examine:* Access control policy; information flow control policies; procedures addressing information flow enforcement; information system design documentation; information system configuration settings and associated documentation; information system audit records; other relevant documents or records. *Interview:* System/network administrators; organizational personnel with information security responsibilities; system developers. *Test:* Automated mechanisms implementing information flow enforcement policy.
AC-4(5)	Information flow enforcement: Embedded data types	Review documentation to ensure embedded data types, such as inserting executable files as objects within word	*Examine:* Access control policy; procedures addressing information flow enforcement; information system design documentation; information system configuration settings and associated documentation;

(Continued)

Control number	Control name	Notes and guidance	Assessment methods	SP 800-53A Guidance
			processing files, inserting references or descriptive information into a media file, and compressed or archived data types that may include multiple embedded data types are reviewed and limited to organizationally defined levels. Test levels with samples of embedded data types to ensure tools decipher data correctly. Discuss with System Owner, Security Officer, and security staff.	list of limitations to be enforced on embedding data types within other data types; information system audit records; other relevant documents or records. *Interview:* System/network administrators; organizational personnel with information security responsibilities; system developers. *Test:* Automated mechanisms implementing information flow enforcement policy.
AC-4(6)	Information flow enforcement: Metadata		Review documentation for metadata, data about the data, attached and associated with the information on the system. Review integrity, accuracy, and binding of metadata to data system components. Review sample metadata components for completeness, accuracy, and trustworthiness of metadata. Discuss with System Owner, data owner(s), Security Officer, and security staff.	*Examine:* Access control policy; information flow control policies; procedures addressing information flow enforcement; information system design documentation; information system configuration settings and associated documentation; types of metadata used to enforce information flow control decisions; information system audit records; other relevant documents or records. *Interview:* System/network administrators; organizational personnel with information security responsibilities; system developers. *Test:* Automated mechanisms implementing information flow enforcement policy.
AC-4(7)	Information flow enforcement: One-way flow mechanisms		Review system documentation for implementation of one-way hardware-based flow control mechanisms. Discuss with Security Officer, System Owner, and security staff.	*Examine:* Access control policy; information flow control policies; procedures addressing information flow enforcement; information system design documentation; information system configuration settings and associated documentation; information system hardware mechanisms and associated configurations; information system audit records; other relevant documents or records. *Interview:* System/network administrators; organizational personnel with information security responsibilities;

AC-4(8)	Information flow enforcement: Security policy filters	Review system-level documentation to determine the implementation of security policy filters for the flow control of information. Review documentation for filter settings and criteria to ensure assignment and applicability of flow control filtering activities. Discuss with Security Officer, security staff, and operations staff.	system developers. *Test:* Hardware mechanisms implementing information flow enforcement policy. *Examine:* Access control policy; procedures addressing information flow enforcement; information system design documentation; information system configuration settings and associated documentation; list of security policy filters regulating flow control decisions; information system audit records; other relevant documents or records. *Interview:* System/network administrators; organizational personnel with information security responsibilities; system developers. *Test:* Automated mechanisms implementing information flow enforcement policy.
AC-4(9)	Information flow enforcement: Human reviews	Review documentation to ensure that the organization employs human filtering processes and procedures, when automated filtering mechanisms cannot be fully accomplished. Discuss methods and procedures with System Owner, Security Officer, and security staff.	*Examine:* Access control policy; procedures addressing information flow enforcement; information system design documentation; information system configuration settings and associated documentation; records of human reviews regarding information flows; list of conditions requiring human reviews for information flows; information system audit records; other relevant documents or records. *Interview:* System/network administrators; organizational personnel with information flow enforcement responsibilities; system developers. *Test:* Automated mechanisms enforcing the use of human reviews.
AC-4(10)	Information flow enforcement: Enable/disable security policy filters	Review access control documentation to determine organizational criteria for enabling or disabling of security policy filters. Ensure only authorized administrators can enable security policy filters to accommodate approved data	*Examine:* Access control policy; procedures addressing information flow enforcement; information system design documentation; information system configuration settings and associated documentation; list of security policy filters enabled/disabled by privileged administrators; information system audit records; other relevant documents or records. *Interview:* Organizational personnel with responsibilities

(Continued)

Control number	Control name	Notes and guidance	Assessment methods	SP 800-53A Guidance
			types. Discuss with System Owner, Information Owner(s), security staff, and Security Officer.	for enabling/disabling security policy filters; system/network administrators; organizational personnel with information security responsibilities; system developers. *Test:* Automated mechanisms implementing information flow enforcement policy.
AC-4(11)	Information flow enforcement: Configuration of security policy filters		Review access control documentation to determine the level of control allowed system administrators to configure security policy filters. Ensure the processes for configuration, such as administrators changing the list of "dirty words" that security policy mechanisms check in accordance with the definitions provided by organization is monitored and controlled. Discuss with operations staff, System Owner, Information Owner(s), security staff, and Security Officer.	*Examine:* Access control policy; information flow control policies; procedures addressing information flow enforcement; information system design documentation; information system configuration settings and associated documentation; list of security policy filters; information system audit records; other relevant documents or records. *Interview:* Organizational personnel with responsibilities for configuring security policy filters; system/network administrators; organizational personnel with information security responsibilities; system developers. *Test:* Automated mechanisms implementing information flow enforcement policy.
AC-4(12)	Information flow enforcement: Data type identifiers		Review access control documentation to determine, if organization has defined the various allowed data type identifiers for filtering, such as filenames, file types, file signatures/tokens, and multiple internal file signatures/tokens. Ensure enforcement mechanisms are active and functional through testing of data types. Discuss with System Owner, security staff, operations staff, Information Owner(s) and Security Officer.	*Examine:* Access control policy; information flow control policies; procedures addressing information flow enforcement; information system design documentation; information system configuration settings and associated documentation; list of data type identifiers; information system audit records; other relevant documents or records. *Interview:* System/network administrators; organizational personnel with information security responsibilities; system developers. *Test:* Automated mechanisms implementing information flow enforcement policy.

AC-4(13)	Information flow enforcement: Decomposition into policy-relevant subcomponents	Review access control documentation to determine the level of decomposition and filtering employed by system by filtering, inspection, and/or sanitization rules being enforced. Discuss with security staff, operations staff, information owner(s). System Owner and Security Officer.	*Examine:* Access control policy; information flow control policies; procedures addressing information flow enforcement; information system design documentation; information system configuration settings and associated documentation; information system audit records; other relevant documents or records. *Interview:* System/network administrators; organizational personnel with information security responsibilities; system developers. *Test:* Automated mechanisms implementing information flow enforcement policy.
AC-4(14)	Information flow enforcement: Security policy filter constraints	Review access control documentation to determine the level of filter constraints utilized, such as data structure and content restrictions, which reduce the range of potential malicious and/or unsanctioned content in cross-domain transactions. Test with scripts and sample data inputs to verify that filtering is active and functioning correctly. Discuss with System Owner, information(s), operations staff, security staff, and Security Officer.	*Examine:* Access control policy; information flow control policies; procedures addressing information flow enforcement; information system design documentation; information system configuration settings and associated documentation; list of security policy filters; list of data content policy filters; information system audit records; other relevant documents or records. *Interview:* System/network administrators; organizational personnel with information security responsibilities; system developers. *Test:* Automated mechanisms implementing information flow enforcement policy.
AC-4(15)	Information flow enforcement: Detection of unsanctioned information	Review access control documentation to ensure that the detection of unacceptable information is not allowed within system. Detection of unsanctioned information includes, for example, checking all information to be transferred for malicious code and dirty words. Verify these detection actions with sample	*Examine:* Access control policy; information flow control policies; procedures addressing information flow enforcement; information system design documentation; information system configuration settings and associated documentation; list of unsanctioned information types and associated information; information system audit records; other relevant documents or records. *Interview:* Organizational personnel with information security responsibilities; system developers. *Test:* Automated mechanisms implementing information flow enforcement policy.

(Continued)

Control number	Control name	Assessment methods	Notes and guidance	SP 800-53A Guidance
		input of test data. Discuss with Information Owner(s), System Owner, operations staff, security staff, and Security Officer.		
AC-4(16)	Information flow enforcement: Information transfers on interconnected systems		Withdrawn: Incorporated into AC-4	
AC-4(17)	Information flow enforcement: Domain authentication	Review documentation for system to ensure that domain authentication is performed for all transactions on the system. This authentication requires information system labels distinguish among systems, organizations, and individuals involved in preparing, sending, receiving, or disseminating information to provide proper security levels by maintaining the confidentiality and integrity of the information. Test via sample inputs of false data and verification of system responses. Discuss with System Owner, operations staff, security staff, Information Owner(s) and Security Officer.		*Examine:* Access control policy; information flow control policies; procedures addressing information flow enforcement; procedures addressing source and destination domain identification and authentication; information system design documentation; information system configuration settings and associated documentation; information system audit records; other relevant documents or records. *Interview:* System/network administrators; organizational personnel with information security responsibilities; system developers. *Test:* Automated mechanisms implementing information flow enforcement policy.
AC-4(18)	Information flow enforcement: Security attribute binding	Review access control documentation to determine the level of security label binding to all information		*Examine:* Information flow enforcement policy; information flow control policies; procedures addressing information flow enforcement; information system design documentation;

	flowing within system. Discuss with System Owner, Information Owner(s), security staff, and Security Office.		information system configuration settings and associated documentation; list of binding techniques to bind security attributes to information; information system audit records; other relevant documents or records. *Interview:* Organizational personnel with information flow enforcement responsibilities; system/network administrators; organizational personnel with information security responsibilities; system developers. *Test:* Automated mechanisms implementing information flow enforcement functions.
AC-4(19)	Information flow enforcement: Validation of metadata	Review access control documentation to ensure that the system validates metadata along with the actual data, when enforcing all security filtering and flow controls. Discuss with System Owner, Information Owner(s), security staff, and Security Officer.		*Examine:* Information flow enforcement policy; information flow control policies; procedures addressing information flow enforcement; information system design documentation; information system configuration settings and associated documentation; list of security policy filtering criteria applied to metadata and data payloads; information system audit records; other relevant documents or records. *Interview:* Organizational personnel with information flow enforcement responsibilities; system/network administrators; organizational personnel with information security responsibilities; system developers. *Test:* Automated mechanisms implementing information flow enforcement functions.
AC-4(20)	Information flow enforcement: Approved solutions	Review documentation to ensure that organization provides approved solutions and configurations in cross-domain policies and guidance in accordance with the types of information flows across classification boundaries for system when required. Review CDS documentation to ensure that overlay for	Unified cross domain management office (UCDMO) documentation, CNSSI 1253, Appendix F for CDS systems	*Examine:* Information flow enforcement policy; information flow control policies; procedures addressing information flow enforcement; information system design documentation; information system configuration settings and associated documentation; list of solutions in approved configurations; approved configuration baselines; information system audit records; other relevant documents or records. *Interview:* Organizational personnel with information flow enforcement responsibilities; system/network administrators; organizational personnel with

(Continued)

Control number	Control name	Assessment methods	Notes and guidance	SP 800-53A Guidance
		CDS is applied appropriately. Discuss with FSO, security staff, System Owner, Information Owner(s) and Security Officer.		information security responsibilities. *Test*: Automated mechanisms implementing information flow enforcement functions.
AC-4(21)	Information flow enforcement: Physical/logical separation of information flows	Review documentation to determine the separation for information flows within system meet data classification requirements, such as inbound and outbound communications traffic, service requests and responses, and information of differing security categories. Test separation with test data inputs and resultant reporting outputs showing maintenance of separation. Discuss with security staff, Information Owner(s), System Owner, operations staff, and Security Officer.		*Examine*: Information flow enforcement policy; information flow control policies; procedures addressing information flow enforcement; information system design documentation; information system configuration settings and associated documentation; list of required separation of information flows by information types; list of mechanisms and/or techniques used to logically or physically separate information flows; information system audit records; other relevant documents or records. *Interview*: Organizational personnel with information flow enforcement responsibilities; system/network administrators; organizational personnel with information security responsibilities; system developers. *Test*: Automated mechanisms implementing information flow enforcement functions.
AC-4(22)	Information flow enforcement: Access only	Review documentation for use and employment of access only devices, such as KVM switches, to maintain separation between different information types. Such devices provide a desktop for users to access each connected security domain without providing any mechanisms to allow transfer of information between the different security domains. Observe use and operation of these devices		*Examine*: information flow enforcement policy; procedures addressing information flow enforcement; information system design documentation; information system configuration settings and associated documentation; information system audit records; other relevant documents or records. *Interview*: Organizational personnel with information flow enforcement responsibilities; system/network administrators; organizational personnel with information security responsibilities. *Test*: Automated mechanisms implementing information flow enforcement functions.

		tc maintain separation. Discuss with System Owner, operations staff, security staff, Information Owner(s), FSO, ar d Security Officer.	
AC-5	Separation of duties	Review documentation of separation of duties within system to provide fraud and collusion protection. Test roles and responsibilities implementation of access control system to evaluate separation criteria and privilege use for administrative tasks and events. Discuss with Security Officer, security staff, FSO, System Owner, operations staff, and Information Owner(s).	*Examine:* Access control policy; procedures addressing divisions of responsibility and separation of duties; information system configuration settings and associated documentation; list of divisions of responsibility and separation of duties; information system access authorizations; information system audit records; other relevant documents or records. *Interview:* Organizational personnel with responsibilities for defining appropriate divisions of responsibility and separation of duties; organizational personnel with information security responsibilities; system/network administrators. *Test:* Automated mechanisms implementing separation of duties policy.
AC-6	Least privilege	Review documentation for system to determine the implementation of the principle of least privilege is employed, where only authorized accesses for users (or processes acting on behalf of users), which are necessary to accomplish assigned tasks in accordance with organizational missions and business functions. Review all roles and responsibilities for users to ensure least privilege is applied. Discuss with System Owrer, Information Owner(s), security staff, operations staff, and Security Officer	*Examine:* Access control policy; procedures addressing least privilege; list of assigned access authorizations (user privileges); information system configuration settings and associated documentation; information system audit records; other relevant documents or records. *Interview:* Organizational personnel with responsibilities for defining least privileges necessary to accomplish specified tasks; organizational personnel with information security responsibilities; system/network administrators. *Test:* Automated mechanisms implementing least privilege functions.

(Continued)

Control number	Control name	Assessment methods	Notes and guidance	SP 800-53A Guidance
AC-6(1)	Least privilege: Authorize access to security functions	Review documentation to determine the least privilege requirements apply to establishing system accounts, configuring access authorizations (i.e., permissions, privileges), setting events to be audited, and setting intrusion detection parameters, during normal system functioning and operations. Evaluate application to obtain proof of least privilege is applied and active. Discuss with security staff, operations staff, System Owner, Information Owner(s), and Security Officer.		*Examine:* Access control policy; procedures addressing least privilege; list of security functions (deployed in hardware, software, and firmware) and security-relevant information for which access must be explicitly authorized; information system configuration settings and associated documentation; information system audit records; other relevant documents or records. *Interview:* Organizational personnel with responsibilities for defining least privileges necessary to accomplish specified tasks; organizational personnel with information security responsibilities; system/network administrators. *Test:* Automated mechanisms implementing least privilege functions.
AC-6(2)	Least privilege: Nonprivileged access for nonsecurity functions	Review documentation to ensure that organization employs nonprivileged access controls when performing nonadministrative functions and activities, such as normal email actions and simple user activities. Discuss with System Owner, operations staff, security staff, and Security Officer.		*Examine:* Access control policy; procedures addressing least privilege; list of system-generated security functions or security-relevant information assigned to information system accounts or roles; information system configuration settings and associated documentation; information system audit records; other relevant documents or records. *Interview:* Organizational personnel with responsibilities for defining least privileges necessary to accomplish specified tasks; organizational personnel with information security responsibilities; system/network administrators. *Test:* Automated mechanisms implementing least privilege functions.
AC-6(3)	Least privilege: Network access to privileged commands	Review documentation to ensure domain access privileges and network privilege access events are monitored and controlled at same level as local		*Examine:* Access control policy; procedures addressing least privilege; security plan; information system configuration settings and associated documentation; information system audit records; list of operational needs for authorizing network access to privileged commands; other relevant documents or records.

		administrative access privileges. Review roles and responsibilities within system to ensure compliance. Discuss with System Owner, security staff, operations staff, and Security Officer.	*Interview:* Organizational personnel with responsibilities for defining least privileges necessary to accomplish specified tasks; organizational personnel with information security responsibilities. *Test:* Automated mechanisms implementing least privilege functions.
AC-6(4)	Least privilege: Separate processing domains	Review documentation for system to ensure finer-grained allocation of user privileges is provided, when processing privileged-based actions in multiple domain environments, such as in virtualization computing and cross-domain system. Discuss with System Owner, Information Owner(s), security staff, operations staff, and Security Officer.	*Examine:* Access control policy; procedures addressing least privilege; information system design documentation; information system configuration settings and associated documentation; information system audit records; other relevant documents or records. *Interview:* Organizational personnel with responsibilities for defining least privileges necessary to accomplish specified tasks; organizational personnel with information security responsibilities; system developers. *Test:* Automated mechanisms implementing least privilege functions.
AC-6(5)	Least privilege: Privileged accounts	Review documentation for system to ensure that privilege account status is explicitly assigned and actions are tracked and logged for all administrative actions. Review logs to ensure actions are logged and evaluated by management. Discuss with System Owner, Information Owner(s), security staff, operations staff, and Security Officer.	*Examine:* Access control policy; procedures addressing least privilege; list of system- generated privileged accounts; list of system administration personnel; information system configuration settings and associated documentation; information system audit records; other relevant documents or records. *Interview:* Organizational personnel with responsibilities for defining least privileges necessary to accomplish specified tasks; organizational personnel with information security responsibilities; system/network administrators. *Test:* Automated mechanisms implementing least privilege functions.
AC-6(6)	Least privilege: Privileged access by nonorganizational users	Review documentation to ensure that the organization prohibits privileged access to the system by noncrganizational users.	*Examine:* Access control policy; procedures addressing least privilege; list of system-generated privileged accounts; list of nonorganizational users; information system configuration settings and associated documentation; information system audit records;

(Continued)

Control number	Control name	Assessment methods	Notes and guidance	SP 800-53A Guidance
		Review logs to ensure compliance. Discuss with Information Owner(s), System Owner, security staff, operations staff, and Security Officer.		other relevant documents or records. *Interview:* Organizational personnel with responsibilities for defining least privileges necessary to accomplish specified tasks; organizational personnel with information security responsibilities; system/network administrators. *Test:* Automated mechanisms prohibiting privileged access to the information system.
AC-6(7)	Least privilege: Review of user privileges	Review access control documentation to ensure that organization conducts periodic review of assigned user privileges to determine if the rationale for assigning such privileges remains valid for mission/business functions. Review logs to ensure compliance and reviews are conducted and approved. Discuss with System Owner, Information Owner(s), security staff, operations staff, and Security Officer.		*Examine:* Access control policy; procedures addressing least privilege; list of system-generated roles or classes of users and assigned privileges; information system design documentation; information system configuration settings and associated documentation; validation reviews of privileges assigned to roles or classes or users; records of privilege removals or reassignments for roles or classes of users; information system audit records; other relevant documents or records. *Interview:* Organizational personnel with responsibilities for reviewing least privileges necessary to accomplish specified tasks; organizational personnel with information security responsibilities; system/network administrators. *Test:* Automated mechanisms implementing review of user privileges.
AC-6(8)	Least privilege: Privilege levels for code execution	Review access control documentation for system to ensure that software applications/programs need to execute with elevated privileges to perform required functions is only implemented for elevated privilege account holders and administrators. Review logs to ensure actions are maintained and operated correctly. Discuss with operations staff, Information Owner(s), System Owner, security staff, and Security Officer.		*Examine:* Access control policy; procedures addressing least privilege; list of software that should not execute at higher privilege levels than users executing software; information system design documentation; information system configuration settings and associated documentation; information system audit records; other relevant documents or records. *Interview:* Organizational personnel with responsibilities for defining least privileges necessary to accomplish specified tasks; organizational personnel with information security responsibilities; system/network administrators; system developers. *Test:* Automated mechanisms implementing least privilege functions for software execution.

AC-6(9)	Least privilege: Auditing use of privileged functions	Review documentation of system to ensure that only privilege account holders have proper permissions to perform elevated privilege actions. Review logs and audit reports to ensure organization monitors and tracks all elevated privilege account usage. Discuss with audit staff, operations staff, Information Owner(s), System, Owner, security staff, and Security Officer.	*Examine:* Access control policy; procedures addressing least privilege; information system design documentation; information system configuration settings and associated documentation; list of privileged functions to be audited; list of audited events; information system audit records; other relevant documents or records. *Interview:* Organizational personnel with responsibilities for reviewing least privileges necessary to accomplish specified tasks; organizational personnel with information security responsibilities; system/network administrators; system developers. *Test:* Automated mechanisms auditing the execution of least privilege functions.
AC-6(10)	Least privilege: Prohibit nonprivileged users from executing privileged functions	Review access control documentation to ensure that system only implements elevated privilege actions to be performed only by approved account holders and restricts nonprivilege users from performing privilege actions. Review logs and access control methodologies to ensure restricts are consistent and fully functional. Discuss with operations staff, security staff, Security Officer and System Owner.	*Examine:* Access control policy; procedures addressing least privilege; information system design documentation; information system configuration settings and associated documentation; list of privileged functions and associated user account assignments; information system audit records; other relevant documents or records. *Interview:* Organizational personnel with responsibilities for defining least privileges necessary to accomplish specified tasks; organizational personnel with information security responsibilities; system developers. *Test:* Automated mechanisms implementing least privilege functions for nonprivileged users.
AC-7	Unsuccessful login attempts	Review documentation to determine the organizational criteria for unsuccessful login attempts and actions to be taken when threshold is reached. The organizational criteria are selectable based on security requirements	*Examine:* Access control policy; procedures addressing unsuccessful logon attempts; security plan; information system design documentation; information system configuration settings and associated documentation; information system audit records; other relevant documents or records. *Interview:* Organizational personnel with information security responsibilities; system developers; system /

(Continued)

Control number	Control name	Assessment methods	Notes and guidance	SP 800-53A Guidance
		for system. Test using both unsuccessful login actions and observe the results and successful login attempts and results. Discuss with System Owner, security staff, operations staff, and Security Officer.		network administrators. *Test:* Automated mechanisms implementing access control policy for unsuccessful logon attempts.
AC-7(1)	Unsuccessful logon attempts: Automatic account lock		Withdrawn: Incorporated into AC-7	
AC-7(2)	Unsuccessful logon attempts: Purge/ wipe mobile device	Review documentation to determine organizational implementation for unsuccessful login attempts on mobile devices and resultant actions. Organizations define information to be purged/ wiped carefully in order to avoid over purging/wiping, which may result in devices becoming unusable in accordance to organizational and agency requirements. Discuss with System Owner, security staff, operations staff, and Security Officer.		*Examine:* Access control policy; procedures addressing unsuccessful login attempts on mobile devices; information system design documentation; information system configuration settings and associated documentation; list of mobile devices to be purged/wiped after organization-defined consecutive, unsuccessful device logon attempts; list of purging/wiping requirements or techniques for mobile devices; information system audit records; other relevant documents or records. *Interview:* System/network administrators; organizational personnel with information security responsibilities. *Test:* Automated mechanisms implementing access control policy for unsuccessful device logon attempts.
AC-8	System use notification	Review documentation to ensure that system implements login banners and displays as necessary for human-based logins onto system. System use notifications can be implemented using messages or warning banners displayed		*Examine:* Access control policy; privacy and security policies; procedures addressing system use notification; documented approval of information system use notification messages or banners; information system audit records; user acknowledgements of notification message or banner; information system design documentation; information system configuration settings and associated documentation; information system use

notification messages; other relevant documents or records. *Interview*: System/network administrators; organizational personnel with information security responsibilities; organizational personnel with responsibility for providing legal advice; system developers. *Test*: Automated mechanisms implementing system use notification.

...before individuals log in to information systems are to be reviewed and evaluated for compliance to legal and operational requirements. Discuss with System Owner, legal staff, operations staff, and Security Officer.

ID	Control	Assessment	Review documentation
AC-9	Previous logon (access) notification	*Examine*: Access control policy; procedures addressing previous logon notification; information system design documentation; information system configuration settings and associated documentation; information system notification messages; other relevant documents or records. *Interview*: System/network administrators; organizational personnel with information security responsibilities; system developers. *Test*: Automated mechanisms implementing access control policy for previous logon notification.	Review documentation for system to determine the implementation of the notification of the user, upon successful logon (access) to the system, of the date, and time of the last logon (access) onto system. Review output for access to confirm implementation utilizing test login actions. Discuss with System Owner, security staff, operations staff and Security Officer.
AC-9(1)	Previous logon notification: Unsuccessful logons	*Examine*: Access control policy; procedures addressing previous logon notification; information system design documentation; information system configuration settings and associated documentation; information system audit records; other relevant documents or records. *Interview*: System/network administrators; organizational personnel with information security responsibilities; system developers. *Test*: Automated mechanisms implementing access control policy for previous logon notification.	Review documentation for system to ensure that it notifies the user, upon successful logon/access, of the number of unsuccessful logon/access attempts, since the last successful logon/access. Review logs to ensure compliance for notifications. Discuss with System Owner, operations staff, security staff, and Security Officer.
AC-9(2)	Previous logon notification: Successful/unsuccessful logons	*Examine*: Access control policy; procedures addressing previous logon notification; information system design documentation; information system configuration settings and associated	Review documentation for system to ensure that it notifies the user of the number of successful and unsuccessful

(Continued)

Control number	Control name	Notes and guidance	Assessment methods	SP 800-53A Guidance
			login attempts during the organizational defined time period. Review logs to ensure compliance for notifications. Discuss with System Owner, operations staff, security staff, and Security Officer.	documentation; information system audit records; other relevant documents or records. *Interview:* System/network administrators; organizational personnel with information security responsibilities; system developers. *Test:* Automated mechanisms implementing access control policy for previous logon notification.
AC-9(3)	Previous logon notification: Notification of account changes		Review documentation for system to ensure that it notifies the user of account changes during the organizational defined time period. Review logs to ensure compliance for notifications. Discuss with System Owner, operations staff, security staff, and Security Officer.	*Examine:* Access control policy; procedures addressing previous logon notification; information system design documentation; information system configuration settings and associated documentation; information system audit records; other relevant documents or records. *Interview:* System/network administrators; organizational personnel with information security responsibilities; system developers. *Test:* Automated mechanisms implementing access control policy for previous logon notification.
AC-9(4)	Previous logon notification: Additional logon information		Review documentation for system to determine what additional information and notification criteria are displayed, when users log into system. This is used to track locations for previous logins and potential areas of concern. Review notification outputs to verify outputs. Discuss with security staff, Security Officer, and System Owner.	*Examine:* Access control policy; procedures addressing previous logon notification; information system design documentation; information system configuration settings and associated documentation; information system audit records; other relevant documents or records. *Interview:* System/network administrators; organizational personnel with information security responsibilities; system developers. *Test:* Automated mechanisms implementing access control policy for previous logon notification.
AC-10	Concurrent session control		Review documentation for system to determine implementation of concurrent session allowances by user type. Review output logs to ensure maximum number	*Examine:* Access control policy; procedures addressing concurrent session control; information system design documentation; information system configuration settings and associated documentation; security plan; other relevant documents or records. *Interview:* System/network administrators; organizational

Control	Name	Reference	Assessment	Assessment methods
			of concurrent sessions for information system accounts globally, by account type (e.g., privileged user, nonprivileged user, domain, specific application), by account, or a combination is defined and implemented. Discuss with operations staff, security staff, System Owner, and Security Officer.	personnel with information security responsibilities; system developers. *Test:* Automated mechanisms implementing access control policy for concurrent session control.
AC-11	Session lock	OMB M06-16	Review documentation for system to determine implementation of session lock on system. Review implementation documents to verify session lock efforts, which are temporary actions taken when users stop work and move away from the immediate vicinity of information systems but do not want to log out because of the temporary nature of their absences; usually implemented with time criteria defined by the organization. Discuss with System Owner, security staff, operations staff, and Security Officer.	*Examine:* Access control policy; procedures addressing session lock; procedures addressing identification and authentication; information system design documentation; information system configuration settings and associated documentation; security plan; other relevant documents or records. *Interview:* System/network administrators; organizational personnel with information security responsibilities; system developers. *Test:* Automated mechanisms implementing access control policy for session lock.
AC-11(1)	Session lock: Pattern-hiding displays	OMB M06-16	Review documentation for system to determine what type of publicly viewable images, such as static or dynamic images, for example, patterns used with screen savers, photographic images,	*Examine:* Access control policy; procedures addressing session lock; display screen with session lock activated; information system design documentation; information system configuration settings and associated documentation; other relevant documents or records. *Interview:* System/network administrators; organizational personnel with information security

(Continued)

Control number	Control name	Assessment methods	Notes and guidance	SP 800-53A Guidance
		solid colors, clock, battery life indicator, or a blank screen, with the additional caveat that none of the images convey sensitive information, are implemented when session lock is invoked on system. Verify by observing displays of images when session lock is triggered. Discuss with System Owner, operations staff, security staff, and Security Officer.		responsibilities; system developers. *Test:* Information system session lock mechanisms.
AC-12	Session termination	Review documentation to ensure that system performs termination of user-initiated logical sessions within organizational defined criteria, such as organization-defined periods of user inactivity, targeted responses to certain types of incidents, time-of-day restrictions on information system use. Verify termination events through testing of input criteria defined by organization and resultant system actions. Discuss with operations staff, security staff, System Owner, and Security Officer.	SC-10	*Examine:* Access control policy; procedures addressing session termination; information system design documentation; information system configuration settings and associated documentation; list of conditions or trigger events requiring session disconnect; information system audit records; other relevant documents or records. *Interview:* System/network administrators; organizational personnel with information security responsibilities; system developers. *Test:* Automated mechanisms implementing user session termination.
AC-12(1)	Session termination: User-initiated logouts/message displays	Review documentation for system to determine the methods and criteria for display messages when logout events occur on the system, such as sending logout		*Examine:* Access control policy; procedures addressing session termination; user logout messages; information system design documentation; information system configuration settings and associated documentation; information system audit records; other relevant documents or records.

Control	Name	Discussion	Withdrawn	Assessment
AC-13	Supervision and review – access control	messages as final messages prior to terminating sessions. Verify output when invoked via logout of user sessions. Discuss with System Owner, operations staff, security staff, and Security Officer.	Withdrawn: Incorporated into AC-2 and AU-6	*Interview:* System/network administrators; organizational personnel with information security responsibilities; system developers. *Test:* Information system session lock mechanisms.
AC-14	Permitted actions without identification or authentication	Review documentation for organization to determine techniques and criteria for when users are permitted onto system without identification or authentication. Review criteria to ensure that proper restrictions are in place and active on these types of logins and access. Discuss with System Owner, security staff, operations staff, and Security Owner.		*Examine:* Access control policy; procedures addressing permitted actions without identification or authentication; information system configuration settings and associated documentation; security plan; list of user actions that can be performed without identification or authentication; information system audit records; other relevant documents or records. *Interview:* System/network administrators; organizational personnel with information security responsibilities.
AC-14(1)	Permitted actions without identification or authentication: Necessary uses		Withdrawn: Incorporated into AC-14	
AC-15	Automated marking		Withdrawn: Incorporated into MP-3	
AC-16	Security attributes	Review documentation for system and organization to ensure implementation of security labeling of information and its		*Examine:* Access control policy; procedures addressing the association of security attributes to information in storage, in process, and in transmission; information system design documentation; information system configuration settings and associated

(Continued)

Control number	Control name	Assessment methods	Notes and guidance	SP 800-53A Guidance
		components to institute mandatory access controls (MAC) on system. Verify implementation through review of all labeling efforts and outputs for each type of user on system. Discuss with Information Owner(s). System Owner, security staff, FSO, operations staff, and Security Officer.		documentation; information system audit records; other relevant documents or records. *Interview:* System/network administrators; organizational personnel with information security responsibilities; system developers. *Test:* Organizational capability supporting and maintaining the association of security attributes to information in storage, in process, and in transmission.
AC-16(1)	Security attributes: Dynamic attribute association	Review documentation for system to determine the extent to which system allows dynamic attribute variables into system due to information aggregation issues (i.e., the security characteristics of individual information elements are different from the combined elements), changes in individual access authorizations (i.e., privileges), and changes in the security category of information. Perform detailed testing of variables of changing MAC levels to ensure full security is maintained. Discuss with Information Owner(s), System Owner, security staff, operations staff, FSO, and Security Officer.		*Examine:* Access control policy; procedures addressing dynamic association of security attributes to information; information system design documentation; information system configuration settings and associated documentation; information system audit records; other relevant documents or records. *Interview:* System/network administrators; organizational personnel with information security responsibilities; system developers. *Test:* Automated mechanisms implementing dynamic association of security attributes to information.

AC-16(2)	Security attributes: Attribute value changes by authorized individuals	Review Access Control documentation to ensure that only authorized privilege account holders can change any security attributes. Review change control documentation to ensure criteria is met. Discuss with System Owner, Information Owner(s), security staff, operations staff, and Security Officer.	*Examine:* Access control policy; procedures addressing the change of security attribute values; information system design documentation; information system configuration settings and associated documentation; list of individuals authorized to change security attributes; information system audit records; other relevant documents or records. *Interview:* Organizational personnel with responsibilities for changing values of security attributes; organizational personnel with information security responsibilities; system developers. *Test:* Automated mechanisms permitting changes to values of security attributes.
AC-16(3)	Security attributes: Maintenance of attribute associations by information system	Review documentation for system to ensure that system automated policy processes are maintained to enforce security attributes. Discuss with System Owner, operations staff, security staff, Information Owner(s), and Security Officer.	*Examine:* Access control policy; procedures addressing the association of security attributes to information; information system design documentation; information system configuration settings and associated documentation; other relevant documents or records. *Interview:* Organizational personnel with information security responsibilities; system developers. *Test:* Automated mechanisms maintaining association and integrity of security attributes to information.
AC-16(4)	Security attributes: Association of attributes by authorized individuals	Review documentation to ensure that individual privilege account holders are required to maintain associations of security attributes with subjects and objects. Discuss with System Owner, Information Owner(s), operations staff, security staff, and Security Officer.	*Examine:* Access control policy; procedures addressing the association of security attributes to information; information system design documentation; information system configuration settings and associated documentation; list of users authorized to associate security attributes to information; information system audit records; other relevant documents or records. *Interview:* Organizational personnel with responsibilities for associating security attributes to information; organizational personnel with information security responsibilities; system developers. *Test:* Automated mechanisms supporting user associations of security attributes to information.
AC-16(5)	Security attributes: Attribute displays for output devices	Review documentation to ensure that system provides outputs with security attributes	*Examine:* Access control policy; procedures addressing display of security attributes in human-readable form; special dissemination, handling, or distribution

(Continued)

Control number	Control name	Notes and guidance	SP 800-53A Guidance
		displayed appropriately for information being displayed, printed, and labeled. Discuss with System Owner, security staff, information(s), operations staff and Security Officer.	instructions; types of human-readable, standard naming conventions; information system design documentation; information system configuration settings and associated documentation; information system audit records; other relevant documents or records. *Interview:* Organizational personnel with information security responsibilities; system developers. *Test:* System output devices displaying security attributes in human-readable form on each object.
AC-16(6)	Security attributes: Maintenance of attribute association by organization	Review documentation to ensure that the system is required to maintain associations of security attributes with subjects and objects. Discuss with System Owner, Information Owner(s), operations staff, security staff, and Security Officer.	*Examine:* Access control policy; procedures addressing association of security attributes with subjects and objects; other relevant documents or records. *Interview:* Organizational personnel with responsibilities for associating and maintaining association of security attributes with subjects and objects; organizational personnel with information security responsibilities; system developers. *Test:* Automated mechanisms supporting associations of security attributes to subjects and objects.
AC-16(7)	Security attributes: Consistent attribute interpretation	Review documentation to determine when system is in distributed environment, the consistent interpretation of security attributes that are used in access enforcement and flow enforcement decisions are being successfully made and applied. Review log reports and active labeling to ensure attributes are correctly applied. Discuss with operations staff, security staff, System Owner, Information Owner(s), and Security Officer.	*Examine:* Access control policy; procedures addressing consistent interpretation of security attributes transmitted between distributed information system components; procedures addressing access enforcement; procedures addressing information flow enforcement; information system design documentation; information system configuration settings and associated documentation; information system audit records; other relevant documents or records. *Interview:* Organizational personnel with responsibilities for providing consistent interpretation of security attributes used in access enforcement and information flow enforcement actions; organizational personnel with information security responsibilities; system developers. *Test:* Automated mechanisms implementing access enforcement and information flow enforcement functions.

| AC-16(8) | Security attributes: Association techniques/ technologies | Review documentation to determine the employed technologies for binding of security attributes to the information, such as cryptographically bind security attributes to information using digital signatures with the supporting cryptographic keys protected by hardware devices. Test automated binding with test data inputs and review of resultant outputs. Discuss with Information Owner(s), System Owner, operations staff, security staff, and Security Officer. | *Examine:* Access control policy; procedures addressing association of security attributes to information; information system design documentation; information system configuration settings and associated documentation; information system audit records; other relevant documents or records. *Interview:* Organizational personnel with responsibilities for associating security attributes to information; organizational personnel with information security responsibilities; system developers. *Test:* Automated mechanisms implementing techniques or technologies associating security attributes to information. |
| AC-16(9) | Security attributes: Attribute reassignment | Review documentation to determine level and actions implemented for the reassignment of security attributes for information. This is required to give validated re-grading mechanisms to achieve the requisite levels of assurance for security attribute reassignment activities, which is verified by testing reassignment functions with test data and review of resultant outputs. Discuss with System Owner, Information Owner(s), security staff, operations staff, and Security Officer. | *Examine:* Access control policy; procedures addressing reassignment of security attributes to information; information system design documentation; information system configuration settings and associated documentation; information system audit records; other relevant documents or records. *Interview:* Organizational personnel with responsibilities for reassigning association of security attributes to information; organizational personnel with information security responsibilities; system developers. *Test:* Automated mechanisms implementing techniques or procedures for reassigning association of security attributes to information. |

(Continued)

Control number	Control name	Assessment methods	Notes and guidance	SP 800-53A Guidance
AC-16(10)	Security attributes: Attribute configuration by authorized individuals	Review documentation to determine the limited field of authorized personnel who can assign and configure the security attribute mechanisms in system. Review list with System Owner, Information Owner(s), security staff, and Security Officer.		*Examine:* Access control policy; procedures addressing configuration of security attributes by authorized individuals; information system design documentation; information system configuration settings and associated documentation; information system audit records; other relevant documents or records. *Interview:* Organizational personnel with responsibilities for defining or changing security attributes associated with information; organizational personnel with information security responsibilities; system developers. *Test:* Automated mechanisms implementing capability for defining or changing security attributes.
AC-17	Remote access	Review documentation to determine remote access criteria for system and authorization prior to allowing remote access without specifying the formats for such authorization necessary for remote access. Test remote access events of various types, based upon differing methods allowed in system. Discuss with System Owner, security staff, operations staff, and Security Officer.	SP 800-46, SP 800-77, SP 800-113, SP 800-114, SP 800-121	*Examine:* Access control policy; procedures addressing remote access implementation and usage (including restrictions); configuration management plan; security plan; information system configuration settings and associated documentation; remote access authorizations; information system audit records; other relevant documents or records. *Interview:* Organizational personnel with responsibilities for managing remote access connections; system/network administrators; organizational personnel with information security responsibilities. *Test:* Remote access management capability for the information system.
AC-17(1)	Remote access: Automated monitoring/control	Review documentation to ensure automated methods for monitoring remote access are employed within system. Automated monitoring and control of remote access sessions allows organizations to detect cyber-attacks and also ensure ongoing compliance with remote access policies by auditing	SP 800-46, SP 800-77, SP 800-113, SP 800-114, SP 800-121	*Examine:* Access control policy; procedures addressing remote access to the information system; information system design documentation; information system configuration settings and associated documentation; information system audit records; information system monitoring records; other relevant documents or records. *Interview:* System/network administrators; organizational personnel with information security responsibilities; system developers. *Test:* Automated mechanisms monitoring and controlling remote access methods.

	Control	Assessment/Test	References	Examine / Interview / Test
		connection activities of remote users on a variety of information system components, therefore testing of each method used is employed and validated. Discuss with System Owner, security staff, operations staff, and Security Officer.		
AC-17(2)	Remote access: Protection of confidentiality/integrity using encryption	Review documentation to ensure that encryption mechanism is employed based on the security categorization of the information on the system being accessed. Test to ensure encryption is active and functioning correctly. Discuss with System Owner, security staff, operations staff, and Security Officer.	SP 800-46, SP 800-77, SP 800-113, SP 800-114, SP 800-121	*Examine:* Access control policy; procedures addressing remote access to the information system; information system design documentation; information system configuration settings and associated documentation; cryptographic mechanisms and associated configuration documentation; information system audit records; other relevant documents or records. *Interview:* System/network administrators; organizational personnel with information security responsibilities; system developers. *Test:* Cryptographic mechanisms protecting confidentiality and integrity of remote access sessions.
AC-17(3)	Remote access: Managed access control points	Review documentation to determine the limitation of the number of access control points allowed for remote access since this reduces the attack surface for organizations and systems. Discuss with System Owner, operations staff, security staff, and Security Officer.	SP 800-46, SP 800-77, SP 800-113, SP 800-114, SP 800-121, TIC (Trusted Internet Connections) Initiative	*Examine:* Access control policy; procedures addressing remote access to the information system; information system design documentation; list of all managed network access control points; information system configuration settings and associated documentation; information system audit records; other relevant documents or records. *Interview:* System/network administrators; organizational personnel with information security responsibilities. *Test:* Automated mechanisms routing all remote accesses through managed network access control points.
AC-17(4)	Remote access: Privileged commands/access	Review documentation to ensure that the organization authorizes the execution of privileged commands and access to security-relevant information via remote access	SP 800-46, SP 800-77, SP 800-113, SP 800-114, SP 800-121	*Examine:* Access control policy; procedures addressing remote access to the information system; information system configuration settings and associated documentation; security plan; information system audit records; other relevant documents or records. *Interview:* System/network administrators;

(Continued)

Control number	Control name	Assessment methods	Notes and guidance	SP 800-53A Guidance
		only for specified pre-defined functions and events on the system. Review logs to determine compliance and validate processes. Discuss with operations staff, security staff, System Owner, and Security Officer.		organizational personnel with information security responsibilities. *Test:* Automated mechanisms implementing remote access management.
AC-17(5)	Remote access: Monitoring for unauthorized connections		Withdrawn: Incorporated into SI-4	
AC-17(6)	Remote access: Protection of information	Review documentation to ensure that users are advised to protect information about remote access mechanisms from unauthorized use and disclosure. Review documentation signed by users with remote access to determine compliance and use. Discuss with System Owner, security staff, operations staff, and Security Officer.	SP 800-46, SP 800-77, SP 800-113, SP 800-114, SP 800-121	*Examine:* Access control policy; procedures addressing remote access to the information system; other relevant documents or records. *Interview:* Organizational personnel with responsibilities for implementing or monitoring remote access to the information system; information system users with knowledge of information about remote access mechanisms; organizational personnel with information security responsibilities.
AC-17(7)	Remote access: Additional protection for security function access		Withdrawn: Incorporated into AC-3 (10)	
AC-17(8)	Remote access: Disable nonsecure network protocols		Withdrawn: Incorporated into CM-7	
AC-17(9)	Remote access: Disconnect/disable access	Review documentation to ensure that organization has provided for rapid disconnection of remote	SP 800-46, SP 800-77, SP 800-113, SP 800-114, SP 800-121	*Examine:* Access control policy; procedures addressing disconnecting or disabling remote access to the information system; information system design documentation; information system configuration

Number	Name	Review/Discuss guidance	References	Examine/Interview/Test
	(continued from previous page)	access and remote sessions on system. Test remote access rapid disconnect process with test session and review results with System Owner, operations staff, security staff, and Security Officer.		settings and associated documentation; security plan, information system audit records; other relevant documents or records. *Interview:* System/network administrators; organizational personnel with information security responsibilities; system developers. *Test:* Automated mechanisms implementing capability to disconnect or disable remote access to information system.
AC-18	Wireless access	Review documentation to ensure that organization provides for establishment of wireless usage restrictions, configuration/connection requirements, and implementation guidance for wireless access including authorization of wireless access prior to allowing such access. Discuss with System Owner, operations staff, security staff, and Security Officer.	SP 800-48, SP 800-94, SP 800-97, SP 800-120, SP 800-153	*Examine:* Access control policy; procedures addressing wireless access implementation and usage (including restrictions); configuration management plan; security plan; information system design documentation; information system configuration settings and associated documentation; wireless access authorizations; information system audit records; other relevant documents or records. *Interview:* Organizational personnel with responsibilities for managing wireless access connections; organizational personnel with information security responsibilities. *Test:* Wireless access management capability for the information system.
AC-18(1)	Wireless access: Authentication and encryption	Review documentation to ensure that organization requires encryption and authentication for wireless access of devices and by users. Test using wireless device to ensure actual process is functional and correctly operating. Discuss with System Owner, security staff, operations staff, and Security Officer.	SP 800-48, SP 800-94, SP 800-97, SP 800-120, SP 800-153	*Examine:* Access control policy; procedures addressing wireless implementation and usage (including restrictions); information system design documentation; information system configuration settings and associated documentation; information system audit records; other relevant documents or records. *Interview:* System/network administrators; organizational personnel with information security responsibilities; system developers. *Test:* Automated mechanisms implementing wireless access protections to the information system.
AC-18(2)	Wireless access: Monitoring unauthorized connections		Withdrawn: Incorporated into SI-4	

(Continued)

Control number	Control name	Assessment methods	Notes and guidance	SP 800-53A Guidance
AC-18(3)	Wireless access: Disable wireless networking	Review documentation for the organization to ensure that the system disables, when not intended for use, wireless-networking capabilities internally embedded within the system components prior to issuance and deployment of wireless components of system. Test disablement with wireless device onto a disabled component and discuss results with System Owner, operations staff, security staff, and Security Officer.	SP 800-48, SP 800-94, SP 800-97, SP 800-120, SP 800-153	*Examine*: Access control policy; procedures addressing wireless implementation and usage (including restrictions); information system design documentation; information system configuration settings and associated documentation; information system audit records; other relevant documents or records. *Interview*: System/network administrators; organizational personnel with information security responsibilities. *Test*: Automated mechanisms managing the disabling of wireless networking capabilities internally embedded within information system components.
AC-18(4)	Wireless access: Restrict configurations by users	Review documentation to determine, which users are allowed to configure wireless components of system and change wireless configurations of system. Discuss with System Owner, security staff, operations staff, and Security Officer.	SP 800-48, SP 800-94, SP 800-97, SP 800-120, SP 800-153	*Examine*: Access control policy; procedures addressing wireless implementation and usage (including restrictions); information system design documentation; information system configuration settings and associated documentation; information system audit records; other relevant documents or records. *Interview*: System/network administrators; organizational personnel with information security responsibilities. *Test*: Automated mechanisms authorizing independent user configuration of wireless networking capabilities.
AC-18(5)	Wireless access: Antennas/ transmission power levels	Review documentation to ensure the organization selects radio antennas and calibrates transmission power levels to reduce the probability that usable signals can be received outside of organization-controlled boundaries in support of emanation security. Test emanations with wireless test equipment to ensure	SP 800-48, SP 800-94, SP 800-97, SP 800-120, SP 800-153, PE-19	*Examine*: Access control policy; procedures addressing wireless implementation and usage (including restrictions); information system design documentation; information system configuration settings and associated documentation; information system audit records; other relevant documents or records. *Interview*: System/network administrators; organizational personnel with information security responsibilities. *Test*: Wireless access capability protecting usable signals from unauthorized access outside organization-controlled boundaries.

Control	Name	Guidance	References	Assessment
AC-19	Access control for mobile devices	compliance to pre-determined power levels. Discuss with System Owner, operations staff, security staff, and Security Officer. Review documentation for organization to determine the requirements to establish usage restrictions, configuration requirements, connection requirements, and implementation guidance for organization-controlled mobile devices that are authorized to access the system under review. Ensure organization defines all mobile access and authentication requirements for mobile usage for system. Discuss with System Owner, security staff, operations staff, and Security Officer.	OMB M06-16, SP 800-114, SP 800-124, SP 800-164	*Examine:* Access control policy; procedures addressing access control for mobile device usage (including restrictions); configuration management plan; security plan; information system design documentation; information system configuration settings and associated documentation; authorizations for mobile device connections to organizational information systems; information system audit records; other relevant documents or records. *Interview:* Organizational personnel using mobile devices to access organizational information systems; system/network administrators; organizational personnel with information security responsibilities. *Test:* Access control capability authorizing mobile device connections to organizational information systems.
AC-19(1)	Access control for mobile devices: Use of writable/portable storage devices		Withdrawn: Incorporated into MP-7	
AC-19(2)	Access control for mobile devices: Use of personally owned portable storage devices		Withdrawn: Incorporated into MP-7	
AC-19(3)	Access control for mobile devices: Use of portable storage devices with no identifiable owner		Withdrawn: Incorporated into MP-7	

(Continued)

Control number	Control name	Assessment methods	Notes and guidance	SP 800-53A Guidance
AC-19(4)	Access control for mobile devices: Restrictions for classified information	Review documentation to ensure that unclassified mobile devices are not allowed access to classified system and reverse (classified devices on unclassified system). All appropriate classified data handled is performed in accordance with FSO and organizational requirements. Discuss with FSO, System Owner, Information Owner(s), security staff, operations staff, and Security Officer.	OMB M06-16, SP 800-114, SP 800-124, SP 800-164	*Examine:* Access control policy; incident handling policy; procedures addressing access control for mobile devices; information system design documentation; information system configuration settings and associated documentation; evidentiary documentation for random inspections and reviews of mobile devices; information system audit records; other relevant documents or records. *Interview:* Organizational personnel responsible for random reviews/inspections of mobile devices; organizational personnel using mobile devices in facilities containing information systems processing, storing, or transmitting classified information; organizational personnel with incident response responsibilities; system/network administrators; organizational personnel with information security responsibilities. *Test:* Automated mechanisms prohibiting the use of internal or external modems or wireless interfaces with mobile devices.
AC-19(5)	Access control for mobile devices: Full device/container-based encryption	Review documentation to determine the level of mobile device container-based encryption, such as encrypting selected data structures such as files, records, or fields is employed on system. Evaluate mobile device by testing container controls on device and discuss results with System Owner, FSO, security staff, operations staff, Information Owner(s), and Security Officer.	OMB M06-16, SP 800-114, SP 800-124, SP 800-164	*Examine:* Access control policy; procedures addressing access control for mobile devices; information system design documentation; information system configuration settings and associated documentation; encryption mechanisms and associated configuration documentation; information system audit records; other relevant documents or records. *Interview:* Organizational personnel with access control responsibilities for mobile devices; system/network administrators; organizational personnel with information security responsibilities. *Test:* Encryption mechanisms protecting confidentiality and integrity of information on mobile devices.
AC-20	Use of external information systems	Review documentation to determine the organizational criteria for access to, process, store, or transmit	FIPS-199, SP 800-47	*Examine:* Access control policy; procedures addressing the use of external information systems; external information systems terms and conditions; list of types of applications accessible

	organization-controlled information using external information systems. Ensure all interconnection documentation is developed and approved for interfaces and interconnects to/from system. Discuss with FSO, System Owner, security staff, operations staff, risk management staff, and Security Officer.		from external information systems; maximum security categorization for information processed, stored, or transmitted on external information systems; information system configuration settings and associated documentation; other relevant documents or records. *Interview:* Organizational personnel with responsibilities for defining terms and conditions for use of external information systems to access organizational systems; system/network administrators; organizational personnel with information security responsibilities. *Test:* Automated mechanisms implementing terms and conditions on use of external information systems.	
AC-20(1)	Use of external information systems: Limits on authorized use	Review documentation for temporary access to system by individuals using external information systems (e.g., contractors, coalition partners) needing to access system under review. Ensure external system meets security requirements through various methods, such as third-party reviews, attestations, and independent reviews. Discuss results with System Owner, security staff, operations staff, and Security Officer.	FIPS-199, SP 800-47	*Examine:* Access control policy; procedures addressing the use of external information systems; security plan; information system connection or processing agreements; account management documents; other relevant documents or records. *Interview:* System/ network administrators; organizational personnel with information security responsibilities. *Test:* Automated mechanisms implementing limits on use of external information systems.
AC-20(2)	Use of external information systems: Portable storage devices	Review documentation to determine the organizational restrictions on use of organization-controlled portable storage devices in external information systems. Discuss with System Owner, security staff, operations staff, and Security Officer.	FIPS-199, SP 800-47	*Examine:* Access control policy; procedures addressing the use of external information systems; security plan; information system configuration settings and associated documentation; information system connection or processing agreements; account management documents; other relevant documents or records. *Interview:* Organizational personnel with responsibilities for restricting or prohibiting use of organization-controlled storage devices on external information systems; system/network

(Continued)

Control number	Control name	Assessment methods	Notes and guidance	SP 800-53A Guidance
				administrators; organizational personnel with information security responsibilities. *Test:* Automated mechanisms implementing restrictions on use of portable storage devices.
AC-20(3)	Use of external information systems: Nonorganizationally owned systems/components/devices	Review documentation on organizational use of nonowned devices and components connected to system, such as other organizational equipment of personally owned devices (BYOD) or components. Discuss with System Owner, operations staff, security staff, legal staff, and Security Officer.	FIPS-199, SP 800-47	*Examine:* Access control policy; procedures addressing the use of external information systems; security plan; information system design documentation; information system configuration settings and associated documentation; information system connection or processing agreements; account management documents; information system audit records, other relevant documents or records. *Interview:* Organizational personnel with responsibilities for restricting or prohibiting use of nonorganizationally owned information systems, system components, or devices; system/network administrators; organizational personnel with information security responsibilities. *Test:* Automated mechanisms implementing restrictions on the use of nonorganizationally owned systems/components/devices.
AC-20(4)	Use of external information systems: Network accessible storage devices	Review documentation for organization to determine use of external network storage mechanisms, such as online storage devices in public, hybrid, or community cloud-based systems. Review controls and legal requirements with legal staff, operations staff, security staff, System Owner, and Security Officer.	FIPS-199, SP 800-47	*Examine:* Access control policy; procedures addressing use of network accessible storage devices in external information systems; security plan, information system design documentation; information system configuration settings and associated documentation; information system connection or processing agreements; list of network accessible storage devices prohibited from use in external information systems; information system audit records; other relevant documents or records. *Interview:* Organizational personnel with responsibilities for prohibiting use of network accessible storage devices in external information systems; system/network administrators; organizational personnel with information security responsibilities. *Test:* Automated mechanisms prohibiting the use of network accessible storage devices in external information systems.

AC-21	Information sharing	Review documentation for information sharing requirements and restrictions, such as content, type, security category, or special access program/compartmentation on information retained within system. Review standards and organizational guidelines with legal staff, FSO, operations staff, security staff, System Owner, Information Owner(s), and Security Officer.	*Examine:* Access control policy; procedures addressing user-based collaboration and information sharing (including restrictions); information system design documentation; information system configuration settings and associated documentation; list of users authorized to make information sharing/collaboration decisions; list of information sharing circumstances requiring user discretion; other relevant documents or records. *Interview:* Organizational personnel responsible for making information sharing/collaboration decisions; system/network administrators; organizational personnel with information security responsibilities. *Test:* Automated mechanisms or manual process implementing access authorizations supporting information sharing/user collaboration decisions.
AC-21(1)	Information sharing: Automated decision support	Review documentation to ensure that organization enforces information-sharing decisions by authorized users based on access authorizations of sharing partners and access restrictions on the information to be shared. Discuss criteria with legal staff, FSO, operations staff, security staff, System Owner, Information Owner(s), and Security Officer	*Examine:* Access control policy; procedures addressing user-based collaboration and information sharing (including restrictions); information system design documentation; information system configuration settings and associated documentation; system-generated list of users authorized to make information sharing/collaboration decisions; system-generated list of sharing partners and access authorizations; system-generated list of access restrictions regarding information to be shared; other relevant documents or records. *Interview:* System/network administrators; organizational personnel with information security responsibilities; system developers. *Test:* Automated mechanisms implementing access authorizations supporting information sharing/user collaboration decisions.
AC-21(2)	Information sharing: Information search and retrieval	Review documentation to ensure the system implements information search and retrieval services that enforce	*Examine:* Access control policy; procedures addressing user-based collaboration and information sharing (including restrictions); information system design documentation; information system

(Continued)

Control number	Control name	Notes and guidance	Assessment methods	SP 800-53A Guidance
			organizational access and sharing standards. Discuss criteria with legal staff, FSO, operations staff, security staff, System Owner, Information Owner(s), and Security Officer.	configuration settings and associated documentation; system-generated list of access restrictions regarding information to be shared; information search and retrieval records; information system audit records; other relevant documents or records. *Interview:* Organizational personnel with access enforcement responsibilities for information system search and retrieval services; system/network administrators; organizational personnel with information security responsibilities; system developers. *Test:* Information system search and retrieval services enforcing information sharing restrictions.
AC-22	Publicly accessible content		Review documentation to determine, if system under review is considered a publicly accessible system, therefore has limited or no identification or authentication requirements. Review results of analysis with System Owner, operations staff, security staff, legal staff, and Security Officer.	*Examine:* Access control policy; procedures addressing publicly accessible content; list of users authorized to post publicly accessible content on organizational information systems; training materials and/or records; records of publicly accessible information reviews; records of response to nonpublic information on public websites; system audit logs; security awareness training records; other relevant documents or records. *Interview:* Organizational personnel with responsibilities for managing publicly accessible information posted on organizational information systems; organizational personnel with information security responsibilities. *Test:* Automated mechanisms implementing management of publicly accessible content.
AC-23	Data mining protection		Review documentation to determine level of protection the system implements to protect organizational information from data mining, while such information resides in organizational data stores. Test protection methods with test queries and selection code. Review results with System Owner, security	*Examine:* Access control policy; procedures addressing data mining techniques; procedures addressing protection of data storage objects against data mining; information system design documentation; information system configuration settings and associated documentation; information system audit logs; information system audit records; other relevant documents or records. *Interview:* Organizational personnel with responsibilities for implementing data mining detection and prevention techniques for data storage objects; organizational

...personnel with information security responsibilities; system developers. *Test:* Automated mechanisms implementing data mining prevention and detection.

	staff, operations staff, and Security Officer.		
AC-24	Access control decisions	Review documentation to ensure organization defined and enforces access control decisions (also known as authorization decisions), which occur when authorization information is applied to specific accesses, rather than enforcement. Discuss with System Owner, security staff, operations staff, and Security Officer.	*Examine:* Access control policy; procedures addressing access control decisions; information system design documentation; information system configuration settings and associated documentation; information system audit records; other relevant documents or records. *Interview:* Organizational personnel with responsibilities for establishing procedures regarding access control decisions to the information system; organizational personnel with information security responsibilities. *Test:* Automated mechanisms applying established access control decisions and procedures.
AC-24(1)	Access control decisions: Transmit access authorization information	Review documentation to ensure that systems in distributed environments transmit access authorization information correctly and completely to other systems and components. Review logs to determine full transmissions are correctly formatted and sent appropriately and discuss with System Owner, security staff, operations staff, and Security Officer.	*Examine:* Access control policy; procedures addressing access enforcement; information system design documentation; information system configuration settings and associated documentation; information system audit records; other relevant documents or records. *Interview:* Organizational personnel with access enforcement responsibilities; system/network administrators; organizational personnel with information security responsibilities; system developers. *Test:* Automated mechanisms implementing access enforcement functions.
AC-24(2)	Access control decisions: No user or process identity	Review documentation to determine if system requires special privacy protection with respect to access control, decisions can be made without information regarding the identity of the users issuing the requests. Discuss with security staff,	*Examine:* Access control policy; procedures addressing access enforcement; information system design documentation; information system configuration settings and associated documentation; information system audit records; other relevant documents or records. *Interview:* Organizational personnel with access enforcement responsibilities; system/network administrators; organizational personnel with information security responsibilities;

(Continued)

Control number	Control name	Notes and guidance	SP 800-53A Guidance
			system developers. *Test*: Automated mechanisms implementing access enforcement functions.
AC-25	Reference monitor	Review documentation to ensure that system utilizes the reference monitor construct, which is tamperproof, always invoked, and small enough to be subject to analysis and testing, the completeness of which can be assured. Discuss with security staff, operations staff, System Owner, and Security Officer.	*Examine*: Access control policy; procedures addressing access enforcement; information system design documentation; information system configuration settings and associated documentation; information system audit records; other relevant documents or records. *Interview*: Organizational personnel with access enforcement responsibilities; system/network administrators; organizational personnel with information security responsibilities; system developers. *Test*: Automated mechanisms implementing access enforcement functions.

legal staff, operations staff, System Owner, and Security Officer.

B. *Awareness and training (AT) family*

FIPS-200 provides the following criteria for this family of controls: "Organizations must: (i) ensure that managers and users of organizational information systems are made aware of the security risks associated with their activities and of the applicable laws, Executive Orders, directives, policies, standards, instructions, regulations, or procedures related to the security of organizational information systems; and (ii) ensure that organizational personnel are adequately trained to carry out their assigned information security-related duties and responsibilities."

The primary assessment areas for these controls include:

a. Review training elements so that managers and users of organizational information systems are made aware of the security risks associated with their activities.

b. Assess training elements that promote managers and users awareness of the applicable laws, executive orders, directives, policies, standards, instructions, regulations, or procedures related to the security of organizational information systems.

c. Inspect training elements that validate organizational personnel are adequately trained to carry out their assigned information security-related duties and responsibilities.

Control number	Control name	Assessment methods	Notes and guidance	SP 800-53A guidance
AT-1	Security awareness and training policy and procedures	Review organizational IT and security policies for training coverage for users, administrators, executives, and security personnel. Discuss training with System Owner and Security Officer to ensure policy is being adhered to by the organization.	SP 800-12, SP 800-16, SP 800-50, SP 800-100	*Examine:* Security awareness and training policy and procedures; other relevant documents or records. *Interview:* Organizational personnel with security awareness and training responsibilities; organizational personnel with information security responsibilities.
AT-2	Security awareness training	Review training as delivered to users for appropriateness and applicability. Check and review training records of the users and staff to ensure training has occurred and is valid. Review the training topics delivered to ensure validity and relevance.	SP 800-16, SP 800-50, E.O 13587, 5 CFR 930.301	*Examine:* Security awareness and training policy; procedures addressing security awareness training implementation; appropriate codes of federal regulations; security awareness training curriculum; security awareness training materials; security plan; training records; other relevant documents or records. *Interview:* Organizational personnel with responsibilities for security awareness training; organizational personnel with information security responsibilities; organizational personnel comprising the general information system user community. *Test:* Automated mechanisms managing security awareness training.
AT-2(1)	Security awareness training: Practical exercise	Verify training topics delivered for validity and relevance. Interview System Owner and Security Officer to gain knowledge of delivery and timing activities.	SP 800-16, SP 800-50, E.O 13587, 5 CFR 930.301	*Examine:* Security awareness and training policy; procedures addressing security awareness training implementation; security awareness training curriculum; security awareness training materials; security plan; other relevant documents or records. *Interview:* Organizational personnel that participate in security awareness training; organizational personnel with responsibilities for security awareness training; organizational personnel with information security responsibilities. *Test:* Automated mechanisms implementing cyber-attack simulations in practical exercises.
AT-2(2)	Security awareness training: Insider threat	Verify training topics delivered for validity and relevance. Interview System Owner and Security Officer	SP 800-16, SP 800-50, E.O 13587, 5 CFR 930.301	*Examine:* Security awareness and training policy; procedures addressing security awareness training implementation; security awareness training curriculum; security awareness training materials;

		to gain knowledge of delivery and timing activities.		security plan; other relevant documents or records. *Interview:* Organizational personnel that participate in security awareness training; organizational personnel with responsibilities for basic security awareness training; organizational personnel with information security responsibilities.
AT-3	Role-based security training	Verify training topics delivered for validity and relevance. Interview System Owner and Security Officer to gain knowledge of delivery and timing activities.	SP 800-16, SP 800-50, 5 CFR 930.301	*Examine:* Security awareness and training policy; procedures addressing security training implementation; codes of federal regulations; security training curriculum; security training materials; security plan; training records; other relevant documents or records. *Interview:* Organizational personnel with responsibilities for role-based security training; organizational personnel with assigned information system security roles and responsibilities. *Test:* Automated mechanisms managing role-based security training.
AT-3(1)	Role-based security training: Environmental controls	Verify training topics delivered for validity and relevance. Interview System Owner and Security Officer to gain knowledge of delivery and timing activities.	SP 800-16, SP 800-50, 5 CFR 930.301	*Examine:* Security awareness and training policy; procedures addressing security training implementation; security training curriculum; security training materials; security plan; training records; other relevant documents or records. *Interview:* Organizational personnel with responsibilities for role-based security training; organizational personnel with responsibilities for employing and operating environmental controls.
AT-3(2)	Role-based security training: Physical security controls	Verify training topics delivered for validity and relevance. Interview System Owner and Security Officer to gain knowledge of delivery and timing activities.	SP 800-16, SP 800-50, 5 CFR 930.301	*Examine:* Security awareness and training policy; procedures addressing security training implementation; security training curriculum; security training materials; security plan; training records; other relevant documents or records. *Interview:* Organizational personnel with responsibilities for role-based security training; organizational personnel with responsibilities for employing and operating physical security controls.
AT-3(3)	Role-based security training: Practical exercises	Verify training topics delivered for validity and relevance. Interview System Owner and Security Officer	SP 800-16, SP 800-50, 5 CFR 930.301	*Examine:* Security awareness and training policy; procedures addressing security awareness training implementation; security awareness training curriculum; security awareness training materials;

(Continued)

Control number	Control name	Assessment methods	Notes and guidance	SP 800-53A guidance
		to gain knowledge of delivery and timing activities.		security plan; other relevant documents or records. *Interview:* Organizational personnel with responsibilities for role-based security training; organizational personnel that participate in security awareness training.
AT-3(4)	Role-based security training; Suspicious communications and anomalous system behavior	Verify training topics delivered for validity and relevance. Interview System Owner and Security Officer to gain knowledge of delivery and timing activities.	SP 800-16, SP 800-50, 5 CFR 930.301	*Examine:* Security awareness and training policy; procedures addressing security training implementation; security training curriculum; security training materials; security plan; training records; other relevant documents or records. *Interview:* Organizational personnel with responsibilities for role-based security training; organizational personnel that participate in security awareness training.
AT-4	Security training records	Check and review training records of the users and staff to ensure that training has occurred and is valid. Review the training topics delivered to ensure validity and relevance. Interview System Owner and Security Officer to gain knowledge of delivery and timing activities.	SP 800-16, SP 800-50	*Examine:* Security awareness and training policy; procedures addressing security training records; security awareness and training records; security plan; other relevant documents or records. *Interview:* Organizational personnel with security training record retention responsibilities. *Test:* Automated mechanisms supporting management of security training records.
AT-5	Contacts with security groups and associations		Withdrawn: Incorporated into PM-15	

C. *Audit and accountability (AU) family*

FIPS-200 provides the following criteria for this family of controls: "Organizations must: (i) create, protect, and retain information system audit records to the extent needed to enable the monitoring, analysis, investigation, and reporting of unlawful, unauthorized, or inappropriate information system activity; and (ii) ensure that the actions of individual information system users can be uniquely traced to those users, so they can be held accountable for their actions."

The primary assessment areas for these controls include:

a. Review controls in a system that facilitate the creation, protection, and retention of information system audit records to the extent needed to enable the monitoring, analysis, and investigation of the system.

b. Inspect security elements in a system to enable the reporting of unlawful, unauthorized, or inappropriate information system activity.

c. Audit controls in a system to facilitate that the actions of individual information system users can be uniquely traced to those users, so that they can be held accountable for their actions.

Control number	Control name	Assessment methods	Notes and guidance	SP 800-53A Guidance
AU-1	Audit and accountability policy and procedures	Review audit policy and procedures, organizational security program guidance. Interview System Owner and Security Officer.	SP 800-12, SP 800-100, GAO-12-331G	*Examine:* Audit and accountability policy and procedures; other relevant documents or records. *Interview:* Organizational personnel with audit and accountability responsibilities; organizational personnel with information security responsibilities.
AU-2	Audit events	Review documentation for identification and selection of auditable events for system. Review system security plan for auditing criteria and requirements to ensure that auditable events are accounted for and monitored. Discuss with System Owner, organizational auditors, and Security Officer.	SP 800-92, GAO-12-331G	*Examine:* Audit and accountability policy; procedures addressing auditable events; security plan; information system design documentation; information system configuration settings and associated documentation; information system audit records; information system auditable events; other relevant documents or records. *Interview:* Organizational personnel with audit and accountability responsibilities; organizational personnel with information security responsibilities; system/network administrators. *Test:* Automated mechanisms implementing information system auditing.
AU-2(1)	Audit events: Compilation of audit records from multiple sources		Withdrawn: Incorporated into AU-12	
AU-2(2)	Audit events: Selection of audit events by component		Withdrawn: Incorporated into AU-12	
AU-2(3)	Audit events: Reviews and updates	Review documentation for identification, selection, and updating of auditable events for system. Review system security plan for auditing criteria and requirements to ensure that auditable events are accounted for and monitored. Discuss with System Owner, organizational auditors, and Security Officer.	SP 800-92	*Examine:* Audit and accountability policy; procedures addressing auditable events; security plan; list of organization-defined auditable events; auditable events review and update records; information system audit records; information system incident reports; other relevant documents or records. *Interview:* Organizational personnel with audit and accountability responsibilities; organizational personnel with information security responsibilities. *Test:* Automated mechanisms supporting review and update of auditable events.
AU-2(4)	Audit events: Privileged functions		Withdrawn: Incorporated into AC-6(9)	

AU-3	Content of audit records	Review output of auditing records to determine if records appropriately record who, what, when, where, and how of each event recorded. Discuss with System Owner, System Developers, and Security Officer.	SP 800-92, GAO-12-331G	*Examine:* Audit and accountability policy; procedures addressing content of audit records; information system design documentation; information system configuration settings and associated documentation; list of organization-defined auditable events; information system audit records; information system incident reports; other relevant documents or records. *Interview:* Organizational personnel with audit and accountability responsibilities; organizational personnel with information security responsibilities; system/network administrators. *Test:* Automated mechanisms implementing information system auditing of auditable events.
AU-3(1)	Content of audit records: Additional audit information	Review system documentation and auditing requirements to determine if additional organizational-defined information is available and recorded in audit records, as needed. Discuss with System Owner and Security Officer.	SP 800-92	*Examine:* Audit and accountability policy; procedures addressing content of audit records; information system design documentation; information system configuration settings and associated documentation; list of organization-defined auditable events; information system audit records; other relevant documents or records. *Interview:* Organizational personnel with audit and accountability responsibilities; organizational personnel with information security responsibilities; system/network administrators; system developers. *Test:* Information system audit capability.
AU-3(2)	Content of audit records: Centralized management of planned audit record content	Review documentation for central management requirements for audit records and logs. If required, verify and test central audit record repository and log management system. Discuss with System Owner and Security Officer.	SP 800-92	*Examine:* Audit and accountability policy; procedures addressing content of audit records; information system design documentation; information system configuration settings and associated documentation; list of organization-defined auditable events; information system audit records; other relevant documents or records. *Interview:* Organizational personnel with audit and accountability responsibilities; organizational personnel with information security responsibilities; system/network administrators; system developers. *Test:* Information system capability implementing centralized management and configuration of audit record content.

(Continued)

Control number	Control name	Assessment methods	Notes and guidance	SP 800-53A Guidance
AU-4	Audit storage capacity	Review documentation to ensure that audit log capacity requirements are defined and operationally maintained for system. Discuss with System Owner and Security Officer.	SP 800-92, GAO-12-331G	*Examine:* Audit and accountability policy; procedures addressing audit storage capacity; information system design documentation; information system configuration settings and associated documentation; audit record storage capability for information system components; information system audit records; other relevant documents or records. *Interview:* Organizational personnel with audit and accountability responsibilities; organizational personnel with information security responsibilities; system/network administrators; system developers. *Test:* Audit record storage capacity and related configuration settings.
AU-4(1)	Audit storage capacity: Transfer to alternate storage	Review documentation to determine audit record and logs transfer requirements to external storage location/system. Test privileges during access control testing to ensure only appropriate system personnel can move, transfer, and maintain audit records and logs on alternate storage location/system. Discuss with System Owner, operations personnel, and Security Officer.	SP 800-92	*Examine:* Audit and accountability policy; procedures addressing audit storage capacity; procedures addressing transfer of information system audit records to secondary or alternate systems; information system design documentation; information system configuration settings and associated documentation; logs of audit record transfers to secondary or alternate systems; information system audit records transferred to secondary or alternate systems; other relevant documents or records. *Interview:* Organizational personnel with audit storage capacity planning responsibilities; organizational personnel with information security responsibilities; system/network administrators. *Test:* Automated mechanisms supporting transfer of audit records onto a different system.
AU-5	Response to audit processing failures	Review system documentation to determine system failure criteria for audit processing and logic behind criteria. Test system with automated scan tools to validate failure settings and events. Discuss with System Owner, system developers,	SP 800-92, GAO-12-331G	*Examine:* Audit and accountability policy; procedures addressing response to audit processing failures; information system design documentation; security plan; information system configuration settings and associated documentation; list of personnel to be notified in case of an audit processing failure; information system audit records; other relevant documents or records. *Interview:* Organizational

Control	Name	Guidance	Reference	Assessment
		system administrators, and Security Officer.		personnel with audit and accountability responsibilities; organizational personnel with information security responsibilities; system/network administrators; system developers. *Test:* Automated mechanisms implementing information system response to audit processing failures.
AU-5(1)	Response to audit processing failures: Audit storage capacity	Review documents for audit log storage capacity determinations. Review volume metrics to determine if capacity sizing is adequate. Test system for storage warnings at appropriate thresholds. Discuss with System Owner, System Administrators, and Security Officer.	SP 800-92	*Examine:* Audit and accountability policy; procedures addressing response to audit processing failures; information system design documentation; security plan; information system configuration settings and associated documentation; information system audit records; other relevant documents or records. *Interview:* Organizational personnel with audit and accountability responsibilities; organizational personnel with information security responsibilities; system/network administrators; system developers. *Test:* Automated mechanisms implementing audit storage limit warnings.
AU-5(2)	Response to audit processing failures: Real-time alerts	Review documentation to determine what alerts are provided automatically, when control is triggered and to which personnel are they provided when triggered. Discuss with System Owner, System Administrators, and Security Officer.	SP 800-92	*Examine:* Audit and accountability policy; procedures addressing response to audit processing failures; information system design documentation; security plan; information system configuration settings and associated documentation; records of notifications or real-time alerts when audit processing failures occur; information system audit records; other relevant documents or records. *Interview:* Organizational personnel with audit and accountability responsibilities; organizational personnel with information security responsibilities; system/network administrators; system developers. *Test:* Automated mechanisms implementing real-time audit alerts when organization-defined audit failure events occur.
AU-5(3)	Response to audit processing failures: Configurable traffic volume thresholds	Review system and network documentation to determine what criteria is used to reject or delay the processing of network communications	SP 800-92	*Examine:* Audit and accountability policy; procedures addressing response to audit processing failures; information system design documentation; security plan; information system configuration settings and associated documentation;

(Continued)

Control number	Control name	Assessment methods	Notes and guidance	SP 800-53A Guidance
		traffic, if auditing such traffic is determined to exceed the storage capacity of the information system audit function. Determine what actual threshold settings are implemented. Validate thresholds with metrics and testing. Discuss with System Owner, Network Administrators, and Security Officer.		configuration of network communications traffic volume thresholds; information system audit records; other relevant documents or records. *Interview:* Organizational personnel with audit and accountability responsibilities; organizational personnel with information security responsibilities; system/network administrators; system developers. *Test:* Information system capability implementing configurable traffic volume thresholds.
AU-5(4)	Response to audit processing failures: Shutdown on failure	Review documentation for criteria definition of when the system under review would perform an automatic shutdown or partial shutdown. Discuss with System Owner and Security Officer.	SP 800-92	*Examine:* Audit and accountability policy; procedures addressing response to audit processing failures; information system design documentation; security plan; information system configuration settings and associated documentation; information system audit records; other relevant documents or records. *Interview:* Organizational personnel with audit and accountability responsibilities; organizational personnel with information security responsibilities; system/network administrators; system developers. *Test:* Information system capability invoking system shutdown or degraded operational mode in the event of an audit processing failure.
AU-6	Audit review, analysis, and reporting	Review documentation and audit records to determine processes and procedures performed by operational and security personnel during monitoring of system activities and status, as well as the governmental mandated continuous monitoring activities. Determine areas of review conducted by organization and adequacy of meeting monitoring needs and criteria. Discuss with System	SP 800-92, GAO-12-331G	*Examine:* Audit and accountability policy; procedures addressing audit review, analysis, and reporting; reports of audit findings; records of actions taken in response to reviews/analyses of audit records; other relevant documents or records. *Interview:* Organizational personnel with audit review, analysis, and reporting responsibilities; organizational personnel with information security responsibilities.

Control			
	Owner, System Administrators, and Security Officer.		
AU-6(1)	Audit review, analysis, and reporting: Process integration	Review documentation for inclusion of system audit reports into organization-wide integrated audit reviews, continuous monitoring activities, and IG reporting. Discuss with System Owner, Organizational Auditors, and Security Officer.	SP 800-92	*Examine:* Audit and accountability policy; procedures addressing audit review, analysis, and reporting; procedures addressing investigation and response to suspicious activities; information system design documentation; information system configuration settings and associated documentation; information system audit records; other relevant documents or records. *Interview:* Organizational personnel with audit review, analysis, and reporting responsibilities; organizational personnel with information security responsibilities. *Test:* Automated mechanisms integrating audit review, analysis, and reporting processes.
AU-6(2)	Audit review, analysis, and reporting: Automated security alerts		Withdrawn: Incorporated into SI-4	
AU-6(3)	Audit review, analysis, and reporting: Correlate audit repositories	Review system and organizational documentation to ensure that system audit reporting is included into organizational level risk reviews and situational awareness reporting. Discuss with System Owner and Security Officer.	SP 800-92	*Examine:* Audit and accountability policy; procedures addressing audit review, analysis, and reporting; information system design documentation; information system configuration settings and associated documentation; information system audit records across different repositories; other relevant documents or records. *Interview:* Organizational personnel with audit review, analysis, and reporting responsibilities; organizational personnel with information security responsibilities. *Test:* Automated mechanisms supporting analysis and correlation of audit records.
AU-6(4)	Audit review, analysis, and reporting: Central review and analysis	Review documentation to determine if system provides methods to combine and correlate audit information for various components of system. Discuss with System Owner, operations staff, and Security Officer.	SP 800-92	*Examine:* Audit and accountability policy; procedures addressing audit review, analysis, and reporting; information system design documentation; information system configuration settings and associated documentation; security plan; information system audit records; other relevant documents or records. *Interview:*

(Continued)

Control number	Control name	Assessment methods	Notes and guidance	SP 800-53A Guidance
				Organizational personnel with audit review, analysis, and reporting responsibilities; organizational personnel with information security responsibilities; system developers. *Test:* Information system capability to centralize review and analysis of audit records.
AU-6(5)	Audit review, analysis, and reporting: Integration/scanning and monitoring capabilities	Review documentation for system to validate, if needed, the process of integration of security information on system with the audit information for the system into a central process, such as an SIEM (security information and event monitoring) tool. Discuss with System Owner, Security Officer, and other security staff.	SP 800-92	*Examine:* Audit and accountability policy; procedures addressing audit review, analysis, and reporting; information system design documentation; information system configuration settings and associated documentation; integrated analysis of audit records, vulnerability scanning information, performance data, network monitoring information and associated documentation; other relevant documents or records. *Interview:* Organizational personnel with audit review, analysis, and reporting responsibilities; organizational personnel with information security responsibilities. *Test:* Automated mechanisms implementing capability to integrate analysis of audit records with analysis of data/information sources.
AU-6(6)	Audit review, analysis, and reporting: Correlation with physical monitoring	Review documentation for system logging and auditing support and reporting inputs to organizational investigations into suspicious activities and events. Discuss with System Owner and Security Officer.	SP 800-92	*Examine:* Audit and accountability policy; procedures addressing audit review, analysis, and reporting; procedures addressing physical access monitoring; information system design documentation; information system configuration settings and associated documentation; documentation providing evidence of correlated information obtained from audit records and physical access monitoring records; security plan; other relevant documents or records. *Interview:* Organizational personnel with audit review, analysis, and reporting responsibilities; organizational personnel with physical access monitoring responsibilities; organizational personnel with information security responsibilities. *Test:* Automated mechanisms implementing capability to correlate information

Control	Description	References	Assessment
AU-6(7)	Audit review, analysis, and reporting; Permitted actions	SP 800-92, AC-5	Review documentation of permissions and privileges of users and administrators allowed access to audit records. Ensure permissions are enforced concerning read, write, and alteration of records to properly enforce Control AC-5 Separation of Duties requirements. Discuss with System Owner, Organizational Auditors, and Security Officer. *Examine:* Audit and accountability policy; procedures addressing process, role and/or user permitted actions from audit review, analysis, and reporting; security plan; other relevant documents or records. *Interview:* Organizational personnel with audit review, analysis, and reporting responsibilities; organizational personnel with information security responsibilities. *Test:* Automated mechanisms supporting permitted actions for review, analysis, and reporting of audit information.
AU-6(8)	Audit review, analysis, and reporting; Full text analysis of privileged commands	SP 800-92	Review documentation for system to ensure that separate repository is maintained for audit review and analysis of audit records. Full test search capabilities to include pattern matching and heuristics should be included in this capability. Discuss with System Owner, Auditors, and Security Officer. Test search capabilities with selected audit records and test case inputs. *Examine:* Audit and accountability policy; procedures addressing audit review, analysis, and reporting; information system design documentation; information system configuration settings and associated documentation; text analysis tools and techniques; text analysis documentation of audited privileged commands; security plan; other relevant documents or records. *Interview:* Organizational personnel with audit review, analysis, and reporting responsibilities; organizational personnel with information security responsibilities. *Test:* Automated mechanisms implementing capability to perform a full text analysis of audited privilege commands.
AU-6(9)	Audit review, analysis, and reporting; Correlation with information from nontechnical sources	SP 800-92	Review documentation to determine the correlation processes between system audit records and nontechnical records from outside sources while conducting investigations and insider threat reviews. Discuss with System Owner, security personnel, and Security Officer. *Examine:* Audit and accountability policy; procedures addressing audit review, analysis, and reporting; information system design documentation; information system configuration settings and associated documentation; documentation providing evidence of correlated information obtained from audit records and organization-defined nontechnical sources; list of information types from nontechnical sources for correlation with audit information; other relevant documents or records. *Interview:* Organizational

from audit records with information from monitoring physical access.

(Continued)

Control number	Control name	Assessment methods	Notes and guidance	SP 800-53A Guidance
				personnel with audit review, analysis, and reporting responsibilities; organizational personnel with information security responsibilities. *Test:* Automated mechanisms implementing capability to correlate information from nontechnical sources.
AU-6(10)	Audit review, analysis, and reporting: Audit level adjustment	Review documentation to ensure that periodic audit level adjustment reviews are performed and documented. The frequency, scope, and / or depth of the audit review, analysis, and reporting may be adjusted to meet organizational needs based on new information received. Discuss this process with System Owner and Security Officer.	SP 800-92	*Examine:* Audit and accountability policy; procedures addressing audit review, analysis, and reporting; organizational risk assessment; security control assessment; vulnerability assessment; security plan; other relevant documents or records. *Interview:* Organizational personnel with audit review, analysis, and reporting responsibilities; organizational personnel with information security responsibilities. *Test:* Automated mechanisms supporting review, analysis, and reporting of audit information.
AU-7	Audit reduction and report generation	Review processes and documentation for system audit record reduction and summarization for meaningful analysis efforts. Determine processes, procedures, and criteria for reduction efforts and needs for reduction actions. Discuss with System Owner and Security Officer, as well as Security analysts performing audit analysis.	SP 800-92, GAO-12-331G	*Examine:* Audit and accountability policy; procedures addressing audit reduction and report generation; information system design documentation; information system configuration settings and associated documentation; audit reduction, review, analysis, and reporting tools; information system audit records; other relevant documents or records. *Interview:* Organizational personnel with audit reduction and report generation responsibilities; organizational personnel with information security responsibilities. *Test:* Audit reduction and report generation capability.
AU-7(1)	Audit reduction and report generation: Automatic processing	Review documentation to ensure that automated processing of audit records is defined by organizational criteria and current events of interest. Organizations may define audit event criteria to any degree of granularity required	SP 800-92	*Examine:* Audit and accountability policy; procedures addressing audit reduction and report generation; information system design documentation; information system configuration settings and associated documentation; audit reduction, review, analysis, and reporting tools; audit record criteria (fields) establishing events of interest; information system audit records; other relevant documents or

AU-7(2)	Audit reduction and report generation: Automatic sort and search	SP 800-92	Review documentation for audit records to ensure that system allows for sorting and searching of audit records, which can be based upon the contents of audit record fields of interest. Discuss with Security Analysts, System Owner, and Security Officer.	*Examine:* Audit and accountability policy; procedures addressing audit reduction and report generation; information system design documentation; information system configuration settings and associated documentation; audit reduction, review, analysis, and reporting tools; audit record criteria (fields) establishing events of interest; information system audit records; other relevant documents or records. *Interview:* Organizational personnel with audit reduction and report generation responsibilities; organizational personnel with information security responsibilities; system developers. *Test:* Audit reduction and report generation capability.
AU-8	Time stamps	SP 800-92, GAO-12-331G	Review documentation to ensure that time stamps and time-based system critical audit functions are active and functioning correctly. Verify with automated scan tools, which will validate system time settings. Discuss with System Owner and Security Officer.	*Examine:* Audit and accountability policy; procedures addressing time stamp generation; information system design documentation; information system configuration settings and associated documentation; information system audit records; other relevant documents or records. *Interview:* Organizational personnel with information security responsibilities; system/network administrators; system developers. *Test:* Automated mechanisms implementing time stamp generation.
AU-8(1)	Time stamps: Synchronization with authoritative time source	SP 800-92	Review documentation to ensure that system or network functions are synchronized with an official governmental time source. This synchronization provides uniformity of time stamps for information systems with multiple system clocks and systems connected over a network. Validate with automated scan tools. Discuss	*Examine:* Audit and accountability policy; procedures addressing time stamp generation; information system design documentation; information system configuration settings and associated documentation; information system audit records; other relevant documents or records. *Interview:* Organizational personnel with information security responsibilities; system/network administrators; system developers. *Test:* Automated mechanisms implementing internal information system clock synchronization.

(Continued)

(First partial row at top, continuation of previous page): ...records. *Interview:* Organizational personnel with audit reduction and report generation responsibilities; organizational personnel with information security responsibilities; system developers. *Test:* Audit reduction and report generation capability. ...to conduct reviews, analysis, and evaluations. Discuss with Security Analysts, System Owner, and Security Officer.

Control number	Control name	Assessment methods	Notes and guidance	SP 800-53A Guidance
AU-8(2)	Time stamps: Secondary authoritative time source	with System Owner, Network Administrators, and Security Officer. Review documentation to check on the system utilizing a secondary time source outside the local geographic area for redundancy and reliability purposes. Discuss with System Owner and Security Officer.	SP 800-92	*Examine:* Audit and accountability policy; procedures addressing time stamp generation; information system design documentation; information system configuration settings and associated documentation; information system audit records; other relevant documents or records. *Interview:* Organizational personnel with information security responsibilities; system/network administrators; system developers. *Test:* Automated mechanisms implementing internal information system clock authoritative time sources.
AU-9	Protection of audit information	Review the system documentation to ensure the technical protection for all audit information is in place and active. Test via automated scan tools and manual records checks. Discuss with System Owner and Security Officer.	SP 800-92, GAO-12-331G	*Examine:* Audit and accountability policy; access control policy and procedures; procedures addressing protection of audit information; information system design documentation; information system configuration settings and associated documentation, information system audit records; audit tools; other relevant documents or records. *Interview:* Organizational personnel with audit and accountability responsibilities; organizational personnel with information security responsibilities; system/network administrators; system developers. *Test:* Automated mechanisms implementing audit information protection.
AU-9(1)	Protection of audit information: Hardware write-once media	Review documentation to ensure that the storage process for all audit records provides the record are backed up onto write once read many (WORM) type(s) of media for long term retention. Verify storage media is WORM type such as CD-R or DVD-R. Discuss with System Owner and Security Officer.	SP 800-92	*Examine:* Audit and accountability policy; access control policy and procedures; procedures addressing protection of audit information; information system design documentation; information system hardware settings; information system configuration settings and associated documentation; information system storage media; information system audit records; other relevant documents or records. *Interview:* Organizational personnel with audit and accountability responsibilities; organizational personnel with

(Continued)

information security responsibilities; system/network administrators; system developers. *Test*: Information system media storing audit trails.

Control	Name	Ref.	Assessment	Examine / Interview / Test
AU-9(2)	Protection of audit information: Audit backup on separate physical systems/components	SP 800-92	Review documentation to ensure that audit backups are conducted on a physically different system, the system under review for security and recovery purposes. Validate back-up process and location by observation. Discuss with System Owner and Security Officer.	*Examine*: Audit and accountability policy; procedures addressing protection of audit information; information system design documentation; information system configuration settings and associated documentation, system or media storing backups of information system audit records; information system audit records; other relevant documents or records. *Interview*: Organizational personnel with audit and accountability responsibilities; organizational personnel with information security responsibilities; system/network administrators; system developers. *Test*: Automated mechanisms implementing the backing up of audit records.
AU-9(3)	Protection of audit information: Cryptographic protection	SP 800-92	Review documentation to ensure that system provides cryptographic protection for audit records and write activities. Typically, systems will utilize signed hash functions using asymmetric cryptography enabling distribution of the public key to verify the hash information while maintaining the confidentiality of the secret key used to generate the hash. Verify using automated scan tools. Discuss with System Owner and Security Officer.	*Examine*: Audit and accountability policy; access control policy and procedures; procedures addressing protection of audit information; information system design documentation; information system hardware settings; information system configuration settings and associated documentation, information system audit records; other relevant documents or records. *Interview*: Organizational personnel with audit and accountability responsibilities; organizational personnel with information security responsibilities; system/network administrators; system developers. *Test*: Cryptographic mechanisms protecting integrity of audit information and tools.
AU-9(4)	Protection of audit information: Access by subset of privileged users	SP 800-92	Review documentation to ensure audit-related actions including audit reduction are only performed by select subset of elevated privilege holders. Validate via access control records review. Discuss with System Owner and Security Officer.	*Examine*: Audit and accountability policy; access control policy and procedures; procedures addressing protection of audit information; information system design documentation; information system configuration settings and associated documentation, system-generated list of privileged users with access to management of audit functionality; access authorizations; access control list; information system

Control number	Control name	Assessment methods	Notes and guidance	SP 800-53A Guidance
				audit records; other relevant documents or records. *Interview:* Organizational personnel with audit and accountability responsibilities; organizational personnel with information security responsibilities; system/network administrators. *Test:* Automated mechanisms managing access to audit functionality.
AU-9(5)	Protection of audit information: Dual authorization	Review documentation to ensure, when defined, the system requires dual authorization to perform certain audit related actions with audit records. Discuss with System Owner and Security Officer.	SP 800-92	*Examine:* Audit and accountability policy; access control policy and procedures; procedures addressing protection of audit information; information system design documentation; information system configuration settings and associated documentation, access authorizations; information system audit records; other relevant documents or records. *Interview:* Organizational personnel with audit and accountability responsibilities; organizational personnel with information security responsibilities; system/network administrators. *Test:* Automated mechanisms implementing enforcement of dual authorization.
AU-9(6)	Protection of audit information: Read only access	Review documentation for limitations provided on elevated privilege account holders to ensure that they or their accounts cannot alter audit logs if compromised or maliciously used. Discuss with System Owner and Security Officer.	SP 800-92	*Examine:* Audit and accountability policy; access control policy and procedures; procedures addressing protection of audit information; information system design documentation; information system configuration settings and associated documentation, system-generated list of privileged users with read only access to audit information; access authorizations; access control list; information system audit records; other relevant documents or records. *Interview:* Organizational personnel with audit and accountability responsibilities; organizational personnel with information security responsibilities; system/network administrators. *Test:* Automated mechanisms managing access to audit information.
AU-10	Nonrepudiation	Review documentation to ensure that system provides methods to identify an individual account or process as actually having accomplished some action or	FIPS 186-3, GAO-12-331G	*Examine:* Audit and accountability policy; procedures addressing nonrepudiation; information system design documentation; information system configuration settings and associated documentation; information system audit records; other relevant documents or

		task. This prevents an individual (or process acting on behalf of an individual) falsely denying having performed the defined action. Discuss with System Owner and Security Officer.		records. *Interview:* Organizational personnel with information security responsibilities; system/network administrators; system developers. *Test:* Automated mechanisms implementing nonrepudiation capability.
AU-10(1)	Nonrepudiation: Association of identities	Review documentation to ensure that the system provides organizational personnel with the means to identify who produced the specific information in the event of an information transfer. Discuss this binding with the System Owner and Security Officer.	FIPS 186-3	*Examine:* Audit and accountability policy; procedures addressing nonrepudiation; information system design documentation; information system configuration settings and associated documentation; information system audit records; other relevant documents or records. *Interview:* Organizational personnel with information security responsibilities; system/network administrators; system developers. *Test:* Automated mechanisms implementing nonrepudiation capability.
AU-10(2)	Nonrepudiation: Validate binding of information producer identity	Review documentation to ensure that the system is designed and operating to prevent the modification of information between production and review, typically, with the use of cryptographic checksums on records. Test via automated scan tools. Discuss with System Owner, System developers, and Security Officer.	FIPS 186-3	*Examine:* Audit and accountability policy; procedures addressing nonrepudiation; information system design documentation; information system configuration settings and associated documentation; validation records; information system audit records; other relevant documents or records. *Interview:* Organizational personnel with information security responsibilities; system/network administrators; system developers. *Test:* Automated mechanisms implementing nonrepudiation capability.
AU-10(3)	Nonrepudiation: Chain of custody	Review documentation to ensure proper control and oversight of all audit evidence is maintained throughout the lifecycle of the evidence. This process is known as chain of custody and is vial to security and validity of audit evidence for further investigations and organizational actions. Discuss with System Owner, Organizational Auditors, and Security Officer.	FIPS 186-3	*Examine:* Audit and accountability policy; procedures addressing nonrepudiation; information system design documentation; information system configuration settings and associated documentation; records of information reviews and releases; information system audit records; other relevant documents or records. *Interview:* Organizational personnel with information security responsibilities; system/network administrators; system developers. *Test:* Automated mechanisms implementing nonrepudiation capability.

(Continued)

Control number	Control name	Assessment methods	Notes and guidance	SP 800-53A Guidance
AU-10(4)	Nonrepudiation: Validate binding of information reviewer identity	Review documentation to ensure that the system is designed and operating to prevent the modification of information between review and transfer/release, typically, with the use of cryptographic checksums on records. Test via automated scan tools. Discuss with System Owner, System Developers, and Security Officer.	FIPS 186-3	*Examine:* Audit and accountability policy; procedures addressing nonrepudiation; information system design documentation; information system configuration settings and associated documentation; validation records; information system audit records; other relevant documents or records. *Interview:* Organizational personnel with information security responsibilities; system/network administrators; system developers. *Test:* Automated mechanisms implementing nonrepudiation capability.
AU-10(5)	Nonrepudiation: Digital signatures		Withdrawn: Incorporated into SI-7	
AU-11	Audit record retention	Review documentation to ensure that audit records are retained in accordance with organizational and operational requirements. Records are to be retained until it is determined that they are no longer needed for administrative, legal, audit, or other operational purposes, such as investigations, FOIA actions, and record retention requirements from NARA. Discuss with System Owner and Security Officer.	NARA/GRS 24, GAO-12-331G	*Examine:* Audit and accountability policy; audit record retention policy and procedures; security plan; organization-defined retention period for audit records; audit record archives; audit logs; audit records; other relevant documents or records. *Interview:* Organizational personnel with audit record retention responsibilities; organizational personnel with information security responsibilities; system/network administrators.
AU-11(1)	Audit record retention: Long-term retrieval capability	Review documentation for audit record retrieval processes to ensure that data in records maintained in long-term storage are available whenever needed. This process will include methods and techniques for data transfer to new media, encryption methods, and storage media requirements.	NARA/GRS 24	*Examine:* Audit and accountability policy; audit record retention policy and procedures; information system design documentation; information system configuration settings and associated documentation; audit record archives; audit logs; audit records; other relevant documents or records. *Interview:* Organizational personnel with audit record retention responsibilities; organizational personnel with information security responsibilities; system/

		Discuss with System Owner and Security Officer.		network administrators. *Test:* Automated mechanisms implementing audit record retention capability.
AU-12	Audit generation	Review documentation to ensure that system audit records contain the proper event (defined in Control AU-2) with the proper context (defined in Control AU-3). Ensure organization defined these parameters in documentation and system contains the ability to record all possible events. Validate through verifying events in records. Discuss with System Owner and Security Officer.	GAO-12-331G	*Examine:* Audit and accountability policy; procedures addressing audit record generation; security plan; information system design documentation; information system configuration settings and associated documentation; list of auditable events; information system audit records; other relevant documents or records. *Interview:* Organizational personnel with audit record generation responsibilities; organizational personnel with information security responsibilities; system/network administrators; system developers. *Test:* Automated mechanisms implementing audit record generation capability.
AU-12(1)	Audit generation: System-wide/time-correlated audit trail	Review documentation for audit record generation to ensure that the audit trails are time-correlated, if the time stamps in the individual audit records can be reliably related to the time stamps in other audit records to achieve a time ordering of the records within the required documented organizational tolerances. Discuss with System Owner and Security Officer.		*Examine:* Audit and accountability policy; procedures addressing audit record generation; information system design documentation; information system configuration settings and associated documentation; system-wide audit trail (logical or physical); information system audit records; other relevant documents or records. *Interview:* Organizational personnel with audit record generation responsibilities; organizational personnel with information security responsibilities; system/network administrators; system developers. *Test:* Automated mechanisms implementing audit record generation capability.
AU-12(2)	Audit generation: Standardized formats	Review documentation to ensure that audit record data is normalized to organizational standard to ensure correlation with other audit records for other systems. Discuss with System Owner and Security Officer.		*Examine:* Audit and accountability policy; procedures addressing audit record generation; information system design documentation; information system configuration settings and associated documentation; system-wide audit trail (logical or physical); information system audit records; other relevant documents or records. *Interview:* Organizational personnel with audit record generation responsibilities; organizational personnel with information security responsibilities; system/network administrators; system developers. *Test:* Automated mechanisms implementing audit record generation capability.

(Continued)

Control number	Control name	Assessment methods	Notes and guidance	SP 800-53A Guidance
AU-12(3)	Audit generation: Changes by authorized individuals	Review documentation for the system audit process to ensure that it allows for limitation or modification to audit process in case of organizational requirements. Discuss process with System Owner, Organizational Auditors, and Security Officer.		*Examine:* Audit and accountability policy; procedures addressing audit record generation; information system design documentation; information system configuration settings and associated documentation; system-generated list of individuals or roles authorized to change auditing to be performed; information system audit records; other relevant documents or records. *Interview:* Organizational personnel with audit record generation responsibilities; organizational personnel with information security responsibilities; system/network administrators; system developers. *Test:* Automated mechanisms implementing audit record generation capability.
AU-13	Monitoring for information disclosure	Review documentation and processes for monitoring of open source and public information locations about system and its mission. Discuss efforts with System Owner, Security staff, and Security Officer.	GAO-12-331G	*Examine:* Audit and accountability policy; procedures addressing information disclosure monitoring; information system design documentation; information system configuration settings and associated documentation; monitoring records; information system audit records; other relevant documents or records. *Interview:* Organizational personnel with responsibilities for monitoring open source information and/or information sites; organizational personnel with information security responsibilities. *Test:* Automated mechanisms implementing monitoring for information disclosure.
AU-13(1)	Monitoring for information disclosure: Use of automated tools	Review documentation to determine what automated mechanisms are being used to monitor open source and public informational websites and data feeds. Review and discuss these efforts with System Owner and Security Officer.		*Examine:* Audit and accountability policy; procedures addressing information disclosure monitoring; information system design documentation; information system configuration settings and associated documentation; automated monitoring tools; information system audit records; other relevant documents or records. *Interview:* Organizational personnel with responsibilities for monitoring information disclosures; organizational personnel with information security responsibilities. *Test:* Automated mechanisms implementing monitoring for information disclosure.

AU-13(2)	Monitoring for information disclosure: Review of monitored sites	Review documentation to determine frequency of review of monitored locations and data feeds. Discuss with System Owner and Security Officer.	*Examine:* Audit and accountability policy; procedures addressing information disclosure monitoring; information system design documentation; information system configuration settings and associated documentation; reviews for open source information sites being monitored; information system audit records; other relevant documents or records. *Interview:* Organizational personnel with responsibilities for monitoring open source information sites; organizational personnel with information security responsibilities. *Test:* Automated mechanisms implementing monitoring for information disclosure.
AU-14	Session audit	SP 800-92, GAO-12-331G	Review documentation for system, which allow select monitoring of user sessions. Discuss with System Owner, Organizational Counsel, and Security Officer.	*Examine:* Audit and accountability policy; procedures addressing user session auditing; information system design documentation; information system configuration settings and associated documentation; information system audit records; other relevant documents or records. *Interview:* Organizational personnel with information security responsibilities; system/network administrators; system developers. *Test:* Automated mechanisms implementing user session auditing capability.
AU-14(1)	Session audit: System startup	SP 800-92	Review documentation to determine system capability to start monitoring of select user session upon system start-up. Discuss with System Owner and Security Officer.	*Examine:* Audit and accountability policy; procedures addressing user session auditing; information system design documentation; information system configuration settings and associated documentation; information system audit records; other relevant documents or records. *Interview:* Organizational personnel with information security responsibilities; system/network administrators; system developers. *Test:* Automated mechanisms implementing user session auditing capability.
AU-14(2)	Session audit: Capture/record and log content	SP 800-92	Review documentation to determine system capability to capture/record and log content related to a user session. Discuss with System Owner, Organizational Counsel, and Security Officer.	*Examine:* Audit and accountability policy; procedures addressing user session auditing; information system design documentation; information system configuration settings and associated documentation; information system audit records; other relevant documents or records. *Interview:* Organizational personnel with information security responsibilities;

(Continued)

Control number	Control name	Assessment methods	Notes and guidance	SP 800-53A Guidance
				system/network administrators; system developers. *Test:* Automated mechanisms implementing user session auditing capability.
AU-14(3)	Session audit: Remote viewing/listening	Review documentation to determine system capability to view/hear remotely all content related to an established user session in real time. Discuss with System Owner, Organizational Counsel, and Security Officer.	SP 800-92	*Examine:* Audit and accountability policy; procedures addressing user session auditing; information system design documentation; information system configuration settings and associated documentation; information system audit records; other relevant documents or records. *Interview:* Organizational personnel with information security responsibilities; system/network administrators; system developers. *Test:* Automated mechanisms implementing user session auditing capability.
AU-15	Alternate audit capability	Review documentation to determine what audit criteria are maintained during alternate auditing implementation. Discuss with System Owner and Security Officer.	GAO-12-331G	*Examine:* Audit and accountability policy; procedures addressing alternate audit capability; information system design documentation; information system configuration settings and associated documentation; test records for alternate audit capability; information system audit records; other relevant documents or records. *Interview:* Organizational personnel responsible for providing alternate audit capability; organizational personnel with information security responsibilities. *Test:* Automated mechanisms implementing alternative audit capability.
AU-16	Cross-organizational auditing	Review documentation and organizational audit policies to determine when cross-organizational auditing (e.g., SOA-based auditing) simply captures the identity of individuals issuing requests at the initial information system, and subsequent systems record that the requests emanated from authorized individuals. Test the capability through manual and	GAO-12-331G	*Examine:* Audit and accountability policy; procedures addressing methods for coordinating audit information among external organizations; information system design documentation; information system configuration settings and associated documentation; methods for coordinating audit information among external organizations; information system audit records; other relevant documents or records. *Interview:* Organizational personnel with responsibilities for coordinating audit information among external organizations; organizational personnel with information security responsibilities. *Test:* Automated

AU-16(1)	Cross-organizational auditing: Identity preservation	automated audit captures and reviews in organizational SIEM monitoring system. Discuss with System Owner, System Developers, and Security Officer. Review documentation to determine the methods for tracing actions across system boundaries to an individual user. Verify traceability via tracking users in the organizational SIEM monitoring system. Discuss with System Owner and Security Officer.	mechanisms implementing cross-organizational auditing (if applicable). *Examine:* Audit and accountability policy; procedures addressing cross-organizational audit trails; information system design documentation; information system configuration settings and associated documentation; information system audit records; other relevant documents or records. *Interview:* Organizational personnel with cross-organizational audit responsibilities; organizational personnel with information security responsibilities. *Test:* Automated mechanisms implementing cross-organizational auditing (if applicable).
AU-16(2)	Cross-organizational auditing: Sharing of audit information	Review documentation to determine level of sharing of the audit information across system boundaries for traceability and investigative purposes. Discuss with System Owner and Security Officer.	*Examine:* Audit and accountability policy; procedures addressing cross-organizational sharing of audit information; cross-organizational sharing agreements; data sharing agreements; other relevant documents or records. *Interview:* Organizational personnel with responsibilities for sharing cross-organizational audit information; organizational personnel with information security responsibilities.

D. *Assessment and authorization (CA) family*

FIPS-200 provides the following criteria for this family of controls: "Organizations must: (i) periodically assess the security controls in organizational information systems to determine if the controls are effective in their application; (ii) develop and implement plans of action designed to correct deficiencies and reduce or eliminate vulnerabilities in organizational information systems; (iii) authorize the operation of organizational information systems and any associated information system connections; and (iv) monitor information system security controls on an ongoing basis to ensure the continued effectiveness of the controls."

The primary assessment areas for these controls include:

a. Review processes that facilitate the periodic assessment of the security controls in organizational information systems to determine if the controls are effective in their application.

b. Assess and implement plans of action designed to correct deficiencies and reduce or eliminate vulnerabilities in organizational information systems.

c. Inspect mechanisms that authorize the operation of organizational information systems and any associated information system connections.

d. Evaluate processes that facilitate the monitoring of information system security controls on an ongoing basis to ensure the continued effectiveness of the controls.

Control number	Control name	Assessment methods	Notes and guidance documents	SP 800-53A guidance
CA-1	Security assessment and authorization policy and procedures	Review organizational documents, policies, and procedures for adherence to RMF criteria and organizational standards. Interview System Owner, agency executives, and Security Officer to gain understanding of agency's view and application of RMF, authorization processes, and C&A planning efforts.	SP 800-37, rev.1, SP 800-12, SP 800-53A, SP 800-100	*Examine:* Security assessment and authorization policy and procedures; other relevant documents or records. *Interview:* Organizational personnel with security assessment and authorization responsibilities; organizational personnel with information security responsibilities.
CA-2	Security assessments	Review organizational documents, policies, and procedures for adherence to RMF-based assessments of systems. Interview System Owner, agency executives and Security Officer to gain understanding of agency's view and application of RMF-based assessment processes efforts.	SP 800-37, rev.1, SP 800-53A, E.O. 13587	*Examine:* Security assessment and authorization policy; procedures addressing security assessment planning; procedures addressing security assessments; security assessment plan; other relevant documents or records. *Interview:* Organizational personnel with security assessment responsibilities; organizational personnel with information security responsibilities. *Test:* Automated mechanisms supporting security assessment, security assessment plan development, and/or security assessment reporting.
CA-2(1)	Security assessments: Independent assessors	Review records and procedures for the selection and monitoring of the independent assessors used by the organization. Discuss these efforts with System Owner and Security Officer to gain understanding of support efforts and results of the independent assessor actions.	SP 800-37, rev.1, SP 800-53A, E.O. 13587	*Examine:* Security assessment and authorization policy; procedures addressing security assessments; security authorization package (including security plan, security assessment report, plan of action and milestones, authorization statement); other relevant documents or records. *Interview:* Organizational personnel with security assessment responsibilities; organizational personnel with information security responsibilities.
CA-2(2)	Security assessments: Specialized assessments	Review records and procedures for the selection and monitoring of the specialized assessments conducted by the organization. Discuss these efforts	SP 800-37, rev.1, SP 800-53A, E.O. 13587	*Examine:* Security assessment and authorization policy; procedures addressing security assessments; security plan; security assessment report; security

(Continued)

Control number	Control name	Assessment methods	Notes and guidance documents	SP 800-53A guidance
		with System Owner and Security Officer to gain understanding of support efforts and results of the specialized assessment activities.		assessment evidence; other relevant documents or records. *Interview:* Organizational personnel with security assessment responsibilities; organizational personnel with information security responsibilities. *Test:* Automated mechanisms supporting security control assessment.
CA-2(3)	Security assessments: External organizations	Review records and procedures for the selection and monitoring of the external organization assessors used by the organization. Discuss these efforts with System Owner and Security Officer to gain understanding of support efforts and results of the external organization assessor activities.	SP 800-37, rev.1, SP 800-53A, E.O. 13587	*Examine:* Security assessment and authorization policy; procedures addressing security assessments; security plan; security assessment requirements; security assessment plan; security assessment report; security assessment evidence; plan of action and milestones; other relevant documents or records. *Interview:* Organizational personnel with security assessment responsibilities; organizational personnel with information security responsibilities; personnel performing security assessments for the specified external organization.
CA-3	System interconnections	Review system interconnect documentation, such as interface documents, drawings, technical specifications, information flow diagrams, for their completeness and validity. Identify and review the appropriate MOU/As and ISAs for each interconnect. Interview System Owner, AO, and Security Officer about interconnections and their use between system and external organization.	FIPS-199, SP 800-37, rev.1, SP 800-47	*Examine:* Access control policy; procedures addressing information system connections; system and communications protection policy; information system interconnection security agreements; security plan; information system design documentation; information system configuration settings and associated documentation; other relevant documents or records. *Interview:* Organizational personnel with responsibility for developing, implementing, or approving information system interconnection agreements; organizational personnel with information security responsibilities; personnel managing the system(s) to which the interconnection security agreement applies.
CA-3(1)	System interconnections: Unclassified	Review system interconnect documentation, such as interface documents, drawings, technical	FIPS-199, SP 800-37, rev.1, SP 800-47	*Examine:* Access control policy; procedures addressing information system connections; system and communications protection

	national security system connections	specifications, information flow diagrams, for their completeness and validity. Identify and review the appropriate MOU/As and ISAs for each interconnect. Interview System Owner, AO, and Security Officer about unclassified NSS interconnections and their use between system and external organization.		policy; information system interconnection security agreements; security plan; information system design documentation; information system configuration settings and associated documentation; security assessment report; information system audit records; other relevant documents or records. *Interview:* Organizational personnel with responsibility for managing direct connections to external networks; network administrators; organizational personnel with information security responsibilities; personnel managing directly connected external networks. *Test:* Automated mechanisms supporting the management of external network connections.
CA-3(2)	System interconnections: Classified national security system connections	Review system interconnect documentation, such as interface documents, drawings, technical specifications, information flow diagrams, for their completeness and validity. Identify and review the appropriate MOU/As and ISAs for each interconnect. Interview System Owner, AO, and Security Officer about classified NSS interconnections and their use between system and external organization. Review oversight and classified control with Information Owner(s) as relevant.	FIPS-199, SP 800-37, rev.1, SP 800-47	*Examine:* Access control policy; procedures addressing information system connections; system and communications protection policy; information system interconnection security agreements; security plan; information system design documentation; information system configuration settings and associated documentation; security assessment report; information system audit records; other relevant documents or records. *Interview:* Organizational personnel with responsibility for managing direct connections to external networks; network administrators; organizational personnel with information security responsibilities; personnel managing directly connected external networks. *Test:* Automated mechanisms supporting the management of external network connections.
CA-3(3)	System interconnections: Unclassified nonnational security system connections	Review system interconnect documentation, such as interface documents, drawings, technical specifications, information flow diagrams, for their completeness	FIPS-199, SP 800-37, rev.1, SP 800-47	*Examine:* Access control policy; procedures addressing information system connections; system and communications protection policy; information system interconnection security agreements; security plan; information

(Continued)

Control number	Control name	Assessment methods	Notes and guidance documents	SP 800-53A guidance
		and validity. Identify and review the appropriate MOU/As and ISAs for each interconnect. Interview System Owner, AO, and Security Officer about unclassified non-NSS interconnections and their use between system and external organization.		system design documentation; information system configuration settings and associated documentation; security assessment report; information system audit records; other relevant documents or records. *Interview:* Organizational personnel with responsibility for managing direct connections to external networks; network administrators; organizational personnel with information security responsibilities; personnel managing directly connected external networks. *Test:* Automated mechanisms supporting the management of external network connections.
CA-3(4)	System interconnections: Connections to public networks	Review system interconnect documentation, such as interface documents, drawings, technical specifications, information flow diagrams, for their completeness and validity. Identify and review the appropriate MOU/As and ISAs for each interconnect. Interview System Owner, AO, and Security Officer about public-facing interconnections and their use.	FIPS-199, SP 800-37, rev.1, SP 800-47	*Examine:* Access control policy; procedures addressing information system connections; system and communications protection policy; information system interconnection security agreements; security plan; information system design documentation; information system configuration settings and associated documentation; security assessment report; information system audit records; other relevant documents or records. *Interview:* Network administrators; organizational personnel with information security responsibilities. *Test:* Automated mechanisms supporting the management of public network connections.
CA-3(5)	System interconnections: Restrictions on external system connections	Review system interconnect documentation, such as interface documents, drawings, technical specifications, information flow diagrams, for their completeness and validity. Identify and review the appropriate MOU/As and ISAs for each interconnect. Interview System Owner, AO, and Security Officer about external	FIPS-199, SP 800-37, rev.1, SP 800-47	*Examine:* Access control policy; procedures addressing information system connections; system and communications protection policy; information system interconnection agreements; security plan; information system design documentation; information system configuration settings and associated documentation; security assessment report; information system audit records; other relevant

		interconnections, specialized restrictions for these interconnections and their use. Review special exceptions criteria for appropriateness to organizational requirements.		documents or records. *Interview:* Organizational personnel with responsibility for managing connections to external information systems; network administrators; organizational personnel with information security responsibilities. *Test:* Automated mechanisms implementing restrictions on external system connections.
CA-4	Security certification		Withdrawn: Incorporated into CA-2	
CA-5	Plan of action and milestones	Review the POA&M register for system. Check for currency of entries, the entry status for each POA&M item, and the accuracy of the entries. Review the supporting organizational documentation and guidance for POA&M use, entries and management of items. Interview System Owner and Security Officer about POA&M actions and activities, tracking efforts, and reporting on status of POA&M items. Review automated mechanisms used by organization for POA&M management, if available and used.	SP 800-37, rev.1, OMB M02-01	*Examine:* Security assessment and authorization policy; procedures addressing plan of action and milestones; security plan; security assessment plan; security assessment report; security assessment evidence; plan of action and milestones; other relevant documents or records. *Interview:* Organizational personnel with plan of action and milestones development and implementation responsibilities; organizational personnel with information security responsibilities. *Test:* Automated mechanisms for developing, implementing, and maintaining plan of action and milestones.
CA-5(1)	Plan of action and milestones: Automation support for accuracy/currency	Review the POA&M register for system and check for currency of entries, the entry status for each POA&M item, and the accuracy of the entries. Review the supporting organizational documentation and guidance for automated control of POA&Ms entries and management of items. Interview System Owner and Security Officer about POA&M actions and activities, tracking efforts and reporting on status of POA&M items. Test and evaluate automated mechanisms used by organization for POA&M management.	SP 800-37, rev.1, OMB M02-01	*Examine:* Security assessment and authorization policy; procedures addressing plan of action and milestones; information system design documentation, information system configuration settings and associated documentation; information system audit records; plan of action and milestones; other relevant documents or records. *Interview:* Organizational personnel with plan of action and milestones development and implementation responsibilities; organizational personnel with information security responsibilities. *Test:* Automated mechanisms for developing, implementing, and maintaining plan of action and milestones.

(Continued)

Control number	Control name	Assessment methods	Notes and guidance documents	SP 800-53A guidance
CA-6	Security authorization	Review all authorization processes and procedures for system. Ensure the authorization official is assigned and active in the operation and management of system. Interview the AO to ensure that the active reviews of risks are being conducted in accordance with SP 800-37 requirements. Check documentation for authorizations for currency and accuracy in authorization efforts. Interview System Owner and Security Officer for efforts in support of authorization of system. Test automated authorization systems employed by organization, if available and used.	SP 800-37, rev.1, OMB A-130, OMB M11-33	*Examine:* Security assessment and authorization policy; procedures addressing security authorization; security authorization package (including security plan; security assessment report; plan of action and milestones; authorization statement); other relevant documents or records. *Interview:* Organizational personnel with security authorization responsibilities; organizational personnel with information security responsibilities. *Test:* Automated mechanisms that facilitate security authorizations and updates.
CA-7	Continuous monitoring	Review records and procedures for the selection and continuous monitoring of the security controls conducted by the organization. Review the continuous monitoring solution employed by the organization with the metric inputs from the controls, the handling of the monitoring process, and the reports and outputs of the continuous monitoring system feeds to the organizational components and departments. Discuss these efforts with System Owner and Security Officer to gain understanding of the support efforts and results of the continuous monitoring activities to ensure that both the actual monitoring results and the compliance reporting portions of the continuous monitoring system.	SP 800-37, rev.1, SP 800-39, SP 800-137, OMB M11-33	*Examine:* Security assessment and authorization policy; procedures addressing continuous monitoring of information system security controls; procedures addressing configuration management; security plan; security assessment report; plan of action and milestones; information system monitoring records; configuration management records; security impact analyses; status reports; other relevant documents or records. *Interview:* Organizational personnel with continuous monitoring responsibilities; organizational personnel with information security responsibilities; system/network administrators. *Test:* Mechanisms implementing continuous monitoring.
CA-7(1)	Continuous monitoring: Independent assessment	Review records and procedures for the assessment process of the continuous monitoring conducted by the organization. Review the continuous	SP 800-37, rev.1, SP 800-39, SP 800-137, OMB M11-33	*Examine:* Security assessment and authorization policy; procedures addressing continuous monitoring of information system security controls; security plan; security assessment

			References	Assessment
		monitoring solution assessment employed by the organization. Discuss these assessment efforts with System Owner and Security Officer to gain understanding of support efforts and results of the continuous monitoring activities to ensure both the actual monitoring results and the compliance reporting portions of the continuous monitoring system.		report; plan of action and milestones; information system monitoring records; security impact analyses; status reports; other relevant documents or records. *Interview:* Organizational personnel with continuous monitoring responsibilities; organizational personnel with information security responsibilities.
CA-7(2)	Continuous monitoring: Types of assessments		Withdrawn: Incorporated into CA-2	
CA-7(3)	Continuous monitoring: Trend analysis	Review the original monitoring strategy developed for system and compare it against the continuous monitoring efforts to ensure that compliance and criteria are being met successfully. Discuss with System Owner and Security Officer to ensure trend analysis and review efforts are being conducted.	SP 800-37, rev.1, SP 800-39, SP 800-137, OMB M11-33	*Examine:* Continuous monitoring strategy; security assessment and authorization policy; procedures addressing continuous monitoring of information system security controls; security plan; security assessment report; plan of action and milestones; information system monitoring records; security impact analyses; status reports; other relevant documents or records. *Interview:* Organizational personnel with continuous monitoring responsibilities; organizational personnel with information security responsibilities.
CA-8	Penetration testing	Review organizational criteria, defined documentation, and actual penetration testing requirements for system-level and network-level testing events, as they are required. Review testing documentation to ensure events are conducted, successfully completed and appropriately reviewed by the organization. Discuss penetration-testing activities with System Owner, Security Officer, and other appropriate organization personnel.	SP 800-37, rev.1, SP 800-115	*Examine:* Security assessment and authorization policy; procedures addressing penetration testing; security assessment plan; penetration test report; security assessment report; security assessment evidence; other relevant documents or records. *Interview:* Organizational personnel with security assessment responsibilities; organizational personnel with information security responsibilities; system/network administrators. *Test:* Automated mechanisms supporting penetration testing.

(Continued)

Control number	Control name	Assessment methods	Notes and guidance documents	SP 800-53A guidance
CA-8(1)	Penetration testing: Independent penetration agent or team	Review organizational criteria, defined documentation, and actual penetration testing requirements for system-level and network-level testing events, as they are required. Review testing documentation to ensure events are conducted, successfully completed by the defined testing organization. Discuss penetration-testing activities with System owner, Security Officer, and other appropriate organization personnel.	SP 800-37, rev.1, SP 800-115	*Examine:* Security assessment and authorization policy; procedures addressing penetration testing; security plan; security assessment plan; penetration test report; security assessment report; security assessment evidence; other relevant documents or records. *Interview:* Organizational personnel with security assessment responsibilities; organizational personnel with information security responsibilities.
CA-8(2)	Penetration testing: Red Team exercises	Review organizational criteria, defined documentation, and actual Red Team penetration testing for system-level and network-level testing events, as they are required. Review testing documentation to ensure events are conducted, successfully completed and appropriately reviewed by the organization. Discuss Red Team activities with System Owner, Security Officer, and other appropriate organization personnel.	SP 800-37, rev.1, SP 800-115	*Examine:* Security assessment and authorization policy; procedures addressing penetration testing; procedures addressing Red Team exercises; security plan; security assessment plan; results of Red Team exercise; penetration test report; security assessment report; rules of engagement; security assessment evidence; other relevant documents or records. *Interview:* Organizational personnel with security assessment responsibilities; organizational personnel with information security responsibilities; system/network administrators. *Test:* Automated mechanisms supporting employment of Red Team exercises.
CA-9	Internal system connections	Review all system connection information for internal connections to ensure that data, information, and the actual connections meet connection criteria, interface needs, security objectives, and defined information exchange requirements. Discuss these connections with System Owner, Security Officer, and other appropriate personnel to ensure needs and requirements are being met by defined system actions.	SP 800-37, rev.1	*Examine:* Access control policy; procedures addressing information system connections; system and communications protection policy; security plan; information system design documentation; information system configuration settings and associated documentation; list of components or classes of components authorized as internal system connections; security assessment report; information system audit records; other relevant documents or records. *Interview:*

| CA-9(1) | Internal system connections: Security compliance checks | Review all system connection information for internal connections to ensure that compliance requirements for data, information, and the actual connections are being met successfully under federal and local governance regulations, laws and reporting needs. Discuss these compliance criteria with System Owner, Security Officer, and other appropriate personnel to ensure needs and requirements are being met by defined system actions. | SP 800-47 | *Examine:* Access control policy; procedures addressing information system connections; system and communications protection policy; security plan; information system design documentation; information system configuration settings and associated documentation; list of components or classes of components authorized as internal system connections; security assessment report; information system audit records; other relevant documents or records. *Interview:* Organizational personnel with responsibility for developing, implementing, or authorizing internal system connections; organizational personnel with information security responsibilities. *Test:* Automated mechanisms supporting compliance checks. | Organizational personnel with responsibility for developing, implementing, or authorizing internal system connections; organizational personnel with information security responsibilities. |

E. *Configuration management (CM) family*

FIPS-200 provides the following criteria for this family of controls: "Organizations must: (i) establish and maintain baseline configurations and inventories of organizational information systems (including hardware, software, firmware, and documentation) throughout the respective system development life cycles; and (ii) establish and enforce security configuration settings for information technology products employed in organizational information systems."

The primary assessment areas for these controls include:

a. Audit baseline configurations to ensure maintenance throughout the respective system development life cycles (SDLC).
b. Review inventories of organizational information systems (including hardware, software, firmware, and documentation) throughout the respective system development life cycles.
c. Evaluate plans that establishes and enforces the security configuration settings for information technology products employed in organizational information systems.

Control number	Control name	Assessment methods	Notes and guidance documents	SP 800-53A guidance
CM-1	Configuration management policy and procedures	Review agency configuration management (CM) policy and procedures. Check for the defined change request (CR) procedures. Review the organizational change request tracking system. Discuss these processes with the System Owner and Security Officer.	SP 800-12, SP 800-100, SP 800-128	*Examine:* Configuration management policy and procedures; other relevant documents or records. *Interview:* Organizational personnel with configuration management responsibilities; organizational personnel with information security responsibilities; system/network administrators.
CM-2	Baseline configuration	Review the defined configuration of system. Ensure the system baseline inventory meets the defined baseline. Review the system documentation and architecture for conformance to baseline. Review system configuration settings. Discuss these documents and their maintenance with System Owner, Security Officer, system developers, and other CM personnel.	SP 800-128	*Examine:* Configuration management policy; procedures addressing the baseline configuration of the information system; configuration management plan; enterprise architecture documentation; information system design documentation; information system configuration documentation; information system configuration settings and associated documentation; change control records; other relevant documents or records. *Interview:* Organizational personnel with configuration management responsibilities; organizational personnel with information security responsibilities; system/network administrators. *Test:* Organizational processes for managing baseline configurations; automated mechanisms supporting configuration control of the baseline configuration.
CM-2(1)	Baseline configuration: Reviews and updates	Review the defined configuration of system. Ensure the system baseline inventory meets the defined baseline. Review the system documentation and architecture for conformance to baseline. Review system configuration settings. Discuss these documents and their maintenance with System Owner, Security Officer, system developers, and other CM personnel.	SP 800-128	*Examine:* Configuration management policy; configuration management plan; procedures addressing the baseline configuration of the information system; procedures addressing information system component installations and upgrades; information system architecture and configuration documentation; information system configuration settings and associated documentation; records of information system baseline configuration reviews and updates; information system component installations/upgrades and associated records; change control records; other relevant documents or records. *Interview:* Organizational personnel with configuration

(Continued)

Control number	Control name	Assessment methods	Notes and guidance documents	SP 800-53A guidance
				management responsibilities; organizational personnel with information security responsibilities; system/network administrators. *Test:* Organizational processes for managing baseline configurations; automated mechanisms supporting review and update of the baseline configuration.
CM-2(2)	Baseline configuration: Automation support for accuracy/currency	Review organizational employed automated CM system for conformance to agency requirements and system utilization. Discuss use of automated CM system with System Owner, Security Officer, and CM Manager/Coordinator.	SP 800-128	*Examine:* Configuration management policy; procedures addressing the baseline configuration of the information system; configuration management plan; information system design documentation; information system architecture and configuration documentation; information system configuration settings and associated documentation; configuration change control records; other relevant documents or records. *Interview:* Organizational personnel with configuration management responsibilities; organizational personnel with information security responsibilities; system/network administrators. *Test:* Organizational processes for managing baseline configurations; automated mechanisms implementing baseline configuration maintenance.
CM-2(3)	Baseline configuration: Retention of previous configurations	Review CM documentation for configuration documentation from pre-change configurations and retention of this documentation. Review retention policies and practices for baseline configuration documentation. Discuss with System Owner, Security Officer, and CM Manager/Coordinator.	SP 800-128	*Examine:* Configuration management policy; procedures addressing the baseline configuration of the information system; configuration management plan; information system architecture and configuration documentation; information system configuration settings and associated documentation; copies of previous baseline configuration versions; other relevant documents or records. *Interview:* Organizational personnel with configuration management responsibilities; organizational personnel with information security responsibilities; system/network administrators. *Test:* Organizational processes for managing baseline configurations.
CM-2(4)	Baseline configuration: Unauthorized software		Withdrawn: Incorporated into CM-7	

Control	Name	Guidance	Reference	Assessment
CM-2(5)	Baseline configuration: Authorized software		Withdrawn: Incorporated into CM-7	
CM-2(6)	Baseline configuration: Development and test environments	Review system baseline operating environment for development and testing of changes. Ensure these environments are separate for the operating environment. Discuss with System Owner, Security Officer, developers, and CM Manager/Coordinator.	SP 800-128	*Examine:* Configuration management policy; procedures addressing the baseline configuration of the information system; configuration management plan; information system design documentation; information system architecture and configuration documentation; information system configuration settings and associated documentation; other relevant documents or records. *Interview:* Organizational personnel with configuration management responsibilities; organizational personnel with information security responsibilities; system/network administrators. *Test:* Organizational processes for managing baseline configurations; automated mechanisms implementing separate baseline configurations for development, test, and operational environments.
CM-2(7)	Baseline configuration: Configure systems, components, or devices for high-risk areas	Review documentation related to system and users equipment travelling to high-risk areas. Ensure systems are reviewed and evaluated prior to travel for baseline configuration settings and security status. Discuss with System Owner and Security Officer.	SP 800-128	*Examine:* Configuration management policy; configuration management plan; procedures addressing the baseline configuration of the information system; procedures addressing information system component installations and upgrades; information system architecture and configuration documentation; information system configuration settings and associated documentation; records of information system baseline configuration reviews and updates; information system component installations/upgrades and associated records; change control records; other relevant documents or records. *Interview:* Organizational personnel with configuration management responsibilities; organizational personnel with information security responsibilities; system/network administrators. *Test:* Organizational processes for managing baseline configurations.
CM-3	Configuration change control	Review configuration change requests submitted for system under review. Check them for review approvals, engineering	SP 800-128	*Examine:* Configuration management policy; procedures addressing information system configuration change control; configuration management plan; information system architecture and configuration documentation;

(Continued)

Control number	Control name	Assessment methods	Notes and guidance documents	SP 800-53A guidance
		analysis, security reviews and developmental analysis, and costing attachments. Ensure CR is documented as going through the CCB for approval, application and final review after completion. Discuss CR process with System Owner, Security Officer, CM Manager/Coordinator and other interested users and department staff. Conduct sample evaluation using a random sample of CRs and trace process through full CM process and documentation.		security plan; change control records; information system audit records; change control audit and review reports; agenda/minutes from configuration change control oversight meetings; other relevant documents or records. *Interview:* Organizational personnel with configuration change control responsibilities; organizational personnel with information security responsibilities; system/network administrators; members of change control board or similar. *Test:* Organizational processes for configuration change control; automated mechanisms that implement configuration change control.
CM-3(1)	Configuration change control: Automated document/ notification/ prohibition of changes	Review configuration change requests submitted for system under review in the automated CM application. Check them for review approvals, engineering analysis, security reviews and developmental analysis, and costing attachments. Ensure CR is documented as going through the CCB for approval, application and final review after completion. Discuss CR process with System Owner, Security Officer, CM Manager/Coordinator and other interested users and department staff.	SP 800-128	*Examine:* Configuration management policy; procedures addressing information system configuration change control; configuration management plan; information system design documentation; information system architecture and configuration documentation; automated configuration control mechanisms; information system configuration settings and associated documentation; change control records; information system audit records; change approval requests; change approvals; other relevant documents or records. *Interview:* Organizational personnel with configuration change control responsibilities; organizational personnel with information security responsibilities; system/network administrators; system developers. *Test:* Organizational processes for configuration change control; automated mechanisms implementing configuration change control activities.
CM-3(2)	Configuration change control: Test/validate/ document changes	Review configuration change requests submitted for system under review. Check them for review approvals, engineering analysis, security reviews and developmental analysis, and	SP 800-128	*Examine:* Configuration management policy; procedures addressing information system configuration change control; information system design documentation; information system architecture and configuration documentation; information system configuration settings and associated documentation;

		costing attachments. Ensure CR is documented as going through the CCB for approval, application and final review after completion. Discuss CR process with System Owner, Security Officer, CM Manager/Coordinator and other interested users and department staff. Conduct sample evaluation using a random sample of CRs and trace process through full CM process and documentation.		test records; validation records; change control records; information system audit records; other relevant documents or records. *Interview:* Organizational personnel with configuration change control responsibilities; organizational personnel with information security responsibilities; system/network administrators. *Test:* Organizational processes for configuration change control; automated mechanisms supporting and/or implementing testing, validating, and documenting information system changes.
CM-3(3)	Configuration change control: Automated change implementation	Review configuration change requests submitted for system under review in the automated CM application. Check them for review approvals, engineering analysis, security reviews and developmental analysis, and costing attachments. Ensure CR is documented as going through the CCB for approval, application and final review after completion. Discuss CR process with System Owner, Security Officer, CM Manager/Coordinator and other interested users and department staff. Conduct sample evaluation using a random sample of CRs and trace process through full CM process and documentation.	SP 800-128	*Examine:* Configuration management policy; procedures addressing information system configuration change control; information system design documentation; information system architecture and configuration documentation; automated configuration control mechanisms; change control records; information system audit records; other relevant documents or records. *Interview:* Organizational personnel with configuration change control responsibilities; organizational personnel with information security responsibilities; system/network administrators; system developers. *Test:* Organizational processes for configuration change control; automated mechanisms implementing changes to current information system baseline.
CM-3(4)	Configuration change control Security representative	Check a random sample of CR requests for security approvals and reviews. Discuss these CRs with System Owner and Security Officer.	SP 800-128	*Examine:* Configuration management policy; procedures addressing information system configuration change control; configuration management plan; security plan; other relevant documents or records. *Interview:* Organizational personnel with configuration change control responsibilities; organizational personnel with information security responsibilities. *Test:* Organizational processes for configuration change control.

(Continued)

Control number	Control name	Assessment methods	Notes and guidance documents	SP 800-53A guidance
CM-3(5)	Configuration change control: Automated security response	Check a random sample of CR requests in the automated CM application for security approvals and reviews. Check to validate system automatically notified security personnel, if the system under review has unauthorized changes applied. Discuss these CRs with System Owner and Security Officer.	SP 800-128	*Examine:* Configuration management policy; procedures addressing information system configuration change control; configuration management plan; security plan; information system design documentation; information system architecture and configuration documentation; information system configuration settings and associated documentation; alerts/notifications of unauthorized baseline configuration changes; information system audit records; other relevant documents or records. *Interview:* Organizational personnel with configuration change control responsibilities; organizational personnel with information security responsibilities; system/network administrators; system developers. *Test:* Organizational processes for configuration change control; automated mechanisms implementing security responses to changes to the baseline configurations.
CM-3(6)	Configuration change control Cryptography management	Review CRs applied to system to verify if any have applied changes to the cryptological functions resident in system. If so, verify security approval was obtained prior to implementation. Discuss any relevant CRs with System Owner and Security Officer to validate change requests and actions taken.	SP 800-128	*Examine:* Configuration management policy; procedures addressing information system configuration change control; configuration management plan; security plan; information system design documentation; information system architecture and configuration documentation; information system configuration settings and associated documentation; other relevant documents or records. *Interview:* Organizational personnel with configuration change control responsibilities; organizational personnel with information security responsibilities; system/network administrators. *Test:* Organizational processes for configuration change control; cryptographic mechanisms implementing organizational security safeguards.
CM-4	Security impact analysis	Review documentation for security impact of changes. Confirm security impact analysis (SIA) was performed for each change. Review with System Owner and Security Officer that	SP 800-128	*Examine:* Configuration management policy; procedures addressing security impact analysis for changes to the information system; configuration management plan; security impact analysis documentation; analysis tools and associated outputs; change control records; information system audit records; other relevant documents or records.

		the process and procedures for SIA is active for all changes.		*Interview:* Organizational personnel with responsibility for conducting security impact analysis; organizational personnel with information security responsibilities; system/network administrators. *Test:* Organizational processes for security impact analysis.
CM-4(1)	Security impact analysis: Separate test environments	Review all documents related to SIA on testing of changes. Ensure SIAs are conducted which review impacts, malicious code, flaws, and potential weaknesses, which could be introduced by changes. Discuss and interview System Owner, Security Officer, and developers related to testing of changes and test environment.	SP 800-128	*Examine:* Configuration management policy; procedures addressing security impact analysis for changes to the information system; configuration management plan; security impact analysis documentation; analysis tools and associated outputs information system design documentation; information system architecture and configuration documentation; change control records; information system audit records; documentation evidence of separate Test and operational environments; other relevant documents or records. *Interview:* Organizational personnel with responsibility for conducting security impact analysis; organizational personnel with information security responsibilities; system/network administrators. *Test:* Organizational processes for security impact analysis; automated mechanisms supporting and/or implementing security impact analysis of changes.
CM-4(2)	Security impact analysis: Verification of security functions	Review documents, which reflect results of testing after changes to ensure security controls are maintained or enhanced by changes. Discuss with System Owner, Security Officer, and development staff.	SP 800-128	*Examine:* Configuration management policy; procedures addressing security impact analysis for changes to the information system; configuration management plan; security impact analysis documentation; analysis tools and associated outputs; change control records; information system audit records; other relevant documents or records. *Interview:* Organizational personnel with responsibility for conducting security impact analysis; organizational personnel with information security responsibilities; system/network administrators. *Test:* Organizational processes for security impact analysis; automated mechanisms supporting and/or implementing verification of security functions.
CM-5	Access restrictions for change	Review documentation to ensure all change activities are controlled in which access is defined,	SP 800-128	*Examine:* Configuration management policy; procedures addressing access restrictions for changes to the information system; configuration management plan;

(Continued)

Control number	Control name	Assessment methods	Notes and guidance documents	SP 800-53A guidance
		documented, controlled, and restricted appropriately based on physical and logical access to the system and application. Discuss with System Owner, development staff, and Security Officer.		information system design documentation; information system architecture and configuration documentation; information system configuration settings and associated documentation; logical access approvals; physical access approvals; access credentials; change control records; information system audit records; other relevant documents or records. *Interview:* Organizational personnel with logical access control responsibilities; organizational personnel with physical access control responsibilities; organizational personnel with information security responsibilities; system/network administrators. *Test:* Organizational processes for managing access restrictions to change; automated mechanisms supporting/implementing/enforcing access restrictions associated with changes to the information system.
CM-5(1)	Access restrictions for change: Automated access enforcement/auditing	Review system and documentation to ensure that it enforces access restrictions based on organizational-defined criteria and enforces these controls automatically. Discuss with System Owner and Security Officer.	SP 800-128	*Examine:* Configuration management policy; procedures addressing access restrictions for changes to the information system; information system design documentation; information system architecture and configuration documentation; information system configuration settings and associated documentation; change control records; information system audit records; other relevant documents or records. *Interview:* Organizational personnel with information security responsibilities; system/network administrators; system developers. *Test:* Organizational processes for managing access restrictions to change; automated mechanisms implementing enforcement of access restrictions for changes to the information system; automated mechanisms supporting auditing of enforcement actions.
CM-5(2)	Access restrictions for change: Review system changes	Review system documentation to ensure organization controls and reviews all system changes for proper actions and development activities. Discuss with System	SP 800-128	*Examine:* Configuration management policy; procedures addressing access restrictions for changes to the information system; configuration management plan; security plan; reviews of information system changes; audit and review reports; change control records;

information system audit records; other relevant documents or records. *Interview:* Organizational personnel with information security responsibilities; system/network administrators. *Test:* Organizational processes for managing access restrictions to change; automated mechanisms supporting/implementing information system reviews to determine whether unauthorized changes have occurred.

Owner, Security Officer, and development staff.

Control	Name	Review	Ref.	Assessment
CM-5(3)	Access restrictions for change: Signed components	Review documentation to ensure all software loads are conducted with signed or verified components and certificates. Discuss with System Owner, development staff, and Security Officer. Test, if available, methods for software management to ensure only signed code components are installed.	SP 800-128	*Examine:* Configuration management policy; procedures addressing access restrictions for changes to the information system; configuration management plan; security plan; list of software and firmware components to be prohibited from installation without a recognized and approved certificate; information system design documentation; information system architecture and configuration documentation; information system configuration settings and associated documentation; change control records; information system audit records; other relevant documents or records. *Interview:* Organizational personnel with information security responsibilities; system/network administrators; system developers. *Test:* Organizational processes for managing access restrictions to change; automated mechanisms preventing installation of software and firmware components not signed with an organization-recognized and approved certificate.
CM-5(4)	Access restrictions for change: Dual authorization	Review documentation to ensure all change activities are controlled, in which access is required to have dual authorizations and this dual authorization is enacted. Discuss with System Owner, development staff, and Security Officer.	SP 800-128	*Examine:* Configuration management policy; procedures addressing access restrictions for changes to the information system; configuration management plan; security plan; information system design documentation; information system architecture and configuration documentation; information system configuration settings and associated documentation; change control records; information system audit records; other relevant documents or records. *Interview:* Organizational personnel with dual authorization enforcement responsibilities for implementing information system changes; organizational personnel with information security responsibilities; system/network administrators.

(Continued)

Control number	Control name	Assessment methods	Notes and guidance documents	SP 800-53A guidance
CM-5(5)	Access restrictions for change: Limit production/ operational privileges	Review documents, which reflect limitations for privileged user accounts in reference to changes to ensure that security controls are maintained or enhanced by changes. Discuss with System Owner, Security Officer, and development staff.	SP 800-128	*Examine:* Configuration management policy; procedures addressing access restrictions for changes to the information system; configuration management plan; security plan; information system design documentation; information system architecture and configuration documentation; information system configuration settings and associated documentation; user privilege reviews; user privilege re-certifications; change control records; information system audit records; other relevant documents or records. *Interview:* Organizational personnel with information security responsibilities; system/network administrators. *Test:* Organizational processes for managing access restrictions to change; automated mechanisms supporting and/or implementing access restrictions for change. *Test:* Organizational processes for managing access restrictions to change; automated mechanisms implementing dual authorization enforcement.
CM-5(6)	Access restrictions for change: Limit library privileges	Review system and documentation to ensure that it enforces software library access restrictions based on the organizational-defined criteria and enforces these controls automatically. Discuss with System Owner and Security Officer.	SP 800-128	*Examine:* Configuration management policy; procedures addressing access restrictions for changes to the information system; configuration management plan; information system design documentation; information system architecture and configuration documentation; information system configuration settings and associated documentation; change control records; information system audit records; other relevant documents or records. *Interview:* Organizational personnel with information security responsibilities; system/network administrators. *Test:* Organizational processes for managing access restrictions to change; automated mechanisms supporting and/or implementing access restrictions for change.
CM-5(7)	Access restrictions for change: Automatic implementation of security safeguards		Withdrawn: Incorporated into SI-7	

CM-6	Configuration settings	Review configuration checklists utilized to setup and configure system. Identify and review additional checklists used. Check configuration policy and procedures for system. Review and confirm configurations are defined and delineated in SSP. Discuss all with System Owner and Security Officer, along with implementation Security Engineer and other members of security staff.	SP 800-70, SP 800-128, OMB M07-11, OMB M07-18, OMB M08-22	*Examine:* Configuration management policy; procedures addressing configuration settings for the information system; configuration management plan; security plan; information system design documentation; information system configuration settings and associated documentation; security configuration checklists; evidence supporting approved deviations from established configuration settings; change control records; information system audit records; other relevant documents or records. *Interview:* Organizational personnel with security configuration management responsibilities; organizational personnel with information security responsibilities; system/network administrators. *Test:* Organizational processes for managing configuration settings; automated mechanisms that implement, monitor, and/or control information system configuration settings; automated mechanisms that identify and/or document deviations from established configuration settings.
CM-6(1)	Configuration settings: Automated central management/ application/ verification	Review configuration checklist automated implementation processes and control mechanisms. Identify and review additional checklist automated mechanisms used. Verify configuration policy and procedures for system. Review and confirm configurations are defined and installed correctly as delineated in SSP. Discuss all with System Owner and Security Officer, along with implementation Security Engineer and other members of security staff.	SP 800-70, SP 800-128, OMB M07-11, OMB M07-18, OMB M08-22	*Examine:* Configuration management policy; procedures addressing configuration settings for the information system; configuration management plan; information system design documentation; information system configuration settings and associated documentation; security configuration checklists; change control records; information system audit records; other relevant documents or records. *Interview:* [Organizational personnel with security configuration management responsibilities; organizational personnel with information security responsibilities; system/network administrators; system developers. *Test:* Organizational processes for managing configuration settings; automated mechanisms implemented to centrally manage, apply, and verify information system configuration settings.
CM-6(2)	Configuration settings: Respond to unauthorized changes	Review policies and procedures for methods of response to unauthorized changes to system/ application. Determine method of response and activities instituted	SP 800-70, SP 800-128, OMB M07-11, OMB M07-18, OMB M08-22	*Examine:* Configuration management policy; procedures addressing configuration settings for the information system; configuration management plan; security plan; information system design documentation; information system configuration settings and associated

(Continued)

Control number	Control name	Assessment methods	Notes and guidance documents	SP 800-53A guidance
		for response when detected. Discuss with Security Officer on actual response efforts and activities, if any, and installed safeguards for configuration settings modification.		documentation; alerts/notifications of unauthorized changes to information system configuration settings; documented responses to unauthorized changes to information system configuration settings; change control records; information system audit records; other relevant documents or records. *Interview:* Organizational personnel with security configuration management responsibilities; organizational personnel with information security responsibilities; system/network administrators. *Test:* Organizational process for responding to unauthorized changes to information system configuration settings; automated mechanisms supporting and/or implementing security safeguards for response to unauthorized changes.
CM-6(3)	Configuration settings: Unauthorized change detection		Withdrawn: Incorporated into SI-7	
CM-6(4)	Configuration settings: Conformance demonstration		Withdrawn: Incorporated into CM-4	
CM-7	Least functionality	Review system documentation for determination of what services are to be provided by system under review. Determine what restrictions are defined for system with respect to active ports, protocols, and services on the system. Test via automated scan tools to identify open ports and configurations for system. Discuss with System Owner, System Administrators, and Security Officer.	SP 800-128, DODI 8551.01	*Examine:* Configuration management policy; configuration management plan; procedures addressing least functionality in the information system; security plan; information system design documentation; information system configuration settings and associated documentation; security configuration checklists; other relevant documents or records. *Interview:* Organizational personnel with security configuration management responsibilities; organizational personnel with information security responsibilities; system/network administrators. *Test:* Organizational processes prohibiting or restricting functions, ports, protocols, and/or services; automated mechanisms implementing restrictions or prohibition of functions, ports, protocols, and/or services.

CM-7(1)	Least functionality: Periodic review	SP 800-128, DODI 8551.01	Review system documentation for the determination of how often the ports, protocols, and services are to be provided by system under review are to be reviewed. Determine which ports, protocols, and services are disabled on system. Test via automated scan tools to identify open ports and configurations for system. Discuss with System Owner, System Administrators, and Security Officer.	*Examine:* Configuration management policy; procedures addressing least functionality in the information system; configuration management plan; security plan; information system design documentation; information system configuration settings and associated documentation; security configuration checklists; documented reviews of functions, ports, protocols, and/or services; change control records; information system audit records; other relevant documents or records. *Interview:* Organizational personnel with responsibilities for reviewing functions, ports, protocols, and services on the information system; organizational personnel with information security responsibilities; system/network administrators. *Test:* Organizational processes for reviewing/disabling nonsecure functions, ports, protocols, and/or services; automated mechanisms implementing review and disabling of nonsecure functions, ports, protocols, and/or services.
CM-7(2)	Least functionality: Prevent program execution	SP 800-128, DODI 8551.01	Review documentation for the system under review to determine how the system prevents program execution of certain designated software components and packages. Test system by attempting to run one of the restricted programs and observing the results. Discuss with System Owner and Security Officer.	*Examine:* Configuration management policy; procedures addressing least functionality in the information system; configuration management plan; security plan; information system design documentation; specifications for preventing software program execution; information system configuration settings and associated documentation; change control records; information system audit records; other relevant documents or records. *Interview:* Organizational personnel with information security responsibilities; system/network administrators; system developers. *Test:* Organizational processes preventing program execution on the information system; organizational processes for software program usage and restrictions; automated mechanisms preventing program execution on the information system; automated mechanisms supporting and/or implementing software program usage and restrictions.
CM-7(3)	Least functionality: Registration compliance	SP 800-128, DODI 8551.01	Review documentation for system to ensure that system enacts the registration process to manage, track, and provide oversight	*Examine:* Configuration management policy; procedures addressing least functionality in the information system; configuration management plan; security plan; information system configuration settings and associated

(Continued)

Control number	Control name	Assessment methods	Notes and guidance documents	SP 800-53A guidance
		for information systems and implemented functions, ports, protocols, and services. Review with the System Owner and Security Officer.		documentation; audit and compliance reviews; information system audit records; other relevant documents or records. *Interview:* Organizational personnel with information security responsibilities; system/network administrators. *Test:* Organizational processes ensuring compliance with registration requirements for functions, ports, protocols, and/or services; automated mechanisms implementing compliance with registration requirements for functions, ports, protocols, and/or services.
CM-7(4)	Least functionality: Unauthorized software (blacklisting)	Review documentation to identify all software, which are not authorized to run on system. The process used to identify software programs that are not authorized to execute on organizational information systems is commonly referred to as blacklisting. Test via attempting to run one of the restricted software packages and observing the results. Discuss with System Owner and Security Officer.	SP 800-128, DODI 8551.01	*Examine:* Configuration management policy; procedures addressing least functionality in the information system; configuration management plan; information system design documentation; information system configuration settings and associated documentation; list of software programs not authorized to execute on the information system; security configuration checklists; review and update records associated with list of unauthorized software programs; change control records; information system audit records; other relevant documents or records. *Interview:* Organizational personnel with responsibilities for identifying software not authorized to execute on the information system; organizational personnel with information security responsibilities; system/network administrators. *Test:* Organizational process for identifying, reviewing, and updating programs not authorized to execute on the information system; organizational process for implementing blacklisting; automated mechanisms supporting and/or implementing blacklisting.
CM-7(5)	Least functionality: Authorized software (whitelisting)	Review documentation to identify only the software authorized to run on system. The process used to identify software programs that are authorized to execute on organizational information systems is commonly referred to as whitelisting. Ensure policy	SP 800-128, DODI 8551.01	*Examine:* Configuration management policy; procedures addressing least functionality in the information system; configuration management plan; information system design documentation; information system configuration settings and associated documentation; list of software programs authorized to execute on the information system; security configuration checklists; review and update records associated with list of authorized software

Control	Name	Reference	Discussion	Assessment
			is defined as deny by default, allow by policy for all software. If software is on list, it can run; otherwise, it cannot run. Discuss with System Owner and Security Officer.	programs; change control records; information system audit records; other relevant documents or records. *Interview:* Organizational personnel with responsibilities for identifying software authorized to execute on the information system; organizational personnel with information security responsibilities; system/network administrators. *Test:* Organizational process for identifying, reviewing, and updating programs authorized to execute on the information system; organizational process for implementing whitelisting; automated mechanisms implementing whitelisting.
CM-8	Information system component inventory	SP 800-128	Review documentation to ensure that the system has a complete and accurate component inventory of all hardware and software associated with the system, which is periodically reviewed and updated as needed. Discuss with System Owner, CM staff, and Security Officer.	*Examine:* Configuration management policy; procedures addressing information system component inventory; configuration management plan; security plan; information system inventory records; inventory reviews and update records; other relevant documents or records. *Interview:* Organizational personnel with responsibilities for information system component inventory; organizational personnel with information security responsibilities; system/network administrators. *Test:* Organizational processes for developing and documenting an inventory of information system components; automated mechanisms supporting and/or implementing the information system component inventory.
CM-8(1)	Information system component inventory: Updates during installations/removals	SP 800-128	Review documentation and inventory of system during update activities of the system. Discuss each update as needed with System Owner and Security Officer.	*Examine:* Configuration management policy; procedures addressing information system component inventory; configuration management plan; security plan; information system inventory records; inventory reviews and update records; component installation records; component removal records; other relevant documents or records. *Interview:* Organizational personnel with responsibilities for updating the information system component inventory; organizational personnel with information security responsibilities; system/network administrators. *Test:* Organizational processes for updating inventory of information system components; automated mechanisms implementing updating of the information system component inventory.

(Continued)

Control number	Control name	Assessment methods	Notes and guidance documents	SP 800-53A guidance
CM-8(2)	Information system component inventory: Automated maintenance	Review documentation for automated system inventory, and where possible, baseline configuration. Review output from automated mechanism to ensure up-to-date, accurate, and complete inventory is maintained. Discuss with System Owner, CM staff and Security Officer.	SP 800-128	*Examine:* Configuration management policy; configuration management plan; procedures addressing information system component inventory; information system design documentation; information system configuration settings and associated documentation; information system inventory records; change control records; information system maintenance records; information system audit records; other relevant documents or records. *Interview:* Organizational personnel with responsibilities for managing the automated mechanisms implementing the information system component inventory; organizational personnel with information security responsibilities; system/network administrators; system developers. *Test:* Organizational processes for maintaining the inventory of information system components; automated mechanisms implementing the information system component inventory.
CM-8(3)	Information system component inventory: Automated unauthorized component detection	Review documentation to ensure an automated detection monitoring effort is active for unauthorized components in the system. Monitoring for unauthorized system components may be accomplished on an ongoing basis or by the periodic scanning of system for that purpose. Automated mechanisms can be implemented within information systems or in other separate devices. Isolation can be achieved, for example, by placing unauthorized information system components in separate domains or subnets or otherwise quarantining such components. This type of component isolation	SP 800-128	*Examine:* Configuration management policy; procedures addressing information system component inventory; configuration management plan; security plan; information system design documentation; information system configuration settings and associated documentation; information system inventory records; alerts/notifications of unauthorized components within the information system; information system monitoring records; change control records; information system audit records; other relevant documents or records. *Interview:* Organizational personnel with responsibilities for managing the automated mechanisms implementing unauthorized information system component detection; organizational personnel with information security responsibilities; system/network administrators; system developers. *Test:* Organizational processes for detection of unauthorized information system components; automated mechanisms implementing the detection of unauthorized information system components.

CM-8(4)	Information system component inventory: Accountability information	is commonly referred to as sandboxing. Discuss with System Owner and Security Officer. Review documentation to determine who is identified as accountable and responsible for the various components of the system. Discuss with System Owner and Security Officer.	SP 800-128	*Examine:* Configuration management policy; procedures addressing information system component inventory; configuration management plan; security plan; information system inventory records; other relevant documents or records. *Interview:* Organizational personnel with responsibilities for managing the information system component inventory; organizational personnel with information security responsibilities; system/ network administrators. *Test:* Organizational processes for maintaining the inventory of information system components; automated mechanisms implementing the information system component inventory.
CM-8(5)	Information system component inventory: No duplicate accounting of components	Review documentation to ensure that no duplicate accounting exists for system components. Discuss with System Owner and inventory control staff.	SP 800-128	*Examine:* Configuration management policy; procedures addressing information system component inventory; configuration management plan; security plan; information system inventory records; other relevant documents or records. *Interview:* Organizational personnel with information system inventory responsibilities; organizational personnel with responsibilities for defining information system components within the authorization boundary of the system; organizational personnel with information security responsibilities; system/ network administrators. *Test:* Organizational processes for maintaining the inventory of information system components; automated mechanisms implementing the information system component inventory.
CM-8(6)	Information system component inventory: Assessed configurations/ approved deviations	Review documentation to ensure that system configuration settings are established by organization for information system components, the specific components that have been assessed to determine compliance with the required configuration settings, and any approved deviations from	SP 800-128	*Examine:* Configuration management policy; procedures addressing information system component inventory; configuration management plan; security plan; information system design documentation; information system configuration settings and associated documentation; information system inventory records; other relevant documents or records. *Interview:* [Organizational personnel with inventory management and assessment responsibilities for information system

(Continued)

Control number	Control name	Assessment methods	Notes and guidance documents	SP 800-53A guidance
		established configuration settings are documented. Discuss with System Owner, CM Staff, and Security Officer.		components; organizational personnel with information security responsibilities; system/network administrators. *Test:* Organizational processes for maintaining the inventory of information system components; automated mechanisms implementing the information system component inventory.
CM-8(7)	Information system component inventory: Centralized repository	Review documentation to determine if the system is included in organizational central repository tracking system. If so, review records to ensure accuracy and completeness. Discuss with System Owner and Security Officer.	SP 800-128	*Examine:* Configuration management policy; procedures addressing information system component inventory; configuration management plan; information system design documentation; information system inventory records; other relevant documents or records. *Interview:* Organizational personnel with inventory management responsibilities for information system components; organizational personnel with information security responsibilities. *Test:* Automated mechanisms implementing the information system component inventory in a centralized repository.
CM-8(8)	Information system component inventory: Automated location tracking	Review documentation to determine if the system is included in organizational automated location tracking system. If so, review records to ensure accuracy and completeness. Discuss with System Owner and Security Officer.	SP 800-128	*Examine:* Configuration management policy; procedures addressing information system component inventory; configuration management plan; information system design documentation; information system configuration settings and associated documentation; information system inventory records; information system audit records; other relevant documents or records. *Interview:* Organizational personnel with inventory management responsibilities for information system components; organizational personnel with information security responsibilities; system/network administrators; system developers. *Test:* Automated mechanisms implementing the information system component inventory; automated mechanisms supporting tracking of information system components by geographic location.
CM-8(9)	Information system component inventory: Assignment of	Review documentation for system to determine the criteria for types of information system components (e.g., microprocessors, motherboards,	SP 800-128	*Examine:* Configuration management policy; procedures addressing information system component inventory; configuration management plan; security plan; information system design documentation; acknowledgements of information system component assignments; information

Control	Name	Guidance	Reference	Assessment
	components to systems	software, programmable logic controllers, and network devices) that are subject to specific assignment. Discuss with System Owner, CM staff and Security Officer.		system inventory records; other relevant documents or records. *Interview:* Organizational personnel with inventory management responsibilities for information system components; information system owner; organizational personnel with information security responsibilities; system/network administrators. *Test:* Organizational processes for assigning components to systems; organizational processes for acknowledging assignment of components to systems; automated mechanisms implementing assignment of acquired components to the information system; automated mechanisms implementing acknowledgment of assignment of acquired components to the information system.
CM-9	Configuration management plan	Review system documentation to determine the existence of the system configuration management plan (CMP). Ensure CMP is accurate, up-to-date and being followed for all changes, as they are applied to the system. Ensure completeness of plan in accordance with SP 800-128 and organizations configuration management policy. Discuss with System Owner, CM staff, and Security Officer.	SP 800-128	*Examine:* Configuration management policy; procedures addressing configuration management planning; configuration management plan; security plan; other relevant documents or records. *Interview:* Organizational personnel with responsibilities for developing the configuration management plan; organizational personnel with responsibilities for implementing and managing processes defined in the configuration management plan; organizational personnel with responsibilities for protecting the configuration management plan; organizational personnel with information security responsibilities; system/network administrators. *Test:* Organizational processes for developing and documenting the configuration management plan; organizational processes for identifying and managing configuration items; organizational processes for protecting the configuration management plan; automated mechanisms implementing the configuration management plan; automated mechanisms for managing configuration items; automated mechanisms for protecting the configuration management plan.
CM-9(1)	Configuration management plan: Assignment of responsibility	Review documentation of CMP to determine if the system developers may be tasked to develop configuration	SP 800-128	*Examine:* Configuration management policy; procedures addressing responsibilities for configuration management process development; configuration management plan; security plan; other relevant documents or records.

(Continued)

Control number	Control name	Assessment methods	Notes and guidance documents	SP 800-53A guidance
		management processes using personnel, who are not directly involved in system development or integration. If so, identify assigned responsibilities and actions. Discuss with System Owner, CM staff, and Security Officer.		*Interview:* Organizational personnel with responsibilities for configuration management process development; organizational personnel with information security responsibilities.
CM-10	Software usage restrictions	Review all documentation to determine proper software licensing and usage is active and being performed correctly for system under review. Discuss with System Owner, acquisition staff, CM staff, and Security Officer.	SP 800-128	*Examine:* Configuration management policy; procedures addressing software usage restrictions; configuration management plan; security plan; software contract agreements and copyright laws; site license documentation; list of software usage restrictions; software license tracking reports; other relevant documents or records. *Interview:* Organizational personnel with information security responsibilities; system/network administrators; organizational personnel operating, using, and/or maintaining the information system; organizational personnel with software license management responsibilities. *Test:* Organizational process for tracking the use of software protected by quantity licenses; organization process for controlling/documenting the use of peer-to-peer file sharing technology; automated mechanisms implementing software license tracking; automated mechanisms implementing and controlling the use of peer-to-peer files sharing technology.
CM-10(1)	Software usage restrictions: Open source software	Review documentation for system to determine if open source software is active on system, and if so, the proper restrictions are in place for its usage. Discuss with System Owner and Security Officer.	SP 800-128	*Examine:* Configuration management policy; procedures addressing restrictions on use of open source software; configuration management plan; security plan; other relevant documents or records. *Interview:* Organizational personnel with responsibilities for establishing and enforcing restrictions on use of open source software; organizational personnel with information security responsibilities; system/network administrators. *Test:* Organizational process for restricting the use of open source software; automated mechanisms implementing restrictions on the use of open source software.

CM-11	User-installed software	SP 800-128	Review documentation to determine what level of software installation is permitted for normal system users. To maintain control over the types of software installed, determine if the organization has identified permitted and prohibited actions regarding software installation. Discuss with System Owner and Security Officer.	*Examine:* Configuration management policy; procedures addressing user installed software; security plan; information system configuration management plan; information system design documentation; information system configuration settings and associated documentation; list of rules governing user installed software; information system monitoring records; information system audit records; other relevant documents or records; continuous monitoring strategy. *Interview:* Organizational personnel with responsibilities for governing user-installed software; organizational personnel operating, using, and/or maintaining the information system; organizational personnel monitoring compliance with user-installed software policy; organizational personnel with information security responsibilities; system/network administrators. *Test:* Organizational processes governing user-installed software on the information system; automated mechanisms enforcing rules/methods for governing the installation of software by users; automated mechanisms monitoring policy compliance.
CM-11(1)	User-installed software: Alerts for unauthorized installations	SP 800-128	Review documentation to determire if the system alerts appropriate personnel, when a user attempts to load unauthorized software onto system. Test by performing test software load effort and observing the results. Discuss with System Owner and Security Officer.	*Examine:* Configuration management policy; procedures addressing user installed software; security plan; information system configuration management plan; information system design documentation; information system configuration settings and associated documentation; information system audit records; other relevant documents or records. *Interview:* Organizational personnel with responsibilities for governing user-installed software; organizational personnel operating, using, and/or maintaining the information system; organizational personnel with information security responsibilities; system/network administrators; system developers. *Test:* Organizational processes governing user-installed software on the information system; automated mechanisms for alerting personnel/roles when unauthorized installation of software is detected.

(Continued)

Control number	Control name	Assessment methods	Notes and guidance documents	SP 800-53A guidance
CM-11(2)	User-installed software: Prohibit installation without privileged status	Review documentation to determine if only privilege account holders can load software onto the system. If so, test by attempting a software load and observing the results. Discuss with System Owner and Security Officer.	SP 800-128	*Examine:* Configuration management policy; procedures addressing user installed software; configuration management plan; security plan; information system design documentation; information system configuration settings and associated documentation; alerts/notifications of unauthorized software installations; information system audit records; other relevant documents or records. *Interview:* Organizational personnel with responsibilities for governing user-installed software; organizational personnel operating, using, and/or maintaining the information system. *Test:* Organizational processes governing user-installed software on the information system; automated mechanisms for prohibiting installation of software without privileged status (e.g., access controls).

F. *Contingency planning family*

FIPS-200 provides the following criteria for this family of controls: Contingency planning (CP): Organizations must establish, maintain, and effectively implement plans for emergency response, backup operations, and post-disaster recovery for organizational information systems to ensure the availability of critical information resources and continuity of operations in emergency situations.

The primary assessment areas for these controls include:

Audit plans that establish and maintain effective implementation plans for emergency response, backup operations, and post-disaster recovery for organizational information systems to ensure the availability of critical information resources and continuity of operations in emergency situations

Control number	Control name	Assessment methods	Notes and guidance documents	SP 800-53A guidance
CP-1	Contingency planning policy and procedures	Review documentation for organization to determine the contingency and recovery process, policies and procedures implemented by the organization. Discuss with System Owner, operations staff, and Security Officer.	SP 800-12, SP 800-34, SP 800-100, FCD-1	*Examine:* Contingency planning policy and procedures; other relevant documents or records. *Interview:* Organizational personnel with contingency planning responsibilities; organizational personnel with information security responsibilities.
CP-2	Contingency plan	Review documentation for system to ensure the contingency plan (CP) is defined, developed, written, and instituted for system under review. Review CP to ensure all component parts are in place and reviewed. Ensure CP is signed and appropriately approved by management of organization and Authorizing Official (AO) of system. Discuss with System Owner and Security Officer.	SP 800-34, FCD-1	*Examine:* Contingency planning policy; procedures addressing contingency operations for the information system; contingency plan; security plan; evidence of contingency plan reviews and updates; other relevant documents or records. *Interview:* Organizational personnel with contingency planning and plan implementation responsibilities; organizational personnel with incident handling responsibilities; organizational personnel with information security responsibilities. *Test:* Organizational processes for contingency plan development, review, update, and protection; automated mechanisms for developing, reviewing, updating and/or protecting the contingency plan.
CP-2(1)	Contingency plan: Coordinate with related plans	Review documentation for organization to ensure CP is coordinated with and correlated to other organizational continuity plans and actions. Discuss with System Owner, COOP staff, and Security Officer.	SP 800-34, FCD-1	*Examine:* Contingency planning policy; procedures addressing contingency operations for the information system; contingency plan; business contingency plans; disaster recovery plans; continuity of operations plans; crisis communications plans; critical infrastructure plans; cyber incident response plan; insider threat implementation plans; occupant emergency plans; security plan; other relevant documents or records. *Interview:* Organizational personnel with contingency planning and plan implementation responsibilities; organizational personnel with information

(Continued)

			security responsibilities; personnel with responsibility for related plans.
CP-2(2)	Contingency plan: Capacity planning	Review documentation for organization to ensure that organization accounted for potential capacity reduction during contingency operations. Review capacity planning documents used to support CP development. Discuss with Operations staff, Security Engineer, COOP staff, System Owner, and Security Officer.	SP 800-34, FCD-1	*Examine:* Contingency planning policy; procedures addressing contingency operations for the information system; contingency plan; capacity planning documents; other relevant documents or records. *Interview:* Organizational personnel with contingency planning and plan implementation responsibilities; organizational personnel with information security responsibilities.
CP-2(3)	Contingency plan: Resume essential missions/business functions	Review documentation for system to determine the recovery time objective (RTO) for system and all actions to support this essential mission resumption time are defined and operational. Ensure RTO defined in CP is consistent with RTO defined in organizational BCP and BIA. Discuss with operations staff, Security Engineer, COOP staff, System Owner, and Security Officer.	SP 800-34, FCD-1	*Examine:* Contingency planning policy; procedures addressing contingency operations for the information system; contingency plan; security plan; business impact assessment; other related plans; other relevant documents or records. *Interview:* Organizational personnel with contingency planning and plan implementation responsibilities; organizational personnel with information security responsibilities. *Test:* Organizational processes for resumption of missions and business functions.
CP-2(4)	Contingency plan: Resume all missions/business functions	Review documentation for system to determine the maximum tolerable outage (MTO) for system and all actions to support this full mission resumption time are defined and operational. Ensure MTO defined in CP is consistent with MTO defined in organizational BCP and BIA. Discuss with operations staff, Security Engineer, COOP staff, System Owner, and Security Officer.	SP 800-34, FCD-1	*Examine:* Contingency planning policy; procedures addressing contingency operations for the information system; contingency plan; security plan; business impact assessment; other relevant documents or records. *Interview:* Organizational personnel with contingency planning and plan implementation responsibilities; organizational personnel with information security responsibilities. *Test:* Organizational processes for resumption of missions and business functions.

Control number	Control name	Assessment methods	Notes and guidance documents	SP 800-53A guidance
CP-2(5)	Contingency plan: Continue essential missions/business functions	Review documentation for system to ensure system essential functions will continue in contingency situations including alternate processing locations being able to sustain full operational capabilities. Discuss with operations staff, Security Engineer, COOP staff, System Owner, and Security Officer.	SP 800-34, FCD-1	*Examine:* Contingency planning policy; procedures addressing contingency operations for the information system; contingency plan; business impact assessment; primary processing site agreements; primary storage site agreements; alternate processing site agreements; alternate storage site agreements; contingency plan Test documentation; contingency plan Test results; other relevant documents or records. *Interview:* Organizational personnel with contingency planning and plan implementation responsibilities; organizational personnel with information security responsibilities. *Test:* Organizational processes for continuing missions and business functions.
CP-2(6)	Contingency plan: Alternate processing/storage site	Review documentation to ensure alternate processing facilities and alternate storage facilities are defined and active. Discuss with operations staff, Security Engineer, COOP staff, System Owner, and Security Officer.	SP 800-34, FCD-1	*Examine:* Contingency planning policy; procedures addressing contingency operations for the information system; contingency plan; business impact assessment; alternate processing site agreements; alternate storage site agreements; contingency plan testing documentation; contingency plan test results; other relevant documents or records. *Interview:* Organizational personnel with contingency planning and plan implementation responsibilities; organizational personnel with information security responsibilities. *Test:* Organizational processes for transfer of essential missions and business functions to alternate processing/storage sites.
CP-2(7)	Contingency plan: Coordinate with external service providers	Review documentation for organization to ensure contingency operations and CP are coordinated with and correlated to other organizational and external service	SP 800-34, FCD-1	*Examine:* Contingency planning policy; procedures addressing contingency operations for the information system; contingency plan; contingency plans of

			References	
		provider continuity plans and actions. Discuss with System Owner, COOP staff, acquisition staff, operations staff, and Security OFFICER.		external; service providers; service level agreements; security plan; contingency plan requirements; other relevant documents or records. *Interview:* Organizational personnel with contingency planning and plan implementation responsibilities; external service providers; organizational personnel with information security responsibilities.
CP-2(8)	Contingency plan: Identify critical assets	Review documentation to ensure that organization has defined and identified all critical assets of system and its operations so that additional safeguards and countermeasures can be employed within the BCP and BIA organizational efforts. This process should be reviewed to ensure operational and management approvals are included within the documentation. Discuss with System Owner, Security Engineer, COOP staff, operations staff, and Security Officer.	SP 800-34, FCD-1	*Examine:* Contingency planning policy; procedures addressing contingency operations for the information system; contingency plan; business impact assessment; security plan; other relevant documents or records. *Interview:* Organizational personnel with contingency planning and plan implementation responsibilities; organizational personnel with information security responsibilities.
CP-3	Contingency training	Review documentation for system level contingency testing to ensure all roles and responsibilities needed for proper operation of system are included, defined and tested during test events and activities. Review CP test results to ensure actual testing has occurred and what the lessons learned were from test events. Discuss with COOP staff, operations staff, System Owner and Security Officer.	SP 800-34, FCD-1, SP 800-50, SP 800-16	*Examine:* Contingency planning policy; procedures addressing contingency training; contingency plan; contingency training curriculum; contingency training material; security plan; contingency training records; other relevant documents or records. *Interview:* Organizational personnel with contingency planning, plan implementation, and training responsibilities; organizational personnel with information security responsibilities. *Test:* Organizational processes for contingency training.
CP-3(1)	Contingency training: Simulated events	Review documentation for system level contingency testing to ensure all actions necessary for proper operation of system are included, defined, and tested during simulated test events and activities. Review CP simulated test results to ensure	SP 800-34, FCD-1, SP 800-50, SP 800-16	*Examine:* Contingency planning policy; procedures addressing contingency training; contingency plan; contingency training curriculum; contingency training material; other relevant documents or records. *Interview:* Organizational personnel with contingency

(Continued)

Control number	Control name	Assessment methods	Notes and guidance documents	SP 800-53A guidance
		testing has occurred and what the lessons learned were from test events. Discuss with COOP staff, operations staff, System Owner, and Security Officer.		planning, plan implementation, and training responsibilities; organizational personnel with information security responsibilities. *Test:* Organizational processes for contingency training; automated mechanisms for simulating contingency events.
CP-3(2)	Contingency training: Automated training environments	Review documentation for system level contingency training to ensure all actions necessary for proper operation of system are included, defined, and tested during automated test events and activities. Review CP automated training environment to ensure it has included proper and thorough system-level components. Discuss with COOP staff, operations staff, System Owner, and Security Officer.	SP 800-34, FCD-1, SP 800-50, SP 800-16	*Examine:* Contingency planning policy; procedures addressing contingency training; contingency plan; contingency training curriculum; contingency training material; other relevant documents or records. *Interview:* Organizational personnel with contingency planning, plan implementation, and training responsibilities; organizational personnel with information security responsibilities. *Test:* Organizational processes for contingency training; automated mechanisms for providing contingency training environments.
CP-4	Contingency plan testing	Review documentation for organization to ensure CP testing is conducted on periodic basis. Discuss with System Owner, COOP staff, and Security Officer.	SP 800-34, FCD-1, SP 800-84	*Examine:* Contingency planning policy; procedures addressing contingency plan testing; contingency plan; security plan; contingency plan test documentation; contingency plan test results; other relevant documents or records. *Interview:* Organizational personnel with responsibilities for contingency plan testing, reviewing or responding to contingency plan tests; organizational personnel with information security responsibilities. *Test:* Organizational processes for contingency plan testing; automated mechanisms supporting the contingency plan and/or contingency plan testing.
CP-4(1)	Contingency plan testing; Coordinate with related plans	Review documentation for organization to ensure CP testing is coordinated with other organizational-wide testing	SP 800-34, FCD-1, SP 800-84	*Examine:* Contingency planning policy; incident response policy; procedures addressing contingency plan testing;

			Assessment	
			contingency plan testing documentation; contingency plan; business continuity plans; disaster recovery plans; continuity of operations plans; crisis communications plans; critical infrastructure plans; cyber incident response plans; occupant emergency plans; security plan; other relevant documents or records. *Interview:* Organizational personnel with contingency plan testing responsibilities; organizational personnel; personnel with responsibilities for related plans; organizational personnel with information security responsibilities.	activities, such as IR testing, DRP testing, or OEP testing. Discuss with System Owner, COOP staff, and Security Officer.
CP-4(2)	Contingency plan testing; Alternate processing site	SP 800-34, FCD-1, SP 800-84	*Examine:* Contingency planning policy; procedures addressing contingency plan testing; contingency plan; contingency plan test documentation; contingency plan test results; alternate processing site agreements; service-level agreements; other relevant documents or records. *Interview:* Organizational personnel with contingency planning and plan implementation responsibilities; organizational personnel with information security responsibilities. *Test:* Organizational processes for contingency plan testing; automated mechanisms supporting the contingency plan and/or contingency plan testing.	Review documentation to ensure organization tests and evaluates the alternate processing site for compatibility, work performance, applicability, and usability when actually processing information and performing work. Review lessons learned documentation from tests to ensure updates are provided to CP. Discuss with operations staff, COOP staff, Security Officer, and System Owner.
CP-4(3)	Contingency plan testing; Automated testing	SP 800-34, FCD-1, SP 800-84	*Examine:* Contingency planning policy; procedures addressing contingency plan testing; contingency plan; automated mechanisms supporting contingency plan testing; contingency plan test documentation; contingency plan test results; other relevant documents or records. *Interview:* Organizational personnel with contingency plan testing responsibilities; organizational personnel with information security	Review documentation to determine if organization utilizes and has implemented automated CP testing. Discuss with System Owner, COOP staff, and Security Officer.

(Continued)

Control number	Control name	Assessment methods	Notes and guidance documents	SP 800-53A guidance
				responsibilities. *Test*: Organizational processes for contingency plan testing; automated mechanisms supporting contingency plan testing.
CP-4(4)	Contingency plan testing: Full recovery/ reconstitution	Review documentation to determine the organizational testing for full resumption testing for system. Review lessons learned documentation to ensure updates are provided to CP and operations. Discuss with COOP staff, Security Officer, operations staff, and System Owner.	SP 800-34, FCD-1, SP 800-84	*Examine*: Contingency planning policy; procedures addressing information system recovery and reconstitution; contingency plan; contingency plan test documentation; contingency plan test results; other relevant documents or records. *Interview*: Organizational personnel with contingency plan testing responsibilities; organizational personnel with information system recovery and reconstitution responsibilities; organizational personnel with information security responsibilities. *Test*: Organizational processes for contingency plan testing; automated mechanisms supporting contingency plan testing; automated mechanisms supporting recovery and reconstitution of the information system.
CP-5	Contingency plan update		Withdrawn: Incorporated into CP-2	
CP-6	Alternate storage site	Review documentation to ensure the organization maintains an alternate storage facility, which stores or maintains duplicate copies of information and data in the event that the primary storage site is not available due to an event. Ensure all criteria for alternate facility is updated, current, and applicable. Discuss with COOP staff, operations staff, System Owner, and Security Officer.	SP 800-34, FCD-1	*Examine*: Contingency planning policy; procedures addressing alternate storage sites; contingency plan; alternate storage site agreements; primary storage site agreements; other relevant documents or records. *Interview*: Organizational personnel with contingency plan alternate storage site responsibilities; organizational personnel with information system recovery responsibilities; organizational personnel with information security responsibilities.

			Test: Organizational processes for storing and retrieving information system backup information at the alternate storage site; automated mechanisms supporting and/or implementing storage and retrieval of information system backup information at the alternate storage site.
CP-6(1)	Alternate storage site: Separation from primary site	Review documentation for organization to ensure alternate site location is geographically separate from primary location for types of events the site is supporting. Discuss with COOP staff, operations staff, System Owner, and Security Officer.	SP 800-34, FCD-1	*Examine:* Contingency planning policy; procedures addressing alternate storage sites; contingency plan; alternate storage site; alternate storage site agreements; primary storage site agreements; other relevant documents or records. *Interview:* Organizational personnel with contingency plan alternate storage site responsibilities; organizational personnel with information system recovery responsibilities; organizational personnel with information security responsibilities.
CP-6(2)	Alternate storage site: Recovery time/point objectives	Review documentation for organization to ensure all time and recovery objectives are being met by alternate storage facility and its use. Discuss with COOP staff, System Owner, operations staff, and Security Officer.	SP 800-34, FCD-1	*Examine:* Contingency planning policy; procedures addressing alternate storage sites; contingency plan; alternate storage site; alternate storage site agreements; alternate storage site configurations; other relevant documents or records. *Interview:* Organizational personnel with contingency plan testing responsibilities; organizational personnel with responsibilities for testing related plans; organizational personnel with information security responsibilities. *Test:* Organizational processes for contingency plan testing; automated mechanisms supporting recovery time/point objectives.
CP-6(3)	Alternate storage site: Accessibility	Review documentation to determine the extent the organization accounts for area-wide disruptions and storage of information. Evaluate area-wide disruption plans and procedures to ensure	SP 800-34, FCD-1	*Examine:* Contingency planning policy; procedures addressing alternate storage sites; contingency plan; alternate storage site; list of potential accessibility problems to alternate storage site; mitigation actions for accessibility

(Continued)

Control number	Control name	Assessment methods	Notes and guidance documents	SP 800-53A guidance
		additional alternate storage is provided in geographically dispersed location. Discuss with COOP staff, System Owner, and Security Officer.		problems to alternate storage site; organizational risk assessments; other relevant documents or records. *Interview:* Organizational personnel with contingency plan alternate storage site responsibilities; organizational personnel with information system recovery responsibilities; organizational personnel with information security responsibilities.
CP-7	Alternate processing site	Review documentation for alternate processing facility for organization and system. An alternate processing site provides processing capability in the event that the primary processing site is not available, especially focused on being geographically located away from primary facility. Review all processes and procedures for operations at alternate facility to ensure full capability is provided. Discuss with operations staff, COOP staff, System Owner, and Security Officer.	SP 800-34, FCD-1	*Examine:* Contingency planning policy; procedures addressing alternate processing sites; contingency plan; alternate processing site agreements; primary processing site agreements; spare equipment and supplies inventory at alternate processing site; equipment and supply contracts; service-level agreements; other relevant documents or records. *Interview:* Organizational personnel with responsibilities for contingency planning and/or alternate site arrangements; organizational personnel with information security responsibilities. *Test:* Organizational processes for recovery at the alternate site; automated mechanisms supporting and/or implementing recovery at the alternate processing site.
CP-7(1)	Alternate processing site: Separation from primary site	Review documentation for alternate processing facility, geographically located away from primary facility, for organization and system. Ensure considerations for full impact separation at alternate facility are accounted for and considered. Discuss with operations staff, COOP staff, System Owner, and Security Officer.	SP 800-34, FCD-1	*Examine:* Contingency planning policy; procedures addressing alternate processing sites; contingency plan; alternate processing site; alternate processing site agreements; primary processing site agreements; other relevant documents or records. *Interview:* Organizational personnel with contingency plan alternate processing site responsibilities; organizational personnel with information system recovery responsibilities;

CP-7(2)	Alternate processing site: Accessibility	Review documentation to ensure organization has considered potential accessibility problems to the alternate processing site. Ensure all management decisions have had appropriate risk informational inputs to process. Discuss with operations staff, COOP staff, System Owner, and Security Officer.	SP 800-34, FCD-1	organizational personnel with information security responsibilities. *Examine:* Contingency planning policy; procedures addressing alternate processing sites; contingency plan; alternate processing site; alternate processing site agreements; primary processing site agreements; other relevant documents or records. *Interview:* Organizational personnel with contingency plan alternate processing site responsi bilities; organizational personnel with information system recovery responsibilities; organizational personnel with information security responsibilities.
CP-7(3)	Alternate processing site: Priority of service	Review documentation for organization and its service providers to ensure negotiated agreements include provision that organizations receive priority treatment consistent with their availability requirements and the availability of information resources when necessary. Discuss with COOP staff, acquisition staff, operations staff, Security Officer, and System Owner.	SP 800-34, FCD-1	*Examine:* Contingency planning policy; procedures addressing alternate processing sites; contingency plan; alternate processing site agreements; service-level agreements; other relevant documents or records. *Interview:* Organizational personnel with contingency plan alternate processing site responsibilities; organizational personnel with information system recovery responsibilities; organizational personnel with information security responsibilities; organizational personnel with responsibility for acquisitions/contractual agreements.
CP-7(4)	Alternate processing site: Preparation for use	Review documentation to ensure organization has properly prepared all documents, operations and support elements to provide full operational support at alternate processing facility when primary facility experiences an event disruption. Discuss with COOP staff, operation staff, System Owner, and Security Officer.	SP 800-34, FCD-1	*Examine:* Contingency planning policy; procedures addressing alternate processing sites; contingency plan; alternate processing site; alternate processing site agreements; alternate processing site configurations; other relevant documents or records. *Interview:* Organizational personnel with contingency plan alternate processing site responsibilities; organizational personnel with information system recovery responsibilities; organizational personnel with information

(Continued)

Control number	Control name	Assessment methods	Notes and guidance documents	SP 800-53A guidance
				security responsibilities. *Test:* Automated mechanisms supporting and/or implementing recovery at the alternate processing site.
CP-7(5)	Alternate processing site: Equivalent information security safeguards		Withdrawn: Incorporated into CP-7	
CP-7(6)	Alternate processing site: Inability to return to primary site	Review documentation to determine the preparations for full support at alternate facility when events preclude returning to primary facility. Events could include natural disasters and full military engagements. Discuss with System Owner, COOP staff, operations staff, and Security Officer.	SP 800-34, FCD-1	*Examine:* Contingency planning policy; procedures addressing alternate processing sites; contingency plan; alternate processing site; alternate processing site agreements; alternate processing site configurations; other relevant documents or records. *Interview:* Organizational personnel with information system reconstitution responsibilities; organizational personnel with information security responsibilities.
CP-8	Telecommunications services	Review documentation to ensure organization accounts for alternate telecommunications providers during outages or events. Alternate telecommunications services reflect the continuity requirements in contingency plans to maintain essential missions/business functions despite the loss of primary telecommunications services. Discuss with COOP staff, acquisition staff, operations staff, System Owner, and Security Officer.	SP 800-34, FCD-1, NCSD 3-10	*Examine:* Contingency planning policy; procedures addressing alternate telecommunications services; contingency plan; primary and alternate telecommunications service agreements; other relevant documents or records. *Interview:* Organizational personnel with contingency plan telecommunications responsibilities; organizational personnel with information system recovery responsibilities; organizational personnel with information security responsibilities; organizational personnel with responsibility for acquisitions/contractual agreements. *Test:* Automated mechanisms supporting telecommunications.

CP-8(1)	Telecommunications services: Priority of service provisions	Review documentation for organization to ensure that considerations for alternate providers consider the potential mission/business impact in situations, where telecommunications service providers are servicing other organizations with similar priority-of-service provisions. Review with acquisition staff, COOP staff, operations staff, Security Officer, and System Owner.	SP 800-34, FCD-1, NCSD 3-10	*Examine:* Contingency planning policy; procedures addressing primary and alternate telecommunications services; contingency plan; primary and alternate telecommunications service agreements; telecommunications service priority documentation; other relevant documents or records. *Interview:* Organizational personnel with contingency plan telecommunications responsibilities; organizational personnel with information system recovery responsibilities; organizational personnel with responsibility for acquisitions/contractual agreements. *Test:* Automated mechanisms supporting telecommunications.
CP-8(2)	Telecommunications services: Single points of failure	Review documentation for organization to ensure alternate providers are obtained to avoid single point of failure issues during support efforts. Discuss with COOP staff, operations staff, acquisition staff, System Owner, and Security Officer.	SP 800-34, FCD-1, NCSD 3-10	*Examine:* Contingency planning policy; procedures addressing primary and alternate telecommunications services; contingency plan; primary and alternate telecommunications service agreements; other relevant documents or records. *Interview:* Organizational personnel with contingency plan telecommunications responsibilities; organizational personnel with information system recovery responsibilities; primary and alternate telecommunications service providers; organizational personnel with information security responsibilities.
CP-8(3)	Telecommunications services: Separation of primary/alternate providers	Review documentation to ensure that organization provides processes for minimizing shared infrastructure among telecommunications service providers and achieving sufficient geographic separation between services. Review telecommunication contract documents and SLA's to ensure compliance. Discuss with operations staff, COOP staff,	SP 800-34, FCD-1, NCSD 3-10	*Examine:* Contingency planning policy; procedures addressing primary and alternate telecommunications services; contingency plan; primary and alternate telecommunications service agreements; alternate telecommunications service provider site; primary telecommunications service provider site; other relevant documents or records. *Interview:* Organizational personnel

(Continued)

Control number	Control name	Assessment methods	Notes and guidance documents	SP 800-53A guidance
		acquisition staff, Security Officer, and System Owner.		with contingency plan telecommunications responsibilities; organizational personnel with information system recovery responsibilities; primary and alternate telecommunications service providers; organizational personnel with information security responsibilities.
CP-8(4)	Telecommunications services: Provider contingency plan	Review documentation for organization to ensure service providers have provided account contingency plans for their service delivery. Review plans for applicability, completeness, and support provisions. Discuss with acquisition staff, COOP staff, operations staff, System Owner, and Security Officer.	SP 800-34, FCD-1, NCSD 3-10	*Examine:* Contingency planning policy; procedures addressing primary and alternate telecommunications services; contingency plan; provider contingency plans; evidence of contingency testing/training by providers; primary and alternate telecommunications service agreements; other relevant documents or records. *Interview:* Organizational personnel with contingency planning, plan implementation, and testing responsibilities; primary and alternate telecommunications service providers; organizational personnel with information security responsibilities; organizational personnel with responsibility for acquisitions/contractual agreements.
CP-8(5)	Telecommunications services: Alternate telecommunication service testing	Review documentation for organization to ensure service providers have tested alternate services and have documented testing with organization. Discuss with operations staff, COOP staff, acquisition staff, Security Officer, and System Owner.	SP 800-34, FCD-1, NCSD 3-10	*Examine:* Contingency planning policy; procedures addressing alternate telecommunications services; contingency plan; evidence of testing alternate telecommunications services; alternate telecommunications service agreements; other relevant documents or records. *Interview:* Organizational personnel with contingency planning, plan implementation, and testing responsibilities; alternate telecommunications service providers; organizational personnel with information security responsibilities. *Test:* Automated mechanisms supporting Testing alternate telecommunications services.

CP-9	Information system backup	Review documentation to determine the system backup methodologies and practices, which the system employs and utilizes. All areas for backup are considered including system-state information, operating system and application software, and licenses. Full backup documentation to be review and tested on periodic basis. Discuss with System Owner, security staff, operations staff, and Security Officer.	SP 800-34, FCD-1	*Examine:* Contingency planning policy; procedures addressing information system backup; contingency plan; backup storage location(s); information system backup logs or records; other relevant documents or records. *Interview:* Organizational personnel with information system backup responsibilities; organizational personnel with information security responsibilities. *Test:* Organizational processes for conducting information system backups; automated mechanisms supporting and/or implementing information system backups.
CP-9(1)	Information system backup: Testing for reliability/integrity	Review documentation for organization to ensure verification and validation of backup processes and procedures are conducted on periodic basis. Test backups to ensure proper and full completion of process is evaluated. Discuss with operations staff, security staff, System Owner, and Security Officer.	SP 800-34, FCD-1	*Examine:* [Contingency planning policy; procedures addressing information system backup; contingency plan; information system backup test results; contingency plan test documentation; contingency plan test results; other relevant documents or records. *Interview:* Organizational personnel with information system backup responsibilities; organizational personnel with information security responsibilities. *Test:* Organizational processes for conducting information system backups; automated mechanisms supporting and/or implementing information system backups.
CP-9(2)	Information system backup: Test restoration using sampling	Review documentation to ensure organization conducts sampling of backups to ensure full restoration is possible with current backup methodology. Discuss with System Owner, operations staff, and Security Officer.	SP 800-34, FCD-1	*Examine:* Contingency planning policy; procedures addressing information system backup; contingency plan; information system backup test results; contingency plan test documentation; contingency plan test results; other relevant documents or records. *Interview:* Organizational personnel with information system backup responsibilities; organizational personnel with contingency planning/contingency plan esting responsibilities; organizational personnel with information security responsibilities.

(Continued)

Control number	Control name	Assessment methods	Notes and guidance documents	SP 800-53A guidance
				Test: Organizational processes for conducting information system backups; automated mechanisms supporting and/or implementing information system backups.
CP-9(3)	Information system backup: Separate storage for critical information	Review documentation for organization to ensure storage of critical and security information are maintained separately from normal backup storage media. Critical information system software includes, for example, operating systems, cryptographic key management systems, and intrusion detection/prevention systems. Security-related information includes, for example, organizational inventories of hardware, software, and firmware components. Discuss with System Owner, security staff, operations staff, and Security Officer.	SP 800-34, FCD-1	*Examine*: Contingency planning policy; procedures addressing information system backup; contingency plan; backup storage location(s); information system backup configurations and associated documentation; information system backup logs or records; other relevant documents or records. *Interview*: Organizational personnel with contingency planning and plan implementation responsibilities; organizational personnel with information system backup responsibilities; organizational personnel with information security responsibilities.
CP-9(4)	Information system backup: Protection from unauthorized modification		Withdrawn: Incorporated into CP-9	
CP-9(5)	Information system backup: Transfer to alternate storage site	Review documentation for organization to ensure transfer of information to alternate storage facility is periodically accomplished sites, either electronically or by physical shipment of storage media. Discuss with System Owner, security staff, operations staff, and Security Officer.	SP 800-34, FCD-1	*Examine*: Contingency planning policy; procedures addressing information system backup; contingency plan; information system backup logs or records; evidence of system backup information transferred to alternate storage site; alternate storage site agreements; other relevant documents or records. *Interview*: Organizational personnel with information system backup responsibilities; organizational personnel with information security responsibilities. *Test*: Organizational processes for transferring information system backups to the alternate

			storage site; automated mechanisms supporting and/or implementing information system backups; automated mechanisms supporting and/or implementing information transfer to the alternate storage site.
CP-9(6)	Information system backup: Redundant secondary system	SP 800-34, FCD-1	Review documentation for organization to determine criteria for system mirror location and criteria for short-term RTP and RPO for system. Review and discuss with System Owner, COOP staff, operations staff, security staff, and Security Officer.	*Examine:* Contingency planning policy; procedures addressing information system backup; contingency plan; information system backup test results; contingency plan test results; contingency plan test documentation; redundant secondary system for information system backups; location(s) of redundant secondary backup system(s); other relevant documents or records. *Interview:* Organizational personnel with information system backup responsibilities; organizational personnel with information security responsibilities; organizational personnel with responsibility for the redundant secondary system. *Test:* Organizational processes for maintaining redundant secondary systems; automated mechanisms supporting and/or implementing information system backups; automated mechanisms supporting and/or implementing information transfer to a redundant secondary system.
CP-9(7)	Information system backup: Dual authorization	SP 800-34, FCD-1	Review documentation for organization to ensure dual control for all deletion and destruction of backup information and storage media. Discuss with System Owner, Security Officer, security staff, and operations staff.	*Examine:* Contingency planning policy; procedures addressing information system backup; contingency plan; information system design documentation; information system configuration settings and associated documentation; system generated list of dual authorization credentials or rules; logs or records of deletion or destruction of backup information; other relevant documents or records. *Interview:* Organizational personnel with information system backup

(Continued)

Control number	Control name	Assessment methods	Notes and guidance documents	SP 800-53A guidance
				responsibilities; organizational personnel with information security responsibilities. *Test:* Automated mechanisms supporting and/or implementing dual authorization; automated mechanisms supporting and/or implementing deletion/destruction of backup information.
CP-10	Information system recovery and reconstitution	Review documentation for organization to ensure full state recovery and reconstitution to known state after a disruption, compromise, or failure is assured. Verify and validate full state recovery with recovery of sample files and software from backup media. Discuss with System Owner, security staff, operations staff, and Security Officer.	SP 800-34, FCD-1	*Examine:* Contingency planning policy; procedures addressing information system backup; contingency plan; information system backup test results; contingency plan test results; contingency plan test documentation; redundant secondary system for information system backups; location(s) of redundant secondary backup system(s); other relevant documents or records. *Interview:* Organizational personnel with contingency planning, recovery, and/or reconstitution responsibilities; organizational personnel with information security responsibilities. *Test:* Organizational processes implementing information system recovery and reconstitution operations; automated mechanisms supporting and/or implementing information system recovery and reconstitution operations.
CP-10(1)	Information system recovery and reconstitution: Contingency plan testing		Withdrawn: Incorporated into CP-4	
CP-10(2)	Information system recovery and reconstitution: Transaction recovery	Review documentation for organization to ensure all transaction-based actions for system are backed up independently and fully for all required components and information. Test transaction backups with sample from active system files. Discuss	SP 800-34, FCD-1	*Examine:* Contingency planning policy; procedures addressing information system recovery and reconstitution; contingency plan; information system design documentation; information system configuration settings and associated

Control	Name	Reference / Withdrawn	Guidance	Assessment
			documentation; contingency plan test documentation; contingency plan test results; information system transaction recovery records; information system audit records; other relevant documents or records. *Interview:* Organizational personnel with responsibility for transaction recovery; organizational personnel with information security responsibilities. *Test:* Automated mechanisms supporting and/or implementing transaction recovery capability.	with operations staff, security staff, System Owner, and Security Officer.
CP-10(3)	Information system recovery and reconstitution: Compensating security controls	Withdrawn: Addressed through the tailoring procedures		
CP-10(4)	Information system recovery and reconstitution: Restore within time period	SP 800-34, FCD-1	*Examine:* Contingency planning policy; procedures addressing information system recovery and reconstitution; contingency plan; information system design documentation; information system configuration settings and associated documentation; contingency plan test documentation; contingency plan test results; evidence of information system recovery and reconstitution operations; other relevant documents or records. *Interview:* Organizational personnel with information system recovery and reconstitution responsibilities; organizational personnel with information security responsibilities. *Test:* Automated mechanisms supporting and/or implementing recovery/reconstitution of information system information.	Review documentation to ensure that organization can restore system to known state in accordance with defined RTO, as defined in BIA and BCP for organization. Test recovery mechanism and review test results for periodic evaluations for RTO of system information. Discuss with System Owner, operations staff, security staff, and Security Officer.
CP-10(5)	Information system recovery and reconstitution: Failover capability	Withdrawn: Incorporated into SI-13		

(Continued)

Control number	Control name	Assessment methods	Notes and guidance documents	SP 800-53A guidance
CP-10(6)	Information system recovery and reconstitution: Component protection	Review documentation for organization to ensure the protection and security of backup mechanisms, hardware, software, and various components are maintained and enforced throughout the organization. Discuss with Security Officer, security staff, operations staff, and System Owner.	SP 800-34, FCD-1	*Examine:* Contingency planning policy; procedures addressing information system recovery and reconstitution; contingency plan; information system design documentation; information system configuration settings and associated documentation; logical access credentials; physical access credentials; logical access authorization records; physical access authorization records; other relevant documents or records. *Interview:* Organizational personnel with information system recovery and reconstitution responsibilities; organizational personnel with information security responsibilities. *Test:* Organizational processes for protecting backup and restoration hardware, firmware, and software; automated mechanisms supporting and/or implementing protection of backup and restoration hardware, firmware, and software.
CP-11	Alternate communications protocols	Review documentation for organization to ensure consideration for instituting alternate communications protocols, such as switching from transmission control protocol/Internet protocol (TCP/IP) Version 4 to TCP/IP Version 6, defined, designed, documented, and installed for system. Discuss with Security Engineer, COOP staff, developers, operations staff, System Owner, and Security Officer.	SP 800-34, FCD-1	*Examine:* Contingency planning policy; procedures addressing alternative communications protocols; contingency plan; continuity of operations plan; information system design documentation; information system configuration settings and associated documentation; list of alternative communications protocols supporting continuity of operations; other relevant documents or records. *Interview:* Organizational personnel with contingency planning and plan implementation responsibilities; organizational personnel with continuity of operations planning and plan implementation responsibilities; organizational personnel with information security responsibilities; system/network administrators; system developers. *Test:*

			Automated mechanisms employing alternative communications protocols.
CP-12	Safe mode	Review documentation for organization to determine if system requires safe mode support due to mission or safety requirements. If so, determine safe mode methodologies and techniques employed by system and staff. Discuss with security staff, COOP staff, operations staff, Security Engineer, Security Officer, and System Owner.	SP 800-34, FCD-1	*Examine:* Contingency planning policy; procedures addressing safe mode of operation for the information system; contingency plan; information system design documentation; information system configuration settings and associated documentation; information system administration manuals; information system operation manuals; information system installation manuals; contingency plan test records; incident handling records; information system audit records; other relevant documents or records. *Interview:* Organizational personnel with information system operation responsibilities; organizational personnel with information security responsibilities; system/network administrators; system developers. *Test:* Automated mechanisms implementing safe mode of operation.
CP-13	Alternative security mechanisms	Review documentation for organization to determine if additional recovery techniques and processes have been identified for use in case original methods cannot or will not work appropriately. Test resiliency capability with test information or evaluation technique on critical system components. Discuss with COOP staff, security staff, operations staff, Security Officer, and System Owner.	SP 800-34, FCD-1	*Examine:* Contingency planning policy; procedures addressing alternate security mechanisms; contingency plan; continuity of operations plan; information system design documentation; information system configuration settings and associated documentation; contingency plan test records; contingency plan test results; other relevant documents or records. *Interview:* Organizational personnel with information system operation responsibilities; organizational personnel with information security responsibilities. *Test:* Information system capability implementing alternative security mechanisms.

G. *Identification and authentication family*

FIPS-200 provides the following criteria for this family of controls: Identification and authentication (IA): Organizations must identify information system users, processes acting on behalf of users, or devices and authenticate (or verify) the identities of those users, processes, or devices, as a prerequisite to allowing access to organizational information systems.

The primary assessment areas for these controls include:

a. Inspect identification mechanisms for users of information systems and authenticate (or verify) the identities of those users as a prerequisite to allowing access to organizational information systems.

b. Review the identification of processes in information systems acting on behalf of users, and authenticate (or verify) the identities of those processes as a prerequisite to allowing access to organizational information systems.

c. Audit identification mechanisms for devices and authenticate (or verify) the identities of those devices as a prerequisite to allowing access to organizational information systems.

Control number	Control name	Assessment methods	Notes and guidance documents	SP 800-53A guidance
IA-1	Identification and authentication policy and procedures	Review all organizational identification and authorization (IA) policies. Identify the organizational frequencies for updating the IA policies and procedures. Discuss implementation with System Owner and Security Officer.	FIPS-190, FIPS-201, SP 800-12, SP 800-63, SP 800-73, SP 800-76, SP 800-78, OMB M04-04	*Examine:* Identification and authentication policy and procedures; other relevant documents or records. *Interview:* Organizational personnel with identification and authentication responsibilities; organizational personnel with information security responsibilities.
IA-2	Identification and authentication (organizational users)	Review all organizational documents, policies, and procedures for all users of system (both standard users and privileged users). Check review policies for all PIV card implementation efforts and actions. Discuss all authentication activities with System Owner and Security officer.	HSPD-12, FIPS-190, FIPS-201, SP 800-63, SP 800-73, SP 800-76, SP 800-78, OMB M04-04, OMB M06-16, OMB M07-11	*Examine:* Identification and authentication policy; procedures addressing user identification and authentication; information system design documentation; information system configuration settings and associated documentation; information system audit records; list of information system accounts; other relevant documents or records. *Interview:* Organizational personnel with information system operations responsibilities; organizational personnel with information security responsibilities; system/network administrators; organizational personnel with account management responsibilities; system developers. *Test:* Organizational processes for uniquely identifying and authenticating users; automated mechanisms supporting and/or implementing identification and authentication capability.
IA-2(1)	Identification and authentication: Network access to privileged accounts	Review documentation for network access for privileged users. Ensure system is required for privileged users through testing. Discuss with System Owner, Security Officer, and Operations Chief.	HSPD-12, FIPS-190, FIPS-201, SP 800-63, SP 800-73, SP 800-76, SP 800-78, OMB M04-04, OMB M06-16, OMB M07-11	*Examine:* Identification and authentication policy; procedures addressing user identification and authentication; information system design documentation; information system configuration settings and associated documentation; information system audit records; list of information system accounts; other relevant documents or records. *Interview:* Organizational personnel with information system operations responsibilities; organizational personnel with account management responsibilities; organizational personnel with information security responsibilities; system/network

(Continued)

Control number	Control name	Assessment methods	Notes and guidance documents	SP 800-53A guidance
				administrators; system developers. *Test:* Automated mechanisms supporting and/or implementing multifactor authentication capability.
IA-2(2)	Identification and authentication: Network access to nonprivileged accounts	Review documentation for network access for nonprivileged users. Ensure system is required for nonprivileged users through testing. Discuss with System Owner, Security Officer, and Operations Chief.	HSPD-12, FIPS-190, FIPS-201, SP 800-63, SP 800-73, SP 800-76, SP 800-78, OMB M04-04, OMB M06-16, OMB M07-11	*Examine:* Identification and authentication policy; procedures addressing user identification and authentication; information system design documentation; information system configuration settings and associated documentation; information system audit records; list of information system accounts; other relevant documents or records. *Interview:* Organizational personnel with information system operations responsibilities; organizational personnel with account management responsibilities; organizational personnel with information security responsibilities; system/network administrators; system developers. *Test:* Automated mechanisms supporting and/or implementing multifactor authentication capability.
IA-2(3)	Identification and authentication: Local access to privileged accounts	Review documentation for local access for privileged users. Ensure system is required for privileged users through testing. Discuss with System Owner, Security Officer, and Operations Chief.	HSPD-12, FIPS-190, FIPS-201, SP 800-63, SP 800-73, SP 800-76, SP 800-78, OMB M04-04, OMB M06-16, OMB M07-11	*Examine:* Identification and authentication policy; procedures addressing user identification and authentication; information system design documentation; information system configuration settings and associated documentation; information system audit records; list of information system accounts; other relevant documents or records. *Interview:* Organizational personnel with information system operations responsibilities; organizational personnel with account management responsibilities; organizational personnel with information security responsibilities; system/network administrators; system developers. *Test:* Automated mechanisms supporting and/or implementing multifactor authentication capability.
IA-2(4)	Identification and authentication: Local access to nonprivileged accounts	Review documentation for local access for nonprivileged users. Ensure system is required for nonprivileged users through testing. Discuss with System Owner,	HSPD-12, FIPS-190, FIPS-201, SP 800-63, SP 800-73, SP 800-76, SP 800-78, OMB M04-04, OMB M06-16, OMB M07-11	*Examine:* Identification and authentication policy; procedures addressing user identification and authentication; information system design documentation; information system configuration settings and associated documentation; information system audit records; list of information system accounts; other relevant documents or records. *Interview:* Organizational personnel with information system operations

	Security Officer, and Operations Chief.			responsibilities; organizational personnel with account management responsibilities; organizational personnel with information security responsibilities; system/network administrators; system developers. *Test:* Automated mechanisms supporting and/or implementing multifactor authentication capability.
IA-2(5)	Identification and authentication: Group authentication	Review documentation for group authentication to ensure that it requires individual identification as additional identification and authentication. Discuss with System Owner and Security Officer. Test authentication system for actual usage of both methods of authentication on all members of group authentication groups.	HSPD-12, FIPS-190, FIPS-201, SP 800-63, SP 800-73, SP 800-76, SP 800-78, OMB M04-04, OMB M06-16, OMB M07-11	*Examine:* Identification and authentication policy; procedures addressing user identification and authentication; information system design documentation; information system configuration settings and associated documentation; information system audit records; list of information system accounts; other relevant documents or records. *Interview:* Organizational personnel with information system operations responsibilities; organizational personnel with account management responsibilities; organizational personnel with information security responsibilities; system/network administrators; system developers. *Test:* Automated mechanisms supporting and/or implementing authentication capability for group accounts.
IA-2(6)	Identification and authentication: Network access to privileged accounts – separate device	Review documentation for network access for privileged users utilizing separate device from network. Ensure system is required for privileged users through testing. Discuss with System Owner, Security Officer, and Operations Chief.	HSPD-12, FIPS-190, FIPS-201, SP 800-63, SP 800-73, SP 800-76, SP 800-78, OMB M04-04, OMB M06-16, OMB M07-11	*Examine:* Identification and authentication policy; procedures addressing user identification and authentication; information system design documentation; information system configuration settings and associated documentation; information system audit records; list of information system accounts; other relevant documents or records. *Interview:* Organizational personnel with information system operations responsibilities; organizational personnel with account management responsibilities; organizational personnel with information security responsibilities; system/network administrators; system developers. *Test:* Automated mechanisms supporting and/or implementing multifactor authentication capability.
IA-2(7)	Identification and authentication: Network access to nonprivileged accounts – separate device	Review documentation for network access for nonprivileged users utilizing separate device from network. Ensure system is required for	HSPD-12, FIPS-190, FIPS-201, SP 800-63, SP 800-73, SP 800-76, SP 800-78, OMB M04-04,	*Examine:* Identification and authentication policy; procedures addressing user identification and authentication; information system design documentation; information system configuration settings and associated documentation; information system audit records; list of information system accounts; other relevant documents or records. *Interview:*

(Continued)

Control number	Control name	Assessment methods	Notes and guidance documents	SP 800-53A guidance
		nonprivileged users through testing. Discuss with System Owner, Security Officer, and Operations Chief.	OMB M06-16, OMB M07-11	Organizational personnel with information system operations responsibilities; organizational personnel with account management responsibilities; organizational personnel with information security responsibilities; system/network administrators; system developers. *Test:* Automated mechanisms supporting and/or implementing multifactor authentication capability.
IA-2(8)	Identification and authentication: Network access to privileged accounts – replay resistant	Review documentation for network access for privileged users utilizing replay-resistant technologies, such as challenge-based TLS or protocols using nonce. Ensure system is required for privileged users through testing. Discuss with System Owner, Security Officer, and Operations Chief.	HSPD-12, FIPS-190, FIPS-201, SP 800-63, SP 800-73, SP 800-76, SP 800-78, OMB M04-04, OMB M06-16, OMB M07-11	*Examine:* Identification and authentication policy; procedures addressing user identification and authentication; information system design documentation; information system configuration settings and associated documentation; information system audit records; list of privileged information system accounts; other relevant documents or records. *Interview:* Organizational personnel with information system operations responsibilities; organizational personnel with account management responsibilities; organizational personnel with information security responsibilities; system/network administrators; system developers. *Test:* Automated mechanisms supporting and/or implementing identification and authentication capability; automated mechanisms supporting and/or implementing replay resistant authentication mechanisms.
IA-2(9)	Identification and authentication: Network access to nonprivileged accounts – replay resistant	Review documentation for network access for nonprivileged users utilizing replay-resistant technologies, such as challenge-based TLS or protocols using nonce. Ensure system is required for nonprivileged users through testing. Discuss with System Owner, Security Officer, and Operations Chief.	HSPD-12, FIPS-190, FIPS-201, SP 800-63, SP 800-73, SP 800-76, SP 800-78, OMB M04-04, OMB M06-16, OMB M07-11	*Examine:* Identification and authentication policy; procedures addressing user identification and authentication; information system design documentation; information system configuration settings and associated documentation; information system audit records; list of nonprivileged information system accounts; other relevant documents or records. *Interview:* Organizational personnel with information system operations responsibilities; organizational personnel with account management responsibilities; organizational personnel with information security responsibilities; system/network administrators; system developers. *Test:* Automated mechanisms supporting and/or implementing identification and authentication capability; automated mechanisms supporting and/or implementing replay resistant authentication mechanisms.

IA-2(10)	Identification and authentication: Single sign-on	Review documentation for access for all users utilizing single sign-on technologies. Ensure system is required to provide additional verification requirements through use of multi-factor authentication for all users through testing. Discuss with System Owner, Security Officer, and Operations Chief.	HSPD-12, FIPS-190, FIPS-201, SP 800-63, SP 800-73, SP 800-76, SP 800-78, OMB M04-04, OMB M06-16, OMB M07-11	*Examine:* Identification and authentication policy; procedures addressing single sign-on capability for information system accounts and services; procedures addressing identification and authentication; information system design documentation; information system configuration settings and associated documentation; information system audit records; list of information system accounts and services requiring single sign-on capability; other relevant documents or records. *Interview:* Organizational personnel with information system operations responsibilities; organizational personnel with account management responsibilities; organizational personnel with information security responsibilities; system network administrators; system developers. *Test:* Automated mechanisms supporting and/or implementing identification and authentication capability; automated mechanisms supporting and/or implementing single sign-on capability for information system accounts and services.
IA-2(11)	Identification and authentication: remote access – separate device	Review documentation for remote access for all users utilizing a separate access device or mechanism. Ensure system is required to provide additional verification requirements through use of multi-factor authentication for all users through testing. Discuss with System Owner, Security Officer, and Operations Chief.	HSPD-12, FIPS-190, FIPS-201, SP 800-63, SP 800-73, SP 800-76, SP 800-78, OMB M04-04, OMB M06-16, OMB M07-11	*Examine:* Identification and authentication policy; procedures addressing user identification and authentication; information system design documentation; information system configuration settings and associated documentation; information system audit records; list of privileged and nonprivileged information system accounts; other relevant documents or records. *Interview:* Organizational personnel with information system operations responsibilities; organizational personnel with account management responsibilities; organizational personnel with information security responsibilities; system/network administrators; system developers. *Test:* Automated mechanisms supporting and/or implementing identification and authentication capability.
IA-2(12)	Identification and authentication: Acceptance of PIV credentials	Review documentation for access for all users utilizing PIV access credentials. Ensure system is required to provide USG approved validation and verification methods and techniques for all users through	HSPD-12, FIPS-190, FIPS-201, SP 800-63, SP 800-73, SP 800-76, SP 800-78, OMB M04-04, OMB M06-16, OMB M07-11	*Examine:* Identification and authentication policy; procedures addressing user identification and authentication; information system design documentation; information system configuration settings and associated documentation; information system audit records; PIV verification records; evidence of PIV credentials; PIV credential authorizations; other relevant documents or records. *Interview:* Organizational personnel with information system operations responsibilities;

(Continued)

Control number	Control name	Assessment methods	Notes and guidance documents	SP 800-53A guidance
		testing. Discuss with System Owner, Security Officer, and Operations Chief.		organizational personnel with account management responsibilities; organizational personnel with information security responsibilities; system/network administrators; system developers. *Test:* Automated mechanisms supporting and/or implementing acceptance and verification of PIV credentials.
IA-2(13)	Identification and authentication: Out-of-band authentication	Review documentation for access for all users or actions, which require OOBA for activities on the system. Test the in-band identification methodology and the OOBA authentication methodology via automated testing and system-level exercises of the OOBA system. Discuss with System Owner, Security Officer, and Operations Chief.	HSPD-12, FIPS-190, FIPS-201, SP 800-63, SP 800-73, SP 800-76, SP 800-78, OMB M04-04, OMB M06-16, OMB M07-11	*Examine:* Identification and authentication policy; procedures addressing user identification and authentication; information system design documentation; information system configuration settings and associated documentation; information system audit records; system-generated list of out-of-band authentication paths; other relevant documents or records. *Interview:* Organizational personnel with information system operations responsibilities; organizational personnel with account management responsibilities; organizational personnel with information security responsibilities; system/network administrators; system developers. *Test:* Automated mechanisms supporting and/or implementing out-of-band authentication capability.
IA-3	Device identification and authentication	Review organizational documentation to ensure requirements for this type of device to device authentication is required. Test this capability with automated scan tools. Interview System Owner, CISO office personnel, and Security Officer.	SP 800-63, OMB M04-04	*Examine:* Identification and authentication policy; procedures addressing device identification and authentication; information system design documentation; list of devices requiring unique identification and authentication; device connection reports; information system configuration settings and associated documentation; other relevant documents or records. *Interview:* Organizational personnel with operational responsibilities for device identification and authentication; organizational personnel with information security responsibilities; system/network administrators; system developers. *Test:* Automated mechanisms supporting and/or implementing device identification and authentication capability.
IA-3(1)	Device identification and authentication:	Review organizational documentation to ensure requirements for this type	SP 800-63, OMB M04-04	*Examine:* Identification and authentication policy; procedures addressing device identification and authentication; information system design documentation; list of devices

	Control	Assessment	References	Examine/Interview/Test
	Cryptographic bidirectional authentication	of bidirectional device to device authentication is required. Test this capability with automated scan tools and manual tests. Interview System Owner, CISO office personnel, and Security Officer.		requiring unique identification and authentication; device connection reports; information system configuration settings and associated documentation; other relevant documents or records. *Interview:* Organizational personnel with operational responsibilities for device identification and authentication; organizational personnel with information security responsibilities; system/network administrators; system developers. *Test:* Automated mechanisms supporting and/or implementing device authentication capability; cryptographically based bidirectional authentication mechanisms.
IA-3(2)	Device identification and authentication: Cryptographic bidirectional network authentication		Withdrawn: Incorporated into IA-3(1)	
IA-3(3)	Device identification and authentication: Dynamic address allocation	Review organizational documentation to ensure requirements for this type of device to device DHCP authentication is required. Test this DHCP capability with automated scan tools. Interview System Owner, CISO office personnel, and Security Officer.	SP 800-63, OMB M04-04	*Examine:* Identification and authentication policy; procedures addressing device identification and authentication; information system design documentation; information system configuration settings and associated documentation; evidence of lease information and lease duration assigned to devices; device connection reports; information system audit records; other relevant documents or records. *Interview:* Organizational personnel with operational responsibilities for device identification and authentication; organizational personnel with information security responsibilities; system/network administrators; system developers. *Test:* Automated mechanisms supporting and/or implementing device identification and authentication capability; automated mechanisms supporting and/or implementing dynamic address allocation; automated mechanisms supporting and/or implanting auditing of lease information.
IA-3(4)	Device identification and authentication: Device attestation	Review organizational documentation to ensure requirements for this type of device to device cryptographic hash-based	SP 800-63, OMB M04-04	*Examine:* Identification and authentication policy; procedures addressing device identification and authentication; procedures addressing device configuration management; information system design documentation; information system configuration settings and associated documentation;

(Continued)

Control number	Control name	Assessment methods	Notes and guidance documents	SP 800-53A guidance
		authentication is required. Test this capability with automated scan tools and with manual hash-based logic code review. Interview System Owner, CISO office personnel, and Security Officer.		configuration management records; change control records; information system audit records; other relevant documents or records. *Interview:* Organizational personnel with operational responsibilities for device identification and authentication; organizational personnel with information security responsibilities; system/network administrators. *Test:* Automated mechanisms supporting and/or implementing device identification and authentication capability; automated mechanisms supporting and/or implementing configuration management; cryptographic mechanisms supporting device attestation.
IA-4	Identifier management	Review organizational account management documentation to ensure individual identifiers are required for each user and device account. Interview System Owner, operational staff, System Administrators, and Security Officer.	FIPS-190, FIPS-201, SP 800-73, SP 800-76, SP 800-78	*Examine:* Identification and authentication policy; procedures addressing identifier management; procedures addressing account management; security plan; information system design documentation; information system configuration settings and associated documentation; list of information system accounts; list of identifiers generated from physical access control devices; other relevant documents or records. *Interview:* Organizational personnel with identifier management responsibilities; organizational personnel with information security responsibilities; system/network administrators; system developers. *Test:* Automated mechanisms supporting and/or implementing identifier management.
IA-4(1)	Identifier management: Prohibit account identifiers as public identifiers	Review documentation for access account management to ensure account identifiers are NOT used as email address identifiers. Test via automated tools for access reviews. Interview System Owner and System Administrators.	FIPS-190, FIPS-201, SP 800-73, SP 800-76, SP 800-78	*Examine:* Identification and authentication policy; procedures addressing identifier management; procedures addressing account management; information system design documentation; information system configuration settings and associated documentation; information system audit records; other relevant documents or records. *Interview:* Organizational personnel with identifier management responsibilities; organizational personnel with information security responsibilities; system/network administrators. *Test:* Automated mechanisms supporting and/or implementing identifier management.

IA-4(2)	Identifier management: Supervisor authorization	Review documentation for account management to ensure account creation process, which includes supervisory approval for each account. Review account creation forms to verify approvals. Interview System Owner, System Administrators, and Security Officer.	FIPS-190, FIPS-201, SP 800-73, SP 800-76, SP 800-78	*Examine:* Identification and authentication policy; procedures addressing identifier management; information system design documentation; information system configuration settings and associated documentation; information system audit records; other relevant documents or records. *Interview:* Organizational personnel with identifier management responsibilities; supervisors responsible for authorizing identifier registration; organizational personnel with information security responsibilities; system/network administrators. *Test:* Automated mechanisms supporting and/or implementing identifier management.
IA-4(3)	Identifier management: Multiple forms of certification	Review documentation to ensure users are required to present multiple forms of identification to obtain a system identifier. Discuss with System Owner and Security Officer.	FIPS-190, FIPS-201, SP 800-73, SP 800-76, SP 800-78	*Examine:* Identification and authentication policy; procedures addressing identifier management; information system design documentation; information system configuration settings and associated documentation; information system audit records; other relevant documents or records. *Interview:* Organizational personnel with identifier management responsibilities; organizational personnel with information security responsibilities. *Test:* Automated mechanisms supporting and/or implementing identifier management.
IA-4(4)	Identifier management: Identify user status	Review documentation to ensure organization requires unique identifier characteristics for special users, such as identification of user being a contractor or a guest. Discuss with System Owner, CISO staff, and Security Officer. Test by manually reviewing these types of accounts and their associated identifiers.	FIPS-190, FIPS-201, SP 800-73, SP 800-76, SP 800-78	*Examine:* Identification and authentication policy; procedures addressing identifier management; list of characteristics identifying individual status; other relevant documents or records. *Interview:* Organizational personnel with identifier management responsibilities; organizational personnel with information security responsibilities; system/network administrators. *Test:* Automated mechanisms supporting and/or implementing identifier management.
IA-4(5)	Identifier management: Dynamic management	Review documentation for dynamic system-generated identifier creation and use. Automatically test	FIPS-190, FIPS-201, SP 800-73, SP 800-76, SP 800-78	*Examine:* Identification and authentication policy; procedures addressing identifier management; information system design documentation; information system configuration settings

(Continued)

Control number	Control name	Assessment methods	Notes and guidance documents	SP 800-53A guidance
		using access control-based tools. Discuss with System Owner and Security Officer.		and associated documentation; information system audit records; other relevant documents or records. *Interview:* Organizational personnel with identifier management responsibilities; organizational personnel with information security responsibilities; system/network administrators; system developers. *Test:* Automated mechanisms supporting and/or implementing dynamic identifier management.
IA-4(6)	Identifier management: Cross-organization management	Review documentation for cross-organizational usage of single identifiers, especially in single sign-on (SSO) implementations. Ensure proper identification and authentication criteria are identified and utilized for all accounts of this type. Discuss with System Owner, System Administrators, and Security Officer.	FIPS-190, FIPS-201, SP 800-73, SP 800-76, SP 800-78	*Examine:* Identification and authentication policy; procedures addressing identifier management; procedures addressing account management; security plan; other relevant documents or records. *Interview:* Organizational personnel with identifier management responsibilities; organizational personnel with information security responsibilities. *Test:* Automated mechanisms supporting and/or implementing identifier management.
IA-4(7)	Identifier management: In-person registration	Review documentation for in-person requirements and process flow for all users requiring identification and authentication in person. Discuss process and requirements with System Owner and Security Officer.	FIPS-190, FIPS-201, SP 800-73, SP 800-76, SP 800-78	*Examine:* Identification and authentication policy; procedures addressing identifier management; procedures addressing account management; information system design documentation; information system configuration settings and associated documentation; information system audit records; other relevant documents or records. *Interview:* Organizational personnel with identifier management responsibilities; organizational personnel with information security responsibilities.
IA-5	Authenticator management	Review all account and access documentation for authentication requirements, process flow and practices to ensure all means of authentication	FIPS-190, FIPS-201, SP 800-63, SP 800-73, SP 800-76, SP 800-78, OMB M04-04, OMB M11-11	*Examine:* Identification and authentication policy; procedures addressing authenticator management; information system design documentation; information system configuration settings and associated documentation; list of information system authenticator types; change control records associated with managing information system authenticators;

	Control	Assessment Procedure	References	Assessment Methods
		are employed and utilized. Test via automated tools to ensure all identifiers require authentication prior to access being granted. Discuss with System Owner, operations personnel, System Administrators, and Security Officer.		information system audit records; other relevant documents or records. *Interview:* Organizational personnel with authenticator management responsibilities; organizational personnel with information security responsibilities; system/network administrators. *Test:* Automated mechanisms supporting and/or implementing authenticator management capability.
IA-5(1)	Authenticator management: Password-based authentication	Review documentation for authentication via passwords only process and procedures. Test via automated scan tools to ensure no authentication is performed without passwords being installed and active. Discuss with System Owner, System Administrators, and Security Officer.	FIPS-190, FIPS-201, SP 800-63, SP 800-73, SP 800-76, SP 800-78, OMB M04-04, OMB M11-11	*Examine:* Identification and authentication policy; password policy; procedures addressing authenticator management; security plan; information system design documentation; information system configuration settings and associated documentation; password configurations and associated documentation; other relevant documents or records. *Interview:* Organizational personnel with authenticator management responsibilities; organizational personnel with information security responsibilities; system/network administrators; system developers. *Test:* Automated mechanisms supporting and/or implementing password-based authenticator management capability.
IA-5(2)	Authenticator management: PKI-based authentication	Review documentation for authentication via PKI-based tokens and PIV cards process and procedures. Test via automated scan tools to ensure no authentication is performed without PIV Cards or PKI-based tokens being installed and active. Discuss with System Owner, System Administrators, and Security Officer.	FIPS-190, FIPS-201, SP 800-63, SP 800-73, SP 800-76, SP 800-78, OMB M04-04, OMB M11-11	*Examine:* Identification and authentication policy; procedures addressing authenticator management; security plan; information system design documentation; information system configuration settings and associated documentation; PKI certification validation records; PKI certification revocation lists; other relevant documents or records. *Interview:* Organizational personnel with PKI-based, authenticator management responsibilities; organizational personnel with information security responsibilities; system/network administrators; system developers. *Test:* Automated mechanisms supporting and/or implementing PKI-based, authenticator management capability.
IA-5(3)	Authenticator management: In-person or	Review documentation to ensure all user and system authentication criteria be	FIPS-190, FIPS-201, SP 800-63, SP 800-73, SP 800-76,	*Examine:* Identification and authentication policy; procedures addressing authenticator management; registration process for receiving information system authenticators; list of

(Continued)

Control number	Control name	Assessment methods	Notes and guidance documents	SP 800-53A guidance
	trusted third-party registration	conducted through trusted registration process and organizations, either via in-person review or by trusted third-party organizations. Discuss with System Owner, operational personnel, and Security Officer.	SP 800-78, OMB M04-04, OMB M11-11	authenticators requiring in-person registration; list of authenticators requiring trusted third party registration; authenticator registration documentation; other relevant documents or records. *Interview:* Organizational personnel with authenticator management responsibilities; registration authority; organizational personnel with information security responsibilities.
IA-5(4)	Authenticator management: Automated support for password strength determination	Review authentication and password policy documents to ensure appropriate password strength requirements are defined and implemented within system under review. Test password strength via automated scan tools to ensure all passwords meet strength requirements. Discuss with System Owner and Security Officer.	FIPS-190, FIPS-201, SP 800-63, SP 800-73, SP 800-76, SP 800-78, OMB M04-04, OMB M11-11	*Examine:* Identification and authentication policy; procedures addressing authenticator management; information system design documentation; information system configuration settings and associated documentation; automated tools for evaluating password authenticators; password strength assessment results; other relevant documents or records. *Interview:* Organizational personnel with authenticator management responsibilities; organizational personnel with information security responsibilities; system/network administrators. *Test:* Automated mechanisms supporting and/or implementing password-based authenticator management capability; automated tools for determining password strength.
IA-5(5)	Authenticator management: Change authenticators prior to delivery	Review documentation and configuration settings for system under review to ensure default authenticators, such as passwords, are changed upon receipt or delivery of system. Test system with automated tools to ensure passwords are not in default configuration. Discuss with System Owner, System Administrators, and Security Officer.	FIPS-190, FIPS-201, SP 800-63, SP 800-73, SP 800-76, SP 800-78, OMB M04-04, OMB M11-11	*Examine:* Identification and authentication policy; system and services acquisition policy; procedures addressing authenticator management; procedures addressing the integration of security requirements into the acquisition process; acquisition documentation; acquisition contracts for information system procurements or services; other relevant documents or records. *Interview:* Organizational personnel with authenticator management responsibilities; organizational personnel with information system security, acquisition, and contracting responsibilities; system developers. *Test:* Automated mechanisms supporting and/or implementing authenticator management capability.

IA-5(6)	Authenticator management: Protection of authenticators	Review documentation for systems with multiple levels of security to ensure proper protection, at the highest level of security, is maintained for all authenticators on the system. Discuss with System Owner and Security Officer.	FIPS-190, FIPS-201, SP 800-63, SP 800-73, SP 800-76, SP 800-78, OMB M04-04, OMB M11-11	*Examine:* Identification and authentication policy; procedures addressing authenticator management; security categorization documentation for the information system; risk assessment results; security plan; other relevant documents or records. *Interview:* Organizational personnel with authenticator management responsibilities; organizational personnel implementing and/or maintaining authenticator protections; organizational personnel with information security responsibilities; system/network administrators. *Test:* Automated mechanisms supporting and/or implementing authenticator management capability; automated mechanisms protecting authenticators.
IA-5(7)	Authenticator management: No embedded unencrypted static authenticators	Review documentation and configuration files and scripts to ensure no storage of embedded authenticators (i.e., passwords) is maintained on the system. Test via automated scan tools to verify no embedded passwords are used. Discuss with System Owner, Developmental personnel, and Security Officer.	FIPS-190, FIPS-201, SP 800-63, SP 800-73, SP 800-76, SP 800-78, OMB M04-04, OMB M11-11	*Examine:* Identification and authentication policy; procedures addressing authenticator management; information system design documentation; information system configuration settings and associated documentation; logical access scripts; application code reviews for detecting unencrypted static authenticators; other relevant documents or records. *Interview:* Organizational personnel with authenticator management responsibilities; organizational personnel with information security responsibilities; system/network administrators; system developers. *Test:* Automated mechanisms supporting and/or implementing authenticator management capability; automated mechanisms implementing authentication in applications.
IA-5(8)	Authenticator management: Multiple information system accounts	Review documentation and policies for the system to ensure users, which have accounts on multiple systems, use the appropriate authentication methods and techniques for maintaining separation of authenticators. Discuss with System Owner and Security Officer.	FIPS-190, FIPS-201, SP 800-63, SP 800-73, SP 800-76, SP 800-78, OMB M04-04, OMB M11-11	*Examine:* Identification and authentication policy; procedures addressing authenticator management; security plan; list of individuals having accounts on multiple information systems; list of security safeguards intended to manage risk of compromise due to individuals having accounts on multiple information systems; other relevant documents or records. *Interview:* Organizational personnel with authenticator management responsibilities; organizational personnel with information security responsibilities; system/network administrators. *Test:* Automated mechanisms supporting and/or implementing safeguards for authenticator management.

(Continued)

Control number	Control name	Assessment methods	Notes and guidance documents	SP 800-53A guidance
IA-5(9)	Authenticator management: Cross-organizational credential management	Review documentation for cross-organizational usage of single credentials, especially in single sign-on (SSO) implementations. Ensure proper identification and authentication criteria are identified and utilized for all accounts of this type. Discuss with System Owner, System Administrators, and Security Officer.	FIPS-190, FIPS-201, SP 800-63, SP 800-73, SP 800-76, SP 800-78, OMB M04-04, OMB M11-11	*Examine*: Identification and authentication policy; procedures addressing authenticator management; procedures addressing account management; security plan; information security agreements; other relevant documents or records. *Interview*: Organizational personnel with authenticator management responsibilities; organizational personnel with information security responsibilities; system/network administrators. *Test*: Automated mechanisms supporting and/or implementing safeguards for authenticator management.
IA-5(10)	Authenticator management: Dynamic credential association	Review documentation for dynamic system-generated authenticator creation and use. Ensure any trust authentication criteria for identifiers is established and operational. Automatically test using access control-based tools. Discuss with System Owner and Security Officer.	FIPS-190, FIPS-201, SP 800-63, SP 800-73, SP 800-76, SP 800-78, OMB M04-04, OMB M11-11	*Examine*: Identification and authentication policy; procedures addressing identifier management; security plan; information system design documentation; automated mechanisms providing dynamic binding of identifiers and authenticators; information system configuration settings and associated documentation; information system audit records; other relevant documents or records. *Interview*: Organizational personnel with identifier management responsibilities; organizational personnel with information security responsibilities; system/network administrators. *Test*: Automated mechanisms implementing identifier management capability; automated mechanisms implementing dynamic provisioning of identifiers.
IA-5(11)	Authenticator management: Hardware token-based authentication	Review documentation for PKI-based authentication processing and provisioning as well as operations on the system. Validate using automated scan tools. Discuss with System Owner and Security Officer.	FIPS-190, FIPS-201, SP 800-63, SP 800-73, SP 800-76, SP 800-78, OMB M04-04, OMB M11-11	*Examine*: Identification and authentication policy; procedures addressing authenticator management; security plan; information system design documentation; automated mechanisms employing hardware token-based authentication for the information system; list of token quality requirements; information system configuration settings and associated documentation; information system audit records; other relevant documents or records. *Interview*: Organizational personnel with authenticator management responsibilities; organizational personnel with information security responsibilities; system/

IA-5(12)	Authenticator management: Biometric authentication	Review documentation, policies and procedures to ensure biometric based authentication, when required, is installed and implemented correctly. Validate biometric CER criteria for system with tools and tests. Discuss with System Owner, System Developers, and Security Officer.	FIPS-190, FIPS-201, SP 800-63, SP 800-73, SP 800-76, SP 800-78, OMB M04-04, OMB M11-11	network administrators; system developers. *Test:* Automated mechanisms supporting and/or implementing hardware token-based authenticator management capability. *Examine:* Identification and authentication policy; procedures addressing authenticator management; security plan; information system design documentation; automated mechanisms employing biometric-based authentication for the information system; list of biometric quality requirements; information system configuration settings and associated documentation; information system audit records; other relevant documents or records. *Interview:* Organizational personnel with authenticator management responsibilities; organizational personnel with information security responsibilities; system/network administrators; system developers. *Test:* Automated mechanisms supporting and/or implementing biometric-based authenticator management capability.
IA-5(13)	Authenticator management: Expiration of cached authenticators	Review documentation to ensure expiration dates for stored authenticators are maintained and checked during authentication actions by the system. Test via scan tools and manual tests of expired authenticators. Discuss with System Owner, System Developers, and Security Officer.	FIPS-190, FIPS-201, SP 800-63, SP 800-73, SP 800-76, SP 800-78, OMB M04-04, OMB M11-11	*Examine:* Identification and authentication policy; procedures addressing authenticator management; security plan; information system design documentation; information system configuration settings and associated documentation; information system audit records; other relevant documents or records. *Interview:* Organizational personnel with authenticator management responsibilities; organizational personnel with information security responsibilities; system/network administrators; system developers. *Test:* Automated mechanisms supporting and/or implementing authenticator management capability.
IA-5(14)	Authenticator management: Managing content of PKI trust stores	Review documentation to ensure system PKI-based activities are based on connections with the organization-wide PKI trust methodology and systems. Discuss with System Owner, System Developers, and Security	FIPS-190, FIPS-201, SP 800-63, SP 800-73, SP 800-76, SP 800-78, OMB M04-04, OMB M11-11	*Examine:* Identification and authentication policy; procedures addressing authenticator management; security plan; organizational methodology for managing content of PKI trust stores across installed all platforms; information system design documentation; information system configuration settings and associated documentation; enterprise security architecture documentation; enterprise architecture documentation; other relevant documents or records. *Interview:* Organizational personnel with authenticator management

(Continued)

Control number	Control name	Assessment methods	Notes and guidance documents	SP 800-53A guidance
		Officer. Validate using external PKI-based authenticator to ensure communications is active and verified.		responsibilities; organizational personnel with information security responsibilities; system/network administrators; system developers. *Test:* Automated mechanisms supporting and/or implementing PKI-based authenticator management capability; automated mechanisms supporting and/or implementing the PKI trust store capability.
IA-5(15)	Authenticator management: FICAM-approved products and services	Review documentation to ensure system is utilizing the federal identity, credential, and access management (FICAM)-approved path discovery and validation methodologies and services. Discuss with System Owner, System Developers, and Security Officer.	FIPS-190, FIPS-201, SP 800-63, SP 800-73, SP 800-76, SP 800-78, OMB M04-04, OMB M11-11, HSPD-12, http://www.idmanagement.gov	*Examine:* Identification and authentication policy; procedures addressing identifier management; security plan; information system design documentation; automated mechanisms providing dynamic binding of identifiers and authenticators; information system configuration settings and associated documentation; information system audit records; other relevant documents or records. *Interview:* Organizational personnel with identification and authentication management responsibilities; organizational personnel with information security responsibilities; system/network administrators. *Test:* Automated mechanisms supporting and/or implementing account management capability; automated mechanisms supporting and/or implementing identification and authentication management capability for the information system.
IA-6	Authenticator feedback	Review documentation to ensure system is obscuring the authenticators upon entry. This blanking out of passwords is typically tested by entering the password and observing the blanking out process. Discuss with System Owner and Security Officer.	FIPS-190, FIPS-191, SP 800-63, OMB M04-04	*Examine:* Identification and authentication policy; procedures addressing authenticator feedback; information system design documentation; information system configuration settings and associated documentation; information system audit records; other relevant documents or records. *Interview:* Organizational personnel with information security responsibilities; system/network administrators; system developers. *Test:* Automated mechanisms supporting and/or implementing the obscuring of feedback of authentication information during authentication.
IA-7	Cryptographic module authentication	Review documentation for system to ensure authentication for cryptographic modules is performed in	FIPS 140-2, http://csrc.nist.gov/groups/STM/cmvp/index.html	*Examine:* Identification and authentication policy; procedures addressing cryptographic module authentication; information system design documentation; information system configuration settings and associated documentation; information system audit records; other relevant documents

			or records. *Interview:* Organizational personnel with responsibility for cryptographic module authentication; organizational personnel with information security responsibilities; system/network administrators; system developers. *Test:* Automated mechanisms supporting and/or implementing cryptographic module authentication.
IA-8	Identification and authentication (nonorganizational users)	FIPS-190, FIPS-201, SP 800-63, SP 800-116, OMB M04-04, OMB M11-11	Review system documentation and requirements for nonorganizational users of system to ensure the same requirements are being met as found in control IA-2 for organizational users. Validate via automated scan tools for access and authentication actions. Discuss with System Owner, System Administrators, and Security Officer. / *Examine:* Identification and authentication policy; procedures addressing user identification and authentication; information system design documentation; information system configuration settings and associated documentation; information system audit records; list of information system accounts; other relevant documents or records. *Interview:* Organizational personnel with information system operations responsibilities; organizational personnel with information security responsibilities; system/network administrators; organizational personnel with account management responsibilities. *Test:* Automated mechanisms supporting and/or implementing identification and authentication capability.
IA-8(1)	Identification and authentication: Acceptance of PIV credentials from other agencies	FIPS-190, FIPS-201, SP 800-63, SP 800-116, OMB M04-04, OMB M11-11	Review documentation to ensure system accepts and processes FIPS-201 based PIV cards and credentials as issued by other governmental agencies. Test via use of external PIV card and successful authentication of same card. Discuss with System Owner, System Developers, and Security Officer. / *Examine:* Identification and authentication policy; procedures addressing user identification and authentication; information system design documentation; information system configuration settings and associated documentation; information system audit records; PIV verification records; evidence of PIV credentials; PIV credential authorizations; other relevant documents or records. *Interview:* Organizational personnel with information system operations responsibilities; organizational personnel with information security responsibilities; system/network administrators; system developers; organizational personnel with account management responsibilities. *Test:* Automated mechanisms supporting and/or implementing identification and authentication capability; automated mechanisms that accept and verify PIV credentials.

(Continued)

Control number	Control name	Assessment methods	Notes and guidance documents	SP 800-53A guidance
IA-8(2)	Identification and authentication: Acceptance of third-party credentials	Review documentation for system to ensure that it provides for authentication of third-party FICAM-based credentials. This control typically applies to organizational information systems that are accessible to the general public, for example, public-facing websites. Verify by testing using an external FICAM-based card. Discuss with System Owner, System Developers, System Administrators, and Security Officer.	FIPS-190, FIPS-201, SP 800-63, SP 800-116, OMB M04-04, OMB M11-11	*Examine:* Identification and authentication policy; procedures addressing user identification and authentication; information system design documentation; information system configuration settings and associated documentation; information system audit records; list of FICAM-approved, third-party credentialing products, components, or services procured and implemented by organization; third-party credential verification records; evidence of FICAM-approved third-party credentials; third-party credential authorizations; other relevant documents or records. *Interview:* Organizational personnel with information system operations responsibilities; organizational personnel with information security responsibilities; system/network administrators; system developers; organizational personnel with account management responsibilities. *Test:* Automated mechanisms supporting and/or implementing identification and authentication capability; automated mechanisms that accept FICAM-approved credentials.
IA-8(3)	Identification and authentication: Use of FICAM-approved products	Review documentation for system to ensure that it provides for authentication of FICAM-based credentials. This control typically applies to organizational information systems that are accessible to the general public, for example, public-facing websites. Verify by testing using an external FICAM-based card. Discuss with System Owner, System Developers, System Administrators, and Security Officer.	FIPS-190, FIPS-201, SP 800-63, SP 800-116, OMB M04-04, OMB M11-11	*Examine:* Identification and services acquisition policy; system and services acquisition policy; procedures addressing user identification and authentication; procedures addressing the integration of security requirements into the acquisition process; information system design documentation; information system configuration settings and associated documentation; information system audit records; third-party credential validations; third-party credential authorizations; third-party credential records; list of FICAM-approved information system components procured and implemented by organization; acquisition documentation; acquisition contracts for information system procurements or services; other relevant documents or records. *Interview:* Organizational personnel with information system operations responsibilities; system/network administrators; organizational personnel with account management responsibilities; organizational personnel with information system security, acquisition, and contracting responsibilities. *Test:* Automated mechanisms supporting and/or implementing identification and authentication capability.

IA-8(4)	Identification and authentication: use of FICAM-issued profiles	Review documentation for system to ensure that it provides for authentication of FICAM-based credential of organizational open identity profiles. This control typically applies to organizational information systems that are accessible to the general public, for example, public-facing websites. Verify by testing using an external FICAM-based card. Discuss with System Owner, System Developers, System Administrators, and Security Officer.	FIPS-190, FIPS-201, SP 800-63, SP 800-116, OMB M04-04, OMB M11-11	*Examine:* Identification and authentication policy; system and services acquisition policy; procedures addressing user identification and authentication; procedures addressing the integration of security requirements into the acquisition process; information system design documentation; information system configuration settings and associated documentation; information system audit records; list of FICAM-issued profiles and associated, approved protocols; acquisition documentation; acquisition contracts for information system procurements or services; other relevant documents or records. *Interview:* Organizational personnel with information system operations responsibilities; organizational personnel with information security responsibilities; system/network administrators; system developers; organizational personnel with account management responsibilities. *Test:* Automated mechanisms supporting and/or implementing identification and authentication capability; automated mechanisms supporting and/or implementing conformance with FICAM-issued profiles.
IA-8(5)	Identification and authentication: Acceptance of PIV-I credentials	Review documentation for system to ensure that it provides for authentication of nonfederal users of identity cards. Verify by testing using an external PIV-I based card. Discuss with System Owner, System Developers, System Administrators, and Security Officer.	FIPS-190, FIPS-201, SP 800-63, SP 800-116, OMB M04-04, OMB M11-11	*Examine:* Identification and authentication policy; procedures addressing user identification and authentication; information system design documentation; information system configuration settings and associated documentation; information system audit records; PIV-I verification records; evidence of PIV-I credentials; PIV-I credential authorizations; other relevant documents or records. *Interview:* Organizational personnel with information system operations responsibilities; organizational personnel with information security responsibilities; system/network administrators; system developers; organizational personnel with account management responsibilities. *Test:* Automated mechanisms supporting and/or implementing identification and authentication capability; automated mechanisms that accept and verify PIV-I credentials.
IA-9	Service identification and authentication	Review documentation to ensure that information systems can determine in a dynamic manner, if external	FIPS-190, FIPS-191, SP 800-63, OMB M04-04	*Examine:* Identification and authentication policy; procedures addressing service identification and authentication; security plan; information system design documentation; security safeguards used to identify and authenticate information

(Continued)

Control number	Control name	Assessment methods	Notes and guidance documents	SP 800-53A guidance
		providers and associated services are authentic, when authenticating. This control relates to SOA-based web services for authentication, and as, such, must be reviewed with System Developers during design and implementation. Discuss with System Developers, System Owner, and Security Officer to ensure need, validation processes and implementation procedures.		system services; information system configuration settings and associated documentation; information system audit records; other relevant documents or records. *Interview:* Organizational personnel with information system operations responsibilities; organizational personnel with information security responsibilities; system/network administrators; system developers; organizational personnel with identification and authentication responsibilities. *Test:* Security safeguards implementing service identification and authentication capability.
IA-9(1)	Service identification and authentication: Information exchange	Review documentation to ensure system provides correct information for service-based information exchanges of authentication data. Discuss with System Developers, System Owner, and Security Officer.	FIPS-190, FIPS-191, SP 800-63, OMB M04-04	*Examine:* Identification and authentication policy; procedures addressing service identification and authentication; security plan; information system design documentation; information system configuration settings and associated documentation; information system audit records; other relevant documents or records. *Interview:* Organizational personnel with identification and authentication responsibilities; organizational personnel with information security responsibilities; system/network administrators; service providers. *Test:* Automated mechanisms implementing service identification and authentication capabilities.
IA-9(2)	Service identification and authentication: Transmission of decisions	Review documentation for system to ensure validation authentication decisions made by system are performed separately from actions of validated user. Discuss with System Developers, System Owner, and Security Officer.	FIPS-190, FIPS-191, SP 800-63, OMB M04-04	*Examine:* Identification and authentication policy; procedures addressing service identification and authentication; security plan; information system design documentation; information system configuration settings and associated documentation; information system audit records; transmission records; rules for identification and authentication transmission decisions between organizational services; other relevant documents or records. *Interview:* Organizational personnel with identification and authentication responsibilities; organizational personnel

IA-10	Adaptive identification and authentication	Review documentation for system to ensure that when defined threat conditions exist, the system will require additional identification and authentication actions in order to validate user and actions. Discuss these criteria with System Owner and Security Officer.	FIPS-190, FIPS-191, SP 800-63, OMB M04-04	*Examine*: Identification and authentication policy; procedures addressing adaptive/supplemental identification and authentication techniques or mechanisms; security plan; information system design documentation; information system configuration settings and associated documentation; supplemental identification and authentication techniques or mechanisms; information system audit records; other relevant documents or records. *Interview*: Organizational personnel with information system operations responsibilities; with information security responsibilities; system/network administrators. *Test*: Automated mechanisms implementing service identification and authentication capabilities.
IA-11	Re-authentication	Review documentation to determine, when the additional authentication requirements are enacted and what criteria causes these actions to be required. Discuss with System Owner and Security Officer.	FIPS-190, FIPS-191, SP 800-63, OMB M04-04	*Examine*: Identification and authentication policy; procedures addressing user and device re-authentication; security plan; information system design documentation; information system configuration settings and associated documentation; list of circumstances or situations requiring re-authentication; information system audit records; other relevant documents or records. *Interview*: Organizational personnel with information system operations responsibilities; organizational personnel with information security responsibilities; system/network administrators; system developers; organizational personnel with identification and authentication responsibilities. *Test*: Automated mechanisms supporting and/or implementing identification and authentication capability.

H. *Incident response family*

FIPS-200 provides the following criteria for this family of controls: Incident response (IR): Organizations must: (i) establish an operational incident handling capability for organizational information systems that includes adequate preparation, detection, analysis, containment, recovery, and user response activities; and (ii) track, document, and report incidents to appropriate organizational officials and/or authorities.

The primary assessment areas for these controls include:

a. Inspect the establishment of an operational incident handling capability for organizational information systems that includes adequate preparation, detection, analysis, containment, recovery, and user response activities.

b. Audit the tracking, documenting, and reporting of incidents to appropriate organizational officials and/or authorities.

Control number	Control name	Assessment methods	Notes and guidance documents	SP 800-53A guidance
IR-1	Incident response policy and procedures	Review documentation for system and organization. Review organizational IR policy and various procedures. Discuss with System Owner and Security Officer.	SP 800-12, SP 800-61, rev. 2, SP 800-83, SP 800-100, DOD CJCSM 6510.01	*Examine:* Incident response policy and procedures; other relevant documents or records. *Interview:* Organizational personnel with incident response responsibilities; organizational personnel with information security responsibilities.
IR-2	Incident response training	Review documentation for IR training of users, administrators, and security staff. Ensure that incident response training includes user training in the identification and reporting of suspicious activities, both from external and internal sources. Review training documents for all users to ensure correct training is provided for each level of user. Discuss with System Owner and Security Officer.	SP 800-16, SP 800-50, SP 800-61, rev. 2	*Examine:* Incident response policy; procedures addressing incident response training; incident response training curriculum; incident response training materials; security plan; incident response plan; security plan; incident response training records; other relevant documents or records. *Interview:* Organizational personnel with incident response training and operational responsibilities; organizational personnel with information security responsibilities.
IR-2(1)	Incident response training: Simulated events	Review training documentation for IR training of organizational users. Determine if training includes simulated IR events and scenarios. Discuss with System Owner and Security Officer.	SP 800-16, SP 800-50, SP 800-61, rev. 2	*Examine:* Incident response policy; procedures addressing incident response training; incident response training curriculum; incident response training materials; incident response plan; security plan; other relevant documents or records. *Interview:* Organizational personnel with incident response training and operational responsibilities; organizational personnel with information security responsibilities. *Test:* Automated mechanisms that support and/or implement simulated events for incident response training.
IR-2(2)	Incident response training: Automated training environments	Review documentation of IR training for organizational users to determine if training system is automated with standardized IR training modules and components.	SP 800-16, SP 800-50, SP 800-61, rev. 2	*Examine:* Incident response policy; procedures addressing incident response training; incident response training curriculum; incident response training materials; automated mechanisms supporting incident response training; incident response plan; security plan; other relevant documents or records. *Interview:*

(Continued)

Control number	Control name	Assessment methods	Notes and guidance documents	SP 800-53A guidance
		Discuss with System Owner and Security Officer.		Organizational personnel with incident response training and operational responsibilities; organizational personnel with information security responsibilities. *Test*: Automated mechanisms that provide a thorough and realistic incident response training environment.
IR-3	Incident response testing	Review documentation and test results to determine the organization's IR testing capabilities and activities. Discuss with System Owner, CP testing Coordinator, and Security Officer.	SP 800-61, rev. 2, SP 800-84, SP 800-115	*Examine*: Incident response policy; contingency planning policy; procedures addressing incident response testing; procedures addressing contingency plan testing; incident response testing material; incident response test results; incident response test plan; incident response plan; contingency plan; security plan; other relevant documents or records. *Interview*: Organizational personnel with incident response testing responsibilities; organizational personnel with information security responsibilities.
IR-3(1)	Incident response testing: Automated testing	Review IR test plans and results to determine the organizational and system-level IR testing utilizing automated test mechanisms. Determine the extent, the organization use automated mechanisms to more thoroughly and effectively test incident response capabilities. Review results with System Owner and Security Officer.	SP 800-61, rev. 2, SP 800-84, SP 800-115	*Examine*: Incident response policy; contingency planning policy; procedures addressing incident response testing; procedures addressing contingency plan testing; incident response testing documentation; incident response test results; incident response test plan; incident response plan; contingency plan; security plan; automated mechanisms supporting incident response tests; other relevant documents or records. *Interview*: Organizational personnel with incident response testing responsibilities; organizational personnel with information security responsibilities. *Test*: Automated mechanisms that more thoroughly and effectively test the incident response capability.
IR-3(2)	Incident response testing: Coordination with related plans	Review documentation to determine coordination and correlation of IR testing with other organizational-wide test events and activities, such as contingency testing, BCP testing, DRP testing, and other type events. Review with System Owner and Security Officer.	SP 800-61, rev. 2, SP 800-84, SP 800-115	*Examine*: Incident response policy; contingency planning policy; procedures addressing incident response testing; incident response testing documentation; incident response plan; business continuity plans; contingency plans; disaster recovery plans; continuity of operations plans; crisis communications plans; critical infrastructure plans; occupant emergency plans; security plan; other relevant documents or records. *Interview*: Organizational personnel with incident response

IR-4	Incident handling	Review documentation to ensure that organization has an incident handling capability in place for system covering security incidents, their eradication and lessons learned process to update the incident response efforts and training. Test the incident response management system associated with system or organization to ensure all areas of IR are addressed and reported. Discuss with System Owner and Security Officer.	SP 800-61, rev. 2, E.O. 13587	testing responsibilities; organizational personnel with responsibilities for testing organizational plans related to incident response testing; organizational personnel with information security responsibilities. *Examine:* Incident response policy; contingency planning policy; procedures addressing incident handling; incident response plan; contingency plan; security plan; other relevant documents or records. *Interview:* Organizational personnel with incident handling responsibilities; organizational personnel with contingency planning responsibilities; organizational personnel with information security responsibilities. *Test:* Incident handling capability for the organization.
IR-4(1)	Incident handling: Automated incident handling processes	Review documentation to determine the automated incident handling capability tools employed by system and organization. Discuss with System Owner and Security Officer.	SP 800-61, rev. 2, E.O. 13587	*Examine:* Incident response policy; procedures addressing incident handling; automated mechanisms supporting incident handling; information system design documentation; information system configuration settings and associated documentation; information system audit records; incident response plan; security plan; other relevant documents or records. *Interview:* Organizational personnel with incident handling responsibilities; organizational personnel with information security responsibilities. *Test:* Automated mechanisms that support and/or implement the incident handling process.
IR-4(2)	Incident handling: Dynamic reconfiguration	Review documentation for the automated reconfiguration mechanisms in place for the organizational security components, such as changes to router rules, access control lists, intrusion detection/prevention	SP 800-61, rev. 2, E.O. 13587	*Examine:* Incident response policy; procedures addressing incident handling; automated mechanisms supporting incident handling; list of system components to be dynamically reconfigured as part of incident response capability; information system design documentation; information system configuration settings and associated documentation; information

(Continued)

Control number	Control name	Assessment methods	Notes and guidance documents	SP 800-53A guidance
		system parameters, and filter rules for firewalls and gateways. Test dynamic reconfiguration processes with test data inputs designed to cause system to respond. Discuss with System Owner, security staff, and Security Officer.		system audit records; incident response plan; security plan; other relevant documents or records. *Interview:* Organizational personnel with incident handling responsibilities; organizational personnel with information security responsibilities. *Test:* Automated mechanisms that support and/or implement dynamic reconfiguration of components as part of incident response.
IR-4(3)	Incident handling; Continuity of operations	Review documentation to determine defined classes of events, which trigger COOP actions and which actions are defined to occur upon receipt of triggers. Discuss with System Owner, operations staff, and Security Officer.	SP 800-61, rev. 2, E.O. 13587	*Examine:* Incident response policy; procedures addressing incident handling; incident response plan; security plan; list of classes of incidents; list of appropriate incident response actions; other relevant documents or records. *Interview:* Organizational personnel with incident handling responsibilities; organizational personnel with information security responsibilities. *Test:* Automated mechanisms that support and/or implement continuity of operations.
IR-4(4)	Incident handling; Information correlation	Review documentation to determine scope and process for organizational wide event correlation activities. Discuss with System Owner and Security Officer.	SP 800-61, rev. 2, E.O. 13587	*Examine:* Incident response policy; procedures addressing incident handling; incident response plan; security plan; automated mechanisms supporting incident and event correlation; information system design documentation; information system configuration settings and associated documentation; incident management correlation logs; event management correlation logs; security information and event management logs; incident management correlation reports; event management correlation reports; security information and event management reports; audit records; other relevant documents or records. *Interview:* Organizational personnel with incident handling responsibilities; organizational personnel with information security responsibilities; organizational personnel with whom incident information and individual incident responses are to be correlated. *Test:* Organizational processes for correlating incident information and individual incident responses; automated mechanisms that support and or implement

				correlation of incident response information with individual incident responses.
IR-4(5)	Incident handling: Automatic disabling of information system	Review documentation to determine which events trigger the automated disabling of system upon receipt of trigger. Test system with test code simulating such an event. Discuss with System Owner and Security Officer.	SP 800-61, rev. 2, E.O. 13587	*Examine:* Incident response policy; procedures addressing incident handling; automated mechanisms supporting incident handling; information system design documentation; information system configuration settings and associated documentation; incident response plan; security plan; other relevant documents or records. *Interview:* Organizational personnel with incident handling responsibilities; organizational personnel with information security responsibilities; system developers. *Test:* Incident handling capability for the organization; automated mechanisms supporting and/or implementing automatic disabling of the information system.
IR-4(6)	Incident handling: Insider threats – specific capabilities	Review documentation to determine specific insider threat response capabilities, the organization has instituted with system. Discuss with System Owner and Security Officer.	SP 800-61, rev. 2, E.O. 13587	*Examine:* Incident response policy; procedures addressing incident handling; automated mechanisms supporting incident handling; information system design documentation; information system configuration settings and associated documentation; incident response plan; security plan; audit records; other relevant documents or records. *Interview:* Organizational personnel with incident handling responsibilities; organizational personnel with information security responsibilities. *Test:* Incident handling capability for the organization.
IR-4(7)	Incident handling: Insider threats – intraorganization coordination	Review documentation to determine scope and process for organizational wide event correlation activities. Review which organizational components and personnel are involved with coordination. Discuss with System Owner and Security Officer.	SP 800-61, rev. 2, E.O. 13587	*Examine:* Incident response policy; procedures addressing incident handling; incident response plan; security plan; other relevant documents or records. *Interview:* Organizational personnel with incident handling responsibilities; organizational personnel with information security responsibilities; organizational personnel/elements with whom incident handling capability is to be coordinated. *Test:* Organizational processes for coordinating incident handling.
IR-4(8)	Incident handling: Correlation	Review documentation to determine scope and process for external organizational	SP 800-61, rev. 2, E.O. 13587	*Examine:* Incident response policy; procedures addressing incident handling; list of external organizations; records of incident handling

(Continued)

Control number	Control name	Assessment methods	Notes and guidance documents	SP 800-53A guidance
	with external organizations	event correlation activities. Discuss with System Owner and Security Officer.		coordination with external organizations; incident response plan; security plan; other relevant documents or records. *Interview:* Organizational personnel with incident handling responsibilities; organizational personnel with information security responsibilities; personnel from external organizations with whom incident response information is to be coordinated / shared/correlated. *Test:* Organizational processes for coordinating incident handling information with external organizations.
IR-4(9)	Incident handling: Dynamic response capability	Review documentation to determine what new or replacement capabilities are designated for automatic deployment during incidents. Test dynamic response capability with test code simulating one of designated events. Discuss with System Owner and Security Officer.	SP 800-61, rev. 2, E.O. 13587	*Examine:* Incident response policy; procedures addressing incident handling; automated mechanisms supporting dynamic response capabilities; information system design documentation; information system configuration settings and associated documentation; incident response plan; security plan; audit records; other relevant documents or records. *Interview:* Organizational personnel with incident handling responsibilities; organizational personnel with information security responsibilities. *Test:* Organizational processes for dynamic response capability; automated mechanisms supporting and/or implementing the dynamic response capability for the organization.
IR-4(10)	Incident handling: Supply chain coordination	Review documentation to determine which supply chain organizations, personnel, and vendors are designated to assist in incident handling events. Discuss with System Owner, acquisition staff, and Security officer.	SP 800-61, rev. 2, E.O. 13587	*Examine:* Incident response policy; procedures addressing supply chain coordination; acquisition contracts; service-level agreements; incident response plan; security plan; incident response plans of other organization involved in supply chain activities; other relevant documents or records. *Interview:* Organizational personnel with incident handling responsibilities; organizational personnel with information security responsibilities; organizational personnel with supply chain responsibilities.
IR-5	Incident monitoring	Review documentation of various incidents on system and determine extent and	SP 800-61, rev. 2	*Examine:* Incident response policy; procedures addressing incident monitoring; incident response records and documentation; incident response plan;

				security plan; other relevant documents or records. *Interview:* Organizational personnel with incident monitoring responsibilities; organizational personnel with information security responsibilities. *Test:* Incident monitoring capability for the organization; automated mechanisms supporting and/or implementing tracking and documenting of system security incidents.
IR-5(1)	Incident monitoring; Automated tracking/data collection/analysis	Review documentation for automated tracking of incidents and response efforts. Select sample incident event and trace all documentation generated for incident, its handling and response in automated system. Discuss with System Owner and Security Officer.	SP 800-61, rev. 2	*Examine:* Incident response policy; procedures addressing incident monitoring; automated mechanisms supporting incident monitoring; information system design documentation; information system configuration settings and associated documentation; incident response plan; security plan; audit records; other relevant documents or records. *Interview:* Organizational personnel with incident monitoring responsibilities; organizational personnel with information security responsibilities. *Test:* Automated mechanisms assisting in tracking of security incidents and in the collection and analysis of incident information.
IR-6	Incident reporting	Review documentation for reporting of incidents to determine both the specific incident reporting requirements within an organization and the formal incident reporting requirements for federal agencies and their subordinate organizations. Review external reports and documentation to satisfy this review. Discuss with System Owner, operational staff, and Security Officer.	SP 800-61, rev. 2, CJCSM 6510.01	*Examine:* Incident response policy; procedures addressing incident reporting; incident reporting records and documentation; incident response plan; security plan; other relevant documents or records. *Interview:* Organizational personnel with incident reporting responsibilities; organizational personnel with information security responsibilities; personnel who have/should have reported incidents; personnel (authorities) to whom incident information is to be reported. *Test:* Organizational processes for incident reporting; automated mechanisms supporting and/or implementing incident reporting.
IR-6(1)	Incident reporting; Automated reporting	Review documentation and automated reporting mechanisms deployed by organization for reporting of system related incidents.	SP 800-61, rev. 2	*Examine:* Incident response policy; procedures addressing incident reporting; automated mechanisms supporting incident reporting; information system design documentation; information system configuration settings and associated documentation;

(*Continued*)

Control number	Control name	Assessment methods	Notes and guidance documents	SP 800-53A guidance
		Discuss with System Owner and Security Officer.		incident response plan; security plan; other relevant documents or records. *Interview:* Organizational personnel with incident reporting responsibilities; organizational personnel with information security responsibilities. *Test:* Organizational processes for incident reporting; automated mechanisms supporting and/or implementing reporting of security incidents.
IR-6(2)	Incident reporting; Vulnerabilities related to incidents	Review documentation to ensure that the incident reporting of discovered vulnerabilities are assigned to appropriate security and operational personnel for mitigation. Discuss with System Owner, security staff, and Security Officer.	SP 800-61, rev. 2	*Examine:* Incident response policy; procedures addressing incident reporting; incident response plan; security plan; security incident reports and associated information system vulnerabilities; other relevant documents or records. *Interview:* Organizational personnel with incident reporting responsibilities; organizational personnel with information security responsibilities; system/network administrators; personnel to whom vulnerabilities associated with security incidents are to be reported. *Test:* Organizational processes for incident reporting; automated mechanisms supporting and/or implementing reporting of vulnerabilities associated with security incidents.
IR-6(3)	Incident reporting; Coordination with supply chain	Review documentation to determine which supply chain organizations, personnel, and vendors are designated to receive incident reports. Discuss with System Owner, acquisition staff, and Security Officer.	SP 800-61, rev. 2	*Examine:* Incident response policy; procedures addressing supply chain coordination; acquisition contracts; service-level agreements; incident response plan; security plan; plans of other organization involved in supply chain activities; other relevant documents or records. *Interview:* Organizational personnel with incident reporting responsibilities; organizational personnel with information security responsibilities; organizational personnel with supply chain responsibilities. *Test:* Organizational processes for incident reporting; automated mechanisms supporting and/or implementing reporting of incident information involved in the supply chain.
IR-7	Incident response assistance	Review documentation to ensure that the organization has provided for external assistance	SP 800-61, rev. 2	*Examine:* Incident response policy; procedures addressing incident response assistance; incident response plan; security plan; other relevant documents

			in specified instances and incidents. Discuss with System Owner, acquisition staff, and Security Officer.	or records. *Interview:* Organizational personnel with incident response assistance and support responsibilities; organizational personnel with access to incident response support and assistance capability; organizational personnel with information security responsibilities. *Test:* Organizational processes for incident response assistance; automated mechanisms supporting and/or implementing incident response assistance.
IR-7(1)	Incident response assistance: Automation support for availability of information/support	SP 800-61, rev. 2	Review documentation for automated implementation of both reception and transmission of relevant information and support efforts during incident response activities. Discuss with System Owner and Security Officer.	*Examine:* Incident response policy; procedures addressing incident response assistance; automated mechanisms supporting incident response support and assistance; information system design documentation; information system configuration settings and associated documentation; incident response plan; security plan; other relevant documents or records. *Interview:* Organizational personnel with incident response support and assistance responsibilities; organizational personnel with access to incident response support and assistance capability; organizational personnel with information security responsibilities. *Test:* Organizational processes for incident response assistance; automated mechanisms supporting and/or implementing an increase in the availability of incident response information and support.
IR-7(2)	Incident response assistance: Coordination with external providers	SP 800-61, rev. 2	Review documentation and agreements, the organization has for external provider support during incident handling and response efforts. Discuss with System Owner, operations staff, and Security Officer.	*Examine:* Incident response policy; procedures addressing incident response assistance; incident response plan; security plan; other relevant documents or records. *Interview:* Organizational personnel with incident response support and assistance responsibilities; external providers of information system protection capability; organizational personnel with information security responsibilities.
IR-8	Incident response plan	SP 800-61, rev. 2	Review documentation and specifically the system IRP for validity, applicability, and currency of plan and its defined actions. Review IRP for	*Examine:* Incident response policy; procedures addressing incident response planning; incident response plan; records of incident response plan reviews and approvals; other relevant documents or records. *Interview:* Organizational personnel

(Continued)

Control number	Control name	Assessment methods	Notes and guidance documents	SP 800-53A guidance
		completeness and validity within organizational documentation requirements. Discuss with Security Officer and System Owner.		with incident response planning responsibilities; organizational personnel with information security responsibilities. *Test:* Organizational incident response plan and related organizational processes.
IR-9	Information spillage response	Review documentation for information spillage incident handling events. Ensure that not all reporting requirements are dependent on classification of data involved in the event. Discuss with System Owner, FSO, and Security Officer.	SP 800-61, rev. 2	*Examine:* Incident response policy; procedures addressing information spillage; incident response plan; records of information spillage alerts/notifications, list of personnel who should receive alerts of information spillage; list of actions to be performed regarding information spillage; other relevant documents or records. *Interview:* Organizational personnel with incident response responsibilities; organizational personnel with information security responsibilities. *Test:* Organizational processes for information spillage response; automated mechanisms supporting and/or implementing information spillage response actions and related communications.
IR-9(1)	Information spillage response: Responsible personnel	Review documentation to ensure that appropriate personnel are assigned to each information spillage incident. Discuss with System Owner, Data Custodian, Information Owner, and Security Officer.	SP 800-61, rev. 2	*Examine:* Incident response policy; procedures addressing information spillage; incident response plan; list of personnel responsible for responding to information spillage; other relevant documents or records. *Interview:* Organizational personnel with incident response responsibilities; organizational personnel with information security responsibilities.
IR-9(2)	Information spillage response: Training	Review documentation to ensure that the information spillage assigned personnel have sufficient specialized handling training. Discuss with System Owner, Information Owner, and Security Officer.	SP 800-61, rev. 2	*Examine:* Incident response policy; procedures addressing information spillage response training; information spillage response training curriculum; information spillage response training materials; incident response plan; information spillage response training records; other relevant documents or records. *Interview:* Organizational personnel with incident response training responsibilities; organizational personnel with information security responsibilities.

IR-9(3)	Information spillage response: Post-spill operations	Review documentation to determine the potential extent of operational interrupts during spillage clean-up actions. Ensure operational staff are notified during events. Discuss with System Owner, operations staff, security staff, Information Owner, and Security Officer.	SP 800-61, rev. 2	*Examine:* Incident response policy; procedures addressing incident handling; procedures addressing information spillage; incident response plan; other relevant documents or records. *Interview:* Organizational personnel with incident response responsibilities; organizational personnel with information security responsibilities. *Test:* Organizational processes for post-spill operations.
IR-9(4)	Information spillage response: Exposure to unauthorized personnel	Review documentation to ensure proper notification and identification of exposed unauthorized personnel is defined and procedural in form. Discuss with System Owner, Information Owner, and Security Officer.	SP 800-61, rev. 2	*Examine:* [Incident response policy; procedures addressing incident handling; procedures addressing information spillage; incident response plan; security safeguards regarding information spillage/exposure to unauthorized personnel; other relevant documents or records. *Interview:* Organizational personnel with incident response responsibilities; organizational personnel with information security responsibilities. *Test:* Organizational processes for dealing with information exposed to unauthorized personnel; automated mechanisms supporting and/or implementing safeguards for personnel exposed to information not within assigned access authorizations.
IR-10	Integrated information security analysis team	Review documentation to determine if organization has instituted and integrated team of forensic/malicious code analysts, tool developers, and real-time operations personnel to assist in support and analysis efforts for incident response. Discuss with System Owner and Security Officer.	SP 800-61, rev. 2	*Examine:* Incident response policy; procedures addressing incident response planning and security analysis team integration; incident response plan; other relevant documents or records. *Interview:* Organizational personnel with incident response and information security analysis responsibilities; organizational personnel with information security responsibilities; organizational personnel participating on integrated security analysis teams.

I. *Maintenance family*

FIPS-200 provides the following criteria for this family of controls: Maintenance (MA):
Organizations must: (i) perform periodic and timely maintenance on organizational
information systems; and (ii) provide effective controls on the tools, techniques,
mechanisms, and personnel used to conduct information system maintenance.

The primary assessment areas for these controls include:

a. Review processes that perform periodic and timely maintenance on organizational information systems.
b. Evaluate processes that provide effective controls on the tools, techniques, mechanisms,
and personnel used to conduct information system maintenance.

Control number	Control name	Assessment methods	Notes and guidance documents	SP 800-53A guidance
MA-1	System maintenance policy and procedures	Review organizational and system documentation to determine that proper maintenance policies and procedures are in effect for system under review. Discuss with System Owner, Operational Manager, and Security Officer.	SP 800-12, SP 800-100	*Examine:* Maintenance policy and procedures; other relevant documents or records. *Interview:* Organizational personnel with maintenance responsibilities; organizational personnel with information security responsibilities.
MA-2	Controlled maintenance	Review documentation to ensure that the maintenance records for all types of maintenance are maintained for system. This control addresses the information security aspects of the information system maintenance program and applies to all types of maintenance to any system component (including applications) conducted by any local or nonlocal entity (e.g., in-contract, warranty, in-house, software maintenance agreement). Review all records and documented results for accuracy and completeness. Discuss with System Owner and Security Officer.		*Examine:* Information system maintenance policy; procedures addressing controlled information system maintenance; maintenance records; manufacturer/vendor maintenance specifications; equipment sanitization records; media sanitization records; other relevant documents or records. *Interview:* Organizational personnel with information system maintenance responsibilities; organizational personnel with information security responsibilities; organizational personnel responsible for media sanitization; system/network administrators. *Test:* Organizational processes for scheduling, performing, documenting, reviewing, approving, and monitoring maintenance and repairs for the information system; organizational processes for sanitizing information system components; automated mechanisms supporting and/or implementing controlled maintenance; automated mechanisms implementing sanitization of information system components.
MA-2(1)	Controlled maintenance: record content		Withdrawn: Incorporated into MA-2	
MA-2(2)	Controlled maintenance: Automated maintenance activities	Review documentation to ensure that maintenance is scheduled automatically, records for all maintenance performed are controlled automatically and		*Examine:* Information system maintenance policy; procedures addressing controlled information system maintenance; automated mechanisms supporting information system maintenance activities; information system configuration settings and

(Continued)

Control number	Control name	Assessment methods	Notes and guidance documents	SP 800-53A guidance
		reports are generated from automatic system. Test maintenance system by generating automatic report and verifying maintenance performed. Discuss with System Owner and Security Officer.		associated documentation; maintenance records; other relevant documents or records. *Interview:* Organizational personnel with information system maintenance responsibilities; organizational personnel with information security responsibilities; system/network administrators. *Test:* Automated mechanisms supporting and/or implementing controlled maintenance; automated mechanisms supporting and/or implementing production of records of maintenance and repair actions.
MA-3	Maintenance tools	Review the documentation for the use of maintenance tools on system. These maintenance tools can include hardware/software diagnostic test equipment and hardware/software packet sniffers, which could have potential security implications for the system. Review and test the on-hand maintenance tools and review policies for the use of these tools. Discuss with System Owner and Security Officer.	SP 800-88, rev. 1	*Examine:* Information system maintenance policy; procedures addressing information system maintenance tools; information system maintenance tools and associated documentation; maintenance records; other relevant documents or records. *Interview:* Organizational personnel with information system maintenance responsibilities; organizational personnel with information security responsibilities. *Test:* Organizational processes for approving, controlling, and monitoring maintenance tools; automated mechanisms supporting and/or implementing approval, control, and/or monitoring of maintenance tools.
MA-3(1)	Maintenance tools: Inspect tools	Review documentation for inspection of all maintenance tools brought into facility for use on system. Verify inspection reports. Discuss with System Owner and Security Officer.	SP 800-88, rev. 1	*Examine:* Information system maintenance policy; procedures addressing information system maintenance tools; information system maintenance tool inspection records; maintenance records; other relevant documents or records. *Interview:* Organizational personnel with information system maintenance responsibilities; organizational personnel with information security responsibilities. *Test:* Organizational processes for inspecting maintenance tools; automated mechanisms supporting and/or implementing inspection of maintenance tools.

MA-3(2)	Maintenance tools: Inspect media	Review documentation for the inspection of all maintenance media brought into facility for use on system. Verify inspection reports. Discuss with System Owner and Security Officer.	SP 800-88, rev. 1	*Examine:* Information system maintenance policy; procedures addressing information system maintenance tools; information system maintenance tools and associated documentation; maintenance records; other relevant documents or records. *Interview:* Organizational personnel with information system maintenance responsibilities; organizational personnel with information security responsibilities. *Test:* Organizational process for inspecting media for malicious code; automated mechanisms supporting and/or implementing inspection of media used for maintenance.
MA-3(3)	Maintenance tools: Prevent unauthorized removal	Review documentation for the inspection of all maintenance tools removed from facility. Review documentation of the inspection reports verifying checks for organizational data were performed. Discuss with System Owner and Security Officer.	SP 800-88, rev. 1	*Examine:* Information system maintenance policy; procedures addressing information system maintenance tools; information system maintenance tools and associated documentation; maintenance records; equipment sanitization records; media sanitization records; exemptions for equipment removal; other relevant documents or records. *Interview:* Organizational personnel with information system maintenance responsibilities; organizational personnel with information security responsibilities; organizational personnel responsible for media sanitization. *Test:* Organizational process for preventing unauthorized removal of information; automated mechanisms supporting media sanitization or destruction of equipment; automated mechanisms supporting verification of media sanitization.
MA-3(4)	Maintenance tools: Restricted tool use	Review documentation, which stipulates only authorized personnel, may conduct maintenance activities on system. Confirm actions via maintenance reports and inspections. Discuss with System Owner and Security Officer.	SP 800-88, rev. 1	*Examine:* Information system maintenance policy; procedures addressing information system maintenance tools; information system maintenance tools and associated documentation; list of personnel authorized to use maintenance tools; maintenance tool usage records; maintenance records; other relevant documents or records. *Interview:* Organizational personnel with information system maintenance responsibilities; organizational personnel with information security responsibilities. *Test:* Organizational process for restricting use of maintenance tools; automated

(Continued)

Control number	Control name	Assessment methods	Notes and guidance documents	SP 800-53A guidance
				mechanisms supporting and/or implementing restricted use of maintenance tools.
MA-4	Nonlocal maintenance	Review documentation to ensure only authorized nonlocal maintenance is conducted with Control IA-2 requirements. Nonlocal maintenance and diagnostic activities are those activities conducted by individuals communicating through a network, either an external network (e.g., the Internet) or an internal network. Confirm via maintenance reports, inspections, and log reviews of maintenance activities. Discuss with System Owner and Security Officer.	FIPS 140-2, FIPS-197, FIPS-201, SP 800-63, SP 800-88, rev.1, CNSSP 15	*Examine:* Information system maintenance policy; procedures addressing nonlocal information system maintenance; security plan; information system design documentation; information system configuration settings and associated documentation; maintenance records; diagnostic records; other relevant documents or records. *Interview:* Organizational personnel with information system maintenance responsibilities; organizational personnel with information security responsibilities; system/network administrators. *Test:* Organizational processes for managing nonlocal maintenance; automated mechanisms implementing, supporting, and/or managing nonlocal maintenance; automated mechanisms for strong authentication of nonlocal maintenance diagnostic sessions; automated mechanisms for terminating nonlocal maintenance sessions and network connections.
MA-4(1)	Nonlocal maintenance: Auditing and review	Review documentation to ensure only authorized nonlocal maintenance is conducted with Control IA-2 requirements and this maintenance is audited and reviewed by the organization. Confirm via maintenance reports, inspections and log reviews of maintenance activities. Discuss with System Owner and Security Officer.	FIPS 140-2, FIPS-197, FIPS-201, SP 800-63, SP 800-88, rev.1, CNSSP 15	*Examine:* Information system maintenance policy; procedures addressing nonlocal information system maintenance; list of audit events; information system configuration settings and associated documentation; maintenance records; diagnostic records; audit records; reviews of maintenance and diagnostic session records; other relevant documents or records. *Interview:* Organizational personnel with information system maintenance responsibilities; organizational personnel with information security responsibilities; organizational personnel with audit and review responsibilities; system/network administrators. *Test:* Organizational processes for audit and review of nonlocal maintenance; automated mechanisms supporting and/or implementing audit and review of nonlocal maintenance.

MA-4(2)	Nonlocal maintenance: Document nonlocal maintenance	Review system security plan to ensure that it documents the policies and procedures for the establishment and use of nonlocal maintenance and diagnostic connections. Discuss with System Owner and Security Officer.	FIPS 140-2, FIPS-197, FIPS-201, SP 800-63, SP 800-88, rev.1, CNSSP 15	*Examine*: Information system maintenance policy; procedures addressing nonlocal information system maintenance; security plan; maintenance records; diagnostic records; audit records; other relevant documents or records. *Interview*: Organizational personnel with information system maintenance responsibilities; organizational personnel with information security responsibilities.
MA-4(3)	Nonlocal maintenance: Comparable security/sanitization	Review documentation to ensure the nonlocal maintenance system employed has at least comparable level of security as system undergoing maintenance. Identify security level of nonlocal maintenance and confirm its level of security. Discuss with System Owner and Security Officer.	FIPS 140-2, FIPS-197, FIPS-201, SP 800-63, SP 800-88, rev.1, CNSSP 15	*Examine*: Information system maintenance policy; procedures addressing nonlocal information system maintenance; service provider contracts and/or service-level agreements; maintenance records; inspection records; audit records; equipment sanitization records; media sanitization records; other relevant documents or records. *Interview*: Organizational personnel with information system maintenance responsibilities; information system maintenance provider; organizational personnel with information security responsibilities; organizational personnel responsible for media sanitization; system/network administrators. *Test*: Organizational processes for comparable security and sanitization for nonlocal maintenance; organizational processes for removal, sanitization, and inspection of components serviced via nonlocal maintenance; automated mechanisms supporting and/or implementing component sanitization and inspection.
MA-4(4)	Nonlocal maintenance Authentication/separation of maintenance sessions	Review documentation to ensure maintenance sessions are isolated from other network session when active. Verify via logs and observation. Discuss with System Owner, Network Administrators, and Security Officer.	FIPS 140-2, FIPS-197, FIPS-201, SP 800-63, SP 800-88, rev.1, CNSSP 15	*Examine*: Information system maintenance policy; procedures addressing nonlocal information system maintenance; information system design documentation; information system configuration settings and associated documentation; maintenance records; audit records; other relevant documents or records. *Interview*: Organizational personnel with information system maintenance responsibilities; network engineers; organizational personnel with information security responsibilities; system/network administrators. *Test*: Organizational processes for protecting nonlocal maintenance sessions; automated

(Continued)

Control number	Control name	Assessment methods	Notes and guidance documents	SP 800-53A guidance
				mechanisms implementing replay resistant authenticators; automated mechanisms implementing logically separated/encrypted communications paths.
MA-4(5)	Nonlocal maintenance: Approvals and notifications	Review documentation to ensure appropriate notification and approvals are conducted and received by organizational personnel and the System Owner. Discuss with System Owner and Security Officer.	FIPS 140-2, FIPS-197, FIPS-201, SP 800-63, SP 800-88, rev.1, CNSSP 15	*Examine:* Information system maintenance policy; procedures addressing nonlocal information system maintenance; security plan; notifications supporting nonlocal maintenance sessions; maintenance records; audit records; other relevant documents or records. *Interview:* Organizational personnel with information system maintenance responsibilities; organizational personnel with notification responsibilities; organizational personnel with approval responsibilities; organizational personnel with information security responsibilities. *Test:* Organizational processes for approving and notifying personnel regarding nonlocal maintenance; automated mechanisms supporting notification and approval of nonlocal maintenance.
MA-4(6)	Nonlocal maintenance: Cryptographic protection	Review documentation to ensure that the system implements cryptographic mechanisms to protect the integrity and confidentiality of nonlocal maintenance and diagnostic communications. Verify via system review of maintenance actions. Discuss with Security Officer.	FIPS 140-2, FIPS-197, FIPS-201, SP 800-63, SP 800-88, rev.1, CNSSP 15	*Examine:* Information system maintenance policy; procedures addressing nonlocal information system maintenance; information system design documentation; information system configuration settings and associated documentation; cryptographic mechanisms protecting nonlocal maintenance activities; maintenance records; diagnostic records; audit records; other relevant documents or records. *Interview:* Organizational personnel with information system maintenance responsibilities; network engineers; organizational personnel with information security responsibilities; system/network administrators. *Test:* Cryptographic mechanisms protecting nonlocal maintenance and diagnostic communications.
MA-4(7)	Nonlocal maintenance: Remote disconnect verification	Review documentation to ensure that the system provides for full disconnect when maintenance is completed and remote access is terminated. Verify via logs and session termination notices.	FIPS 140-2, FIPS-197, FIPS-201, SP 800-63, SP 800-88, rev.1, CNSSP 15	*Examine:* Information system maintenance policy; procedures addressing nonlocal information system maintenance; information system design documentation; information system configuration settings and associated documentation; crypto graphic mechanisms protecting nonlocal maintenance activities;

Control	Name	Guidance	Assessment
		Discuss with System Owner and Security Officer.	maintenance records; diagnostic records; audit records; other relevant documents or records. *Interview:* Organizational personnel with information system maintenance responsibilities; network engineers; organizational personnel with information security responsibilities; system/network administrators. *Test:* Automated mechanisms implementing remote disconnect verifications of terminated nonlocal maintenance and diagnostic sessions.
MA-5	Maintenance personnel	Review documentation for maintenance personnel and their system level access to the components of the system. Discuss access process and system-level criteria with System Owner, security staff, operations staff, and Security Officer.	*Examine:* Information system maintenance policy; procedures addressing maintenance personnel; service provider contracts; service-level agreements; list of authorized personnel; maintenance records; access control records; other relevant documents or records. *Interview:* Organizational personnel with information system maintenance responsibilities; organizational personnel with information security responsibilities. *Test:* Organizational processes for authorizing and managing maintenance personnel; automated mechanisms supporting and/or implementing authorization of maintenance personnel.
MA-5(1)	Maintenance personnel: Individuals without appropriate access	Review documentation for use of noncleared personnel on system. This control denies individuals who lack appropriate security clearances (i.e., individuals who do not possess security clearances or possess security clearances at a lower level than required) or who are not the US citizens, visual and electronic access to any classified information, controlled unclassified information (CUI), or any other sensitive information contained on organizational information systems when it is installed. Discuss with security staff, operations staff, facility	*Examine:* Information system maintenance policy; procedures addressing maintenance personnel; information system media protection policy; physical and environmental protection policy; security plan; list of maintenance personnel requiring escort/supervision; maintenance records; access control records; other relevant documents or records. *Interview:* Organizational personnel with information system maintenance responsibilities; organizational personnel with personnel security responsibilities; organizational personnel with physical access control responsibilities; organizational personnel with information security responsibilities; organizational personnel responsible for media sanitization; system/network administrators. *Test:* Organizational processes for managing maintenance personnel without appropriate access; automated mechanisms supporting

(Continued)

Control number	Control name	Assessment methods	Notes and guidance documents	SP 800-53A guidance
		security staff, System Owner, and Security Officer.		and/or implementing alternative security safeguards; automated mechanisms supporting and/or implementing information storage component sanitization.
MA-5(2)	Maintenance personnel: Security clearances for classified systems	Review documentation to ensure that personnel performing maintenance and diagnostic activities on an information system processing, storing, or transmitting classified information possess security clearances and formal access approvals for at least the highest classification level and for all compartments of information on the system. Discuss with security staff, operations staff, facility security staff, System Owner, and Security Officer.		*Examine:* Information system maintenance policy; procedures addressing maintenance personnel; personnel records; maintenance records; access control records; access credentials; access authorizations; other relevant documents or records. *Interview:* Organizational personnel with information system maintenance responsibilities; organizational personnel with personnel security responsibilities; organizational personnel with physical access control responsibilities; organizational personnel with information security responsibilities. *Test:* Organizational processes for managing security clearances for maintenance personnel.
MA-5(3)	Maintenance personnel: Citizenship requirements for classified systems	Review documentation to ensure that personnel performing maintenance and diagnostic activities on an information system processing, storing, or transmitting classified information are the US citizens. Discuss with security staff, operations staff, facility security staff, System Owner, and Security Officer.		*Examine:* Information system maintenance policy; procedures addressing maintenance personnel; personnel records; maintenance records; access control records; access credentials; access authorizations; other relevant documents or records. *Interview:* Organizational personnel with information system maintenance responsibilities; organizational personnel with personnel security responsibilities; organizational personnel with information security responsibilities.
MA-5(4)	Maintenance personnel: Foreign nationals	Review documentation to ensure that cleared foreign nationals are used to conduct maintenance and diagnostic activities on classified information systems only when the systems are jointly owned and operated by the United States and foreign allied governments		*Examine:* Information system maintenance policy; procedures addressing maintenance personnel; information system media protection policy; access control policy and procedures; physical and environmental protection policy and procedures; memorandum of agreement; maintenance records; access control records; access credentials; access authorizations; other relevant documents or records.

		or owned by foreign allied governments. Discuss with security staff, operations staff, facility ecurity staff, System Owner, and Security Officer.	*Interview:* Organizational personnel with information system maintenance responsibilities, organizational personnel with personnel security responsibilities; organizational personnel managing memoranda of agreements; organizational personnel with information security responsibilities. *Test:* Organizational processes for managing foreign national maintenance personnel.
MA-5(5)	Maintenance personnel: Nonsystem-related maintenance	Review documentation to ensure personnel performing maintenance activities in other capacities not directly related to the information system include, for example, physical plant personnel and janitorial personnel have appropriate access. Discuss with security staff, operations staff, facility security staff, System Owner, and Security Officer.	*Examine:* Information system maintenance policy; procedures addressing maintenance personnel; information system media protection policy; access control policy and procedures; physical and environmental protection policy and procedures; maintenance records; access control records; access authorizations; other relevant documents or records. *Interview:* Organizational personnel with information system maintenance responsibilities; organizational personnel with personnel security responsibilities; organizational personnel with physical access control responsibilities; organizational personnel with information security responsibilities.
MA-6	Timely maintenance	Review documentation and contracts in place to ensure appropriate levels of maintenance can be accomplished within specified time frames, as determined by the organization. Discuss with System Owner, operations staff, and Security Officer.	*Examine:* Information system maintenance policy; procedures addressing information system maintenance; service provider contracts; service-level agreements; inventory and availability of spare parts; security plan; other relevant documents or records. *Interview:* Organizational personnel with information system maintenance responsibilities; organizational personnel with acquisition responsibilities; organizational personnel with information security responsibilities; system/network administrators. *Test:* Organizational processes for ensuring timely maintenance.
MA-6(1)	Timely maintenance: Preventive maintenance	Review documentation to ensure that the preventive maintenance (PM) processes and procedures are being accomplished appropriately and within time-based criteria for the system. Review PM sheets, procedures and reports. Discuss	*Examine:* Information system maintenance policy; procedures addressing information system maintenance; service provider contracts; service-level agreements; security plan; maintenance records; list of system components requiring preventive maintenance; other relevant documents or records. *Interview:* Organizational personnel with information system

(Continued)

Control number	Control name	Assessment methods	Notes and guidance documents	SP 800-53A guidance
		with operations staff, maintenance staff, System Owner, and Security Officer.		maintenance responsibilities; organizational personnel with information security responsibilities; system/ network administrators. *Test:* Organizational processes for preventive maintenance; automated mechanisms supporting and/or implementing preventive maintenance.
MA-6(2)	Timely maintenance: Predictive maintenance	Review documentation to ensure that the predictive maintenance actions are being conducted appropriately for the system. Predictive maintenance, or condition-based maintenance, attempts to evaluate the condition of equipment by performing periodic or continuous (online) equipment condition monitoring. Discuss with System Owner, maintenance staff, and Security Officer.		*Examine:* Information system maintenance policy; procedures addressing information system maintenance; service provider contracts; service-level agreements; security plan; maintenance records; list of system components requiring predictive maintenance; other relevant documents or records. *Interview:* Organizational personnel with information system maintenance responsibilities; organizational personnel with information security responsibilities; system/ network administrators. *Test:* Organizational processes for predictive maintenance; automated mechanisms supporting and/or implementing predictive maintenance.
MA-6(3)	Timely maintenance: Automated support for predictive maintenance	Review documentation to ensure the organization employs automated mechanisms to transfer predictive maintenance data to a computerized maintenance management system. Review output reports and trigger cards for maintenance actions from automated system to ensure proper operation. Discuss with System Owner, maintenance staff, operations staff, and Security Officer.		*Examine:* Information system maintenance policy; procedures addressing information system maintenance; service provider contracts; service-level agreements; security plan; maintenance records; list of system components requiring predictive maintenance; other relevant documents or records. *Interview:* Organizational personnel with information system maintenance responsibilities; organizational personnel with information security responsibilities; system/ network administrators. *Test:* Automated mechanisms implementing the transfer of predictive maintenance data to a computerized maintenance management system; operations of the computer maintenance management system.

J. *Media protection family*

FIPS-200 provides the following criteria for this family of controls: Media protection (MP):
Organizations must: (i) protect information system media, both paper and digital;
(ii) limit access to information on information system media to authorized users; and
(iii) sanitize or destroy information system media before disposal or release for reuse.

The primary assessment areas for these controls include:

a. Audit mechanisms that facilitate the protection of paper information system media.
b. Review system controls that facilitate the protection of digital information system media.
c. Assess system safeguards that enable the limitation of access to information on information system media to authorized users.
d. Evaluate systems mechanisms that enable the sanitization or destruction of information system media before disposal or release for reuse.

Control number	Control name	Assessment methods	Notes and guidance documents	SP 800-53A guidance
MP-1	Media protection policy and procedures	Review documentation for organization to ensure all media protection policies and procedures are defined and in practice within the organization. Discuss with operations staff, security staff, System Owner, and Security Officer.	SP 800-12, SP 800-88, rev. 1, SP 800-100	*Examine:* Media protection policy and procedures; other relevant documents or records. *Interview:* Organizational personnel with media protection responsibilities; organizational personnel with information security responsibilities.
MP-2	Media access	Review documentation for organization to ensure that appropriate media access actions are active. Media includes both digital and nondigital media, which require controlled access in accordance with organizational and legal requirements. Discuss with operations staff, System Owner, and Security Officer.	FIPS-199, SP 800-111	*Examine:* Information system media protection policy; procedures addressing media access restrictions; access control policy and procedures; physical and environmental protection policy and procedures; media storage facilities; access control records; other relevant documents or records. *Interview:* Organizational personnel with information system media protection responsibilities; organizational personnel with information security responsibilities; system/network administrators. *Test:* Organizational processes for restricting information media; automated mechanisms supporting and/or implementing media access restrictions.
MP-2(1)	Media access: Automated restricted access		Withdrawn: Incorporated into MP-4(2)	
MP-2(2)	Media access: Cryptographic protection		Withdrawn: Incorporated into SC-28(1)	
MP-3	Media marking	Review documentation of organization to ensure that media marking is practiced for appropriate media used. Media security marking refers to the application/use of human-readable security attributes. Media security labeling refers to the application/use of security attributes with regard to internal data structures	FIPS-199, AC-16	*Examine:* Information system media protection policy; procedures addressing media marking; physical and environmental protection policy and procedures; security plan; list of information system media marking security attributes; designated controlled areas; other relevant documents or records. *Interview:* Organizational personnel with information system media protection and marking responsibilities; organizational personnel

			within information systems. Test both types of marking to ensure appropriate actions are taken with each type. Discuss with operations staff, Security Officer, and System Owner.	with information security responsibilities. *Test:* Organizational processes for marking information media; automated mechanisms supporting and/or implementing media marking.
MP-4	Media storage	FIPS-199, SP 800-56, SP 800-57, SP 800-111	Review documentation for the system to ensure that media used for the system is stored properly in accordance with data sensitivity criteria, classification requirements, physical needs, and informational usage actions. Observe storage locations and methods to determine compliance with federal, legal and information regulations, and standards. Discuss with operations staff, Security Officer, and System Owner.	*Examine:* Information system media protection policy; procedures addressing media storage; physical and environmental protection policy and procedures; access control policy and procedures; security plan; information system media; designated controlled areas; other relevant documents or records. *Interview:* Organizational personnel with information system media protection and storage responsibilities; organizational personnel with information security responsibilities. *Test:* Organizational processes for storing information media; automated mechanisms supporting and/or implementing secure media storage/media protection.
MP-4(1)	Media storage: Cryptographic protection	Withdrawn: Incorporated into SC-28(1)		
MP-4(2)	Media storage: Automated restricted access	FIPS-199, SP 800-56, SP 800-57, SP 800-111	Review documentation for organization to ensure storage and operational areas for media are utilizing a controlled access method for security of media. Observe storage controlled access area to ensure implementation and operation. Discuss with System Owner, operations staff, and Security Officer.	*Examine:* Information system media protection policy; procedures addressing media storage; access control policy and procedures; physical and environmental protection policy and procedures; information system design documentation; information system configuration settings and associated documentation; media storage facilities; access control devices; access control records; audit records; other relevant documents or records. *Interview:* Organizational personnel with information system media protection and storage responsibilities; organizational personnel with information security responsibilities; system/network administrators. *Test:* Automated mechanisms restricting access to media storage areas; automated mechanisms auditing access attempts and access granted to media storage areas.

(Continued)

Control number	Control name	Assessment methods	Notes and guidance documents	SP 800-53A guidance
MP-5	Media transport	Review documentation for organization to determine the control mechanisms in place and active for media transport external to organization. Observe organizational actions with methods and techniques for controlled transport, such as locked containers or encryption of media to verify safe and secure transport by both internal parties and external third-party transport organizations. Discuss with operations staff, System Owner, and Security Officer.	FIPS-199, SP 800-60	*Examine:* Information system media protection policy; procedures addressing media storage; physical and environmental protection policy and procedures; access control policy and procedures; security plan; information system media; designated controlled areas; other relevant documents or records. *Interview:* Organizational personnel with information system media protection and storage responsibilities; organizational personnel with information security responsibilities; system/network administrators. *Test:* Organizational processes for storing information media; automated mechanisms supporting and/or implementing media storage/media protection.
MP-5(1)	Media transport: Protection outside of controlled areas		Withdrawn: Incorporated into MP-5	
MP-5(2)	Media transport: Documentation of activities		Withdrawn: Incorporated into MP-5	
MP-5(3)	Media transport: Custodians	Review documentation for organization to ensure that use of identified media custodians is enforced, which provides specific points of contact during the media transport process and facilitate individual accountability. Observe process during transport for verification of implementation. Discuss with System Owner, operations staff, and Security Officer.	FIPS-199, SP 800-60	*Examine:* Information system media protection policy; procedures addressing media transport; physical and environmental protection policy and procedures; information system media transport records; audit records; other relevant documents or records. *Interview:* Organizational personnel with information system media transport responsibilities; organizational personnel with information security responsibilities.
MP-5(4)	Media transport: Cryptographic protection	Review documentation for organization to determine the extent of implementation of encryption for	FIPS-199, SP 800-60	*Examine:* Information system media protection policy; procedures addressing media transport; information system design documentation;

		media transport components and devices, such as portable storage devices (e.g., USB memory sticks, compact disks, digital video disks, external/removable hard disk drives) and mobile devices with storage capability (e.g., smart phones, tablets, E-readers). Observe encryption of media process to verify implementation. Discuss with operations staff, System Owner, and Security Officer.		information system configuration settings and associated documentation; information system media transport records; audit records; other relevant documents or records. *Interview:* Organizational personnel with information system media transport responsibilities; organizational personnel with information security responsibilities. *Test:* Cryptographic mechanisms protecting information on digital media during transportation outside controlled areas.
MP-6	Media sanitization	Review documentation for organization to determine extent of sanitation efforts implemented controlling the information used, stored, and saved by the system. Observe all potential locations of information media, such as found in scanners, copiers, printers, notebook computers, workstations, network components, and mobile devices for sanitation efforts. Observe sanitation actions to ensure efforts provide for the removal of information from the media such that the information cannot be retrieved or reconstructed. Sanitization techniques, including clearing, purging, cryptographic erase, and destruction, prevent the disclosure of information to unauthorized individuals, when such media is reused or released for disposal should all be utilized as appropriate for information requirements. Discuss with System Owner, security staff, Operations staff, and Security Officer.	FIPS-199, SP 800-60, SP 800-88, rev. 1	*Examine:* Information system media protection policy; procedures addressing media sanitization and disposal; applicable federal standards and policies addressing media sanitization; media sanitization records; audit records; information system design documentation; information system configuration settings and associated documentation; other relevant documents or records. *Interview:* Organizational personnel with media sanitization responsibilities; organizational personnel with information security responsibilities; system/network administrators. *Test:* Organizational processes for media sanitization; automated mechanisms supporting and/or implementing media sanitization.

(Continued)

Control number	Control name	Assessment methods	Notes and guidance documents	SP 800-53A guidance
MP-6(1)	Media sanitization: Review/ approve/track/ document/verify	Review documentation for organization on sanitation processes and procedures to determine compliance with records-retention policies and requirements. Review results and reports defining the various sanitation efforts for completeness and accuracy. Discuss with operations staff, System Owner, and Security Officer.	FIPS-199, SP 800-60, SP 800-88, rev. 1	*Examine:* Information system media protection policy; procedures addressing media sanitization and disposal; media sanitization and disposal records; review records for media sanitization and disposal actions; approvals for media sanitization and disposal actions; tracking records; verification records; audit records; other relevant documents or records. *Interview:* Organizational personnel with information system media sanitization and disposal responsibilities; organizational personnel with information security responsibilities; system/network administrators. *Test:* Organizational processes for media sanitization; automated mechanisms supporting and/or implementing media sanitization.
MP-6(2)	Media sanitization: Equipment testing	Review documentation of organization to determine the testing of sanitation equipment is verified and validated as fully functional and complete. Discuss with operations staff, System Owner, and Security Officer.	FIPS-199, SP 800-60, SP 800-88, rev. 1	*Examine:* Information system media protection policy; procedures addressing media sanitization and disposal; procedures addressing testing of media sanitization equipment; results of media sanitization equipment and procedures testing; audit records; other relevant documents or records. *Interview:* Organizational personnel with information system media sanitization responsibilities; organizational personnel with information security responsibilities. *Test:* Organizational processes for media sanitization; automated mechanisms supporting and/or implementing media sanitization.
MP-6(3)	Media sanitization: Nondestructive techniques	Review documentation for organization to determine the extent of nondestructive sanitation performed on various media, especially portable media, during initial usage efforts. This is focused on media to be utilized for media containing classified information and controlled unclassified information (CUI). Observe sanitation actions to	FIPS-199, SP 800-60, SP 800-88, rev. 1	*Examine:* Information system media protection policy; procedures addressing media sanitization and disposal; list of circumstances requiring sanitization of portable storage devices; media sanitization records; audit records; other relevant documents or records. *Interview:* Organizational personnel with information system media sanitization responsibilities; organizational personnel with information security responsibilities. *Test:* Organizational processes for media sanitization of

MP-6(4)	Media sanitization: Controlled unclassified information	ensure that proper results and actions are correct and complete. Discuss with System Owner, operations staff, security staff, and Security Officer.	Withdrawn: Incorporated into MP-6	portable storage devices; automated mechanisms supporting and/or implementing media sanitization.
MP-6(5)	Media sanitization: Classified information		Withdrawn: Incorporated into MP-6	
MP-6(6)	Media sanitization: Media destruction		Withdrawn: Incorporated into MP-6	
MP-6(7)	Media sanitization: Dual authorization	Review documentation for organization to determine the process and implementation of dual control of sanitation efforts to ensure that media sanitization cannot occur unless two technically qualified individuals conduct the task jointly. Observe process to ensure implementation and completeness of actions. Discuss with operations staff, System Owner, Information Owner(s), and Security Officer.	FIPS-199, SP 800-60, SP 800-88, rev. 1	*Examine:* Information system media protection policy; procedures addressing media sanitization and disposal; list of information system media requiring dual authorization for sanitization; authorization records; media sanitization records; audit records; other relevant documents or records. *Interview:* Organizational personnel with information system media sanitization responsibilities; organizational personnel with information security responsibilities; system/network administrators. *Test:* Organizational processes requiring dual authorization for media sanitization; automated mechanisms supporting and/or implementing media sanitization; automated mechanisms supporting and/or implementing dual authorization.
MP-6(8)	Media sanitization: Remote purging/wiping of information	Review documentation for organization on usage and actions for remote purging of media components in order to protect data/information on organizational information	FIPS-199, SP 800-60, SP 800-88, rev. 1	*Examine:* Information system media protection policy; procedures addressing media sanitization and disposal; information system design documentation; information system configuration settings and associated documentation; media

(Continued)

Control number	Control name	Assessment methods	Notes and guidance documents	SP 800-53A guidance
		systems, system components, or devices (e.g., mobile devices), if such systems, components, or devices are obtained by unauthorized individuals This process includes mobile remote wipe and utilization of complete purging of storage devices. Evaluate capabilities through enacting test purge sample of select devices or components. Discuss with security staff, Security Officer, operations staff, and System Owner.		sanitization records; audit records; other relevant documents or records. *Interview:* Organizational personnel with information system media sanitization responsibilities; organizational personnel with information security responsibilities; system/ network administrators. *Test:* Organizational processes for purging/wiping media; automated mechanisms supporting and/or implementing purge/wipe capabilities.
MP-7	Media use	Review documentation for organization use of certain types of media devices on information systems, such as restricting/ prohibiting the use of flash drives or external hard disk drives or even portable devices and smart devices. Observe implementation by testing connections of restricted devices in test environment. Discuss with System Owner, operations staff, and Security Officer.	FIPS-199, SP 800-111	*Examine:* Information system media protection policy; system use policy; procedures addressing media usage restrictions; security plan; rules of behavior; information system design documentation; information system configuration settings and associated documentation; audit records; other relevant documents or records. *Interview:* Organizational personnel with information system media use responsibilities; organizational personnel with information security responsibilities; system/ network administrators. *Test:* Organizational processes for media use; automated mechanisms restricting or prohibiting use of information system media on information systems or system components.
MP-7(1)	Media use: Prohibit use without owner	Review documentation for organization to ensure that all devices and media has assigned ownership. Review assignment documentation to verify ownership and responsibilities are defined and officially assigned. Discuss with System Owner, operations staff, and Security Officer.	FIPS-199, SP 800-111	*Examine:* Information system media protection policy; system use policy; procedures addressing media usage restrictions; security plan; rules of behavior; information system design documentation; information system configuration settings and associated documentation; audit records; other relevant documents or records. *Interview:* Organizational personnel with information system media use responsibilities; organizational personnel

MP-7(2)	Media use: Prohibit use of sanitization-resistant media	Review documentation to ensure that organization implements sanitation-resistant media for use on system, such as compact flash, embedded flash on boards and devices, solid state drives, or USB removable media. Test methods by attempting to purge these types of media and review results. Discuss with System Owner, security staff, and Security Officer.	FIPS-199, SP 800-111	with information security responsibilities; system/network administrators. *Test:* Organizational processes for media use; automated mechanisms prohibiting use of media on information systems or system components. *Examine:* Information system media protection policy; system use policy; procedures addressing media usage restrictions; rules of behavior; audit records; other relevant documents or records. *Interview:* Organizational personnel with information system media use responsibilities; organizational personnel with information security responsibilities; system/network administrators. *Test:* Organizational processes for media use; automated mechanisms prohibiting use of media on information systems or system components.
MP-8	Media downgrading	Review documentation for organization to determine use and implementation of media downgrading efforts for media subject to release outside of the organization, whether or not the media is considered removable. Ensure downgrading efforts implement complete purging of media to include slack space and other system level areas of media. Test by evaluating subject media to forensics evaluation to ensure all data, sensitive or otherwise, is removed from media. Discuss with System Owner, security staff, and Security Officer.	SP 800-88, rev. 1	*Examine:* Information system media protection policy; procedures addressing media downgrading; system categorization documentation; list of media requiring downgrading; records of media downgrading; audit records; other relevant documents or records. *Interview:* Organizational personnel with information system media downgrading responsibilities; organizational personnel with information security responsibilities; system/network administrators. *Test:* Organizational processes for media downgrading; automated mechanisms supporting and/or implementing media downgrading.
MP-8(1)	Media downgrading: Documentation of process	Review documentation for organizational efforts of downgrading media, such as providing information such as the downgrading technique employed, the identification number of the downgraded media, and	SP 800-88, rev. 1	*Examine:* Information system media protection policy; procedures addressing media downgrading; list of media requiring downgrading; records of media downgrading; audit records; other relevant documents or records. *Interview:* Organizational personnel with information system media

(Continued)

Control number	Control name	Assessment methods	Notes and guidance documents	SP 800-53A guidance
		the identity of the individual that authorized and/or performed the downgrading action. Review in detail the processes, procedures and implementation guidelines for these events. Discuss with System Owner, security staff, operations staff, and Security Officer.		downgrading responsibilities; organizational personnel with information security responsibilities. *Test:* Organizational processes for media downgrading; automated mechanisms supporting and/or implementing media downgrading.
MP-8(2)	Media downgrading: Equipment testing	Review documentation for organization to ensure that all required testing of downgrading equipment is performed in accordance with organizational standards, vendor specifications, and agency regulations. Discuss with System Owner, security staff, and Security Officer.	SP 800-88, rev. 1	*Examine:* Information system media protection policy; procedures addressing media downgrading; procedures addressing testing of media downgrading equipment; results of downgrading equipment and procedures testing; audit records: other relevant documents or records. *Interview:* Organizational personnel with information system media downgrading responsibilities; organizational personnel with information security responsibilities. *Test:* Organizational processes for media downgrading; automated mechanisms supporting and/or implementing media downgrading; automated mechanisms supporting and/or implementing tests for downgrading equipment.
MP-8(3)	Media downgrading: Controlled unclassified information	Review documentation for organization to ensure all downgrading efforts for CUI information are conducted in accordance with federal guidelines, agency regulations, and organizational requirements. Discuss with System Owner, Information Owner(s), operations staff, and Security Officer.	SP 800-88, rev. 1	*Examine:* Information system media protection policy; access authorization policy; procedures addressing downgrading of media containing CUI; applicable federal and organizational standards and policies regarding protection of CUI; media downgrading records; other relevant documents or records. *Interview:* Organizational personnel with information system media downgrading responsibilities; organizational personnel with information security responsibilities. *Test:* Organizational processes for media downgrading; automated mechanisms supporting and/or implementing media downgrading.

| MP-8(4) | Media downgrading: Classified information | Review documentation for organization to ensure that all downgrading efforts for classified information are conducted in accordance with NSA instructions, federal guidelines, agency regulations, and organizational requirements. Discuss with System Owner, Information Owner(s), operations staff, and Security Officer. | SP 800-88, rev. 1 | *Examine:* Information system media protection policy; access authorization policy; procedures addressing downgrading of media containing classified information; procedures addressing handling of classified information; NSA standards and policies regarding protection of classified information; media downgrading records; other relevant documents or records. *Interview:* Organizational personnel with information system media downgrading responsibilities; organizational personnel with information security responsibilities. *Test:* Organizational processes for media downgrading; automated mechanisms supporting and/or implementing media downgrading. |

K. *Physical and environmental family*

FIPS-200 provides the following criteria for this family of controls: Physical and environmental protection (PE): Organizations must: (i) limit physical access to information systems, equipment, and the respective operating environments to authorized individuals; (ii) protect the physical plant and support infrastructure for information systems; (iii) provide supporting utilities for information systems; (iv) protect information systems against environmental hazards; and (v) provide appropriate environmental controls in facilities containing information systems.

The primary assessment areas for these controls include:

a. Review security mechanisms that limit the physical access to information systems, equipment, and the respective operating environments to authorized individuals.
b. Assess protection mechanisms that protect the physical plant and support infrastructure for information systems.
c. Audit plans for the provision of supporting utilities for information systems.
d. Evaluate controls that protect information systems against environmental hazards.
e. Inspect the appropriate environmental controls in facilities containing information systems.

Control number	Control name	Assessment methods	Notes and guidance documents	SP 800-53A guidance
PE-1	Physical and environmental protection policy and procedures	Review documentation for organization to ensure all physical and environmental security components are defined in the PE policy and procedures. Discuss with the System Owner and Security Officer.	SP 800-12, SP 800-100	*Examine:* Physical and environmental protection policy and procedures; other relevant documents or records. *Interview:* Organizational personnel with physical and environmental protection responsibilities; organizational personnel with information security responsibilities.
PE-2	Physical access authorizations	Review documentation to ensure that the organizational workers, users, and employees are required to follow the defined organizational physical access process and all procedures to include physical access to facility, access to specialized processing areas within facility and access to controlled environment surrounding the facility, but not the public areas of the facility, if any. Discuss with Facility Official, System Owner, and Security Officer.		*Examine:* Physical and environmental protection policy; procedures addressing physical access authorizations; security plan; authorized personnel access list; authorization credentials; physical access list reviews; physical access termination records and associated documentation; other relevant documents or records. *Interview:* Organizational personnel with physical access authorization responsibilities; organizational personnel with physical access to information system facility; organizational personnel with information security responsibilities. *Test:* Organizational processes for physical access authorizations; automated mechanisms supporting and/or implementing physical access authorizations.
PE-2(1)	Physical access authorizations: Access by position/role	Review documentation to ensure that organization has defined all roles and access is granted based on roles assigned. Discuss with System Owner, FSO, and Security Officer.		*Examine:* Physical and environmental protection policy; procedures addressing physical access authorizations; physical access control logs or records; list of positions/roles and corresponding physical access authorizations; information system entry and exit points; other relevant documents or records. *Interview:* Organizational personnel with physical access authorization responsibilities; organizational personnel with physical access to information system facility; organizational personnel with information security responsibilities. *Test:* Organizational processes for physical access authorizations; automated mechanisms supporting and/or implementing physical access authorizations.

(Continued)

Control number	Control name	Assessment methods	Notes and guidance documents	SP 800-53A guidance
PE-2(2)	Physical access authorizations: Two forms of identification	Review documentation to ensure that physical security personnel require two forms of government issues identification to enter the facility. Observe the access control area of facility during normal operations to verify process is active. Discuss with FSO, System Owner, and Security Officer.	HSPD-12, FIPS-201	*Examine*: Physical and environmental protection policy; procedures addressing physical access authorizations; list of acceptable forms of identification for visitor access to the facility where information system resides; access authorization forms; access credentials; physical access control logs or records; other relevant documents or records. *Interview*: Organizational personnel with physical access authorization responsibilities; organizational personnel with physical access to information system facility; organizational personnel with information security responsibilities. *Test*: Organizational processes for physical access authorizations; automated mechanisms supporting and/or implementing physical access authorizations.
PE-2(3)	Physical access authorizations: Restrict unescorted access	Review documentation to ensure facility access for uncleared personnel is restricted and requires escort of visitors and uncleared entrants. Observe escorts in progress to verify process and procedures. Discuss with FSO, System Owner, and Security Officer.		*Examine*: Physical and environmental protection policy; procedures addressing physical access authorizations; authorized personnel access list; security clearances; access authorizations; access credentials; physical access control logs or records; other relevant documents or records. *Interview*: Organizational personnel with physical access authorization responsibilities; organizational personnel with physical access to information system facility; organizational personnel with information security responsibilities. *Test*: Organizational processes for physical access authorizations; automated mechanisms supporting and/or implementing physical access authorizations.
PE-3	Physical access control	Review documentation for facility to ensure full physical access control mechanisms and process are defined, active, and in process at all times for facility entrance of all personnel entering the facility. Observe access control processes around the facility to verify all procedures and access activities.	FIPS-201, SP 800-73, SP 800-76, SP 800-78, SP 800-116, ICD 704, ICD 705, DODI 5200.39	*Examine*: Physical and environmental protection policy; procedures addressing physical access control; security plan; physical access control logs or records; inventory records of physical access control devices; information system entry and exit points; records of key and lock combination changes; storage locations for physical access control devices; physical access control devices; list of security safeguards controlling access to designated publicly accessible areas within facility; other relevant documents or records. *Interview*: Organizational personnel

	Discuss with facilities staff, FSO, physical security staff, System Owner, and Security Officer.		with physical access control responsibilities; organizational personnel with information security responsibilities. *Test:* Organizational processes for physical access control; automated mechanisms supporting and/or implementing physical access control devices.
PE-3(1)	Physical access control: Information system access	Review documentation to ensure that the information systems areas have enhanced access controls for physical access to the location, such as the server room or the data center. Discuss with facilities staff, FSO, security staff, System Owner, and Security Officer.	FIPS-201, SP 800-73, SP 800-76, SP 800-116, ICD 704, ICD 705, DODI 5200.39	*Examine:* Physical and environmental protection policy; procedures addressing physical access control; physical access control logs or records; physical access control devices; access authorizations; access credentials; information system entry and exit points; list of areas within the facility containing concentrations of information system components or information system components requiring additional physical protection; other relevant documents or records. *Interview:* Organizational personnel with physical access authorization responsibilities; organizational personnel with information security responsibilities. *Test:* Organizational processes for physical access control to the information system/components; automated mechanisms supporting and/or implementing physical access control for facility areas containing information system components.
PE-3(2)	Physical access control: Facility/information system boundaries	Review the documentation for the organization to determine the extent, frequency, and/or randomness of security checks to adequately mitigate risk associated with exfiltration. Review the results of these checks to determine their validity and input into risk assessments for the organization. Discuss with System Owner, Security Officer, and FSO.	FIPS-201, SP 800-73, SP 800-76, SP 800-116, ICD 704, ICD 705, DODI 5200.39	*Examine:* Physical and environmental protection policy; procedures addressing physical access control; physical access control logs or records; records of security checks; security audit reports; security inspection reports; facility layout documentation; information system entry and exit points; other relevant documents or records. *Interview:* Organizational personnel with physical access control responsibilities; organizational personnel with information security responsibilities. *Test:* Organizational processes for physical access control to the facility and/or information system; automated mechanisms supporting and/or implementing physical access control for the facility or information system; automated mechanisms supporting and/or implementing security checks for unauthorized exfiltration of information.

(Continued)

Control number	Control name	Assessment methods	Notes and guidance documents	SP 800-53A guidance
PE-3(3)	Physical access control: Continuous guards/alarms/monitoring	Review documentation to ensure that organization employs methods for monitoring physical access to location/facility on a 24 h basis, as required. Discuss with security staff, System Owner, Security Officer, and physical security staff.	FIPS-201, SP 800-73, SP 800-76, SP 800-78, SP 800-116, ICD 704, ICD 705, DODI 5200.39	*Examine:* Physical and environmental protection policy; procedures addressing physical access control; physical access control logs or records; physical access control devices; facility surveillance records; facility layout documentation; information system entry and exit points; other relevant documents or records. *Interview:* Organizational personnel with physical access control responsibilities; organizational personnel with information security responsibilities. *Test:* Organizational processes for physical access control to the facility where the information system resides; automated mechanisms supporting and/or implementing physical access control for the facility where the information system resides.
PE-3(4)	Physical access control: Lockable casings	Review documentation to ensure that organization has implemented lockable mechanisms for movable devices and components. Observe lockable casings in action. Discuss with System Owner, FSO, and Security Officer.	FIPS-201, SP 800-73, SP 800-76, SP 800-78, SP 800-116, ICD 704, ICD 705, DODI 5200.39	*Examine:* Physical and environmental protection policy; procedures addressing physical access control; security plan; list of information system components requiring protection through lockable physical casings; lockable physical casings; other relevant documents or records. *Interview:* Organizational personnel with physical access control responsibilities; organizational personnel with information security responsibilities. *Test:* Lockable physical casings.
PE-3(5)	Physical access control: Tamper protection	Review documentation to determine the organizational implementation of tamper protection mechanisms, such as tamper detection/prevention at selected hardware components or tamper detection at some components and tamper prevention at other components. Discuss with System Owner, security staff and Security Officer.	FIPS-201, SP 800-73, SP 800-76, SP 800-78, SP 800-116, ICD 704, ICD 705, DODI 5200.39	*Examine:* Physical and environmental protection policy; procedures addressing physical access control; list of security safeguards to detect/prevent physical tampering or alteration of information system hardware components; other relevant documents or records. *Interview:* Organizational personnel with physical access control responsibilities; organizational personnel with information security responsibilities. *Test:* [Organizational processes to detect/prevent physical tampering or alteration of information system hardware components; automated mechanisms/security safeguards supporting and/or implementing detection/prevention of physical tampering/alternation of information system hardware components.

(Continued)

PE-3(6)	Physical access control: Facility penetration testing	Review documentation to ensure that the facility periodically tests the physical access to facility through scheduled and unscheduled penetration testing. Review results and lessons learned from such events to ensure application of repairs and remediation efforts are applied. Discuss with FSO, facilities staff, Security Officer, and System Owner.	FIPS-201, SP 800-73, SP 800-76, SP 800-78, SP 800-116, ICD 704, ICD 705, DODI 5200.39	*Examine:* Physical and environmental protection policy; procedures addressing physical access control; procedures addressing penetration testing; rules of engagement and associated documentation; penetration test results; security plan; other relevant documents or records. *Interview:* Organizational personnel with physical access control responsibilities; organizational personnel with information security responsibilities. *Test:* Organizational processes for facility penetration testing; automated mechanisms supporting and/or implementing facility penetration testing.
PE-4	Access control for transmission medium	Review documentation to ensure that the organization and facility have implemented methods and techniques for protection of the various transmission medium components implemented in facility, such as cable trays, conduits for cabling, shielding techniques, and other types of control. Ensure, when required, TEMPEST type controls are also implemented. Discuss with FSO, facility staff, System Owner, and Security Officer.	NSTISSI No. 7003	*Examine:* Physical and environmental protection policy; procedures addressing access control for transmission medium; information system design documentation; facility communications and wiring diagrams; list of physical security safeguards applied to information system distribution and transmission lines; other relevant documents or records. *Interview:* Organizational personnel with physical access control responsibilities; organizational personnel with information security responsibilities. *Test:* Organizational processes for access control to distribution and transmission lines; automated mechanisms/security safeguards supporting and/or implementing access control to distribution and transmission lines.
PE-5	Access control for output devices	Review documentation to ensure that the organization controls the access to various output devices and components, such as monitors, printers, copiers, scanners, facsimile machines, and audio devices, to protect output from unauthorized access or disclosure. Observe such protection mechanisms		*Examine:* Physical and environmental protection policy; procedures addressing access control for display medium; facility layout of information system components; actual displays from information system components; other relevant documents or records. *Interview:* Organizational personnel with physical access control responsibilities; organizational personnel with information security responsibilities. *Test:* Organizational processes for access control to output devices; automated mechanisms supporting and/or implementing access control to output devices.

Control number	Control name	Assessment methods	Notes and guidance documents	SP 800-53A guidance
		such as lockable rooms and devices. Discuss with System Officer, System Owner, and FSO.		
PE-5(1)	Access control for output devices: Access to output by authorized individuals	Review documentation to ensure facility and organization has implemented additional physical access controls for output devices to include placing printers, copiers, and facsimile machines in controlled areas with keypad access controls or limiting access to individuals with certain types of badges. Observe such access controls in operation. Discuss with FSO, facilities staff, System Owner, and Security Officer.		*Examine:* Physical and environmental protection policy; procedures addressing physical access control; list of output devices and associated outputs requiring physical access controls; physical access control logs or records for areas containing output devices and related outputs; other relevant documents or records. *Interview:* Organizational personnel with physical access control responsibilities; organizational personnel with information security responsibilities. *Test:* Organizational processes for access control to output devices; automated mechanisms supporting and/or implementing access control to output devices.
PE-5(2)	Access control for output devices: Access to output by individual identity	Review documentation to ensure facility and organization has implemented additional physical access controls for individual access, such as installing security functionality on printers, copiers, and facsimile machines that allows organizations to implement authentication (e.g., using a Pin or hardware token) on output devices prior to the release of output to individuals. Observe such access controls in operation. Discuss with FSO, facilities staff, System Owner, and Security Officer.		*Examine:* Physical and environmental protection policy; procedures addressing physical access control; information system design documentation; information system configuration settings and associated documentation; list of output devices and associated outputs requiring physical access controls; physical access control logs or records for areas containing output devices and related outputs; information system audit records; other relevant documents or records. *Interview:* Organizational personnel with physical access control responsibilities; organizational personnel with information security responsibilities; system/network administrators; system developers. *Test:* Organizational processes for access control to output devices; automated mechanisms supporting and/or implementing access control to output devices.
PE-5(3)	Access control for output	Review documentation to ensure that the organization		*Examine:* Physical and environmental protection policy; procedures addressing physical access control; security

devices: Marking output devices	Has marked output devices as related to the information system. Observe labeling and marking as appropriate on output devices. Discuss with System Owner, facilities staff, FSO, and Security Officer.	markings for information types permitted as output from information system output devices; other relevant documents or records. *Interview:* Organizational personnel with physical access control responsibilities; organizational personnel with information security responsibilities. *Test:* Organizational processes for marking output devices.
PE-6	Monitoring physical access	Review documentation to ensure that the organization monitors physical access to facility on consistent and regular basis to include review of access logs, unauthorized access attempts into locations not authorized, long-term access into areas not authorized and access at unauthorized times. Discuss with facilities staff, FSO, System Owner, and Security Officer.	*Examine:* Physical and environmental protection policy; procedures addressing physical access monitoring; security plan; physical access logs or records; physical access monitoring records; physical access log reviews; other relevant documents or records. *Interview:* Organizational personnel with physical access monitoring responsibilities; organizational personnel with incident response responsibilities; organizational personnel with information security responsibilities. *Test:* Organizational processes for monitoring physical access; automated mechanisms supporting and/or implementing physical access monitoring; automated mechanisms supporting and/or implementing reviewing of physical access logs.
PE-6(1)	Monitoring physical access: Intrusion alarms/surveillance equipment	Review documentation to ensure that facilities staff monitor surveillance system and monitors as well as physical intrusion systems and alarms. Observe monitoring efforts to ensure monitoring is active. Discuss with FSO, System Owner, and Security Officer.	*Examine:* Physical and environmental protection policy; procedures addressing physical access monitoring; security plan; physical access logs or records; physical access monitoring records; physical access log reviews; other relevant documents or records. *Interview:* Organizational personnel with physical access monitoring responsibilities; organizational personnel with incident response responsibilities; organizational personnel with information security responsibilities. *Test:* Organizational processes for monitoring physical intrusion alarms and surveillance equipment; automated mechanisms supporting and/or implementing physical access monitoring; automated mechanisms supporting and/or implementing physical intrusion alarms and surveillance equipment.
PE-6(2)	Monitoring physical access: Automated intrusion	Review documentation to determine organizational efforts with automated intrusion recognition systems. Observe	*Examine:* Physical and environmental protection policy; procedures addressing physical access monitoring; information system design documentation; information system configuration settings and associated

(Continued)

Control number	Control name	Assessment methods	Notes and guidance documents	SP 800-53A guidance
	recognition/ responses	system in operation to ensure proper usage and monitoring is active. Discuss with facilities staff, FSO, Security Officer, and System Owner.		documentation; information system audit records; list of response actions to be initiated when specific classes/types of intrusions are recognized; other relevant documents or records. *Interview:* Organizational personnel with physical access monitoring responsibilities; organizational personnel with information security responsibilities. *Test:* Organizational processes for monitoring physical access; automated mechanisms supporting and/or implementing physical access monitoring; automated mechanisms supporting and/or implementing recognition of classes/types of intrusions and initiation of a response.
PE-6(3)	Monitoring physical access: Video surveillance	Review documentation to determine the video surveillance system active within facility, which records surveillance video for purposes of subsequent review when necessary. Observe system to ensure usage and activities are monitored and reviewed. Discuss with FSO, facilities physical security staff, System Owner, and Security Officer.		*Examine:* Physical and environmental protection policy; procedures addressing physical access monitoring; video surveillance equipment used to monitor operational areas; video recordings of operational areas where video surveillance is employed; video surveillance equipment logs or records; other relevant documents or records. *Interview:* Organizational personnel with physical access monitoring responsibilities; organizational personnel with information security responsibilities. *Test:* Organizational processes for monitoring physical access; automated mechanisms supporting and/or implementing physical access monitoring; automated mechanisms supporting and/or implementing video surveillance.
PE-6(4)	Monitoring physical access: Monitoring physical access to information systems	Review documentation to determine extent of usage of additional monitoring for those areas within facilities, where there is a concentration of information system components such as data center, server rooms, media storage areas, and communications centers. Observe monitoring efforts to ensure active and		*Examine:* Physical and environmental protection policy; procedures addressing physical access monitoring; physical access control logs or records; physical access control devices; access authorizations; access credentials; list of areas within the facility containing concentrations of information system components or information system components requiring additional physical access monitoring; other relevant documents or records. *Interview:* Organizational personnel with physical access monitoring responsibilities; organizational personnel with information security responsibilities. *Test:* Organizational

PE-7	Visitor control	physical reviews are being conducted on an on-going basis. Discuss with facility physical security staff, FSO, System Owner, and Security Officer.	processes for monitoring physical access to the information system; automated mechanisms supporting and/or implementing physical access monitoring for facility areas containing information system components.
		Withdrawn: Incorporated into PE-2 and PE-3	
PE-8	Visitor access records	Review documentation to ensure that visitor access is recorded and monitored for access to nonpublic areas of facility. Review records to determine full documentation is maintained, which includes names and organizations of persons visiting, visitor signatures, forms of identification, dates of access, entry and departure times, purposes of visits, and names and organizations of persons visited. Discuss with facilities staff, FSO, Security Officer, and System Owner.	*Examine:* Physical and environmental protection policy; procedures addressing visitor access records; security plan; visitor access control logs or records; visitor access record or log reviews; other relevant documents or records. *Interview:* Organizational personnel with visitor access records responsibilities; organizational personnel with information security responsibilities. *Test:* Organizational processes for maintaining and reviewing visitor access records; automated mechanisms supporting and/or implementing maintenance and review of visitor access records.
PE-8(1)	Visitor access records: Automated records maintenance/review	Review documentation to ensure that organization has implemented automated visitor records system for facility. Review automated records and observe system utilized to ensure proper use is active. Discuss with System Owner, FSO, facilities staff, and Security Officer.	*Examine:* Physical and environmental protection policy; procedures addressing visitor access records; automated mechanisms supporting management of visitor access records; visitor access control logs or records; other relevant documents or records. *Interview:* Organizational personnel with visitor access records responsibilities; organizational personnel with information security responsibilities. *Test:* Organizational processes for maintaining and reviewing visitor access records; automated mechanisms supporting and/or implementing maintenance and review of visitor access records.

(Continued)

Control number	Control name	Assessment methods	Notes and guidance documents	SP 800-53A guidance
PE-8(2)	Visitor access records: Physical access records		Withdrawn: Incorporated into PE-2	
PE-9	Power equipment and cabling	Review documentation to ensure that protection and installation of power equipment is correct and functional. Such equipment like generators and power cabling outside of buildings, internal cabling, and uninterruptible power sources within an office or data center, and power sources for self-contained entities, such as vehicles and satellites all need protection from internal; and external threats. Observe equipment and security while conducting a security walk-through inspection. Discuss with facilities staff, System Owner, FSO, and Security Officer.		*Examine:* Physical and environmental protection policy; procedures addressing power equipment/cabling protection; facilities housing power equipment/cabling; other relevant documents or records. *Interview:* Organizational personnel with responsibility for protecting power equipment/cabling; organizational personnel with information security responsibilities. *Test:* Automated mechanisms supporting and/or implementing protection of power equipment/cabling.
PE-9(1)	Power equipment and cabling: Redundant cabling	Review documentation to ensure that redundant power delivery cabling is installed and active as necessary. Observe redundant cabling for proper installation and maintenance. Discuss with facilities staff, Security Officer, and System Owner.		*Examine:* Physical and environmental protection policy; procedures addressing power equipment/cabling protection; facilities housing power equipment/cabling; other relevant documents or records. *Interview:* Organizational personnel with responsibility for protecting power equipment/cabling; organizational personnel with information security responsibilities. *Test:* Automated mechanisms supporting and/or implementing protection of power equipment/cabling.
PE-9(2)	Power equipment and cabling: Automatic voltage controls	Review documentation for power delivery equipment to ensure that automated switching and voltage delivery is installed and maintained. Observe installed switching		*Examine:* Physical and environmental protection policy; procedures addressing voltage control; security plan; list of critical information system components requiring automatic voltage controls; automatic voltage control mechanisms and associated configurations; other relevant documents or records. *Interview:* Organizational

		mechanisms for proper usage. Discuss with facilities staff, System Owner, and Security Officer.	personnel with responsibility for environmental protection of information system components; organizational personnel with information security responsibilities. *Test:* Automated mechanisms supporting and/or implementing automatic voltage controls.
PE-10	Emergency shutoff	Review documentation to ensure that emergency power shut-off mechanism is installed and active for safety purposes in areas of high concern, such as data centers, server rooms, and mainframe computing facilities. Observe emergency switch location to ensure protection from inadvertent engagement is installed. Discuss with facilities staff, System Owner, and Security officer.	*Examine:* Physical and environmental protection policy; procedures addressing power source emergency shutoff; security plan; emergency shutoff controls or switches; locations housing emergency shutoff switches and devices; security safeguards protecting emergency power shutoff capability from unauthorized activation; other relevant documents or records. *Interview:* Organizational personnel with responsibility for emergency power shutoff capability (both implementing and using the capability); organizational personnel with information security responsibilities. *Test:* Automated mechanisms supporting and/or implementing emergency power shutoff.
PE-10(1)	Emergency shutoff: Accidental/unauthorized activation		Withdrawn: Incorporated into PE-10
PE-11	Emergency power	Review documentation to ensure that facilities supply short-term uninterruptible power supply (UPS) mechanisms for use in case the primary power source is interrupted for any reason. Observe UPS and ensure its capabilities are sufficient for equipment it is supporting. Discuss with System Owner, facilities staff, and Security Officer.	*Examine:* Physical and environmental protection policy; procedures addressing emergency power; uninterruptible power supply; uninterruptible power supply documentation; uninterruptible power supply test records; other relevant documents or records. *Interview:* Organizational personnel with responsibility for emergency power and/or planning; organizational personnel with information security responsibilities. *Test:* Automated mechanisms supporting and/or implementing uninterruptible power supply; the uninterruptible power supply.

(Continued)

Control number	Control name	Assessment methods	Notes and guidance documents	SP 800-53A guidance
PE-11(1)	Emergency power: Long-term alternate power supply – minimal operational capability	Review documentation to ensure that organization has implemented an alternate method for long-term power delivery as redundant power with the use of a secondary commercial power supply or other external power supply. Methods of engagement of alternate power can be manual or automatic. Observe alternate power source equipment to ensure adequacy and installation. Discuss with facilities staff, System Owner, and Security Officer.		*Examine:* Physical and environmental protection policy; procedures addressing emergency power; alternate power supply; alternate power supply documentation; alternate power supply test records; other relevant documents or records. *Interview:* Organizational personnel with responsibility for emergency power and/or planning; organizational personnel with information security responsibilities. *Test:* Automated mechanisms supporting and/or implementing alternate power supply; the alternate power supply.
PE-11(2)	Emergency power: Long-term alternate power supply – self-contained	Review documentation to ensure that organization has implemented an alternate method for long-term power delivery as redundant power through by the use of one or more generators with sufficient capacity to meet the needs of the organization. Methods of engagement of alternate power can be manual or automatic. Observe alternate power source equipment to ensure adequacy and installation. Discuss with facilities staff, System Owner, and Security Officer.		*Examine:* Physical and environmental protection policy; procedures addressing emergency power; alternate power supply; alternate power supply documentation; alternate power supply test records; other relevant documents or records. *Interview:* Organizational personnel with responsibility for emergency power and/or planning; organizational personnel with information security responsibilities. *Test:* Automated mechanisms supporting and/or implementing alternate power supply; the alternate power supply.
PE-12	Emergency lighting	Review documentation to ensure that organization employs emergency lighting for facilities to include coverage of emergency exits and evacuation		*Examine:* Physical and environmental protection policy; procedures addressing emergency lighting; emergency lighting documentation; emergency lighting test records; emergency exits and evacuation routes; other relevant documents or records. *Interview:* Organizational

		routes. Observe lighting during security walk-through inspection. Discuss with facilities staff, FSO, Security Officer, and System Owner.	personnel with responsibility for emergency lighting and/or planning; organizational personnel with information security responsibilities. *Test:* Automated mechanisms supporting and/or implementing emergency lighting capability.
PE-12(1)	Emergency lighting; Essential missions/business functions	Review documentation to ensure that organization employs emergency lighting for facilities to include coverage of critical and essential mission/business functional areas of operations. Observe lighting during security walk-through inspection. Discuss with Facilities staff, FSO, Security Officer, and System Owner.	*Examine:* Physical and environmental protection policy; procedures addressing emergency lighting; emergency lighting documentation; emergency lighting test records; emergency exits and evacuation routes; areas/locations within facility supporting essential missions and business functions; other relevant documents or records. *Interview:* Organizational personnel with responsibility for emergency lighting and/or planning; organizational personnel with information security responsibilities. *Test:* Automated mechanisms supporting and/or implementing emergency lighting capability.
PE-13	Fire protection	Review documentation for facility to ensure that fire suppression and detection devices/systems include, for example, sprinkler systems, handheld fire extinguishers, fixed fire hoses, and smoke detectors, are deployed throughout the facility as required by local fire regulations and code. Observe fire equipment during security walk-through inspection. Discuss with facilities staff, FSO, Security Officer, and System Owner.	*Examine:* Physical and environmental protection policy; procedures addressing fire protection; fire suppression and detection devices/systems; fire suppression and detection devices/systems documentation; test records of fire suppression and detection devices/systems; other relevant documents or records. *Interview:* Organizational personnel with responsibilities for fire detection and suppression devices/systems; organizational personnel with information security responsibilities. *Test:* Automated mechanisms supporting and/or implementing fire suppression/detection devices/systems.
PE-13(1)	Fire protection: Detection devices/systems	Review documentation to ensure that automated fire suppression and detection equipment is deployed throughout the facility. Observe automated equipment during security walk-through	*Examine:* Physical and environmental protection policy; procedures addressing fire protection; facility housing the information system; alarm service-level agreements; test records of fire suppression and detection devices/systems; fire suppression and detection devices/systems documentation; alerts/notifications of fire events; other relevant documents or records. *Interview:* Organizational

(Continued)

Control number	Control name	Assessment methods	Notes and guidance documents	SP 800-53A guidance
		inspection. Discuss with facilities staff, FSO, Security Officer, and System Owner.		personnel with responsibilities for fire detection and suppression devices/systems; organizational personnel with responsibilities for notifying appropriate personnel, roles, and emergency responders of fires; organizational personnel with information security responsibilities. *Test:* Automated mechanisms supporting and/or implementing fire detection devices/systems; activation of fire detection devices/systems (simulated); automated notifications.
PE-13(2)	Fire protection: Suppression devices/systems	Review documentation to ensure fire suppression and detection equipment is set to notify automatically appropriate personnel, if activated. Observe automated equipment during security walk-through inspection. Discuss with facilities staff, FSO, Security Officer, and System Owner.		*Examine:* Physical and environmental protection policy; procedures addressing fire protection; fire suppression and detection devices/systems documentation; facility housing the information system; alarm service-level agreements; test records of fire suppression and detection devices/systems; other relevant documents or records. *Interview:* Organizational personnel with responsibilities for fire detection and suppression devices/systems; organizational personnel with responsibilities for providing automatic notifications of any activation of fire suppression devices/systems to appropriate personnel, roles, and emergency responders; organizational personnel with information security responsibilities. *Test:* Automated mechanisms supporting and/or implementing fire suppression devices/systems; activation of fire suppression devices/systems (simulated); automated notifications.
PE-13(3)	Fire protection: Automatic fire suppression	Review documentation to ensure that automated fire suppression and detection equipment is deployed throughout the facility, when it is not occupied. Observe automated equipment during security walk-through inspection. Discuss with facilities staff, FSO, Security Officer, and System Owner.		*Examine:* Physical and environmental protection policy; procedures addressing fire protection; fire suppression and detection devices/systems documentation; facility housing the information system; alarm service-level agreements; test records of fire suppression and detection devices/systems; other relevant documents or records. *Interview:* Organizational personnel with responsibilities for fire detection and suppression devices/systems; organizational personnel with responsibilities for providing automatic notifications of any activation of fire suppression devices/systems to appropriate personnel, roles, and emergency responders; organizational

PE-13(4)	Fire protection: Inspections	Review documentation to ensure that fire detection and suppression equipment is periodically inspected and approved by appropriate personnel. Observe inspection stickers while conducting security walk-through inspection. Discuss with facilities staff, FSO, Security Officer, and System Owner.	personnel with information security responsibilities. *Test:* Automated mechanisms supporting and/or implementing fire suppression devices/systems; activation of fire suppression devices/systems (simulated). *Examine:* Physical and environmental protection policy; procedures addressing fire protection; security plan; facility housing the information system; inspection plans; inspection results; inspect reports; test records of fire suppression and detection devices/systems; other relevant documents or records. *Interview:* Organizational personnel with responsibilities for planning, approving, and executing fire inspections; organizational personnel with information security responsibilities.
PE-14	Temperature and humidity controls	Review documentation for all temperature and humidity control activities to ensure proper settings are applied for all focus areas, such as data centers, server rooms, and mainframe computer rooms. Ensure settings are appropriate for local and environmental conditions for system. Observe settings and controls during security walk-through inspection. Discuss with security staff, System Owner, facilities staff, and Security Officer.	*Examine:* Physical and environmental protection policy; procedures addressing temperature and humidity control; security plan; temperature and humidity controls; facility housing the information system; temperature and humidity controls documentation; temperature and humidity records; other relevant documents or records. *Interview:* Organizational personnel with responsibilities for information system environmental controls; organizational personnel with information security responsibilities. *Test:* Automated mechanisms supporting and/or implementing maintenance and monitoring of temperature and humidity levels.
PE-14(1)	Temperature and humidity controls: Automatic controls	Review documentation for all automatic temperature and humidity control activities to ensure proper settings are applied for all focus areas, such as data centers, server rooms, and mainframe computer	*Examine:* Physical and environmental protection policy; procedures addressing temperature and humidity controls; facility housing the information system; automated mechanisms for temperature and humidity; temperature and humidity controls; temperature and humidity documentation; other relevant documents or records. *Interview:* Organizational personnel with

(Continued)

Control number	Control name	Notes and guidance documents	SP 800-53A guidance
			responsibilities for information system environmental controls; organizational personnel with information security responsibilities. *Test:* Automated mechanisms supporting and/or implementing temperature and humidity levels.
PE-14(2)	Temperature and humidity controls: Monitoring with alarms/notifications	Review documentation for all temperature and humidity control activities to ensure that monitoring mechanisms alert appropriate personnel when necessary. Observe settings and controls during security walk-through inspection. Discuss with security staff, System Owner, facilities staff, and Security Officer.	*Examine:* Physical and environmental protection policy; procedures addressing temperature and humidity monitoring; facility housing the information system; logs or records of temperature and humidity monitoring; records of changes to temperature and humidity levels that generate alarms or notifications; other relevant documents or records. *Interview:* Organizational personnel with responsibilities for information system environmental controls; organizational personnel with information security responsibilities. *Test:* Automated mechanisms supporting and/or implementing temperature and humidity monitoring.
PE-15	Water damage protection	Review documentation to ensure that system employs water damage protection, such as emergency shutoff valves, when deployed in concentrated areas such as data centers, server rooms, or mainframe computer rooms. Isolation valves can be employed in addition to or in lieu of master shutoff valves to shut off water supplies in specific areas of concern, without affecting entire organizations. Discuss with facilities staff, FSO, System Owner, and Security Officer.	*Examine:* Physical and environmental protection policy; procedures addressing water damage protection; facility housing the information system; master shutoff valves; list of key personnel with knowledge of location and activation procedures for master shutoff valves for the plumbing system; master shutoff valve documentation; other relevant documents or records. *Interview:* Organizational personnel with responsibilities for information system environmental controls; organizational personnel with information security responsibilities. *Test:* Master water-shutoff valves; organizational process for activating master water shutoff.
PE-15(1)	Water damage protection:	Review documentation for system to ensure that it uses	*Examine:* Physical and environmental protection policy; procedures addressing water damage protection; facility

	Automation support	automatic water detection sensors. Observe sensors during security walk-through inspection. Discuss with facilities staff, FSO, System Owner, and Security Officer.	housing the information system; automated mechanisms for water shutoff valves; automated mechanisms detecting presence of water in vicinity of information system; alerts/notifications of water detection in information system facility; other relevant documents or records. *Interview:* Organizational personnel with responsibilities for information system environmental controls; organizational personnel with information security responsibilities. *Test:* Automated mechanisms supporting and/or implementing water detection capability and alerts for the information system.
PE-16	Delivery and removal	Review documentation to ensure that organization authorizes, monitors, and controls system equipment entering and exiting the facility and maintains records of those items. Review all logs for completeness, time of entry, item involved, employee approval and who brought/carried it out. Discuss with facilities staff, physical security staff, FSO, System Owner, and Security Officer.	*Examine:* Physical and environmental protection policy; procedures addressing delivery and removal of information system components from the facility; security plan; facility housing the information system; records of items entering and exiting the facility; other relevant documents or records. *Interview:* Organizational personnel with responsibilities for controlling information system components entering and exiting the facility; organizational personnel with information security responsibilities. *Test:* Organizational process for authorizing, monitoring, and controlling information system-related items entering and exiting the facility; automated mechanisms supporting and/or implementing authorizing, monitoring, and controlling information system-related items entering and exiting the facility.
PE-17	Alternate work site	SP 800-46, SP 800-34, CP-7, AC-17	Review documentation to determine if organization allows alternate work sites, besides the standard alternate processing facility in the CP family of controls. If so, review documentation, approval, IT support documentation, and employee requirements for work area and requirements. Discuss with System Owner, COOP staff, and Security Officer.	*Examine:* Physical and environmental protection policy; procedures addressing alternate work sites for organizational personnel; security plan; list of security controls required for alternate work sites; assessments of security controls at alternate work sites; other relevant documents or records. *Interview:* Organizational personnel approving use of alternate work sites; organizational personnel using alternate work sites; organizational personnel assessing controls at alternate work sites; organizational personnel with information security responsibilities. *Test:* Organizational processes for security at alternate work sites; automated

(Continued)

Control number	Control name	Assessment methods	Notes and guidance documents	SP 800-53A guidance
				mechanisms supporting alternate work sites; security controls employed at alternate work sites; means of communications between personnel at alternate work sites and security personnel.
PE-18	Location of information system components	Review documentation to determine the physical and environmental hazards considered during location selection process for system and its operations. Discuss with acquisition staff, operations staff, security staff, FSO, facilities staff, System Owner, and Security Officer.		*Examine:* Physical and environmental protection policy; procedures addressing positioning of information system components; documentation providing the location and position of information system components within the facility; locations housing information system components within the facility; list of physical and environmental hazards with potential to damage information system components within the facility; other relevant documents or records. *Interview:* Organizational personnel with responsibilities for positioning information system components; organizational personnel with information security responsibilities. *Test:* Organizational processes for positioning information system components.
PE-18(1)	Location of information system components: Facility site	Review documentation to determine the organization planning efforts for the location or site of the facility, where the information system resides with regard to physical and environmental hazards and for existing facilities and considered the physical and environmental hazards in its risk mitigation strategy and planning. Discuss with System Owner, operations staff, acquisition staff, facilities staff, security staff, FSO, and Security Officer.	PM-8	*Examine:* Physical and environmental protection policy; physical site planning documents; organizational assessment of risk, contingency plan; risk mitigation strategy documentation; other relevant documents or records. *Interview:* Organizational personnel with site selection responsibilities for the facility housing the information system; organizational personnel with risk mitigation responsibilities; organizational personnel with information security responsibilities. *Test:* Organizational processes for site planning.
PE-19	Information leakage	Review documentation for organization to determine the emanation (electromagnetic)	FIPS-199	*Examine:* Physical and environmental protection policy; procedures addressing information leakage due to electromagnetic signals emanations; mechanisms

		security requirements for system and their implementation. Ensure the security categories or classifications of information systems (with respect to confidentiality) and organizational security policies are defined and guide the selection of security controls employed to protect systems against information leakage due to electromagnetic signals emanations. Discuss with FSO, security staff, facilities staff, Security Officer, and System Owner.		protecting the information system against electronic signals emanation; facility housing the information system; records from electromagnetic signals emanation tests; other relevant documents or records. *Interview:* Organizational personnel with responsibilities for information system environmental controls; organizational personnel with information security responsibilities. *Test:* Automated mechanisms supporting and/or implementing protection from information leakage due to electromagnetic signals emanations.
PE-19(1)	Information leakage: National emissions/ TEMPESTt policies and procedures	Review documentation to ensure the organization reviews the information system components, associated data communications, and networks such that they are protected in accordance with national emissions and TEMPEST policies and procedures based on the security category or classification of the information. This control is focused for DOD and IC in their Tempest Program activities. Special review criteria are defined in the associated program documentation. Discuss with facilities staff, security staff, ESO, System Owner, and Security Officer.	FIPS-199, CNSSI-7000	*Examine:* Physical and environmental protection policy; procedures addressing information leakage that comply with national emissions and TEMPEST policies and procedures; information system component design documentation; information system configuration settings and associated documentation other relevant documents or records. *Interview:* Organizational personnel with responsibilities for information system environmental controls; organizational personnel with information security responsibilities. *Test:* Information system components for compliance with national emissions and TEMPEST policies and procedures.

(Continued)

Control number	Control name	Assessment methods	Notes and guidance documents	SP 800-53A guidance
PE-20	Asset monitoring and tracking	Review documentation to determine the organizational implementation of asset tracking mechanisms and components for the information system. Verify asset tracking components, such as RFID tags or GPS signal tracking devices are functional and required. Discuss with FSO, acquisition staff, legal staff, operations staff, System Owner, and Security Officer.		*Examine:* Physical and environmental protection policy; procedures addressing asset monitoring and tracking; asset location technologies and associated configuration documentation; list of organizational assets requiring tracking and monitoring; asset monitoring and tracking records; other relevant documents or records. *Interview:* Organizational personnel with asset monitoring and tracking responsibilities; organizational personnel with information security responsibilities. *Test:* Organizational processes for tracking and monitoring assets; automated mechanisms supporting and/or implementing tracking and monitoring of assets.

L. *Planning family*

FIPS-200 provides the following criteria for this family of controls: Planning (PL): Organizations must develop, document, periodically update, and implement security plans for organizational information systems that describe the security controls in place or planned for the information systems and the rules of behavior for individuals accessing the information systems.

The primary assessment areas for these controls include:

a. Audit security plans for organizational information systems that describe the security controls in place or planned for the information systems and the rules of behavior for individuals accessing the information systems.

b. Review documentation of the security plans for organizational information systems that describes the security controls in place or planned for the information systems and the rules of behavior for individuals accessing the information systems.

c. Inspect processes to facilitate the periodic update of security plans for organizational information systems that describe the security controls in place or planned for the information systems and the rules of behavior for individuals accessing the information systems.

d. Assess processes to handle the implementation of security plans for organizational information systems that describe the security controls in place or planned for the information systems and the rules of behavior for individuals accessing the information systems.

Control number	Control name	Assessment methods	Notes and guidance documents	SP 800-53A guidance
PL-1	Security planning policy and procedures	Review the security planning policy and procedures for organization. Determine the extent the planning process aligns with organizational criteria and compliance requirements for agency. Interview System Owner and Security Officer to determine planning efforts of organization and planning processes as implemented.	SP 800-12, SP 800-18, rev. 1, SP 800-100	*Examine:* Planning policy and procedures; other relevant documents or records. *Interview:* Organizational personnel with planning responsibilities; organizational personnel with information security responsibilities.
PL-2	System security plan	Review the system security plan (SSP) for accuracy, completeness and scope. Ensure that planning activities for system are coordinated via all relevant sections and departments with areas of focus on system and its inputs/outputs. Discuss roles and responsibilities for sections of SSP with System Owner and Security Officer. Review organizational planning efforts and documentation to ensure the agency provides for and conducts all required planning for security for system.	SP 800-18, rev. 1, OMB A-130	*Examine:* Security planning policy; procedures addressing security plan development and implementation; procedures addressing security plan reviews and updates; enterprise architecture documentation; security plan for the information system; records of security plan reviews and updates; other relevant documents or records. *Interview:* Organizational personnel with security planning and plan implementation responsibilities; organizational personnel with information security responsibilities. *Test:* Organizational processes for security plan development/review/update/approval; automated mechanisms supporting the information system security plan.
PL-2(1)	System security plan: Concept of operations		Withdrawn: Incorporated into PL-7	
PL-2(2)	System security plan: Functional architecture		Withdrawn: Incorporated into PL-8	
PL-2(3)	System security plan: Plan/coordinate with other organizational entities	Review the SSP for interface and coordination efforts between departments and other components and agencies as necessary. Ensure that planning activities for system	SP 800-18, rev. 1	*Examine:* Security planning policy; access control policy; contingency planning policy; procedures addressing security-related activity planning for the information system; security plan for the information system; contingency plan for the

Control	Name	Guidance	Reference	Assessment
		are coordinated via all relevant sections and departments with areas of focus on system and its inputs/outputs. Discuss coordination efforts with System Owner and Security Officer.		information system; information system design documentation; other relevant documents or records. *Interview:* Organizational personnel with security planning and plan implementation responsibilities; organizational individuals or groups with whom security-related activities are to be planned and coordinated; organizational personnel with information security responsibilities.
PL-3	System security plan update		Withdrawn: Incorporated into PL-2	
PL-4	Rules of behavior	Review inputs from Information Owners and Data Custodians for Rules of Behavior (ROB) section of SSP to ensure that they are incorporated and provided to all system users as appropriate. Discuss ROB with all relevant owners (information and system) as well as the Data Custodians for IC, NSS, and Classified systems.	SP 800-18, rev. 1, OMB A-130	*Examine:* Security planning policy; procedures addressing rules of behavior for information system users; rules of behavior; signed acknowledgements; records for rules of behavior reviews and updates; other relevant documents or records. *Interview:* Organizational personnel with responsibility for establishing, reviewing, and updating rules of behavior; organizational personnel who are authorized users of the information system and have signed and resigned rules of behavior; organizational personnel with information security responsibilities. *Test:* Organizational processes for establishing, reviewing, disseminating, and updating rules of behavior; automated mechanisms supporting and/or implementing the establishment, review, dissemination, and update of rules of behavior.
PL-4(1)	Rules of behavior: Social media and networking restrictions	Review all documentation and ROB for explicit restrictions on the use of social media/networking sites and posting organizational information on public websites by users. Discuss these requirements and their adherence with the System Owner and Security Officer.	SP 800-18, rev. 1	*Examine:* Security planning policy; procedures addressing rules of behavior for information system users; rules of behavior; other relevant documents or records. *Interview:* Organizational personnel with responsibility for establishing, reviewing, and updating rules of behavior; organizational personnel, who are authorized users of the information system and have signed rules of behavior; organizational personnel with information security responsibilities. *Test:* Organizational processes for establishing rules of

(Continued)

Control number	Control name	Assessment methods	Notes and guidance documents	SP 800-53A guidance
PL-5	Privacy impact assessment		Withdrawn: Incorporated into Appendix J, AR-2	behavior; automated mechanisms supporting and/or implementing the establishment of rules of behavior.
PL-6	Security-related activity planning		Withdrawn: Incorporated into PL-2	
PL-7	Security concept of operations	Review the security concept of operations (CONOPS) document for the information system to ensure that it contains discussion of how the organization intends to operate the system from the perspective of information security. Interview the CONOPS author, System Owner, and Security Officer to ensure organizational compliance with the CONOPS.	SP 800-18, rev. 1	*Examine:* Security planning policy; procedures addressing security CONOPS development; procedures addressing security CONOPS reviews and updates; security CONOPS for the information system; security plan for the information system; records of security CONOPS reviews and updates; other relevant documents or records. *Interview:* Organizational personnel with security planning and plan implementation responsibilities; organizational personnel with information security responsibilities. *Test:* Organizational processes for developing, reviewing, and updating the security CONOPS; automated mechanisms supporting and/or implementing the development, review, and update of the security CONOPS.
PL-8	Information security architecture	Review the organizational segment or solution architecture documents for the system under review to verify that system is architecturally covered and addressed by the external security features, which it inherits. Review architecture documents to ensure that they include an architectural description, the placement/allocation of security functionality (including	SP 800-18, rev. 1	*Examine:* Security planning policy; procedures addressing information security architecture development; procedures addressing information security architecture reviews and updates; enterprise architecture documentation; information security architecture documentation; security plan for the information system; security CONOPS for the information system; records of information security architecture reviews and updates; other relevant documents or records. *Interview:* Organizational personnel with security planning and plan

	Description	References	Assessment
	security controls), security-related information for external interfaces, information being exchanged across the interfaces, and the protection mechanisms associated with each interface. Discuss architecture and the process with the Security Officer, System Owner, and the Security Architect.		implementation responsibilities; organizational personnel with information security architecture development responsibilities; organizational personnel with information security responsibilities. *Test:* Organizational processes for developing, reviewing, and updating the information security architecture; automated mechanisms supporting and/or implementing the development, review, and update of the information security architecture.
PL-8(1)	Information security architecture: Defense-in-depth	Review architecture documents to ensure that the security design for the system is designed to allocate the security controls are operating in a coordinated and mutually reinforcing manner. Discuss this process with the Security Architect for the system under review.	SP 800-18, rev. 1, IATF 3.1, SP 800-160	*Examine:* Security planning policy; procedures addressing information security architecture development; enterprise architecture documentation; information security architecture documentation; security plan for the information system; security CONOPS for the information system; other relevant documents or records. *Interview:* Organizational personnel with security planning and plan implementation responsibilities; organizational personnel with information security architecture development responsibilities; organizational personnel with information security responsibilities. *Test:* Organizational processes for designing the information security architecture; automated mechanisms supporting and/or implementing the design of the information security architecture.
PL-8(2)	Information security architecture: Supplier diversity	Review system security controls, their vendors, and the acquisition process to ensure that the security control components and equipment are purchased from various different vendors and suppliers. Discuss this requirement with both the security staff and the acquisition staff of the organization.	SP 800-18, rev. 1	*Examine:* Security planning policy; procedures addressing information security architecture development; enterprise architecture documentation; information security architecture documentation; security plan for the information system; security CONOPS for the information system; other relevant documents or records. *Interview:* Organizational personnel with security planning and plan implementation responsibilities; organizational personnel with information security architecture development responsibilities; organizational personnel with acquisition responsibilities;

(Continued)

Control number	Control name	Assessment methods	Notes and guidance documents	SP 800-53A guidance
				organizational personnel with information security responsibilities. *Test:* Organizational processes for obtaining information security safeguards from different suppliers.
PL-9	Central management	Review the common controls and their implementation to ensure that the control sets are managed centrally to provide economies, efficiencies and control effectiveness for the system. Discuss the implementation of this central control management with the System Owner, Security Officer, and the CCP for each control set inherited by the system.	SP 800-18, rev. 1, SP 800-37, rev. 1	*Examine:* Security planning policy; procedures addressing security plan development and implementation; security plan for the information system; other relevant documents or records. *Interview:* Organizational personnel with security planning and plan implementation responsibilities; organizational personnel with responsibilities for planning/implementing central management of security controls and related processes; organizational personnel with information security responsibilities. *Test:* Organizational processes for central management of security controls and related processes; automated mechanisms supporting and/or implementing central management of security controls and related processes.

M. *Program management family*

This family of controls was added to the SP 800-53 in revision 3 due to the need to reflect the organizational commitment and requirement for support and oversight of the security program components in each agency.

The primary assessment areas for these controls include:

Audit processes and controls that are compatible and consistent with an organization's information security program

Control number	Control name	Assessment methods	Notes and guidance documents	SP 800-53A guidance
PM-1	Information security program plan	Review the organizational security program policy, program documents, agency directives, and program guidance. Discuss program guidance with agency executives, System Owner, and security officials to determine status and general agency focus on security.	SP 800-12, SP 800-100	*Examine:* Information security program plan; procedures addressing program plan development and implementation; procedures addressing program plan reviews and updates; procedures addressing coordination of the program plan with relevant entities; procedures for program plan approvals; records of program plan reviews and updates; other relevant documents or records. *Interview:* Organizational personnel with information security program planning and plan implementation responsibilities; organizational personnel with information security responsibilities. *Test:* Organizational processes for information security program plan development/review/update/approval; automated mechanisms supporting and/or implementing the information security program plan.
PM-2	Senior Information Security Officer	Review documents and assignment letters to ensure that the organization has assigned a senior information security officer to coordinate, develop, implement, and maintain an organization-wide information security program.	SP 800-37, rev. 1	*Examine:* Information security program plan; procedures addressing program plan development and implementation; procedures addressing program plan reviews and updates; procedures addressing coordination of the program plan with relevant entities; other relevant documents or records. *Interview:* Organizational personnel with information security program planning and plan implementation responsibilities; senior information security officer; organizational personnel with information security responsibilities.
PM-3	Information security resources	Review all capital planning and investment request documents (Business Cases, Exhibit 300, Exhibit 53) to ensure that the organization is including security resources requirements and that resources are available for expenditure as planned.	OMB A-11, Clinger-Cohen Act, OMB M00-07, SP 800-65	*Examine:* Information security program plan; Exhibits 300; Exhibits 53; business cases for capital planning and investment; procedures for capital planning and investment; documentation of exceptions to capital planning requirements; other relevant documents or records. *Interview:* Organizational personnel with information security program planning responsibilities; organizational personnel responsible for capital planning and investment; organizational personnel with information security responsibilities. *Test:* Organizational processes for capital planning and investment; organizational processes for business case/Exhibit 300/Exhibit 53 development; automated mechanisms supporting the capital planning and investment process.

PM-4	Plan of action and milestones process	Review POA&M Register for accuracy and currency of entries. Verify security plans and activities are being conducted in support of POA&M items.	OMB M02-01, SP 800-37 rev. 1	*Examine:* Information security program plan; plans of action and milestones; procedures addressing plans of action and milestones development and maintenance; procedures addressing plans of action and milestones reporting; procedures for review of plans of action and milestones for consistency with risk management strategy and risk response priorities; results of risk assessments associated with plans of action and milestones; OMB FISMA reporting requirements; other relevant documents or records. *Interview:* Organizational personnel with responsibility for developing, maintaining, reviewing, and reporting plans of action and milestones; organizational personnel with information security responsibilities. *Test:* Organizational processes for plan of action and milestones development, review, maintenance, reporting; automated mechanisms supporting plans of action and milestones.
PM-5	Information system inventory	Review system hardware and software inventory lists.	Annual OMB FISMA reporting memoranda	*Examine:* Information security program plan; information system inventory; procedures addressing information system inventory development and maintenance; OMB FISMA reporting guidance; other relevant documents or records. *Interview:* Organizational personnel with information security program planning and plan implementation responsibilities; organizational personnel responsible for developing and maintaining the information system inventory; organizational personnel with information security responsibilities. *Test:* Organizational processes for information system inventory development and maintenance; automated mechanisms supporting the information system inventory.
PM-6	Information security measures of performance	Review reports and reporting guidance for security metrics and measures of performance delivered to agency by organization under review. Ensure data reported is accurate and relevant. Discuss these reports with System Owner and Security Officer to determine validity and accuracy. Test automated	SP 800-55	*Examine:* Information security program plan; procedures addressing development, monitoring, and reporting of information security measures of performance; other relevant documents or records. *Interview:* Organizational personnel with information security program planning and plan implementation responsibilities; organizational personnel responsible for developing, monitoring, and reporting information security measures of performance; organizational personnel with information security responsibilities. *Test:* Organizational processes for developing, monitoring, and reporting information security measures of performance; automated mechanisms supporting the development, monitoring, and reporting of information security measures of performance.

(Continued)

Control number	Control name	Assessment methods	Notes and guidance documents	SP 800-53A guidance
		reporting system for reporting requirements and delivery of reports.		
PM-7	Enterprise architecture	Review architecture documents for system and organization to ensure that security architecture components are included and valid for system under review. Discuss architecture approach with System Owner, Security Architect, and Security Officer.	SP 800-39, CIO Council's FEA/FSAM guidance, DODAF 2.0 (DOD)	*Examine:* Information security program plan; enterprise architecture documentation; procedures addressing enterprise architecture development; results of risk assessment of enterprise architecture; other relevant documents or records. *Interview:* Organizational personnel with information security program planning and plan implementation responsibilities; organizational personnel responsible for developing enterprise architecture; organizational personnel responsible for risk assessment of enterprise architecture; organizational personnel with information security responsibilities. *Test:* Organizational processes for enterprise architecture development; automated mechanisms supporting the enterprise architecture and its development.
PM-8	Critical infrastructure plan	Review organizational and system-level critical infrastructure requirements documentation. Determine if system is considered part of CIKR (Critical Infrastructure and Key Resources) domain. If so, ensure CIKR Protection Plan is documented and active. Discuss these criteria and documents with organization's key executives, System Owner, AO, and Security Officer for validity and accuracy, along with key resource allocations and budgeting requirements.	HSPD-7, NIPP with Sector extensions	*Examine:* Information security program plan; critical infrastructure and key resources protection plan; procedures addressing development, documentation, and updating of the critical infrastructure and key resources protection plan; HSPD 7; National Infrastructure Protection Plan; other relevant documents or records. *Interview:* Organizational personnel with information security program planning and plan implementation responsibilities; organizational personnel responsible for developing, documenting, and updating the critical infrastructure and key resources protection plan; organizational personnel with information security responsibilities. *Test:* Organizational processes for developing, documenting, and updating the critical infrastructure and key resources protection plan; automated mechanisms supporting the development, documentation, and updating of the critical infrastructure and key resources protection plan.

PM-9	Risk management strategy	Review agency requirements and documentation for risk management and guidance provided to organization. Discuss risk management practices and procedures with senior and key personnel within organization.	SP 800-39, SP 800-37 rev. 1, SP 800-30 rev. 1	*Examine:* Information security program plan; risk management strategy; procedures addressing development, implementation, review, and update of the risk management strategy; risk assessment results relevant to the risk management strategy; other relevant documents or records. *Interview:* Organizational personnel with information security program planning and plan implementation responsibilities; organizational personnel responsible for development, implementation, review, and update of the risk management strategy; organizational personnel with information security responsibilities. *Test:* Organizational processes for development, implementation, review, and update of the risk management strategy; automated mechanisms supporting the development, implementation, review, and update of the risk management strategy.
PM-10	Security authorization process	Review agency guidance for authorizations and the RMF process. Review risk executive guidance provided to the AO during the authorization process. Review this documentation and guidance with the AO, System Owner, and Security Officer to determine relevance and appropriateness of the documentation. Test the automated authorization system, if provided by agency, to determine the viability, accuracy, and functionality of the system in support of the authorization efforts.	SP 800-37 rev. 1, SP 800-39	*Examine:* Information security program plan; procedures addressing management (i.e., documentation, tracking, and reporting) of the security authorization process; security authorization documents; lists or other documentation about security authorization process roles and responsibilities; risk assessment results relevant to the security authorization process and the organization-wide risk management program; organizational risk management strategy; other relevant documents or records. *Interview:* Organizational personnel with information security program planning and plan implementation responsibilities; organizational personnel responsible for management of the security authorization process; authorizing officials; system owners, senior information security officer; organizational personnel with information security responsibilities. *Test:* Organizational processes for security authorization; automated mechanisms supporting the security authorization process. PM-11
PM-11	Mission/business process definition	Review agency cocumentation to cetermine, if system level protection requirements	FIPS-199, SP 800-60	*Examine:* Information security program plan; risk management strategy; procedures for determining mission/business protection needs; risk assessment results relevant to determination of mission/business protection needs; other relevant documents

(Continued)

Control number	Control name	Assessment methods	Notes and guidance documents	SP 800-53A guidance
		are derived from the agency needs. Review documents and criteria to ensure protection needs are continually revised as new protection needs are identified by the agency. Discuss these protection efforts with System Owner and Security Officer to determine the validity of requirements and protection needs as identified by the agency.		or records. *Interview:* Organizational personnel with information security program planning and plan implementation responsibilities; organizational personnel responsible for mission/business processes; organizational personnel responsible for determining information protection needs for mission/business processes; organizational personnel with information security responsibilities. *Test:* Organizational processes for defining mission/business processes and their information protection needs.
PM-12	Insider threat program	Review agency documentation to determine if the agency has implemented an insider threat program that includes a cross-discipline insider threat incident handling team. Discuss these efforts with AO, System Owner, and Security Officer to determine applicability and validity of program to organization and system.	E.O. 13587	*Examine:* Information security program plan; insider threat program documentation; procedures for the insider threat program; risk assessment results relevant to insider threats; list or other documentation on the cross-discipline insider threat incident handling team; other relevant documents or records. *Interview:* Organizational personnel with information security program planning and plan implementation responsibilities; organizational personnel responsible for the insider threat program; members of the cross-discipline insider threat incident handling team; organizational personnel with information security responsibilities. *Test:* Organizational processes for implementing the insider threat program and the cross-discipline insider threat incident handling team; automated mechanisms supporting and/or implementing the insider threat program and the cross-discipline insider threat incident handling team.
PM-13	Information security workforce	Review workforce and training documentation and program for the agency to ensure that these needs are being implemented within the organization. Discuss these	DOD Specific (DOD 8570.01M), DHS NICE Guidance	*Examine:* Information security program plan; information security workforce development and improvement program documentation; procedures for the information security workforce development and improvement program; other relevant documents or records. *Interview:* Organizational personnel with information security program planning and plan implementation responsibilities; organizational personnel responsible for the

information security workforce development and improvement program; organizational personnel with information security responsibilities. *Test:* Organizational processes for implementing information security workforce development and improvement program; automated mechanisms supporting and/or implementing the information security workforce development and improvement program.

PM-14	Testing, training, and monitoring	*Examine:* Information security program plan; plans for conducting security testing, training, and monitoring activities; organizational procedures addressing development and maintenance of plans for conducting security testing, training, and monitoring activities; risk management strategy; procedures for review of plans for conducting security testing, training, and monitoring activities for consistency with risk management strategy and risk response priorities; results of risk assessments associated with conducting security testing, training, and monitoring activities; evidence that plans for conducting security testing, training, and monitoring activities are executed in a timely manner; other relevant documents or records. *Interview:* Organizational personnel with responsibility for developing and maintaining plans for conducting security testing, training, and monitoring activities; organizational personnel with information security responsibilities. *Test:* Organizational processes for development and maintenance of plans for conducting security testing, training, and monitoring activities; automated mechanisms supporting development and maintenance of plans for conducting security testing, training, and monitoring activities.	SP 800-82, SP 800-16, SP 800-37, rev.1, SP 800-53A, SAP 800-137
		Review agency documentation to ensure the security testing, training, and monitoring requirements are being achieved. Discuss these with the senior security officials and the Security Officer.	
PM-15	Contacts with security groups and associations	*Examine:* Information security program plan; risk management strategy; procedures for contacts with security groups and associations; evidence of established and institutionalized contact with security groups and associations; lists or other documentation about contact with and/or membership in security groups and associations; other relevant documents or records. *Interview:* Organizational personnel with information security program planning and plan implementation responsibilities; organizational personnel responsible for establishing and institutionalizing contact with security groups and associations; organizational personnel with information security responsibilities; personnel	
		Review agency requirements for external security training and interface activities and support. Ensure the agency supports the exchange of best practices and learning for the security staff of the organization. Discuss these needs with the senior security staff and the	

efforts with organization senior officials, AO, System Owner, and Security Officer to ensure implementation has occurred within the organization.

(Continued)

Control number	Control name	Assessment methods	Notes and guidance documents	SP 800-53A guidance
		Security Officer to ensure implementation and support are active.		from selected groups and associations with which the organization has established and institutionalized contact. *Test:* Organizational processes for establishing and institutionalizing contact with security groups and associations; automated mechanisms supporting contacts with security groups and associations.
PM-16	Threat awareness program	Review agency documentation of threat and vulnerability information sharing within the agency, among the departments, and across the security domains. Discuss these information-sharing efforts with the AO, System Owner, and the Security Officer to ensure implementation and sharing is actually occurring and active.		*Examine:* Information security program plan; threat awareness program documentation; procedures for the threat awareness program; risk assessment results relevant to threat awareness; list or other documentation on the cross-organization information-sharing capability; other relevant documents or records. *Interview:* Organizational personnel with information security program planning and plan implementation responsibilities; organizational personnel responsible for the threat awareness program; organizational personnel with responsibility for the cross-organization information sharing capability; organizational personnel with information security responsibilities; personnel with whom threat awareness information is shared by the organization. *Test:* Organizational processes for implementing the threat awareness program; Organizational processes for implementing the cross-organization information-sharing capability; automated mechanisms supporting and/or implementing the threat awareness program; automated mechanisms supporting and/or implementing the cross-organization information-sharing capability.

N. *Personnel security family*

FIPS-200 provides the following criteria for this family of controls: Personnel security (PS): Organizations must: (i) ensure that individuals occupying positions of responsibility within organizations (including third-party service providers) are trustworthy and meet established security criteria for those positions; (ii) ensure that organizational information and information systems are protected during and after personnel actions such as terminations and transfers; and (iii) employ formal sanctions for personnel failing to comply with organizational security policies and procedures.

The primary assessment areas for these controls include:

a. Audit controls that ensure individuals occupying positions of responsibility within organizations (including third-party service providers) are trustworthy.
b. Review security mechanisms that ensure that organizational information and information systems are protected during and after personnel actions, such as terminations and transfers.
c. Assess formal sanctions for personnel failing to comply with organizational security policies and procedures.

Control number	Control name	Assessment methods	Notes and guidance documents	SP 800-53A guidance
PS-1	Personnel security policy and procedures	Review documentation for policies and procedures for personnel actions with staff, contractors and users. Discuss with System Owner and Security Officer.	SP 800-12, SP 800-100	*Examine:* Personnel security policy and procedures; other relevant documents or records. *Interview:* Organizational personnel with access control responsibilities; organizational personnel with information security responsibilities.
PS-2	Position risk designation	Review documentation for risk and position screen requirement, which the organization implements for users and staff. Discuss with operations staff, personnel staff, System Owner, and Security Officer.	5 C.F.R. 731.106	*Examine:* Personnel security policy; procedures addressing position categorization; appropriate codes of federal regulations; list of risk designations for organizational positions; security plan; records of position risk designation reviews and updates; other relevant documents or records. *Interview:* Organizational personnel with personnel security responsibilities; organizational personnel with information security responsibilities. *Test:* Organizational processes for assigning, reviewing, and updating position risk designations; organizational processes for establishing screening criteria.
PS-3	Personnel screening	Review documentation of organization to determine screening requirements for users of system and rescreen actions implemented for personnel accessing information systems based on types of information processed, stored, or transmitted by the systems. Discuss with operations staff, personnel staff, System Owner and Security Officer.	5 C.F.R. 731.106, FIPS-199, FIPS-201, SP 800-60, SP 800-73, SP 800-76, SP 800-78, ICD 704	*Examine:* Personnel security policy; procedures addressing personnel screening; records of screened personnel; security plan; other relevant documents or records. *Interview:* Organizational personnel with personnel security responsibilities; organizational personnel with information security responsibilities. *Test:* Organizational processes for personnel screening.
PS-3(1)	Personnel screening: Classified information	Review documentation for the organization to determine processes implemented for accessing an information system processing, storing, or transmitting classified information are cleared and indoctrinated to the highest classification level of the information to which users have access on	5 C.F.R. 731.106, FIPS-199, FIPS-201, SP 800-60, SP 800-73, SP 800-76, SP 800-78, ICD 704	*Examine:* Personnel security policy; procedures addressing personnel screening; records of screened personnel; other relevant documents or records. *Interview:* Organizational personnel with personnel security responsibilities; organizational personnel with information security responsibilities. *Test:* Organizational processes for clearing and indoctrinating personnel for access to classified information.

	the system. Discuss with System Owner, Information Owner(s), personnel staff, operations staff, and Security Officer.		
PS-3(2)	Personnel screening: Formal indoctrination	Review documentation of organization to ensure that formal indoctrination actions are instituted for all of the relevant types of information to which specified users have access on the system. Verify formal records of indoctrination are records and maintained by appropriate staff. Discuss with System Owner, Information Owner(s), personnel staff, operations staff, and Security Officer.	5 C.F.R. 731.106, FIPS-199, FIPS-201, SP 800-60, SP 800-73, SP 800-76, SP 800-78, ICD 704	*Examine:* Personnel security policy; procedures addressing personnel screening; records of screened personnel; other relevant documents or records. *Interview:* Organizational personnel with personnel security responsibilities; organizational personnel with information security responsibilities. *Test:* Organizational processes for formal indoctrination for all relevant types of information to which personnel have access.
PS-3(3)	Personnel screening: Information with special protection measures	Review documentation for organization to determine processes implemented for accessing an information system processing, storing, or transmitting classified information are cleared and indoctrinated to the special protected information required for their positon. Special protected information, which requires this treatment, may include controlled unclassified information (CUI) or sources and methods information (SAMI). Discuss with System Owner, Information Owner(s), personnel staff, operations staff, and Security Officer.	5 C.F.R. 731.106, FIPS-199, FIPS-201, SP 800-60, SP 800-73, SP 800-76, SP 800-78, ICD 704	*Examine:* Personnel security policy; access control policy, procedures addressing personnel screening; records of screened personnel; screening criteria; records of access authorizations; other relevant documents or records. *Interview:* Organizational personnel with personnel security responsibilities; organizational personnel with information security responsibilities. *Test:* Organizational processes for ensuring valid access authorizations for information requiring special protection; organizational process for additional personnel screening for information requiring special protection.
PS-4	Personnel termination	Review documentation for organization to determine full termination actions, which transpire when user is terminated. Actions		*Examine:* Personnel security policy; procedures addressing personnel termination; records of personnel termination actions; list of information system accounts; records of terminated or revoked

(Continued)

Control number	Control name	Assessment methods	Notes and guidance documents	SP 800-53A guidance
		will include exit interviews, disabling of accounts, returning of organizational property, revoking authentication credentials, and other selectable activities. Ensure termination activities are formally documented for each user terminated in accordance with laws, regulations and EO's as required. Discuss with System Owner, Operations Managers, Security Officer, and personnel staff.		authenticators/credentials; records of exit interviews; other relevant documents or records. *Interview:* Organizational personnel with personnel security responsibilities; organizational personnel with account management responsibilities; system/network administrators; organizational personnel with information security responsibilities. *Test:* Organizational processes for personnel termination; automated mechanisms supporting and/or implementing personnel termination notifications; automated mechanisms for disabling information system access/revoking authenticators.
PS-4(1)	Personnel termination: Post-employment requirements	Review documentation to ensure that the organization has consulted with the legal staff/office of the General Counsel regarding matters of post-employment requirements on terminated individuals. Discuss with personnel staff, System Owner, and Security Officer.		*Examine:* Personnel security policy; procedures addressing personnel termination; signed post-employment acknowledgement forms; list of applicable, legally binding postemployment requirements; other relevant documents or records. *Interview:* [Organizational personnel with personnel security responsibilities; organizational personnel with information security responsibilities. *Test:* Organizational processes for post-employment requirements.
PS-4(2)	Personnel termination: Automated notification	Review documentation for organization to determine the extent of automated mechanisms are used for termination actions. Automated mechanisms can be used to send automatic alerts or notifications to specific organizational personnel or roles, when users are terminated. Discuss with personnel staff, System Owner, and Security Officer.		*Examine:* Personnel security policy; procedures addressing personnel termination; information system design documentation; information system configuration settings and associated documentation; records of personnel termination actions; automated notifications of employee terminations; other relevant documents or records. *Interview:* Organizational personnel with personnel security responsibilities; organizational personnel with information security responsibilities. *Test:* Organizational processes for personnel termination; automated mechanisms supporting and/or implementing personnel termination notifications.

PS-5	Personnel transfer	Review documentation for the organization to determine the system-based actions invoked, when users are transferred to another organization, either permanently or for long-term assignments. Discuss with personnel staff, System Owner, operations staff, and Security Officer	*Examine:* Personnel security policy; procedures addressing personnel transfer; security plan; records of personnel transfer actions; list of information system and facility access authorizations; other relevant documents or records. *Interview:* Organizational personnel with personnel security responsibilities organizational personnel with account management responsibilities; system/network administrators; organizational personnel with information security responsibilities. *Test:* Organizational processes for personnel transfer; automated mechanisms supporting and/or implementing personnel transfer notifications; automated mechanisms for disabling information system access/revoking authenticators.
PS-6	Access agreements	Review documentation to ensure that the organization has developed and requires all users to read, understand, and sign all appropriate assess agreements for system such as nondisclosure agreements, acceptable use agreements, rules of behavior, and conflict-of-interest agreements. Review these agreements for appropriate coverage and applicability. Discuss with personnel staff, System Owner, and Security Officer.	*Examine:* Personnel security policy; procedures addressing access agreements for organizational information and information systems; security plan; access agreements; records of access agreement reviews and updates; other relevant documents or records. *Interview:* Organizational personnel with personnel security responsibilities; organizational personnel who have signed/resigned access agreements; organizational personnel with information security responsibilities. *Test:* Organizational processes for access agreements; automated mechanisms supporting access agreements.
PS-6(1)	Access agreements: Information requiring special protection		Withdrawn: Incorporated into PS-3
PS-6(2)	Access agreements: Classified information	Review documentation for the organization to determine processes implemented for formal user agreements necessary accessing	*Examine:* Personnel security policy; procedures addressing access agreements for organizational information and information systems; access agreements; access authorizations; personnel

(Continued)

Control number	Control name	Assessment methods	Notes and guidance documents	SP 800-53A guidance
	requiring special protection	an information system processing, storing, or transmitting classified information to which users have access on the system. Discuss with System Owner, Information Owner(s), personnel staff, operations staff and Security Officer.		security criteria; signed nondisclosure agreements; other relevant documents or records. *Interview:* Organizational personnel with personnel security responsibilities; organizational personnel who have signed nondisclosure agreements; organizational personnel with information security responsibilities. *Test:* Organizational processes for access to classified information requiring special protection.
PS-6(3)	Access agreements: Post-employment requirements	Review documentation to ensure that the organization has consulted with the legal staff/Office of the General Counsel regarding matters of post-employment agreement requirements on terminated individuals. Ensure these agreements are enacted by sampling the terminated user records for completeness and accuracy. Discuss with personnel staff, System Owner, and Security Officer.		*Examine:* Personnel security policy; procedures addressing access agreements for organizational information and information systems; signed post-employment acknowledgement forms; access agreements; list of applicable, legally binding postemployment requirements; other relevant documents or records. *Interview:* Organizational personnel with personnel security responsibilities; organizational personnel who have signed access agreements that include post-employment requirements; organizational personnel with information security responsibilities. *Test:* Organizational processes for post-employment requirements; automated mechanisms supporting notifications and individual acknowledgements of post-employment requirements.
PS-7	Third-party personnel security	Review documentation for the organization to ensure that all personnel security requirements for third-party or contract users are maintained at same level as all other users of system. Discuss with acquisition staff, Contract Administrators, personnel staff, System Owner, and Security Officer.	SP 800-35	*Examine:* Personnel security policy; procedures addressing third-party personnel security; list of personnel security requirements; acquisition documents; service-level agreements; compliance monitoring process; other relevant documents or records. *Interview:* Organizational personnel with personnel security responsibilities; third-party providers; system/network administrators; organizational personnel with account management responsibilities; organizational personnel with information security responsibilities. *Test:* Organizational processes for managing and

| PS-8 | Personnel sanctions | Review documentation for the organization to ensure that personnel sanctions are maintained and enforced to the legal and regulatory levels required for system. Sanctions processes are described in access agreements and can be included as part of general personnel policies and procedures for organizations. Organizations consult with the legal staff/Office of the General Counsel regarding matters of user sanctions. Discuss with legal staff, personnel staff, operations staff, System Owner, and Security Officer. | monitoring third-party personnel security; automated mechanisms supporting and/or implementing monitoring of provider compliance. *Examine:* Personnel security policy; procedures addressing personnel sanctions; rules of behavior; records of formal sanctions; other relevant documents or records. *Interview:* Organizational personnel with personnel security responsibilities; organizational personnel with information security responsibilities. *Test:* Organizational processes for managing personnel sanctions; automated mechanisms supporting and/or implementing notifications. |

O. *Risk assessment family*

FIPS-200 provides the following criteria for this family of controls: Risk assessment (RA): Organizations must periodically assess the risk to organizational operations (including mission, functions, image, or reputation), organizational assets, and individuals, resulting from the operation of organizational information systems and the associated processing, storage, or transmission of organizational information.

The primary assessment areas for these controls include:

Audit the necessary mechanisms to ensure periodic assessment of risk to organizational operations (including mission, functions, image, or reputation), organizational assets, and individuals, resulting from the operation of organizational information systems and the associated processing, storage, or transmission of organizational information.

Control number	Control name	Assessment methods	Notes and guidance documents	SP 800-53A guidance
RA-1	Risk assessment policy and procedures	Review risk management policy and procedures, risk assessment guidance for organization, and risk tolerance guidance from Risk Executive. Check for accuracy, currently, and relevance to program, project and system. Discuss risk assessment process with Security Officer and System Owner.	SP 800-12, SP 800-30, rev. 1, SP 800-37, rev. 1, SP 800-100	*Examine:* Risk assessment policy and procedures; other relevant documents or records. *Interview:* Organizational personnel with risk assessment responsibilities; organizational personnel with information security responsibilities.
RA-2	Security categorization	Review Categorization documents for system to ensure that the categories are set and justifications are documented for each information type utilized in the system under review. Discuss categorization with AO, System Owner, and Security Officer for applicability and status reporting.	FIPS-199, SP 800-37, rev. 1, SP 800-39, SP 800-60	*Examine:* Risk assessment policy; security planning policy and procedures; procedures addressing security categorization of organizational information and information systems; security plan; security categorization documentation; other relevant documents or records. *Interview:* Organizational personnel with security categorization and risk assessment responsibilities; organizational personnel with information security responsibilities. *Test:* Organizational processes for security categorization.
RA-3	Risk assessment	Review all risk assessments for system for completeness, impact, and likelihood determinations based upon potential loss resulting from loss of confidentiality, integrity or availability. Review and discuss risk assessments with AO, System Owner, and Security Officer for use, process flow, and applicability to system.	SP 800-37, rev. 1, SP 800-30, rev. 1	*Examine:* [Risk assessment policy; security planning policy and procedures; procedures addressing organizational assessments of risk; security plan; risk assessment; risk assessment results; risk assessment reviews; risk assessment updates; other relevant documents or records. *Interview:* Organizational personnel with risk assessment responsibilities; organizational personnel with information security responsibilities. *Test:* Organizational processes for risk assessment; automated mechanisms supporting and/or for conducting, documenting, reviewing, disseminating, and updating the risk assessment.
RA-4	Risk assessment update		Withdrawn: Incorporated into RA-3	

(Continued)

Control number	Control name	Assessment methods	Notes and guidance documents	SP 800-53A guidance
RA-5	Vulnerability scanning	Review organizational documentation for vulnerability scan events and activities. Verify scan activities with Security Officer are conducted on an organizational defined schedule. Confirm results of scans are reviewed by Security Officer and System Owner. Test vulnerability scanning tool(s) utilized by organization.	SP 800-37, rev. 1, SP 800-40, SP 800-70, SP 800-115	*Examine:* Risk assessment policy; procedures addressing vulnerability scanning; risk assessment; security plan; security assessment report; vulnerability scanning tools and associated configuration documentation; vulnerability scanning results; patch and vulnerability management records; other relevant documents or records. *Interview:* Organizational personnel with risk assessment, security control assessment and vulnerability scanning responsibilities; organizational personnel with vulnerability scan analysis responsibilities; organizational personnel with vulnerability remediation responsibilities; organizational personnel with information security responsibilities; system/network administrators. *Test:* Organizational processes for vulnerability scanning, analysis, remediation, and information sharing; automated mechanisms supporting and/or implementing vulnerability scanning, analysis, remediation, and information sharing.
RA-5(1)	Vulnerability scanning; Update tool capability	Test vulnerability scanning tool(s) for automatic/manual update capabilities. Confirm periodic updates are performed by security staff prior to conducting each scan event.	SP 800-37, rev. 1, SP 800-40, SP 800-70, SP 800-115	*Examine:* Procedures addressing vulnerability scanning; security plan; security assessment report; vulnerability scanning tools and associated configuration documentation; vulnerability scanning results; patch and vulnerability management records; other relevant documents or records. *Interview:* Organizational personnel with vulnerability scanning responsibilities; organizational personnel with information security responsibilities. *Test:* Organizational processes for vulnerability scanning; automated mechanisms/tools supporting and/or implementing vulnerability scanning.
RA-5(2)	Vulnerability scanning; Update by frequency/prior to new	Test vulnerability scanning tool(s) for update capabilities on an organizational-defined frequency. Ensure that each scan tool vendor provides updates	SP 800-37, rev. 1, SP 800-40, SP 800-70, SP 800-115	*Examine:* Procedures addressing vulnerability scanning; security plan; security assessment report; vulnerability scanning tools and associated configuration documentation; vulnerability scanning results; patch and vulnerability management records;

	scan/when identified	based upon new vulnerabilities identified for system/operating system under review. Confirm periodic updates are performed by security staff prior to conducting each scan event.		other relevant documents or records. *Interview:* Organizational personnel with vulnerability scanning responsibilities; organizational personnel with vulnerability scan analysis responsibilities; organizational personnel with information security responsibilities; system/network administrators. *Test:* Organizational processes for vulnerability scanning; automated mechanisms/tools supporting and/or implementing vulnerability scanning.
RA-5(3)	Vulnerability scanning: Breadth/depth of coverage	Verify scan tool(s) used to cover all components, which are scanned (breadth) and whose vulnerabilities are identified during scans (depth). Confirm security personnel review depth and breadth of scan event, each time a scan is conducted. Discussions with Security Officer and review of scan result documentation and reports.	SP 800-37, rev. 1, SP 800-40, SP 800-70, SP 800-115	*Examine:* Procedures addressing vulnerability scanning; security plan; security assessment report; vulnerability scanning tools and associated configuration documentation; vulnerability scanning results; patch and vulnerability management records; other relevant documents or records. *Interview:* Organizational personnel with vulnerability scanning responsibilities; organizational personnel with vulnerability scan analysis responsibilities; organizational personnel with information security responsibilities. *Test:* Organizational processes for vulnerability scanning; automated mechanisms/tools supporting and/or implementing vulnerability scanning.
RA-5(4)	Vulnerability scanning: Discoverable information	Review documentation from scan events to ensure that organization reviews results and documents anomalies and issues are identified and acted upon by the organization through items added to POA&M register and other methods of issue identification. Confirm process with System Owner and Security Officer.	SP 800-37, rev. 1, SP 800-40, SP 800-70, SP 800-115	*Examine:* Procedures addressing vulnerability scanning; security assessment report; penetration test results; vulnerability scanning results; risk assessment report; records of corrective actions taken; incident response records; audit records; other relevant documents or records. *Interview:* Organizational personnel with vulnerability scanning and/or penetration testing responsibilities; organizational personnel with vulnerability scan analysis responsibilities; organizational personnel responsible for risk response; organizational personnel responsible for incident management and response; organizational personnel with information security responsibilities. *Test:* Organizational processes for vulnerability scanning; organizational processes for risk response; organizational processes for incident management

(Continued)

Control number	Control name	Assessment methods	Notes and guidance documents	SP 800-53A guidance
				and response; automated mechanisms/tools supporting and/or implementing vulnerability scanning; automated mechanisms supporting and/or implementing risk response; automated mechanisms supporting and/or implementing incident management and response.
RA-5(5)	Vulnerability scanning: Privileged access	Review the vulnerability scan requirements for privileged credential access and scanning efforts. Ensure all requirements and procedures for privileged access scan events are documented and approved by System Owner. Confirm in discussions with System Owner and Security Officer.	SP 800-37, rev. 1, SP 800-40, SP 800-70, SP 800-115	*Examine:* Risk assessment policy; procedures addressing vulnerability scanning; security plan; information system design documentation; information system configuration settings and associated documentation; list of information system components for vulnerability scanning; personnel access authorization list; authorization credentials; access authorization records; other relevant documents or records. *Interview:* Organizational personnel with vulnerability scanning responsibilities; system/network administrators; organizational personnel responsible for access control to the information system; organizational personnel responsible for configuration management of the information system; system developers; organizational personnel with information security responsibilities. *Test:* Organizational processes for vulnerability scanning; organizational processes for access control; automated mechanisms supporting and/or implementing access control; automated mechanisms/tools supporting and/or implementing vulnerability scanning.
RA-5(6)	Vulnerability scanning: Automated trend analyses	Review output documentation from vulnerability scanning to ensure that trend analysis evaluations are conducted by relevant staff. Confirm through discussions with System Owner and Security Officer.	SP 800-37, rev. 1, SP 800-40, SP 800-70, SP 800-115	*Examine:* Risk assessment policy; procedures addressing vulnerability scanning; information system design documentation; vulnerability scanning tools and techniques documentation; vulnerability scanning results; other relevant documents or records. *Interview:* Organizational personnel with vulnerability scanning responsibilities; organizational personnel with vulnerability scan analysis responsibilities; organizational personnel with information security responsibilities. *Test:* Organizational processes for

RA-5(7)	Vulnerability scanning; Automated detection and notification of unauthorized components	Withdrawn: Incorporated into CM-8		vulnerability scanning; automated mechanisms/tools supporting and/or implementing vulnerability scanning; automated mechanisms supporting and/or implementing trend analysis of vulnerability scan results.
RA-5(8)	Vulnerability scanning; Review historic audit logs	Review output documentation from vulnerability scanning to ensure that historical analysis and event evaluations are conducted by relevant staff. Confirm through discussions with System Owner and Security Officer.	SP 800-37, rev. 1, SP 800-40, SP 800-70, SP 800-115	*Examine*: Risk assessment policy; procedures addressing vulnerability scanning; audit logs; records of audit log reviews; vulnerability scanning results; patch and vulnerability management records; other relevant documents or records. *Interview*: Organizational personnel with vulnerability scanning responsibilities; organizational personnel with vulnerability scan analysis responsibilities; organizational personnel with audit record review responsibilities; system/network administrators; organizational personnel with information security responsibilities. *Test*: Organizational processes for vulnerability scanning; organizational process for audit record review and response; automated mechanisms/tools supporting and/or implementing vulnerability scanning; automated mechanisms supporting and/or implementing audit record review.
RA-5(9)	Vulnerability scanning; Penetration testing and analyses	Withdrawn: Incorporated into CA-8		
RA-5(10)	Vulnerability scanning; Correlate	Review output scan results analysis documentation to determine the organization	SP 800-37, rev. 1, SP 800-40, SP 800-70, SP 800-115	*Examine*: Risk assessment policy; procedures addressing vulnerability scanning; risk assessment; security plan; vulnerability scanning tools and

(Continued)

Control number	Control name	Assessment methods	Notes and guidance documents	SP 800-53A guidance
	scanning information	correlates the output from vulnerability scanning tools to determine the presence of multi-vulnerability/multi-hop attack vectors. Discuss events and results with System Owner and Security Officer to determine depth of analysis conducted and any resultant actions taken as a result of correlated information.		techniques documentation; vulnerability scanning results; vulnerability management records; audit records; event/vulnerability correlation logs; other relevant documents or records. *Interview*: Organizational personnel with vulnerability scanning responsibilities; organizational personnel with vulnerability scan analysis responsibilities; organizational personnel with information security responsibilities. *Test*: Organizational processes for vulnerability scanning; automated mechanisms/tools supporting and/or implementing vulnerability scanning; automated mechanisms implementing correlation of vulnerability scan results.
RA-6	Technical surveillance countermeasures survey	Review documentation to determine the scope and conduct of the technical countermeasures evaluations conducted by the organization and outside entities. This process involves scanning for electronic listening devices and components. Confirm the requirements, actions, and support activities with System Owner, Security Officer and the Facility Security Officer during interviews.	SP 800-37, rev. 1	*Examine*: Risk assessment policy; procedures addressing technical surveillance countermeasures surveys; security plan; audit records/event logs; other relevant documents or records. *Interview*: Organizational personnel with technical surveillance countermeasures surveys responsibilities; system/network administrators; organizational personnel with information security responsibilities. *Test*: Organizational processes for technical surveillance countermeasures surveys; automated mechanisms/tools supporting and/or implementing technical surveillance countermeasures surveys.

P. *Systems acquisition family*
FIPS-200 provides the following criteria for this family of controls: System and services acqui-sition (SA): Organizations must: (i) allocate sufficient resources to adequately protect organizational information systems; (ii) employ system development life cycle processes that incorporate information security considerations; (iii) employ software usage and installation restrictions; and (iv) ensure that third-party providers employ adequate security measures to protect information, applications, and/or services outsourced from the organization.

The primary assessment areas for these controls include:

a. Audit strategies for the allocation of sufficient resources to adequately protect the organizational information systems.
b. Review mechanisms that ensure the use of system development life cycle processes that incorporate information security considerations.
c. Assess software usage and installation restrictions on information systems.
d. Evaluate processes that ensure that third-party providers employ adequate security measures to protect information, applications, and/or services outsourced from the organization.

Control number	Control name	Assessment methods	Notes and guidance documents	SP 800-53A guidance
SA-1	System and services acquisition policy and procedures	Review documentation for organization to determine the acquisition processes, policies, and procedures in place for systems, components, and services in support of system under review. Discuss with System Owner, acquisition staff, operations staff, and Security Officer.	SP 800-12, SP 800-37, rev. 1, SP 800-64, SP 800-100	*Examine:* System and services acquisition policy and procedures; other relevant documents or records. *Interview:* Organizational personnel with system and services acquisition responsibilities; organizational personnel with information security responsibilities.
SA-2	Allocation of resources	Review documentation for organization to determine the acquisition methods and techniques for the allocation of various resources for system and system components with both initial acquisition and sustainment activities are to be reviewed. Discuss with System Owner, acquisition staff, operations staff, and Security Officer.	SP 800-37, rev. 1, SP 800-64, SP 800-65, OMB A-11, OMB M-00-07	*Examine:* System and services acquisition policy; procedures addressing the allocation of resources to information security requirements; procedures addressing capital planning and investment control; organizational programming and budgeting documentation; other relevant documents or records. *Interview:* Organizational personnel with capital planning, investment control, organizational programming and budgeting responsibilities; organizational personnel responsible for determining information security requirements for information systems/services; organizational personnel with information security responsibilities. *Test:* Organizational processes for determining information security requirements; organizational processes for capital planning, programming, and budgeting; automated mechanisms supporting and/or implementing organizational capital planning, programming, and budgeting.
SA-3	System development life cycle	Review documentation for organization to ensure that a fully developed system development life cycle (SDLC) approach to acquisition is in place and operational, since this sets the foundation for the successful	SP 800-37, rev. 1, SP 800-64, OMB A-11, OMB M-00-07	*Examine:* System and services acquisition policy; procedures addressing the integration of information security into the system development life cycle process; information system development life cycle documentation; information security risk management strategy/program documentation; other relevant

		documents or records. *Interview:* Organizational personnel with information security and system life cycle development responsibilities; organizational personnel with information security risk management responsibilities; organizational personnel with information security responsibilities. *Test:* Organizational processes for defining and documenting the SDLC; organizational processes for identifying SDLC roles and responsibilities; organizational process for integrating information security risk management into the SDLC; automated mechanisms supporting and/or implementing the SDLC.		development, implementation, and operation of organizational information systems. Review processes, procedures and SDLC products for system to determine extent of compliance and conformity of system acquisition to organizational requirements. Discuss with System Owner, Security Officer, acquisition staff and operations staff.
SA-4	Acquisition process	*Examine:* System and services acquisition policy; procedures addressing the integration of information security requirements, descriptions, and criteria into the acquisition process; acquisition contracts for the information system, system component, or information system service; information system design documentation; other relevant documents or records. *Interview:* Organizational personnel with acquisition/contracting responsibilities; organizational personnel with responsibility for determining information system security functional, strength, and assurance requirements; system/network administrators; organizational personnel with information security responsibilities. *Test:* Organizational processes for determining information system security functional, strength, and assurance requirements; organizational processes for developing acquisition contracts; automated mechanisms supporting and/or implementing acquisitions and inclusion of security requirements in contracts.	HSPD-12, FIPS-140-2, FIPS-201, SP 800-23, SP 800-35, SP 800-36, SP 800-37, rev. 1, SP 800-64, SP 800-70, SP 800-137, ISO 15408	Review documentation for organization to ensure that all required documents, acquisition documents, and acceptance testing documents are complete, compliant with defined SDLC, and accurate. Review test results to ensure that proper verification and validation efforts were applied during acceptance testing of system. Discuss with System Owner, Security Officer, acquisition staff, and operations staff.
SA-4(1)	Acquisition process: Functional	*Examine:* System and services acquisition policy; procedures addressing the integration of information security requirements,	HSPD-12, FIPS-140-2, FIPS-201, SP 800-23, SP 800-35, SP	Review documentation for organization to ensure the interface functionality of the

(Continued)

Control number	Control name	Assessment methods	Notes and guidance documents	SP 800-53A guidance
	properties of security controls	security controls for the system. Evaluate the visible functionality, rather than the internal functionality of the controls through tests and examinations. Discuss with Security Officer, acquisition staff, Developers, operations staff, and System Owner.	800-36, SP 800-37, rev. 1, SP 800-64, SP 800-70, SP 800-137, ISO 15408	descriptions, and criteria into the acquisition process; solicitation documents; acquisition documentation; acquisition contracts for the information system, system component, or information system services; other relevant documents or records. *Interview:* Organizational personnel with acquisition/contracting responsibilities; organizational personnel with responsibility for determining information system security functional requirements; information system developer or service provider; organizational personnel with information security responsibilities. *Test:* Organizational processes for determining information system security functional, requirements; organizational processes for developing acquisition contracts; automated mechanisms supporting and/or implementing acquisitions and inclusion of security requirements in contracts.
SA-4(2)	Acquisition process: Design/implementation information for security controls	Review documentation to determine the extent the organization requires different levels of detail in design and implementation documentation for security controls employed in the system, system components, or system services based on mission/business requirements, requirements for trustworthiness/resiliency, and requirements for analysis and testing. Evaluate documents to ensure that compliance and full explanations are produced to support analysis. Discuss with Developers, System Owner, acquisition staff, operations staff, and Security Officer.	HSPD-12, FIPS-140-2, FIPS-201, SP 800-23, SP 800-35, SP 800-37, rev. 1, SP 800-64, SP 800-70, SP 800-137, ISO 15408	*Examine:* System and services acquisition policy; procedures addressing the integration of information security requirements, descriptions, and criteria into the acquisition process; solicitation documents; acquisition documentation; acquisition contracts for the information system, system components, or information system services; design and implementation information for security controls employed in the information system, system component, or information system service; other relevant documents or records. *Interview:* Organizational personnel with acquisition/contracting responsibilities; organizational personnel with responsibility for determining information system security requirements; information system developer or service provider; organizational personnel with information security responsibilities. *Test:*

				[Organizational processes for determining level of detail for system design and security controls; organizational processes for developing acquisition contracts; automated mechanisms supporting and/or implementing development of system design details.
SA-4(3)	Acquisition process: Development methods/ techniques/ practices	Review documentation for the organization to ensure that development activities to reduce errors in system SDLC include state-of-the-practice software development methods, systems/ security engineering methods, quality control processes, and testing, evaluation, and validation techniques. Validate documentation through observing the coding methodologies, practices, and testing events. Discuss with System Owner, Developers, acquisition staff, operations staff, and Security Officer.	HSPD-12, FIPS-140-2, FIPS-201, SP 800-23, SP 800-35, SP 800-36, SP 800-37, rev. 1, SP 800-64, SP 800-70, SP 800-137, ISO 15408	Examine: System and services acquisition policy; procedures addressing the integration of information security requirements, descriptions, and criteria into the acquisition process; solicitation documents; acquisition documentation; acquisition contracts for the information system, system component, or information system service; list of system/ security engineering methods to be included in developer's system development life cycle process; list of software development methods to be included in developer's system development life cycle process; list of testing/ evaluation/validation techniques to be included in developer's system development life cycle process; list of quality control processes to be included in developer's system development life cycle process; other relevant documents or records. Interview: Organizational personnel with acquisition/contracting responsibilities; organizational personnel with responsibility for determining information system security requirements; organizational personnel with information security and system life cycle responsibilities; information system developer or service provider. Test: Organizational processes for development methods, techniques, and processes.
SA-4(4)	Acquisition process: Assignment of components to systems		Withdrawn: Incorporated into CM-8(9)	

Control number	Control name	Assessment methods	Notes and guidance documents	SP 800-53A guidance
SA-4(5)	Acquisition process: System/component/service configurations	Review documentation to ensure that the organization requires full configuration for all security components in accordance with federal guidelines, regulations, and agency directives. Special testing for ports, protocols, and services active on system is one area of review for delivery of system. Discuss with Developers, acquisition staff, operations staff, System Owner, and Security Officer.	HSPD-12, FIPS-140-2, FIPS-201, SP 800-23, SP 800-35, SP 800-36, SP 800-37, rev. 1, SP 800-64, SP 800-70, SP 800-137, ISO 15408, DODI 8551.01	*Examine:* System and services acquisition policy; procedures addressing the integration of information security requirements, descriptions, and criteria into the acquisition process; solicitation documents; acquisition documentation; acquisition contracts for the information system, system component, or information system service; security configurations to be implemented by developer of the information system, system component, or information system service; service-level agreements; other relevant documents or records. *Interview:* Organizational personnel with acquisition/contracting responsibilities; organizational personnel with responsibility for determining information system security requirements; information system developer or service provider; organizational personnel with information security responsibilities. *Test:* Automated mechanisms used to verify that the configuration of the information system, component, or service, as delivered, is as specified.
SA-4(6)	Acquisition process: Use of information assurance products	Review documentation for organization to ensure that the system under review utilized approved IA products in accordance with ISO 15408 Evaluated Products List (EPL), as directed by the National Information Assurance Program (NIAP). Evaluate documentation for products to ensure proper reviews, tests, and approvals are present for IA products, especially encryption products for sensitive or classified information processing. Discuss with Developers,	HSPD-12, FIPS-140-2, FIPS-201, SP 800-23, SP 800-35, SP 800-36, SP 800-37, rev. 1, SP 800-64, SP 800-70, SP 800-137, ISO 15408	*Examine:* System and services acquisition policy; procedures addressing the integration of information security requirements, descriptions, and criteria into the acquisition process; solicitation documents; acquisition documentation; acquisition contracts for the information system, system component, or information system service; security configurations to be implemented by developer of the information system, system component, or information system service; service-level agreements; other relevant documents or records. *Interview:* Organizational personnel with acquisition/contracting responsibilities; organizational personnel with responsibility

for determining information system security requirements; organizational personnel responsible for ensuring information assurance products are NSA-approved and are evaluated and/or validated products in accordance with NSA-approved procedures; organizational personnel with information security responsibilities. *Test:* Organizational processes for selecting and employing evaluated and/or validated information assurance products and services that compose an NSA-approved solution to protect classified information.

acquisition staff, System Owner, security staff, operations staff, and Security Officer.

| SA-4(7) | Acquisition process: NIAP-approved protection profiles | Review documentation for the organization to ensure that the system under review utilized approved IA products in accordance with ISO 15408 Evaluated Products List (EPL), as directed by the National Information Assurance Program (NIAP). Evaluate documentation for products to ensure proper reviews, tests, and approvals are present for IA products, especially product protection profiles for sensitive or classified information processing components. Discuss with Developers, acquisition staff, System Owner, security staff, operations staff, and Security Officer. | HSPD-12, FIPS-140-2, FIPS-201, SP 800-23, SP 800-35, SP 800-36, SP 800-37, rev. 1, SP 800-64, SP 800-70, SP 800-137, ISO 15408 | *Examine:* System and services acquisition policy; procedures addressing the integration of information security requirements, descriptions, and criteria into the acquisition process; solicitation documents; acquisition documentation; acquisition contracts for the information system, system component, or information system service; NIAP-approved protection profiles; FIPS-validation information for cryptographic functionality; other relevant documents or records. *Interview:* Organizational personnel with acquisition/contracting responsibilities; organizational personnel with responsibility for determining information system security requirements; organizational personnel responsible for ensuring information assurance products are have been evaluated against a NIAP-approved protection profile or for ensuring products relying on cryptographic functionality are FIPS-validated; organizational personnel with information security responsibilities. *Test:* Organizational processes for selecting and employing products/services evaluated against a NIAP-approved protection profile or FIPS-validated products. |

(Continued)

Control number	Control name	Assessment methods	Notes and guidance documents	SP 800-53A guidance
SA-4(8)	Acquisition process: Continuous monitoring plan	Review documentation for the organization to ensure that continuous monitoring of documents and strategies developed by development staff are incorporated into system continuous monitoring activities. This documentation will include a complete set of planned, required, and deployed security controls within the information system, system component, or information system service to ensure they continue to be effective over time based on the inevitable changes that occur. Discuss with Developers, acquisition staff, operations staff, security staff, Security Officer, and System Owner.	HSPD-12, FIPS-140-2, FIPS-201, SP 800-23, SP 800-35, SP 800-36, SP 800-37, rev. 1, SP 800-64, SP 800-70, SP 800-137, ISO 15408	*Examine:* System and services acquisition policy; procedures addressing developer continuous monitoring plans; procedures addressing the integration of information security requirements, descriptions, and criteria into the acquisition process; developer continuous monitoring plans; security assessment plans; acquisition contracts for the information system, system component, or information system service; acquisition documentation; solicitation documentation; service-level agreements; other relevant documents or records. *Interview:* Organizational personnel with acquisition/contracting responsibilities; organizational personnel with responsibility for determining information system security requirements; information system developers; organizational personnel with information security responsibilities. *Test:* Vendor processes for continuous monitoring; automated mechanisms supporting and/or implementing developer continuous monitoring.
SA-4(9)	Acquisition process: Functions/ports/protocols/services in use	Review documentation to ensure that the organization enacts procedures and actions requiring various ports, protocols, and services (PPS) for system server(s) are reviewed and determined to be necessary for proper operation of system. Evaluate full developer documentation and use cases to ensure PPS are periodically review and recertified as necessary. Discuss with Developers, acquisition staff, operations staff, System Owner, and Security Officer.	HSPD-12, FIPS-140-2, FIPS-201, SP 800-23, SP 800-35, SP 800-36, SP 800-37, rev. 1, SP 800-64, SP 800-70, SP 800-137, ISO 15408, DODI 8551.01	*Examine:* System and services acquisition policy; procedures addressing the integration of information security requirements, descriptions, and criteria into the acquisition process; information system design documentation; information system documentation including functions, ports, protocols, and services intended for organizational use; acquisition contracts for information systems or services; acquisition documentation; solicitation documentation; service-level agreements; organizational security requirements, descriptions, and criteria for developers of information systems, system components, and information system services; other relevant documents or records. *Interview:* Organizational personnel with

SA-4(10)	Acquisition process: Use of approved PIV products	Review documentation to ensure that the federal PIV authentication requirements (FIPS-201) for systems is installed and active on system. Test system to ensure PIV-authenticated access is active. Discuss with Developers, acquisition staff, operations staff, security staff, System Owner, and Security Officer.	HSPD-12, FIPS-140-2, FIPS-201, SP 800-23, SP 800-35, SP 800-36, SP 800-37, rev. 1, SP 800-64, SP 800-70, SP 800-137, ISO 15408	acquisition/contracting responsibilities; organizational personnel with responsibility for determining information system security requirements; system/network administrators; organizational personnel operating, using, and/or maintaining the information system; information system developers; organizational personnel with information security responsibilities. *Examine*: System and services acquisition policy; procedures addressing the integration of information security requirements, descriptions, and criteria into the acquisition process; solicitation documentation; acquisition documentation; acquisition contracts for the information system, system component, or information system service; service-level agreements; other relevant documents or records. *Interview*: Organizational personnel with acquisition/contracting responsibilities; organizational personnel with responsibility for determining information system security requirements; organizational personnel with responsibility for ensuring only FIPS 201 approved products are implemented; organizational personnel with information security responsibilities. *Test*: Organizational processes for selecting and employing FIPS 201-approved products.
SA-5	Information system documentation	Review documentation for system to ensure its completeness and accuracy for security components, services and controls installed on the system. Discuss with Security Officer, security staff, System Owner, and Developers.	SP 800-37, rev. 1, SP 800-64	*Examine*: System and services acquisition policy; procedures addressing information system documentation; information system documentation including administrator and user guides; records documenting attempts to obtain unavailable or nonexistent information system documentation; list of actions to be taken in response to documented attempts to obtain information system, system component, or information system service documentation;

(Continued)

Control number	Control name	Assessment methods	Notes and guidance documents	SP 800-53A guidance
				risk management strategy documentation; other relevant documents or records. *Interview:* Organizational personnel with acquisition/contracting responsibilities; organizational personnel with responsibility for determining information system security requirements; system administrators; organizational personnel operating, using, and/or maintaining the information system; information system developers; organizational personnel with information security responsibilities. *Test:* Organizational processes for obtaining, protecting, and distributing information system administrator and user documentation.
SA-5(1)	Information system documentation: Functional properties of security controls		Withdrawn: Incorporated into SA-4(1)	
SA-5(2)	Information system documentation: Security-relevant external system interfaces		Withdrawn: Incorporated into SA-4(2)	
SA-5(3)	Information system documentation: High-level design		Withdrawn: Incorporated into SA-4(2)	
SA-5(4)	Information system documentation: Low-level design		Withdrawn: Incorporated into SA-4(2)	

SA-5(5)	Information system documentation: Source code	Withdrawn: Incorporated into SA-4(2)		
SA-6	Software usage restrictions	Withdrawn: Incorporated into CM-10 and SI-7		
SA-7	User installed software	Withdrawn: Incorporated into CM-11 and SI-7		
SA-8	Security engineering principles	SP 800-27, SP 800-160	Review documentation for organization to ensure that the security engineering principles, such as layered defenses and security architectures, are applied for all areas of system design and operations. Review design documents for new systems to ensure further that full security engineering principles are considered in all designs. Discuss with Developers, System Owner, acquisition staff, and Security Officer.	*Examine:* System and services acquisition policy; procedures addressing security engineering principles used in the specification, design, development, implementation, and modification of the information system; information system design documentation; information security requirements and specifications for the information system; other relevant documents or records. *Interview:* Organizational personnel with acquisition/contracting responsibilities; organizational personnel with responsibility for determining information system security requirements; organizational personnel with information system specification, design, development, implementation, and modification responsibilities; information system developers; organizational personnel with information security responsibilities. *Test:* Organizational processes for applying security engineering principles in information system specification, design, development, implementation, and modification; automated mechanisms supporting the application of security engineering principles in information system specification, design, development, implementation, and modification.
SA-9	External information system services	SP 800-35, SP 800-47, SP 800-161, SP 800-171	Review documentation for organization to ensure that all external providers and interfacing	*Examine:* System and services acquisition policy; procedures addressing external information system services; procedures addressing

(Continued)

Control number	Control name	Assessment methods	Notes and guidance documents	SP 800-53A guidance
		systems are providing risk, security, and controls information for their components and systems. Ensure full SLA's and ISA's, as appropriate, are provided to organization for risk management purposes. Discuss with Developers, Service Providers, acquisition staff, operations staff, System Owner, and Security Officer.		methods and techniques for monitoring security control compliance by external service providers of information system services; acquisition contracts, service-level agreements; organizational security requirements and security specifications for external provider services; security control assessment evidence from external providers of information system services; other relevant documents or records. *Interview:* Organizational personnel with system and services acquisition responsibilities; external providers of information system services; organizational personnel with information security responsibilities. *Test:* Organizational processes for monitoring security control compliance by external service providers on an ongoing basis; automated mechanisms for monitoring security control compliance by external service providers on an ongoing basis.
SA-9(1)	External information system services: Risk assessments/ organizational approvals	Review the documentation the organization maintains on the dedicated security services and their operations. Ensure all services are appropriately authorized and approved for use. Discuss with System Owner, Security Officer, security staff, acquisition staff, and the operations staff.	SP 800-35, SP 800-47, SP 800-161, SP 800-171	*Examine:* System and services acquisition policy; procedures addressing external information system services; acquisition documentation; acquisition contracts for the information system, system component, or information system service; risk assessment reports; approval records for acquisition or outsourcing of dedicated information security services; other relevant documents or records. *Interview:* Organizational personnel with system and services acquisition responsibilities; organizational personnel with information system security responsibilities; external providers of information system services; organizational personnel with information security responsibilities. *Test:* Organizational processes for conducting a risk assessment prior to acquiring or outsourcing dedicated information security services;

organizational processes for approving the outsourcing of dedicated information security services; automated mechanisms supporting and/or implementing risk assessment; automated mechanisms supporting and/or implementing approval processes.

SA-9(2)	External information system services: Identification of functions/ports/protocols/services	Review documentation from external service providers to evaluate it with relation to the specific functions, ports, protocols, and services, used in the provision of such services, which can be particularly useful when the need arises to understand the trade-offs involved in restricting certain functions/services or blocking certain ports/protocols. Discuss with acquisition staff, operations staff, Security Officer, and System Owner.	SP 800-35, SP 800-47, SP 800-161, SP 800-171

Examine: System and services acquisition policy; procedures addressing external information system services; acquisition contracts for the information system, system component, or information system service; acquisition documentation; solicitation documentation, service-level agreements; organizational security requirements and security specifications for external service providers; list of required functions, ports, protocols, and other services; other relevant documents or records. *Interview:* Organizational personnel with system and services acquisition responsibilities; system/network administrators; external providers of information system services.

SA-9(3)	External information system services: Establish/maintain trust relationship with providers	Evaluate the system documentation for the trust levels between the organization and its external providers. Review documents for any issues with trust relationships and areas of concern. Discuss with operations staff, acquisition staff, security staff, System Owner, and Security Officer.	SP 800-35, SP 800-47, SP 800-161, SP 800-171

Examine: System and services acquisition policy; procedures addressing external information system services; acquisition contracts for the information system, system component, or information system service; acquisition documentation; solicitation documentation; service-level agreements; organizational security requirements, properties, factors, or conditions defining acceptable trust relationships; documentation of trust relationships with external service providers; other relevant documents or records. *Interview:* Organizational personnel with system and services acquisition responsibilities; organizational personnel with information security responsibilities; external providers of information system services.

(Continued)

Control number	Control name	Assessment methods	Notes and guidance documents	SP 800-53A guidance
SA-9(4)	External information system services: Consistent interests of consumers and providers	Review documentation for system, which reflects service provider support for organization with focus on the interests of the service providers, which may diverge from organizational interests. Test by observing service provider at their facility during assessment/audit visit. Discuss results with System Owner, Security Officer, acquisition staff, and operations staff.	SP 800-35, SP 800-47, SP 800-161, SP 800-171	*Examine:* System and services acquisition policy; procedures addressing external information system services; acquisition contracts for the information system, system component, or information system service; solicitation documentation; acquisition documentation; service-level agreements; organizational security requirements/safeguards for external service providers; personnel security policies for external service providers; assessments performed on external service providers; other relevant documents or records. *Interview:* Organizational personnel with system and services acquisition responsibilities; organizational personnel with information security responsibilities; external providers of information system services. *Test:* Organizational processes for defining and employing safeguards to ensure consistent interests with external service providers; automated mechanisms supporting and/or implementing safeguards to ensure consistent interests with external service providers.
SA-9(5)	External information system services: Processing, storage, and service location	Review documentation for external service provider to ensure that location criteria are carefully considered during selection process. Discuss with operations staff and acquisition staff to ensure that statutory and regulatory considerations for operating in vendor locations are included in all operational and mission related decision-making processes. Discuss with security staff, Security Officer, and System Owner.	SP 800-35, SP 800-47, SP 800-161, SP 800-171	*Examine:* System and services acquisition policy; procedures addressing external information system services; acquisition contracts for the information system, system component, or information system service; solicitation documentation; acquisition documentation; service-level agreements; restricted locations for information processing; information/data and/or information system services; information processing, information/data, and/or information system services to be maintained in restricted locations; organizational security requirements or conditions for external providers; other relevant documents or records. *Interview:* Organizational personnel with system and services acquisition

				responsibilities; organizational personnel with information security responsibilities; external providers of information system services. *Test:* Organizational processes for defining requirements to restrict locations of information processing, information/data, or information services; organizational processes for ensuring the location is restricted in accordance with requirements or conditions.
SA-10	Developer configuration management	Review developer provided documentation for system to ensure that the quality and completeness of the configuration management activities conducted by developers is considered as evidence of applying effective security safeguards in support of system. Review all provided documentation with acquisition staff, Developers, security staff, operations staff, System Owner, and Security Officer.	SP 800-37, rev. 1, SP 800-64, SP 800-128	*Examine:* System and services acquisition policy; procedures addressing system developer configuration management; solicitation documentation; acquisition documentation; service-level agreements; acquisition contracts for the information system, system component, or information system service; system developer configuration management plan; security flaw and flaw resolution tracking records; system change authorization records; change control records; configuration management records; other relevant documents or records. *Interview:* Organizational personnel with system and services acquisition responsibilities; organizational personnel with information security responsibilities; organizational personnel with configuration management responsibilities; system developers. *Test:* Organizational processes for monitoring developer configuration management; automated mechanisms supporting and/or implementing the monitoring of developer configuration management.
SA-10(1)	Developer configuration management: Software/firmware integrity verification	Review documentation from developers of system to ensure that they provide methodologies used to detect unauthorized changes to software and firmware components with the use of tools, techniques, and/or mechanisms	SP 800-37, rev. 1, SP 800-64, SP 800-128	*Examine:* System and services acquisition policy; procedures addressing system developer configuration management; solicitation documentation; acquisition documentation; service-level agreements; acquisition contracts for the information system; system component, or information system service; system developer

(Continued)

Control number	Control name	Assessment methods	Notes and guidance documents	SP 800-53A guidance
		as provided by developers. Ensure that the organizations maintain use and proficiency of these vendor-provided tools for integrity checking of code. Discuss with acquisition staff, operations staff, security staff, Security Officer, and System Owner.		configuration management plan; software and firmware integrity verification records; system change authorization records; change control records; configuration management records; other relevant documents or records. *Interview:* Organizational personnel with system and services acquisition responsibilities; organizational personnel with information security responsibilities; organizational personnel with configuration management responsibilities; system developers. *Test:* Organizational processes for monitoring developer configuration management; automated mechanisms supporting and/or implementing the monitoring of developer configuration management.
SA-10(2)	Developer configuration management: Alternative configuration management processes	Review documentation for alternative forms of CM used with COTS products and updates. SIA forms, discussed in CM family, are used here in detail and reviewed by assessment. Discuss with System Owner, CM staff, acquisition staff, Security Officer, and System Owner.	SP 800-37, rev. 1, SP 800-64, SP 800-128	*Examine:* System and services acquisition policy; procedures addressing system developer configuration management; procedures addressing configuration management; solicitation documentation; acquisition documentation; service-level agreements; acquisition contracts for the information system; system component, or information system service; system developer configuration management plan; other relevant documents or records. *Interview:* Organizational personnel with system and services acquisition responsibilities; organizational personnel with information security responsibilities; organizational personnel with configuration management responsibilities; system developers. *Test:* Organizational processes for monitoring developer configuration management; automated mechanisms supporting and/or implementing the monitoring of developer configuration management.
SA-10(3)	Developer configuration	Review documentation from developers of system to ensure,	SP 800-37, rev. 1, SP 800-64, SP 800-128	*Examine:* System and services acquisition policy; procedures addressing system developer

	management: Hardware integrity verification	they provided methodologies used to detect unauthorized changes to hardware components with the use of tools, techniques, and/or mechanisms as provided by developers. Ensure that the organizations maintain use and proficiency of these vendor-provided tools for integrity checking of components. Discuss with acquisition staff, security staff, operations staff, Security Officer, and System Owner.		configuration management; solicitation documentation; acquisition documentation; service-level agreements; acquisition contracts for the information system, system component, or information system service; system developer configuration management plan; hardware integrity verification records; other relevant documents or records. *Interview:* Organizational personnel with system and services acquisition responsibilities; organizational personnel with information security responsibilities; organizational personnel with configuration management responsibilities; system developers. *Test:* Organizational processes for monitoring developer configuration management; automated mechanisms supporting and/or implementing the monitoring of developer configuration management.
SA-10(4)	Developer configuration management: Trusted generation	Review documentation provided by developers for changes to hardware, software, and firmware components between versions during the development and their configuration management of these versions. Discuss with acquisition staff, Developers, System Owner, and Security Officer.	SP 800-37, rev. 1, SP 800-64, SP 800-128	*Examine:* System and services acquisition policy; procedures addressing system developer configuration management; solicitation documentation; acquisition documentation; service-level agreements; acquisition contracts for the information system, system component, or information system service; system developer configuration management plan; change control records; configuration management records; configuration control audit records; other relevant documents or records. *Interview:* Organizational personnel with system and services acquisition responsibilities; organizational personnel with information security responsibilities; organizational personnel with configuration management responsibilities; system developers. *Test:* Organizational processes for monitoring developer configuration management; automated mechanisms supporting and/or implementing the monitoring of developer configuration management.

(Continued)

Control number	Control name	Assessment methods	Notes and guidance documents	SP 800-53A guidance
SA-10(5)	Developer configuration management: Mapping integrity for version control	Review documentation for the development of CM processes, where changes to hardware, software, and firmware components during initial development and during system life cycle updates by the development staff/organization. Review change requests, change documentation, and approval processes to ensure full integrity between the master copies of security-relevant hardware, software, and firmware (including designs and source code) and the equivalent data in master copies on-site in operational environments and compliance with documented CM procedures. Discuss with Developers, operations staff, Security Officer, acquisition staff, and System Owner.	SP 800-37, rev. 1, SP 800-64, SP 800-128	*Examine:* System and services acquisition policy; procedures addressing system developer configuration management; solicitation documentation; acquisition documentation; service-level agreements; acquisition contracts for the information system, system component, or information system service; system developer configuration management plan; change control records; configuration management records; version control change/update records; integrity verification records between master copies of security-relevant hardware, software, and firmware (including designs and source code); other relevant documents or records. *Interview:* Organizational personnel with system and services acquisition responsibilities; organizational personnel with information security responsibilities; organizational personnel with configuration management responsibilities; system developers. *Test:* Organizational processes for monitoring developer configuration management; automated mechanisms supporting and/or implementing the monitoring of developer configuration management.
SA-10(6)	Developer configuration management: Trusted distribution	Review documentation to ensure that distribution of developed changes, software, hardware, and configuration criteria is trusted and temper resistant. Discuss with Developers, acquisition staff, operations staff, System Owner, and Security Officer.	SP 800-37, rev. 1, SP 800-64, SP 800-128	*Examine:* System and services acquisition policy; procedures addressing system developer configuration management; solicitation documentation; acquisition documentation; service-level agreements; acquisition contracts for the information system, system component, or information system service; system developer configuration management plan; change control records; configuration management records; other relevant documents or records. *Interview:* Organizational personnel with system and services acquisition responsibilities; organizational personnel with information

SA-11	Developer security testing and evaluation	Review that development test and evaluation (DT&E) actions are in accordance with mission and organizational requirements, security criteria, and contractual guidelines. Review testing documentation and plans to ensure that full coverage of all components and functions is evaluated. The depth of T&E refers to the rigor and level of detail associated with the assessment process (e.g., black box, gray box, or white box testing). The coverage of T&E refers to the scope (i.e., number and type) of the artifacts included in the assessment process. Discuss with Developers, acquisition staff, operations staff, Security Officer, and System Owner.	SP 800-37, rev. 1, SP 800-53A, SP 800-64, ISO 15408	security responsibilities; organizational personnel with configuration management responsibilities; organizational personnel with configuration management responsibilities; system developers. *Test:* Organizational processes for monitoring developer configuration management; automated mechanisms supporting and/or implementing the monitoring of developer configuration management. *Examine:* System and services acquisition policy; procedures addressing system developer security testing; procedures addressing flaw remediation; solicitation documentation; acquisition documentation; service-level agreements; acquisition contracts for the information system, system component, or information system service; system developer security test plans; records of developer security testing results for the information system, system component, or information system service; security flaw and remediation tracking records; other relevant documents or records. *Interview:* Organizational personnel with system and services acquisition responsibilities; organizational personnel with information security responsibilities; organizational personnel with developer security testing responsibilities; system developers. *Test:* Organizational processes for monitoring developer security testing and evaluation; automated mechanisms supporting and/or implementing the monitoring of developer security testing and evaluation.
SA-11(1)	Developer security testing and evaluation: Static code analysis	Review documentation to ensure static code analysis for software of system was performed during development. Identify and review the aggregate defect density for critical defect types, evidence that defects were inspected by developers, and evidence that	SP 800-37, rev. 1, SP 800-53A, SP 800-64, ISO 15408	*Examine:* System and services acquisition policy; procedures addressing system developer security testing; procedures addressing flaw remediation; solicitation documentation; acquisition documentation; service-level agreements; acquisition contracts for the information system, system component, or information system service; system developer security test plans; system

(Continued)

Control number	Control name	Assessment methods	Notes and guidance documents	SP 800-53A guidance
		defects were fixed appropriately. Review defect documentation for methods and techniques employed to identify and fix code issues and "bugs." Discuss with acquisition staff, Developers, operations staff, Security Officer, and System Owner.		developer security testing results; security flaw and remediation tracking records; other relevant documents or records. *Interview:* Organizational personnel with system and services acquisition responsibilities; organizational personnel with information security responsibilities; organizational personnel with developer security testing responsibilities; organizational personnel with configuration management responsibilities; system developers. *Test:* Organizational processes for monitoring developer security testing and evaluation; automated mechanisms supporting and/or implementing the monitoring of developer security testing and evaluation; static code analysis tools.
SA-11(2)	Developer security testing and evaluation: Threat and vulnerability analyses	Review documentation to ensure the organization required and the development staff conducted threat and vulnerability analyses of information systems, system components, and information system services prior to delivery. Review documentation and scan results to ensure completeness and coverage of analyses conducted. Discuss with Developers, acquisition staff, security staff, System Owner, and Security Officer.	SP 800-37, rev. 1, SP 800-53A, SP 800-64, ISO 15408	*Examine:* System and services acquisition policy; procedures addressing system developer security testing; solicitation documentation; acquisition documentation; service-level agreements; acquisition contracts for the information system, system component, or information system service; system developer security test plans; records of developer security testing results for the information system, system component, or information system service; vulnerability scanning results; information system risk assessment reports; threat and vulnerability analysis reports; other relevant documents or records. *Interview:* Organizational personnel with system and services acquisition responsibilities; organizational personnel with information security responsibilities; organizational personnel with developer security testing responsibilities; system developers. *Test:* Organizational processes for monitoring developer security testing and evaluation; automated mechanisms supporting and/or implementing the monitoring of developer security testing and evaluation.

SA-11(3)	Developer security testing and evaluation: Independent verification of assessment plans/evidence	Review documentation and reports from independent assessor for DT&E efforts and assessments to ensure that all areas for security controls and components were verified and validated successfully. Discuss with Independent Assessor, Developers, acquisition staff, security staff, System Owner, and Security Officer.	SP 800-37, rev. 1, SP 800-53A, SP 800-64, ISO 15408	*Examine:* System and services acquisition policy; procedures addressing system developer security testing; solicitation documentation; acquisition documentation; service-level agreements; acquisition contracts for the information system, system component, or information system service; independent verification and validation reports; security test and evaluation plans; security test and evaluation results for the information system, system component, or information system service; other relevant documents or records. *Interview:* Organizational personnel with system and services acquisition responsibilities; organizational personnel with information security responsibilities; organizational personnel with developer security testing responsibilities; system developers; independent verification agent. *Test:* Organizational processes for monitoring developer security testing and evaluation; automated mechanisms supporting and/or implementing the monitoring of developer security testing and evaluation.
SA-11(4)	Developer security testing and evaluation: Manual code reviews	Review documentation for developer-based manual code reviews of software for system. Ensure that code reviews include verifying access control matrices against application controls, memory management processing, and reviewing more detailed aspects of cryptographic implementations and controls. Review results of code reviews for completeness and accuracy. Discuss with Security Officer, Developers, acquisition staff, and System Owner.	SP 800-37, rev. 1, SP 800-53A, SP 800-64, ISO 15408	*Examine:* System and services acquisition policy; procedures addressing system developer security testing; processes, procedures, and/or techniques for performing manual code reviews; solicitation documentation; acquisition documentation; service-level agreements; acquisition contracts for the information system, system component, or information system service; system developer security testing and evaluation plans; system developer security testing and evaluation results; list of code requiring manual reviews; records of manual code reviews; other relevant documents or records. *Interview:* Organizational personnel with system and services acquisition responsibilities; organizational personnel with information security responsibilities; organizational personnel with developer

(Continued)

Control number	Control name	Assessment methods	Notes and guidance documents	SP 800-53A guidance
				security testing responsibilities; system developers; independent verification agent. *Test:* Organizational processes for monitoring developer security testing and evaluation; automated mechanisms supporting and/or implementing the monitoring of developer security testing and evaluation.
SA-11(5)	Developer security testing and evaluation: Penetration testing/analysis	Review documentation for testing and evaluation of system externally through use of penetration test methodologies. Ensure that penetration testing covered all external connections and techniques following defined by NIST guidance found in SP 800-115. Discuss results with Developers, acquisition staff, System Owner, and Security Officer.	SP 800-37, rev. 1, SP 800-53A, SP 800-64, SP 800-115, ISO 15408	*Examine:* System and services acquisition policy; procedures addressing system developer security testing; solicitation documentation; acquisition documentation; service-level agreements; acquisition contracts for the information system, system component, or information system service; system developer penetration testing and evaluation plans; system developer penetration testing and evaluation results; other relevant documents or records. *Interview:* Organizational personnel with system and services acquisition responsibilities; organizational personnel with information security responsibilities; organizational personnel with developer security testing responsibilities; system developers; independent verification agent. *Test:* Organizational processes for monitoring developer security testing and evaluation; automated mechanisms supporting and/or implementing the monitoring of developer security testing and evaluation.
SA-11(6)	Developer security testing and evaluation: Attack surface reviews	Review documentation for organization to ensure that attack surface vulnerabilities are identified and corrected during development of system. Ensure reviews cover cyber-attack areas of interest and concern, as identified in system risk analysis documents. Discuss with Developers, System	SP 800-37, rev. 1, SP 800-53A, SP 800-64, ISO 15408	*Examine:* System and services acquisition policy; procedures addressing system developer security testing; solicitation documentation; acquisition documentation; service-level agreements; acquisition contracts for the information system, system component, or information system service; system developer security testing and evaluation plans; system developer security testing and evaluation results; records of attack

		Owner, acquisition staff, and Security Officer.		surface reviews; other relevant documents or records. *Interview:* Organizational personnel with system and services acquisition responsibilities; organizational personnel with information security responsibilities; organizational personnel with developer security testing responsibilities; organizational personnel with configuration management responsibilities; system developers. *Test:* Organizational processes for monitoring developer security testing and evaluation; automated mechanisms supporting and/or implementing the monitoring of developer security testing and evaluation.
SA-11(7)	Developer security testing and evaluation: Verify scope of testing/evaluation	Review documentation to ensure full and complete coverage of DT&E and other testing activities on the system during its development. Review results for complete coverage of required security controls and total security requirements coverage. Discuss with System Owner, acquisition staff, Developers, and Security Officer.	SP 800-37, rev. 1, SP 800-53A, SP 800-64, SP 800-115, ISO 15408	*Examine:* System and services acquisition policy; procedures addressing system developer security testing; solicitation documentation; acquisition documentation; service-level agreements; acquisition contracts for the information system, system component, or information system service; system developer security testing and evaluation plans; system developer security testing and evaluation results; other relevant documents or records. *Interview:* Organizational personnel with system and services acquisition responsibilities; organizational personnel with information security responsibilities; organizational personnel with developer security testing responsibilities; system developers; independent verification agent. *Test:* Organizational processes for monitoring developer security testing and evaluation; automated mechanisms supporting and/or implementing the monitoring of developer security testing and evaluation.
SA-11(8)	Developer security testing and evaluation: Dynamic code analysis	Review documentation to ensure that dynamic code analysis techniques and procedures are utilized to evaluate code and software components for system.	SP 800-37, rev. 1, SP 800-53A, SP 800-64, SP 800-115, ISO 15408	*Examine:* System and services acquisition policy; procedures addressing system developer security testing; procedures addressing flaw remediation; solicitation documentation; acquisition documentation; service-level agreements;

(Continued)

Control number	Control name	Assessment methods	Notes and guidance documents	SP 800-53A guidance
		Typical dynamic code analysis methods include run-time verification of software programs, using tools capable of monitoring programs for memory corruption, user privilege issues, and other potential security problems, such as fuzz testing, code coverage analysis, and/or concordance analysis. Review results of testing with System Owner, Developers, acquisition staff, and Security Officer.		acquisition contracts for the information system, system component, or information system service; system developer security test and evaluation plans; security test and evaluation results; security flaw and remediation tracking reports; other relevant documents or records. *Interview:* Organizational personnel with system and services acquisition responsibilities; organizational personnel with information security responsibilities; organizational personnel with developer security testing responsibilities; organizational personnel with configuration management responsibilities; system developers. *Test:* Organizational processes for monitoring developer security testing and evaluation; automated mechanisms supporting and/or implementing the monitoring of developer security testing and evaluation.
SA-12	Supply chain protection	Review documentation to ensure organization requires supplier of service or component to meet all system protection needs throughout the SDLC (i.e., during design, development, manufacturing, packaging, assembly, distribution, system integration, operations, maintenance, and retirement). All acquisition and operational uses of products and/or services from external providers will match the documented security requirements, needs, and designs for the system. Verify documentation conforms to operational and organizational policies and procedures. Discuss with acquisition staff, Developers,	SP 800-161, NISTIR 7622	*Examine:* System and services acquisition policy; procedures addressing supply chain protection; procedures addressing the integration of information security requirements into the acquisition process; solicitation documentation; acquisition documentation; service-level agreements; acquisition contracts for the information system, system component, or information system service; list of supply chain threats; list of security safeguards to be taken against supply chain threats; system development life cycle documentation; other relevant documents or records. *Interview:* Organizational personnel with system and services acquisition responsibilities; organizational personnel with information security responsibilities; organizational personnel with supply chain protection responsibilities. *Test:* Organizational processes for defining

Control	Title	Guidance	Assessment methods	References
		operational staff, security staff, System Owner, and Security Officer.	safeguards for and protecting against supply chain threats; automated mechanisms supporting and/or implementing safeguards for supply chain threats.	
SA-12(1)	Supply chain protection: Acquisition strategies/tools/methods	Review documentation for sensitive system acquisition activities such as incentives for suppliers, who provide additional vetting of the processes and security practices of subordinate suppliers, critical information system components, and services or minimizing the time between purchase decisions and required delivery to limit opportunities for adversaries to corrupt information system components or products. Additional areas to review would include requiring use of trusted/controlled distribution, delivery, and warehousing options to reduce supply chain risk (e.g., requiring tamper-evident packaging of information system components during shipping and warehousing). Review organizational requirements to ensure acquisition processes include these organizational components. Discuss with acquisition staff, operations staff, Security Officer, and System Owner.	*Examine:* System and services acquisition policy; procedures addressing supply chain protection; procedures addressing the integration of information security requirements into the acquisition process; procedures addressing the integration of acquisition strategies, contract tools, and procure methods into the acquisition process; solicitation documentation; acquisition documentation; service-level agreements; acquisition contracts for information systems or services; purchase orders/requisitions for the information system; system component; or information system service from suppliers; other relevant documents or records. *Interview:* Organizational personnel with system and services acquisition responsibilities; organizational personnel with information security responsibilities; organizational personnel with supply chain protection responsibilities. *Test:* Organizational processes for defining and employing tailored acquisition strategies, contract tools, and procurement methods; automated mechanisms supporting and/or implementing the definition and employment of tailored acquisition strategies, contract tools, and procurement methods.	SP 800-161, NISTIR 7622
SA-12(2)	Supply chain protection: Supplier reviews	Review documentation to ensure that acquisition activities include analysis of supplier processes used to design, develop, test, implement, verify, deliver, and support information systems,	*Examine:* System and services acquisition policy; procedures addressing supply chain protection; procedures addressing the integration of information security requirements into the acquisition process; records of supplier due diligence reviews; other relevant documents or	SP 800-161, NISTIR 7622

(Continued)

Control number	Control name	Assessment methods	Notes and guidance documents	SP 800-53A guidance
		system components, and information system services and their training and developmental standards and procedures. Discuss with acquisition staff, operations staff, Developers, System Owner, and Security Officer.		records. *Interview:* Organizational personnel with system and services acquisition responsibilities; organizational personnel with information security responsibilities; organizational personnel with supply chain protection responsibilities. *Test:* Organizational processes for conducting supplier reviews; automated mechanisms supporting and/or implementing supplier reviews.
SA-12(3)	Supply chain protection: Trusted shipping and warehousing		Withdrawn: Incorporated into SA-12(1)	
SA-12(4)	Supply chain protection: Diversity of suppliers		Withdrawn: Incorporated into SA-12(13)	
SA-12(5)	Supply chain protection: Limitation of harm	Review documentation to ensure acquisition actions provide for avoiding the purchase of custom configurations to reduce the risk of acquiring information systems, components, or products that have been corrupted via supply chain actions targeted at specific organizations, using vendors on pre-approved supplier activities, and/or employing a diverse set of suppliers for services, or components acquired for system. Review with acquisition staff, operations staff, security staff, Security Officer, and System Owner.	SP 800-161, NISTIR 7622	*Examine:* System and services acquisition policy; configuration management policy; procedures addressing supply chain protection; procedures addressing the integration of information security requirements into the acquisition process; procedures addressing the baseline configuration of the information system; configuration management plan; information system design documentation; information system architecture and associated configuration documentation; solicitation documentation; acquisition documentation; acquisition contracts for the information system, system component, or information system service; list of security safeguards to be taken to protect organizational supply chain against potential supply chain threats; other relevant documents or records. *Interview:* Organizational personnel with system and services acquisition responsibilities; organizational personnel with information

security responsibilities; organizational personnel with supply chain protection responsibilities. *Test:* Organizational processes for defining and employing safeguards to limit harm from adversaries of the organizational supply chain; automated mechanisms supporting and/or implementing the definition and employment of safeguards to protect the organizational supply chain.

SA-12(6)	Supply chain protection: Minimizing procurement time	Withdrawn: Incorporated into SA-12(1)		
SA-12(7)	Supply chain protection: Assessments prior to selection/acceptance/update	SP 800-161, NISTIR 7622	Review documentation to ensure that the organization acquisition process includes testing of components during or before acceptance of system components. Review these testing, evaluations, reviews, and analyses results. Independent, third-party entities or organizational personnel conducts assessment of systems, components, products, tools, and services can provide some or all of these documents. Discuss with System Owner, Security Officer, acquisition staff, and Developers.	*Examine:* System and services acquisition policy; procedures addressing supply chain protection; procedures addressing the integration of information security requirements into the acquisition process; security test and evaluation results; vulnerability assessment results; penetration testing results; organizational risk assessment results; other relevant documents or records. *Interview:* Organizational personnel with system and services acquisition responsibilities; organizational personnel with information security responsibilities; organizational personnel with supply chain protection responsibilities. *Test:* Organizational processes for conducting assessments prior to selection, acceptance, or update; automated mechanisms supporting and/or implementing the conducting of assessments prior to selection, acceptance, or update.
SA-12(8)	Supply chain protection: Use of all-source intelligence	SP 800-161, NISTIR 7622	Review documentation to ensure acquisition and operations staff utilizes all-source intelligence during sensitive component acquisition process. These documents inform engineering,	*Examine:* System and services acquisition policy; procedures addressing supply chain protection; solicitation documentation; acquisition documentation; acquisition contracts for the information system, system component, or information system service; records of all-source

(Continued)

Control number	Control name	Assessment methods	Notes and guidance documents	SP 800-53A guidance
		acquisition, and risk management decisions. Ensure the all-source intelligence documentation consists of intelligence products and/or organizations and activities that incorporate all sources of information, most frequently including human intelligence, imagery intelligence, measurement and signature intelligence, signals intelligence, and open source data in the production of finished intelligence. Discuss with acquisitions staff, operations staff, development staff, Security Officer, FSO, and System Owner.		intelligence analyses; other relevant documents or records. *Interview:* Organizational personnel with system and services acquisition responsibilities; organizational personnel with information security responsibilities; organizational personnel with supply chain protection responsibilities. *Test:* Organizational processes for use of an all-source analysis of suppliers and potential suppliers; automated mechanisms supporting and/or implementing the use of all-source analysis of suppliers and potential suppliers.
SA-12(9)	Supply chain protection: Operations security	Review documentation for acquisitions to ensure that all of the following OPSEC components are reviewed: user identities; uses for information systems, information system components, and information system services; supplier identities; supplier processes; security requirements; design specifications; testing and evaluation results; and system/component configurations. Following standard USG OPSEC guidelines for system is modified to include suppliers and their activities. Discuss with acquisitions staff, operations staff, development staff, System Owner, Security Officer, and FSO.	SP 800-161, NISTIR 7622	*Examine:* System and services acquisition policy; procedures addressing supply chain protection; solicitation documentation; acquisition documentation; acquisition contracts for the information system, system component, or information system service; records of all-source intelligence analyses; other relevant documents or records. *Interview:* Organizational personnel with system and services acquisition responsibilities; organizational personnel with information security responsibilities; organizational personnel with supply chain protection responsibilities. *Test:* Organizational processes for defining and employing OPSEC safeguards; automated mechanisms supporting and/or implementing the definition and employment of OPSEC safeguards.

SA-12(10)	Supply chain protection: Validate as genuine and not altered	Review documentation provided by supplier to ensure that methodologies are employed to validate hardware and software components as genuine. Ensure security safeguards used to validate the authenticity of information systems and information system components include, for example, optical/nanotechnology tagging and side-channel analysis have been utilized. Verify documentation through searches and retrieval of validation certifications and documentation obtained via independent sources. Discuss with acquisition staff, operations staff, security staff, System Owner, and Security Officer.	SP 800-161, NISTIR 7622	*Examine:* System and services acquisition policy; procedures addressing supply chain protection; procedures address the integration of information security requirements into the acquisition process; solicitation documentation; acquisition documentation; service-level agreements; acquisition contracts for the information system, system component, or information system service; evidentiary documentation (including applicable configurations) indicating the information system, system component, or information system service are genuine and have not been altered; other relevant documents or records. *Interview:* Organizational personnel with system and services acquisition responsibilities; organizational personnel with information security responsibilities; organizational personnel with supply chain protection responsibilities. *Test:* Organizational processes for defining and employing validation safeguards; automated mechanisms supporting and/or implementing the definition and employment of validation safeguards.
SA-12(11)	Supply chain protection: Penetration testing/analysis of elements, processes, and actors	Review documentation and penetration test results to ensure testing addresses analysis and/or testing of the supply chain, not just delivered items and components, such as supplier channels, supplier locations and developmental environment. Discuss with System Owner, acquisition staff, Developers, security staff, System Owner, and Security Officer.	SP 800-115, SP 800-161, NISTIR 7622	*Examine:* System and services acquisition policy; procedures addressing supply chain protection; evidence of organizational analysis, independent third-party analysis, organizational penetration testing, and/or independent third-party penetration testing; list of supply chain elements, processes, and actors (associated with the information system, system component, or information system service) subject to analysis and/or testing; other relevant documents or records. *Interview:* Organizational personnel with system and services acquisition responsibilities; organizational personnel with information security responsibilities; organizational personnel with supply chain protection responsibilities; organizational personnel with responsibilities for

(Continued)

Control number	Control name	Assessment methods	Notes and guidance documents	SP 800-53A guidance
				analyzing and/or testing supply chain elements, processes, and actors. *Test:* Organizational processes for defining and employing methods of analysis/testing of supply chain elements, processes, and actors; automated mechanisms supporting and/or implementing the analysis/testing of supply chain elements, processes, and actors.
SA-12(12)	Supply chain protection: Inter-organizational agreements	Review documentation for inter-organizational agreements related to supplier compromise events, which provides for early notification of supply chain compromises that can potentially adversely affect or have adversely affected organizational information systems, including critical system components, so organizations can provide appropriate responses to such incidents. Discuss with System Owner, acquisition staff, Security Officer, and security staff.	SP 800-161, NISTIR 7622, SP 800-61, rev. 2	*Examine:* System and services acquisition policy; procedures addressing supply chain protection; acquisition documentation; service-level agreements; acquisition contracts for the information system, system component, or information system service; inter-organizational agreements and procedures; other relevant documents or records. *Interview:* Organizational personnel with system and services acquisition responsibilities; organizational personnel with information security responsibilities; organizational personnel with supply chain protection responsibilities. *Test:* Organizational processes for establishing inter-organizational agreements and procedures with supply chain entities.
SA-12(13)	Supply chain protection: Critical information system components	Review documentation to ensure that the organization has accounted for possible supplier disruption and lack of potential support for critical system components. Discuss with acquisition staff, operations staff, security staff, System Owner, and Security Officer.	SP 800-161, NISTIR 7622	*Examine:* System and services acquisition policy; procedures addressing supply chain protection; physical inventory of critical information system components; inventory records of critical information system components; list of security safeguards ensuring adequate supply of critical information system components; other relevant documents or records. *Interview:* Organizational personnel with system and services acquisition responsibilities; organizational personnel with information security responsibilities; organizational personnel with supply chain protection responsibilities. *Test:* Organizational processes for defining and employing security safeguards to ensure an adequate supply of critical

		information system components; automated mechanisms supporting and/or implementing the security safeguards that ensure an adequate supply of critical information system components.	
SA-12(14)	Supply chain protection: Identity and traceability	Review documentation to ensure that the organization maintains visibility into what is happening within such supply chains, as well as monitoring and identifying high-risk events and activities. Evaluate various hardware and software items and components, which provide independent visibility to organization on supplier components and activities, such as RFID tags, serial number labels, and other tracking components. Discuss with acquisition staff, development organization, security staff, operations staff, System Owner, and Security Officer.	*Examine:* System and services acquisition policy; procedures addressing supply chain protection; procedures addressing the integration of information security requirements into the acquisition process; list of supply chain elements, processes, and actors (associated with the information system, system component, or information system service) requiring implementation of unique identification processes, procedures, tools, mechanisms, equipment, techniques and/or configurations; other relevant documents or records. *Interview:* Organizational personnel with system and services acquisition responsibilities; organizational personnel with information security responsibilities; organizational personnel with supply chain protection responsibilities; organizational personnel with responsibilities for establishing and retaining unique identification of supply chain elements, processes, and actors. *Test:* Organizational processes for defining, establishing, and retaining unique identification for supply chain elements, processes, and actors; automated mechanisms supporting and/or implementing the definition, establishment, and retention of unique identification for supply chain elements, processes, and actors.	SP 800-161, NISTIR 7622
SA-12(15)	Supply chain protection: Processes to address weaknesses or deficiencies	Review documentation to ensure that suppliers are implementing recommendations and repairs to system components based upon independent testing and evaluation actions taken previously. Discuss with	*Examine:* System and services acquisition policy; procedures addressing supply chain protection; procedures addressing weaknesses or deficiencies in supply chain elements; results of independent or organizational assessments of supply chain controls and processes; acquisition contracts, service-level agreements; other relevant	SP 800-161, NISTIR 7622

(Continued)

Control number	Control name	Assessment methods	Notes and guidance documents	SP 800-53A guidance
		Developers, acquisition staff, System Owner, and Security Officer.		documents or records. *Interview:* Organizational personnel with system and services acquisition responsibilities; organizational personnel with information security responsibilities; organizational personnel with supply chain protection responsibilities. *Test:* Organizational processes for addressing weaknesses or deficiencies in supply chain elements; automated mechanisms supporting and/or implementing the addressing of weaknesses or deficiencies in supply chain elements.
SA-13	Trustworthiness	Review documentation for system to ensure that security functionality and security assurance are obtained through proper installation and implementation of all security components, controls and functionalities themselves. Discuss with System Owner, operations staff, security staff, and Security Officer.	FIPS-199, FIPS-200, SP 800-37, rev. 1, SP 800-53, SP 800-64	*Examine:* System and services acquisition policy; procedures addressing trustworthiness requirements for the information system, system component, or information system service; security plan; information system design documentation; information system configuration settings and associated documentation; security categorization documentation/results; security authorization package for the information system, system component, or information system service; other relevant documents or records. *Interview:* Organizational personnel with system and services acquisition responsibilities; organizational personnel with information security responsibilities; authorizing official.
SA-14	Criticality analysis	Review documentation to ensure that the organization conduct criticality analysis for all system components and security functionality. Such analysis, like end-to-end functional decomposition of an information system to identify mission-critical functions and components, provides detailed documentation on security components and their	SP 800-37, rev. 1, SP 800-64	*Examine:* System and services acquisition policy; procedures addressing criticality analysis requirements for information systems, security plan; contingency plan; list of information systems, information system components, or information system services requiring criticality analyses; list of critical information system components and functions identified by criticality analyses; criticality analysis documentation; business impact analysis documentation; system development life cycle documentation; other

	Control	Discussion	References	Assessment
SA-14(1)	Criticality analysis: Critical components with no viable alternative sourcing	use within the system. Discuss with Security Engineer, security staff, Security Architect, operations staff, Security Officer, acquisition staff, and System Owner.	Withdrawn: Incorporated into SA-20	relevant documents or records. *Interview:* Organizational personnel with system and services acquisition responsibilities; organizational personnel with information security responsibilities; organizational personnel with responsibilities for performing criticality analysis for the information system.
SA-15	Development process, standards, and tools	Review documentation to ensure that developmental tools and techniques are used to ensure proper security functionality and engineering techniques are employed during development of system. Such activities and tools, like programming languages and computer-aided design (CAD) systems and methods like the use of maturity models to determine the potential effectiveness of such processes aid assurance requirement evaluations and testing. Review these components and tools to validate use, application, and results. Discuss with acquisition staff, development staff, security staff, operations staff, System Owner, and Security Officer.	SP 800-37, rev. 1, SP 800-64	*Examine:* System and services acquisition policy; procedures addressing development process, standards, and tools; procedures addressing the integration of security requirements during the development process; solicitation documentation; acquisition documentation; service-level agreements; acquisition contracts for the information system, system component, or information system service; system developer documentation listing tool options/configuration guides; configuration management records; change control records; configuration control records; documented reviews of development process, standards, tools, and tool options/configurations; other relevant documents or records. *Interview:* Organizational personnel with system and services acquisition responsibilities; organizational personnel with information security responsibilities; system developer.
SA-15(1)	Development process, standards, and	Review documentation to ensure that use of metrics for development and testing result	SP 800-37, rev. 1, SP 800-64	*Examine:* System and services acquisition policy; procedures addressing development process, standards, and tools; procedures addressing the

(Continued)

Control number	Control name	Assessment methods	Notes and guidance documents	SP 800-53A guidance
	tools: Quality metrics	produce validated results, such as quality metrics to establish minimum acceptable levels of information system quality. Evaluate metric results with independent validation testing of metrics and results. Discuss with acquisition staff, development staff, security staff, operations staff, System Owner, and Security Officer.		integration of security requirements into the acquisition process; solicitation documentation; acquisition documentation; service level agreements; acquisition contracts for the information system, system component, or information system service; list of quality metrics; documentation evidence of meeting quality metrics; other relevant documents or records. *Interview:* Organizational personnel with system and services acquisition responsibilities; organizational personnel with information security responsibilities; system developer.
SA-15(2)	Development process, standards, and tools: Security tracking tools	Review documentation from developer on the employment and use of security tracking tools. Ensure that the organization required development organization to select and deploy security tracking tools, which includes, for example, vulnerability/work item tracking systems that facilitate assignment, sorting, filtering, and tracking of completed work items or tasks associated with system development processes. Discuss with acquisition staff, development staff, security staff, operations staff, System Owner, and Security Officer.	SP 800-37, rev. 1, SP 800-64	*Examine:* System and services acquisition policy; procedures addressing development process, standards, and tools; procedures addressing the integration of security requirements into the acquisition process; solicitation documentation; acquisition documentation; service level agreements; acquisition contracts for the information system, system component, or information system service; list of quality metrics; documentation evidence of meeting quality metrics; other relevant documents or records. *Interview:* Organizational personnel with system and services acquisition responsibilities; organizational personnel with information security responsibilities; system developer.
SA-15(3)	Development process, standards, and tools: Criticality analysis	Review documentation to ensure that development team provides developer input to the criticality analysis performed by organizations as found in Control SA-14. The criticality analysis provided in areas such as	SP 800-37, rev. 1, SP 800-64	*Examine:* System and services acquisition policy; procedures addressing development process, standards, and tools; procedures addressing criticality analysis requirements for the information system, system component, or information system service; solicitation documentation; acquisition documentation;

			service-level agreements; acquisition contracts for the information system, system component, or information system service; criticality analysis documentation; business impact analysis documentation; software development life cycle documentation; other relevant documents or records. *Interview:* Organizational personnel with system and services acquisition responsibilities; organizational personnel with information security responsibilities; organizational personnel responsible for performing criticality analysis; system developer. *Test:* Organizational processes for performing criticality analysis; automated mechanisms supporting and/or implementing criticality analysis.
SA-15(4)	Development process, standards, and tools: Threat modeling/ vulnerability analysis	Review documentation to ensure that the organization receives developmental derived threat modeling and vulnerability analysis guidance for operations and maintenance of system. These techniques, as delivered by development staff, provide methods to system utilization for increased security functionality and assurance. Discuss with acquisition staff, development staff, security staff, operations staff, System Owner, and Security Officer.	SP 800-37, rev. 1, SP 800-64	*Examine:* System and services acquisition policy; procedures addressing development process, standards, and tools; solicitation documentation; acquisition documentation; service level agreements; acquisition contracts for the information system, system component, or information system service; threat modeling documentation; vulnerability analysis results; organizational risk assessments; acceptance criteria for evidence produced from threat modeling and vulnerability analysis; other relevant documents or records. *Interview:* Organizational personnel with system and services acquisition responsibilities; organizational personnel with information security responsibilities; system developer. *Test:* Organizational processes for performing development threat modeling and vulnerability analysis; automated mechanisms supporting and/or implementing development threat modeling and vulnerability analysis.
SA-15(5)	Development process,	Review documentation to ensure that the organization receives development	SP 800-37, rev. 1, SP 800-64	*Examine:* System and services acquisition policy; procedures addressing development

(Continued)

Control number	Control name	Assessment methods	Notes and guidance documents	SP 800-53A guidance
	standards, and tools: Attack surface reduction	developmental derived threat reduction guidance, such as applying the principle of least privilege, employing layered defenses, applying the principle of least functionality (i.e., restricting ports, protocols, functions, and services), deprecating unsafe functions, and eliminating application programming interfaces (APIs) that are vulnerable to cyber-attacks. These techniques, as delivered by development staff, provide methods to system utilization for increased security functionality and assurance. Discuss with acquisition staff, development staff, security staff, operations staff, System Owner, and Security Officer.		process, standards, and tools; procedures addressing attack surface reduction; solicitation documentation; acquisition documentation; service-level agreements; acquisition contracts for the information system, or information system service; information system design documentation; network diagram; information system configuration settings and associated documentation establishing/enforcing organization-defined thresholds for reducing attack surfaces; list of restricted ports, protocols, functions and services; other relevant documents or records. *Interview:* Organizational personnel with system and services acquisition responsibilities; organizational personnel with information security responsibilities; organizational personnel responsibility for attack surface reduction thresholds; system developer. *Test:* Organizational processes for defining attack surface reduction thresholds.
SA-15(6)	Development process, standards, and tools: Continuous improvement	Review documentation received from development team to ensure consideration was given to the effectiveness/efficiency of current development processes for meeting quality objectives and addressing security capabilities in current threat environments. Ensure that the resultant documentation reflects development level of compliance to CMMI and other quality-based evaluation criteria. Discuss with acquisition staff, development staff, security staff, operations staff, System Owner, and Security Officer.	SP 800-37, rev. 1, SP 800-64	*Examine:* System and services acquisition policy; procedures addressing development process, standards, and tools; solicitation documentation; acquisition documentation; service level agreements; acquisition contracts for the information system, system component, or information system service; quality goals and metrics for improving system development process; security assessments and/or quality control reviews of system development process; plans of action and milestones for improving system development process; other relevant documents or records. *Interview:* Organizational personnel with system and services acquisition responsibilities; organizational personnel with information security responsibilities; system developer.

| SA-15(7) | Development process, standards, and tools: Automated vulnerability analysis | Review documentation to ensure that developmental vulnerability analysis techniques were performed in compliance with federal guidelines and security control RA-5. Review scan reports and results to validate results and compliance. Discuss with acquisition staff, development staff, security staff, operations staff, System Owner, and Security Officer. | SP 800-37, rev. 1, SP 800-64 | *Examine:* System and services acquisition policy; procedures addressing development process, standards, and tools; solicitation documentation; acquisition documentation; service level agreements; acquisition contracts for the information system, system component, or information system service; vulnerability analysis tools and associated documentation; risk assessment reports; vulnerability analysis results; vulnerability mitigation reports; risk mitigation strategy documentation; other relevant documents or records. *Interview:* Organizational personnel with system and services acquisition responsibilities; organizational personnel with information security responsibilities; system developer; organizational personnel performing automated vulnerability analysis on the information system. *Test:* Organizational processes for vulnerability analysis of information systems, system components, or information system services under development; automated mechanisms supporting and/or implementing vulnerability analysis of information systems, system components, or information system services under development. |
| SA-15(8) | Development process, standards, and tools: Reuse of threat/vulnerability information | Review documentation to determine, if development organization used similar software applications to identify potential design or implementation issues for information systems under development. Evaluate received documents to validate such activities and analysis. Discuss with acquisition staff, development staff, security staff, operations staff, System Owner, and Security Officer. | SP 800-37, rev. 1, SP 800-64, NVD (National Vulnerability Database) | *Examine:* System and services acquisition policy; procedures addressing development process, standards, and tools; solicitation documentation; acquisition documentation; service level agreements; acquisition contracts for the information system, system component, or information system service; threat modeling and vulnerability analyses from similar information systems, system components, or information system service; other relevant documents or records. *Interview:* Organizational personnel with system and services acquisition responsibilities; organizational personnel with information security responsibilities; system developer. |

(Continued)

Control number	Control name	Assessment methods	Notes and guidance documents	SP 800-53A guidance
SA-15(9)	Development process, standards, and tools: Use of live data	Review documentation to determine if developers used live data for testing and evaluation of system under development. Mitigation of live data usage risks is major area of concern and needs justification and AO approval before use, so the use of dummy or redacted data provides additional mitigation of potential risk. Discuss with acquisition staff, development staff, security staff, operations staff, System Owner, and Security Officer.	SP 800-37, rev. 1, SP 800-64	*Examine:* System and services acquisition policy; procedures addressing development process, standards, and tools; solicitation documentation; acquisition documentation; service level agreements; acquisition contracts for the information system, system component, or information system service; information system design documentation; information system configuration settings and associated documentation; documentation authorizing use of live data in development and test environments; other relevant documents or records. *Interview:* Organizational personnel with system and services acquisition responsibilities; organizational personnel with information security responsibilities; system developer. *Test:* Organizational processes for approving, documenting, and controlling the use of live data in development and test environments; automated mechanisms supporting and/or implementing the approval, documentation, and control of the use of live data in development and test environments.
SA-15(10)	Development process, standards, and tools: Incident response plan	Review documentation for developer-based incident response plan (IRP) implementation during developmental process. Review IRP for applicability and IR-8 control compliance. Discuss with acquisition staff, development staff, security staff, operations staff, System Owner, and Security Officer.	SP 800-37, rev. 1, SP 800-64, Security Control IR-8	*Examine:* System and services acquisition policy; procedures addressing development process, standards, and tools; solicitation documentation; acquisition documentation; service level agreements; acquisition contracts for the information system, or services; acquisition documentation; solicitation documentation; service-level agreements; developer incident response plan; other relevant documents or records. *Interview:* Organizational personnel with system and services acquisition responsibilities; organizational personnel with information security responsibilities; system developer.

SA-15(11)	Development process, standards, and tools: Archive information system/component	Review documentation for the organization to determine if development staff provided additional documentation of system components and implementation actions. Archiving relevant documentation from the development process can provide a readily available baseline of information that can be helpful during information system/component upgrades or modifications. Discuss with acquisition staff, development staff, security staff, operations staff, System Owner, and Security Officer.	SP 800-37, rev. 1, SP 800-64	*Examine:* System and services acquisition policy; procedures addressing development process, standards, and tools; solicitation documentation; acquisition documentation; service level agreements; acquisition contracts for the information system, or services; acquisition documentation; solicitation documentation; service-level agreements; developer incident response plan; other relevant documents or records. *Interview:* Organizational personnel with system and services acquisition responsibilities; organizational personnel with information security responsibilities; system developer.
SA-16	Developer-provided training	Review documentation to determine the developer-based training components delivered, which cover the correct use and operation of the implemented security functions, controls, and/or mechanisms. Discuss with acquisition staff, development staff, security staff, operations staff, System Owner, and Security Officer.	SP 800-37, rev. 1, SP 800-64	*Examine:* System and services acquisition policy; procedures addressing developer provided training; solicitation documentation; acquisition documentation; service-level agreements; acquisition contracts for the information system, system component, or information system service; developer-provided training materials; training records; other relevant documents or records. *Interview:* Organizational personnel with system and services acquisition responsibilities; organizational personnel with information system security responsibilities; system developer; organizational or third-party developers with training responsibilities for the information system, system component, or information system service.
SA-17	Developer security architecture and design	Review documentation to determine the external developer delivered security architecture documents and concepts. This control covers external development activities, whereas PL-8	SP 800-37, rev. 1, SP 800-64	*Examine:* System and services acquisition policy; enterprise architecture policy; procedures addressing developer security architecture and design specification for the information system; solicitation documentation; acquisition documentation; service-level agreements;

(Continued)

Control number	Control name	Assessment methods	Notes and guidance documents	SP 800-53A guidance
		covers security architecture components for internal developers. Discuss with acquisition staff, development staff, security staff, operations staff, System Owner, and Security Officer.		acquisition contracts for the information system, system component, or information system service; design specification and security architecture documentation for the system; information system design documentation; information system configuration settings and associated documentation; other relevant documents or records. *Interview:* Organizational personnel with system and services acquisition responsibilities; organizational personnel with information security responsibilities; system developer; organizational personnel with security architecture and design responsibilities.
SA-17(1)	Developer security architecture and design: Formal policy model	Review documentation to determine the developer produced formal models for system, which provide specific behaviors or security policies using formal languages, thus enabling the correctness of those behaviors/policies to be formally proven. Discuss with acquisition staff, development staff, security staff, operations staff, System Owner, and Security Officer.	SP 800-37, rev. 1, SP 800-64	*Examine:* System and services acquisition policy; enterprise architecture policy; procedures addressing developer security architecture and design specification for the information system; solicitation documentation; acquisition documentation; service-level agreements; acquisition contracts for the information system, system component, or information system service; design specification and security architecture documentation for the system; information system design documentation; information system configuration settings and associated documentation; other relevant documents or records. *Interview:* Organizational personnel with system and services acquisition responsibilities; organizational personnel with information security responsibilities; system developer; organizational personnel with security architecture and design responsibilities.
SA-17(2)	Developer security architecture and design: Security-	Review documentation to determine the security components and items, which provide the actual security for the	SP 800-37, rev. 1, SP 800-64	*Examine:* System and services acquisition policy; enterprise architecture policy; procedures addressing developer security architecture and design specification for the information

relevant components		system. Discuss with acquisition staff, development staff, security staff, operations staff, System Owner, and Security Officer.	system; solicitation documentation; acquisition documentation; service-level agreements; acquisition contracts for the information system, system component, or information system service; list of security-relevant hardware, software, and firmware components; documented rationale of completeness regarding definitions provided for security-relevant hardware, software, and firmware; other relevant documents or records. *Interview:* Organizational personnel with system and services acquisition responsibilities; organizational personnel with information security responsibilities; system developers; organizational personnel with security architecture and design responsibilities.
SA-17(3)	Developer security architecture and design: Formal correspondence	SP 800-37, rev. 1, SP 800-64	Review documentation for development staff to ensure that formal correspondence is provided and produced for system under review. Correspondence is an important part of the assurance gained through modeling, since it demonstrates that the implementation is an accurate transformation of the model, and that any additional code or implementation details present have no impact on the behaviors or policies being modeled. Discuss with acquisition staff, development staff, security staff, operations staff, System Owner, and Security Officer.	*Examine:* System and services acquisition policy; enterprise architecture policy; formal policy model; procedures addressing developer security architecture and design specification for the information system; solicitation documentation; acquisition documentation; service level agreements; acquisition contracts for the information system, system component, or information system service; formal top-level specification documentation; information system security architecture and design documentation; information system design documentation; information system configuration settings and associated documentation; documentation describing security-relevant hardware, software and firmware mechanisms not addressed in the formal top-level specification documentation; other relevant documents or records. *Interview:* Organizational personnel with system and services acquisition responsibilities; organizational personnel with information security responsibilities; system developer; organizational personnel with security architecture and design responsibilities.

(Continued)

Control number	Control name	Assessment methods	Notes and guidance documents	SP 800-53A guidance
SA-17(4)	Developer security architecture and design: Informal correspondence	Review documentation from development staff, which produces the informal correspondence on the security structures of the system. Verify the informal correspondence includes hardware, software, and firmware mechanisms strictly internal to security-relevant hardware, software, and firmware include, for example, mapping registers and direct memory input/output. Discuss with acquisition staff, development staff, security staff, operations staff, System Owner, and Security Officer.	SP 800-37, rev. 1, SP 800-64	*Examine:* System and services acquisition policy; enterprise architecture policy; formal policy model; procedures addressing developer security architecture and design specification for the information system; solicitation documentation; acquisition documentation; service level agreements; acquisition contracts for the information system, system component, or information system service; informal descriptive top-level specification documentation; information system security architecture and design documentation; information system design documentation; information system configuration settings and associated documentation; documentation describing security-relevant hardware, software and firmware mechanisms not addressed in the informal descriptive top-level specification documentation; other relevant documents or records. *Interview:* Organizational personnel with system and services acquisition responsibilities; organizational personnel with information security responsibilities; system developer; organizational personnel with security architecture and design responsibilities.
SA-17(5)	Developer security architecture and design: Conceptually simple design	Review development documentation for evidence of a simple protection mechanism with precisely defined semantics. Discuss with acquisition staff, development staff, security staff, operations staff, System Owner, and Security Officer.	SP 800-37, rev. 1, SP 800-64	*Examine:* System and services acquisition policy; enterprise architecture policy; procedures addressing developer security architecture and design specification for the information system; solicitation documentation; acquisition documentation; service-level agreements; acquisition contracts for the information system, system component, or information system service; information system design documentation; information system security architecture documentation; information system configuration settings and associated

		documentation; developer documentation describing design and structure of security-relevant hardware, software, and firmware components; other relevant documents or records. *Interview:* Organizational personnel with system and services acquisition responsibilities; organizational personnel with information security responsibilities; system developer; organizational personnel with security architecture and design responsibilities.		
SA-17(6)	Developer security architecture and design: Structure for testing	Review development documentation to ensure that security-relevant hardware, software, and firmware has been designed to facilitate testing and security metrics outputs for verification of the security functions. Discuss with acquisition staff, development staff, security staff, operations staff, System Owner, and Security Officer.	SP 800-37, rev. 1, SP 800-64	*Examine:* System and services acquisition policy; enterprise architecture policy; procedures addressing developer security architecture and design specification for the information system; solicitation documentation; acquisition documentation; service-level agreements; acquisition contracts for the information system, system component, or information system service; information system design documentation; information system security architecture documentation; information system configuration settings and associated documentation; developer documentation describing design and structure of security-relevant hardware, software, and firmware components to facilitate testing; other relevant documents or records. *Interview:* Organizational personnel with system and services acquisition responsibilities; organizational personnel with information security responsibilities; system developer; organizational personnel with security architecture and design responsibilities.
SA-17(7)	Developer security architecture and design: Structure for least privilege	Review documentation to ensure that the principle of least privilege was accounted for and designed into the security structures of the system under review. Discuss with acquisition staff, development	SP 800-37, rev. 1, SP 800-64	*Examine:* System and services acquisition policy; enterprise architecture policy; procedures addressing developer security architecture and design specification for the information system; solicitation documentation; acquisition documentation; service-level agreements;

(Continued)

Control number	Control name	Assessment methods	Notes and guidance documents	SP 800-53A guidance
		staff, security staff, operations staff, System Owner, and Security Officer.		acquisition contracts for the information system, system component, or information system service; information system design documentation; information system security architecture documentation; information system configuration settings and associated documentation; developer documentation describing design and structure of security-relevant hardware, software, and firmware components to facilitate controlling access with least privilege; other relevant documents or records. *Interview:* Organizational personnel with system and services acquisition responsibilities; organizational personnel with information security responsibilities; system developer; organizational personnel with security architecture and design responsibilities.
SA-18	Tamper resistance and detection	Review documentation to ensure that antitamper technologies and techniques provide a level of protection for critical information systems, system components, and information technology products against a number of related threats including modification, reverse engineering, and substitution have been implemented within the security controls of the system under review. Discuss with acquisition staff, developers, security staff, System Owner, and Security Officer.	SP 800-37, rev. 1, SP 800-64	*Examine:* System and services acquisition policy; procedures addressing tamper resistance and detection; tamper protection program documentation; tamper protection tools and techniques documentation; tamper resistance and detection tools and techniques documentation; other relevant documents or records. *Interview:* Organizational personnel with system and services acquisition responsibilities; organizational personnel with information security responsibilities; organizational personnel with responsibility for the tamper protection program. *Test:* Organizational processes for implementation of the tamper protection program; automated mechanisms supporting and/or implementing the tamper protection program.
SA-18(1)	Tamper resistance and detection: Multiple phases of SDLC	Review documentation to ensure that tamper resistant technologies and coding techniques are implemented throughout the SDLC of the system to include design,	SP 800-37, rev. 1, SP 800-64	*Examine:* System and services acquisition policy; procedures addressing tamper resistance and detection; tamper protection program documentation; tamper protection tools and techniques documentation; tamper resistance

		development, integration, operations, and maintenance activities and phases. Discuss with acquisition staff, development staff, security staff, System Owner, and Security Officer.		and detection tools (technologies) and techniques documentation; system development life cycle documentation; other relevant documents or records. *Interview:* Organizational personnel with system and services acquisition responsibilities; organizational personnel with information security responsibilities; organizational personnel with responsibility for the tamper protection program; organizational personnel with SDLC responsibilities. *Test:* Organizational processes for employing anti-tamper technologies; automated mechanisms supporting and/or implementing anti-tamper technologies.
SA-18(2)	Tamper resistance and detection: Inspection of information systems, components, or devices	Review documentation to ensure that tamper resistant components and requirements address both physical and logical tampering, and are typically applied to mobile devices, notebook computers, or other system components taken out of organization-controlled areas. Discuss with acquisition staff, development staff, operations staff, security staff, Security Officer, FSO, and System Owner.	SP 800-37, rev. 1, SP 800-64	*Examine:* System and services acquisition policy; procedures addressing tamper resistance and detection; records of random inspections; inspection reports/results; assessment reports/results; other relevant documents or records. *Interview:* Organizational personnel with system and services acquisition responsibilities; organizational personnel with information security responsibilities; organizational personnel with responsibility for the tamper protection program. *Test:* Organizational processes for inspecting information systems, system components, or devices to detect tampering; automated mechanisms supporting and/or implementing tampering detection.
SA-19	Component authenticity	Review documentation for organization to ensure that the organization has and implements anti-counterfeiting policy and procedures support tamper resistance and provide a level of protection against the introduction of malicious code into system. Discuss with operations staff, System Owner, Security Officer, and legal staff.	SP 800-37, rev. 1, SP 800-64	*Examine:* System and services acquisition policy; anti-counterfeit policy and procedures; media disposal policy; media protection policy; incident response policy; training materials addressing counterfeit information system components; training records on detection and prevention of counterfeit components from entering the information system; reports notifying developers/manufacturers/vendors/contractors and/or external reporting organizations of counterfeit information system components;

(Continued)

Control number	Control name	Assessment methods	Notes and guidance documents	SP 800-53A guidance
				other relevant documents or records. *Interview:* Organizational personnel with system and services acquisition responsibilities; organizational personnel with information security responsibilities; organizational personnel with responsibility for anti-counterfeit policy, procedures, and reporting. *Test:* Organizational processes for anti-counterfeit detection, prevention, and reporting; automated mechanisms supporting and/or implementing anti-counterfeit detection, prevention, and reporting.
SA-19(1)	Component authenticity: Anti-counterfeit training	Review documentation to ensure that the organization provides counterfeit component awareness training for system hardware, software, and firmware. Discuss with security staff, operations staff, System Owner, and Security Officer.	SP 800-37, rev. 1, SP 800-64	*Examine:* System and services acquisition policy; anti-counterfeit policy and procedures; media disposal policy; media protection policy; incident response policy; training materials addressing counterfeit information system components; training records on detection of counterfeit information system components; other relevant documents or records. *Interview:* Organizational personnel with system and services acquisition responsibilities; organizational personnel with information security responsibilities; organizational personnel with responsibility for anti-counterfeit policy, procedures, and training. *Test:* Organizational processes for anti-counterfeit training.
SA-19(2)	Component authenticity: Configuration control for component service/repair	Review documentation to ensure that the organization maintains configuration management of system components during repair actions and activities. Discuss with security staff, System Owner, operations staff, and Security Officer.	SP 800-37, rev. 1, SP 800-64	*Examine:* System and services acquisition policy; anti-counterfeit policy and procedures; media protection policy; configuration management plan; information system design documentation; information system configuration settings and associated documentation; configuration control records for components awaiting service/repair; configuration control records for serviced/repaired components awaiting return to service; information system maintenance records; information system audit records; inventory

				management records; other relevant documents or records. *Interview:* Organizational personnel with system and services acquisition responsibilities; organizational personnel with information security responsibilities; organizational personnel with responsibility for anti-counterfeit policy and procedures; organizational personnel with responsibility for configuration management. *Test:* Organizational processes for configuration management; automated mechanisms supporting and/or implementing configuration management.
SA-19(3)	Component authenticity: Component disposal	Review documentation to ensure that the organization performs proper disposal of system components to maintain integrity and full destruction of sensitive items. Discuss with operations staff, security staff, Security Officer, and System Owner.	SP 800-37, rev. 1, SP 800-64	*Examine:* System and services acquisition policy; anti-counterfeit policy and procedures; media disposal policy; media protection policy; disposal records for information system components; documentation of disposal techniques and methods employed for information system components; other relevant documents or records. *Interview:* Organizational personnel with system and services acquisition responsibilities; organizational personnel with information security responsibilities; organizational personnel with responsibility for anti-counterfeit policy and procedures; organizational personnel with responsibility for disposal of information system components. *Test:* Organizational techniques and methods for information system component disposal; automated mechanisms supporting and/or implementing system component disposal.
SA-19(4)	Component authenticity: Anti-counterfeit scanning	Review documentation to ensure that the organization conducts periodic scanning for counterfeit components and parts used on system. Discuss with security staff, Security Officer, and System Owner.	SP 800-37, rev. 1, SP 800-64	*Examine:* System and services acquisition policy; anti-counterfeit policy and procedures; information system design documentation; information system configuration settings and associated documentation; scanning tools and associated documentation; scanning results; other relevant documents or records. *Interview:* Organizational personnel with system and

(Continued)

Control number	Control name	Assessment methods	Notes and guidance documents	SP 800-53A guidance
				services acquisition responsibilities; organizational personnel with information security responsibilities; organizational personnel with responsibility for anti-counterfeit policy and procedures; organizational personnel with responsibility for anti-counterfeit scanning. *Test:* Organizational processes for anti-counterfeit scanning; automated mechanisms supporting and/or implementing anti-counterfeit scanning.
SA-20	Customized development of critical components	Review documentation for specialized system components, which have high criticality for system operations and low tolerance for failure. Reimplementation or custom development of such components helps to satisfy requirements for higher assurance. This is accomplished by initiating changes to system components (including hardware, software, and firmware). Discuss with System Owner, development staff, acquisition staff, security staff, and Security Officer.	SP 800-37, rev. 1, SP 800-64	*Examine:* System and services acquisition policy; procedures addressing customized development of critical information system components; information system design documentation; information system configuration settings and associated documentation; system development life cycle documentation addressing custom development of critical information system components; configuration management records; information system audit records; other relevant documents or records. *Interview:* Organizational personnel with system and services acquisition responsibilities; organizational personnel with information security responsibilities; organizational personnel with responsibility for reimplementation or customized development of critical information system components. *Test:* Organizational processes for reimplementing or customized development of critical information system components; automated mechanisms supporting and/or implementing reimplementation or customized development of critical information system components.
SA-21	Developer screening	Review documentation for organization to ensure that the development staff is vetted and screened in accordance with the security requirements for system to include authorization and	SP 800-37, rev. 1, SP 800-64	*Examine:* System and services acquisition policy; personnel security policy and procedures; procedures addressing personnel screening; information system design documentation; information system configuration settings and associated documentation; list of appropriate

Control	Name	Description	References	Assessment
		personnel screening criteria, such as clearance requirements, satisfactory background checks, citizenship, and nationality. Trustworthiness of developers may also include a review and analysis of company ownership and any relationships, the company has with entities potentially affecting the quality/reliability of the systems, components, or services being developed for system or organization. Discuss with acquisition staff, development staff, security staff, operations staff, System Owner, and Security Officer.		access authorizations required by developers of the information system; personnel screening criteria and associated documentation; other relevant documents or records. *Interview:* Organizational personnel with system and services acquisition responsibilities; organizational personnel with information security responsibilities; organizational personnel with responsibility for developer screening. *Test:* Organizational processes for developer screening; automated mechanisms supporting developer screening.
SA-21(1)	Developer screening; Validation of screening	Review documentation to ensure that the development staff meets all criteria for valid background screening and authorization verification efforts. Discuss with acquisition staff, development staff, security staff, operations staff, System Owner, and Security Officer.	SP 800-37, rev. 1, SP 800-64	*Examine:* System and services acquisition policy; personnel security policy and procedures; procedures addressing personnel screening; information system design documentation; information system configuration settings and associated documentation; list of appropriate access authorizations required by developers of the information system; personnel screening criteria and associated documentation; list of actions ensuring required access authorizations and screening criteria are satisfied; other relevant documents or records. *Interview:* Organizational personnel with system and services acquisition responsibilities; organizational personnel with information security responsibilities; organizational personnel with responsibility for developer screening; system developer. *Test:* Organizational processes for developer screening; automated mechanisms supporting developer screening.
SA-22	Unsupported system components	Review documentation to ensure that the system and organization is not utilizing unsupported	SP 800-37, rev. 1, SP 800-64	*Examine:* System and services acquisition policy; procedures addressing replacement or continued use of unsupported information system

(Continued)

Control number	Control name	Assessment methods	Notes and guidance documents	SP 800-53A guidance
		components (e.g., when vendors are no longer providing critical software patches), which can provide a substantial opportunity for adversaries to exploit new weaknesses discovered in the currently installed components. Typically, this is called the EOL (End Of Life) threshold (in the software industry), and requires justification and documents approval for the continued use of unsupported system components required to satisfy mission/business needs. Discuss with System Owner, operations staff, and Security Officer.		components; documented evidence of replacing unsupported information system components; documented approvals (including justification) for continued use of unsupported information system components; other relevant documents or records. *Interview:* Organizational personnel with system and services acquisition responsibilities; organizational personnel with information security responsibilities; organizational personnel with responsibility system development life cycle; organizational personnel responsible for configuration management. *Test:* Organizational processes for replacing unsupported system components; automated mechanisms supporting and/or implementing replacement of unsupported system components.
SA-22(1)	Unsupported system components: Alternative sources for continued support	Review documentation to ensure that the organization has provisioned for continued support for selected information system components that are no longer supported by the original developers, vendors, or manufacturers, when such components remain essential to mission/business operations. Both in-house development staff and external third-party system support organizations can meet these criteria and validate such documentation and support agreements. Discuss with acquisition staff, security staff, operations staff, System Owner, and Security Officer.	SP 800-37, rev. 1, SP 800-64	*Examine:* System and services acquisition policy; procedures addressing support for unsupported information system components; solicitation documentation; acquisition documentation; acquisition contracts; service-level agreements; other relevant documents or records. *Interview:* Organizational personnel with system and services acquisition responsibilities; organizational personnel with information security responsibilities; organizational personnel with responsibility system development life cycle; organizational personnel or third-party external providers supporting information system components no longer supported by original developers, vendors, or manufacturers. *Test:* Organizational processes for supporting system components no longer supported by original developers, vendors, or manufacturers; automated mechanisms providing support for system components no longer supported by original developers, vendors, or manufacturers.

Q. *Systems and communication protection family*

FIPS-200 provides the following criteria for this family of controls: System and communications protection (SC): Organizations must: (i) monitor, control, and protect organizational communications (i.e., information transmitted or received by organizational information systems) at the external boundaries and key internal boundaries of the information systems; and (ii) employ architectural designs, software development techniques, and systems engineering principles that promote effective information security within organizational information systems.

The primary assessment areas for these controls include:

a. Audit processes that monitor, control, and protect organizational communications (i.e., information transmitted or received by organizational information systems) at the external boundaries and key internal boundaries of the information systems.

b. Review techniques that employ architectural designs, software development techniques, and systems engineering principles that promote effective information security within organizational information systems.

Control number	Control name	Assessment methods	Notes and guidance documents	SP 800-53A guidance
SC-1	System and communications protection policy and procedures	Review documentation for organization to ensure that the protection policies and procedures are developed, installed, active, and followed by users and organization. Discuss with System Owner, operations staff, and Security Officer.	SP 800-12, SP 800-100	*Examine:* System and communications protection policy and procedures; other relevant documents or records. *Interview:* Organizational personnel with system and communications protection responsibilities; organizational personnel with information security responsibilities.
SC-2	Application partitioning	Review documentation to ensure that the system separates user functionality from information system management functionality, either, physically or logically or both ways. Observe separated functions between user and management activities. Discuss with System Owner, security staff, operations staff, and Security Officer.		*Examine:* System and communications protection policy; procedures addressing application partitioning; information system design documentation; information system configuration settings and associated documentation; information system audit records; other relevant documents or records. *Interview:* System/network administrators; organizational personnel with information security responsibilities; system developer. *Test:* Separation of user functionality from information system management functionality.
SC-2(1)	Application partitioning: Interfaces for nonprivileged users	Review documentation to ensure that the system prevents normal users from accessing or being presented with administrative functions during normal operations. Observe such separation during normal operations to ensure that separation is active and functioning correctly. Discuss with operations staff, security staff, System Owner, and Security Officer.		*Examine:* System and communications protection policy; procedures addressing application partitioning; information system design documentation; information system configuration settings and associated documentation; information system audit records; other relevant documents or records. *Interview:* System/network administrators; organizational personnel with information security responsibilities; nonprivileged users of the information system; system developer. *Test:* Separation of user functionality from information system management functionality.
SC-3	Security function isolation	Review documentation to ensure that the system provides isolation between security functions and nonsecurity		*Examine:* System and communications protection policy; procedures addressing security function isolation; list of security functions to be isolated from nonsecurity functions; information system

Control	Name	Procedure	Related	Assessment
		functions, such as protection rings or isolation boundaries. Test with script or test code to attempt crossing boundary and discuss results with System Owner, operations staff, and Security Officer.		design documentation; information system configuration settings and associated documentation; information system audit records; other relevant documents or records. *Interview:* System/network administrators; organizational personnel with information security responsibilities; system developer. *Test:* Separation of security functions from nonsecurity functions within the information system.
SC-3(1)	Security function isolation: Hardware separation	Review documentation to ensure that the system provides hardware-based isolation between security functions and nonsecurity functions, such as protection rings or hardware address segmentation. Test with script or test code to attempt crossing rings or segments and discuss results with System Owner, operations staff, and Security Officer.		*Examine:* System and communications protection policy; procedures addressing security function isolation; information system design documentation; hardware separation mechanisms; information system configuration settings and associated documentation; information system audit records; other relevant documents or records. *Interview:* System/network administrators; organizational personnel with information security responsibilities; system developer. *Test:* Separation of security functions from nonsecurity functions within the information system.
SC-3(2)	Security function isolation: Access/flow control functions	Review documentation to ensure that the security functions, such as AV, intrusion detection, and auditing are separated via access and flow control mechanisms from nonsecurity functions. Confirm isolation on system via review of configuration files, access control roles, and testing of security functions from nonsecurity logins. Discuss with System Owner, security staff, operations staff, and Security Officer.	AC-4	*Examine:* System and communications protection policy; procedures addressing security function isolation; list of critical security functions; information system design documentation; information system configuration settings and associated documentation; information system audit records; other relevant documents or records. *Interview:* System/network administrators; organizational personnel with information security responsibilities; system developer. *Test:* Isolation of security functions enforcing access and information flow control.
SC-3(3)	Security function isolation: Minimize	Review documentation to ensure that the organization minimizes the nonsecurity-relevant		*Examine:* System and communications protection policy; procedures addressing security function isolation; information system design

(Continued)

Control number	Control name	Assessment methods	Notes and guidance documents	SP 800-53A guidance
	nonsecurity functionality	functions within the security function boundary. Review design documents to determine level of minimization achieved versus what is measured on the system. Discuss results with development staff, operations staff, security staff, System Owner, and Security Officer.		documentation; information system configuration settings and associated documentation; information system audit records; other relevant documents or records. *Interview:* System/network administrators; organizational personnel with information security responsibilities. *Test:* Automated mechanisms supporting and/or implementing an isolation boundary.
SC-3(4)	Security function isolation: Module coupling and cohesiveness	Review documentation to determine level of cohesion and coupling within the software modules within system. Ensure development efforts provide modular decomposition, layering, and minimization to reduce and manage complexity, thus producing software modules that are highly cohesive and loosely coupled. Discuss with System Owner, Security Officer, security staff, development staff, and operations staff.	SP 800-64	*Examine:* System and communications protection policy; procedures addressing security function isolation; information system design documentation; information system configuration settings and associated documentation; information system audit records; other relevant documents or records. *Interview:* System/network administrators; organizational personnel with information security responsibilities. *Test:* Organizational processes for maximizing internal cohesiveness within modules and minimizing coupling between modules; automated mechanisms supporting and/or implementing security functions as independent modules.
SC-3(5)	Security function isolation: Layered structures	Review documentation to ensure that the system provides layered structures within code to enhance the layered security structures with minimized interactions among security functions and nonlooping layers. Evaluate specific design documentation and code to ensure compliance. Discuss with development staff, operations staff, security staff, System Owner, and Security Officer.	SP 800-64	*Examine:* System and communications protection policy; procedures addressing security function isolation; information system design documentation; information system configuration settings and associated documentation; information system audit records; other relevant documents or records. *Interview:* System/network administrators; organizational personnel with information security responsibilities. *Test:* Organizational processes for implementing security functions as a layered structure that minimizes interactions between layers and avoids dependence by lower layers on functionality/correctness of higher layers; automated mechanisms supporting and/or

implementing security functions as a layered structure.

SC-4	Information in shared resources	SP 800-64	Review documentation to ensure that the system controls shared resources in a secure manner through use of object reuse and residual information protection of roles within objects in code. Discuss with System Owner, operations staff, development staff, security staff, and Security Officer.	*Examine:* System and communications protection policy; procedures addressing information protection in shared system resources; information system design documentation; information system configuration settings and associated documentation; information system audit records; other relevant documents or records. *Interview:* System/network administrators; organizational personnel with information security responsibilities; system developer. *Test:* Automated mechanisms preventing unauthorized and unintended transfer of information via shared system resources.
SC-4(1)	Information in shared resources: Security levels	Withdrawn: Incorporated into SC-4		
SC-4(2)	Information in shared resources: Periods processing	SP 800-64	Review documentation to ensure that when changes are made explicitly in security levels, such as during multilevel processing and periods processing with information at different classification levels or security categories, the system prevents transfer of unauthorized data through multiple means, including approved sanitization processes for electronically stored information. Discuss with development staff, security staff, operations staff, Security Officer, and System Owner.	*Examine:* System and communications protection policy; procedures addressing information protection in shared system resources; information system design documentation; information system configuration settings and associated documentation; information system audit records; other relevant documents or records. *Interview:* System/network administrators; organizational personnel with information security responsibilities; system developer. *Test:* Automated mechanisms preventing unauthorized transfer of information via shared system resources.
SC-5	Denial of service protection		Review documentation to ensure the system protects against or limits the effects of denial of	*Examine:* System and communications protection policy; procedures addressing denial of service protection; information system design documentation;

(Continued)

Control number	Control name	Assessment methods	Notes and guidance documents	SP 800-53A guidance
		service (DOS) attacks, such as boundary protection devices, which can filter certain types of packets to protect information system components on internal organizational networks. Review design specifications, equipment operating systems, and filtering components for DOS protection. Review logs to ensure operational functioning of DOS protection mechanisms. Discuss with security staff, operations staff, System Owner, and Security Officer.		security plan; list of denial of services attacks requiring employment of security safeguards to protect against or limit effects of such attacks; list of security safeguards protecting against or limiting the effects of denial of service attacks; information system configuration settings and associated documentation; information system audit records; other relevant documents or records. *Interview:* System/network administrators; organizational personnel with information security responsibilities; organizational personnel with incident response responsibilities; system developer. *Test:* Automated mechanisms protecting against or limiting the effects of denial of service attacks.
SC-5(1)	Denial of service protection: Restrict internal users	Review documentation to determine the level of restriction on users to transmit or initiate other communication methods within the system. Test via scripting test communications and reviewing results with System Owner, security staff, operations staff, and Security Officer.		*Examine:* System and communications protection policy; procedures addressing denial of service protection; information system design documentation; security plan; list of denial of service attacks launched by individuals against information systems; information system configuration settings and associated documentation; information system audit records; other relevant documents or records. *Interview:* System/network administrators; organizational personnel with information security responsibilities; organizational personnel with incident response responsibilities; system developer. *Test:* Automated mechanisms restricting the ability to launch denial of service attacks against other information systems.
SC-5(2)	Denial of service protection: Excess capacity/ bandwidth/ redundancy	Review documentation to ensure that the system automatically limits excess usage of capability or bandwidth by applying various techniques, such as establishing selected usage priorities, quotas, or partitioning.		*Examine:* System and communications protection policy; procedures addressing denial of service protection; information system design documentation; information system configuration settings and associated documentation; information system audit records; other relevant documents or records. *Interview:* System/network administrators;

		Discuss with operation staff, security staff, Security Officer, and System Owner.	organizational personnel with information security responsibilities; organizational personnel with incident response responsibilities; system developer. *Test:* Automated mechanisms implementing management of information system bandwidth, capacity, and redundancy to limit the effects of information flooding denial of service attacks.
SC-5(3)	Denial of service protection: Detection/monitoring	Review documentation to determine the level of detection and monitoring for DOS attacks is implemented within the system. Evaluate to response mechanisms implemented for DOS attacks on the storage components of the system such as, instituting disk quotas, configuring information systems to automatically alert administrators, when specific storage capacity thresholds are reached, using file compression technologies to maximize available storage space, and imposing separate partitions for system and user data. Discuss with System Owner, operations staff, security staff, and Security Officer.	*Examine:* System and communications protection policy; procedures addressing denial of service protection; information system design documentation; information system monitoring tools and techniques documentation; information system configuration settings and associated documentation; information system audit records; other relevant documents or records. *Interview:* System/network administrators; organizational personnel with information security responsibilities; organizational personnel with detection and monitoring responsibilities. *Test:* Automated mechanisms/tools implementing information system monitoring for denial of service attacks.
SC-6	Resource availability	Review documentation for multi-user system allocations and components to ensure that the system assigns priorities for resources, which prevents lower-priority processes from delaying or interfering with the information system servicing any higher-priority processes. Review logs and account activities to ensure priorities	*Examine:* System and communications protection policy; procedures addressing prioritization of information system resources; information system design documentation; information system configuration settings and associated documentation; information system audit records; other relevant documents or records. *Interview:* System/network administrators; organizational personnel with information security responsibilities; system developer. *Test:* Automated mechanisms supporting and/or implementing resource

(Continued)

Control number	Control name	Assessment methods	Notes and guidance documents	SP 800-53A guidance
		and allocations are functioning correctly. Discuss with System Owner, operations staff, security staff, and Security Officer.		allocation capability; safeguards employed to protect availability of resources.
SC-7	Boundary protection	Review documentation for boundary or edge protection mechanisms and methods employed to protect the interfaces for the system. Such components, like gateways, routers, firewalls, guards, network-based malicious code analysis, and virtualization systems, or encrypted tunnels, all provide differing levels and types of protection and review engineering and operational documents to verify applicability and functional requirements. Discuss with Security Engineer, Security Architect, security staff, operations staff, acquisition staff, System Owner, and Security Officer.	FIPS-199, SP 800-41, SP 800-77	*Examine:* System and communications protection policy; procedures addressing boundary protection; list of key internal boundaries of the information system; information system design documentation; boundary protection hardware and software; information system configuration settings and associated documentation; enterprise security architecture documentation; information system audit records; other relevant documents or records. *Interview:* System/network administrators; organizational personnel with information security responsibilities; system developer; organizational personnel with boundary protection responsibilities. *Test:* Automated mechanisms implementing boundary protection capability.
SC-7(1)	Boundary protection: Physically separated subnetworks		Withdrawn: Incorporated into SC-7	
SC-7(2)	Boundary protection: Public access		Withdrawn: Incorporated into SC-7	
SC-7(3)	Boundary protection Access points	Review documentation to ensure that the system limits number of access points into system since control of these connections facilitates more comprehensive	FIPS-199, SP 800-41, SP 800-77, TIC Initiative	*Examine:* System and communications protection policy; procedures addressing boundary protection; information system design documentation; boundary protection hardware and software; information system architecture and configuration documentation;

		monitoring of inbound and outbound communications traffic. Discuss with Security Engineer, Security Architect, security staff, operations staff, acquisition staff, System Owner, and Security Officer.		information system configuration settings and associated documentation; communications and network traffic monitoring logs; information system audit records; other relevant documents or records. *Interview:* System/network administrators; organizational personnel with information security responsibilities; organizational personnel with boundary protection responsibilities. *Test:* Automated mechanisms implementing boundary protection capability; automated mechanisms limiting the number of external network connections to the information system.
SC-7(4)	Boundary protection: External telecommunications services	Review documentation to ensure that the external interfaces and traffic flow policies for telecommunications are defined and monitored. Review logs and monitoring outputs to verify monitoring. Discuss with operations staff, security staff, acquisition staff, security staff, System Owner, and Security Officer.	FIPS-199, SP 800-41, SP 800-47, SP 800-77	*Examine:* System and communications protection policy; traffic flow policy; information flow control policy; procedures addressing boundary protection; information system security architecture; information system design documentation; boundary protection hardware and software; information system architecture and configuration documentation; information system configuration settings and associated documentation; records of traffic flow policy exceptions; information system audit records; other relevant documents or records. *Interview:* System/network administrators; organizational personnel with information security responsibilities; organizational personnel with boundary protection responsibilities. *Test:* Organizational processes for documenting and reviewing exceptions to the traffic flow policy; organizational processes for removing exceptions to the traffic flow policy; automated mechanisms implementing boundary protection capability; managed interfaces implementing traffic flow policy.
SC-7(5)	Boundary protection: Deny by default/allow by exception	Review documentation to ensure that both inbound and outbound network communications traffic is monitored and controlled. Ensure a deny-all, permit-by-	FIPS-199, SP 800-41, SP 800-77	*Examine:* System and communications protection policy; procedures addressing boundary protection; information system design documentation; information system configuration settings and associated documentation; information system

(Continued)

Control number	Control name	Assessment methods	Notes and guidance documents	SP 800-53A guidance
		exception (AKA as DD-AE deny by default - allow by exception) network communications traffic policy so that only those connections, which are essential and approved are allowed. Discuss with Security Architect, Security Engineer, operations staff, System Owner, security staff, and Security Officer.		audit records; other relevant documents or records. *Interview:* System/network administrators; organizational personnel with information security responsibilities; system developer; organizational personnel with boundary protection responsibilities. *Test:* Automated mechanisms implementing traffic management at managed interfaces.
SC-7(6)	Boundary protection: Response to recognized failures		Withdrawn: Incorporated into SC-7(18)	
SC-7(7)	Boundary protection: Prevent split tunneling for remote devices	Review documentation to ensure that the organization implements within remote devices (e.g., notebook computers) through configuration settings, the disabling of ability to disable split tunneling in those devices, and by preventing those configuration settings from being readily configurable by users. Evaluate sample remote device to verify disabling. Discuss with security staff, Security Officer, operations staff, and System Owner.	FIPS-199, SP 800-41, SP 800-77	*Examine:* System and communications protection policy; procedures addressing boundary protection; information system design documentation; information system hardware and software; information system architecture; information system configuration settings and associated documentation; information system audit records; other relevant documents or records. *Interview:* System/network administrators; organizational personnel with information security responsibilities; system developer; organizational personnel with boundary protection responsibilities. *Test:* Automated mechanisms implementing boundary protection capability; automated mechanisms supporting/restricting nonremote connections.
SC-7(8)	Boundary protection: Route traffic to authenticated proxy servers	Review documentation to ensure that the system provides for user requests get established through an initial connection to the proxy server, so these requests are evaluated to manage complexity and to provide additional	FIPS-199, SP 800-41, SP 800-77	*Examine:* System and communications protection policy; procedures addressing boundary protection; information system design documentation; information system hardware and software; information system architecture; information system configuration settings and associated documentation; information system audit records;

	protection by limiting direct connectivity to user machine from outside the system. Test proxy mechanism with sample requests and review results with System Owner, operations staff, Security Engineer, security staff, and Security Officer.		other relevant documents or records. *Interview:* System/network administrators; organizational personnel with information security responsibilities; system developer; organizational personnel with boundary protection responsibilities. *Test:* Automated mechanisms implementing traffic management through authenticated proxy servers at managed interfaces.
SC-7(9)	Boundary protection: Restrict threatening outgoing communications traffic	Review documentation for system to ensure that extrusion detection is installed and implemented. Test extrusion detection method to ensure detection at system boundaries as part of managed interfaces, which includes the analysis of incoming and outgoing communications traffic searching for indications of internal threats to the security of external systems. Discuss with Security Architect, Security Engineer, security staff, Security Officer, and System Owner.	FIPS-199, SP 800-41, SP 800-77	*Examine:* System and communications protection policy; procedures addressing boundary protection; information system design documentation; information system hardware and software; information system architecture; information system configuration settings and associated documentation; information system audit records; other relevant documents or records. *Interview:* System/network administrators; organizational personnel with information security responsibilities; system developer; organizational personnel with boundary protection responsibilities. *Test:* Automated mechanisms implementing boundary protection capability; automated mechanisms implementing detection and denial of threatening outgoing communications traffic; automated mechanisms implementing auditing of outgoing communications traffic.
SC-7(10)	Boundary protection: Prevent unauthorized exfiltration	Review documentation to ensure that the data loss prevention methods for the prevention of unauthorized exfiltration of information are installed and implemented. Test using restricted information and discuss with System Owner, Security Engineer, security staff, FSO (if necessary), and Security Officer.	FIPS-199, SP 800-41, SP 800-77	*Examine:* System and communications protection policy; procedures addressing boundary protection; information system design documentation; information system configuration settings and associated documentation; information system audit records; other relevant documents or records. *Interview:* System/network administrators; organizational personnel with information security responsibilities; organizational personnel with boundary protection responsibilities. *Test:* Automated mechanisms implementing boundary protection

(Continued)

Control number	Control name	Assessment methods	Notes and guidance documents	SP 800-53A guidance
				capability; preventing unauthorized exfiltration of information across managed interfaces.
SC-7(11)	Boundary protection: Restrict incoming communications traffic	Review documentation to ensure that the system allows only source and destination address pairs representing authorized/allowed communications in exchange of information across interfaces. Test using restricted communications and discuss results with System Owner, security staff, operations staff, and Security Office.r	FIPS-199, SP 800-41, SP 800-77	*Examine:* System and communications protection policy; procedures addressing boundary protection; information system design documentation; information system configuration settings and associated documentation; information system audit records; other relevant documents or records. *Interview:* System/network administrators; organizational personnel with information security responsibilities; system developer; organizational personnel with boundary protection responsibilities. *Test:* Automated mechanisms implementing boundary protection capabilities with respect to source/destination address pairs.
SC-7(12)	Boundary protection: Host-based protection	Review documentation to ensure that the system utilizes host-based protection methods, such as host-based firewalls to provide further protection. Review and test protection methods employed and discuss with Security Engineer, security staff, operations staff, System Owner, and Security Officer.	FIPS-199, SP 800-41, SP 800-77	*Examine:* System and communications protection policy; procedures addressing boundary protection; information system design documentation; boundary protection hardware and software; information system configuration settings and associated documentation; information system audit records; other relevant documents or records. *Interview:* System/network administrators; organizational personnel with information security responsibilities; organizational personnel with boundary protection responsibilities; information system users. *Test:* Automated mechanisms implementing host-based boundary protection capabilities.
SC-7(13)	Boundary protection: Isolation of security tools/mechanisms/support components	Review documentation to determine the system use of physically separated subnets and other methods of isolation, such as isolating computer network defenses from critical operational processing networks to prevent adversaries from discovering the	FIPS-199, SP 800-41, SP 800-77	*Examine:* System and communications protection policy; procedures addressing boundary protection; information system design documentation; information system hardware and software; information system architecture; information system configuration settings and associated documentation; list of security tools and support components to be isolated from other internal

			References	Assessment
		analysis and forensics techniques of organizations, to ensure protection. Test with methods of system and network mapping and discuss results with Security Architect, Security Engineer, security staff, operations staff, System Owner, and Security Officer.		information system components; information system audit records; other relevant documents or records. *Interview:* System/network administrators; organizational personnel with information security responsibilities; organizational personnel with boundary protection responsibilities. *Test:* Automated mechanisms supporting and/or implementing isolation of information security tools, mechanisms, and support components.
SC-7(14)	Boundary protection: Protects against unauthorized physical connections	Review documentation and identify physical components for separation protection, such as employing clearly identified and physically separated cable trays, connection frames, and patch panels for each side of managed interfaces with physical access controls enforcing limited authorized access to these items. Observe these physical isolation protection methods and components. Discuss with facilities staff, FSO, security staff, operations staff, System Owner, and Security Officer.	FIPS-199, SP 800-41, SP 800-77	*Examine:* System and communications protection policy; procedures addressing boundary protection; information system design documentation; information system hardware and software; information system architecture; information system configuration settings and associated documentation; facility communications and wiring diagram; other relevant documents or records. *Interview:* System/network administrators; organizational personnel with information security responsibilities; organizational personnel with boundary protection responsibilities. *Test:* Automated mechanisms supporting and/or implementing protection against unauthorized physical connections.
SC-7(15)	Boundary protection: Route privileged network accesses	Review documentation to determine the implementation of system routing all networked, privileged accesses through a dedicated, managed interface for purposes of access control and auditing. Review audit logs to ensure full implementation and activities recorded. Discuss with Security Engineer, operations staff, security staff, System Owner, and Security Officer.	FIPS-199, SP 800-41, SP 800-77	*Examine:* System and communications protection policy; procedures addressing boundary protection; information system design documentation; information system hardware and software; information system architecture; information system configuration settings and associated documentation; audit logs; other relevant documents or records. *Interview:* System/network administrators; organizational personnel with information security responsibilities; system developer; organizational personnel with boundary protection responsibilities. *Test:* Automated mechanisms supporting and/or implementing the

(Continued)

Control number	Control name	Assessment methods	Notes and guidance documents	SP 800-53A guidance
				routing of networked, privileged access through dedicated managed interfaces.
SC-7(16)	Boundary protection: Prevent discovery of components/devices	Review documentation to determine the level of protection provided for prevention of network discovery methods being successful on system. Review techniques utilized and discuss results of review with security staff, System Owner, operations staff, and Security Officer.	FIPS-199, SP 800-41, SP 800-77	*Examine:* System and communications protection policy; procedures addressing boundary protection; information system design documentation; information system hardware and software; information system architecture; information system configuration settings and associated documentation; information system audit records; other relevant documents or records. *Interview:* System/network administrators; organizational personnel with information security responsibilities; system developer; organizational personnel with boundary protection responsibilities. *Test:* Automated mechanisms supporting and/or implementing the prevention of discovery of system components at managed interfaces.
SC-7(17)	Boundary protection: Automated enforcement of protocol formats	Review documentation to ensure that the system requires adherence to specified protocol formats through components like deep packet inspection firewalls and XML gateways. Test with sample inputs and review results with Security Engineer, security staff, operations staff, System Owner, and Security Officer.	FIPS-199, SP 800-41, SP 800-77	*Examine:* System and communications protection policy; procedures addressing boundary protection; information system design documentation; information system architecture; information system configuration settings and associated documentation; information system audit records; other relevant documents or records. *Interview:* System/network administrators; organizational personnel with information security responsibilities; system developer; organizational personnel with boundary protection responsibilities. *Test:* Automated mechanisms supporting and/or implementing enforcement of adherence to protocol formats.
SC-7(18)	Boundary protection: Fail secure	Review documentation to ensure that all the protection components for system, such as routers, firewalls, guards, and application gateways, when failed, do not cause information	FIPS-199, SP 800-41, SP 800-77	*Examine:* System and communications protection policy; procedures addressing boundary protection; information system design documentation; information system architecture; information system configuration settings and associated documentation; information system audit

	to be inadvertently release or otherwise compromise. Test with intentional failure of one component and review results with Security Engineer, security staff, operations staff, System Owner, and Security Officer.		records; other relevant documents or records. *Interview:* System/network administrators; organizational personnel with information security responsibilities; system developer; organizational personnel with boundary protection responsibilities. *Test:* Automated mechanisms supporting and/or implementing secure failure.
SC-7(19)	Boundary protection: Blocks communication from nonorganizationally configured hosts	Review documentation to ensure that the system controls and blocks communications from IM clients and other user installed components as defined by organization. Test IM capability to institute communications and review with security staff, operations staff, Security Officer, and System Owner.	FIPS-199, SP 800-41, SP 800-77	*Examine:* System and communications protection policy; procedures addressing boundary protection; information system design documentation; information system hardware and software; information system architecture; information system configuration settings and associated documentation; list of communication clients independently configured by end users and external service providers; information system audit records; other relevant documents or records. *Interview:* System/network administrators; organizational personnel with information security responsibilities; organizational personnel with boundary protection responsibilities. *Test:* Automated mechanisms supporting and/or implementing the blocking of inbound and outbound communications traffic between communication clients independently configured by end users and external service providers.
SC-7(20)	Boundary protection: Dynamic isolation/segregation	Review documentation to ensure that the system dynamically isolates or segregates certain internal components of system in order to partition or separate certain components of dubious origin from those components possessing greater trustworthiness, which reduces the attack surface of the system. Discuss with Security Architect, Security Engineer, operations	FIPS-199, SP 800-41, SP 800-77	*Examine:* System and communications protection policy; procedures addressing boundary protection; information system design documentation; information system hardware and software; information system architecture; information system configuration settings and associated documentation; list of information system components to be dynamically isolated/segregated from other components of the system; information system audit records; other relevant documents or records. *Interview:* System/network administrators; organizational personnel

(Continued)

Control number	Control name	Assessment methods	Notes and guidance documents	SP 800-53A guidance
		staff, security staff, System Owner, and Security Officer.		with information security responsibilities; system developer; organizational personnel with boundary protection responsibilities. *Test:* Automated mechanisms supporting and/or implementing the capability to dynamically isolate/segregate information system components.
SC-7(21)	Boundary protection: Isolation of information system components	Review documentation to ensure that the system isolates different system components performing differing missions and functions from each other to limit unauthorized information flows from occurring within system. These various techniques, such as routers, gateways, and firewalls separating system components into physically separate networks or subnetworks, cross-domain devices separating subnetworks, virtualization techniques, and encrypting information flows among system components using distinct encryption keys are tested to ensure isolation and discussed with Security Engineer, security staff, operations staff, System Owner, and Security Officer.	FIPS-199, SP 800-41, SP 800-77	*Examine:* System and communications protection policy; procedures addressing boundary protection; information system design documentation; information system hardware and software; enterprise architecture documentation; information system architecture; information system configuration settings and associated documentation; information system audit records; other relevant documents or records. *Interview:* System/network administrators; organizational personnel with information security responsibilities; organizational personnel with boundary protection responsibilities. *Test:* Automated mechanisms supporting and/or implementing the capability to separate information system components supporting organizational missions and/or business functions.
SC-7(22)	Boundary protection: Separate subnets for connecting to different security domains	Review documentation to ensure that the system implements separate network addresses (i.e., different subnets) to connect to systems in different security domains for information flow control, cross domain actions and data classification control. Evaluate implementation and	FIPS-199, SP 800-41, SP 800-77, UCDMO	*Examine:* System and communications protection policy; procedures addressing boundary protection; information system design documentation; information system hardware and software; information system architecture; information system configuration settings and associated documentation; information system audit records; other relevant documents or records. *Interview:* System/network administrators; organizational

		discuss with Security Engineer, FSO, operations staff, and Security Officer.		personnel with information security responsibilities; system developer; organizational personnel with boundary protection responsibilities. *Test:* Automated mechanisms supporting and/or implementing separate network addresses/different subnets.
SC-7(23)	Boundary protection: Disable sender feedback or protocol validation failure	Review documentation for system to ensure that the system disables feedback to senders on protocol format validation failure to restrict potential notification of additional data about system used for enumeration purposes. Discuss with Security Engineer, development staff, security staff, and Security Officer.	FIPS-199, SP 800-41, SP 800-77	*Examine:* System and communications protection policy; procedures addressing boundary protection; information system design documentation; information system hardware and software; information system architecture; information system configuration settings and associated documentation; information system audit records; other relevant documents or records. *Interview:* System/network administrators; organizational personnel with information security responsibilities; system developer; organizational personnel with boundary protection responsibilities. *Test:* Automated mechanisms supporting and/or implementing the disabling of feedback to senders on protocol format validation failure.
SC-8	Transmission confidentiality and integrity	Review documentation to determine the levels of confidentiality and integrity from external providers and organizations. Review specific system level requirements and ensure that providers are delivering these required levels. Protecting the confidentiality and/or integrity of organizational information can be accomplished by physical or by logical means and test each area with sample data transmissions to determine level of compliance. Discuss results with operations staff, acquisition	FIPS 140-2, FIPS-197, SP 800-52, SP 800-77, SP 800-81, SP 800-113, CNSSP 15, NSTISSI No. 7003	*Examine:* System and communications protection policy; procedures addressing transmission confidentiality and integrity; information system design documentation; information system configuration settings and associated documentation; information system audit records; other relevant documents or records. *Interview:* System/network administrators; organizational personnel with information security responsibilities; system developer. *Test:* Automated mechanisms supporting and/or implementing transmission confidentiality and/or integrity.

(Continued)

Control number	Control name	Assessment methods	Notes and guidance documents	SP 800-53A guidance
		staff, security staff, System Owner, and Security Officer.		
SC-8(1)	Transmission confidentiality and integrity: Cryptographic or alternate physical protection	Review documentation to determine cryptographic or alternate physical security criteria for system. Ensure system is receiving appropriate levels of security by testing these documented methods and discuss with operations staff, security staff, System Owner, and Security Officer.	FIPS 140-2, FIPS-197, SP 800-52, SP 800-77, SP 800-81, SP 800-113, CNSSP 15, NSTISSI No. 7003	*Examine:* System and communications protection policy; procedures addressing transmission confidentiality and integrity; information system design documentation; information system configuration settings and associated documentation; information system audit records; other relevant documents or records. *Interview:* System/network administrators; organizational personnel with information security responsibilities; system developer. *Test:* Cryptographic mechanisms supporting and/or implementing transmission confidentiality and/or integrity; automated mechanisms supporting and/or implementing alternative physical safeguards; organizational processes for defining and implementing alternative physical safeguards.
SC-8(2)	Transmission confidentiality and integrity: Pre/post transmission handling	Review documentation to determine the security controls needed and installed, when the system is sending or receiving information, such as during aggregation efforts, at protocol transformation points, and during packing/unpacking periods. Evaluate the results of testing these process points with System Owner, security staff, Security Officer, and Operations staff.	FIPS 140-2, FIPS-197, SP 800-52, SP 800-77, SP 800-81, SP 800-113, CNSSP 15, NSTISSI No. 7003	*Examine:* System and communications protection policy; procedures addressing transmission confidentiality and integrity; information system design documentation; information system configuration settings and associated documentation; information system audit records; other relevant documents or records. *Interview:* System/network administrators; organizational personnel with information security responsibilities; system developer. *Test:* Automated mechanisms supporting and/or implementing transmission confidentiality and/or integrity.
SC-8(3)	Transmission confidentiality and integrity: Cryptographic protection for message externals	Review documentation to ensure that the encryption is used on message headers/routing information for each transmission. Test transmission with test messages and evaluate results	FIPS 140-2, FIPS-197, SP 800-52, SP 800-77, SP 800-81, SP 800-113, CNSSP 15, NSTISSI No. 7003	*Examine:* System and communications protection policy; procedures addressing transmission confidentiality and integrity; information system design documentation; information system configuration settings and associated documentation; information system audit

Control			References	
		with System Owner, Security Officer, and security staff.		records; other relevant documents or records. *Interview:* System/network administrators; organizational personnel with information security responsibilities; system developer. *Test:* Cryptographic mechanisms supporting and/or implementing transmission confidentiality and/or integrity for message externals; automated mechanisms supporting and/or implementing alternative physical safeguards; organizational processes for defining and implementing alternative physical safeguards.
SC-8(4)	Transmission confidentiality and integrity: Conceal/randomize communications	Review documentation to ensure that the system randomizes and conceals communications patterns to ensure integrity and confidentiality of information being transmitted. Communication patterns to be altered include frequency, periods, amount, and predictability and require encrypting the links and transmitting in continuous, fixed/random patterns. Test randomization with sample communications and discuss results with security staff, FSO, operations staff, System Owner, and Security Officer.	FIPS 140-2, FIPS-197, SP 800-52, SP 800-77, SP 800-81, SP 800-113, CNSSP 15, NSTISSI No. 7003	*Examine:* System and communications protection policy; procedures addressing transmission confidentiality and integrity; information system design documentation; information system configuration settings and associated documentation; information system audit records; other relevant documents or records. *Interview:* System/network administrators; organizational personnel with information security responsibilities; system developer. *Test:* Cryptographic mechanisms supporting and/or implementing concealment or randomization of communications patterns; automated mechanisms supporting and/or implementing alternative physical safeguards; organizational processes for defining and implementing alternative physical safeguards.
SC-9	Transmission confidentiality	Withdrawn: Incorporated into SC-8		
SC-10	Network disconnect	Review documentation to ensure that the system implements network termination actions, such as deallocating associated TCP/IP address/port pairs at the operating system level,		*Examine:* System and communications protection policy; procedures addressing network disconnect; information system design documentation; security plan; information system configuration settings and associated documentation; information system audit records; other relevant documents or

(Continued)

Control number	Control name	Assessment methods	Notes and guidance documents	SP 800-53A guidance
		or deallocating networking assignments at the application level, if multiple application sessions are using a single, operating system-level network connection, when the organizationally defined time period is met. Test by submitting network access efforts, which exceed time period and discuss results with System Owner, operations staff, security staff, and Security Officer.		records. *Interview:* System/network administrators; organizational personnel with information security responsibilities; system developer. *Test:* Automated mechanisms supporting and/or implementing network disconnect capability.
SC-11	Trusted path	Review documentation to ensure that the user interaction with the system security functions are controlled and assured. Evaluate trusted path through testing connections and examining architecture. Discuss with Security Architect, security staff, operations staff, System Owner, and Security Officer.	TIC Initiative, AC-25	*Examine:* System and communications protection policy; procedures addressing trusted communications paths; security plan; information system design documentation; information system configuration settings and associated documentation; assessment results from independent, testing organizations; information system audit records; other relevant documents or records. *Interview:* System/network administrators; organizational personnel with information security responsibilities; system developer. *Test:* Automated mechanisms supporting and/or implementing trusted communications paths.
SC-11(1)	Trusted path: Logical isolation	Review documentation to ensure that the system provides a trusted communications path that is logically isolated and distinguishable from other paths. Evaluate trusted path through testing connections and examining architecture. Discuss with Security Architect, security staff, operations staff, System Owner, and Security Officer.	TIC Initiative, AC-25	*Examine:* System and communications protection policy; procedures addressing trusted communications paths; security plan; information system design documentation; information system configuration settings and associated documentation; assessment results from independent, testing organizations; information system audit records; other relevant documents or records. *Interview:* System/network administrators; organizational personnel with information security responsibilities; system developer. *Test:* Automated

mechanisms supporting and/or implementing trusted communications paths.

SC-12	Cryptographic key establishment and management	Review documentation to ensure that the system implementation of all cryptographic actions are performed correctly and completely. Review guidance and implementation to validate compliance. Discuss with Security Engineer, security staff, operations staff, System Owner, and Security Officer.	FIPS 140-2, SP 800-56, SP 800-57	*Examine:* System and communications protection policy; procedures addressing cryptographic key establishment and management; information system design documentation; cryptographic mechanisms; information system configuration settings and associated documentation; information system audit records; other relevant documents or records. *Interview:* System/network administrators; organizational personnel with information security responsibilities; organizational personnel with responsibilities for cryptographic key establishment and/or management. *Test:* Automated mechanisms supporting and/or implementing cryptographic key establishment and management.
SC-12(1)	Cryptographic key establishment and management: Availability	Review documentation to ensure that active use of cryptographic key control mechanism and key escrow actions are controlled and assured. Ensure all cryptographic actions are in accordance with federal directives. Discuss with System Owner, FSO, Security Engineer, security staff, operations staff, and Security Officer.	FIPS 140-2, SP 800-56, SP 800-57	*Examine:* System and communications protection policy; procedures addressing cryptographic key establishment, management, and recovery; information system design documentation; information system configuration settings and associated documentation; information system audit records; other relevant documents or records. *Interview:* System/network administrators; organizational personnel with information security responsibilities; organizational personnel with responsibilities for cryptographic key establishment or management. *Test:* Automated mechanisms supporting and/or implementing cryptographic key establishment and management.
SC-12(2)	Cryptographic key establishment and management: Symmetric keys	Review documentation for encryption use on system to ensure full compliance with federal requirements in use of symmetric encryption on system. Discuss with System Owner, FSO, Security Engineer, security	FIPS 140-2, SP 800-56, SP 800-57	*Examine:* System and communications protection policy; procedures addressing cryptographic key establishment and management; information system design documentation; information system configuration settings and associated documentation; information system audit records; list of FIPS validated cryptographic products; list of

(Continued)

Control number	Control name	Assessment methods	Notes and guidance documents	SP 800-53A guidance
		staff, operations staff, and Security Officer.		NSA-approved cryptographic products; other relevant documents or records. *Interview:* System/network administrators; organizational personnel with information security responsibilities; system developer; organizational personnel with responsibilities for cryptographic key establishment or management. *Test:* Automated mechanisms supporting and/or implementing symmetric cryptographic key establishment and management.
SC-12(3)	Cryptographic key establishment and management: Asymmetric keys	Review documentation for encryption use on system to ensure full compliance with federal requirements in use of asymmetric encryption on system. Discuss with System Owner, FSO, Security Engineer, security staff, operations staff, and Security Officer.	FIPS 140-2, SP 800-56, SP 800-57	*Examine:* System and communications protection policy; procedures addressing cryptographic key establishment and management; information system design documentation; information system configuration settings and associated documentation; information system audit records; list of NSA-approved cryptographic products; list of approved PKI Class 3 and Class 4 certificates; other relevant documents or records. *Interview:* System/network administrators; organizational personnel with information security responsibilities; system developer; organizational personnel with responsibilities for cryptographic key establishment or management; organizational personnel with responsibilities for PKI certificates. *Test:* Automated mechanisms supporting and/or implementing asymmetric cryptographic key establishment and management.
SC-12(4)	Cryptographic key establishment and management: PKI certificates		Withdrawn: Incorporated into SC-12	
SC-12(5)	Cryptographic key establishment and management: PKI certificates/hardware tokens		Withdrawn: Incorporated into SC-12	

SC-13	Cryptographic protection	Review documentation to ensure that the system employs either FIPS-validated cryptography or NSA-approved cryptography, when implementing use of encryption on the system. Review detailed documentation for architecture and system use to ensure compliance. Discuss with Security Architect, Security Engineer, FSO, security staff, operations staff, System Owner, and Security Officer.	FIPS 140-2	*Examine:* System and communications protection policy; procedures addressing cryptographic protection; information system design documentation; information system configuration settings and associated documentation; cryptographic module validation certificates; list of FIPS validated cryptographic modules; information system audit records; other relevant documents or records. *Interview:* System/network administrators; organizational personnel with information security responsibilities; system developer; organizational personnel with responsibilities for cryptographic protection. *Test:* Automated mechanisms supporting and/or implementing cryptographic protection.
SC-13(1)	Cryptographic protection: FIPS-validated cryptography		Withdrawn: Incorporated into SC-13
SC-13(2)	Cryptographic protection: NSA-approved cryptography		Withdrawn: Incorporated into SC-13
SC-13(3)	Cryptographic protection: Individuals without formal access approvals		Withdrawn: Incorporated into SC-13
SC-13(4)	Cryptographic protection: Digital signatures		Withdrawn: Incorporated into SC-13
SC-14	Public access protections		Withdrawn: Capability provided by AC-2, AC-3, AC-5, AC-6, SI-3, SI-4, SI-5, SI-7, SI-10

(Continued)

Control number	Control name	Assessment methods	Notes and guidance documents	SP 800-53A guidance
SC-15	Collaborative computing devices	Review documentation to ensure that all collaborative computing on system is defined, approved, installed, and implemented in accordance with system requirements and federal directives for remote communications and interchange of information. Ensure collaborative components, such as networked white boards, cameras, and microphones, are identified and controlled appropriately. Discuss with System Owner, operations staff, security staff, and Security Officer.		*Examine:* System and communications protection policy; procedures addressing collaborative computing; access control policy and procedures; information system design documentation; information system configuration settings and associated documentation; information system audit records; other relevant documents or records. *Interview:* System/network administrators; organizational personnel with information security responsibilities; system developer; organizational personnel with responsibilities for managing collaborative computing devices. *Test:* Automated mechanisms supporting and/or implementing management of remote activation of collaborative computing devices; automated mechanisms providing an indication of use of collaborative computing devices.
SC-15(1)	Collaborative computing devices: Physical disconnect	Review documentation to determine system methods for physically disconnecting collaborative computing components. Observe disconnect actions and activities to ensure completeness and full disconnect actions. Discuss with FSO, security staff, operations staff, System Owner, and Security Officer.		*Examine:* System and communications protection policy; procedures addressing collaborative computing; access control policy and procedures; information system design documentation; information system configuration settings and associated documentation; information system audit records; other relevant documents or records. *Interview:* System/network administrators; organizational personnel with information security responsibilities; system developer; organizational personnel with responsibilities for managing collaborative computing devices. *Test:* Automated mechanisms supporting and/or implementing physical disconnect of collaborative computing devices.
SC-15(2)	Collaborative computing devices: Blocking inbound/outbound communications traffic		Withdrawn: Incorporated into SC-7	

SC-15(3)	Collaborative computing devices: Disabling/removal in secure work areas	Review documentation to ensure that full disconnect or disabling of collaborative components is accomplished, when not in use on system. Observe disconnect process to ensure compliance. Discuss with FSO, operations staff, security staff, System Owner, and Security Officer.	*Examine:* System and communications protection policy; procedures addressing collaborative computing; access control policy and procedures; information system design documentation; information system configuration settings and associated documentation; information system audit records; list of secure work areas; information systems or information system components in secured work areas where collaborative computing devices are to be disabled or removed; other relevant documents or records. *Interview:* System/network administrators; organizational personnel with information security responsibilities; organizational personnel with responsibilities for managing collaborative computing devices. *Test:* Automated mechanisms supporting and/or implementing the capability to disable collaborative computing devices.
SC-15(4)	Collaborative computing devices: Explicitly indicate current participants	Review documentation to ensure the system indicates all participants during collaborative activities. Observe indications on system or by system when participants join collaborative events. Discuss with FSO, operations staff, security staff, System Owner, and Security Officer.	*Examine:* System and communications protection policy; procedures addressing collaborative computing; access control policy and procedures; information system design documentation; information system configuration settings and associated documentation; information system audit records; list of types of meetings and teleconferences requiring explicit indication of current participants; other relevant documents or records. *Interview:* System/network administrators; organizational personnel with information security responsibilities; organizational personnel with responsibilities for managing collaborative computing devices. *Test:* Automated mechanisms supporting and/or implementing the capability to indicate participants on collaborative computing devices.
SC-16	Transmission of security attributes	Review documentation to ensure the system assigns appropriate security attributes to each information transaction and	*Examine:* System and communications protection policy; procedures addressing transmission of security attributes; access control policy and procedures; information system design

(Continued)

Control number	Control name	Assessment methods	Notes and guidance documents	SP 800-53A guidance
		component. Discuss with Security Engineer, security staff, System Owner, and Security Officer.		documentation; information system configuration settings and associated documentation; information system audit records; other relevant documents or records. *Interview:* System/network administrators; organizational personnel with information security responsibilities. *Test:* Automated mechanisms supporting and/or implementing transmission of security attributes between information systems.
SC-16(1)	Transmission of security attributes: Integrity validation	Review documentation to ensure that assigned security attributes are validated for integrity, when assigned and in transit. Review logs to verify assignment and use of security attributes for information components. Discuss with security staff, System Owner, and Security Officer.		*Examine:* System and communications protection policy; procedures addressing transmission of security attributes; access control policy and procedures; information system design documentation; information system configuration settings and associated documentation; information system audit records; other relevant documents or records. *Interview:* System/network administrators; organizational personnel with information security responsibilities. *Test:* Automated mechanisms supporting and/or implementing validation of the integrity of transmitted security attributes.
SC-17	Public key infrastructure certificates	Review documentation to ensure that all PKI certificates are appropriately obtained or purchased from trusted vendors or providers. Review certificates to ensure, they are either certificates with visibility external to organizational information systems or certificates related to the internal operations of systems, such as application-specific time services. Discuss with Security Engineer, security staff, operations staff, System Owner, and Security Officer.	SP 800-32, SP 800-63, OMB M05-24	*Examine:* System and communications protection policy; procedures addressing public key infrastructure certificates; public key certificate policy or policies; public key issuing process; other relevant documents or records. *Interview:* System/network administrators; organizational personnel with information security responsibilities; organizational personnel with responsibilities for issuing public key certificates; service providers. *Test:* Automated mechanisms supporting and/or implementing the management of public key infrastructure certificates.

Control	Name	Assessment	Reference	Procedures
SC-18	Mobile code	Review documentation to determine the use and acceptance of mobile in system under review. Ensure that organizational criteria for mobile code is verified and validated for the various types of mobile code, such as Java, JavaScript, ActiveX, Postscript, PDF, Shockwave movies, Flash animations, and VBScript. Validate usage of mobile code by testing components and observing usage during operations. Discuss with System Owner, operations staff, Security Engineer, security staff, and Security Officer.	SP 800-28, DODI 8552.01	*Examine:* System and communications protection policy; procedures addressing mobile code; mobile code usage restrictions, mobile code implementation policy and procedures; list of acceptable mobile code and mobile code technologies; list of unacceptable mobile code and mobile technologies; authorization records; information system monitoring records; information system audit records; other relevant documents or records. *Interview:* System/network administrators; organizational personnel with information security responsibilities; organizational personnel with responsibilities for managing mobile code. *Test:* Organizational process for controlling, authorizing, monitoring, and restricting mobile code; automated mechanisms supporting and/or implementing the management of mobile code; automated mechanisms supporting and/or implementing the monitoring of mobile code.
SC-18(1)	Mobile code: Identify unacceptable code/ take correction actions	Review documentation to determine system actions required, when unacceptable mobile code is processed by system. Verify actions to be taken, such as blocking, quarantine, or alerting administrators by testing with test code of unacceptable type and review results with System Owner, operations staff, security staff, and Security Officer.	SP 800-28, DODI 8552.01	*Examine:* System and communications protection policy; procedures addressing mobile code; mobile code usage restrictions, mobile code implementation policy and procedures; information system design documentation; information system configuration settings and associated documentation; list of unacceptable mobile code; list of corrective actions to be taken when unacceptable mobile code is identified; information system monitoring records; information system audit records; other relevant documents or records. *Interview:* System/network administrators; organizational personnel with information security responsibilities; system developer; organizational personnel with responsibilities for managing mobile code. *Test:* Automated mechanisms supporting and/or implementing mobile code detection, inspection, and corrective capability.

(Continued)

Control number	Control name	Assessment methods	Notes and guidance documents	SP 800-53A guidance
SC-18(2)	Mobile code: Acquisition/development/use	Review documentation to determine the use and acceptance of mobile in system under review. Ensure that organizational criteria for mobile code is verified and validated for the various types of mobile code, such as Java, JavaScript, ActiveX, Postscript, PDF, Shockwave movies, Flash animations, and VBScript. Validate usage of mobile code by testing components and observing usage during operations. Discuss with System Owner, operations staff, Security Engineer, security staff, and Security Officer.	SP 800-28, DODI 8552.01	*Examine:* System and communications protection policy; procedures addressing mobile code; mobile code requirements; mobile code usage restrictions, mobile code implementation policy and procedures; acquisition documentation; acquisition contracts for information system, system component, or information system service; system development life cycle documentation; other relevant documents or records. *Interview:* System/network administrators; organizational personnel with information security responsibilities; organizational personnel with responsibilities for managing mobile code; organizational personnel with acquisition and contracting responsibilities. *Test:* Organizational processes for the acquisition, development, and use of mobile code.
SC-18(3)	Mobile code: Prevent downloading/execution	Review documentation to determine the use and acceptance of mobile in system under review. Ensure that unacceptable mobile code is not allowed for download or execution on system. Validate usage of mobile code by testing components and observing usage during operations. Discuss with System Owner, operations staff, Security Engineer, security staff, and Security Officer.	SP 800-28, DODI 8552.01	*Examine:* System and communications protection policy; procedures addressing mobile code; mobile code usage restrictions, mobile code implementation policy and procedures; information system design documentation; information system configuration settings and associated documentation; information system audit records; other relevant documents or records. *Interview:* System/network administrators; organizational personnel with information security responsibilities; system developer; organizational personnel with responsibilities for managing mobile code. *Test:* Automated mechanisms preventing download and execution of unacceptable mobile code.
SC-18(4)	Mobile code: Prevent automatic execution	Review documentation to determine the use and acceptance of mobile in system under review. Ensure that unacceptable mobile code is	SP 800-28, DODI 8552.01	*Examine:* System and communications protection policy; procedures addressing mobile code; mobile code usage restrictions; mobile code implementation policy and procedures; information system design documentation; information system

Control	Name	Reference	Assessment	Examine / Interview / Test
			automatically not allowed for execution on system. Validate usage of mobile code by testing components and observing usage during operations. Discuss with System Owner, operations staff, Security Engineer, security staff, and Security Officer.	configuration settings and associated documentation; list of software applications for which automatic execution of mobile code must be prohibited; list of actions required before execution of mobile code; other relevant documents or records. *Interview:* System/network administrators; organizational personnel with information security responsibilities; system developer; organizational personnel with responsibilities for managing mobile code. *Test:* Automated mechanisms preventing automatic execution of unacceptable mobile code; automated mechanisms enforcing actions to be taken prior to the execution of the mobile code.
SC-18(5)	Mobile code: Allow execution only in confined environments	SP 800-28, DODI 8552.01	Review documentation to determine the use and acceptance of mobile in system under review. Ensure that unacceptable mobile code is automatically not allowed for execution on system, such as disabling auto execute features on information system components employing portable storage devices. Discuss with System Owner, operations staff, Security Engineer, security staff, and Security Officer.	*Examine:* System and communications protection policy; procedures addressing mobile code; mobile code usage allowances; mobile code usage restrictions; information system design documentation; information system configuration settings and associated documentation; list of confined virtual machine environments for which execution of organizationally-acceptable mobile code is allowed; information system audit records; other relevant documents or records. *Interview:* System/network administrators; organizational personnel with information security responsibilities; system developer; organizational personnel with responsibilities for managing mobile code. *Test:* Automated mechanisms allowing execution of permitted mobile code in confined virtual machine environments.
SC-19	Voice over internet protocol	SP 800-58	Review documentation to ensure that VOIP components for system under review are verified, validated, and approved. Ensure implementation follows all security criteria for information system. Discuss with security staff, operations staff, System Owner, and Security Officer.	*Examine:* System and communications protection policy; procedures addressing VoIP; VoIP usage restrictions; VoIP implementation guidance; information system design documentation; information system configuration settings and associated documentation; information system monitoring records; information system audit records; other relevant documents or records. *Interview:* System/network administrators;

(Continued)

Control number	Control name	Assessment methods	Notes and guidance documents	SP 800-53A guidance
				organizational personnel with information security responsibilities; organizational personnel with responsibilities for managing VoIP. *Test:* Organizational process for authorizing, monitoring, and controlling VoIP; automated mechanisms supporting and/or implementing authorizing, monitoring, and controlling VoIP.
SC-20	Secure name/address resolution service (authoritative source)	Review documentation to ensure system, when required, is providing name and address resolution services as an authoritative source for the organization. These authenticity and integrity mechanisms will include such items as DNS Security (DNSSEC) digital signatures and cryptographic keys. Verify delivery to the organization of certificates and keys, as appropriate to test and verify system. Discuss with System Owner, security staff, Security Engineer, operations staff, and Security Officer.	SP 800-81, OMB M08-23	*Examine:* System and communications protection policy; procedures addressing secure name/address resolution service (authoritative source); information system design documentation; information system configuration settings and associated documentation; other relevant documents or records. *Interview:* System/network administrators; organizational personnel with information security responsibilities; organizational personnel with responsibilities for managing DNS. *Test:* Automated mechanisms supporting and/or implementing secure name/address resolution service.
SC-20(1)	Secure name/address resolution service (authoritative source): Child subspaces		Withdrawn: Incorporated into SC-20	
SC-20(2)	Secure name/address resolution service (authoritative source): Data origin/data integrity	Review documentation to ensure that the system is providing data origin and integrity protection artifacts for internal name/address resolution queries, when requested or required by the organization. Review output	SP 800-81, OMB M08-23	*Examine:* System and communications protection policy; procedures addressing secure name/address resolution service (authoritative source); information system design documentation; information system configuration settings and associated documentation; information system audit records; other relevant documents or records.

	artifacts to verify authenticity and integrity of outputs. Discuss with System Owner, security staff, Security Engineer, operations staff, and Security Officer.			*Interview:* System/network administrators; organizational personnel with information security responsibilities; organizational personnel with responsibilities for managing DNS. *Test:* Automated mechanisms supporting and/or implementing data origin and integrity protection for internal name/address resolution service queries.
SC-21	Secure name/address resolution service (recursive or caching resolver)	Review documentation to ensure that the name resolution activities are successfully provided by system to the organization, and if applicable, other organizations. Verify the system name resolution services either performs this validation on its own, or has authenticated channels to trusted validation providers by submitting name queries and review results with security staff, Security Engineer, operations staff, System Owner, and Security Officer.	SP 800-81	*Examine:* System and communications protection policy; procedures addressing secure name/address resolution service (recursive or caching resolver); information system design documentation; information system configuration settings and associated documentation; information system audit records; other relevant documents or records. *Interview:* System/network administrators; organizational personnel with information security responsibilities; organizational personnel with responsibilities for managing DNS. *Test:* Automated mechanisms supporting and/or implementing data origin authentication and data integrity verification for name/address resolution services.
SC-21(1)	Secure name/address resolution service (recursive or caching resolver): Data origin/Integrity		Withdrawn: Incorporated into SC-21	
SC-22	Architecture and provisioning for name/address resolution service	Review documentation to ensure that the organization implements name and address resolution services, which include fault tolerance and internal/external role separation, such as disperse locations for primary and secondary servers and redundancy of equipment. Verify	SP 800-81	*Examine:* System and communications protection policy; procedures addressing architecture and provisioning for name/address resolution service; access control policy and procedures; information system design documentation; assessment results from independent, testing organizations; information system configuration settings and associated documentation; information system audit records; other relevant documents or records.

(Continued)

Control number	Control name	Assessment methods	Notes and guidance documents	SP 800-53A guidance
		architectural components and design documentation. Discuss with System Owner, security staff, operations staff, Security Architect, and Security Officer.		*Interview:* System/network administrators; organizational personnel with information security responsibilities; organizational personnel with responsibilities for managing DNS. *Test:* Automated mechanisms supporting and/or implementing name/address resolution service for fault tolerance and role separation.
SC-23	Session authenticity	Review documentation to ensure system protects and authenticates the communications at the session level/layer. To account for and prevent such items as man-in-the-middle attacks/session hijacking and the session insertion of false information. Discuss with operations staff, security staff, Security Engineer, System Owner, and Security Officer.	SP 800-52, SP 800-77, SP 800-95	*Examine:* System and communications protection policy; procedures addressing session authenticity; information system design documentation; information system configuration settings and associated documentation; information system audit records; other relevant documents or records. *Interview:* System/network administrators; organizational personnel with information security responsibilities. *Test:* Automated mechanisms supporting and/or implementing session authenticity.
SC-23(1)	Session authenticity: Invalidate session identifiers at logout	Review documentation to ensure that the system terminates identifiers at session closure or logout to prevent capturing and continuing to employ previously valid session IDs. Test with sample session ID test and review results with System Owner, security staff, operations staff, and Security Officer.	SP 800-52, SP 800-77, SP 800-95	*Examine:* System and communications protection policy; procedures addressing session authenticity; information system design documentation; information system configuration settings and associated documentation; information system audit records; other relevant documents or records. *Interview:* System/network administrators; organizational personnel with information security responsibilities. *Test:* Automated mechanisms supporting and/or implementing session identifier invalidation upon session termination.
SC-23(2)	Session authenticity: User-initiated logouts/message displays		Withdrawn: Incorporated into AC-12(1)	

SC-23(3)	Session authenticity: Unique session identifiers with randomization	Review documentation to ensure that the system generates random session IDs for each session to reduce the reuse previously valid session IDs and prevent brute-force attacks based on session ID numbering schemes. Discuss with System Owner, security staff, operations staff, Security Architect, and Security Officer.	SP 800-52, SP 800-77, SP 800-95	*Examine*: System and communications protection policy; procedures addressing session authenticity; information system design documentation; information system configuration settings and associated documentation; information system audit records; other relevant documents or records. *Interview*: System/network administrators; organizational personnel with information security responsibilities. *Test*: Automated mechanisms supporting and/or implementing generating and monitoring unique session identifiers; automated mechanisms supporting and/or implementing randomness requirements.
SC-23(4)	Session authenticity: Unique session identifiers with randomization		Withdrawn: Incorporated into SC-23(3)	
SC-23(5)	Session authenticity: Allowed certificate authorities	Review documentation to ensure that the organization incorporates and uses secure socket layer (SSL) and/or transport layer security (TLS) certificates for session authenticity activities and actions. Review and test SSL and TLS to ensure, it is at correct release level and implemented correctly. Discuss with Security Architect, Security Engineer, security staff, operations staff, System Owner, and Security Officer.	SP 800-52, SP 800-77, SP 800-95	*Examine*: System and communications protection policy; procedures addressing session authenticity; information system design documentation; information system configuration settings and associated documentation; list of certificate authorities allowed for verification of the establishment of protected sessions; information system audit records; other relevant documents or records. *Interview*: System/network administrators; organizational personnel with information security responsibilities. *Test*: Automated mechanisms supporting and/or implementing management of certificate authorities.
SC-24	Fail in known state	Review documentation to ensure that the system fails into a known state consistently and such state is acceptable to organizational CP criteria and BIA requirements. Test failure mode when possible for	SP 800-34, ISO 15504	*Examine*: System and communications protection policy; procedures addressing information system failure to known state; information system design documentation; information system configuration settings and associated documentation; list of failures requiring information system to fail in a known state; state information to be preserved

(Continued)

Control number	Control name	Assessment methods	Notes and guidance documents	SP 800-53A guidance
		system to ensure failure state is acceptable. Discuss with System Owner, COOP staff, Security Architect, operations staff, security staff, and Security Officer.		in system failure; information system audit records; other relevant documents or records. *Interview:* System/network administrators; organizational personnel with information security responsibilities; system developer. *Test:* Automated mechanisms supporting and/or implementing fail-in-known state capability; automated mechanisms preserving system state information in the event of a system failure.
SC-25	Thin nodes	Review documentation to ensure that the diskless nodes or thin client components are deployed within the system are functioning correctly and within specifications, which reduces the attack surface of the system. Test the nodes and thin clients for reduce security requirements and components. Discuss with System Owner, operations staff, security staff, and Security Officer.		*Examine:* System and communications protection policy; procedures addressing use of thin nodes; information system design documentation; information system configuration settings and associated documentation; information system audit records; other relevant documents or records. *Interview:* System/network administrators; organizational personnel with information security responsibilities. *Test:* Automated mechanisms supporting and/or implementing thin nodes.
SC-26	Honey pots	Review documentation for the system, which employs honeypot based network defenses. Test honeypot to ensure proper deployment and monitoring capabilities. Discuss with operations staff, legal staff, security staff, System Owner, and Security Officer.		*Examine:* System and communications protection policy; procedures addressing use of honeypots; information system design documentation; information system configuration settings and associated documentation; information system audit records; other relevant documents or records. *Interview:* System/network administrators; organizational personnel with information security responsibilities; system developer. *Test:* Automated mechanisms supporting and/or implementing honey pots.
SC-26(1)	Honey pots: Detection of malicious code		Withdrawn: Incorporated into SC-35	

Control	Name	Description	References	Assessment
SC-27	Platform-independent applications	Review documentation for the organization to ensure that platform based independent applications, which can run on multiple platforms or computing devices, are deployed and functional for system and organization. Test each application deployment to ensure full functionality and operation and discuss results with operations staff, System Owner, and Security Officer.		*Examine:* System and communications protection policy; procedures addressing platform-independent applications; information system design documentation; information system configuration settings and associated documentation; list of platform-independent applications; information system audit records; other relevant documents or records. *Interview:* System/network administrators; organizational personnel with information security responsibilities; system developer. *Test:* Automated mechanisms supporting and/or implementing platform-independent applications.
SC-28	Protection of information at rest	Review documentation to ensure system protects the data stored within the system storage components under the data at rest requirements. Test protection for system specific information, such as configurations or rule sets for firewalls, gateways, intrusion detection/prevention systems, filtering routers, and authenticator content. Review results with operations staff, security staff, Security Officer, and System Owner.	SP 800-56, SP 800-57, SP 800-111	*Examine:* System and communications protection policy; procedures addressing protection of information at rest; information system design documentation; information system configuration settings and associated documentation; cryptographic mechanisms and associated configuration documentation; list of information at rest requiring confidentiality and integrity protections; other relevant documents or records. *Interview:* System/network administrators; organizational personnel with information security responsibilities; system developer. *Test:* Automated mechanisms supporting and/or implementing confidentiality and integrity protections for information at rest.
SC-28(1)	Protection of information at rest: Cryptographic protections	Review documentation for system to ensure that encryption mechanisms are installed and operational for all storage media utilized on system, such as significant concentrations of digital media in organizational areas designated for media storage, and also to limit	FIPS 140-2, SP 800-56, SP 800-57, SP 800-111	*Examine:* System and communications protection policy; procedures addressing protection of information at rest; information system design documentation; information system configuration settings and associated documentation; cryptographic mechanisms and associated configuration documentation; information system audit records; other relevant documents or records. *Interview:* System/network administrators;

(Continued)

Control number	Control name	Assessment methods	Notes and guidance documents	SP 800-53A guidance
		quantities of media generally associated with information system components in operational environments, like flash drives and thumb drives. Test storage and encryption process on sample thumb drive and discuss results with operational staff, security staff, System Owner, and Security Officer.		organizational personnel with information security responsibilities; system developer. *Test:* Cryptographic mechanisms implementing confidentiality and integrity protections for information at rest.
SC-28(2)	Protection of information at rest: Off-line storage	Review documentation to determine the organizational deployment of off-line storage of system data employed in system. Organization can move information to off-line storage in lieu of protecting such information in online storage. Test off-line storage mechanisms to ensure that safety and security components are utilized. Discuss with operations staff, System Owner, security staff, and Security Officer.	FIPS 140-2, SP 800-56, SP 800-57, SP 800-111	*Examine:* System and communications protection policy; procedures addressing protection of information at rest; information system design documentation; information system configuration settings and associated documentation; cryptographic mechanisms and associated configuration documentation; off-line storage locations for information at rest; information system audit records; other relevant documents or records. *Interview:* System/network administrators; organizational personnel with information security responsibilities. *Test:* Automated mechanisms supporting and/or implementing removal of information from online storage; automated mechanisms supporting and/or implementing storage of information off-line.
SC-29	Heterogeneity	Review documentation for the organization to determine level of diversity of information technologies within organizational information systems, which reduces the impact of potential exploitations and common vulnerabilities within organization. Discuss with Security Architect, Security		*Examine:* System and communications protection policy; information system design documentation; information system configuration settings and associated documentation; list of technologies deployed in the information system; acquisition documentation; acquisition contracts for information system components or services; other relevant documents or records. *Interview:* System/network administrators; organizational personnel with information security

responsibilities; organizational personnel with information system acquisition, development, and implementation responsibilities. *Test:* Automated mechanisms supporting and/or implementing employment of a diverse set of information technologies.

Engineer, acquisition staff, operations staff, System Owner, and Security Officer.

| SC-29(1) | Heterogeneity: Virtualization techniques | SP 800-125 | Review documentation for the organization to ensure deployment of a diversity of operating systems and applications that are changed periodically include virtual machines and deployments, which can be controlled and changed quickly and easily in high threat environments. Discuss with Security Architect, Security Engineer, security staff, operations staff, System Owner, and Security Officer. | *Examine:* System and communications protection policy; configuration management policy and procedures; information system design documentation; information system configuration settings and associated documentation; information system architecture; list of operating systems and applications deployed using virtualization techniques; change control records; configuration management records; information system audit records; other relevant documents or records. *Interview:* System/network administrators; organizational personnel with information security responsibilities; organizational personnel with responsibilities for implementing approved virtualization techniques to the information system. *Test:* Automated mechanisms supporting and/or implementing employment of a diverse set of information technologies; automated mechanisms supporting and/or implementing virtualization techniques. |
| SC-30 | Concealment and misdirection | | Review documentation for system to ensure, when operating in high threat environment, various deployment techniques, such as, randomness, uncertainty, and virtualization, are used to assist in the security of the system and its operations. Discuss with FSO, Security Architect, Security Engineer, operations staff, System Owner, and Security Officer. | *Examine:* System and communications protection policy; procedures addressing concealment and misdirection techniques for the information system; information system design documentation; information system configuration settings and associated documentation; information system architecture; list of concealment and misdirection techniques to be employed for organizational information systems; information system audit records; other relevant documents or records. *Interview:* System/network administrators; organizational personnel with information security responsibilities; |

(Continued)

Control number	Control name	Assessment methods	Notes and guidance documents	SP 800-53A guidance
				organizational personnel with responsibility for implementing concealment and misdirection techniques for information systems. *Test:* Automated mechanisms supporting and/or implementing concealment and misdirection techniques.
SC-30(1)	Concealment and misdirection: Virtualization techniques		Withdrawn: Incorporated into SC-29(1)	
SC-30(2)	Concealment and misdirection: Randomness	Review documentation to determine the level of misdirection and randomness deployed within system and its operating environment for security purposes. Such efforts employing techniques involving randomness include, for example, performing certain routine actions at different times of day, employing different information technologies (e.g., browsers, search engines), using different suppliers, and rotating roles and responsibilities of organizational personnel, causes attack vectors and surfaces to be monitored and maintained in more effective and efficient ways. Discuss with Security Architect, Security Engineer, System Owner, operations staff, security staff, and Security Officer.		*Examine:* System and communications protection policy; procedures addressing concealment and misdirection techniques for the information system; information system design documentation; information system configuration settings and associated documentation; information system architecture; list of techniques to be employed to introduce randomness into organizational operations and assets; information system audit records; other relevant documents or records. *Interview:* System/network administrators; organizational personnel with information security responsibilities; organizational personnel with responsibility for implementing concealment and misdirection techniques for information systems. *Test:* Automated mechanisms supporting and/or implementing randomness as a concealment and misdirection technique.
SC-30(3)	Concealment and misdirection: Change processing/ storage locations	Review documentation for system and organization to determine the level of deployment for moving target		*Examine:* System and communications protection policy; configuration management policy and procedures; procedures addressing concealment and misdirection techniques for the information

	defense, which addresses the advanced persistent threat (APT) using techniques, such as virtualization, distributed processing, and replication for the system. Discuss with Security Engineer, Security Architect, security staff, operations staff, FSO, System Owner, and Security Officer.	system; list of processing/storage locations to be changed at organizational time intervals; change control records; configuration management records; information system audit records; other relevant documents or records. *Interview:* System/network administrators; organizational personnel with information security responsibilities; organizational personnel with responsibility for changing processing and/or storage locations. *Test:* Automated mechanisms supporting and/or implementing changing processing and/or storage locations.
SC-30(4) Concealment and misdirection: Misleading information	Review documentation to determine the level of realistic but misleading information about system and operations are published and/or deployed. Use of deception is additional component to security posture and uses of the system. Discuss with operations staff, security staff, System Owner, and Security Officer.	*Examine:* System and communications protection policy; configuration management policy and procedures; procedures addressing concealment and misdirection techniques for the information system; information system design documentation; information system configuration settings and associated documentation; information system audit records; other relevant documents or records. *Interview:* System/network administrators; organizational personnel with information security responsibilities; organizational personnel with responsibility for defining and employing realistic, but misleading information about the security posture of information system components. *Test:* Automated mechanisms supporting and/or implementing employment of realistic, but misleading information about the security posture of information system components.
SC-30(5) Concealment and misdirection: Concealment of system components	Review documentation to determine the organizational uses of concealment of system components, to include use of hiding, disguising, or otherwise concealing critical information system components. This process allows the organizations to possibly	*Examine:* System and communications protection policy; configuration management policy and procedures; procedures addressing concealment and misdirection techniques for the information system; information system design documentation; information system configuration settings and associated documentation; list of techniques employed to hide or conceal information system components; list of information

(Continued)

Control number	Control name	Assessment methods	Notes and guidance documents	SP 800-53A guidance
		decrease the probability that adversaries target and successfully compromise those system components. Discuss with System Owner, security staff, Security Architect, operations staff, and Security Officer.		system components to be hidden or concealed; other relevant documents or records. *Interview:* System/network administrators; organizational personnel with information security responsibilities; organizational personnel with responsibility for concealment of system components. *Test:* Automated mechanisms supporting and/or implementing techniques for concealment of system components.
SC-31	Covert channel analysis	Review documentation to determine the level of organizational evaluation of covert channel analysis applied to system under review, such as analysis of unauthorized information flows across security domains, containing export-controlled information and having connections to external networks, MLS systems, and CDS based systems. Review logs and examine output flows from system and discuss with development staff, operations staff, security staff, FSO, System Owner, Information Owner(s), and Security Officer.	UCDMO, CNSSI-1253 App F	*Examine:* System and communications protection policy; procedures addressing covert channel analysis; information system design documentation; information system configuration settings and associated documentation; covert channel analysis documentation; information system audit records; other relevant documents or records. *Interview:* System/network administrators; organizational personnel with information security responsibilities; organizational personnel with covert channel analysis responsibilities; information system developers/integrators. *Test:* Organizational process for conducting covert channel analysis; automated mechanisms supporting and/or implementing covert channel analysis; automated mechanisms supporting and/or implementing the capability to estimate the bandwidth of covert channels.
SC-31(1)	Covert channel analysis: Test covert channels for exploitability	Review documentation to determine the level of organizational evaluation of covert channel analysis applied to the identified covert channels to determine, which channels are exploitable for the system under review. Review logs, and examine output flows from system and discuss with	UCDMO, CNSSI-1253 App F	*Examine:* System and communications protection policy; procedures addressing covert channel analysis; information system design documentation; information system configuration settings and associated documentation; list of covert channels; covert channel analysis documentation; information system audit records; other relevant documents or records. *Interview:* System/network administrators; organizational personnel with information security responsibilities; organizational personnel with

Control	Name	Description	Reference	Assessment
		development staff, operations staff, FSO, System Owner, Information Owner(s), and Security Officer.		covert channel analysis responsibilities. *Test:* Organizational process for testing covert channels; automated mechanisms supporting and/or implementing testing of covert channels analysis.
SC-31(2)	Covert channel analysis: Maximum bandwidth	Review documentation to determine the level of organizational evaluation of covert channel analysis applied to the identified covert channels to determine, which channels are to reduce the maximum bandwidth for identified covert storage and timing channels. Review logs, and examine output flows from system and discuss with development staff, operations staff, security staff, FSO, System Owner, Information Owner(s), and Security Officer.	UCDMO, CNSSI-1253 App F	*Examine:* System and communications protection policy; procedures addressing covert channel analysis; acquisition contracts for information systems or services; acquisition documentation; information system design documentation; information system configuration settings and associated documentation; covert channel analysis documentation; information system audit records; other relevant documents or records. *Interview:* System/network administrators; organizational personnel with information security responsibilities; organizational personnel with covert channel analysis responsibilities; information system developers/integrators. *Test:* Organizational process for conducting covert channel analysis; automated mechanisms supporting and/or implementing covert channel analysis; automated mechanisms supporting and/or implementing the capability to reduce the bandwidth of covert channels.
SC-31(3)	COVERT Channel analysis: Measure bandwidth in operational environments	Review documentation for system to determine the organizational defined measurements for bandwidth usage for covert channels and their security implications on system under review and its mission/operations. Review logs and examine output flows from system and discuss with development staff, operations staff, security staff, FSO, System Owner, Information Owner(s), and Security Officer.	UCDMO, CNSSI-1253 App F	*Examine:* System and communications protection policy; procedures addressing covert channel analysis; information system design documentation; information system configuration settings and associated documentation; covert channel analysis documentation; information system audit records; other relevant documents or records. *Interview:* System/network administrators; organizational personnel with information security responsibilities; organizational personnel with covert channel analysis responsibilities; information system developers/integrators. *Test:* Organizational process for conducting covert channel analysis; automated mechanisms

(Continued)

Control number	Control name	Assessment methods	Notes and guidance documents	SP 800-53A guidance
				supporting and / or implementing covert channel analysis; automated mechanisms supporting and / or implementing the capability to measure the bandwidth of covert channels.
SC-32	Information system partitioning	Review documentation for the organization to determine the level of applied separation to system by degree of physical separation of system components from physically distinct components in separate racks in the same room, to components in separate rooms for the more critical components, to more significant geographical separation of the most critical components. Conduct observational security walk-through to evaluate separation. Discuss results with System Owner, facilities staff, security staff, operations staff, FSO, and Security Officer.	FIPS-199	*Examine:* System and communications protection policy; procedures addressing information system partitioning; information system design documentation; information system configuration settings and associated documentation; information system architecture; list of information system physical domains (or environments); information system facility diagrams; information system network diagrams; other relevant documents or records. *Interview:* System / network administrators; organizational personnel with information security responsibilities; organizational personnel installing, configuring, and / or maintaining the information system; information system developers/integrators. *Test:* Automated mechanisms supporting and / or implementing physical separation of information system components.
SC-33	Transmission preparation integrity		Withdrawn: Incorporated into SC-8	
SC-34	Nonmodifiable executable programs	Review documentation for the organization to determine system installation and operation is loaded and executed for the operating environment and applications from hardware-enforced, read-only media. Observe test load for the system and discuss results with security staff, operations staff, System Owner, and Security Officer.		*Examine:* System and communications protection policy; procedures addressing nonmodifiable executable programs; information system design documentation; information system configuration settings and associated documentation; information system architecture; list of operating system components to be loaded from hardware-enforced, read-only media; list of applications to be loaded from hardware-enforced, read-only media; media used to load and execute information system operating environment; media used to load

and execute information system applications; information system audit records; other relevant documents or records. *Interview:* System/network administrators; organizational personnel with information security responsibilities; system developer; organizational personnel installing, configuring, and/or maintaining the information system; information system developers/integrators. *Test:* Automated mechanisms supporting and/or implementing loading and executing the operating environment from hardware-enforced, read-only media; automated mechanisms supporting and/or implementing loading and executing applications from hardware-enforced, read-only media.

SC-34(1)	Nonmodifiable executable programs: No writable storage	Review documentation to ensure that the organization loads and operates system with no writable storage mechanisms available; this applies to both fixed and removable storage, with the latter being addressed directly or as specific restrictions imposed through access controls for mobile devices. Review observable results of load process with security staff, operations staff, System Owner, and Security Officer.	*Examine:* System and communications protection policy; procedures addressing nonmodifiable executable programs; information system design documentation; information system configuration settings and associated documentation; information system architecture; list of information system components to be employed without writeable storage capability; information system audit records; other relevant documents or records. *Interview:* System/network administrators; organizational personnel with information security responsibilities; organizational personnel installing, configuring, and/or maintaining the information system; information system developers/integrators. *Test:* Automated mechanisms supporting and/or implementing employment of components with no writeable storage; automated mechanisms supporting and/or implementing persistent nonwriteable storage across component restart and power on/off.
SC-34(2)	Nonmodifiable executable programs: Integrity protection/read-only media	Review documentation to ensure that the organizational processes protect the integrity of information prior to storage on read-only media and controls the	*Examine:* System and communications protection policy; procedures addressing nonmodifiable executable programs; information system design documentation; information system configuration settings and associated documentation; information

(Continued)

Control number	Control name	Assessment methods	Notes and guidance documents	SP 800-53A guidance
		media, after such information has been recorded onto the media by preventing substitution of media or reprogramming of code elements during installation and operations. Discuss with development staff, operations staff, security staff, FSO, Security Officer, System Owner, and Information Owner(s).		system architecture; information system audit records; other relevant documents or records. *Interview:* System/network administrators; organizational personnel with information security responsibilities; organizational personnel installing, configuring, and/or maintaining the information system; information system developers/integrators. *Test:* Automated mechanisms supporting and/or implementing capability for protecting information integrity on read-only media prior to storage and after information has been recorded onto the media.
SC-34(3)	Nonmodifiable executable programs: Hardware-based protection	Review documentation to ensure that the organization institutes hardware-based write protection for firmware components used on and in system. Observe hardware instituting protection and discuss the results with FSO, Information Owner(s), System Owner, operations staff, development staff, security staff, and Security Officer.		*Examine:* System and communications protection policy; procedures addressing firmware modifications; information system design documentation; information system configuration settings and associated documentation; information system architecture; information system audit records; other relevant documents or records. *Interview:* System/network administrators; organizational personnel with information security responsibilities; organizational personnel installing, configuring, and/or maintaining the information system; information system developers/integrators. *Test:* Organizational processes for modifying firmware; automated mechanisms supporting and/or implementing hardware-based, write-protection for firmware.
SC-35	Honeyclients	Review documentation to determine the organizational directed activities for system components that proactively seek to identify malicious websites and/or web-based malicious code through by the use of honeyclients on external locations and websites. Discuss with legal staff, operations		*Examine:* System and communications protection policy; procedures addressing honeyclients; information system design documentation; information system configuration settings and associated documentation; information system components deployed to identify malicious websites and/or web-based malicious code; information system audit records; other relevant documents or records. *Interview:* System/network administrators; organizational personnel with

		Assessment Methods	
		information security responsibilities; system developer; organizational personnel installing, configuring, and/or maintaining the information system; information system developers/integrators. *Test:* Automated mechanisms supporting and/or implementing honeyclients.	staff, security staff, FSO, System Owner, and Security Officer.
SC-36	Distributed processing and storage	*Examine:* System and communications protection policy; contingency planning policy and procedures; contingency plan; information system design documentation; information system configuration settings and associated documentation; information system architecture; list of information system physical locations (or environments) with distributed processing and storage; information system facility diagrams; processing site agreements; storage site agreements; other relevant documents or records. *Interview:* System/network administrators; organizational personnel with information security responsibilities; organizational personnel installing, configuring, and/or maintaining the information system; organizational personnel with contingency planning and plan implementation responsibilities; information system developers/integrators. *Test:* Organizational processes for distributing processing and storage across multiple physical locations; automated mechanisms supporting and/or implementing capability for distributing processing and storage across multiple physical locations.	Review documentation to determine the organizational criteria and system implementation of distributed processing and storage capabilities implemented in system, to include parallel processing and storage. Test distributed capabilities with test scripts and processes and review results with development staff, operations staff, security staff, System Owner, and Security Officer.
SC-36(1)	Distributed processing and storage: Polling techniques	*Examine:* System and communications protection policy; information system design documentation; information system configuration settings and associated documentation; information system architecture; list of distributed processing and storage components subject to polling; information system polling techniques and associated documentation or records; information system audit records; other relevant documents or records. *Interview:* System/network administrators;	Review documentation for system to ensure that polling of distributed processes and storage components is implemented, since polling compares the processing results and/or storage content from the various distributed components and subsequently voting on the outcomes and provides

(Continued)

Control number	Control name	Assessment methods	Notes and guidance documents	SP 800-53A guidance
		additional security functions and abilities. Test polling through use of scripts, and test programs and discuss results with System Owner, security staff, development staff, operations staff, and Security Officer.		organizational personnel with information security responsibilities; organizational personnel installing, configuring, and/or maintaining the information system; information system developers/integrators. *Test:* Automated mechanisms supporting and/or implementing polling techniques.
SC-37	Out-of-band channels	Review documentation to determine the use of nonsystem mechanisms of physical and electronic delivery of information from system. These out-of-band methods include local (nonnetwork) accesses to information systems, network paths physically separate from network paths used for operational traffic, or nonelectronic paths, such as the US Postal Service or other bonded delivery service organization. Review logs and observe delivery process and discuss results with System Owner, operations staff, security staff, FSO, and Security Officer.		*Examine:* System and communications protection policy; procedures addressing use of out-of-band channels; access control policy and procedures; identification and authentication policy and procedures; information system design documentation; information system architecture; information system configuration settings and associated documentation; list of out-of-band channels; types of information, information system components, or devices requiring use of out-of-band channels for physical delivery or electronic transmission to authorized individuals or information systems; physical delivery records; electronic transmission records; information system audit records; other relevant documents or records. *Interview:* System/network administrators; organizational personnel with information security responsibilities; organizational personnel installing, configuring, and/or maintaining the information system; organizational personnel authorizing, installing, configuring, operating, and/or using out-of-band channels; information system developers/integrators. *Test:* Organizational processes for use of out-of-band channels; automated mechanisms supporting and/or implementing use of out-of-band channels.
SC-37(1)	Out-of-band channels: Ensure delivery/ transmission	Review documentation to ensure that the organization requires additional criteria for out-of-band delivery services, such		*Examine:* System and communications protection policy; procedures addressing use of out-of-band channels; access control policy and procedures; identification and authentication policy and

(Continued)

procedures; information system design documentation; information system architecture; information system configuration settings and associated documentation; list of security safeguards to be employed to ensure designated individuals or information systems receive organization-defined information, information system components, or devices; list of security safeguards for delivering designated information, information system components, or devices to designated individuals or information systems; list of information, information system components, or devices to be delivered to designated individuals or information systems; information system audit records; other relevant documents or records. *Interview:* System/network administrators; organizational personnel with information security responsibilities; organizational personnel installing, configuring, and/or maintaining the information system; organizational personnel authorizing, installing, configuring, operating, and/or using out-of-band channels; information system developers/integrators. *Test:* Organizational processes for use of out-of-band channels; automated mechanisms supporting and/or implementing use of out-of-band channels; automated mechanisms supporting/implementing safeguards to ensure delivery of designated information, system components, or devices.

as sending authenticators via courier service but requiring recipients to show some form of government-issued photographic identification as a condition of receipt. Observe delivery process to ensure that authentication of delivery is provided, and discuss results with System Owner, operations staff, FSO, security staff, and Security Officer.

SC-38

Operations security

SP 800-64, SP 800-171, RA-2, RA-5, SA-12

Review documentation to ensure that the organization applies the operations security (OPSEC) principles and practices for system through use of identifying, controlling, and protecting generally unclassified information that specifically relates to the planning and execution of

Examine: System and communications protection policy; procedures addressing operations security; security plan; list of operations security safeguards; security control assessments; risk assessments; threat and vulnerability assessments; plans of action and milestones; system development life cycle documentation; other relevant documents or records. *Interview:* System/network administrators; organizational personnel with information security

Control number	Control name	Notes and guidance documents	Assessment methods	SP 800-53A guidance
			sensitive organizational activities. Following the standard OPSEC practices, limits availability of user identities, element uses, suppliers, supply chain processes, functional and security requirements, system design specifications, testing protocols, and security control implementation details to maintain security of system and its operating environment. Review documents, processes, and practices with operations staff, FSO, System Owner, development staff, security staff, and Security Officer.	responsibilities; organizational personnel installing, configuring, and/or maintaining the information system; information system developers/integrators. *Test:* Organizational processes for protecting organizational information throughout the SDLC; automated mechanisms supporting and/or implementing safeguards to protect organizational information throughout the SDLC.
SC-39	Process isolation		Review documentation for the system to ensure that the system maintains separate execution domains for each executing process by assigning each process a separate address space, within the system core processing capability. Review process logs to verify separation and discuss with development staff, security staff, operations staff, System Owner, and Security Officer.	*Examine:* Information system design documentation; information system architecture; independent verification and validation documentation; testing and evaluation documentation, other relevant documents or records. *Interview:* Information system developers/integrators; information system security architect. *Test:* Automated mechanisms supporting and/or implementing separate execution domains for each executing process.
SC-39(1)	Process isolation: Hardware separation		Review documentation for the system to ensure that the system maintains separate execution domains for each executing process by implementing hardware memory management mechanisms within the system	*Examine:* System and communications protection policy; information system design documentation; information system configuration settings and associated documentation; information system architecture; information system documentation for hardware separation mechanisms; information system documentation from vendors,

Control	Name	Assessment	Review	Reference
		manufacturers or developers; independent verification and validation documentation; other relevant documents or records. *Interview:* System/network administrators; organizational personnel with information security responsibilities; system developer; organizational personnel installing, configuring, and/or maintaining the information system; information system developers/integrators. *Test:* Information system capability implementing underlying hardware separation mechanisms for process separation.	hardware components. Review process logs to verify separation and discuss with development staff, security staff, operations staff, System Owner, and Security Officer.	
SC-39(2)	Process isolation: Thread isolation	*Examine:* System and communications protection policy; information system design documentation; information system configuration settings and associated documentation; information system architecture; list of information system execution domains for each thread in multi-threaded processing; information system documentation for multi-threaded processing; information system documentation from vendors, manufacturers or developers; independent verification and validation documentation; other relevant documents or records. *Interview:* System/network administrators; organizational personnel with information security responsibilities; system developer; organizational personnel installing, configuring, and/or maintaining the information system; information system developers/integrators. *Test:* Information system capability implementing a separate execution domain for each thread in multi-threaded processing.	Review documentation to ensure that the system implements and maintains a separate execution domain for each thread in various system-defined multi-threaded processing activities. Review logs to ensure compliance and discuss with development staff, operations staff, security staff, System Owner, and Security Officer.	SP 800-64
SC-40	Wireless link protection	*Examine:* System and communications protection policy; access control policy and procedures; procedures addressing wireless link protection; information system design documentation; wireless network diagrams; information system configuration settings and associated documentation; information system architecture; list or internal and external wireless links; list of	Review documentation to ensure that the system installs and maintains wireless communications protection mechanisms, since internal and external wireless communication links may be visible to	SP 800-153

(Continued)

Control number	Control name	Assessment methods	Notes and guidance documents	SP 800-53A guidance
		individuals, who are not authorized system users through various electromagnetic processes. Conduct electromagnetic scans of operating environment and discuss results with facilities staff, FSO, operations staff, System Owner, and Security Officer.		signal parameter attacks or references to sources for attacks; information system audit records; other relevant documents or records. *Interview:* System/network administrators; organizational personnel with information security responsibilities; system developer; organizational personnel installing, configuring, and/or maintaining the information system; organizational personnel authorizing, installing, configuring and/or maintaining internal and external wireless links. *Test:* Automated mechanisms supporting and/or implementing protection of wireless links.
SC-40(1)	Wireless link protection: Electromagnetic interference	Review documentation to ensure that the system employs various cryptographic enhancements to wireless communication to limit intentional jamming, which might deny or impair communications by ensuring that wireless spread spectrum waveforms used to provide anti-jam protection are not predictable by unauthorized individuals. Test scan environment to ensure encryption is active and discuss results with facilities staff, operations staff, FSO, security staff, Security Officer, and System Owner.	SP 800-153, FIPS 140-2	*Examine:* System and communications protection policy; access control policy and procedures; procedures addressing wireless link protection; information system design documentation; wireless network diagrams; information system configuration settings and associated documentation; information system architecture; information system communications hardware and software; security categorization results; information system audit records; other relevant documents or records. *Interview:* System/network administrators; organizational personnel with information security responsibilities; system developer; organizational personnel installing, configuring, and/or maintaining the information system; organizational personnel authorizing, installing, configuring and/or maintaining internal and external wireless links. *Test:* Cryptographic mechanisms enforcing protections against effects of intentional electromagnetic interference.
SC-40(2)	Wireless link protection: Reduce detection potential	Review documentation to ensure that the system implements spread-spectrum encryption techniques to covert communications and protecting	SP 800-153, FIPS 140-2	*Examine:* System and communications protection policy; access control policy and procedures; procedures addressing wireless link protection; information system design documentation; wireless network diagrams; information system

	configuration settings and associated documentation; information system architecture; information system communications hardware and software; security categorization results; information system audit records; other relevant documents or records. *Interview:* System/network administrators; organizational personnel with information security responsibilities; system developer; organizational personnel installing, configuring, and/or maintaining the information system; organizational personnel authorizing, installing, configuring and/or maintaining internal and external wireless links. *Test:* Cryptographic mechanisms enforcing protections to reduce detection of wireless links.		wireless transmitters from being geo-located by their transmissions. Scan system and operating environment with electromagnetic scanners and discuss results with operations staff, facilities staff, security staff, FSO, System Owner, and Security Officer.
SC-40(3)	Wireless link protection: Imitative or manipulative communications deception	*Examine:* System and communications protection policy; access control policy and procedures; procedures addressing information system design documentation; wireless network diagrams; information system configuration settings and associated documentation; information system architecture; information system communications hardware and software; information system audit records; other relevant documents or records. *Interview:* System/network administrators; organizational personnel with information security responsibilities; system developer; organizational personnel installing, configuring, and/or maintaining the information system; organizational personnel authorizing, installing, configuring and/or maintaining internal and external wireless links. *Test:* Cryptographic mechanisms enforcing wireless link protections against imitative or manipulative communications deception.	SP 800-153, FIPS 140-2	Review documentation to ensure that the system implements spread-spectrum encryption techniques to identify and reject wireless transmissions that deliberate attempts to achieve imitative or manipulative communications deception based on signal parameters. Scan system and operating environment with electromagnetic scanners and discuss results with operations staff, facilities staff, security staff, FSO, System Owner, and Security Officer.
SC-40(4)	Wireless link protection: Signal parameter identification	*Examine:* System and communications protection policy; access control policy and procedures; procedures addressing information system design documentation; wireless network diagrams; information system configuration settings and	SP 800-153, FIPS 140-2	Review documentation to ensure that the system implements encryption techniques to protect against the unique identification

(Continued)

Control number	Control name	Assessment methods	Notes and guidance documents	SP 800-53A guidance
		of wireless transmitters for purposes of intelligence exploitation by ensuring that anti-fingerprinting alterations to signal parameters are not predictable by unauthorized individuals. Scan system and operating environment with electromagnetic scanners and discuss results with operations staff, facilities staff, security staff, FSO, System Owner, and Security Officer.		associated documentation; information system architecture; information system communications hardware and software; information system audit records; other relevant documents or records. *Interview:* System/network administrators; organizational personnel with information security responsibilities; system developer; organizational personnel installing, configuring, and/or maintaining the information system; organizational personnel authorizing, installing, configuring and/or maintaining internal and external wireless links. *Test:* Cryptographic mechanisms preventing the identification of wireless transmitters.
SC-41	Port and I/O device access	Review documentation for the organization to determine requirements and extent of physically disabling or removing connection ports and I/O devices, which allows for the prevention of exfiltration of information from system and the introduction of malicious code into system from those ports/devices. Test these restrictions by attempting load from USB or other restricted device and discuss results with System Owner, operations staff, security staff, FSO, and Security Officer.		*Examine:* System and communications protection policy; access control policy and procedures; procedures addressing port and input/output device access; information system design documentation; information system configuration settings and associated documentation; information system architecture; information systems or information system components list of connection ports or input/output devices to be physically disabled or removed on information systems or information system components; other relevant documents or records. *Interview:* System/network administrators; organizational personnel with information security responsibilities; organizational personnel installing, configuring, and/or maintaining the information system. *Test:* Automated mechanisms supporting and/or implementing disabling of connection ports or input/output devices.
SC-42	Sensor capability and data	Review documentation for the system to ensure that any mobile devices connected to system, prohibit the remote activation of environmental	SP 800-124, SP 800-163	*Examine:* System and communications protection policy; procedures addressing sensor capability and data collection; access control policy and procedures; information system design documentation; information system configuration

Control	Name	Assessment / Review	References
		settings and associated documentation; information system audit records; other relevant documents or records. *Interview:* System/network administrators; organizational personnel with information security responsibilities; system developer; organizational personnel installing, configuring, and/or maintaining the information system; organizational personnel with responsibility for sensor capability. *Test:* Automated mechanisms implementing access controls for remote activation of information system sensor capabilities; automated mechanisms implementing capability to indicate sensor use. sensing capabilities or sensors, such as cameras, microphones, global positioning system (GPS) mechanisms, and accelerometers. Test using sample mobile device and review results with System Owner, facilities staff, operations staff, security staff, and Security Officer.	
SC-42(1)	Sensor capability and data: Reporting to authorized individuals or roles	*Examine:* System and communications protection policy; access control policy and procedures; procedures addressing sensor capability and data collection; information system design documentation; information system configuration settings and associated documentation; information system architecture; information system audit records; other relevant documents or records. *Interview:* System/network administrators; organizational personnel with information security responsibilities; system developer; organizational personnel installing, configuring, and/or maintaining the information system; organizational personnel with responsibility for sensor capability. *Test:* Automated mechanisms restricting reporting of sensor information only to those authorized; sensor data collection and reporting capability for the information system. Review documentation for the system to ensure that sensors, which are activated by authorized individuals (e.g., end users), it is not possible that the data/information collected by the sensors can be sent to unauthorized entities. Test sensor distribution of data and discuss result with operations staff, security staff, System Owner, and Security Officer.	SP 800-124, SP 800-163
SC-42(2)	Sensor capability and data: Authorized use	*Examine:* System and communications protection policy; access control policy and procedures; sensor capability and data collection; information system design documentation; information system configuration settings and associated documentation; information system architecture; list of measures to be employed to ensure data or information collected by sensors is only used for Review documentation for the system to ensure data collected by sensors is utilized for only authorized purposes and actions, which requires additional training to ensure that authorized parties do not abuse their authority, or (in the case	SP 800-124, SP 800-163

(Continued)

Control number	Control name	Assessment methods	Notes and guidance documents	SP 800-53A guidance
		where sensor data/information is maintained by external parties) contractual restrictions on the use of the data/information. Review training material and discuss with operations staff, security staff, System Owner, and Security Officer.		authorized purposes; information system audit records; other relevant documents or records. *Interview:* System/network administrators; organizational personnel with information security responsibilities; organizational personnel with responsibility for sensor capability. *Test:* Automated mechanisms supporting and/or implementing measures to ensure sensor information is only used for authorized purposes; sensor information collection capability for the information system.
SC-42(3)	Sensor capability and data: Prohibit use of devices	Review documentation to ensure that the restriction of external mobile devices is maintained in areas, where regulations or operations requires such restrictions. Test with entry of such devices and discuss results with facilities staff, operations staff, FSO, security staff, System Owner, and Security Officer.	SP 800-124, SP 800-163	*Examine:* System and communications protection policy; access control policy and procedures; procedures addressing sensor capability and data collection; information system design documentation; wireless network diagrams; information system configuration settings and associated documentation; information system architecture; facilities, areas, or systems where use of devices possessing environmental sensing capabilities is prohibited; list of devices possessing environmental sensing capabilities; other relevant documents or records. *Interview:* System/network administrators; organizational personnel with information security responsibilities; organizational personnel installing, configuring, and/or maintaining the information system; organizational personnel with responsibility for sensor capability.
SC-43	Usage restrictions	Review documentation for the system and organization to determine, which kinds of computing devices are restricted within operating environment of system. Test by attempting to engage a restricted computing device and discuss with FSO,		*Examine:* System and communications protection policy; procedures addressing usage restrictions; usage restrictions; implementation policy and procedures; authorization records; information system monitoring records; information system audit records; other relevant documents or records. *Interview:* System/network administrators; organizational personnel with information

| SC-44 | Detonation chambers | Review documentation to determine the level and extent of the use of "sandboxes", also known as detonation chambers, for use with evaluation of external inputs, codes, and information prior to loading the same onto the system. These dynamic execution environments allow the organization to open email attachments, execute untrusted or suspicious applications, and execute universal resource locator (URL) requests in the safety of an isolated environment or virtualized sandbox. Test the sandbox environment and discuss with operations staff, security staff, Security Officer, and System Owner. | *Examine:* System and communications protection policy; procedures addressing detonation chambers; information system design documentation; information system configuration settings and associated documentation; information system audit records; other relevant documents or records. *Interview:* System/network administrators; organizational personnel with information security responsibilities; organizational personnel installing, configuring, and/or maintaining the information system. *Test:* Automated mechanisms supporting and/or implementing detonation chamber capability. |

security responsibilities; organizational personnel installing, configuring, and/or maintaining the information system. *Test:* Organizational processes for authorizing, monitoring, and controlling use of components with usage restrictions; Automated mechanisms supporting and/or implementing authorizing, monitoring, and controlling use of components with usage restrictions.

facilities staff, operations staff, security Staff, Security Officer, and System Owner.

R. *Systems integrity family*

FIPS-200 provides the following criteria for this family of controls: System and information integrity (SI): Organizations must: (i) identify, report, and correct information and information system flaws in a timely manner; (ii) provide protection from malicious code at appropriate locations within the organizational information systems; and (iii) monitor information system security alerts and advisories and take appropriate actions in response.

The primary assessment areas for these controls include:

a. Audit the identification, reporting, and correcting of system flaws, which should be done in a timely manner.
b. Assess processes that provide protection from malicious code at appropriate locations within the organizational information systems.
c. Review mechanisms that monitor information system security alerts and advisories that take appropriate actions in response.

Control number	Control name	Assessment methods	Notes and guidance documents	SP 800-53A guidance
SI-1	System and information integrity policy and procedures	Review the organizational and system documentation to ensure that all system integrity policies and procedures are properly identified and documented. Discuss with System Owner and Security Officer.	SP 800-12, SP 800-100	*Examine:* System and information integrity policy and procedures; other relevant documents or records. *Interview:* Organizational personnel with system and information integrity responsibilities; organizational personnel with information security responsibilities.
SI-2	Flaw remediation	Review documentation to determine the flaw remediation actions, activities and efforts of the organization to meet requirements operationally for system. Determine extent of software update processes and procedures follow defined and documented methods and techniques. Ensure all software patching conforms to organizational frequency and methodology needs. Discuss with Security Officer, System Owner, operational staff, and security staff.	SP 800-40, SP 800-128	*Examine:* System and information integrity policy; procedures addressing flaw remediation; procedures addressing configuration management; list of flaws and vulnerabilities potentially affecting the information system; list of recent security flaw remediation actions performed on the information system (e.g., list of installed patches, service packs, hot fixes, and other software updates to correct information system flaws); test results from the installation of software and firmware updates to correct information system flaws; installation/change control records for security-relevant software and firmware updates; other relevant documents or records. *Interview:* System/network administrators; organizational personnel with information security responsibilities; organizational personnel installing, configuring, and/or maintaining the information system; organizational personnel with responsibility for flaw remediation; organizational personnel with configuration management responsibility. *Test:* Organizational processes for identifying, reporting, and correcting information system flaws; organizational process for installing software and firmware updates; automated mechanisms supporting and/or implementing reporting, and correcting information system flaws; automated mechanisms supporting and/or implementing testing software and firmware updates.

(Continued)

Control number	Control name	Assessment methods	Notes and guidance documents	SP 800-53A guidance
SI-2(1)	Flaw remediation: Central management	Review documentation to determine the implementation of centralized flaw management actions, such as planning, implementing, assessing, authorizing, and monitoring the organization-defined, centrally managed flaw remediation security controls. Review central management system and reporting to ensure that the system is active and operational. Discuss with System Owner, security staff, and Security Officer.	SP 800-40, SP 800-128	*Examine:* System and information integrity policy; procedures addressing flaw remediation; automated mechanisms supporting centralized management of flaw remediation; information system design documentation; information system configuration settings and associated documentation; information system audit records; other relevant documents or records. *Interview:* System/network administrators; organizational personnel with information security responsibilities; organizational personnel installing, configuring, and/or maintaining the information system; organizational personnel with responsibility for flaw remediation. *Test:* Organizational processes for central management of the flaw remediation process; automated mechanisms supporting and/or implementing central management of the flaw remediation process.
SI-2(2)	Flaw remediation: Automated flaw remediation status	Review documentation to ensure that the organization is performing automated reviews for flaw remediation-patching efforts on system. Review reports and outputs from automated system to verify remediation. Test system sample to ensure that remediation has been performed correctly and completely. Discuss with security staff, System Owner, and Security Officer.	SP 800-40, SP 800-128	*Examine:* System and information integrity policy; procedures addressing flaw remediation; automated mechanisms supporting centralized management of flaw remediation; information system design documentation; information system configuration settings and associated documentation; information system audit records; other relevant documents or records. *Interview:* System/network administrators; organizational personnel with information security responsibilities; organizational personnel installing, configuring, and/or maintaining the information system; organizational personnel with responsibility for flaw remediation. *Test:* Automated mechanisms used to determine the state of information system components with regard to flaw remediation.
SI-2(3)	Flaw remediation: Time to remediate flaws/benchmarks for correction actions	Review documentation to determine the organizational requirement for time between issuance of patch and actual loading of patch onto the system. This establishes the	SP 800-40, SP 800-128	*Examine:* System and information integrity policy; procedures addressing flaw remediation; information system design documentation; information system configuration settings and associated documentation; list of benchmarks for taking corrective action on flaws identified; records providing time stamps of flaw identification and subsequent flaw remediation

			benchmark for corrective action. Review output and system logs to determine if the organization is meeting benchmark requirements. Discuss with System Owner, security staff, operations staff, and Security Officer.	activities; other relevant documents or records. *Interview:* System/network administrators; organizational personnel with information security responsibilities; organizational personnel installing, configuring, and/or maintaining the information system; organizational personnel with responsibility for flaw remediation. *Test:* Organizational processes for identifying, reporting, and correcting information system flaws; automated mechanisms used to measure the time between flaw identification and flaw remediation.
SI-2(4)	Flaw remediation: Automated patch management tools			Withdrawn: Incorporated into SI-2
SI-2(5)	Flaw remediation: Automatic software/firmware updates	SP 800-40, SP 800-128	Review documentation on automated updates for system to ensure that operational, configuration management, and security needs are balanced with each other in applying updates and patches to the system in a timely manner. Discuss with System Owner, operations staff, security staff, and Security Officer.	*Examine:* System and information integrity policy; procedures addressing flaw remediation; automated mechanisms supporting flaw remediation and automatic software/firmware updates; information system design documentation; information system configuration settings and associated documentation; records of recent security-relevant software and firmware updates automatically installed to information system components; information system audit records; other relevant documents or records. *Interview:* System/network administrators; organizational personnel with information security responsibilities; organizational personnel installing, configuring, and/or maintaining the information system; organizational personnel with responsibility for flaw remediation. *Test:* Automated mechanisms implementing automatic software/firmware updates.
SI-2(6)	Flaw remediation: Removal of previous versions of software/firmware	SP 800-40, SP 800-128	Review documentation to ensure that the previous versions of software are appropriately removed from system upon new software being applied. Discuss with security staff, System Administrators, Security Officer, and System Owner.	*Examine:* System and information integrity policy; procedures addressing flaw remediation; automated mechanisms supporting flaw remediation; information system design documentation; information system configuration settings and associated documentation; records of software and firmware component removals after updated versions are installed; information system audit records; other relevant documents or records. *Interview:* System/network administrators; organizational personnel with information

(Continued)

Control number	Control name	Assessment methods	Notes and guidance documents	SP 800-53A guidance
				security responsibilities; organizational personnel installing, configuring, and/or maintaining the information system; organizational personnel with responsibility for flaw remediation. *Test:* Automated mechanisms supporting and/or implementing removal of previous versions of software/firmware.
SI-3	Malicious code protection	Review documentation for malicious code control and protection mechanisms installed and applied to system. Various techniques can define actions in response to malicious code detection during periodic scans, actions in response to detection of malicious downloads, and/or actions in response to detection of maliciousness, when attempting to open or execute files. Test various methods of code integrity errors to ensure system responds correctly. Discuss with System Owner, security staff, and Security Officer.	SP 800-83	*Examine:* System and information integrity policy; configuration management policy and procedures; procedures addressing malicious code protection; malicious code protection mechanisms; records of malicious code protection updates; information system design documentation; information system configuration settings and associated documentation; scan results from malicious code protection mechanisms; record of actions initiated by malicious code protection mechanisms in response to malicious code detection; information system audit records; other relevant documents or records. *Interview:* System/network administrators; organizational personnel with information security responsibilities; organizational personnel installing, configuring, and/or maintaining the information system; organizational personnel with responsibility for malicious code protection; organizational personnel with configuration management responsibility. *Test:* Organizational processes for employing, updating, and configuring malicious code protection mechanisms; organizational process for addressing false positives and resulting potential impact; automated mechanisms supporting and/or implementing employing, updating, and configuring malicious code protection mechanisms; automated mechanisms supporting and/or implementing malicious code scanning and subsequent actions.
SI-3(1)	Malicious code protection: Central management	Review documentation to ensure that the organization controls malicious code protection from central system. Central management	SP 800-83	*Examine:* System and information integrity policy; procedures addressing malicious code protection; automated mechanisms supporting centralized management of malicious code protection mechanisms; information system design documentation; information system configuration

Control	Name	Description	Reference	Assessment
		includes planning, implementing, assessing, authorizing, and monitoring the organization-defined, centrally managed flaw malicious code protection security controls. Ensure central management through testing code load and detection actions. Discuss with System Owner, security staff, System Administrators, and Security Officer.		settings and associated documentation; information system audit records; other relevant documents or records. *Interview*: System/network administrators; organizational personnel with information security responsibilities; organizational personnel installing, configuring, and/or maintaining the information system; organizational personnel with responsibility for malicious code protection. *Test*: Organizational processes for central management of malicious code protection mechanisms; automated mechanisms supporting and/or implementing central management of malicious code protection mechanisms.
SI-3(2)	Malicious code protection: Automatic updates	Review documentation for malicious code detection and control to ensure that automated signature processes are enacted and active. Review recent updates to the system to verify process is functioning and active. Discuss with System Owner and Security Officer.	SP 800-83	*Examine*: System and information integrity policy; procedures addressing malicious code protection; automated mechanisms supporting centralized management of malicious code protection mechanisms; information system design documentation; information system configuration settings and associated documentation; information system audit records; other relevant documents or records. *Interview*: System/network administrators; organizational personnel with information security responsibilities; system developers; organizational personnel installing, configuring, and/or maintaining the information system; organizational personnel with responsibility for malicious code protection. *Test*: Automated mechanisms supporting and/or implementing automatic updates to malicious code protection capability.
SI-3(3)	Malicious code protection: Nonprivileged users		Withdrawn: Incorporated into AC-6(10)	
SI-3(4)	Malicious code protection: Updates only by privileged users	Review documentation for malicious code updates to ensure that only elevated privilege users are allowed to perform updates. Verify via operating system or	SP 800-83	*Examine*: System and information integrity policy; procedures addressing malicious code protection; information system design documentation; malicious code protection mechanisms; records of malicious code protection updates; information system configuration settings and associated documentation; information system audit records; other

(*Continued*)

Control number	Control name	Assessment methods	Notes and guidance documents	SP 800-53A guidance
		LDAP account management processes. Test via account management review and test code load processes. Discuss with System Owner, security staff, System Administrators, and Security Officer.		relevant documents or records. *Interview:* System/network administrators; organizational personnel with information security responsibilities; system developers; organizational personnel installing, configuring, and/or maintaining the information system; organizational personnel with responsibility for malicious code protection. *Test:* Automated mechanisms supporting and/or implementing malicious code protection capability.
SI-3(5)	Malicious code protection: Portable storage devices		Withdrawn: Incorporated into MP-7	
SI-3(6)	Malicious code protection: Testing/ verification	Review documentation to ensure that the organizational testing of malicious code detection is performed. Test malicious code detection with test code to verify detection process. Discuss with System Owner and Security Officer.	SP 800-83	*Examine:* System and information integrity policy; procedures addressing malicious code protection; information system design documentation; information system configuration settings and associated documentation; test cases; records providing evidence of test cases executed on malicious code protection mechanisms; information system audit records; other relevant documents or records. *Interview:* System/network administrators; organizational personnel with information security responsibilities; organizational personnel installing, configuring, and/or maintaining the information system; organizational personnel with responsibility for malicious code protection. *Test:* Automated mechanisms supporting and/or implementing testing and verification of malicious code protection capability.
SI-3(7)	Malicious code protection: Nonsignature-based detection	Review documentation to determine the system and organizational utilization of heuristics or other code and to provide safeguards against malicious code for which signatures do not exist yet. Test system with sample malicious code to verify system. Discuss with System	SP 800-83	*Examine:* System and information integrity policy; procedures addressing malicious code protection; information system design documentation; malicious code protection mechanisms; records of malicious code protection updates; information system configuration settings and associated documentation; information system audit records; other relevant documents or records. *Interview:* System/network administrators; organizational personnel with information security responsibilities; system developers; organizational personnel installing, configuring, and/or maintaining

the information system; organizational personnel with responsibility for malicious code protection. *Test*: Automated mechanisms supporting and/or implementing nonsignature-based malicious code protection capability.

			Owner, operational staff, security staff, and Security Officer.	
SI-3(8)	Malicious code protection: Detect unauthorized commands	Review documentation to ensure that the system provides detection of unauthorized commands or requests to kernel, virtualized system, or other protected component of system and its operating system. Discuss with System Owner, security staff, and Security Officer.	*Examine*: System and information integrity policy; procedures addressing malicious code protection; information system design documentation; malicious code protection mechanisms; warning messages sent upon detection of unauthorized operating system command execution; information system configuration settings and associated documentation; information system audit records; other relevant documents or records. *Interview*: System/network administrators; organizational personnel with information security responsibilities; system developers; organizational personnel installing, configuring, and/or maintaining the information system; organizational personnel with responsibility for malicious code protection. *Test*: Automated mechanisms supporting and/or implementing malicious code protection capability; automated mechanisms supporting and/or implementing detection of unauthorized operating system commands through the kernel application programming interface.	SP 800-83
SI-3(9)	Malicious code protection: Authenticate remote commands	Review documentation to ensure that the system protects against unauthorized commands and replay of authorized commands. Test with malicious code sample to verify system reaction to code command. Discuss with System Owner, security staff, and Security Officer.	*Examine*: System and information integrity policy; procedures addressing malicious code protection; information system design documentation; malicious code protection mechanisms; warning messages sent upon detection of unauthorized operating system command execution; information system configuration settings and associated documentation; information system audit records; other relevant documents or records. *Interview*: System/network administrators; organizational personnel with information security responsibilities; system developers; organizational personnel installing, configuring, and/or maintaining the information system; organizational personnel with responsibility for malicious code protection. *Test*: Automated mechanisms supporting and/or implementing malicious code protection capability; automated mechanisms implementing authentication of remote commands;	SP 800-83

(Continued)

Control number	Control name	Assessment methods	Notes and guidance documents	SP 800-53A guidance
				automated mechanisms supporting and/or implementing security safeguards to authenticate remote commands.
SI-3(10)	Malicious code protection: Malicious code analysis	Review documentation to determine the organization's implementation of reverse engineering and other code analysis techniques for review and evaluation of malicious code and code events. Discuss with security Staff, System Owner, and Security Officer.	SP 800-83	*Examine:* System and information integrity policy; procedures addressing malicious code protection; procedures addressing incident response; procedures addressing flaw remediation; information system design documentation; malicious code protection mechanisms, tools, and techniques; information system configuration settings and associated documentation; results from malicious code analyses; records of flaw remediation events resulting from malicious code analyses; information system audit records; other relevant documents or records. *Interview:* System/network administrators; organizational personnel with information security responsibilities; organizational personnel installing, configuring, and/or maintaining the information system; organizational personnel with responsibility for malicious code protection; organizational personnel responsible for flaw remediation; organizational personnel responsible for incident response/management. *Test:* Organizational process for incident response; organizational process for flaw remediation; automated mechanisms supporting and/or implementing malicious code protection capability; tools and techniques for analysis of malicious code characteristics and behavior.
SI-4	Information system monitoring	Review documentation to determine the organizational monitoring of system and operational status. Review techniques and procedures for monitoring, which could include intrusion detection systems, intrusion prevention systems, malicious code protection software, scanning tools, audit record monitoring software, network monitoring software, and other	SP 800-61, rev.2, SP 800-83, SP 800-92, SP 800-94, SP 800-137	*Examine:* Continuous monitoring strategy; system and information integrity policy; procedures addressing information system monitoring tools and techniques; facility diagram/layout; information system design documentation; information system monitoring tools and techniques documentation; locations within information system where monitoring devices are deployed; information system configuration settings and associated documentation; other relevant documents or records. *Interview:* System/network administrators; organizational personnel with information security responsibilities; organizational personnel installing, configuring, and/or maintaining the information system; organizational personnel with responsibility monitoring

		components and methods. Discuss with security staff, operations staff, System Owner, and Security Officer.		the information system. *Test*: Organizational processes for information system monitoring; automated mechanisms supporting and/or implementing information system monitoring capability.
SI-4(1)	Information system monitoring: System-wide intrusion detection system	Review documentation for the system and organizational implementation of IDS and its sensors for the system under review. Ensure that the monitoring of the IDS is active and alarms and alerts are identified and responded to through reviews and observations. Test response times of system IDS with test code and snippets. Discuss with System Owner, security staff, and Security Officer.	SP 800-61, rev.2, SP 800-83,SP 800-92, SP 800-94, SP 800-137	*Examine*: System and information integrity policy; procedures addressing information system monitoring tools and techniques; information system design documentation; information system monitoring tools and techniques documentation; information system configuration settings and associated documentation; information system audit records; other relevant documents or records. *Interview*: System/network administrators; organizational personnel with information security responsibilities; organizational personnel installing, configuring, and/or maintaining the information system; organizational personnel with responsibility for monitoring the information system; organizational personnel with responsibility for the intrusion detection system. *Test*: Organizational processes for intrusion detection/information system monitoring; automated mechanisms supporting and/or implementing intrusion detection capability.
SI-4(2)	Information system monitoring: Automated tools for real-time analysis	Review documentation to ensure that the system is utilizing automated mechanisms for monitoring and evaluation. Automated tools include, for example, host-based, network-based, transport-based, or storage-based event monitoring tools or Security Information and Event Management (SIEM) technologies that provide real time analysis of alerts and/or notifications generated by the organizational information systems. Review outputs from tools to verify actual use and	SP 800-61, rev.2, SP 800-83,SP 800-94, SP 800-137	*Examine*: System and information integrity policy; procedures addressing information system monitoring tools and techniques; information system design documentation; information system monitoring tools and techniques documentation; information system configuration settings and associated documentation; information system audit records; other relevant documents or records. *Interview*: System/network administrators; organizational personnel with information security responsibilities; organizational personnel installing, configuring, and/or maintaining the information system; organizational personnel with responsibility for monitoring the information system; organizational personnel with responsibility for incident response/management. *Test*: Organizational processes for near real-time analysis of events; organizational processes for information system monitoring; automated mechanisms supporting and/or implementing information system

(Continued)

Control number	Control name	Assessment methods	Notes and guidance documents	SP 800-53A guidance
		value of monitoring actions and events. Discuss with System Owner, operations staff, security staff, and Security Officer.		monitoring; automated mechanisms/tools supporting and/or implementing analysis of events.
SI-4(3)	Information system monitoring: Automated tool integration	Review documentation to determine full integration of automatic monitoring tools with intrusion detection tools into access control and flow control mechanisms for rapid response to attacks by enabling reconfiguration of these mechanisms in support of attack isolation and elimination. Verify output from the tools that show rapid response efforts and actions. Discuss with System Owner, security staff, and Security Officer.	SP 800-61, rev.2, SP 800-83, SP 800-92, SP 800-94, SP 800-137	*Examine:* System and information integrity policy; access control policy and procedures; procedures addressing information system monitoring tools and techniques; information system design documentation; information system monitoring tools and techniques documentation; information system configuration settings and associated documentation; information system audit records; other relevant documents or records. *Interview:* System/network administrators; organizational personnel with information security responsibilities; organizational personnel with information installing, configuring, and/or maintaining the information system; organizational personnel with responsibility for monitoring the information system; organizational personnel with responsibility for the intrusion detection system. *Test:* Organizational processes for intrusion detection/information system monitoring; automated mechanisms supporting and/or implementing intrusion detection/information system monitoring capability; automated mechanisms/tools supporting and/or implementing access/flow control capability; automated mechanisms/tools supporting and/or implementing integration of intrusion detection tools into access/flow control mechanisms.
SI-4(4)	Information system monitoring: Inbound and outbound communications traffic	Review documentation for monitoring of internal traffic that indicates the presence of malicious code within the organizational information systems or propagating among system components, the unauthorized exporting of information, or signaling to	SP 800-61, rev.2, SP 800-83, SP 800-92, SP 800-94, SP 800-137	*Examine:* System and information integrity policy; procedures addressing information system monitoring tools and techniques; information system design documentation; information system monitoring tools and techniques documentation; information system configuration settings and associated documentation; information system protocols; information system audit records; other relevant documents or records. *Interview:* System/network administrators; organizational personnel with information security

			external information systems. Discuss with System Owner, security staff, and Security Officer.	responsibilities; organizational personnel installing, configuring, and/or maintaining the information system; organizational personnel with responsibility for monitoring the information system; organizational personnel with responsibility for the intrusion detection system. *Test:* Organizational processes for intrusion detection/information system monitoring; automated mechanisms supporting and/or implementing intrusion detection capability/information system monitoring; automated mechanisms supporting and/or implementing monitoring of inbound/outbound communications traffic.
SI-4(5)	Information system monitoring: System-generated alerts	SP 800-61, rev.2, SP 800-83, SP 800-92, SP 800-94, SP 800-137	Review documentation to ensure that monitoring component provides alarms and alerts, when events are identified or discovered. Verify alert mechanism when triggered through testing with test code. Discuss with System Owner, Security Officer, and security staff.	*Examine:* System and information integrity policy; procedures addressing information system monitoring tools and techniques; information system monitoring tools and techniques documentation; information system configuration settings and associated documentation; alerts/notifications generated based on compromise indicators; information system audit records; other relevant documents or records. *Interview:* System/network administrators; organizational personnel with information security responsibilities; system developers; organizational personnel installing, configuring, and/or maintaining the information system; organizational personnel with responsibility for monitoring the information system; organizational personnel with responsibility for the intrusion detection system. *Test:* Organizational processes for intrusion detection/information system monitoring; automated mechanisms supporting and/or implementing intrusion detection/information system monitoring capability; automated mechanisms supporting and/or implementing alerts for compromise indicators.
SI-4(6)	Information system monitoring: Restrict nonprivileged users	Withdrawn: Incorporated into AC-6(10)		
SI-4(7)	Information system monitoring: Automated	SP 800-61, rev.2, SP 800-83, SP 800-92,	Review documentation for monitoring tool to identify and verify automated	*Examine:* System and information integrity policy; procedures addressing information system monitoring tools and techniques; information system design documentation;

(Continued)

Control number	Control name	Assessment methods	Notes and guidance documents	SP 800-53A guidance
	response to suspicious events	response mechanisms, which are less disruptive. Least-disruptive actions may include, for example, initiating requests for human responses. Verify system provides this notification process. Discuss with System Owner and Security Officer.	SP 800-94, SP 800-137	information system monitoring tools and techniques documentation; information system configuration settings and associated documentation; alerts/notifications generated based on detected suspicious events; records of actions taken to terminate suspicious events; information system audit records; other relevant documents or records. *Interview:* System/network administrators; organizational personnel with information security responsibilities; system developers; organizational personnel installing, configuring, and/or maintaining the information system; organizational personnel with responsibility for monitoring the information system; organizational personnel with responsibility for the intrusion detection system. *Test:* Organizational processes for intrusion detection/information system monitoring; automated mechanisms supporting and/or implementing intrusion detection/information system monitoring capability; automated mechanisms supporting and/or implementing notifications to incident response personnel; automated mechanisms supporting and/or implementing actions to terminate suspicious events.
SI-4(8)	Information system monitoring: Protection of monitoring information		Withdrawn: Incorporated into SI-4	
SI-4(9)	Information system monitoring: Testing of monitoring tools	Review documentation for intrusion monitoring tools. Verify tools through testing each tool, its operation and outputs. Discuss with Security Officer and System Owner.	SP 800-61, rev.2, SP 800-83, SP 800-92, SP 800-94, SP 800-137	*Examine:* System and information integrity policy; procedures addressing testing of information system monitoring tools and techniques; documentation providing evidence of testing intrusion-monitoring tools; other relevant documents or records. *Interview:* System/network administrators; organizational personnel with information security responsibilities; organizational personnel installing, configuring, and/or maintaining the information system; organizational personnel with responsibility for monitoring the information system; organizational personnel with responsibility for the intrusion detection system. *Test:*

Organizational processes for intrusion detection/information system monitoring; automated mechanisms supporting and/or implementing intrusion detection/information system monitoring capability; automated mechanisms supporting and/or implementing testing of intrusion monitoring tools.

SI-4(10)	Information system monitoring: Visibility of encrypted communications	Review documentation for monitoring of the encrypted communications within the system. Ensure documentation defines the organizational balance, the potentially conflicting needs for encrypting communications traffic and for having insight into such traffic from a monitoring perspective that are required for system. Discuss with System Owner, security staff, operations staff, and Security Officer.	SP 800-61, rev.2, SP 800-83, SP 800-92, SP 800-94, SP 800-137	*Examine:* System and information integrity policy; procedures addressing information system monitoring tools and techniques; information system design documentation; information system monitoring tools and techniques documentation; information system configuration settings and associated documentation; information system protocols; other relevant documents or records. *Interview:* System/network administrators; organizational personnel with information security responsibilities; organizational personnel installing, configuring, and/or maintaining the information system; organizational personnel with responsibility for monitoring the information system; organizational personnel with responsibility for the intrusion detection system. *Test:* Organizational processes for intrusion detection/information system monitoring; automated mechanisms supporting and/or implementing intrusion detection/information system monitoring capability; automated mechanisms supporting and/or implementing visibility of encrypted communications traffic to monitoring tools.
SI-4(11)	Information system monitoring: Analyze communications traffic anomalies	Review documentation for system and traffic anomalies such as large file transfers, long-time persistent connections, unusual protocols and ports in use, and attempted communications with suspected malicious external addresses. Verify with testing the notification process with test code. Discuss with System Owner, security staff, and Security Officer.	SP 800-61, rev.2, SP 800-83, SP 800-92, SP 800-94, SP 800-137	*Examine:* System and information integrity policy; procedures addressing information system monitoring tools and techniques; information system design documentation; network diagram; information system monitoring tools and techniques documentation; information system configuration settings and associated documentation; information system monitoring logs or records; other relevant documents or records. *Interview:* System/network administrators; organizational personnel with information security responsibilities; organizational personnel installing, configuring, and/or maintaining the information system; organizational personnel with responsibility for monitoring the information system; organizational personnel with responsibility for the intrusion

(Continued)

Control number	Control name	Assessment methods	Notes and guidance documents	SP 800-53A guidance
				detection system. *Test:* Organizational processes for intrusion detection/information system monitoring; automated mechanisms supporting and/or implementing intrusion detection/information system monitoring capability; automated mechanisms supporting and/or implementing analysis of communications traffic.
SI-4(12)	Information system monitoring: Automated alerts	Review documentation for monitoring the system to verify system reports alarms and alerts from external sources, as well as internal to system sources. Discuss with System Owner and Security Officer.	SP 800-61, rev.2, SP 800-83,SP 800-92, SP 800-94, SP 800-137	*Examine:* System and information integrity policy; procedures addressing information system monitoring tools and techniques; information system design documentation; information system monitoring tools and techniques documentation; information system configuration settings and associated documentation; list of inappropriate or unusual activities (with security implications) that trigger alerts; alerts/notifications provided to security personnel; information system monitoring logs or records; information system audit records; other relevant documents or records. *Interview:* System/network administrators; organizational personnel with information security responsibilities; system developers; organizational personnel installing, configuring, and/or maintaining the information system; organizational personnel with responsibility for monitoring the information system; organizational personnel with responsibility for the intrusion detection system. *Test:* Organizational processes for intrusion detection/information system monitoring; automated mechanisms supporting and/or implementing intrusion detection/information system monitoring capability; automated mechanisms supporting and/or implementing automated alerts to security personnel.
SI-4(13)	Information system monitoring: Analyze traffic/event patterns	Review documentation to determine, what level of traffic analysis on patterns is utilized to define the traffic/event profiles in tuning system-monitoring devices to reduce the number of false positives and the number of	SP 800-61, rev.2, SP 800-83,SP 800-92, SP 800-94, SP 800-137	*Examine:* System and information integrity policy; procedures addressing information system monitoring tools and techniques; information system design documentation; information system monitoring tools and techniques documentation; information system configuration settings and associated documentation; list of profiles representing common traffic patterns and/or events; information system protocols documentation; list of acceptable thresholds

				for false positives and false negatives; other relevant documents or records. *Interview:* System/network administrators; organizational personnel with information security responsibilities; organizational personnel installing, configuring, and/or maintaining the information system; organizational personnel with responsibility for monitoring the information system; organizational personnel with responsibility for the intrusion detection system. *Test:* Organizational processes for intrusion detection/information system monitoring; automated mechanisms supporting and/or implementing intrusion detection/information system monitoring capability; automated mechanisms supporting and/or implementing analysis of communications traffic/event patterns.
SI-4(14)	Information system monitoring: Wireless intrusion detection	Review documentation to determine extent the wireless network deployments within the system are monitored with wireless-based IDS (WIDS) components. WIDS scans are not limited to those areas within facilities containing information systems, but also include areas outside of facilities as needed, to verify that unauthorized wireless access points are not connected to the systems. Test WIDS through injecting a rogue WAP and evaluating the resultant scans and reports. Discuss with System Owner and Security Officer.	SP 800-61, rev.2, SP 800-83, SP 800-92, SP 800-94, SP 800-137	*Examine:* System and information integrity policy; procedures addressing information system monitoring tools and techniques; information system design documentation; information system monitoring tools and techniques documentation; information system configuration settings and associated documentation; information system protocols; information system audit records; other relevant documents or records. *Interview:* System/network administrators; organizational personnel with information security responsibilities; organizational personnel installing, configuring, and/or maintaining the information system; organizational personnel with responsibility for monitoring the information system; organizational personnel with responsibility for the intrusion detection system. *Test:* Organizational processes for intrusion detection; automated mechanisms supporting and/or implementing wireless intrusion detection capability.
SI-4(15)	Information system monitoring: Wireless to wireline communications	Review documentation to determine the monitoring of wireless activity as it travels the wireless to wired connections within the	SP 800-61, rev.2, SP 800-83, SP 800-92, SP 800-94, SP 800-137	*Examine:* System and information integrity policy; procedures addressing information system monitoring tools and techniques; information system design documentation; information system monitoring tools and techniques documentation; information system configuration settings

(Continued)

Control number	Control name	Assessment methods	Notes and guidance documents	SP 800-53A guidance
		system. Discuss with security staff, Security Officer, and System Owner.		and associated documentation; information system protocols documentation; information system audit records; other relevant documents or records. *Interview:* System/network administrators; organizational personnel with information security responsibilities; organizational personnel installing, configuring, and/or maintaining the information system; organizational personnel with responsibility for monitoring the information system; organizational personnel with responsibility for the intrusion detection system. *Test:* Organizational processes for intrusion detection/information system monitoring; automated mechanisms supporting and/or implementing intrusion detection/information system monitoring capability; automated mechanisms supporting and/or implementing wireless intrusion detection capability.
SI-4(16)	Information system monitoring: Correlate monitoring information	Review documentation to determine, if organization provides methods to correlate various monitoring efforts to provide an organizational-wide monitoring capability. Discuss with System Owner, security staff, and Security Officer.	SP 800-61, rev.2, SP 800-83,SP 800-92, SP 800-94, SP 800-137	*Examine:* System and information integrity policy; procedures addressing information system monitoring tools and techniques; information system design documentation; information system monitoring tools and techniques documentation; information system configuration settings and associated documentation; event correlation logs or records; information system audit records; other relevant documents or records. *Interview:* System/network administrators; organizational personnel with information security responsibilities; organizational personnel installing, configuring, and/or maintaining the information system; organizational personnel with responsibility for monitoring the information system; organizational personnel with responsibility for the intrusion detection system. *Test:* Organizational processes for intrusion detection/information system monitoring; automated mechanisms supporting and/or implementing intrusion detection/information system monitoring capability; automated mechanisms supporting and/or implementing correlation of information from monitoring tools.

SI-4(17)	Information system monitoring: Integrated situational awareness	Review documentation to determine, if the organization provides methods to correlate various monitoring efforts, both inclusive to organization as well as external to organization, to provide a larger organizational-wide monitoring capability and situational awareness. Discuss with System Owner, security staff, and Security Officer.	SP 800-61, rev.2, SP 800-83, SP 800-92, SP 800-94, SP 800-137	*Examine:* System and information integrity policy; procedures addressing information system monitoring tools and techniques; information system design documentation; information system monitoring tools and techniques documentation; information system configuration settings and associated documentation; event correlation logs or records resulting from physical, cyber, and supply chain activities; information system audit records; other relevant documents or records. *Interview:* System/network administrators; organizational personnel with information security responsibilities; organizational personnel installing, configuring, and/or maintaining the information system; organizational personnel with responsibility for monitoring the information system; organizational personnel with responsibility for the intrusion detection system. *Test:* Organizational processes for intrusion detection/information system monitoring; automated mechanisms supporting and/or implementing intrusion detection/system monitoring capability; automated mechanisms supporting and/or implementing correlation of information from monitoring tools.
SI-4(18)	Information system monitoring Analyze traffic/covert exfiltration	Review documentation to determine, if the organization has covert exfiltration detection methods and techniques available and deployed within system or organization. Covert means that can be used for the unauthorized exfiltration of organizational information include, for example, steganography. Discuss with security staff, System Owner, and Security Officer.	SP 800-61, rev.2, SP 800-83, SP 800-92, SP 800-94, SP 800-137	*Examine:* System and information integrity policy; procedures addressing information system monitoring tools and techniques; information system design documentation; network diagram; information system monitoring tools and techniques documentation; information system configuration settings and associated documentation; information system monitoring logs or records; information system audit records; other relevant documents or records. *Interview:* System/network administrators; organizational personnel with information security responsibilities; organizational personnel installing, configuring, and/or maintaining the information system; organizational personnel with responsibility for monitoring the information system; organizational personnel with responsibility for the intrusion detection system. *Test:* Organizational processes for intrusion detection/information system monitoring; automated mechanisms supporting and/or implementing intrusion detection/system monitoring capability; automated mechanisms supporting and/or implementing analysis of outbound communications traffic.

(Continued)

Control number	Control name	Assessment methods	Notes and guidance documents	SP 800-53A guidance
SI-4(19)	Information system monitoring: Individuals posing greater risk	Review documentation to determine, if the organization provides monitoring of at-risk or suspect individuals with access to system. Ensure all monitoring is under supervision of appropriate organizational management oversight to include legal staff, management, personnel department, and operations. The monitoring of individuals is closely coordinated with management, legal, security, and human resources officials within organizations conducting such monitoring and complies with federal legislation, Executive Orders, policies, directives, regulations, and standards. Discuss with System Owner and Security Officer.	SP 800-61, rev.2, SP 800-83, SP 800-92, SP 800-94, SP 800-137	*Examine:* System and information integrity policy; procedures addressing information system monitoring; information system design documentation; list of individuals who have been identified as posing an increased level of risk; information system monitoring tools and techniques documentation; information system configuration settings and associated documentation; information system audit records; other relevant documents or records. *Interview:* System/network administrators; organizational personnel with information security responsibilities; organizational personnel installing, configuring, and/or maintaining the information system; organizational personnel with responsibility for monitoring the information system. *Test:* Organizational processes for information system monitoring; automated mechanisms supporting and/or implementing system monitoring capability.
SI-4(20)	Information system monitoring: Privileged users	Review documentation for monitoring efforts on elevated privilege users and their activities. Ensure all monitoring is under supervision of appropriate organizational management oversight to include legal staff, management, personnel department, and operations. The monitoring of individuals is closely coordinated with management, legal, security,	SP 800-61, rev.2, SP 800-83, SP 800-92, SP 800-94, SP 800-137	*Examine:* System and information integrity policy; procedures addressing information system monitoring tools and techniques; information system design documentation; list of privileged users; information system monitoring tools and techniques documentation; information system configuration settings and associated documentation; information system monitoring logs or records; information system audit records; other relevant documents or records. *Interview:* System/network administrators; organizational personnel with information security responsibilities; organizational personnel installing, configuring, and/or maintaining the information system; organizational personnel with responsibility for monitoring the information system. *Test:*

			Organizational processes for information system monitoring; automated mechanisms supporting and/or implementing system monitoring capability.
			and human resources officials within the organizations conducting such monitoring and complies with federal legislation, executive orders, policies, directives, regulations, and standards. Discuss with System Owner and Security Officer.
SI-4(21)	Information system monitoring: Probationary periods	SP 800-61, rev.2, SP 800-83, SP 800-92, SP 800-94, SP 800-137	Review documentation for monitoring efforts on users during the organizationally define probationary period. Ensure all monitoring is under supervision of appropriate organizational management oversight to include legal staff, management, personnel department, and operations. The monitoring of individuals is closely coordinated with management, legal, security, and human resources officials within organizations conducting such monitoring and complies with federal legislation, Executive Orders, policies, directives, regulations, and standards. Discuss with System Owner and Security Officer.	*Examine:* System and information integrity policy; procedures addressing information system monitoring; information system design documentation; information system monitoring tools and techniques documentation; information system configuration settings and associated documentation; information system monitoring logs or records; information system audit records; other relevant documents or records. *Interview:* System/network administrators; organizational personnel with information security responsibilities; organizational personnel installing, configuring, and/or maintaining the information system; organizational personnel with responsibility for monitoring the information system. *Test:* Organizational processes for information system monitoring; automated mechanisms supporting and/or implementing system monitoring capability.
SI-4(22)	Information system monitoring: Unauthorized network services	SP 800-61, rev.2, SP 800-83, SP 800-92, SP 800-94, SP 800-137	Review documentation to determine, how system and organization validate and verify outside or unauthorized network services to ensure their use and lack of malicious	*Examine:* System and information integrity policy; procedures addressing information system monitoring tools and techniques; information system design documentation; information system monitoring tools and techniques documentation; information system configuration settings and associated documentation; documented authorization/approval of network services; notifications or alerts of

(Continued)

Control number	Control name	Assessment methods	Notes and guidance documents	SP 800-53A guidance
		components or software. Test system with test code to verify control. Discuss with System Owner, security staff, and Security Officer.		unauthorized network services; information system monitoring logs or records; information system audit records; other relevant documents or records. *Interview:* System/network administrators; organizational personnel with information security responsibilities; system developer; organizational personnel installing, configuring, and/or maintaining the information system; organizational personnel with responsibility for monitoring the information system. *Test:* Organizational processes for information system monitoring; automated mechanisms supporting and/or implementing system monitoring capability; automated mechanisms for auditing network services; automated mechanisms for providing alerts.
SI-4(23)	Information system monitoring; host-based devices	Review documentation to ensure that host-based monitoring devices are installed and operating correctly. Evaluate with test code to ensure monitoring is functioning and operational. Discuss with Security Officer, security staff, and System Owner.	SP 800-61, rev.2, SP 800-83,SP 800-92, SP 800-94, SP 800-137	*Examine:* System and information integrity policy; procedures addressing information system monitoring tools and techniques; information system design documentation; host-based monitoring mechanisms; information system monitoring tools and techniques documentation; information system configuration settings and associated documentation; list of information system components requiring host-based monitoring; information system monitoring logs or records; information system audit records; other relevant documents or records. *Interview:* System/network administrators; organizational personnel with information security responsibilities; organizational personnel installing, configuring, and/or maintaining the information system; organizational personnel with responsibility for monitoring information system hosts. *Test:* Organizational processes for information system monitoring; automated mechanisms supporting and/or implementing host-based monitoring capability.
SI-4(24)	Information system monitoring; Indicators of compromise	Review documentation for use, if indicators of compromise (IOC) in monitoring efforts. IOC are forensic artifacts from	SP 800-61, rev.2, SP 800-83,SP 800-92, SP 800-94, SP 800-137	*Examine:* System and information integrity policy; procedures addressing information system monitoring; information system design documentation; information system monitoring tools and techniques documentation; information system configuration settings and associated documentation;

information system monitoring logs or records; information system audit records; other relevant documents or records. *Interview:* System/network administrators; organizational personnel with information security responsibilities; system developer; organizational personnel installing, configuring, and/or maintaining the information system; organizational personnel with responsibility for monitoring information system hosts. *Test:* Organizational processes for information system monitoring; organizational processes for discovery, collection, distribution, and use of indicators of compromise; automated mechanisms supporting and/or implementing system monitoring capability; automated mechanisms supporting and/or implementing the discovery, collection, distribution, and use of indicators of compromise.

ID	Control	Assessment	References	Guidance
				intrusions and are often retrieved via forensics methods after an intrusion to be used to help other systems and organizational components, identify potential compromise events. Discuss with Security Officer and System Owner.
SI-5	Security alerts, advisories, and directives	*Examine:* System and information integrity policy; procedures addressing security alerts, advisories, and directives; records of security alerts and advisories; other relevant documents or records. *Interview:* Organizational personnel with security alert and advisory responsibilities; organizational personnel implementing, operating, maintaining, and using the information system; organizational personnel, organizational elements, and/or external organizations to whom alerts, advisories, and directives are to be disseminated; system/network administrators; organizational personnel with information security responsibilities. *Test:* Organizational processes for defining, receiving, generating, disseminating, and complying with security alerts, advisories, and directives; automated mechanisms supporting and/or implementing definition, receipt, generation, and dissemination of security alerts, advisories, and directives; automated mechanisms supporting and/or implementing security directives.	SP 800-137, SP 800-94, SP 800-40	Review documentation to determine receipt and use of external security alerts and advisories from governmental and nongovernmental entities. Discuss with System Owner, security staff, and Security Officer.
SI-5(1)	Security alerts, advisories, and directives: Automated alerts and advisories	*Examine:* System and information integrity policy; procedures addressing security alerts, advisories, and directives; information system design documentation; information system configuration settings and associated documentation; automated mechanisms supporting the distribution of security alert and advisory information; records of	SP 800-137, SP 800-94, SP 800-40	Review documentation to determine receipt and use of external security alerts and advisories from governmental and nongovernmental entities. Ensure automated

(Continued)

Control number	Control name	Notes and guidance documents	Assessment methods	SP 800-53A guidance
			mechanisms are used to disseminate these alerts and advisories. Discuss with System Owner, security staff, and Security Officer.	security alerts and advisories; information system audit records; other relevant documents or records. *Interview:* Organizational personnel with security alert and advisory responsibilities; organizational personnel implementing, operating, maintaining, and using the information system; organizational personnel, organizational elements, and/or external organizations to whom alerts and advisories are to be disseminated; system/network administrators; organizational personnel with information security responsibilities. *Test:* Organizational processes for defining, receiving, generating, and disseminating security alerts and advisories; automated mechanisms supporting and/or implementing dissemination of security alerts and advisories.
SI-6	Security function verification		Review documentation to ensure that the system security functions, such as system startup, restart, shutdown, and abort provide notification to appropriate operational and security staff in a timely manner. Notifications provided by information systems include, for example, electronic alerts to system administrators, messages to local computer consoles, and/or hardware indications such as lights. Discuss with operations staff, security staff, Security Officer, and System Owner.	*Examine:* System and information integrity policy; procedures addressing security function verification; information system design documentation; information system configuration settings and associated documentation; alerts/notifications of failed security verification tests; list of system transition states requiring security functionality verification; information system audit records; other relevant documents or records. *Interview:* Organizational personnel with security function verification responsibilities; organizational personnel implementing, operating, and maintaining the information system; system/network administrators; organizational personnel with information security responsibilities; system developer. *Test:* Organizational processes for security function verification; automated mechanisms supporting and/or implementing security function verification capability.
SI-6(1)	Security function verification: Notification of failed security tests	Withdrawn: Incorporated into SI-6		

SI-6(2)	Security function verification: Automation support for distributed testing		Review documentation to determine the automated mechanisms in place for distributed security testing of system components and functions. Discuss with Security Officer, security staff, and System Owner.	*Examine:* System and information integrity policy; procedures addressing security function verification; information system design documentation; information system configuration settings and associated documentation; information system audit records; other relevant documents or records. *Interview:* Organizational personnel with security function verification responsibilities; organizational personnel implementing, operating, and maintaining the information system; system/network administrators; organizational personnel with information security responsibilities. *Test:* Organizational processes for security function verification; automated mechanisms supporting and/or implementing the management of distributed security testing.
SI-6(3)	Security function verification: Report verification results		Review documentation to ensure that appropriate interested security personnel receive results from security function testing and evaluations. Discuss with security staff, Security Officer, and System Owner.	*Examine:* System and information integrity policy; procedures addressing security function verification; information system design documentation; information system configuration settings and associated documentation; records of security function verification results; information system audit records; other relevant documents or records. *Interview:* Organizational personnel with security function verification responsibilities; organizational personnel with information security responsibilities. *Test:* Organizational processes for reporting security function verification results; automated mechanisms supporting and/or implementing the reporting of security function verification results.
SI-7	Software, firmware, and information integrity	SP 800-147, SP 800-155	Review documentation to determine the level and extent of software and firmware integrity checks employed by system. Test with sample code to ensure accuracy of checks and results reporting of integrity tools employed. Discuss with security staff, Security Officer, and System Owner.	*Examine:* System and information integrity policy; procedures addressing software, firmware, and information integrity; information system design documentation; information system configuration settings and associated documentation; integrity verification tools and associated documentation; records generated/triggered from integrity verification tools regarding unauthorized software, firmware, and information changes; information system audit records; other relevant documents or records. *Interview:* Organizational personnel with responsibility for software, firmware, and/or information integrity; organizational personnel with information security responsibilities; system/network administrators. *Test:* Software, firmware, and information integrity verification tools.

(Continued)

Control number	Control name	Assessment methods	Notes and guidance documents	SP 800-53A guidance
SI-7(1)	Software, firmware, and information integrity: Integrity checks	Review documentation to ensure that integrity check actions are used for all installations of SW and FW at critical points during process. Verify using test code during a test installation. Discuss with security staff, Security Officer, and System Owner.	SP 800-147, SP 800-155	*Examine:* System and information integrity policy; procedures addressing software, firmware, and information integrity; information system design documentation; information system configuration settings and associated documentation; integrity verification tools and associated documentation; records of integrity scans; other relevant documents or records *Interview:* Organizational personnel with responsibility for software, firmware, and / or information integrity; organizational personnel with information security responsibilities; system / network administrators; system developer. *Test:* Software, firmware, and information integrity verification tools.
SI-7(2)	Software, firmware, and information integrity: Automated notifications of integrity violations	Review documentation to ensure that integrity check tools provide automated reporting of integrity violations and notification of appropriate organizational personnel in a timely matter. Review reports and tool results to ensure reporting is provided. Discuss with operations staff, security staff, System Owner, and Security Officer.	SP 800-147, SP 800-155	*Examine:* System and information integrity policy; procedures addressing software, firmware, and information integrity; information system design documentation; information system configuration settings and associated documentation; integrity verification tools and associated documentation; records of integrity scans; automated tools supporting alerts and notifications for integrity discrepancies; alerts / notifications provided upon discovering discrepancies during integrity verifications; information system audit records; other relevant documents or records. *Interview:* Organizational personnel with responsibility for software, firmware, and / or information integrity; organizational personnel with information security responsibilities. *Test:* Software, firmware, and information integrity verification tools; automated mechanisms providing integrity discrepancy notifications.
SI-7(3)	Software, firmware, and information integrity: Centrally-managed integrity tools	Review documentation to determine the organizational use of centrally managed integrity check tools and techniques. Discuss with operations staff, security staff, Security Officer, and System Owner.	SP 800-147, SP 800-155	*Examine:* System and information integrity policy; procedures addressing software, firmware, and information integrity; information system design documentation; information system configuration settings and associated documentation; integrity verification tools and associated documentation; records of integrity scans; other relevant documents or records. *Interview:* Organizational personnel with responsibility for central management of integrity verification tools; organizational personnel with information security responsibilities. *Test:* Automated mechanisms

				supporting and/or implementing central management of integrity verification tools.
SI-7(4)	Security function verification: Tamper-evident packaging		Withdrawn: Incorporated into SA-12	
SI-7(5)	Software, firmware, and information integrity: Automated response to integrity violations	Review documentation to determine the organizational or system use of automatic response mechanisms to integrity violations. Such responses can include reversing the changes, halting the information system, or triggering audit alerts, when unauthorized modifications to critical security files occur. Verify response mechanisms with test code. Discuss with security staff, operations staff, Security Officer, and System Owner.	SP 800-147, SP 800-155	*Examine:* System and information integrity policy; procedures addressing software, firmware, and information integrity; information system design documentation; information system configuration settings and associated documentation; integrity verification tools and associated documentation; records of integrity scans; records of integrity checks and responses to integrity violations; information audit records; other relevant documents or records. *Interview:* Organizational personnel with responsibility for software, firmware, and/or information integrity; organizational personnel with information security responsibilities; system/network administrators; system developer. *Test:* Software, firmware, and information integrity verification tools; automated mechanisms providing an automated response to integrity violations; automated mechanisms supporting and/or implementing security safeguards to be implemented when integrity violations are discovered.
SI-7(6)	Software, firmware, and information integrity: Cryptographic protection	Review documentation to determine use of various cryptographic mechanisms used to protect files and code. Discuss with System Owner, Security Officer, and security staff.	SP 800-147, SP 800-155	*Examine:* System and information integrity policy; procedures addressing software, firmware, and information integrity; information system design documentation; information system configuration settings and associated documentation; cryptographic mechanisms and associated documentation; records of detected unauthorized changes to software, firmware, and information; information system audit records; other relevant documents or records. *Interview:* Organizational personnel with responsibility for software, firmware, and/or information integrity; organizational personnel with information security responsibilities; system/network administrators; system developer. *Test:* Software, firmware, and information integrity verification tools; cryptographic mechanisms implementing software, firmware, and information integrity.

(Continued)

Control number	Control name	Assessment methods	Notes and guidance documents	SP 800-53A guidance
SI-7(7)	Software, firmware, and information integrity: Integration of detection and response	Review documentation to ensure that detected events are tracked, monitored, corrected, and available for historical purposes by the organization or the system. Review reports and event logs to validate retention. Discuss with System Owner, Security Officer, and security staff.	SP 800-147, SP 800-155	*Examine:* System and information integrity policy; procedures addressing software, firmware, and information integrity; procedures addressing incident response; information system design documentation; information system configuration settings and associated documentation; incident response records; information audit records; other relevant documents or records. *Interview:* Organizational personnel with responsibility for software, firmware, and/or information integrity; organizational personnel with information security responsibilities; organizational personnel with incident response responsibilities. *Test:* Organizational processes for incorporating detection of unauthorized security relevant changes into the incident response capability; software, firmware, and information integrity verification tools; automated mechanisms supporting and/or implementing incorporation of detection of unauthorized security-relevant changes into the incident response capability.
SI-7(8)	Software, firmware, and information integrity: Auditing capability for significant events	Review documentation to determine the extent to which the organization reviews results of significant events for evaluation, auditing, and response efforts. Discuss with System Owner and Security Officer.	SP 800-147, SP 800-155	*Examine:* System and information integrity policy; procedures addressing software, firmware, and information integrity; information system design documentation; information system configuration settings and associated documentation; integrity verification tools and associated documentation; records of integrity scans; incident response records, list of security-relevant changes to the information system; automated tools supporting alerts and notifications if unauthorized security changes are detected; information system audit records; other relevant documents or records. *Interview:* Organizational personnel with responsibility for software, firmware, and/or information integrity; organizational personnel with information security responsibilities; system/network administrators; system developer. *Test:* Software, firmware, and information integrity verification tools; automated mechanisms supporting and/or implementing the capability to audit potential integrity violations; automated mechanisms supporting and/or implementing alerts about potential integrity violations.

SI-7(9)	Software, firmware, and information integrity: Verify boot process	Review documentation to determine how the organization or system only allows trusted code to be executed during boot processes. Discuss with System Owner, security staff, and Security Officer.	SP 800-147, SP 800-155	*Examine:* System and information integrity policy; procedures addressing software, firmware, and information integrity; information system design documentation; information system configuration settings and associated documentation; integrity verification tools and associated documentation; documentation; records of integrity verification scans; information system audit records; other relevant documents or records. *Interview:* Organizational personnel with responsibility for software, firmware, and/or information integrity; organizational personnel with information security responsibilities; system developer. *Test:* Software, firmware, and information integrity verification tools; automated mechanisms supporting and/or implementing integrity verification of the boot process.
SI-7(10)	Software, firmware, and information integrity: Protection of boot software	Review documentation to determine the organizational efforts to ensure that only allowable boot firmware is executed during startup of system. Unauthorized modifications to boot firmware may be indicative of a sophisticated, targeted cyber-attack. Review organizational implementation of specialized review processes found in SP 800-155. Discuss with System Owner, security staff, and Security Officer.	SP 800-147, SP 800-155	*Examine:* System and information integrity policy; procedures addressing software, firmware, and information integrity; information system design documentation; information system configuration settings and associated documentation; integrity verification tools and associated documentation; records of integrity verification scans; information system audit records; other relevant documents or records. *Interview:* Organizational personnel with responsibility for software, firmware, and/or information integrity; organizational personnel with information security responsibilities; system/ network administrators; system developer. *Test:* Software, firmware, and information integrity verification tools; automated mechanisms supporting and/or implementing protection of the integrity of boot firmware; safeguards implementing protection of the integrity of boot firmware.
SI-7(11)	Software, firmware, and information integrity: Confined environments with limited privileges	Review documentation to determine the extent that the organization limits user installation of suspect software. Ensure user installations occur in confined environments of operation to limit or contain damage from malicious code that may	SP 800-147, SP 800-155	*Examine:* System and information integrity policy; procedures addressing software, firmware, and information integrity; information system design documentation; information system configuration settings and associated documentation; information system audit records; other relevant documents or records. *Interview:* Organizational personnel with responsibility for software, firmware, and/or information integrity; organizational personnel with information security responsibilities. *Test:* Software, firmware, and information

(Continued)

Control number	Control name	Assessment methods	Notes and guidance documents	SP 800-53A guidance
		be executed. Discuss with operations staff, security staff, System Owner, and Security Officer.		integrity verification tools; automated mechanisms supporting and/or implementing execution of software in a confined environment (physical and/or virtual); automated mechanisms supporting and/or implementing limited privileges in the confined environment.
SI-7(12)	Software, firmware, and information integrity: Integrity verification	Review documentation to determine the organizational process for user installed software to verify the integrity of user-installed software prior to execution to reduce the likelihood of executing malicious code or code that contains errors from unauthorized modifications. Discuss with security staff, System Owner, and Security Officer.	SP 800-147, SP 800-155	*Examine:* System and information integrity policy; procedures addressing software, firmware, and information integrity; information system design documentation; information system configuration settings and associated documentation; integrity verification records; information system audit records; other relevant documents or records. *Interview:* Organizational personnel with responsibility for software, firmware, and/or information integrity; organizational personnel with information security responsibilities. *Test:* Software, firmware, and information integrity verification tools; automated mechanisms supporting and/or implementing verification of the integrity of user-installed software prior to execution.
SI-7(13)	Software, firmware, and information integrity: Code execution in protected environments	Review documentation of system control for all code execution action to ensure that all sources of binary or machine-executable code including, for example, commercial software/ firmware and open source software are controlled and verified. Discuss with Security Officer, security staff, and System Owner.	SP 800-147, SP 800-155	*Examine:* System and information integrity policy; procedures addressing software, firmware, and information integrity; information system design documentation; information system configuration settings and associated documentation; approval records for execution of binary and machine-executable code; information system audit records; other relevant documents or records. *Interview:* Organizational personnel with responsibility for software, firmware, and/ or information integrity; organizational personnel with information security responsibilities; system/network administrators; system developer. *Test:* Software, firmware, and information integrity verification tools; automated mechanisms supporting and/or implementing approvals for execution of binary or machine executable code.
SI-7(14)	Software, firmware, and information integrity: Binary or	Review documentation to determine how the organization limits the use	SP 800-147, SP 800-155	*Examine:* System and information integrity policy; procedures addressing software, firmware, and information integrity; information system design documentation; information system

	Control	Review Documentation	References	Assessment Procedures
	machine executable code	and execution of software and code with limited or no external verification testing results. Discuss with Security Officer and System Owner.		configuration settings and associated documentation; approval records for execution of binary and machine-executable code; information system audit records; other relevant documents or records. *Interview:* Organizational personnel with responsibility for software, firmware, and/or information integrity; organizational personnel with information security responsibilities; authorizing official; system/network administrators; system developer. *Test:* Automated mechanisms supporting and/or implementing prohibition of the execution of binary or machine-executable code.
SI-7(15)	Software, firmware, and information integrity: Code authentication	Review documentation to ensure that the organization uses only proper authenticated software and code on system. Code signing and cryptographic authentication are proper techniques for this process. Discuss with security staff, operations staff, System Owner, and Security Officer.	SP 800-147, SP 800-155	*Examine:* System and information integrity policy; procedures addressing software, firmware, and information integrity; information system design documentation; information system configuration settings and associated documentation; cryptographic mechanisms and associated documentation; information system audit records; other relevant documents or records. *Interview:* Organizational personnel with responsibility for software, firmware, and/or information integrity; organizational personnel with information security responsibilities; system/network administrators; system developer. *Test:* Cryptographic mechanisms authenticating software/firmware prior to installation.
SI-7(16)	Software, firmware, and information integrity: Time limit on process execution without supervision	Review documentation to determine the organizational process for which normal execution periods can be determined and situations, in which organizations exceed such periods. Discuss with System Owner and Security Officer.	SP 800-147, SP 800-155	*Examine:* System and information integrity policy; procedures addressing software and information integrity; information system design documentation; information system configuration settings and associated documentation; information system audit records; other relevant documents or records. *Interview:* Organizational personnel with responsibility for software, firmware, and/or information integrity; organizational personnel with information security responsibilities; system/network administrators; system developer. *Test:* Software, firmware, and information integrity verification tools; automated mechanisms supporting and/or implementing time limits on process execution without supervision.
SI-8	Spam protection	Review documentation to determine the spam protection mechanisms	SP 800-45	*Examine:* System and information integrity policy; configuration management policy and procedures (CM-1); procedures addressing spam protection; spam protection

(Continued)

Control number	Control name	Assessment methods	Notes and guidance documents	SP 800-53A guidance
		employed by the system on the entry and exit points, which could include, for example, firewalls, electronic mail servers, web servers, proxy servers, remote-access servers, workstations, mobile devices, and notebook/laptop computers. Discuss with System Owner, operations staff, security staff, and Security Officer.		mechanisms; records of spam protection updates; information system design documentation; information system configuration settings and associated documentation; information system audit records; other relevant documents or records. *Interview:* Organizational personnel with responsibility for spam protection; organizational personnel with information security responsibilities; system/network administrators; system developer. *Test:* Organizational processes for implementing spam protection; automated mechanisms supporting and/or implementing spam protection.
SI-8(1)	Spam protection: Central management	Review documentation to determine the level of organizational oversight and central management of all spam protection processes and mechanisms employed. Discuss with System Owner, operations staff, security staff, and Security Officer.	SP 800-45	*Examine:* System and information integrity policy; procedures addressing spam protection; spam protection mechanisms; information system design documentation; information system configuration settings and associated documentation; information system audit records; other relevant documents or records. *Interview:* Organizational personnel with responsibility for spam protection; organizational personnel with information security responsibilities; system/network administrators. *Test:* Organizational processes for central management of spam protection; automated mechanisms supporting and/or implementing central management of spam protection.
SI-8(2)	Spam protection: Automatic updates	Review documentation to ensure that all spam protection components employ automatic update features. Discuss with Security officer and System Owner.	SP 800-45	*Examine:* System and information integrity policy; procedures addressing spam protection; spam protection mechanisms; records of spam protection updates; information system design documentation; information system configuration settings and associated documentation; information system audit records; other relevant documents or records. *Interview:* Organizational personnel with responsibility for spam protection; organizational personnel with information security responsibilities; system/network administrators; system developer. *Test:* Organizational processes for spam protection; automated mechanisms supporting and/or implementing automatic updates to spam protection mechanisms.

SI-8(3)	Spam protection: Continuous learning capability	Review documentation to determine the extent, the spam protection process employs various continuous learning techniques, such as Bayesian filters that respond to user inputs, which identifies specific traffic as spam or legitimate by updating algorithm parameters and thereby more accurately separating types of traffic. Discuss with security staff, Security Officer, Security Engineer, and System Owner.	SP 800-45	*Examine:* System and information integrity policy; procedures addressing spam protection; spam protection mechanisms; information system design documentation; information system configuration settings and associated documentation; information system audit records; other relevant documents or records. *Interview:* Organizational personnel with responsibility for spam protection; organizational personnel with information security responsibilities; system/network administrators; system developer. *Test:* Organizational processes for spam protection; automated mechanisms supporting and/or implementing spam protection mechanisms with a learning capability.
SI-9	Information input restrictions		Withdrawn: Incorporated into AC-2, AC-3, AC-5, AC-6	
SI-10	Information input validation	Review documentation to determine the input validation checks performed by system upon data entry. Checking the valid syntax and semantics of information system inputs (e.g., character set, length, numerical range, and acceptable values) verifies that inputs match specified definitions for format and content. Text input process with various input anomalies to verify input validation processes employed by the system. Discuss with System Owner, Developers, security staff, and Security Officer.		*Examine:* System and information integrity policy; access control policy and procedures; separation of duties policy and procedures; procedures addressing information input validation; documentation for automated tools and applications to verify validity of information; list of information inputs requiring validity checks; information system design documentation; information system configuration settings and associated documentation; information system audit records; other relevant documents or records. *Interview:* Organizational personnel with responsibility for information input validation; organizational personnel with information security responsibilities; system/network administrators; system developer. *Test:* Automated mechanisms supporting and/or implementing validity checks on information inputs.

(Continued)

Control number	Control name	Assessment methods	Notes and guidance documents	SP 800-53A guidance
SI-10(1)	Information input validation: Manual override capability	Review documentation to determine the organizational implementation of manual override capabilities for any inputs into system. Review criteria and selection processes and procedures for manual override actions. Discuss with System Owner, operations staff, and Security Officer.		*Examine:* System and information integrity policy; access control policy and procedures; separation of duties policy and procedures; procedures addressing information input validation; information system design documentation; information system configuration settings and associated documentation; information system audit records; other relevant documents or records. *Interview:* Organizational personnel with responsibility for information input validation; organizational personnel with information security responsibilities; system/network administrators; system developer. *Test:* Organizational processes for use of manual override capability; automated mechanisms supporting and/or implementing manual override capability for input validation; automated mechanisms supporting and/or implementing auditing of the use of manual override capability.
SI-10(2)	Information input validation: Review/resolution of errors	Review documentation to evaluate processes and procedures for resolution of errors during input activities, to include correcting systemic causes of errors and resubmitting transactions with corrected input. Discuss with System Owner, Security Officer, and operations staff.		*Examine:* System and information integrity policy; access control policy and procedures; separation of duties policy and procedures; procedures addressing information input validation; information system design documentation; information system configuration settings and associated documentation; review records of information input validation errors and resulting resolutions; information input validation error logs or records; information system audit records; other relevant documents or records. *Interview:* Organizational personnel with responsibility for information input validation; organizational personnel with information security responsibilities; system/network administrators. *Test:* Organizational processes for review and resolution of input validation errors; automated mechanisms supporting and/or implementing review and resolution of input validation errors.
SI-10(3)	Information input validation: Predictable behavior	Review documentation to determine capabilities of the system to resolve issues correctly, when given incorrect inputs. Identify the expected and predictable		*Examine:* System and information integrity policy; procedures addressing information input validation; information system design documentation; information system configuration settings and associated documentation; information system audit records; other relevant documents or records. *Interview:* Organizational personnel with responsibility for information

input validation; organizational personnel with information security responsibilities; system/network administrators; system developer. *Test:* Automated mechanisms supporting and/or implementing predictable behavior when invalid inputs are received.

SI-10(4)	Information input validation: Review/timing interactions	behavior resultant from incorrect inputs. Test system with unexpected inputs and evaluate the results. Discuss with System Owner, Developers, and Security Officer. Review documentation to determine the organizational mechanism for handling and responding to timing of input actions, such as invalid information system inputs received across protocol interfaces, since this causes timing interactions become relevant, where one protocol needs to consider the impact of the error response on other protocols within the protocol stack. Test via test code inputs and review of outputs in response. Discuss with Security Officer, Developers, and System Owner.	*Examine:* System and information integrity policy; procedures addressing information input validation; information system design documentation; information system configuration settings and associated documentation; information system audit records; other relevant documents or records. *Interview:* Organizational personnel with responsibility for information input validation; organizational personnel with information security responsibilities; system/network administrators; system developer. *Test:* Organizational processes for determining appropriate responses to invalid inputs; automated mechanisms supporting and/or implementing responses to invalid inputs.
SI-10(5)	Information input validation: Restrict inputs to trusted sources and approved formats	Review documentation to ensure that the system provides for whitelisting (list of trusted sources and sites) of valid sources of inputs to system. Discuss with Security Officer and System Owner.	*Examine:* System and information integrity policy; procedures addressing information input validation; information system design documentation; information system configuration settings and associated documentation; list of trusted sources for information inputs; list of acceptable formats for input restrictions; information system audit records; other relevant documents or records. *Interview:* Organizational personnel with responsibility for information input validation; organizational personnel with information security responsibilities; system/network administrators; system developer. *Test:* Organizational processes for restricting information inputs; automated mechanisms supporting and/or implementing restriction of information inputs.

(Continued)

Control number	Control name	Assessment methods	Notes and guidance documents	SP 800-53A guidance
SI-11	Error handling	Review documentation for system to determine the error handling routines and messages for system and their required outputs to users. Ensure the structure/content of error messages only provides the needed information and not additional information, which can be used by malicious systems, programs, or attackers. Discuss with Developers, System Owner, and Security Officer.		*Examine:* System and information integrity policy; procedures addressing information system error handling; information system design documentation; information system configuration settings and associated documentation; documentation providing structure/content of error messages; information system audit records; other relevant documents or records. *Interview:* Organizational personnel with responsibility for information input validation; organizational personnel with information security responsibilities; system/network administrators; system developer. *Test:* Organizational processes for error handling; automated mechanisms supporting and/or implementing error handling; automated mechanisms supporting and/or implementing management of error messages.
SI-12	Information handling and retention	Review documentation to ensure that the system and organization is performing information handling and storage actions in compliance of data retention requirements, federal law requirements, and agency regulations. Discuss with System Owner, operations staff, and Security Officer.		*Examine:* System and information integrity policy; federal laws, Executive Orders, directives, policies, regulations, standards, and operational requirements applicable to information handling and retention; media protection policy and procedures; procedures addressing information system output handling and retention; information retention records, other relevant documents or records. *Interview:* Organizational personnel with responsibility for information handling and retention; organizational personnel with information security responsibilities/network administrators. *Test:* Organizational processes for information handling and retention; automated mechanisms supporting and/or implementing information handling and retention.
SI-13	Predictable failure prevention	Review documentation for the organization to determine documented status and repair reports for security equipment and components. Review potential failures of specific information system components that provide		*Examine:* System and information integrity policy; procedures addressing predictable failure prevention; information system design documentation; information system configuration settings and associated documentation; list of MTTF substitution criteria; information system audit records; other relevant documents or records. *Interview:* Organizational personnel with responsibility for MTTF determinations and activities; organizational personnel

with information security responsibilities; system/network administrators; organizational personnel with contingency planning responsibilities. *Test*: Organizational processes for managing MTTF.

		security capability documents and maintenance reports to ensure MTTF (Mean Time To Fail) is with requirements and specifications for the system and organization. Discuss with security staff, System Owner, and Security Officer.		
SI-13(1)	Predictable failure prevention: Transferring component responsibilities	Review documentation for the system to ensure that time limits are set and used for substitution of component functionality, when original system components are experiencing long repair times. Discuss with System Owner and Security Officer		*Examine*: System and information integrity policy; procedures addressing predictable failure prevention; information system design documentation; information system configuration settings and associated documentation; information system audit records; other relevant documents or records. *Interview*: Organizational personnel with responsibility for MTTF activities; organizational personnel with information security responsibilities; system/network administrators; organizational personnel with contingency planning responsibilities. *Test*: Organizational processes for managing MTTF; automated mechanisms supporting and/or implementing transfer of component responsibilities to substitute components.
SI-13(2)	Predictable failure prevention: Time limit on process execution without supervision		Withdrawn: Incorporated into SI-7(16)	
SI-13(3)	Predictable failure prevention: Manual transfer between components	Review documentation to ensure that the organization invokes transfers to standby system or components, if primary component is experiencing long repair times. Discuss with System Owner and Security Officer.		*Examine*: System and information integrity policy; procedures addressing predictable failure prevention; information system design documentation; information system configuration settings and associated documentation; information system audit records; other relevant documents or records. *Interview*: Organizational personnel with responsibility for MTTF activities; organizational personnel with information security responsibilities; system/network administrators; organizational personnel with contingency planning responsibilities. *Test*: Organizational processes for managing MTTF and conducting the manual transfer between active and standby components.

(Continued)

Control number	Control name	Assessment methods	Notes and guidance documents	SP 800-53A guidance
SI-13(4)	Predictable failure prevention: Standby component installation/ notification	Review documentation to ensure that the process for automated or manual transfers of components are defined and instituted, when required. Discuss with System Owner, operations staff, and Security Officer.		*Examine:* System and information integrity policy; procedures addressing predictable failure prevention; information system design documentation; information system configuration settings and associated documentation; list of actions to be taken once information system component failure is detected; information system audit records; other relevant documents or records. *Interview:* Organizational personnel with responsibility for MTTF activities; organizational personnel with information security responsibilities; system/network administrators; organizational personnel with contingency planning responsibilities. *Test:* Organizational processes for managing MTTF; automated mechanisms supporting and/or implementing transparent installation of standby components; automated mechanisms supporting and/or implementing alarms or system shutdown if component failures are detected.
SI-13(5)	Predictable failure prevention: Failover capability	Review documentation to ensure that the process for automated failover transfers of components are defined and instituted, when required. Discuss with System Owner, operations staff, and Security Officer.		*Examine:* System and information integrity policy; procedures addressing predictable failure prevention; information system design documentation; information system configuration settings and associated documentation; documentation describing failover capability provided for the information system; information system audit records; other relevant documents or records. *Interview:* Organizational personnel with responsibility for failover capability; organizational personnel with information security responsibilities; system/network administrators; organizational personnel with contingency planning responsibilities. *Test:* Organizational processes for managing failover capability; automated mechanisms supporting and/or implementing failover capability.
SI-14	Nonpersistence	Review documentation of the organization to ensure that the nonpersistence of select components of system is performed. This risk from advanced persistent threats (APTs) is treated by		*Examine:* System and information integrity policy; procedures addressing nonpersistence for information system components; information system design documentation; information system configuration settings and associated documentation; information system audit records; other relevant documents or records. *Interview:* Organizational personnel with responsibility for nonpersistence;

		significantly reducing the targeting capability of adversaries (i.e., window of opportunity and available attack surface) to initiate and complete cyber-attacks. Ensure system performs nonpersistence by evaluating logs for system, monitoring reports for select components, and access logs for user activities. Discuss with System Owner, security staff, and Security Officer.	organizational personnel with information security responsibilities; system/network administrators; system developer. *Test:* Automated mechanisms supporting and/or implementing initiation and termination of nonpersistent components.
SI-14(1)	Nonpersistence: Refresh from trusted sources	Review documentation for the system to ensure that refresh actions for system are performed with software/data from write-once, read-only media (WORM) or from selected off-line secure storage facilities. Discuss with System Owner, Security Officer, and security staff.	*Examine:* System and information integrity policy; procedures addressing nonpersistence for information system components; information system design documentation; information system configuration settings and associated documentation; information system audit records; other relevant documents or records. *Interview:* Organizational personnel with responsibility for obtaining component and service refreshes from trusted sources; organizational personnel with information security responsibilities. *Test:* Organizational processes for defining and obtaining component and service refreshes from trusted sources; automated mechanisms supporting and/or implementing component and service refreshes.
SI-15	Information output filtering	Review documentation for the system and organization to ensure that the monitoring of outputs from system are consistently being performed to detect extraneous content, preventing such extraneous content from being displayed, and alerting monitoring tools that anomalous behavior has been discovered. Discuss with	*Examine:* System and information integrity policy; procedures addressing information output filtering; information system design documentation; information system configuration settings and associated documentation; information system audit records; other relevant documents or records. *Interview:* Organizational personnel with responsibility for validating information output; organizational personnel with information security responsibilities; system/network administrators; system developer. *Test:* Organizational processes for validating information output; automated mechanisms supporting and/or implementing information output validation.

(Continued)

Control number	Control name	Assessment methods	Notes and guidance documents	SP 800-53A guidance
SI-16	Memory protection	System Owner, operations staff, security staff, and Security Officer. Review documentation to ensure that the system provides memory protection methods to prevent unauthorized code execution. These techniques, such as data execution prevention and address space layout randomization are tested for proper execution via sample test injection tests and subsequent evaluations of results. Discuss with System Owner, security staff, and Security Officer.		*Examine:* System and information integrity policy; procedures addressing memory protection for the information system; information system design documentation; information system configuration settings and associated documentation; list of security safeguards protecting information system memory from unauthorized code execution; information system audit records; other relevant documents or records. *Interview:* Organizational personnel with responsibility for memory protection; organizational personnel with information security responsibilities; system/network administrators; system developer. *Test:* Automated mechanisms supporting and/or implementing safeguards to protect information system memory from unauthorized code execution.
SI-17	Fail-safe procedures	Review documentation to determine failure modes for system and actions to be taken as result of failure, such as do nothing, reestablish system settings, shut down processes, restart the system, or contact designated organizational personnel. Test system by causing an interruption of processing, correlated with operations, to evaluation failure techniques and actions of system. Discuss with operations staff, System Owner, security staff, and Security Officer.		*Examine:* System and information integrity policy; procedures addressing memory protection for the information system; information system design documentation; information system configuration settings and associated documentation; list of security safeguards protecting information system memory from unauthorized code execution; information system audit records; other relevant documents or records. *Interview:* Organizational personnel with responsibility for fail-safe procedures; organizational personnel with information security responsibilities; system/network administrators; system developer. *Test:* Organizational fail-safe procedures; automated mechanisms supporting and/or implementing fail-safe procedures.

S. *Privacy controls*

    a. SP 800-53, rev.4

Appendix J of the SP 800-53 rev. 4 contains the recommended privacy controls for the US Governmental systems broken out into 8 families of 26 specific privacy controls. These controls address the confidentiality and the integrity concerns for assessors to review and test against with respect to information privacy on the data retained by the system under review.

Control number	Control name	Assessment methods	Notes and guidance documents
AP-1	Authority to collect	Review documentation for the organization to determine legal and organizational requirements for PII collection. Ensure organization has assigned senior privacy official for organization and review their authorities and responsibilities. Ensure all privacy-related documentation is filed with appropriate external agencies. Discuss with System Owner, Senior Privacy Official, and Security Officer.	Privacy Act, E-Government Act, A-130, Appendix I
AP-2	Purpose specification	Review documentation to ensure the organization describes the purpose(s) for which personally identifiable information (PII) is collected, used, maintained, and shared in its privacy notices and public documents. Ensure all privacy documents are completed and filed appropriately, such as PTAs, PIAs, and SORNs. Discuss with Senior Privacy Official, System Owner, and Security Officer.	Privacy Act, E-Government Act, A-130, Appendix I
AR-1	Governance and privacy program	Review documentation for organization to ensure the Privacy plan encompasses all privacy considerations, plans, processes, policies and procedures for handling privacy-related information. Discuss with System Owner, Senior Privacy Official, and Security Officer.	Privacy Act, E-Government Act, FISMA, A-130, Appendix I, OMB M-03-22, OMB M-05-08, OMB M-07-16
AR-2	Privacy impact and risk assessment	Review documentation to ensure the organization has completed all privacy risk assessments, privacy threshold analysis documents and privacy impact analysis forms and documents. Review documents for completeness and accuracy. Discuss with Senior Privacy Official, Security Officer, and System Owner.	E-Government Act, FISMA, OMB M-03-22, OMB M-05-08, OMB 10-23, SP 800-30, rev. 1
AR-3	Privacy Requirements for contractors and service providers	Review documentation for organization to ensure all contracting actions, acquisition processes and contractors to organization are instructed in, advised on, and abide by all privacy regulations and guidance for the organization. Discuss with Senior Privacy Official, Acquisition staff, Security Officer, and System Owner.	Privacy Act, FAR, DFAR

(Continued)

Control number	Control name	Assessment methods	Notes and guidance documents
AR-4	Privacy monitoring and auditing	Review documentation for the organization to ensure monitoring of the privacy program and the auditing of the PII utilization is in accordance with federal guidelines and requirements. Review results with System Owner, Senior Privacy Official, and Security Officer.	Privacy Act, E-Government Act, FISMA, A-130, OMB M-03-22, OMB M-05-08, OMB M-07-16, OMB 10-23
AR-5	Privacy awareness and training	Review documentation for proof of training events and activities for all users of system which contains Privacy topics and overviews. Ensure all users receive training through review of training records, online tracking systems and review of educational materials. Discuss with Senior Privacy Official, System Owner, operations staff, and Security Officer.	Privacy Act, FISMA, OMB M-03-22, OMB M-07-16
AR-6	Privacy reporting	Review documentation to ensure all reporting requirements and needs are met and continue throughout the lifecycle of system. Ensure all reports contain correct and accurate data via sampling of reports and criteria from external agency. Discuss with Senior Privacy Official, System Owner, operations staff, Security Officer.	Privacy Act, E-Government Act, FISMA, 9/11 Commission Act, OMB A-130, OMB M-03-22
AR-7	Privacy-enhanced system design and development	Review documentation to verify system has automated privacy controls for the collection, use, retention, and disclosure of personally identifiable information (PII). Ensure automatic controls are appropriate, valid and functional. Discuss with security staff, operations staff, System Owner, Senior Privacy Official, and Security Officer.	Privacy Act, E-Government Act, OMB M-03-22
AR-8	Accounting of disclosures	Review documentation to ensure required accountings of disclosures of records are being properly maintained and provided to persons named in those records consistent with the dictates of the Privacy Act. Review criteria for reporting, based on agency requirements, and ensure organization fulfills these requirements when necessary. Discuss with Senior Privacy Official, System Owner, operations staff and Security Officer.	Privacy Act
DI-1	Data quality	Review documentation to determine the extent the organization reviews and updates the PII retained in system for accuracy, relevance, timeliness, and completeness of that information. Ensure documentation and reporting reflects actions for quality control of retained PII. Discuss with operations staff, Senior Privacy Official, System Owner, and Security Officer.	Privacy Act, Paperwork Reduction Act, OMB M-07-16
DI-1(1)	Data quality: Validate PII	Review documentation to ensure sensitive data quality requirements are reviewed, validated, and instituted by organization. Discuss with Senior Privacy Official, operations staff, Security Officer, and System Owner.	Privacy Act, Paperwork Reduction Act, OMB M-07-16

Control number	Control name	Assessment methods	Notes and guidance documents
DI-1(2)	Data quality: Revalidate PII	Review documentation to ensure sensitive data quality requirements are revalidated by organization on a periodic basis. Discuss with Senior Privacy Official, operations staff, Security Officer, and System Owner.	Privacy Act, Paperwork Reduction Act, OMB M-07-16
DI-2	Data integrity and data integrity board	Review documentation to ensure organization institutes security controls for integrity of PII and creates a data integrity board for PII oversight. Discuss with Senior Privacy Official, System Owner, operations staff, and Security Officer.	Privacy Act, Computer Matching and Privacy Protection Act, OMB A-130, App I
DI-2(1)	Data integrity and data integrity board: Publish agreements on website	Review documentation to ensure organization publishes all computer matching agreements on its public website. Observe agreements posted on website to validate compliance. Discuss with System Owner and Security Officer.	Privacy Act, Computer Matching and Privacy Protection Act, OMB A-130, App I
DM-1	Minimization of personally identifiable information	Review documentation for organization to ensure minimization of retrieved and retained PII is maintained and documented. Ensure organization periodically reviews amount of retained PII and performs minimization when possible. Discuss with Senior Privacy Official, System Owner, operations staff, and Security Officer.	Privacy Act, E-Government Act, OMB M-03-22, OMB M-07-16, NISTIR 8053
DM-1(1)	Minimization of personally identifiable information: Locate/ Remove/ Redact/ Anonymize PII	Review documentation to ensure location and redacting of PII is performed whenever possible in accordance with federal standards and agency requirements. Discuss PII redaction and anonymization efforts with Senior Privacy official, operations staff, System Owner, and Security Officer.	Privacy Act, E-Government Act, OMB M-03-22, OMB M-07-16, SP 800-122, NISTIR 8053
DM-2	Data retention and disposal	Review documentation to ensure organization retains and disposes of PII information utilizing proper agency procedures and policies and in accordance with federal guidelines. Ensure data is stored on appropriate media and marked correctly. Discuss with System Owner, Senior Privacy Official, Security Officer, and operations staff.	Privacy Act, E-Government Act, OMB M-07-16, SP 800-88, NISTIR 8053, NARA Record Retention regulations
DM-2(1)	Data retention and disposal: System configuration	Review documentation for organization to ensure all PII data identified and recorded to include the date PII is collected, created, or updated and when PII is to be deleted or archived. Test the system configuration settings by observing the actual configurations and their system implementation within the organizational system. Discuss with System Owner, Security Officer, operations staff, and security staff.	Privacy Act, E-Government Act, OMB M-07-16, SP 800-88, NISTIR 8053, NARA Record Retention regulations

(*Continued*)

Control number	Control name	Assessment methods	Notes and guidance documents
DM-3	Minimization of PII used in testing, training, and research	Review documentation for organization to ensure use of PII data is minimized during testing and training efforts. Organizations often use PII for testing new applications or information systems prior to deployment, and this practice needs to be reviewed closely to ensure no release of live data occurs during testing, research efforts and training. Discuss with Senior Privacy Official, operations staff, development staff, Security Officer, and System Owner.	SP 800-122
DM-3(1)	Minimization of PII used in testing, training, and research: Risk minimization techniques	Revie documentation to ensure organization uses de-identification techniques to minimize the risk to privacy of using PII for research, testing, or training where and when possible. Discuss with Senior Privacy Official, System Owner, development staff, operations staff, and Security Officer.	SP 800-122, NISTIR 8053, SP 800-82
IP-1	Consent	Review documentation for organization to ensure the practice of obtaining consent to PII collection and data retention is documented for all data and information retained by system. Ensure review of the methods of obtaining consent through opt-in, opt-out, or implied consent are documented, approved and implemented for all users and objects of the system. Review with Senior Privacy Official, System Owner, Security Officer, and operations staff	Privacy Act, E-Government Act, OMB M-03-22, OMB M-10-22
IP-1(1)	Consent: Mechanisms supporting itemized or tiered consent	Review documentation to ensure the organizational process for consent includes options for individuals' itemized choices as to whether they wish to be contacted for any of a variety of purposes. Ensure all policies and procedures for this process are documented and implemented. Discuss with Senior Privacy Official, System Owner, Security Officer, and operations staff.	E-Government Act, Privacy Act, OMB M-03-22, OMB 10-22
IP-2	Individual access	Review documentation to ensure organization enacts methods and techniques for individuals the ability to review PII about them held within organizational systems of records. Ensure all processes and requests for access are processed and appropriately adjudicated by organization. Discuss with System Owner, Security Officer, operations staff, and Senior Privacy Official.	Privacy Act, OMB A-130
IP-3	Redress	Review documentation to ensure organization provides the ability of individuals to ensure the accuracy of PII held by organizations. Effective redress processes demonstrate organizational commitment to data quality especially in those business functions where inaccurate data may result in inappropriate decisions or denial of benefits and services to individuals. This review includes review of PII retention and organizations options for correction or amendment of records of individuals. Discuss with Senior Privacy Official, System Owner, operations staff, legal staff, and Security Officer.	Privacy Act, OMB A-130

Control number	Control name	Assessment methods	Notes and guidance documents
IP-4	Complaint management	Review documentation for organization to ensure all complaints are handled correctly and in accordance with documented procedures. This ability of individuals to ensure the accuracy of PII held by organizations is considered important to help define the effective redress processes which demonstrate organizational commitment to data quality especially in those business functions where inaccurate data may result in inappropriate decisions or denial of benefits and services to individuals. Review and discuss these processes with the Senior Privacy Official, operations staff, legal staff, System Owner, and Security Officer.	OMB A-130, OMB M-07-16, OMB M-08-09
IP-4(1)	Complaint management: Response times	Review documentation to ensure tracking mechanisms to ensure that all complaints received are reviewed and appropriately addressed in a timely manner and appropriate time-frame. Discuss with Senior Privacy Official, operations staff, System Owner, and Security Officer.	OMB A-130, OMB M-07-16, OMB M-08-09
SE-1	Inventory of personally identifiable information	Review documentation to ensure a full and accurate inventory of all PII retained within system is maintained for its accuracy, currency and completeness. Review and discuss with Senior Privacy Official, System Owner, Security Officer, and operations staff.	Privacy Act, E-Government Act, FIPS-199, OMB M-03-22, SP 800-37, rev. 1, SP 800-122
SE-2	Privacy incident response	Review documentation to ensure Incident Response efforts include focus on only those incidents that relate to personally identifiable information (PII). Discuss with operations staff, security staff, Senior Privacy Official, System Owner, and Security Officer.	Privacy Act, FISMA, OMB M-06-19, OMB M-07-16, SP 800-37, rev. 1, SP 800-651, rev. 2
TR-1	Privacy notice	Review documentation to ensure all PII collection is given effective notice to all individuals. Effective notice, by virtue of its clarity, readability, and comprehensiveness, enables individuals to understand how an organization uses PII generally and, where appropriate, to make an informed decision prior to providing PII to an organization. Discuss with System Owner, Security Officer, operations staff, and Senior Privacy Official	Privacy Act, E-Government Act, OMB M-03-22, OMB M-07-16, OMB M-10-22, OMB M-10-23, ISE Guidelines
TR-1(1)	Privacy notice: Real-time or layered notice	Review documentation to ensure appropriate notice is gen at time of collection. Real-time notice is defined as notice at the point of collection. A layered notice approach involves providing individuals with a summary of key points in the organization's privacy policy. Discuss with Senior Privacy Official, operations staff, legal staff, System Owner, and Security Officer.	Privacy Act, E-Government Act, OMB M-03-22, OMB M-07-16, OMB M-10-22, OMB M-10-23, ISE Guidelines

(Continued)

Control number	Control name	Assessment methods	Notes and guidance documents
TR-2	System of records notices and privacy act statements	Review documentation to ensure organizational filing of SORN are accomplished successfully and timely. The organization is required to publish System of Records Notices (SORNs) in the Federal Register, subject to required oversight processes, for systems containing personally identifiable information (PII). Review process, documents and approvals for SORN actions and activities. Discuss with Approving Official (AO), Senior Privacy Official, System Owner, and Security Officer.	Privacy Act, OMB A-130
TR-2(1)	System of records notices and privacy act statements: Public website publication	Review documentation to ensure all SORNs are published publically on agency website for public review. Discuss with Senior Privacy Official, System Owner, operations staff, and Security Officer.	Privacy Act, OMB A-130
TR-3	Dissemination of privacy program information	Review documentation to ensure organization provides the public with information on the privacy requirements and standards it maintains and follows. Method of dissemination include, but not limited to, privacy impact assessments (PIAs), SORNs, privacy reports, publicly available web pages, email distributions, blogs, and periodic publications (e.g., quarterly newsletters). Ensure documents are publically available and verified. Discuss with Senior Privacy Official, System Owner, operations staff, and Security Officer.	Privacy Act, E-Government Act, OMB M-03-22, OMB M-10-23
UL-1	Internal use	Review documentation to ensure all PII in system is used only for authorized and documented usage within the organization. Discuss with Senior Privacy Official, System Owner, operations staff, security staff, legal staff, and Security Officer.	Privacy Act
UL-2	Information sharing with third parties	Review documentation to ensure only approved and appropriate usage of PII is subject to information sharing with other agencies and this external sharing of PII, including with other public, international, or private sector entities, will be consistent with uses described in the existing organizational public notice(s). Discuss with Senior Privacy Official, operations staff, legal staff, System Owner, and Security Officer.	Privacy Act, ISE Guidelines

T. *DOD specific controls*

All DOD security controls from DODI 8500.2 have now been replaced with the SP 800-53, rev. 4 controls throughout all of the services. The DOD RMF transition process for the controls is automated under the DISA E-MASS tool and the controls are defined and discussed on the RMF Knowledge Service run by DISA and OSD. The site is DOD specific and requires a DOD-PKI cert in order to obtain the DOD versions of the SP 800-53 controls and the site is at https://rmfks.osd.mil

U. *DHS EBK controls*

a. Application security family

The primary assessment areas for these controls include:
- ☐ Evaluate security requirements during software development activities on a system
- ☐ Review processes that translate security requirements into application design elements
- ☐ Audit mechanisms that govern the development of secure code and exploit mitigation

b. Data security family
The primary assessment areas for these controls include:
- ☐ Review controls that facilitate the necessary levels of confidentiality of information found within the organization's information system
- ☐ Evaluate safeguards in the system that facilitate the necessary levels of integrity of information found within information systems
- ☐ Audit controls that facilitate the necessary levels of availability of information and information systems

c. Regulatory and standards compliance family

The primary assessment areas for these controls include:
- ☐ Audit strategies for compliance with the organization's information security program
- ☐ Identify and stay current on all laws, regulations, standards, and best practices applicable to the organization
- ☐ Establish relationships with all regulatory information security organizations and appropriate industry groups, forums, and stakeholders
- ☐ Keep informed on pending information security changes, trends, and best practices by participating in collaborative settings
- ☐ Review information security compliance performance measurement components

V. *ISO 27001/27002 specific controls*

There are 114 controls in 14 groups

a. Information security policies – 2 controls
Management should define a set of policies to clarify their direction of, and support for, information security. At the top level, there should be an overall "information security policy."

b. Organization of information security – 7 controls

The organization should define the roles and responsibilities for information security, and allocate them to assigned individuals. Where relevant, duties should be segregated across roles and individuals to avoid potential conflicts of interest and prevent inappropriate activities, such as fraud and collusion. There should be contacts with relevant external authorities on information security matters. Information security should be an integral part of the management of all types of project. There should be security policies and controls for mobile devices and teleworking.

c. Human resources security – 6 controls

Security responsibilities should be taken into account when recruiting permanent employees, contractors and temporary staff (e.g., through adequate job descriptions, pre-employment screening, and background checks) and included in contracts (e.g., terms and conditions of employment and other signed agreements (such as Nondisclosure agreements [NDAs]) on security roles and responsibilities). Managers should ensure that employees and contractors are made aware of and motivated to comply with their information security obligations. A formal disciplinary process is necessary to define and handle information security breaches. Security aspects of a person's exit from the organization or significant changes of roles should be managed, such as returning corporate information and equipment in their possession, updating their access rights, and reminding them of their ongoing obligations under privacy laws, contractual terms, etc.

d. Asset management – 10 controls

All information assets should be inventoried and owners should be identified to be held accountable for their security. "Acceptable use" policies should be defined, and assets should be returned when people leave the organization. Information should be classified and labeled by its owners according to the security protection needed, and handled appropriately. Information storage media should be managed, controlled, moved, and disposed of in such a way that the information content is not compromised.

e. Access control – 14 controls

The organization's requirements to control access to information assets should be clearly documented in an access control policy and procedures. Network access and connections should be restricted. The allocation of access rights to users should be controlled from the initial user registration through the removal of access rights when it is no longer required. This includes special restrictions for privileged access rights and the management of passwords. Plus, regular reviews and updates of access rights. Users should be made aware of their responsibilities toward maintaining effective access controls, for example, choosing strong passwords and keeping them confidential. Information access should be restricted in accordance with the access control policy, for example, through secure log-on, password management, control over privileged utilities, and restricted access to program source code.

f. Cryptography – 2 controls

There should be a policy on the use of encryption, plus cryptographic authentication, and integrity controls such as digital signatures and message authentication codes, and cryptographic key management.

g. Physical and environmental security – 15 controls

Defined physical perimeters and barriers, with physical entry controls and working procedures, should protect the premises, offices, rooms, delivery/loading areas etc. against unauthorized access. Specialist advice should be sought regarding protection against fires, floods, earthquakes, bombs, etc. "Equipment" (meaning ICT equipment, mostly) plus supporting utilities (such as power and air conditioning) and cabling should be secured and maintained. Equipment and information should not be taken off-site unless authorized, and must be adequately protected both on and off-site. Information must be destroyed prior to storage media being disposed of or reused. Unattended equipment must be secured and there should be a clear desk and clear screen policy.

h. Operations security – 14 controls

IT operating responsibilities and procedures should be documented. Changes to IT facilities and systems should be controlled. Capacity and performance should be managed. Development, test, and operational systems should be separated. Malware controls are required, including user awareness. Appropriate backups should be taken and retained in accordance with a backup policy. System user and administrator/operator activities, exceptions, faults, and information security events should be logged and protected. Clocks should be synchronized. Software installation on operational systems should be controlled. Technical vulnerabilities should be patched, and there should be rules in place governing software installation by users. IT audits should be planned and controlled to minimize adverse effects on production systems, or inappropriate data access.

i. Communications security – 7 controls

Networks and network services should be secured, for example, by segregation. There should be policies, procedures, and agreements (e.g., nondisclosure agreements) concerning information transfer to/from third parties, including electronic messaging.

j. System acquisition, development, and maintenance – 13 controls

Security control requirements should be analyzed and specified, including web applications and transactions. Rules governing secure software/systems development should be defined as policy. Changes to systems (both applications and operating systems) should be controlled. Software packages should ideally not be modified, and secure system engineering principles should be followed. The development environment should be secured, and outsourced development should be controlled. System security should be tested and acceptance criteria defined to include security aspects. Test data should be carefully selected/generated and controlled.

k. Supplier relationships – 5 controls

There should be policies, procedures, awareness etc., to protect the organization's information that is accessible to IT outsourcers and other external suppliers throughout the supply chain, agreed within the contracts or agreements. Service delivery by external suppliers should be monitored, and reviewed/audited against the contracts/agreements. Service changes should be controlled.

l. Information security incident management – 7 controls

There should be responsibilities and procedures to manage (report, assess, respond to, and learn from) information security events, incidents, and weaknesses consistently and effectively, and to collect forensic evidence.

m. Business continuity management – 4 controls

The continuity of information security should be planned, implemented, and reviewed as an integral part of the organization's business continuity management systems. IT facilities should have sufficient redundancy to satisfy availability requirements.

n. Compliance – 8 controls

The organization must identify and document its obligations to external authorities and other third parties in relation to information security, including intellectual property, [business] records, privacy/personally identifiable information, and cryptography. The organization's information security arrangements should be independently reviewed (audited) and reported to management. Managers should also routinely review employees' and systems' compliance with security policies, procedures etc. and initiate corrective actions where necessary.

The following spreadsheet lists each of the ISO controls along with the corresponding SP 800-53 control(s) associated with the ISO control. This table, from Appendix H of SP 800-53, provides the correlating test criteria for each control. There are many ISO controls, which cover more than 1 SP 800-53 control, which means when you test these controls, you must review all controls for full evaluation needs. Following the assessment criteria for the SP 800-53 controls will provide an almost complete evaluation criterion, but there are a few controls, which require additional areas for testing. The reference "A." number (i.e., A.6.1.2) in front of the control refers to the ISO 27001 number.

ISO/IEC 27001 controls	NIST SP 800-53 controls
A.5 Information Security Policies	
A.5.1 Management direction for information security	
A.5.1.1 Policies for information security	All XX-1 controls
A.5.1.2 Review of the policies for information security	All XX-1 controls
A.6 Organization of information security	
A.6.1 Internal organization	
A.6.1.1 Information security roles and responsibilities	All XX-1 controls, CM-9, CP-2, PS-7, SA-3, SA-9, PM-2, PM-10
A.6.1.2 Segregation of duties	AC-5
A.6.1.3 Contact with authorities	IR-6
A.6.1.4 Contact with special interest groups	SI-5, PM-15
A.6.1.5 Information security in project management	SA-3, SA-9, SA-15
A.6.2 Mobile devices and teleworking	
A.6.2.1 Mobile device policy	AC-17, AC-18, AC-19
A.6.2.2 Teleworking	AC-3, AC-17, PE-17
A.7 Human Resources Security	
A.7.1 Prior to Employment	
A.7.1.1 Screening	PS-3, SA-21

ISO/IEC 27001 controls	NIST SP 800-53 controls
A.7.1.2 Terms and conditions of employment	PL-4, PS-6
A.7.2 During employment	
A.7.2.1 Management responsibilities	PL-4, PS-6, PS-7, SA-9
A.7.2.2 Information security awareness, education, and training	AT-2, AT-3, CP-3, IR-2, PM-13
A.7.2.3 Disciplinary process	PS-8
A.7.3 Termination and change of employment	
A.7.3.1 Termination or change of employment responsibilities	PS-4, PS-5
A.8 Asset Management	
A.8.1 Responsibility for assets	
A.8.1.1 Inventory of assets	CM-8
A.8.1.2 Ownership of assets	CM-8
A.8.1.3 Acceptable use of assets	PL-4
A.8.1.4 Return of assets	PS-4, PS-5
A.8.2 Information Classification	
A.8.2.1 Classification of information	RA-2
A.8.2.2 Labelling of Information	MP-3
A.8.2.3 Handling of Assets	MP-2, MP-4, MP-5, MP-6, MP-7, PE-16, PE-18, PE-20, SC-8, SC-28
A.8.3 Media Handling	
A.8.3.1 Management of removable media	MP-2, MP-4, MP-5, MP-6, MP-7
A.8.3.2 Disposal of media	MP-6
A.8.3.3 Physical media transfer	MP-5
A.9 Access Control	
A.9.1 Business requirement of access control	
A.9.1.1 Access control policy	AC-1
A.9.1.2 Access to networks and network services	AC-3, AC-6
A.9.2 User access management	
A.9.2.1 User registration and de-registration	AC-2, IA-2, IA-4, IA-5, IA-8
A.9.2.2 User access provisioning	AC-2
A.9.2.3 Management of privileged access rights	AC-2, AC-3, AC-6, CM-5
A.9.2.4 Management of secret authentication information of users	IA-5
A.9.2.5 Review of user access rights	AC-2
A.9.2.6 Removal or adjustment of access rights	AC-2

(Continued)

ISO/IEC 27001 controls	NIST SP 800-53 controls
A.9.3 User responsibilities	
A.9.3.1 Use of secret authentication information	IA-5
A.9.4 System and application access control	
A.9.4.1 Information access restriction	AC-3, AC-24
A.9.4.2 Secure logon procedures	AC-7, AC-8, AC-9, IA-6
A.9.4.3 Password management system	IA-5
A.9.4.4 Use of privileged utility programs	AC-3, AC-6
A.9.4.5 Access control to program source code	AC-3, AC-6, CM-5
A.10 Cryptography	
A.10.1 Cryptographic controls	
A.10.1.1 Policy on the use of cryptographic controls	SC-13
A.10.1.2 Key Management	SC-12, SC-17
A.11 Physical and environmental security	
A.11.1 Secure areas	
A.11.1.1 Physical security perimeter	PE-3*
A.11.1.2 Physical entry controls	PE-2, PE-3, PE-4, PE-5
A.11.1.3 Securing offices, rooms and facilities	PE-3, PE-5
A.11.1.4 Protecting against external and environmental threats	CP-6, CP-7, PE-9, PE-13, PE-14, PE-15, PE-18, PE-19
A.11.1.5 Working in secure areas	SC-42(3)*
A.11.1.6 Delivery and loading areas	PE-16
A.11.2 Equipment	
A.11.2.1 Equipment siting and protection	PE-9, PE-13, PE-14, PE-15, PE-18, PE-19
A.11.2.2 Supporting utilities	CP-8, PE-9, PE-10, PE-11, PE-12, PE-14, PE-15
A.11.2.3 Cabling security	PE-4, PE-9
A.11.2.4 Equipment maintenance	MA-2, MA-6
A.11.2.5 Removal of assets	MA-2, MP-5, PE-16
A.11.2.6 Security of equipment and assets off-premises	AC-19, AC-20, MP-5, PE-17
A.11.2.7 Secure disposal or reuse of equipment	MP-6
A.11.2.8 Unattended user equipment	AC-11
A.11.2.9 Clear desk and clear screen policy	AC-11, MP-2, MP-4
A.12 Operations security	
A.12.1 Operational procedures and responsibilities	
A.12.1.1 Documented operating procedures	All XX-1 controls, SA-5
A.12.1.2 Change management	CM-3, CM-5, SA-10
A.12.1.3 Capacity management	AU-4, CP-2(2), SC-5(2)
A.12.1.4 Separation of development, testing, and operational environments	CM-4(1)*, CM-5*

ISO/IEC 27001 controls	NIST SP 800-53 controls
A.12.2 Protection from malware	
A.12.2.1 Controls against malware	AT-2, SI-3
A.12.3 Backup	
A.12.3.1 Information backup	CP-9
A.12.4 Logging and monitoring	
A.12.4.1 Event logging	AU-3, AU-6, AU-11, AU-12, AU-14
A.12.4.2 Protection of log information	AU-9
A.12.4.3 Administrator and operator logs	AU-9, AU-12
A.12.4.4 Clock synchronization	AU-8
A.12.5 Control of operational software	
A.12.5.1 Installation of software on operational systems	CM-5, CM-7(4), CM-7(5), CM-11
A.12.6 Technical vulnerability management	
A.12.6.1 Management of technical vulnerabilities	RA-3, RA-5, SI-2
A.12.6.2 Restrictions on software installation	CM-11
A.12.7 Information systems audit considerations	
A.12.7.1 Information systems audit controls	AU-5*
A.13 Communications security	
A.13.1 Network security management	
A.13.1.1 Network controls	AC-3, AC-17, AC-18, AC-20, SC-7, SC-8, SC-10
A.13.1.2 Security of network services	CA-3, SA-9
A.13.1.3 Segregation in networks	AC-4, SC-7
A.13.2 Information transfer	
A.13.2.1 Information transfer policies and procedures	AC-4, AC-17, AC-18, AC-19, AC-20, CA-3, PE-17, SC-7, SC-8, SC-15
A.13.2.2 Agreements on information transfer	CA-3, PS-6, SA-9
A.13.2.3 Electronic messaging	SC-8
A.13.2.4 Confidentiality or nondisclosure agreements	PS-6
A.14 System acquisition, development and maintenance	
A.14.1 Security requirements of information systems	
A.14.1.1 Information security requirements analysis and specification	PL-2, PL-7, PL-8, SA-3, SA-4
A.14.1.2 Securing application services on public networks	AC-3, AC-4, AC-17, SC-8, SC-13
A.14.1.3 Protecting application services transactions	AC-3, AC-4, SC-7, SC-8, SC-13
A.14.2 Security in development and support processes	
A.14.2.1 Secure development policy	SA-3, SA-15, SA-17
A.14.2.2 System change control procedures	CM-3, SA-10, SI-2

(*Continued*)

ISO/IEC 27001 controls	NIST SP 800-53 controls
A.14.2.3 Technical review of applications after operating platform changes	CM-3, CM-4, SI-2
A.14.2.4 Restrictions on changes to software packages	CM-3, SA-10
A.14.2.5 Secure system engineering principles	SA-8
A.14.2.6 Secure development environment	SA-3*
A.14.2.7 Outsourced development	SA-4, SA-10, SA-11, SA-12, SA-15
A.14.2.8 System security testing	CA-2, SA-11
A.14.2.9 System acceptance testing	SA-4, SA-12(7)
A.14.3 Test data	
A.14.3.1 Protection of test data	SA-15(9)*
A.15 Supplier Relationships	
A.15.1 Information security in supplier relationships	
A.15.1.1 Information security policy for supplier relationships	SA-12
A.15.1.2 Address security within supplier agreements	SA-4, SA-12
A.15.1.3 Information and communication technology supply chain	SA-12
A.15.2 Supplier service delivery management	
A.15.2.1 Monitoring and review of supplier services	SA-9
A.15.2.2 Managing changes to supplier services	SA-9
A.16 Information security incident management	
A.16.1 Managing of information security incidents and improvements	
A.16.1.1 Responsibilities and procedures	IR-8
A.16.1.2 Reporting information security events	AU-6, IR-6
A.16.1.3 Reporting information security weaknesses	SI-2
A.16.1.4 Assessment of and decision on information security events	AU-6, IR-4
A.16.1.5 Response to information security incidents	IR-4
A.16.1.6 Learning from information security incidents	IR-4
A.16.1.7 Collection of evidence	AU-11*
A.17 Information security aspects of business continuity management	
A.17.1 Information security continuity	
A.17.1.1 Planning information security continuity	CP-2
A.17.1.2 Implementing information security continuity	CP-6, CP-7, CP-8, CP-9, CP-10, CP-11, CP-13
A.17.1.3 Verify, review, and evaluate information security continuity	CP-4

ISO/IEC 27001 controls	NIST SP 800-53 controls
A.17.2 Redundancies	
A.17.2.1 Availability of information processing facilities	CP-2,CP-6, CP-7
A.18 Compliance	
A.18.1 Compliance with legal and contractual requirements	
A.18.1.1 Identification of applicable legislation and contractual requirements	All XX-1 controls
A.18.1.2 Intellectual property rights	CM-10
A.18.1.3 Protection of records	AC-3, AU-9, CP-9
A.18.1.4 Privacy and protection of personal information	Appendix J Privacy controls
A.18.1.5 Regulation of cryptographic controls	IA-7, SC-13
A.18.2 Information security reviews	
A.18.2.1 Independent review of information security	CA-2(1), SA-11(3)
A.18.2.2 Compliance with security policies and standards	All XX-1 controls, CA-2
A.18.2.3 Technical compliance review	CA-2

Note: An asterisk (*) indicates that the NIST control does not fully satisfy the intent of the ISO/IEC control.

CHAPTER

10

System and Network Assessments

Security control assessments are not about checklists, simple pass-fail results, or generating paperwork to pass inspections or audits, rather, security controls assessments are the principal vehicle used to verify that the implementers and operators of information systems are meeting their stated security goals and objectives.[1]

The object of any testing event or activity is to evaluate the item being tested against some set of external criteria to verify and to validate the item under test meets the defined criteria. The needs for running today's complex and disparate systems safely and securely are many and varied. The requirements for testing and evaluating these systems find uses in various areas including:

- *Risk analysis*: The evaluations for risk often require the identified risks be rated according to impact and potential harm they could cause to the organization. These evaluations will often include controls and their methodology of implementation which can be determined by analyzing the effectiveness of the installed controls through use of automated toolsets and scanners.
- *Assessment*: There are many ongoing needs and requirements throughout the federal government where the system which processes the information for the agency needs to be tested for its functionality and for its operations. These assessments will include testing after repairs have been completed to the system, testing when some major event or incident has occurred which calls into question the security of the system, evaluating the system subsequent to an external analysis which indicates some anomalous component, and examining the system when warranted by a reported condition or requested by a senior leadership.
- *Authorization*: Each system that is projected to be on or is already on a Federal Backbone or Network requires, under FISMA law, to be reviewed and analyzed for risks, evaluated and tested to ensure the security controls are working correctly, and then assessed to ensure the system is functioning at an acceptable level of risk to operate relatively securely. These authorization efforts are the basis for the Risk Management Framework criteria for federal Automated Information System (AIS) as defined in OMB Circular A-130 and are closely adhered to by federal agencies and authorizing officials. The independent testing needs for authorization on both Major Applications and General Support Systems, such as networks and data centers, provide many opportunities for

---

[1]SP 800-53A, xiii.

499

testing efforts with various methods and techniques as required by the type of system being evaluated.

- *Security architecture validation*: Within each network are the various components, pieces of hardware, appliances, and software applications which comprise the network-based and system-based security controls. Each of these items is designed to provide some level of security for the system or network component it is protecting. However, there are often areas of interface and interconnections between or among components wherein protection is also needed and required. The designs and constructs for these areas are found in the security architecture documentation and drawings. Security architecture is an architectural subset under the enterprise architecture methodology which has developed over the past 15–20 years. Security architecture documents will include the reference models for the technical and business processes, the conceptual and actual drawings of the security processes for the network or system under review, and the various defined information types used within the system or network.

- *Policy development support*: One of the starting points for any assessment is to verify and validate to overarching corporate or organizational structures for security as they are implemented, the security policies. Each organization needs to have a policy document which covers the security, privacy, and liability needs of the organization with respect to the legal and privacy requirements of the people and the information the organization uses and retains. There are a multitude of privacy and legal requirements, regulations, and industry standards in today's world which all provide guidance for use, retention, transmittal, and storage of these types of data and actions. Assessors need to review the policy documents for the organization to ensure compliance to these various statutory and regulatory needs. As part of the review, assessors should also review the policy development process to verify the organizational efforts to stay current with its regulatory environment and security needs.

- *Develop a cohesive, well-thought-out operational security testing program*: Each organization has many testing and evaluation process events they will be carrying out throughout the year and this program needs to be reviewed and validated. This validation is accomplished to ensure the program performance is providing the right level of information to the decision makers in the organization so they are making their risk-based decision fully informed rather than with only partial data and incomplete testing results. Since these decisions are critical to the organization's business objectives or missions, this process is very important to verify the completeness of the testing, the validity of the tests conducted, and the full scope of the evaluation procedures conducted by the organization.

The benefits of conducting the assessment and test program in a comprehensive and structured way include the following:

- Provides consistency and structure
- Minimizes testing risks
- Expedites transition of new staff
- Addresses resource constraints
- Reuses resources
- Decreases time required
- Reduces cost

Because information security assessment requires resources such as time, staff, hardware, and software, resource availability is often a limiting factor in the type and frequency of security assessments. Evaluating the types of security tests and examinations the organization will execute, developing an appropriate methodology, identifying the resources required, and structuring the assessment process to support expected requirements can mitigate the resource challenge. This gives the organization the ability to reuse pre-established resources such as trained staff and standardized testing platforms; decreases time required to conduct the assessment and the need to purchase testing equipment and software; and reduces overall assessment costs.[2]

Each benefit has its own value and the accumulated gains for the organization add up to full and complete coverage of all areas to provide the assurance to the senior leadership of the organization that the results of the program do indeed provide the needed information to the decision makers on the risks and treatments of these identified risks to make the risk-based decisions about operating and running these systems safely and securely.

- *Security testing program within federal agencies*: Under FISMA requirements, each federal agency is required to evaluate their information systems for security on an annual and on a triannual basis to ensure their viability to keep the information secure and to operate at an acceptable level of risk.

  The annual requirement covers the need to make sure the system is operating as intended and to check the current level of security for adequacy in light of the current threats and vulnerabilities of operating the system. This process has become standardized with OMB providing the listing of the families of security controls to be reviewed and tested each year to go with the high volatility controls and recently installed controls and control fixes the organization has implemented.

  The triannual requirement is for the organization to completely reassess and retest all security components and controls for each system to verify and validate to full scope of control implementation with respect to the security requirements of confidentiality, integrity, and availability for the system.

- *Testing purposes*: The actual testing provides multiple important and positive results when conducted in conjunction with the other parts of the security program and activities. The results often document the purposes behind the testing and include the following areas:

  - *Exploitable flaws*: Weaknesses and flaws within the system are often found by testing of the system and its security controls. This process is critical to the organization since it is the main way these flaws can be determined, remediated, and repaired to keep the system secure and people utilizing the system on track and safe as they conduct the business supported by this system.

  - *Understanding, calibrating, and documenting the operational security posture*: Testing and evaluation provide a means to identify, adjust, and fully document the system, its operating environment, the interfaces to and from the system, and its operating status at the point in time of the test event. As a result of the assessment, the system and its documentation is verified, corrected, and provided to the test results receiver.

  - *Improving the security posture*: The major component for testing is to produce an improved and viable security posture for the system under test. This security result is found in the recommendations of the assessor as documented in the Security

---

[2]SP 800-115, p. 2-1.

Assessment Report (SAR) defined later in this book. The improvement of the security is the goal of any testing event and the testing provides identified areas for improvement.

- *Routine and integral part of the system and network operations*: In today's world with constantly changing operating environments, threat sources consistently changing their methods and techniques of attack, and the consistently changing vulnerability flaws and weaknesses in applications and operating systems, ongoing assessments are necessary to assist the system owners and executives to provide information on the current risks and security of their systems. The following areas and focus points are critical to using the assessment methods mentioned herein for operational utilization:
  - *Most important systems first*: The methods for your business to make money (if it is a for-profit corporation) or for your organization to deliver its service (if it is a not-for-profit organization) are vital to the completion of the business objectives and/or mission of your company or organization. Since that area is true, the most critical systems within that business objective need to be available and active at all the times your organization is conducting its business. The assessment of these critical systems and their risks and security therefore is vital to the organization and its normal operations.
    - Since all systems within the organization are always considered vital to an organization and its business processes, evaluating the most critical systems first provides a baseline to set the core security and privacy assurance for the organization.
    - Always test and evaluate the critical, most important systems first to ensure the business continuity/COOP efforts are focused correctly, and then move on to the essential systems. The organization's business impact analysis Bureau of Indian Affairs (BIA) is a good place to start since that is where the organization itself has identified those systems most vital to the mission and/or business processes of the unit, component, or agency.
  - *Use caution when testing*: During the course of conducting testing on controls and networks, there are instances where the automated tools used can cause interrupts in processing or operations of the system being review. Be careful and understand the tool and its capabilities so as not to cause an unintended denial of service (DOS) or other interrupt of activities on the system.
  - *Security policy accurately reflects the organization's needs*: Reviewing the organizational policies and standards is one of the first and most important steps in conducting any assessment. I have often heard that "security controls are implemented to support security policies" and this is very true. Each policy, as defined by the management and security portions of the agency, provides the basis and foundation for every control implemented in the system. Therefore, these policies set the core requirements for security and assurance which each user and customer of the system expects to be met by the system in its use and implementation. The basic policy sets the needs, requirements, and guidance to the user for use on the system.
    - *Maximize use of common controls*: The agency's use of common controls provides the assessor the basic viewpoint of security within the organization. If there are many Common Control Providers which follow the basic requirements for data centers, physical and environmental security, personnel, facilities maintenance and management, incident response, and other common areas, then the senior

management of the organization is approaching security in a holistic and standardized manner which provides common ground for each department to base their risk and security approaches on for continued assurance and trustworthiness.

- *Share assessment results*: The continued sharing of assessment results within an organization provides the senior leadership with an updated and current view of the risks the organization is currently facing during the accomplishment of its mission or business processes. This is important to maintain the organizational risk tolerance in light of the changing threats to the world and constant vulnerabilities being identified for each type of system and operating system.
- *Develop organization-wide procedures*: When an organization provides the various departments the common security procedures for standardized activities, it is creating a "mind-set" for the use and implementation of security which gives the result of utilizing the industry "best practices" for practices and implementation guidance. These procedures provide the individual security professional and the agencies with the methods and means for conducting the security operations of the unit in accordance with both the agency requirements and the external compliance requirements all agencies must meet in today's world.
- *Provide organization-wide tools, templates, and techniques*: By developing and implementing standard tools, templates, and security techniques, the organization is providing the best practice approach to security and assurance. With templates for forms, plans, and reports, the unit personnel can identify the critical information components and metrics needed to keep focus on during the course of their daily security activities. By defining standard tools for use, the unit is giving the means for continued identification and classification of the data elements needed to provide the senior leadership with the continuous monitoring points for ongoing risk evaluations and decision making.

- *Security testing integrated into the risk management process*: The FISMA-mandated and NIST-designed Risk Management Framework approach to security assurance and evaluations for USG systems demands that security component and system testing be conducted ongoing throughout the system life cycle of the system under evaluation. Testing and evaluation under the Risk Management Framework is defined as the critical independent need for the authorizing official to use as his/her risk-based decision-making input to ensure the operation and maintenance of the system under evaluation is actually safe and secure to operate in the normal course of activities.

- *Ensure system administrators and network managers are trained and capable*: One of the most important areas of continued security of each system is to make sure the elevated privilege account holders for the system are properly trained in their performance of their daily activities. Insider threat in today's world is still the highest impact area of potential issues and security concerns and by providing proper training to these elevated privilege users, the organization is reducing the likelihood of misuse and abuse possibilities.

- *Keep systems up-to-date with patches*: Systems today have many areas of potential flaws and weaknesses in the operating systems and applications that they deploy and use. The software industry has developed a methodology over the past 40 years wherein the end user is the tester of the software, rather than develop their (the vendor) own testing program. All major software vendors utilize this construct and we need to constantly be vigilant with the software to keep it up-to-date in its patching.

- *Capabilities and limitations of vulnerability testing*: Vulnerability testing on systems and networks is a common best practice for organizations to ensure their systems are not vulnerable to some exposure or exploit in the software and systems they employ. However, remember the vulnerability scanning tools that are currently being used throughout the industry do *not* review external mitigation efforts for system weaknesses. For example, a security flaw commonly identified in a system would be a self-signed SSL certificate on a system not externally provided to the organization. However, if the organization utilizes external SSL certificates and the encryption processes are controlled at the entrance to the network, this flaw is not actually visible or exploitable from outside the network. Therefore, this weakness is minor in nature since it is handled externally to the identified server.

800-115 INTRODUCTION

NIST produced SP 800-115 in September 2008 to give guidance to federal agencies in the conduct of testing events for their systems and networks. The intent of this document is as follows:

> The purpose of this document is to provide guidelines for organizations on planning and conducting technical information security testing and assessments, analyzing findings, and developing mitigation strategies. It provides practical recommendations for designing, implementing, and maintaining technical information relating to security testing and assessment processes and procedures, which can be used for several purposes—such as finding vulnerabilities in a system or network and verifying compliance with a policy or other requirements. This guide is not intended to present a comprehensive information security testing or assessment program, but rather an overview of the key elements of technical security testing and assessment with emphasis on specific techniques, their benefits and limitations, and recommendations for their use.[3]

The big picture, the main purpose for assessing, evaluating, and testing systems, is clearly defined as follows:

> This document is a guide to the basic technical aspects of conducting information security assessments. It presents technical testing and examination methods and techniques that an organization might use as part of an assessment, and offers insights to assessors on their execution and the potential impact they may have on systems and networks. For an assessment to be successful and have a positive impact on the security posture of a system (and ultimately the entire organization), elements beyond the execution of testing and examination must support the technical process. Suggestions for these activities—including a robust planning process, root cause analysis, and tailored reporting—are also presented in this guide.
>
> The processes and technical guidance presented in this document enable organizations to:

- Develop information security assessment policy, methodology, and individual roles and responsibilities related to the technical aspects of assessment
- Accurately plan for a technical information security assessment by providing guidance on determining which systems to assess and the approach for assessment, addressing logistical considerations, developing an assessment plan, and ensuring legal and policy considerations are addressed

---

[3]SP 800-115, p. 1-1.

- Safely and effectively execute a technical information security assessment using the presented methods and techniques, and respond to any incidents that may occur during the assessment
- Appropriately handle technical data (collection, storage, transmission, and destruction) throughout the assessment process
- Conduct analysis and reporting to translate technical findings into risk mitigation actions that will improve the organization's security posture.

The information presented in this publication is intended to be used for a variety of assessment purposes. For example, some assessments focus on verifying that a particular security control (or controls) meets requirements, while others are intended to identify, validate, and assess a system's exploitable security weaknesses. Assessments are also performed to increase an organization's ability to maintain a proactive computer network defense. Assessments are not meant to take the place of implementing security controls and maintaining system security.[4]

Now, there are many reasons to conduct technical testing and evaluation activities within an organization or agency. Within the scope of technical testing the criteria for assessments include:

- *Internet change*: The incredible changes which have occurred across the ubiquitous internet in the past several years have created a vast array of new capabilities, technologies, attack methods, and means for exploitation which were never even thought of by the original designers. The full scope of the protocols, services, and activities available today on the internet is mind staggering. You can virtually accomplish any task or perform any endeavor entirely on the internet rapidly and completely.
- *Intruder attacks*: Today the methods and techniques of attack against anyone using the internet are extremely varied and complex. Often many organizations and individuals have no knowledge that they and their data have been compromised and exfiltrated from their systems. The incredible proliferation of malware across the internet has produced a virtual "Wild West" of attackers, "botnets," cybercrime organizations, and "monetization" of many data types which have never been subjected to these uses in the past. "Hacker" tools and tactics have dramatically increased in their use and the standard internet user is the constant victim of these efforts to gain the money and the resultant return from these attacks.
- *Powerful systems today*: The advances in technology for both hardware and software in the modern PC and laptop machines have provided a dramatic expansion of options, available resources, and advances in the abilities and capabilities of these machines. Additionally, with these technological advances, the network computing components (routers, switches, virtualization, cloud, etc.) have added to the capabilities of organizations and agencies to provide services never thought of before. Many of these systems are well advanced of the computing machine just 6 or 8 years ago and give many new methods and techniques available to today's attack-minded hacker.
- *Complex system administration*: With the technological advances mentioned above, the administration of these machines and systems has dramatically advanced as well. Multiple servers with many inputs and outputs to systems both inside a network and outside the organizational boundaries are almost required to have log-ins from multiple users literally all over the world. The control and review of these very active systems has become a full-time job for many system administrators of these systems.

[4]SP 800-115, p. ES-1.

Reasons for conducting technical and nontechnical testing on today's systems are as follows:

- *Highly cost-effective in preventing incidents and uncovering unknown vulnerabilities*: Testing can provide a detailed review of the systems and their vulnerability to both inside and outside attack techniques. This process leads to preventive measures being taken by the organization which both is cost-effective in result and often uncovers previously unknown (to the organization) issues and potential vulnerabilities in the systems under test.
- *Testing – most conclusive determinant*: Testing provides security artifacts and results documentation which can support evaluation efforts, audit findings, and control recommendations with definitive objective documentation in the various security areas of confidentiality, integrity, availability, authentication, and reliability. The objective, scientific basis for the results provides the independent-type reporting necessary for the organizational decision makers to use to make their risk-based decisions on the viability and risk management practices for the system and the agency.
- *Methods for achieving the mission/business goals*: Testing and evaluations support the operations of systems in the areas of verifying configuration changes, providing realistic results in an operational environment, and ensuring the security and safety of the system is being maintained continuously as it is providing the operating results expected and desired by the organization. By performing ongoing testing, the organization is deriving continuous compliance with external requirements and standards.

ASSESSMENT TECHNIQUES

SP 800-115 defines three basic techniques for technical assessments. They are as follows:

- **Review Techniques**. These are examination techniques used to evaluate systems, applications, networks, policies, and procedures to discover vulnerabilities, and are generally conducted manually. They include documentation, log, rule-set, and system configuration review; network sniffing; and file integrity checking.
- **Target Identification and Analysis Techniques**. These testing techniques can identify systems, ports, services, and potential vulnerabilities, and may be performed manually but are generally performed using automated tools. They include network discovery, network port and service identification, vulnerability scanning, wireless scanning, and application security examination.
- **Target Vulnerability Validation Techniques**. These testing techniques corroborate the existence of vulnerabilities, and may be performed manually or by using automatic tools, depending on the specific technique used and the skill of the test team. Target vulnerability validation techniques include password cracking, penetration testing, social engineering, and application security testing.[5]

SP 800-115 goes on and adds the nontechnical means for assessments as follows:

Additionally, there are many non-technical techniques that may be used in addition to or instead of the technical techniques.

One example is physical security testing, which confirms the existence of physical security vulnerabilities by attempting to circumvent locks, badge readers, and other physical security controls, typically to gain unauthorized access to specific hosts.

Another example of a non-technical technique is manual asset identification. An organization may choose to identify assets to be assessed through asset inventories, physical walkthroughs of facilities, and other non-technical means, instead of relying on technical techniques for asset identification.[6]

---

[5]SP 800-115, p. 2–3.
[6]*Ibid.*

SP 800-115 goes on to explain:

Examinations primarily involve the review of documents such as policies, procedures, security plans, security requirements, standard operating procedures, architecture diagrams, engineering documentation, asset inventories, system configurations, rule-sets, and system logs. They are conducted to determine whether a system is properly documented, and to gain insight on aspects of security that are only available through documentation. This documentation identifies the intended design, installation, configuration, operation, and maintenance of the systems and network, and its review and cross-referencing ensures conformance and consistency. For example, an environment's security requirements should drive documentation such as system security plans and standard operating procedures—so assessors should ensure that all plans, procedures, architectures, and configurations are compliant with stated security requirements and applicable policies. Another example is reviewing a firewall's rule-set to ensure its compliance with the organization's security policies regarding Internet usage, such as the use of instant messaging, peer-to-peer (P2P) file sharing, and other prohibited activities.

Examinations typically have no impact on the actual systems or networks in the target environment aside from accessing necessary documentation, logs, or rule-sets. (One passive testing technique that can potentially impact networks is network sniffing, which involves connecting a sniffer to a hub, tap, or span port on the network. In some cases, the connection process requires reconfiguring a network device, which could disrupt operations.) However, if system configuration files or logs are to be retrieved from a given system such as a router or firewall, only system administrators an modified or deleted.

Testing involves hands-on work with systems and networks to identify security vulnerabilities, and can be executed across an entire enterprise or on selected systems. The use of scanning and penetration techniques can provide valuable information on potential vulnerabilities and predict the likelihood that an adversary or intruder will be able to exploit them. Testing also allows organizations to measure levels of compliance in areas such as patch management, password policy, and configuration management.

Although testing can provide a more accurate picture of an organization's security posture than what is gained through examinations, it is more intrusive and can impact systems or networks in the target environment. The level of potential impact depends on the specific types of testing techniques used, which can interact with the target systems and networks in various ways—such as sending normal network packets to determine open and closed ports, or sending specially crafted packets to test for vulnerabilities. Any time that a test or tester directly interacts with a system or network, the potential exists for unexpected system halts and other denial of service conditions. Organizations should determine their acceptable levels of intrusiveness when deciding which techniques to use. Excluding tests known to create denial of service conditions and other disruptions can help reduce these negative impacts.

Testing does not provide a comprehensive evaluation of the security posture of an organization, and often has a narrow scope because of resource limitations—particularly in the area of time. Malicious attackers, on the other hand, can take whatever time they need to exploit and penetrate a system or network. Also, while organizations tend to avoid using testing techniques that impact systems or networks, attackers are not bound by this constraint and use whatever techniques they feel necessary. As a result, testing is less likely than examinations to identify weaknesses related to security policy and configuration. In many cases, combining testing and examination techniques can provide a more accurate view of security.[7]

NETWORK TESTING PURPOSE AND SCOPE

Networking evaluations and testing areas of focus include the following components, equipment, and devices:

- Firewalls
- Routers and switches
- Network-perimeter security systems (Intrusion Detection System (IDS))
- Application servers

[7]SP 800-115, p. 2-3, 2-4.

- Other servers such as for Domain Name System (DNS) or directory servers or file servers (Common Internet File System (CIFS)/Server Message Block (SMB), Network File System (NFS), File Transfer Protocol (FTP), etc.)

These various components are often standardized by the organization with common configurations, formal change management request actions, and continued monitoring and maintenance, all similar to computing equipment residing on the network such as file and application servers and workstations and laptops. Within this normal network view, there are common access controls utilized through the Access Control List (ACL) implementation.

ACL Reviews

A rule-set is a collection of rules or signatures that network traffic or system activity is compared against to determine what action to take—for example, forwarding or rejecting a packet, creating an alert, or allowing a system event. Review of these rule-sets is done to ensure comprehensiveness and identify gaps and weaknesses on security devices and throughout layered defenses such as network vulnerabilities, policy violations, and unintended or vulnerable communication paths. A review can also uncover inefficiencies that negatively impact a rule-set's performance.

Rule-sets to review include network- and host-based firewall and IDS/IPS rule-sets, and router access control lists. The following list provides examples of the types of checks most commonly performed in rule-set reviews:

1. For router access control lists
   - Each rule is still required (for example, rules that were added for temporary purposes are removed as soon as they are no longer needed)
   - Only traffic that is authorized per policy is permitted, and all other traffic is denied by default
2. For firewall rule-sets
   - Each rule is still required
   - Rules enforce least privilege access, such as specifying only required Internet Protocol (IP) addresses and ports
   - More specific rules are triggered before general rules
   - There are no unnecessary open ports that could be closed to tighten the perimeter security
   - The rule-set does not allow traffic to bypass other security defenses
   - For host-based firewall rule-sets, the rules do not indicate the presence of backdoors, spyware activity, or prohibited applications such as peer-to-peer file sharing programs
3. For IDS/IPS rule-sets
   - Unnecessary signatures have been disabled or removed to eliminate false positives and improve performance
   - Necessary signatures are enabled and have been fine-tuned and properly maintained.[8]

System-Defined Reviews

There are many types of configurations for each type of computer and system. With these varied types there comes a strong need to have each system, machine, or device under standard configuration control and management. This process places the system under test in a relatively controlled environment with its configuration files, software leads, and other areas. The machines and devices which should be under this type of control include:

- Computer system (mainframe, minicomputer)
- Network system (LAN)

[8]SP 800-115, p. 3-2, 3-3.

- Network domain
- Host (computer system)
- Network nodes, routers, switches, and firewalls
- Network and/or computer application on each computer system

System configuration review is the process of identifying weaknesses in security configuration controls, such as systems not being hardened or configured according to security policies. For example, this type of review will reveal unnecessary services and applications, improper user account and password settings, and improper logging and backup settings. Examples of security configuration files that may be reviewed are Windows security policy settings and Unix security configuration files such as those in /etc.

Assessors using manual review techniques rely on security configuration guides or checklists to verify that system settings are configured to minimize security risks. To perform a manual system configuration review, assessors access various security settings on the device being evaluated and compare them with recommended settings from the checklist. Settings that do not meet minimum security standards are flagged and reported.

Automated tools are often executed directly on the device being assessed, but can also be executed on a system with network access to the device being assessed. While automated system configuration reviews are faster than manual methods, there may still be settings that must be checked manually. Both manual and automated methods require root or administrator privileges to view selected security settings.

Generally it is preferable to use automated checks instead of manual checks whenever feasible. Automated checks can be done very quickly and provide consistent, repeatable results. Having a person manually checking hundreds or thousands of settings is tedious and error-prone.[9]

TESTING ROLES AND RESPONSIBILITIES

- Take approval of CIO/upper management.
- Alert security officers, management, and users.
- Avoid confusion and unnecessary expense.
- Alert local law enforcement officials, if necessary.

SECURITY TESTING TECHNIQUES

1. Network scanning
2. Vulnerability scanning
3. Password cracking
4. Log review
5. Integrity checkers
6. Virus detection
7. War dialing
8. War driving
9. Penetration testing

1. *Network scanning*:
   a. *Network scanning (sniffing)*:

Network sniffing is a passive technique that monitors network communication, decodes protocols, and examines headers and payloads to flag information of interest. Besides being used as a review technique,

[9]SP 800-115, p. 3-3.

network sniffing can also be used as a target identification and analysis technique. Reasons for using network sniffing include the following:

- Capturing and replaying network traffic
- Performing passive network discovery (e.g., identifying active devices on the network)
- Identifying operating systems, applications, services, and protocols, including unsecured (e.g., telnet) and unauthorized (e.g., peer-to-peer file sharing) protocols
- Identifying unauthorized and inappropriate activities, such as the unencrypted transmission of sensitive information
- Collecting information, such as unencrypted usernames and passwords.

Network sniffing has little impact on systems and networks, with the most noticeable impact being on bandwidth or computing power utilization. The sniffer—the tool used to conduct network sniffing—requires a means to connect to the network, such as a hub, tap, or switch with port spanning. Port spanning is the process of copying the traffic transmitted on all other ports to the port where the sniffer is installed. Organizations can deploy network sniffers in a number of locations within an environment. These commonly include the following:

- At the perimeter, to assess traffic entering and exiting the network
- Behind firewalls, to assess that rule-sets are accurately filtering traffic
- Behind IDSs/IPSs, to determine if signatures are triggering and being responded to appropriately
- In front of a critical system or application to assess activity
- On a specific network segment, to validate encrypted protocols.

One limitation to network sniffing is the use of encryption. Many attackers take advantage of encryption to hide their activities—while assessors can see that communication is taking place, they are unable to view the contents. Another limitation is that a network sniffer is only able to sniff the traffic of the local segment where it is installed. This requires the assessor to move it from segment to segment, install multiple sniffers throughout the network, and/or use port spanning. Assessors may also find it challenging to locate an open physical network port for scanning on each segment. In addition, network sniffing is a fairly labor-intensive activity that requires a high degree of human involvement to interpret network traffic.[10]

b. *Port scanning:*

Network discovery uses a number of methods to discover active and responding hosts on a network, identify weaknesses, and learn how the network operates. Both passive (examination) and active (testing) techniques exist for discovering devices on a network. Passive techniques use a network sniffer to monitor network traffic and record the IP addresses of the active hosts, and can report which ports are in use and which operating systems have been discovered on the network. Passive discovery can also identify the relationships between hosts—including which hosts communicate with each other, how frequently their communication occurs, and the type of traffic that is taking place—and is usually performed from a host on the internal network where it can monitor host communications. This is done without sending out a single probing packet. Passive discovery takes more time to gather information than does active discovery, and hosts that do not send or receive traffic during the monitoring period might not be reported.

Network port and service identification involves using a port scanner to identify network ports and services operating on active hosts—such as FTP and HTTP—and the application that is running each identified service, such as Microsoft Internet Information Server (IIS) or Apache for the HTTP service. Organizations should conduct network port and service identification to identify hosts if this has not already been done by other means (e.g., network discovery), and flag potentially vulnerable services. This information can be used to determine targets for penetration testing.

All basic scanners can identify active hosts and open ports, but some scanners are also able to provide additional information on the scanned hosts. Information gathered during an open port scan can assist in identifying the target operating system through a process called *OS fingerprinting*. For example, if a host has TCP ports 135,

---

[10]SP 800-115, p. 3-4.

139, and 445 open, it is probably a Windows host, or possibly a UNIX host running Samba. Other items—such as the TCP packet sequence number generation and responses to packets—also provide a clue to identifying the OS. But OS fingerprinting is not foolproof. For example, firewalls block certain ports and types of traffic, and system administrators can configure their systems to respond in nonstandard ways to camouflage the true OS.

c. Network services discovery:

Active discovery techniques send various types of network packets, such as Internet Control Message Protocol (ICMP) pings, to solicit responses from network hosts, generally through the use of an automated tool. One activity, known as OS fingerprinting, enables the assessor to determine the system's OS by sending it a mix of normal, abnormal, and illegal network traffic. Another activity involves sending packets to common port numbers to generate responses that indicate the ports are active. The tool analyzes the responses from these activities, and compares them with known traits of packets from specific operating systems and network services—enabling it to identify hosts, the operating systems they run, their ports, and the state of those ports. This information can be used for purposes that include gathering information on targets for penetration testing, generating topology maps, determining firewall and IDS configurations, and discovering vulnerabilities in systems and network configurations.

Network discovery tools have many ways to acquire information through scanning. Enterprise firewalls and intrusion detection systems can identify many instances of scans, particularly those that use the most suspicious packets (e.g., SYN/FIN scan, NULL scan). Assessors who plan on performing discovery through firewalls and intrusion detection systems should consider which types of scans are most likely to provide results without drawing the attention of security administrators, and how scans can be conducted in a more stealthy manner (such as more slowly or from a variety of source IP addresses) to improve their chances of success. Assessors should also be cautious when selecting types of scans to use against older systems, particularly those known to have weak security, because some scans can cause system failures. Typically, the closer the scan is to normal activity, the less likely it is to cause operational problems.

Network discovery may also detect unauthorized or rogue devices operating on a network. For example, an organization that uses only a few operating systems could quickly identify rogue devices that utilize different ones. Once a wired rogue device is identified, 12 it can be located by using existing network maps and information already collected on the device's network activity to identify the switch to which it is connected. It may be necessary to generate additional network activity with the rogue device—such as pings—to find the correct switch. The next step is to identify the switch port on the switch associated with the rogue device, and to physically trace the cable connecting that switch port to the rogue device.

A number of tools exist for use in network discovery, and it should be noted that many active discovery tools can be used for passive network sniffing and port scanning as well. Most offer a graphical user interface (GUI), and some also offer a command-line interface. Command-line interfaces may take longer to learn than GUIs because of the number of commands and switches that specify what tests the tool should perform and which an assessor must learn to use the tool effectively. Also, developers have written a number of modules for open source tools that allow assessors to easily parse tool output. For example, combining a tool's Extensible Markup Language (XML) output capabilities, a little scripting, and a database creates a more powerful tool that can monitor the network for unauthorized services and machines. Learning what the many commands do and how to combine them is best achieved with the help of an experienced security engineer. Most experienced IT professionals, including system administrators and other network engineers, should be able to interpret results, but working with the discovery tools themselves is more efficiently handled by an engineer.

Some of the advantages of active discovery, as compared to passive discovery, are that an assessment can be conducted from a different network and usually requires little time to gather information. In passive discovery, ensuring that all hosts are captured requires traffic to hit all points, which can be time-consuming—especially in larger enterprise networks.

A disadvantage to active discovery is that it tends to generate network noise, which sometimes results in network latency. Since active discovery sends out queries to receive responses, this additional network activity could slow down traffic or cause packets to be dropped in poorly configured networks if performed at high volume. Active discovery can also trigger IDS alerts, since unlike passive discovery it reveals its origination point. The ability to successfully discover all network systems can be affected by environments with protected network segments and perimeter security devices and techniques. For example, an environment using network address translation (NAT)—which allows organizations to have internal, non-publicly routed

IP addresses that are translated to a different set of public IP addresses for external traffic—may not be accurately discovered from points external to the network or from protected segments. Personal and host-based firewalls on target devices may also block discovery traffic. Misinformation may be received as a result of trying to instigate activity from devices. Active discovery presents information from which conclusions must be drawn about settings on the target network.

For both passive and active discovery, the information received is seldom completely accurate. To illustrate, only hosts that are on and connected during active discovery will be identified—if systems or a segment of the network are offline during the assessment, there is potential for a large gap in discovering devices. Although passive discovery will only find devices that transmit or receive communications during the discovery period, products such as network management software can provide continuous discovery capabilities and automatically generate alerts when a new device is present on the network. Continuous discovery can scan IP address ranges for new addresses or monitor new IP address requests. Also, many discovery tools can be scheduled to run regularly, such as once every set amount of days at a particular time. This provides more accurate results than running these tools sporadically.

Some of the tools for conducting these discovery activities include Network Mapper (NMAP) and GFI LanGuard products. Protocols which are observed during scanning and sniffing activities would include:
- Internet Protocol (IP)
- Internet Control Message Protocol (ICMP)
- User Datagram Protocol (UDP)
- Transmission Control Protocol (TCP)

d. *Fingerprinting*: The process of identifying the type of operating system, its current patch level and revision, along with the various additional management data about the system under review is known in this context as "fingerprinting the server."

Knowing the version and type of a running web server allows testers to determine known vulnerabilities and the appropriate exploits to use during testing. There are several different vendors and versions of servers on the market today. Knowing the type of server that you are testing significantly helps in the testing process, and will also change the course of the test. This information can be derived by sending the server specific commands and analyzing the output, as each version of server software may respond differently to these commands. By fingerprinting the target's server and enumerating as much information as possible, an attacker may develop an accurate attack scenario, which will effectively exploit an identified vulnerability in the software type/version being utilized by the target host. This is one of the initial steps involved in penetration testing and the outside attack tactics and techniques hackers use in attempting to gain unauthorized access to systems and servers.

As the *OWASP Testing Guide* defines: "By knowing how each type of web server responds to specific commands and keeping this information in a web server fingerprint database, a penetration tester can send these commands to the web server, analyze the response, and compare it to the database of known signatures. Please note that it usually takes several different commands to accurately identify the web server, as different versions may react similarly to the same command. Rarely, however, different versions react the same to all HTTP commands. So, by sending several different commands, you increase the accuracy of your guess" [1].

e. *Banner grabbing*:
"Some scanners can help identify the application running on a particular port through a process called service identification. Many scanners use a services file that lists common port numbers and typical associated services—for example, a scanner that identifies that

TCP port 80 is open on a host may report that a web server is listening at that port—but additional steps are needed before this can be confirmed. Some scanners can initiate communications with an observed port and analyze its communications to determine what service is there, often by comparing the observed activity to a repository of information on common services and service implementations. These techniques may also be used to identify the service application and application version, such as which Web server software is in use—this process is known as *version scanning*. A well-known form of version scanning, called *banner grabbing*, involves capturing banner information transmitted by the remote port when a connection is initiated. This information can include the application type, application version, and even OS type and version. Version scanning is not foolproof, because a security-conscious administrator can alter the transmitted banners or other characteristics in hopes of concealing the service's true nature. However, version scanning is far more accurate than simply relying on a scanner's services file."[11] An example of an NMAP output is shown as follows:

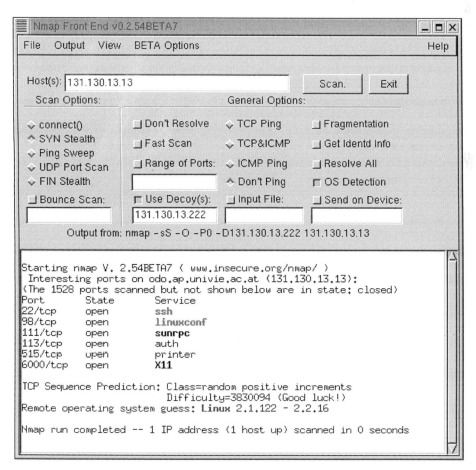

---

[11]SP 800-115.

Common reasons that scanning of networks and machines is conducted include:
- *Check for unauthorized hosts*: Identifying machines, rogue devices, and hosts is commonly a result of scanning. This process helps create a network topology of the active devices and servers on the network, whether they were previously identified or not.
- *Identify vulnerable services*: Each device which is scanned provides output data of all the services, ports, and protocols that device is currently running at the time of the scan. These outputs identify the open areas of access to the device which could be exposed to outside attack or exploitation.
- *Identify deviations from the allowed services defined in the organization's security policy*: The core foundation for any security activity within an organization is the enforcement of the organizational security policy and scanning provides the technical support and evidence that this policy is being correctly adhered to and in place. The scanning gives the tester proof the security components for the policy are in effect and active for the agency or organizations.
- *Prepare for penetration testing*: Penetration testing, as defined below, needs to be focused on the hosts, machines, and devices of the network and the system; therefore, the scanning gives the tester the right machine names, IP addresses, and services which are active. Many times, the penetration testing will identify the deficiencies in the systems by using the scan data to drill into the security of the machines and devices.
- *Configure IDS*: Scanning provides many areas for the security personnel to identify and isolate responses needed for tuning the network IDS (NIDS) devices to properly respond to deficiencies and behavioral patterns.

Potential recommendations for testers to identify corrective actions to results from this type of evaluation include:
- Investigate and disconnect unauthorized hosts.
- Disable or remove unnecessary and vulnerable services.
- Modify hosts to restrict access to vulnerable services to a limited number of required hosts.
- Modify enterprise firewalls to restrict outside access to known vulnerable services.

2. *Vulnerability scanning*:

Like network port and service identification, vulnerability scanning identifies hosts and host attributes (e.g., operating systems, applications, open ports), but it also attempts to identify vulnerabilities rather than relying on human interpretation of the scanning results. Many vulnerability scanners are equipped to accept results from network discovery and network port and service identification, which reduces the amount of work needed for vulnerability scanning. Also, some scanners can perform their own network discovery and network port and service identification. Vulnerability scanning can help identify outdated software versions, missing patches, and misconfigurations, and validate compliance with or deviations from an organization's security policy. This is done by identifying the operating systems and major software applications running on the hosts and matching them with information on known vulnerabilities stored in the scanners' vulnerability databases.[12]

Vulnerability scanning is often used to conduct the following test and evaluation activities:
a. Identify active hosts on network.
b. Define the active and vulnerable services (ports) on hosts.

---

[12]SP 800-115, p. 4-4.

c. Identify applications.
d. Identify the running operating systems.
e. Pinpoint the vulnerabilities associated with discovered OS and applications.
f. Locate misconfigured settings on servers, workstations, and network devices.
g. Track inventory and categorize assets.
h. Verify vulnerabilities against inventory.
i. Classify and rank risks.
j. Identify patches, fixes, and workarounds.
k. Rescan to validate remediation (application of patches, fixes, and workarounds).
l. Test compliance with host application usage/security policies.
m. Establish a baseline for penetration testing.

There are many books and papers available which identify values, techniques, and tactics needed for use of scanning so I will not try to go into detail on those uses of vulnerability scanning here.

a. Potential recommendations for testers to identify corrective actions to results from this type of evaluation include:
   - Upgrade or patch vulnerable systems.
   - Deploy mitigating measures.
   - Improve configuration management program and procedures.
   - Assign a staff member to:
      (i) Monitor vulnerability alerts/mailing lists.
      (ii) Examine applicability to environment.
      (iii) Initiate appropriate system changes.
   - Modify the organization's security policies and architecture.

3. *Password cracking*:

When a user enters a password, a hash of the entered password is generated and compared with a stored hash of the user's actual password. If the hashes match, the user is authenticated. Password cracking is the process of recovering passwords from password hashes stored in a computer system or transmitted over networks. It is usually performed during assessments to identify accounts with weak passwords. Password cracking is performed on hashes that are either intercepted by a network sniffer while being transmitted across a network, or retrieved from the target system, which generally requires administrative-level access on, or physical access to, the target system. Once these hashes are obtained, an automated password cracker rapidly generates additional hashes until a match is found or the assessor halts the cracking attempt.[13]

a. *Identifies weak passwords*:

Password crackers can be run during an assessment to ensure policy compliance by verifying acceptable password composition. For example, if the organization has a password expiration policy, then password crackers can be run at intervals that coincide with the intended password lifetime. Password cracking that is performed offline produces little or no impact on the system or network, and the benefits of this operation include validating the organization's password policy and verifying policy compliance.[14]

---

[13]SP 800-115, p. 5-1.
[14]*Ibid.*

b. *Stored and transmitted in encrypted form*: Hashes of passwords are primarily stored in hash (one-way encryption) format and are often stored in a password hash file on the server (SAM file on Windows boxes, "/etc/password" file on UNIX boxes). These files are usually the first target of malicious attackers to retrieve the passwords and then crack the administrative passwords off the machine so they can then re-enter the machine and use the correct password on the first log-in attempt and bypass the common security tool of locking out the account if incorrectly entering the password three times.

c. *Dictionary attack/hybrid attack/brute force*:

One method for generating hashes is a *dictionary attack*, which uses all words in a dictionary or text file. There are numerous dictionaries available on the Internet that encompass major and minor languages, names, popular television shows, etc. Another cracking method is known as a *hybrid attack*, which builds on the dictionary method by adding numeric and symbolic characters to dictionary words. Depending on the password cracker being used, this type of attack can try a number of variations, such as using common substitutions of characters and numbers for letters (e.g., p@ssword and h4ckme). Some will also try adding characters and numbers to the beginning and end of dictionary words (e.g., password99, password$%).

Yet another password-cracking method is called the *brute force* method. This generates all possible passwords up to a certain length and their associated hashes. Since there are so many possibilities, it can take months to crack a password. Although brute force can take a long time, it usually takes far less time than most password policies specify for password changing. Consequently, passwords found during brute force attacks are still too weak. Theoretically, all passwords can be cracked by a brute force attack, given enough time and processing power, although it could take many years and require serious computing power. Assessors and attackers often have multiple machines over which they can spread the task of cracking passwords, which greatly shortens the time involved.[13]

d. *Theoretically all passwords are "crackable"*:

Password cracking can also be performed with *rainbow tables*, which are lookup tables with pre-computed password hashes. For example, a rainbow table can be created that contains every possible password for a given character set up to a certain character length. Assessors may then search the table for the password hashes that they are trying to crack. Rainbow tables require large amounts of storage space and can take a long time to generate, but their primary shortcoming is that they may be ineffective against password hashing that uses *salting*. Salting is the inclusion of a random piece of information in the password hashing process that decreases the likelihood of identical passwords returning the same hash. Rainbow tables will not produce correct results without taking salting into account—but this dramatically increases the amount of storage space that the tables require. Many operating systems use salted password hashing mechanisms to reduce the effectiveness of rainbow tables and other forms of password cracking.[15]

e. *"LanMan" password hashes*:

The "LanMan" hash is a compromised password hashing function that was the primary hash that Microsoft LAN Manager and Microsoft Windows versions prior to Windows NT used to store user passwords. Support for the legacy LAN Manager protocol continued in later versions of Windows for backward compatibility, but was recommended by Microsoft to be turned off by administrators; as of Windows Vista, the protocol is disabled by default, but continues to be used by some non-Microsoft Common Internet File System (CIFS) implementations.

---

[15]SP 800-115, p. 5-2.

The LM hash is not a true one-way hash encryption function as the password can be determined from the hash because of several weaknesses in its design:

a. Passwords are limited to a maximum of only 14 characters
b. Passwords longer than 7 characters are divided into two pieces and each piece is hashed separately
c. All lower case letters in the password are changed to upper case before the password is hashed
d. The LM hash also does not use cryptographic salt, a standard technique to prevent pre-computed dictionary attacks
e. Implementation issue — since the LanMan Hashes change only when a user changes their password, they can be used to carry out a pass the hash side channel attack.

While LAN Manager is considered obsolete and current Windows operating systems use the stronger NTLMv2 or Kerberos authentication methods, Windows systems before Windows Vista/Windows Server 2008 enabled the LAN Manager hash by default for backward compatibility with legacy LAN Manager and Windows Me or earlier clients, or legacy NetBIOS-enabled applications.[16]

> For many years, LanMan hashes have been identified as weak password implementation techniques, but they persist and continue to be used throughout the server community as people do not often change the server implementation and view them as relatively obscure and difficult to retrieve.

4. *Log reviews*:

Log review determines if security controls are logging the proper information, and if the organization is adhering to its log management policies. As a source of historical information, audit logs can be used to help validate that the system is operating in accordance with established policies. For example, if the logging policy states that all authentication attempts to critical servers must be logged, the log review will determine if this information is being collected and shows the appropriate level of detail. Log review may also reveal problems such as misconfigured services and security controls, unauthorized accesses, and attempted intrusions. For example, if an intrusion detection system (IDS) sensor is placed behind a firewall, its logs can be used to examine communications that the firewall allows into the network. If the sensor registers activities that should be blocked, it indicates that the firewall is not configured securely.

Examples of log information that may be useful when conducting technical security assessments include:

- Authentication server or system logs may include successful and failed authentication attempts.
- System logs may include system and service startup and shutdown information, installation of unauthorized software, file accesses, security policy changes, account changes (e.g., account creation and deletion, account privilege assignment), and privilege use.
- Intrusion detection and prevention system logs may include malicious activity and inappropriate use.
- Firewall and router logs may include outbound connections that indicate compromised internal devices (e.g., rootkits, bots, Trojan horses, spyware).
- Firewall logs may include unauthorized connection attempts and inappropriate use.
- Application logs may include unauthorized connection attempts, account changes, use of privileges, and application or database usage information.
- Antivirus logs may include update failures and other indications of outdated signatures and software.
- Security logs, in particular patch management and some IDS and intrusion prevention system (IPS) products, may record information on known vulnerable services and applications.

Manually reviewing logs can be extremely time-consuming and cumbersome. Automated audit tools are available that can significantly reduce review time and generate predefined and customized reports that summarize log contents and track them to a set of specific activities. Assessors can also use these automated tools to facilitate log analysis by converting logs in different formats to a single, standard format for analysis.

---

[16]Data retrieved from Wikipedia, 10/1/2014.

In addition, if assessors are reviewing a specific action—such as the number of failed logon attempts in an organization—they can use these tools to filter logs based on the activity being checked.[17]

Log management and analysis should be conducted frequently on major servers, firewalls, IDS devices, and other applications. Logs that should be considered for use and review in any log management system include:

a. Firewall logs
b. IDS logs
c. Server logs
d. Other logs that are collecting audit data – especially network devices
e. Snort – free IDS sensors and their data components

5. *File integrity checkers*:

File integrity checkers provide a way to identify that system files have been changed computing and storing a checksum for every guarded file, and establishing a file checksum database. Stored checksums are later recomputed to compare their current value with the stored value, which identifies file modifications. A file integrity checker capability is usually included with any commercial host-based IDS, and is also available as a standalone utility.

Although an integrity checker does not require a high degree of human interaction, it must be used carefully to ensure its effectiveness. File integrity checking is most effective when system files are compared with a reference database created using a system known to be secure—this helps ensure that the reference database was not built with compromised files. The reference database should be stored offline to prevent attackers from compromising the system and covering their tracks by modifying the database. In addition, because patches and other updates change files, the checksum database should be kept up-to-date. For file integrity checking, strong cryptographic checksums such as Secure Hash Algorithm 1 (SHA-1) should be used to ensure the integrity of data stored in the checksum database. Federal agencies are required by Federal Information Processing Standard (FIPS) PUB 140-2, *Security Requirements for Cryptographic Modules*, to use SHA (e.g., SHA-1, SHA-256).[18]

File integrity checkers usually have the following features which provide the tester a specialized method of evaluating the file or directory structures:

a. Compute and store a checksum
b. Recomputed regularly
c. Initial reference database
d. False-positive alarm adjustment

6. *Antivirus protection/virus detectors*: Antivirus (AV) software was originally developed to detect and remove computer viruses. However, with the proliferation of other kinds of malware, AV software started to provide protection from other computer threats. In particular, modern AV software can protect from: backdoors, rootkits, Trojan horses, worms, malicious Layered Service Providers (LSPs), dialers, fraudtools, malicious Browser Helper Objects (BHOs), browser hijackers, ransomware, keyloggers, adware, and spyware. Some virus detector products also include protection from other computer threats, such as infected and malicious URLs, spam, scam and phishing attacks, online identity (privacy), online banking attacks, social engineering techniques, advanced persistent threat (APT), botnets, and even Decision Disk Operating System (DDoS) attacks.

[17]SP 800-115, p. 3-1, 3-2.
[18]SP 800-115, p. 3-5.

It is primarily used to detect and isolate the following types of threats:

a. Virus, Trojan, or worm.
b. Malicious code.
c. More sophisticated programs also look for virus-like activity in an attempt to identify new or mutated viruses.

Two primary types are as follows:

a. Network infrastructure–based AV software
b. End-user machine–based AV software

There are several methods which AV engine can use to identify malware:

a. *Signature-based detection*: Is the most common method. To identify viruses and other malware, the AV engine compares the contents of a file to its database of known malware signatures. Traditionally, AV software heavily relied on signatures to identify malware.
b. *Heuristic-based detection*: Is generally used together with signature-based detection. It detects malware based on characteristics typically used in known malware code.
c. Behavioral-based detection is similar to heuristic-based detection and used also in IDS. The main difference is that, instead of characteristics hardcoded in the malware code itself, it is based on the behavioral fingerprint of the malware at run time. Clearly, this technique is able to detect (known or unknown) malware only after they have starting doing their malicious actions.
d. Sandbox detection is a particular behavioral-based detection technique that, instead of detecting the behavioral fingerprint at run time, executes the programs in a virtual environment, logging what actions the program performs. Depending on the actions logged, the AV engine can determine if the program is malicious or not. If not, then, the program is executed in the real environment. Albeit this technique has shown to be quite effective, given its heaviness and slowness, it is rarely used in end-user AV solutions.
e. Data mining techniques are one of the latest approaches applied in malware detection. Data mining and machine learning algorithms are used to try to classify the behavior of a file (as either malicious or benign) given a series of file features that are extracted from the file itself.

7. *War dialing*:

Several available software packages allow network administrators—and attackers—to dial large blocks of telephone numbers to search for available modems. This process is called *war dialing*. A computer with four modems can dial 10,000 numbers in a matter of days. War dialers provide reports on numbers with modems, and some dialers have the capacity to attempt limited automatic attacks when a modem is discovered. Organizations should conduct war dialing at least once per year to identify their unauthorized and the organization's phone system. (It should be considered, however, that many unauthorized modems may be turned off after hours and might go undetected.) War dialing may also be used to detect fax equipment. Testing should include all numbers that belong to an organization, except those that could be impacted by receiving a large number of calls (e.g., 24-hour operation centers and emergency numbers). Most types of war dialing software allow testers to exempt specific numbers from the calling list.

Skills needed to conduct remote access testing include TCP/IP and networking knowledge; knowledge of remote access technologies and protocols; knowledge of authentication and access control methods; general knowledge of telecommunications systems and modem/PBX operations; and the ability to use scanning and security testing tools such as war dialers.[19]

Some of the criteria for war dialing include:

a. Going after unauthorized modems
b. Dialing large blocks of phone numbers in search of available modems
c. Including all numbers that belong to an organization

8. *Wireless LAN testing*:

Wireless technologies, in their simplest sense, enable one or more devices to communicate without the need for physical connections such as network or peripheral cables. They range from simple technologies like wireless keyboards and mice to complex cell phone networks and enterprise wireless local area networks (WLAN). As the number and availability of wireless-enabled devices continues to increase, it is important for organizations to actively test and secure their enterprise wireless environments. Wireless scans can help organizations determine corrective actions to mitigate risks posed by wireless-enabled technologies.

Wireless scanning should be conducted using a mobile device with wireless analyzer software installed and configured—such as a laptop, handheld device, or specialty device. The scanning software or tool should allow the operator to configure the device for specific scans, and to scan in both passive and active modes. The scanning software should also be configurable by the operator to identify deviations from the organization's wireless security configuration requirements.

The wireless scanning tool should be capable of scanning all Institute of Electrical and Electronics Engineers (IEEE) 802.11a/b/g/n channels, whether domestic or international. In some cases, the device should also be fitted with an external antenna to provide an additional level of radio frequency (RF) capturing capability. Support for other wireless technologies, such as Bluetooth, will help evaluate the presence of additional wireless threats and vulnerabilities. Note that devices using nonstandard technology or frequencies outside of the scanning tool's RF range will not be detected or properly recognized by the scanning tool. A tool such as an RF spectrum analyzer will assist organizations in identifying transmissions that occur within the frequency range of the spectrum analyzer. Spectrum analyzers generally analyze a large frequency range (e.g., 3 to 18 GHz)—and although these devices do not analyze traffic, they enable an assessor to determine wireless activity within a specific frequency range and tailor additional testing and examination accordingly.

Passive scanning should be conducted regularly to supplement wireless security measures already in place, such as WIDPSs. Wireless scanning tools used to conduct completely passive scans transmit no data, nor do the tools in any way affect the operation of deployed wireless devices. By not transmitting data, a passive scanning tool remains undetected by malicious users and other devices. This reduces the likelihood of individuals avoiding detection by disconnecting or disabling unauthorized wireless devices.

Passive scanning tools capture wireless traffic being transmitted within the range of the tool's antenna. Most tools provide several key attributes regarding discovered wireless devices, including service set identifier (SSID), device type, channel, media access control (MAC) address, signal strength, and number of packets being transmitted. This information can be used to evaluate the security of the wireless environment, and to identify potential rogue devices and unauthorized ad hoc networks discovered within range of the scanning device. The wireless scanning tool should also be able to assess the captured packets to determine if any operational anomalies or threats exist.

Wireless scanning tools scan each IEEE 802.11a/b/g/n channel/frequency separately, often for only several hundred milliseconds at a time. The passive scanning tool may not receive all transmissions on a specific channel. For example, the tool may have been scanning channel 1 at the precise moment when a wireless device transmitted a packet on channel 5. This makes it important to set the dwell time of the tool to be long enough to capture packets, yet short enough to efficiently scan each channel. Dwell time configurations will depend on the device or tool used to conduct the wireless scans. In addition, security personnel conducting the scans should slowly move through the area being scanned to reduce the number of devices that go undetected.

[19]SP 800-115, Appendix D, p. D-1, D-2.

Rogue devices can be identified in several ways through passive scanning:

- The MAC address of a discovered wireless device indicates the vendor of the device's wireless interface. If an organization only deploys wireless interfaces from vendors A and B, the presence of interfaces from any other vendor indicates potential rogue devices.
- If an organization has accurate records of its deployed wireless devices, assessors can compare the MAC addresses of discovered devices with the MAC addresses of authorized devices. Most scanning tools allow assessors to enter a list of authorized devices. Because MAC addresses can be spoofed, assessors should not assume that the MAC addresses of discovered devices are accurate—but checking MAC addresses can identify rogue devices that do not use spoofing.
- Rogue devices may use SSIDs that are not authorized by the organization.
- Some rogue devices may use SSIDs that are authorized by the organization but do not adhere to its wireless security configuration requirements.

The signal strength of potential rogue devices should be reviewed to determine whether the devices are located within the confines of the facility or in the area being scanned. Devices operating outside an organization's confines might still pose significant risks because the organization's devices might inadvertently associate to them.

Organizations can move beyond passive wireless scanning to conduct active scanning. This builds on the information collected during passive scans, and attempts to attach to discovered devices and conduct penetration or vulnerability-related testing. For example, organizations can conduct active wireless scanning on their authorized wireless devices to ensure that they meet wireless security configuration requirements—including authentication mechanisms, data encryption, and administration access if this information is not already available through other means.

Organizations should be cautious in conducting active scans to make sure they do not inadvertently scan devices owned or operated by neighboring organizations that are within range. It is important to evaluate the physical location of devices before actively scanning them. Organizations should also be cautious in performing active scans of rogue devices that appear to be operating within the organization's facility. Such devices could belong to a visitor to the organization who inadvertently has wireless access enabled, or to a neighboring organization with a device that is close to, but not within, the organization's facility. Generally, organizations should focus on identifying and locating potential rogue devices rather than performing active scans of such devices.

Organizations may use active scanning when conducting penetration testing on their own wireless devices. Tools are available that employ scripted attacks and functions, attempt to circumvent implemented security measures, and evaluate the security level of devices. For example, tools used to conduct wireless penetration testing attempt to connect to access points (AP) through various methods to circumvent security configurations. If the tool can gain access to the AP, it can obtain information and identify the wired networks and wireless devices to which the AP is connected.

Security personnel who operate the wireless scanning tool should attempt to locate suspicious devices. RF signals propagate in a manner relative to the environment, which makes it important for the operator to understand how wireless technology supports this process. Mapping capabilities are useful here, but the main factors needed to support this capability are a knowledgeable operator and an appropriate wireless antenna.

If rogue devices are discovered and physically located during the wireless scan, security personnel should ensure that specific policies and processes are followed on how the rogue device is handled—such as shutting it down, reconfiguring it to comply with the organization's policies, or removing the device completely. If the device is to be removed, security personnel should evaluate the activity of the rogue device before it is confiscated. This can be done through monitoring transmissions and attempting to access the device.

If discovered wireless devices cannot be located during the scan, security personnel should attempt to use a WIDPS to support the location of discovered devices. This requires the WIDPS to locate a specific MAC address that was discovered during the scan. Properly deployed WIDPSs should have the ability to assist security personnel in locating these devices, and usually involves the use of multiple WIDPS sensors to increase location identification granularity. Because the WIDPS will only be able to locate a device within several feet, a wireless scanning tool may still be needed to pinpoint the location of the device.

For organizations that want to confirm compliance with their Bluetooth security requirements, passive scanning for Bluetooth-enabled wireless devices should be conducted to evaluate potential presence and activity. Because Bluetooth has a very short range (on average 9 meters [30 feet], with some devices having ranges of as little as 1 meter [3 feet]), scanning for devices can be difficult and time-consuming. Assessors should take range limitations into consideration when scoping this type of scanning. Organizations may want to perform scanning only in areas of their facilities that are accessible by the public—to see if attackers could gain access to devices via Bluetooth—or to perform scanning in a sampling of physical locations rather than throughout the entire facility. Because many Bluetooth-enabled devices (such as cell phones and personal digital assistants [PDA]) are mobile, conducting passive scanning several times over a period of time may be necessary. Organizations should also scan any Bluetooth infrastructure, such as access points, that they deploy. If rogue access points are discovered, the organization should handle them in accordance with established policies and processes.

A number of tools are available for actively testing the security and operation of Bluetooth devices. These tools attempt to connect to discovered devices and perform attacks to surreptitiously gain access and connectivity to Bluetooth-enabled devices. Assessors should be extremely cautious of performing active scanning because of the likelihood of inadvertently scanning personal Bluetooth devices, which are found in many environments. As a general rule, assessors should use active scanning only when they are certain that the devices being scanned belong to the organization. Active scanning can be used to evaluate the security mode in which a Bluetooth device is operating, and the strength of Bluetooth password identification numbers (PIN). Active scanning can also be used to verify that these devices are set to the lowest possible operational power setting to minimize their range. As with IEEE 802.11a/b/g rogue devices, rogue Bluetooth devices should be dealt with in accordance with policies and guidance.[20]

Uses for wireless scanning include identifying the following areas for further testing and evaluation:

a. 802.11
b. Serious flaws in its current implementation of Wired Equivalent Privacy (WEP)
c. Default configuration
d. Websites that publish the locations of discovered wireless networks
e. Insertion attacks
f. Interception and monitoring of wireless traffic
g. DOS
h. Client-to-client attacks

9. *Penetration testing*: Penetration testing is security testing in which assessors mimic real-world attacks to identify methods for circumventing the security features of an application, system, or network. It often involves launching real attacks on real systems and data that use tools and techniques commonly used by attackers. Most penetration tests involve looking for combinations of vulnerabilities on one or more systems that can be used to gain more access than could be achieved through a single vulnerability. Penetration testing can also be useful for determining:
a. How well the system tolerates real world–style attack patterns
b. The likely level of sophistication an attacker needs to successfully compromise the system
c. Additional countermeasures that could mitigate threats against the system
d. Defenders' ability to detect attacks and respond appropriately
Penetration testing can be invaluable, but it is labor-intensive and requires great expertise to minimize the risk to targeted systems. Systems may be damaged or

---

[20]SP 800-115, p. 4-6 to 4-10.

otherwise rendered inoperable during the course of penetration testing, even though the organization benefits in knowing how a system could be rendered inoperable by an intruder. Although experienced penetration testers can mitigate this risk, it can never be fully eliminated. Penetration testing should be performed only after careful consideration, notification, and planning.

Penetration testing often includes nontechnical methods of attack. For example, a penetration tester could breach physical security controls and procedures to connect to a network, steal equipment, capture sensitive information (possibly by installing keylogging devices), or disrupt communications. Caution should be exercised when performing physical security testing – security guards should be made aware of how to verify the validity of tester activity, such as via a point of contact or documentation. Another nontechnical means of attack is the use of social engineering, such as posing as a help desk agent and calling to request a user's passwords, or calling the help desk posing as a user and asking for a password to be reset.

The objectives of a penetration test are to simulate an attack using tools and techniques that may be restricted by law. This practice then needs the following areas for consideration and delineation in order to properly conduct this type of testing:

a. Formal permission

b. IP addresses/ranges to be tested

c. Any restricted hosts

d. List of acceptable testing techniques

e. When and how long?

f. IP addresses of the machines launching test

g. POCs for the testing team, targeted systems, and the networks

h. Measures to prevent law enforcement being called with false alarms

i. Handling of info collected by testing team

1. *Overt or covert testing*: There are several ways to conduct these types of tests. Testing can be conducted either overtly (also known as blue team or white-hat testing) or covertly (also known as red team or black-hat testing).

Overt security testing, also known as white hat testing, involves performing external and/or internal testing with the knowledge and consent of the organization's IT staff, enabling comprehensive evaluation of the network or system security posture. Because the IT staff is fully aware of and involved in the testing, it may be able to provide guidance to limit the testing's impact. Testing may also provide a training opportunity, with staff observing the activities and methods used by assessors to evaluate and potentially circumvent implemented security measures. This gives context to the security requirements implemented or maintained by the IT staff, and also may help teach IT staff how to conduct testing.

Covert security testing, also known as black hat testing, takes an adversarial approach by performing testing without the knowledge of the organization's IT staff but with the full knowledge and permission of upper management. Some organizations designate a trusted third party to ensure that the target organization does not initiate response measures associated with the attack without first verifying that an attack is indeed underway (e.g., that the activity being detected does not originate from a test). In such situations, the trusted third party provides an agent for the assessors, the management, the IT staff, and the security staff that mediates activities and facilitates communications. This type of test is useful for testing technical security controls, IT staff response to perceived security incidents, and staff knowledge and implementation of the organization's security policy. Covert testing may be conducted with or without warning.

The purpose of covert testing is to examine the damage or impact an adversary can cause—it does not focus on identifying vulnerabilities. This type of testing does not test every security control, identify each vulnerability, or assess all systems within an organization. Covert testing examines the organization from gain network access. If an organization's goal is to mirror a specific adversary, this type of testing requires special considerations—such as acquiring and modeling threat data. The resulting scenarios provide an overall strategic view of the potential methods of exploit, risk, and impact of an intrusion. Covert testing usually has defined boundaries, such as stopping testing when a certain level of access is achieved or a certain type of damage is achievable as a next step in testing. Having such boundaries prevents damage while still showing that the damage could occur.

   Besides failing to identify many vulnerabilities, covert testing is often time-consuming and costly due to its stealth requirements. To operate in a stealth environment, a test team will have to slow its scans and other actions to stay "under the radar" of the target organization's security staff. When testing is performed in-house, training must also be considered in terms of time and budget. In addition, an organization may have staff trained to perform regular activities such as scanning and vulnerability assessments, but not specialized techniques such as penetration or application security testing. Overt testing is less expensive, carries less risk than covert testing, and is more frequently used—but covert testing provides a better indication of the everyday security of the target organization because system administrators will not have heightened awareness.[21]

   Penetration test scenarios should focus on locating and targeting exploitable defects in the design and implementation of an application, system, or network. Tests should reproduce both the most likely and the most damaging attack patterns – including worst-case scenarios such as malicious actions by administrators. Since a penetration test scenario can be designed to simulate an inside attack, an outside attack, or both, external and internal security testing methods are considered. If both internal and external testing are to be performed, the external testing usually occurs first.

   Outsider scenarios simulate the outsider attacker who has little or no specific knowledge of the target and who works entirely from assumptions. To simulate an external attack, testers are provided with no real information about the target environment other than targeted IP addresses or address ranges, and perform open source research by collecting information on the targets from public web pages, newsgroups, and similar sites. Port scanners and vulnerability scanners are then used to identify target hosts. If given a list of authorized IP addresses to use as targets, assessors should verify that all public addresses (i.e., not private, unroutable addresses) are under the organization's purview before testing begins. Websites that provide domain name registration information (e.g., WHOIS) can be used to determine owners of address spaces. Since the testers' traffic usually goes through a firewall, the amount of information obtained from scanning is far less than if the test were undertaken from an insider perspective. After identifying hosts on the network that can be reached from outside, testers attempt to compromise one of the hosts. If successful, this access may then be used to compromise other hosts that are not generally accessible from outside the network. Penetration testing is an iterative process that leverages minimal access to gain greater access.

   Insider scenarios simulate the actions of a malicious insider. An internal penetration test is similar to an external test, except that the testers are on the internal network (i.e., behind the firewall) and have been granted some level of access to the network or specific network systems. Using this access, the penetration testers try to gain a greater level of access to the network and its systems through privilege escalation. Testers are provided with network

---

[21]SP 800-115, p. 2-5, 2-6.

information that someone with their level of access would normally have – generally as a standard employee, although depending on the goals of the test it could instead be information that a system or network administrator might possess.

Penetration testing is important for determining the vulnerability of an organization's network and the level of damage that can occur if the network is compromised. It is important to be aware that depending on an organization's policies, testers may be prohibited from using particular tools or techniques or may be limited to using them only during certain times of the day or days of the week. Penetration testing also poses a high risk to the organization's networks and systems because it uses real exploits and attacks against production systems and data. Because of its high cost and potential impact, penetration testing of an organization's network and systems on an annual basis may be sufficient. Also, penetration testing can be designed to stop when the tester reaches a point when an additional action will cause damage. The results of penetration testing should be taken seriously, and any vulnerabilities discovered should be mitigated. Results, when available, should be presented to the organization's managers. Organizations should consider conducting less labor-intensive testing activities on a regular basis to ensure that they are maintaining their required security posture. A well-designed program of regularly scheduled network and vulnerability scanning, interspersed with periodic penetration testing, can help prevent many types of attacks and reduce the potential impact of successful ones.[22]

FOUR PHASES OF PENETRATION TESTING

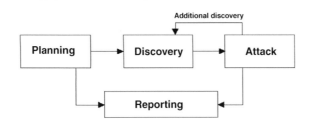

1. *Planning*: "In the planning phase, rules are identified, management approval is finalized and documented, and testing goals are set. The planning phase sets the groundwork for a successful penetration test. No actual testing occurs in this phase."[15] In planning a penetration test, always include a legal review for the test event with the corporate counsel staff of the organization that is being tested, as there are some strong legal issues which need to be identified and documented prior to conducting the testing. These issues include conducting testing on government systems from outside, which under CFAA and CSA is typically considered illegal as well as the actual testing may include breaching a system with sensitive information. These various criteria are included elsewhere in this handbook, but I wish to re-emphasize these again here as a caution.

---

[22]SP 800-115, p. 5-5, 5-6.

2. *Discovery*:

The discovery phase of penetration testing includes two parts. The first part is the start of actual testing, and covers information gathering and scanning. Network port and service identification is conducted to identify potential targets. In addition to port and service identification, other techniques are used to gather information on the targeted network:

a) **Host name and IP address information** can be gathered through many methods, including DNS interrogation, InterNIC (WHOIS) queries, and network sniffing (generally only during internal tests)
b) **Employee names and contact information** can be obtained by searching the organization's Web servers or directory servers
c) **System information, such as names and shares** can be found through methods such as NetBIOS enumeration (generally only during internal tests) and Network Information System (NIS) (generally only during internal tests)
d) **Application and service information,** such as version numbers, can be recorded through banner grabbing.

In some cases, techniques such as dumpster diving and physical walk-throughs of facilities may be used to collect additional information on the targeted network, and may also uncover additional information to be used during the penetration tests, such as passwords written on paper.

The second part of the discovery phase is vulnerability analysis, which involves comparing the services, applications, and operating systems of scanned hosts against vulnerability databases (a process that is automatic for vulnerability scanners) and the testers' own knowledge of vulnerabilities. Human testers can use their own databases – or public databases such as the National Vulnerability Database (NVD) – to identify vulnerabilities manually. Manual processes can identify new or obscure vulnerabilities that automated scanners may miss, but are much slower than an automated scanner.

Some of the various discovery techniques used during penetration testing are identified as follows:

a. DNS queries
b. InterNIC (whois) queries
c. Target organization's website information
d. Social engineering techniques including:
- *Dumpster diving*: Gathering info on a target by digging through what they have thrown out
e. Packet sniffing/capture
f. NetBIOS enumeration
g. Network Information System (NIS)
h. Banner grabbing
i. Vulnerability analysis:
- Services
- Applications
- Operating systems
- Manual
- Automated scanners

3. *Attack*: Executing an attack is at the heart of any penetration test. The figure below represents the individual steps of the attack phase – the process of verifying previously identified potential vulnerabilities by attempting to exploit them. The four steps to any attack are as follows:

a. Gaining access
b. Escalating privilege
c. System browsing
d. Installing additional test software

If an attack is successful, the vulnerability is verified and safeguards are identified to mitigate the associated security exposure. In many cases, exploits that are executed do not grant the maximum level of potential access to an attacker. They may instead result in the testers learning more about the targeted network and its potential vulnerabilities, or induce a change in the state of the targeted network's security. Some exploits enable testers to escalate their privileges on the system or network to gain access to additional resources. If this occurs, additional analysis and testing are required to determine the true level of risk for the network, such as identifying the types of information that can be gleaned, changed, or removed from the system. In the event an attack on a specific vulnerability proves impossible, the tester should attempt to exploit another discovered vulnerability. If testers are able to exploit a vulnerability, they can install more tools on the target system or network to facilitate the testing process. These tools are used to gain access to additional systems or resources on the network, and obtain access to information about the network or organization. Testing and analysis on multiple systems should be conducted during a penetration test to determine the level of access an adversary could gain. This process is represented in the feedback loop in the figure above between the attack and the discovery phase of a penetration test.

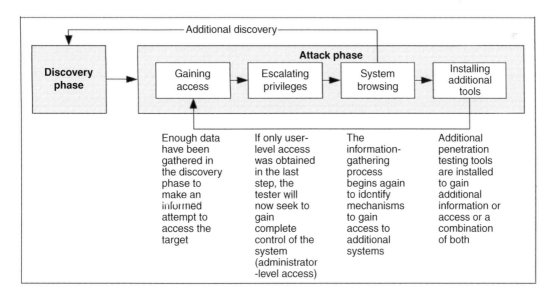

While vulnerability scanners check only for the possible existence of a vulnerability, the attack phase of a penetration test exploits the vulnerability to confirm its existence.

Most vulnerabilities exploited by penetration testing fall into the following categories:

  a. *Misconfigurations*: Misconfigured security settings, particularly insecure default settings, are usually easily exploitable.
  b. *Kernel flaws*: Kernel code is the core of an OS, and enforces the overall security model for the system – so any security flaw in the kernel puts the entire system in danger.
  c. *Buffer overflows*: A buffer overflow occurs when programs do not adequately check input for appropriate length. When this occurs, arbitrary code can be introduced into the system and executed with the privileges – often at the administrative level – of the running program.
  d. *Insufficient input validation*: Many applications fail to fully validate the input they receive from users. An example is a web application that embeds a value from a user in a database query. If the user enters SQL commands instead of or in addition to the requested value, and the web application does not filter the SQL commands, the query may be run with malicious changes that the user requested – causing what is known as a SQL injection attack.
  e. *Symbolic links*: A symbolic link (symlink) is a file that points to another file. Operating systems include programs that can change the permissions granted to a file. If these programs run with privileged permissions, a user could strategically create symlinks to trick these programs into modifying or listing critical system files.
  f. *File descriptor attacks*: File descriptors are numbers used by the system to keep track of files in lieu of filenames. Specific types of file descriptors have implied uses. When a privileged program assigns an inappropriate file descriptor, it exposes that file to compromise.
  g. *Race conditions*: Race conditions can occur during the time a program or process has entered into a privileged mode. A user can time an attack to take advantage of elevated privileges while the program or process is still in the privileged mode.
  h. *Incorrect file and directory permissions*: File and directory permissions control the access assigned to users and processes. Poor permissions could allow many types of attacks, including the reading or writing of password files or additions to the list of trusted remote hosts.

4. *Reporting*: The reporting phase occurs simultaneously with the other three phases of the penetration test. In the planning phase, the assessment plan—or ROE—is developed. In the discovery and attack phases, written logs are usually kept and periodic reports are made to system administrators and/or management. At the conclusion of the test, a report is generally developed to describe identified vulnerabilities, present a risk rating, and give guidance on how to mitigate the discovered weaknesses. Section 8 discusses post-testing activities such as reporting in more detail.[23]

POST-TEST ACTIONS TO BE TAKEN

As a result of the penetration testing, several areas for action by the tester/assessor include:

• Identifying the issues that need to be addressed quickly
• Delineating the how of the test – the most important step in the testing process

[23]SP 800-115, p. 5-2 to 5-5.

- Common causes and methods for addressing them:
  - Lack of (or poorly enforced) organizational security
  - Misconfiguration
  - Software (un)reliability
  - Failure to apply patches

Penetration testing is important for determining the vulnerability of an organization's network and the level of damage that can occur if the network is compromised. It is important to be aware that depending on an organization's policies, testers may be prohibited from using particular tools or techniques or may be limited to using them only during certain times of the day or days of the week. Penetration testing also poses a high risk to the organization's networks and systems because it uses real exploits and attacks against production systems and data. Because of its high cost and potential impact, penetration testing of an organization's network and systems on an annual basis may be sufficient. Also, penetration testing can be designed to stop when the tester reaches a point when an additional action will cause damage. The results of penetration testing should be taken seriously, and any vulnerabilities discovered should be mitigated. Results, when available, should be presented to the organization's managers. Organizations should consider conducting less labor-intensive testing activities on a regular basis to ensure that they are maintaining their required security posture. A well-designed program of regularly scheduled network and vulnerability scanning, interspersed with periodic penetration testing, can help prevent many types of attacks and reduce the potential impact of successful ones.[24]

GENERAL SCHEDULE FOR TESTING CATEGORIES

- *Category 1*: This category tests to verify the systems or activities that *provide security or other critical functions* for the organization or agency:
  - Firewalls, routers, and perimeter defense systems such as for intrusion detection
  - Public access systems such as web and email servers
  - DNS and directory servers, and other internal systems that would likely be intruder targets
- *Category 2*: This category tests *all other systems* besides the critical ones:
  - *Assessment testing*:
    - *Vulnerability scanning*: Vulnerability scanning is designed to allow a cybersecurity analyst to create a prioritized list of vulnerabilities for a customer who is likely already aware that they are not where they need to be in terms of information assurance and computer security. The customer already understands that they have open vulnerabilities (perhaps on new computer systems, networks, etc.) and simply need assistance identifying and prioritizing them.
    Also note that during initial vulnerability scans and assessments, the more potential vulnerabilities identified, the better.
    - *Log review*: Log reviews are important security activity for the purposes of isolating anomalous events, identifying troubles in the system or network, and providing evidence during troubleshooting and incident response actions. SP 800-92 Log Management has many techniques and identified tactics for conducting log reviews.

[24]SP 800-115, p. 5-6.

- *Penetration testing*: Penetration testing is a process designed to simulate a cyber attacker who has a specific goal. Penetrating testing, therefore, is often focused on a particular piece of software or network service.

  These tests are conducted by a cybersecurity analyst for customers who are already compliant with the regulations for cybersecurity and information assurance, but are concerned about vulnerabilities relating to a particular system or part of their network. A typical goal could be to access a new network service like a customer-facing database.

  The standard output for a penetration test is a report detailing how the cybersecurity analyst breached specific cybersecurity defenses during the simulated attack, and suggestions on how to remediate this vulnerability.
- *Configuration checklist review*: The federal government security actions today typically include configuring machines and services in accordance with standard configurations which are defined by checklists for each type of machine and the settings for hardening the system under review. The first level of testing, compliance testing, involves running through the checklists against the actual machine and reviewing these various settings and ensuring they are actually installed correctly. Often the scanning tools mentioned above have these various settings already installed and the report outputs identify any setting which does not meet the criteria.

Reference

[1] OWASP testing guide 4.0, web application fingerprint section; July 2014.

11

Security Component Fundamentals for Assessment

The key to the management, oversight, and governance of the security components and program in the organization is the understanding of the risks involved and how each is treated and tolerated by the organization. As the assessor for a US governmental system, it is important to grasp and work with the fundamental requirements for these systems. With the SP 800-53 structured approach to security controls, the assessor can review each management, technical, and operational area of security directly. NIST SP 800-53, rev. 4, is divided into 18 control families comprising 3 security classes of controls:

1. *Management controls*: Focus on the management of the computer security system and the management of risk for a system. They are techniques and concerns that are normally addressed by management, through policy and documentation.
2. *Operational controls*: Address security issues related to mechanisms primarily implemented and executed by people (as opposed to systems). Often, they require technical or specialized expertise and rely on management activities as well as technical controls.
3. *Technical controls*: Technical controls are security controls that are configured within the system. They can provide automated protection for unauthorized access or misuse, facilitate detection of security violations, and support security requirements for applications and data.

Each family of controls starts with the base "−1" control which defines the policies necessary for the family of controls. All 18 families of controls within the SP 800-53 are defined in this manner. These are commonly known as the "XX 1 Policy and Procedures" controls. An information security policy is an aggregate of directives, rules, and practices that prescribes how an organization manages, protects, and distributes information. Information security policy is an essential component of information security governance – without the policy, governance has no substance and rules to enforce.

Information security policy should be based on a combination of appropriate legislation, such as FISMA; applicable standards, such as NIST Federal Information Processing Standards (FIPS) and guidance; and internal agency requirements. Therefore, the assessor will identify the relevant governmental documents for each policy and then check the system documentation for reference to those documents. Agency information security policy should address the fundamentals of agency information security governance structure, including:

1. Information security roles and responsibilities
2. Statement of security control baseline and rules for exceeding the baseline
3. Rules of behavior that agency users are expected to follow and minimum repercussions for noncompliance

We will discuss each of these families of controls in this chapter, starting with the management controls.

MANAGEMENT AREAS OF CONSIDERATION

There are many areas which the assessor needs to consider when evaluating and testing the various management controls installed on the systems under test as shown below in the listing of the families of controls. The starting point for most of these areas is the oversight and governance requirements. So the first area of management controls to review would be the security program and its operations section.

The management areas covered by SP 800-53 controls are varied and wide in their scope.

The basic ideas behind the controls are to provide direct information security program elements to assist managers in establishing, implementing, and running an information security program. Typically, the organization looks to the program for overall responsibility to ensure the selection and implementation of appropriate security controls and to demonstrate the effectiveness of satisfying their stated security requirements.

As SP 800-100 states: "Federal agencies rely heavily on information technology (IT) to run their daily operations and deliver products and services. With an increasing reliability on IT, a growing complexity of federal government IT infrastructure, and a constantly changing information security threat and risk environment, information security has become a mission-essential function. This function must be managed and governed to reduce the risks to federal government operations and to ensure the federal government's ability to do business and serve the American public."[1]

Key elements to review for any security management program are as follows:

- *Senior management commitment and support*: As the cornerstone for successful establishment and continuance of an information security management program, commitment and support from senior management should exist.
- *Policies and procedures*: As a structured framework, policy and procedures start with a general organization policy providing concise top management declaration of direction.
- *Organization*: Responsibilities for the protection of individual assets and for carrying out specific security processes should be clearly defined. The information security policy should provide general guidance on the allocation of security roles and responsibilities in the organization.

---

[1]SP 800-100, p. 2.

- *Security awareness and education*: All employees of an organization and, where relevant, third-party users should receive appropriate training and regular updates on the importance of security in organizational policies and procedures.
- *Monitoring and compliance*: In assessing the effectiveness of an organization's security program(s) on a continuous basis, IS auditors must have an understanding of the organization's monitoring activities in assessing the effectiveness of security programs and controls established.
- *Incident handling and response*: A computer security incident is an adverse event that threatens some aspect of computer security.

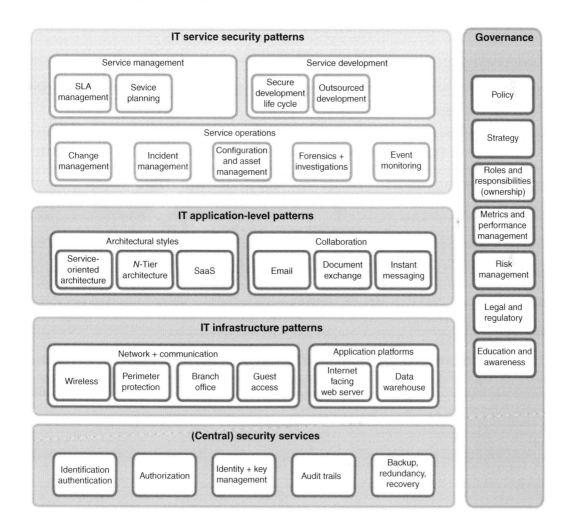

While the standards such as NIST, ISO, and Information Security Forum (ISF) divide their materials into chapters, these do not translate into a security architecture landscape very well.

Therefore, the Open Security Architecture Forum[2] proposes an architecture that identifies topics of poor coverage, determines priorities for new patterns, and helps the community coordinate their risk management (RM) activities. Open Security Architecture (OSA) is a not-for-profit organization, supported by volunteers for the benefit of the security community.

MANAGEMENT CONTROLS

The management controls are defined in SP 800-53 as the overarching controls needed for oversight, compliance, and acquisition of security components, equipment, and processes for security within a federal system. The basic structure of controls is to define the security action to be taken, supplemental guidance for use and installation of the control, any enhancements to each control, references, and then the parameters or variables that the organization can use to install and implement the control.

Program Management (PM)

Information Security Program Plan

The information security program plan can be represented in a single document or compilation of documents at the discretion of the organization. The plan documents the organization-wide PM controls and organization-defined common controls. The security plans for individual information systems and the organization-wide information security program plan together provide complete coverage for all security controls employed within the organization. Common controls are documented in an appendix to the organization's information security program plan unless the controls are included in a separate security plan for an information system (e.g., security controls employed as part of an intrusion detection system (IDS) providing organization-wide boundary protection inherited by one or more organizational information systems). The organization-wide information security program plan will indicate which separate security plans contain descriptions of common controls.

Critical Infrastructure Plan

The organization addresses information security issues in the development, documentation, and updating of a critical infrastructure and key resources (CIKR) protection plan. Critical infrastructure assets are essential for the functioning of a society and economy. Most commonly associated with the term are facilities for:

1. Electricity generation, transmission, and distribution
2. Gas production, transport, and distribution
3. Oil and oil products production, transport, and distribution
4. Telecommunication
5. Water supply (drinking water, waste water/sewage, stemming of surface water (e.g., dikes and sluices))
6. Agriculture, food production and distribution

---

[2]Retrieved from http://www.opensecurityarchitecture.org on 1/21/2015.

7. Heating (e.g., natural gas, fuel oil, district heating)
8. Public health (hospitals, ambulances)
9. Transportation systems (fuel supply, railway network, airports, harbors, inland shipping)
10. Financial services (banking, clearing)
11. Security services (police, military)

The main document of the US government for the critical infrastructure is HSPD-7, *Critical Infrastructure Identification, Prioritization, and Protection*, which references the CIKR of the United States.

Essential Services that Underpin American Society

It is the policy of the United States to enhance the protection of our nation's CIKR against terrorist acts that could:

1. Cause catastrophic health effects or mass casualties comparable to those from the use of a weapon of mass destruction
2. Impair federal departments and agencies' abilities to perform essential missions, or to ensure the public's health and safety
3. Undermine state and local government capacities to maintain order and to deliver minimum essential public services
4. Damage the private sector's capability to ensure the orderly functioning of the economy and delivery of essential services
5. Have a negative effect on the economy through the cascading disruption of other CIKR
6. Undermine the public's morale and confidence in our national economic and political institutions

Industrial Control Systems Characteristics

- Pervasive throughout critical infrastructure
- Need for real-time response
- Extremely high availability, predictability, and reliability

An industrial control system (ICS) is an information system used to control industrial processes such as manufacturing, product handling, production, and distribution. ICSs include supervisory control and data acquisition (SCADA) systems, distributed control systems (DCS), and programmable logic controllers (PLC). ICS are typically found in the electric, water, oil and gas, chemical, pharmaceutical, pulp and paper, food and beverage, and discrete manufacturing (automotive, aerospace, and durable goods) industries as well as in air and rail transportation control systems.

Security PM is designed to and often struggles with meeting several and often conflicting requirements:

- Minimizing risk to the safety of the public
- Preventing serious damage to environment
- Preventing serious production stoppages or slowdowns

- Protecting critical infrastructure from cyber attacks and human error
- Safeguarding against compromise of proprietary information

So the assessor must review the program documents, reports, and reviews to verify the documented requirements are actually being met while the A&A – controls review and implementation process reflects the security is being maintained during operational activities.

INFORMATION SECURITY RESOURCES

The assessor will determine if the organization:

1. Ensures that all capital planning and investment requests include the resources needed to implement the information security program and documents all exceptions to this requirement
2. Employs a business case/Exhibit 300/Exhibit 53 to record the resources required
3. Ensures that information security resources are available for expenditure as planned

Organizations may designate and empower an Investment Review Board (IRB; or similar group) to manage and provide oversight for the information security-related aspects of the capital planning and investment control process. Which ties into the Capital Planning and Investment Control (SP 800-65) criteria of an Exhibit 300 must be submitted for all major investments in accordance with this section.

Major information technology (IT) investments also must be reported on the agency's Exhibit 53. Exhibit 300s and the Exhibit 53, together with the agency's Enterprise Architecture (EA) program, define how to manage the IT Capital Planning and Control Process.

All IT investments must clearly demonstrate the investment is needed to help meet the agency's strategic goals and mission. They should also support the President's Management Agenda (PMA). The capital asset plans and business cases (Exhibit 300) and "Agency IT Investment Portfolio" (Exhibit 53) demonstrate the agency management of IT investments and how these governance processes are used when planning and implementing IT investments within the agency.

Investments in the development of new or the continued operation of existing information systems, both general support systems and major applications, proposed for funding in the President's budget must:

1. Be tied to the agency's information architecture. Proposals should demonstrate that the security controls for components, applications, and systems are consistent with and an integral part of the IT architecture of the agency.
2. Be well planned, by:
    a. Demonstrating that the costs of security controls are understood and are explicitly incorporated in the life-cycle planning of the overall system in a manner consistent with OMB guidance for capital programming
    b. Incorporating a security plan that discusses risk management.
3. Manage risks, by:
    a. Demonstrating specific methods used to ensure that risks and the potential for loss are understood and continually assessed, that steps are taken to maintain risk at an acceptable level, and that procedures are in place to ensure that controls are implemented effectively and remain effective over time

    b. Demonstrating specific methods used to ensure that the security controls are commensurate with the risk and magnitude of harm that may result from the loss, misuse, or unauthorized access to or modification of the system itself or the information it manages

    c. Identifying additional security controls that are necessary to minimize risks to and potential loss from those systems that promote or permit public access, other externally accessible systems, and those systems that are interconnected with systems over which program officials have little or no control

4. Protect privacy and confidentiality, by:

    a. Deploying effective security controls and authentication tools consistent with the protection of privacy, such as public key–based digital signatures, for those systems that promote or permit public access

    b. Ensuring that the handling of personal information is consistent with relevant government-wide and agency policies, such as privacy statements on the agency's websites

5. Account for departures from NIST guidance. For non-national security applications, to ensure the use of risk-based cost-effective security controls, describe each occasion when employing standards and guidance that are more stringent than those promulgated by the NIST.

To promote greater attention to security as a fundamental management priority, OMB continues to take steps to integrate security into the capital planning and budget process. To further assist in this integration, the Plan of Action and Milestones (POAMs; M02-01) and annual security reports and executive summaries must be cross-referenced to the budget materials sent to OMB in the fall including Exhibits 300 and 53.

MEASURES OF PERFORMANCE (SP 800-55)

NIST SP 800-55 is a guide to assist in the development, selection, and implementation of measures to be used at the information system and program levels. These measures indicate the effectiveness of security controls applied to information systems and supporting information security programs. Such measures are used to facilitate decision making, improve performance, and increase accountability through the collection, analysis, and reporting of relevant performance-related data – providing a way to tie the implementation, efficiency, and effectiveness of information system and program security controls to an agency's success in achieving its mission. The performance measures development process described in SP 800-55 will assist agency information security practitioners in establishing a relationship between information system and program security activities under their purview and the agency mission, helping to demonstrate the value of information security to their organization.

Additionally, performance measurements are required to ensure the IT system is in compliance with existing laws, rules, and regulations, such as FISMA.

Factors that must be considered during the development and implementation of an IT measurement program are as follows:

- Measures must yield quantifiable information: percentages, averages, and numbers.
- Data that supports the measures needs to be readily obtainable.

- Only repeatable information security processes should be considered for measurement.
- Measures must be useful for tracking performance and directing resources.

MEASURES OF PERFORMANCE

- Metric types
- Metrics development and implementation approach
- Metrics development process

Metric Types

- "Am I implementing the tasks for which I am responsible?"
- "How efficiently or effectively am I accomplishing those tasks?"
- "What impact are those tasks having on the mission?"

Metrics Development Process

The place of information security metrics within a larger organizational context demonstrates that information security metrics can be used to progressively measure implementation, efficiency, effectiveness, and the business impact of information security activities within organizations or for specific systems.

The information security metrics development process consists of two major activities:

1. Identifying and defining the current information security program
2. Developing and selecting specific metrics to measure implementation, efficiency, effectiveness, and the impact of the security controls

The process steps do not need to be sequential. Rather, the process illustrated in the following diagram provides a framework for thinking about metrics and aids in identifying metrics to be developed for each system. The type of metric depends on where the system is within its life cycle and on the maturity of the information system security program. This framework facilitates tailoring metrics to a specific organization and to the different stakeholder groups present within each organization.

Phases 5, 6, and 7 involve developing metrics that measure process implementation, effectiveness and efficiency, and mission impact, respectively. The specific aspect of information security that metrics will focus on at any given point will depend on information security program maturity. Implementation evidence, required to prove higher levels of effectiveness, will change from establishing existence of policy and procedures to quantifying implementation of these policies and procedures, then to quantifying results of implementation of policies and procedures, and ultimately to identifying the impact of implementation on the organization's mission.

Based on existing policies and procedures, the universe of possible metrics can be prohibitively large; therefore, agencies should prioritize metrics to ensure that the final set selected for initial implementation has the following attributes:

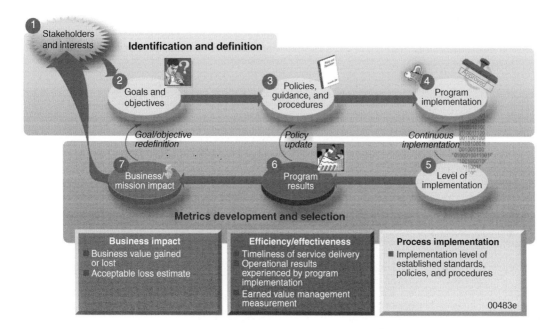

1. **Facilitates improvement of high-priority security control implementation.** High priority may be defined by the latest Government Accountability Office (GAO) or Inspector General (IG) reports, results of a risk assessment, or an internal organizational goal.
2. Uses data that can realistically be obtained from existing processes and data repositories.
3. Measures processes that already exist and are relatively stable. Measuring nonexistent or unstable processes will not provide meaningful information about security performance and will therefore not be useful for targeting specific aspects of performance. On the other hand, attempting such measurement may not be entirely useless, because such a metric will certainly produce poor results and will therefore identify an area that needs improvement.

Metrics can be derived from existing data sources, including security certification and accreditation, security assessments, POAM, incident statistics, and agency-initiated or independent reviews. Agencies may decide to use a weighting scale to differentiate the importance of selected metrics and to ensure that the results accurately reflect existing security program priorities. This process would involve assigning values to each metric based on the importance of a metric in the context of the overall security program. Metrics weighting should be based on the overall risk mitigation goals, is likely to reflect higher criticality of department-level initiatives versus smaller-scale initiatives, and is a useful tool that facilitates integration of information security into the departmental capital planning process.

A phased approach may be required to identify short-, mid-, and long-term metrics in which the implementation time frame depends on a combination of system-level effectiveness, metric priority, data availability, and process stability. Once applicable metrics that contain the qualities described above are identified, they will need to be documented with supporting detail, including frequency of data collection, data source, formula for calculation, implementation evidence for measured activity, and a guide for metric data interpretation. Other information about each metric can be defined based on an organization's processing and business requirements.

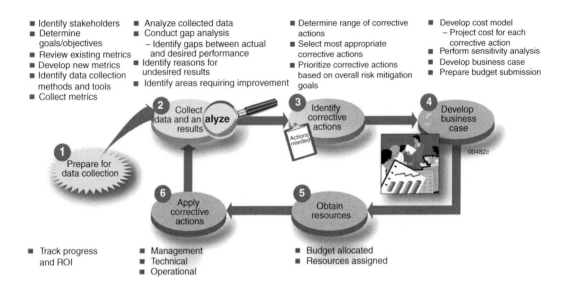

- Identify stakeholders
- Determine goals/objectives
- Review existing metrics
- Develop new metrics
- Identify data collection methods and tools
- Collect metrics

- Analyze collected data
- Conduct gap analysis
  - Identify gaps between actual and desired performance
- Identify reasons for undesired results
- Identify areas requiring improvement

- Determine range of corrective actions
- Select most appropriate corrective actions
- Prioritize corrective actions based on overall risk mitigation goals

- Develop cost model
  - Project cost for each corrective action
- Perform sensitivity analysis
- Develop business case
- Prepare budget submission

- Track progress and ROI

- Management
- Technical
- Operational

- Budget allocated
- Resources assigned

Metrics Program Implementation

- Prepare for data collection.
- Collect data and analyze results.
- Identify corrective actions.
- Develop business case and obtain resources.
- Apply corrective actions.

FEDERAL ENTERPRISE ARCHITECTURE

As part of the management criteria for controls and the system under review, the federal requirement defined in the Clinger Cohen Act of 1996 requires all systems be included in the EA for the agency. This process is identified and delineated in the Federal Enterprise Architecture (FEA) process as adopted by the federal CIO Council.

The FEA practice adopted three core principles to guide its strategic direction. They are as follows:

1. *Business-driven*: The FEA is most useful when it is closely aligned with government strategic plans and executive-level direction. Agency mission statements, presidential management directives, and agency business owners give direction to each agency's EA and to the FEA.

2. *Proactive and collaborative across the federal government*: Adoption of the FEA is achieved through active participation by the EA community in its development and use. The FEA community is responsible for the development, evolution, and adoption of the FEA.

3. *Architecture improves the effectiveness and efficiency of government information resources*: Architecture development is an integral part of the capital investment process. No IT investment should be made without a business-approved architecture.

The FEA consists of a set of interrelated "reference models" designed to facilitate cross-agency analysis and the identification of duplicative investments, gaps, and opportunities for collaboration within and across agencies. Collectively, the reference models comprise a framework for describing important elements of the FEA in a common and consistent way.

Through the use of this common framework and vocabulary, IT portfolios can be better managed and leveraged across the federal government. This chapter introduces the purposes and structures of the five FEA reference models:

1. Performance Reference Model (PRM)
2. Business Reference Model (BRM)
3. Service Component Reference Model (SRM)
4. Technical Reference Model (TRM)
5. Data Reference Model (DRM)

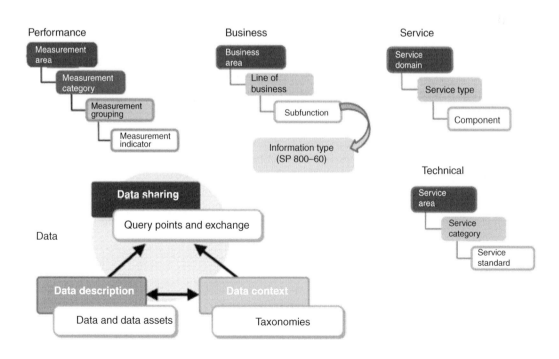

Information protection needs are technology-independent, required capabilities to counter threats to the organization through the compromise of information (i.e., loss of confidentiality, integrity, or availability).

Information protection needs are derived from the mission/business needs defined by the organization, the mission/business processes selected to meet the stated needs, and the organizational RM strategy. Information protection needs determine the required security controls for the organization and the associated information systems supporting the mission/business processes. Inherent in defining an organization's information protection needs is an understanding of the level of adverse impact that could result if a compromise of information occurs.

The security categorization process is used to make such potential impact determinations, which is related to and feeds the development of the security categorization requirements for each system as found in FIPS-199, guided by SP 800-60. These reference the process defined in the first step of the Risk Management Framework (RMF) as for in the previous chapters.

SYSTEM AND SERVICES ACQUISITION (SA)

From OMB Budget Circular A-11, the Exhibit 300 is the capture mechanism for all of the analyses and activities required for full internal review (e.g., IRB, CIO). More importantly, Exhibit 300 is the document that OMB uses to assess investments and ultimately make funding decisions, and therefore should be leveraged by agencies to clearly demonstrate the need for life cycle and annual funding requests. Following selection into the agency's IT portfolio, the agency aggregates Exhibit 300s into the Exhibit 53. The Exhibit 53 provides an overview of the agency's entire IT portfolio by listing every IT investment, life cycle, and budget-year cost information.

Exhibit 300s are companions to an agency's Exhibit 53. Exhibit 300s and the Exhibit 53, together with the agency's EA program, define how to manage the IT Capital Planning and Control Process. Exhibit 53A is a tool for reporting the funding of the portfolio of all IT investments within a department while Exhibit 300A is a tool for detailed justifications of major "IT investments." Exhibit 300B is for the management of the execution of those investments through their project life cycle and into their useful life in production.

By integrating the disciplines of architecture, investment management, and project implementation, these programs provide the foundation for sound IT management practices, end-to-end governance of IT capital assets, and the alignment of IT investments with an agency's strategic goals. As architecture-driven IT investments are funded in the "invest" (development/acquisition) phase, they move forward into the implementation phase where system development life-cycle processes are followed and actual versus planned outputs, schedule, and operational performance expenditures are tracked utilizing performance-based management processes.

SECURITY SERVICES LIFE CYCLE

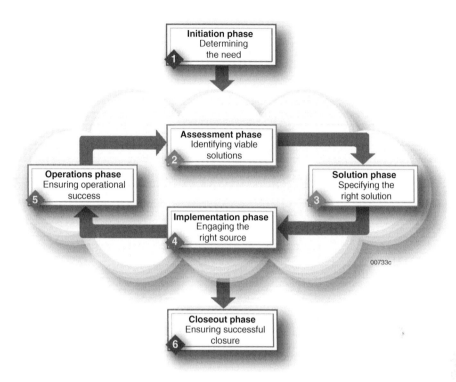

SP 800-14, *Generally Accepted Principles and Practices for Securing Information Technology Systems*, provides a foundation on which organizations can establish and review IT security programs. The eight Generally Accepted System Security Principles in SP 800-14 are designed to provide the public or private sector audience with an organization-level perspective when creating new systems, practices, or policies.

General Considerations for Security Services

- *Strategic/mission*
- *Budgetary/funding*
- *Technical/architectural*
- *Organizational*
- *Personnel*
- *Policy/process*

To facilitate identification and review of these considerations, security program managers may use a set of questions when considering security products for their programs.

1. Identify the user community.
2. Define the relationship between the security product and the organization's mission.
3. Identify data sensitivity.
4. Identify an organization's security requirements.
5. Review security plan.
6. Review policies and procedures.
7. Identify operational issues such as daily operation, maintenance, and training.

This then leads to the assessor reviewing the acquisition criteria for various security components, services, and equipment along with the documentation, contract requirements, and the varied support design reports and analyses to ensure there are considerations defined for selecting the information security products and services from the following viewpoints:

- Organizational
- Product
- Vendor
- Security checklists for IT products
- Organizational conflict of interest

INFORMATION SECURITY AND EXTERNAL PARTIES

The security of the organization's information and information processing facilities that are accessed, processed, communicated to, or managed by external parties should be maintained, and should not be reduced by the introduction of external-party products or services. Any access to the organization's information processing facilities and processing and communication of information by external parties should be controlled. Where there is a business need for working with external parties that may require access to the organization's information and information processing facilities, or in obtaining or providing a product and service from or to an external party, a risk assessment should be carried out to determine security implications and control requirements. Controls should be agreed to and defined in an agreement with the external party.

These external party arrangements can include:

- Service providers, such as internet service providers (ISPs), network providers, telephone services, and maintenance and support services
- Managed security services
- Customers
- Outsourcing facilities and/or operations, for example, IT systems, data collection services, and call center operations
- Management and business consultants, and auditors
- Developers and suppliers, for example, of software products and IT systems
- Cleaning, catering, and other outsourced support services
- Temporary personnel, student placement, and other casual short-term appointments

CA – SECURITY ASSESSMENT AND AUTHORIZATION

This is the control family for the RMF and its implementation. So an assessor will review and identify all the components of the RMF, the identities of the key roles and the people assigned those roles, the process functions, and the key organizational documents which the agency has produced to support these RMF processes as identified in the previous chapters of this book and in SP 800-37, rev. 1.

PL – PLANNING FAMILY AND FAMILY PLANS

The assessor must ensure the organization plans and coordinates security-related activities affecting the information system before conducting such activities in order to reduce the impact on organizational operations (i.e., mission, functions, image, and reputation), organizational assets, and individuals. Security-related activities include, for example, security assessments, audits, system hardware and software maintenance, and contingency plan testing/exercises. Organizational advance planning and coordination includes both emergency and nonemergency (i.e., planned or nonurgent unplanned) situations.

This process is documented in the System Security Plan (SSP) which will include the organizational rules of behavior for each user of the system under review and the system hardware and software inventory.

System Security Plan

The security plan contains sufficient information (including specification of parameters for assignment and selection statements in security controls either explicitly or by reference) to enable an implementation that is unambiguously compliant with the intent of the plan and a subsequent determination of risk to organizational operations and assets, individuals, other organizations, and the nation if the plan is implemented as intended.

Rules of Behavior

These establishes and makes readily available to all information system users the rules that describe their responsibilities and expected behavior with regard to information and information system usage, and receives signed acknowledgment from users indicating that they have read, understand, and agree to abide by the rules of behavior, before authorizing access to information and the information system.

Information Security Hardware

The organization:

1. Develops an information security architecture for the information system that:
   a. Describes the overall philosophy, requirements, and approach to be taken with regard to protecting the confidentiality, integrity, and availability of organizational information

  b. Describes how the information security architecture is integrated into and supports the EA
  c. Describes any information security assumptions about, and dependencies on, external services
2. Reviews and updates the information security architecture periodically to reflect updates in the EA

RA – RISK ASSESSMENT FAMILY

Risk Management

- RM is the process of balancing the risk associated with organizational or business activities with an adequate level of control that will enable the business to meet its mission and/or objectives.
- RM is the identification, assessment, and prioritization of risk followed by coordinated and economical application of resources to minimize, monitor, and control the probability and/or impact of adverse events or to maximize the realization of opportunities.

Holistically, RM covers all concepts and processes affiliated with managing risk, including the systematic application of management policies, procedures, and practices; the tasks of communicating, consulting, and establishing the context; and identifying, analyzing, evaluating, treating, monitoring, and reviewing risk.

As an assessor, one area to always focus on during the review of the policy and procedural documentation, as well as during the key personnel interviews, is the area of responsibility versus accountability. These are typically defined as follows:

- *Responsibility*: Belongs to those who must ensure that the activities are completed successfully
- *Accountability*: Applies to those who either own the required resources or have the authority to approve the execution and/or accept the outcome of an activity within specific RM processes

The risk factors formula is usually a good place to start the review of risks and how they are viewed and treated within the organization. The formula is relatively straightforward for the organization to use and can be a key element to the organizational risk posture as the assessor reviews and interviews the various management staff during the assessment. The formula is as follows: risk $= T \times V \times \$ \times C$, where $C =$ likelihood $\times$ impact. Here:

1. $T =$ threats to the organization
2. $V =$ vulnerabilities within the organization
3. $\$ =$ assets being protected
4. $C =$ consequences of risk

The risk assessment family of controls provides areas of focus for the organization and the assessor to review and update their security posture on an ongoing basis throughout the life cycle of the system under review.

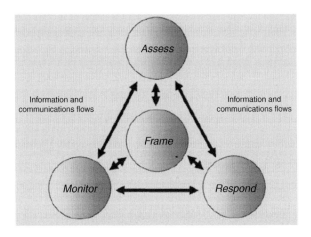

Security Categorization

- A clearly defined authorization boundary is a prerequisite for an effective security categorization. Security categorization describes the potential adverse impacts to organizational operations, organizational assets, and individuals should the information and information system be comprised through a loss of confidentiality, integrity, or availability.
- The organization conducts the security categorization process as an organization-wide activity with the involvement of the chief information officer, senior information security officer, information system owner, mission owners, and information owners/stewards. The organization also considers potential adverse impacts to other organizations and, in accordance with the USA PATRIOT Act of 2001 and Homeland Security Presidential Directives, potential national-level adverse impacts in categorizing the information system. The security categorization process facilitates the creation of an inventory of information assets, and, in conjunction with configuration management (CM)-8, a mapping to the information system components where the information is processed, stored, and transmitted.

Risk and Vulnerability Assessments

- A clearly defined authorization boundary is a prerequisite for an effective risk assessment. Risk assessments take into account vulnerabilities, threat sources, and security controls planned or in place to determine the level of residual risk posed to organization. They also take into account risk posed to organizational operations, organizational assets, or individuals from external parties (e.g., service providers, contractors operating information systems on behalf of the organization, individuals accessing organizational information systems, outsourcing entities).
- In accordance with OMB policy and related e-authentication initiatives, authentication of public users accessing federal information systems may also be required to protect nonpublic or privacy-related information. As such, organizational assessments of risk also address public access to federal information systems. The General Services Administration provides tools supporting that portion of the risk assessment dealing with public access to federal information systems.

- Risk assessments (either formal or informal) can be conducted by organizations at various steps in the RMF including information system categorization, security control selection, security control implementation, security control assessment, information system authorization, and security control monitoring.
- RA-3 is a noteworthy security control in that the control must be partially implemented prior to the implementation of other controls in order to complete the first two steps in the RMF. Risk assessments can play an important role in the security control selection process during the application of tailoring guidance for security control baselines and when considering supplementing the tailored baselines with additional security controls or control enhancements.

RA-5 Vulnerability Scanning

- The security categorization of the information system guides the frequency and comprehensiveness of the vulnerability scans. Vulnerability analysis for custom software and applications may require additional, more specialized techniques and approaches (e.g., web-based application scanners, source code reviews, source code analyzers).
- Vulnerability scanning includes scanning for specific functions, ports, protocols, and services that should not be accessible to users or devices and for improperly configured or incorrectly operating information flow mechanisms.
- The organization considers using tools that express vulnerabilities in the Common Vulnerabilities and Exposures (CVE) naming convention and that use the Open Vulnerability Assessment Language (OVAL) to test for the presence of vulnerabilities.
- The Common Weakness Enumeration (CWE) and the National Vulnerability Database (NVD) are also excellent sources for vulnerability information. In addition, security control assessments such as red team exercises are another source of potential vulnerabilities for which to scan.

The assessor then evaluates the organizational risk tolerance process, usually based on the guidance from SP 800-39 and implemented through the RMF process defined in SP 800-37, rev. 1, for overall treatments of risk within the organization as found through the implementation of the security controls on the system under review. He or she, the assessor, then reviews what is important to the agency and the operations by determining the critical success factors from the management perspective.

CRITICAL SUCCESS FACTORS TO INFORMATION SECURITY MANAGEMENT

- Managers and employees within an organization often tend to consider information security as a secondary priority if compared with their own efficiency or effectiveness matters, because these have a direct and material impact on the outcome of their work.
- For this reason, a strong commitment and support by the senior management on security training is needed, over and above the aforementioned role concerning the information security policy.
- Management must demonstrate a commitment to security by clearly approving and supporting formal security awareness and training (AT). This may require special

management-level training, since security is not necessarily a part of management expertise. The security training for different functions within the organization needs to be customized to address specific security needs. Different functions have different levels of risk. Application developers need technical security training, whereas management requires training that will show the linkage between information security management and the needs of the organization.

- A second vital point is that a professional risk-based approach must be used systematically to identify sensitive and critical information resources and to ensure that there is a clear understanding of threats and risks. Thereafter, appropriate risk assessment activities should be undertaken to mitigate unacceptable risks and ensure that residual risks are at an acceptable level.

OPERATIONAL AREAS OF CONSIDERATION

There are many areas which the assessor needs to consider when evaluating and testing the various operation controls installed on the systems under test as shown below in the listing of the families of controls. The starting point for most of these areas is the user. The user of the system is often, as I teach in my classes, both the first line of defense and the first line of offense with respect to security on the system. So the first area of operational controls to review would be the security awareness, training, and education section.

OPERATIONAL SECURITY CONTROLS KEY CONCEPTS

- AT
- CM
- Contingency planning (CP)
- Incident response (IR)
- Maintenance (MA)
- Media protection (MP)
- Physical and environmental protection (PE)
- Personnel security (PS)
- System and information integrity (SI)

Awareness and Training

With the three areas of awareness, training, and education typically defined in an organizational context by the personnel or human resources department, it is important to focus on the areas of security training being provided to the organization. Concentrate the assessing efforts on the four groups of students for the training. These groups are as follows:

1. End users
2. System administrators – elevated privilege users
3. Security personnel
4. Executives – senior management

Each of these groups has unique security training requirements and we need to ensure these are being addressed by the organization in its training and awareness program. Keep in mind that in several industrial verticals, these training requirements are mandated by either statutory or regulatory requirements, such as the DOD 8570 Workforce regulatory guidance and the end user training requirement found in the Computer Security Act from 1987.

NIST has developed two Special Publications on training of users and support personnel: SP 800-50, *Building an Information Technology Security Awareness and Training Program*, published in October 2003; and SP 800-16, *A Role-Based Model for Federal Information Technology/Cyber Security Training* – third and final draft version from March 2014. Each of these publications provides detailed and explicit information on training and security awareness educational efforts for users, system administrators, security personnel, and executive-level managers.

> A successful IT security program consists of: 1) developing IT security policy that reflects business needs tempered by known risks; 2) informing users of their IT security responsibilities, as documented in agency security policy and procedures; and 3) establishing processes for monitoring and reviewing the program.
>
> Security awareness and training should be focused on the organization's entire user population. Management should set the example for proper IT security behavior within an organization. An awareness program should begin with an effort that can be deployed and implemented in various ways and is aimed at all levels of the organization including senior and executive managers. The effectiveness of this effort will usually determine the effectiveness of the awareness and training program. This is also true for a successful IT security program.
>
> An awareness and training program is crucial in that it is *the* vehicle for disseminating information that users, including managers; need in order to do their jobs. In the case of an IT security program, it is *the* vehicle to be used to communicate security requirements across the enterprise.
>
> An effective IT security awareness and training program explains proper rules of behavior for the use of agency IT systems and information. The program communicates IT security policies and procedures that need to be followed. This must precede and lay the basis for any sanctions imposed due to noncompliance. Users first should be informed of the expectations. Accountability must be derived from a fully informed, well-trained, and aware workforce.[3]

Learning is a continuum; it starts with awareness, builds to training, and evolves into education. The basic construct for this continuum is shown as follows and is found in SP 800-16 and SP 800-50:

Awareness

Security awareness efforts are designed to change behavior or reinforce good security practices. Awareness is defined in NIST Special Publication 800-16 as follows: "Awareness is not training. The purpose of awareness presentations is simply to focus attention on security. Awareness presentations are intended to allow individuals to recognize IT security concerns and respond accordingly. In awareness activities, the learner is the recipient of information, whereas the learner in a training environment has a more active role. Awareness relies on reaching broad audiences with attractive packaging techniques. Training is more formal, having a goal of building knowledge and skills to facilitate the job performance."

An example of a topic for an awareness session (or awareness material to be distributed) is virus protection. The subject can simply and briefly be addressed by describing what a virus is, what can happen if a virus infects a user's system, what the user should do to protect the system, and what the user should do if a virus is discovered.

---

[3]SP 800-50, p. 7.

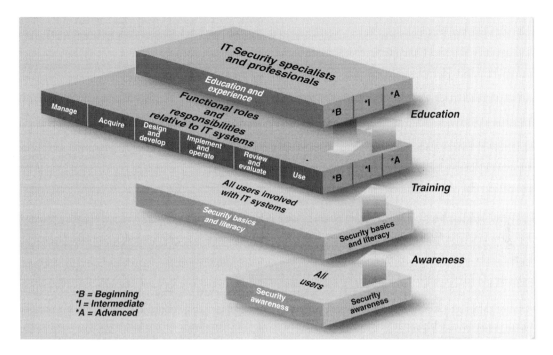

Training

Training is defined in NIST Special Publication 800-16 as follows: "The 'Training' level of the learning continuum strives to produce relevant and needed security skills and competencies by practitioners of functional specialties other than IT security (e.g., management, systems design and development, acquisition, auditing)." The most significant difference between training and awareness is that training seeks to teach skills, which allow a person to perform a specific function, while awareness seeks to focus an individual's attention on an issue or set of issues. The skills acquired during training are built upon the awareness foundation, in particular, upon the security basics and literacy material. A training curriculum must not necessarily lead to a formal degree from an institution of higher learning; however, a training course may contain much of the same material found in a course that a college or university includes in a certificate or degree program.

An example of training is an IT security course for system administrators, which should address in detail the management controls, operational controls, and technical controls that should be implemented. Management controls include policy, IT security PM, RM, and life-cycle security. Operational controls include personnel and user issues, CP, incident handling, AT, computer support and operations, and physical and environmental security issues. Technical controls include identification and authentication (IA), logical Access Controls (ACs), audit trails, and cryptography.

Education

Education is defined in NIST Special Publication 800-16 as follows: "The 'Education' level integrates all of the security skills and competencies of the various functional specialties into a common body of knowledge, adds a multidisciplinary study of concepts, issues, and principles (technological and social), and strives to produce IT security specialists and professionals capable of vision and pro-active response."

An example of education is a degree program at a college or university. Some people take a course or several courses to develop or enhance their skills in a particular discipline. This is training as opposed to education. Many colleges and universities offer certificate programs, wherein a student may take two, six, or eight classes, for example, in a related discipline, and is awarded a certificate on completion. Often, these certificate programs are conducted as a joint effort between schools and software or hardware vendors. These programs are more characteristic of training than education. Those responsible for security training need to assess both types of programs and decide which one better addresses identified needs.[4]

Configuration Management

One of the major areas of focus for any assessor is system changes and CM. There have been many occurrences I have reviewed wherein the development team and the operations team supporting systems have instituted upgrades and changes to system which altered or removed security components with no security review or sign-off on the validity or viability of the change. I have personally seen where the end users requested a change to a processing system to speed up the processing time and the development staff accomplished this through removing the required encryption on the transactional data, and it was approved and installed. The security staff had no idea this change was installed until they scanned the system and found multiple errors in the FIPS-140 and Secure Sockets Layer (SSL) areas where the encryption processing had been removed.

Security CM involves the systems, the hardware and software inventories, the changes to systems, and their interchange with the users on a daily basis. Each change has a security component and all reviews and evaluations of system changes require security checks, configuration reviews, and component evaluations to ensure all the currently installed security controls are maintained and not altered by the proposed change. If a control is modified by the change, detailed engineering and operational examination is needed to make the system safe and secure if the change is approved and installed. All of this activity, usually under the control of the Configuration Control section of the organization, should be defined and documented throughout the system life cycle of the system under review.

NIST SP 800-128, *Guide for Security-Focused Configuration Management of Information Systems*, published in August 2011, provides organizations and assessors with many areas of focus and guidance for security CM actions and activities. It starts out by saying: "An information system is composed of many components4 that can be interconnected in a multitude of arrangements to meet a variety of business, mission, and information security ds. How these information system components are networked, configured, and managed is critical in providing adequate information security and supporting an organization's risk management process.

An information system is typically in a constant state of change in response to new, enhanced, corrected, or updated hardware and software capabilities, patches for correcting software flaws and other errors to existing components, new security threats, changing

---

[4]SP 800-50, p. 8–10.

business functions, etc. Implementing information system changes almost always results in some adjustment to the system configuration. To ensure that the required adjustments to the system configuration do not adversely affect the security of the information system or the organization from operation of the information system, a well-defined configuration management process that integrates information security is needed.

Organizations apply configuration management (CM) for establishing baselines and for tracking, controlling, and managing many aspects of business development and operation (e.g., products, services, manufacturing, business processes, and information technology). Organizations with a robust and effective CM process need to consider information security implications with respect to the development and operation of information systems including hardware, software, applications, and documentation. Effective CM of information systems requires the integration of the management of secure configurations into the organizational CM process or processes. For this reason, this document assumes that information security is an integral part of an organization's overall CM process; however, the focus of this document is on implementation of the information system security aspects of CM, and as such the term *security-focused configuration management* (SecCM) is used to emphasize the concentration on information security. Though both IT business application functions and security-focused practices are expected to be integrated as a single process, *SecCM* in this context is defined as the management and control of configurations for information systems to enable security and facilitate the management of information security risk."[5]

Configuration management has been applied to a broad range of products and systems in subject areas such as automobiles, pharmaceuticals, and information systems. Some basic terms associated with the configuration management discipline are briefly explained below.

- *Configuration Management* (CM) comprises a collection of activities focused on establishing and maintaining the integrity of products and systems, through control of the processes for initializing, changing, and monitoring the configurations of those products and systems.
- A *Configuration Item (CI)* is an identifiable part of a system (e.g., hardware, software, firmware, documentation, or a combination thereof) that is a discrete target of configuration control processes.
- A *Baseline Configuration* is a set of specifications for a system, or CI within a system, that has been formally reviewed and agreed on at a given point in time, and which can be changed only through change control procedures. The baseline configuration is used as a basis for future builds, releases, and/or changes.
- A *Configuration Management Plan* (CM Plan) is a comprehensive description of the roles, responsibilities, policies, and procedures that apply when managing the configuration of products and systems. The basic parts of a CM Plan include:
- *Configuration Control Board (CCB)* – Establishment of and charter for a group of qualified people with responsibility for the process of controlling and approving changes throughout the development and operational lifecycle of products and systems; may also be referred to as a change control board;
- Configuration Item *Identification* – methodology for selecting and naming configuration items that need to be placed under CM;
- Configuration *Change Control* – process for managing updates to the baseline configurations for the configuration items; and
- Configuration *Monitoring* – process for assessing or testing the level of compliance with the established baseline configuration and mechanisms for reporting on the configuration status of items placed under CM.

The configuration of an information system is a representation of the system's components, how each component is configured, and how the components are connected or arranged to implement the information

---

[5]SP 800-128, p. 1.

system. The possible conditions in which an information system or system component can be arranged affect the security posture of the information system. The activities involved in managing the configuration of an information system include development of a configuration management plan, establishment of a configuration control board, development of a methodology for configuration item identification, establishment of the baseline configuration, development of a configuration change control process, and development of a process for configuration monitoring and reporting.[6]

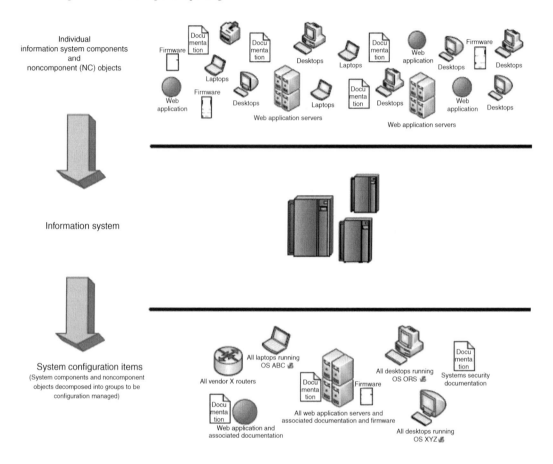

The Phases of Security-Focused Configuration Management

Here are the four defined steps for security CM as found in SP 800-128:

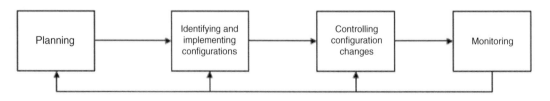

[6]SP 800-128, p. 5–6.

A. **Planning** As a part of planning, the scope or applicability of SecCM processes are identified. Planning includes developing policy and procedures to incorporate SecCM into existing information technology and security programs, and then disseminating the policy throughout the organization. Policy addresses areas such as the implementation of SecCM plans, integration into existing security program plans, Configuration Control Boards (CCBs), configuration change control processes, tools and technology, the use of common secure configurations (A common secure configuration is a recognized, standardized, and established benchmark (e.g., National Checklist Program, DISA STIGs, etc.) that stipulates specific secure configuration settings for a given IT platform.) and baseline configurations, monitoring, and metrics for compliance with established SecCM policy and procedures. It is typically more cost-effective to develop and implement a SecCM plan, policies, procedures, and associated SecCM tools at the organizational level.

B. **Identifying & Implementing Configurations** After the planning and preparation activities are completed, a secure baseline configuration for the information system is developed, reviewed, approved, and implemented. The approved baseline configuration for an information system and associated components represents the most secure state consistent with operational requirements and constraints. For a typical information system, the secure baseline may address configuration settings, software loads, patch levels, how the information system is physically or logically arranged, how various security controls are implemented, and documentation. Where possible, automation is used to enable interoperability of tools and uniformity of baseline configurations across the information system.

C. **Controlling Configuration Changes** In this phase of SecCM, the emphasis is put on the management of change to maintain the secure, approved baseline of the information system. Through the use of SecCM practices, organizations ensure that changes are formally identified, proposed, reviewed, analyzed for security impact, tested, and approved prior to implementation. As part of the configuration change control effort, organizations can employ a variety of access restrictions for change including access controls, process automation, abstract layers, change windows, and verification and audit activities to limit unauthorized and/or undocumented changes to the information system.

D. **Monitoring** Monitoring activities are used as the mechanism within SecCM to validate that the information system is adhering to organizational policies, procedures, and the approved secure baseline configuration. Planning and implementing secure configurations and then controlling configuration change is usually not sufficient to ensure that an information system which was once secure will remain secure. Monitoring identifies undiscovered/undocumented system components, misconfigurations, vulnerabilities, and unauthorized changes, all of which, if not addressed, can expose organizations to increased risk. Using automated tools helps organizations to efficiently identify when the information system is not consistent with the approved baseline configuration and when remediation actions are necessary. In addition, the use of automated tools often facilitates situational awareness and the documentation of deviations from the baseline configuration.[7]

Each area of CM is addressed and covered by security controls identified in SP 800-53 CM family of controls. These areas for assessor focus include:

1. CM Policy and Procedures – CM 1
2. CM Plan – CM 1 and CM 9
3. Configuration Control Board – CM 3
4. Component Inventory – CM 8
5. Configuration Items – CM 3
6. Secure Configurations – CM 6 and CM 7
7. Minimum Security Baseline Configuration – CM 2
8. Configuration Change Control – CM 3 and CM 5
9. Security Impact Analysis – CM 4
10. Configuration Monitoring – all CM controls

[7]SP 800-128, p. 8–9.

Additional guidance for inventory identification and management is also provided in the NIST Interagency Report – NISTIR 7693, *Specifications for Asset Identification.*

Contingency Planning

Information systems are vital elements in most mission/business processes. Because information system resources are so essential to an organization's success, it is critical that identified services provided by these systems are able to operate effectively without excessive interruption. CP supports this requirement by establishing thorough plans, procedures, and technical measures that can enable a system to be recovered as quickly and effectively as possible following a service disruption. It is unique to each system, providing preventive measures, recovery strategies, and technical considerations appropriate to the system's information confidentiality, integrity, and availability requirements and the system impact level.

Evaluating a recovery and preparedness process for a system, an organization or an application can involve many areas of technology, operations, and the personnel identified throughout an organization. There are many focal points of concern which require analysis and attention of the assessor. As the major area for the controls related to the security objective of availability, CP has become a focal point for assessors to determine the commitment of the organization's senior management to the security of their operational systems and applications.

Under Federal Continuity Directive (FCD)-1 and FCD-2 all federal information systems require a contingency plan for recovery and restoration efforts. Additional guidance is provided by NIST is SP 800-34 and templates available on the csrc.nist.gov website.

Information system CP represents a broad scope of activities designed to sustain and recover critical system services following an emergency event. Information system CP fits into a much broader security and emergency management effort that includes organizational and business process continuity, disaster recovery planning, and incident management. Ultimately, an organization would use a suite of plans to properly prepare response, recovery, and continuity activities for disruptions affecting the organization's information systems, mission/business processes, personnel, and the facility. Because there is an inherent relationship between an information system and the mission/business process it supports, there must be coordination between each plan during development and updates to ensure that recovery strategies and supporting resources neither negate each other nor duplicate efforts.

> Continuity and contingency planning are critical components of emergency management and organizational resilience but are often confused in their use. *Continuity planning* normally applies to the mission/business itself; it concerns the ability to continue critical functions and processes during and after an emergency event. *Contingency planning* normally applies to information systems, and provides the steps needed to recover the operation of all or part of designated information systems at an existing or new location in an emergency. *Cyber Incident Response Planning* is a type of plan that normally focuses on detection, response, and recovery to a computer security incident or event.[8]

[8]SP 800-34, p. 7.

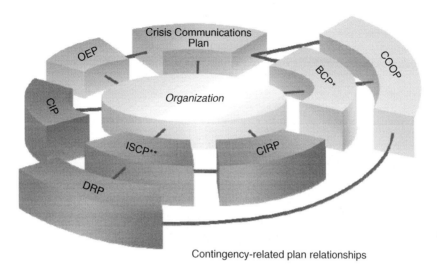

Contingency-related plan relationships

Details for each type of plan and its development, use, and maintenance are found in SP 800-34.

The primary focus of each plan is listed as follows:

Plan	Purpose	Scope	Plan relationship
Business Continuity Plan (BCP)	Provides procedures for sustaining mission/business operations while recovering from a significant disruption	Addresses mission/business processes at a lower or expanded level from Continuity of Operations (COOP) MEFs	Mission/business process focused plan that may be activated in coordination with a COOP plan to sustain non-MEFs
COOP Plan	Provides procedures and guidance to sustain an organization's Metro Ethernet Forums (MEFs) at an alternate site for up to 30 days; mandated by federal directives	Addresses MEFs at a facility; information systems are addressed based only on their support of the mission essential functions	MEF focused plan that may also activate several business unit-level BCPs, Information System Contingency Plans (ISCPs), or Disaster Recovery Plans (DRPs), as appropriate
Crisis Communications Plan	Provides procedures for disseminating internal and external communications; means to provide critical status information and control rumors	Addresses communications with personnel and the public; not information system-focused	Incident-based plan often activated with a COOP or BCP, but may be used alone during a public exposure event

(Continued)

Plan	Purpose	Scope	Plan relationship
Critical Infrastructure Protection (CIP) Plan	Provides policies and procedures for protection of national critical infrastructure components, as defined in the National Infrastructure Protection Plan	Addresses critical infrastructure components that are supported or operated by an agency or organization	Risk management plan that supports COOP plans for organizations with critical infrastructure and key resource assets
Cyber Incident Response Plan	Provides procedures for mitigating and correcting a cyber attack, such as a virus, worm, or Trojan horse	Addresses mitigation and isolation of affected systems, cleanup, and minimizing loss of information	Information system-focused plan that may activate an ISCP or DRP, depending on the extent of the attack
DRP	Provides procedures for relocating information systems operations to an alternate location	Activated after major system disruptions with long-term effects	Information system-focused plan that activates one or more ISCPs for recovery of individual systems
ISCP	Provides procedures and capabilities for recovering an information system	Addresses single information system recovery at the current or, if appropriate, alternate location	Information system-focused plan that may be activated independent from other plans or as part of a larger recovery effort coordinated with a DRP. COOP, and/or BCP
Occupant Emergency Plan (OEP)	Provides coordinated procedures for minimizing loss of life or injury and protecting property damage in response to a physical threat	Focuses on personnel and property particular to the specific facility: not mission/business process or information system-based	Incident-based plan that is initiated immediately after an event, preceding a COOP or DRP activation

Seven Steps to Contingency Planning as Defined in SP 800-34

SP 800-34, rev. 1, provides instructions, recommendations, and considerations for federal information system CP. CP refers to interim measures to recover information system services after a disruption. Interim measures may include relocation of information systems and operations to an alternate site, recovery of information system functions using alternate equipment, or performance of information system functions using manual methods. This guide addresses specific CP recommendations for three platform types and provides strategies and techniques common to all systems:

- Client/server systems
- Telecommunications systems
- Mainframe systems

This guide defines the following seven-step CP process that an organization may apply to develop and maintain a viable CP program for their information systems. These seven progressive steps are designed to be integrated into each stage of the system development life cycle:

1. *Develop the CP policy statement.* A formal policy provides the authority and guidance necessary to develop an effective contingency plan.
2. *Conduct the business impact analysis (BIA).* The BIA helps identify and prioritize information systems and components critical to supporting the organization's mission/ business processes.
3. *Identify preventive controls.* Measures taken to reduce the effects of system disruptions can increase system availability and reduce contingency life-cycle costs.
4. *Create contingency strategies.* Thorough recovery strategies ensure that the system may be recovered quickly and effectively following a disruption.
5. *Develop an information system contingency plan.* The contingency plan should contain detailed guidance and procedures for restoring a damaged system unique to the system's security impact level and recovery requirements.
6. *Ensure plan testing, training, and exercises.* Testing validates recovery capabilities, whereas training prepares recovery personnel for plan activation and exercising the plan identifies planning gaps; combined, the activities improve plan effectiveness and overall organization preparedness.
7. *Ensure plan maintenance.* The plan should be a living document that is updated regularly to remain current with system enhancements and organizational changes.

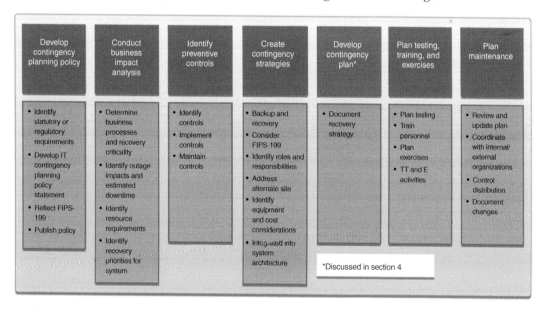

The assessor should be looking for multiple areas of focus which the organization has applied in its CP activities. SP 800-34 provides the agencies and organizations the guidance to conduct these events and the assessor gathers the evidence to ensure these events have been conducted in accordance with these guidelines.

Key points to review and assess include:

1. The CP policy statement:
    a. Policy should define the organization's overall contingency objectives and establish the organizational framework and responsibilities for system CP.
    b. To be successful, senior management, most likely the CIO, must support a contingency program and be included in the process to develop the program policy.
    c. The policy must reflect the FIPS-199 impact levels and the contingency controls that each impact level establishes. Key policy elements are as follows:
       - Roles and responsibilities
       - Scope as applies to common platform types and organization functions (i.e., telecommunications, legal, media relations) subject to CP
       - Resource requirements
       - Training requirements
       - Exercise and testing schedules
       - Plan maintenance schedule
       - Minimum frequency of backups and storage of backup media
2. The ISCPs must be written in coordination with other plans associated with each target system as part of organization-wide resilience strategy. Such plans include the following:
    a. Information SSPs
    b. Facility-level plans, such as the OEP and DRP
    c. MEF support such as the COOP plan
    d. Organization-level plans, such as CIP plans

BIA Requirements

The BIA purpose is to correlate the system with the critical mission/business processes and services provided, and based on that information, characterize the consequences of a disruption. The ISCP Coordinator can use the BIA results to determine contingency planning requirements and priorities. Results from the BIA should be appropriately incorporated into the analysis and strategy development efforts for the organization's COOP, BCPs, and DRP.

Three steps are typically involved in accomplishing the BIA:

1. **Determine mission/business processes and recovery criticality.** Mission/Business processes supported by the system are identified and the impact of a system disruption to those processes is determined **along with outage impacts and estimated downtime.** The downtime should reflect the maximum time that an organization can tolerate while still maintaining the mission.
2. **Identify resource requirements.** Realistic recovery efforts require a thorough evaluation of the resources required to resume mission/business processes and related interdependencies as quickly as possible. Examples of resources that should be identified include facilities, personnel, equipment, software, data files, system components, and vital records.
3. **Identify recovery priorities for system resources.** Based upon the results from the previous activities, system resources can be linked more clearly to critical mission/business processes and functions. Priority levels can be established for sequencing recovery activities and resources.

The sample BIA process and data collection activities, outlined in this section and illustrated below, consisting of a representative information system with multiple components (servers), are designed to help the ISCP Coordinator streamline and focus contingency plan development activities to achieve a more effective plan.[9]

[9]SP 800-34, p. 15–16.

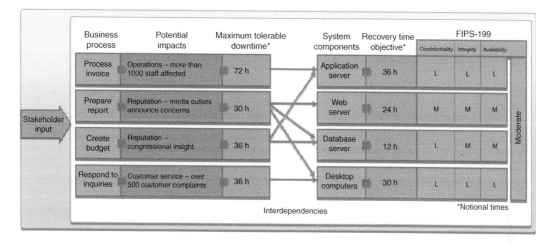

Business process	Potential impacts	Maximum tolerable downtime*		System components	Recovery time objective*	FIPS-199		
						Confidentiality	Integrity	Availability
Process invoice	Operations – more than 1000 staff affected	72 h		Application server	36 h	L	L	L
Prepare report	Reputation – media outlets announce concerns	30 h		Web server	24 h	M	M	M
Create budget	Reputation – congressional insight	36 h		Database server	12 h	L	M	M
Respond to inquiries	Customer service – over 500 customer complaints	36 h		Desktop computers	30 h	L	L	L

Stakeholder input

Interdependencies   *Notional times

Moderate

Numbers that Matter – Critical Recovery Numbers

The assessor always needs to keep the numbers that matter to the business objectives and mission when reviewing the CP and COOP documentation, evidence, and testing results. So, what are these numbers?

- Maximum tolerable downtime (MTD)
- Recovery time objective (RTO)
- Recovery point objective (RPO)

The ISCP Coordinator should next analyze the supported mission/business processes and with the process owners, leadership and business managers determine the acceptable downtime if a given process or specific system data were disrupted or otherwise unavailable. Downtime can be identified in several ways.

- **Maximum Tolerable Downtime (MTD).** The MTD represents the total amount of time the system owner/ authorizing official is willing to accept for a mission/business process outage or disruption and includes all impact considerations. Determining MTD is important because it could leave contingency planners with imprecise direction on (1) selection of an appropriate recovery method, and (2) the depth of detail which will be required when developing recovery procedures, including their scope and content.
- **Recovery Time Objective (RTO).** RTO defines the maximum amount of time that a system resource can remain unavailable before there is an unacceptable impact on other system resources, supported mission/ business processes, and the MTD. Determining the information system resource RTO is important for selecting appropriate technologies that are best suited for meeting the MTD. When it is not feasible to immediately meet the RTO and the MTD is inflexible, a Plan of Action and Milestone should be initiated to document the situation and plan for its mitigation.
- **Recovery Point Objective (RPO).** The RPO represents the point in time, prior to a disruption or system outage, to which mission/business process data can be recovered (given the most recent backup copy of the data) after an outage. Unlike RTO, RPO is not considered as part of MTD. Rather, it is a factor of how much data loss the mission/business process can tolerate during the recovery process.

Because the RTO must ensure that the MTD is not exceeded, the RTO must normally be shorter than the MTD. For example, a system outage may prevent a particular process from being completed, and because it takes time to reprocess the data, that additional processing time must be added to the RTO to stay within the time limit established by the MTD.[10]

[10]SP 800-34, p. 17.

Example:

COOP VERSUS ISCP – THE BASIC FACTS

Recovery times

- COOP functions must be sustained within 12 h and for up to 30 days from an alternate site; ISCP RTOs are determined by the system-based BIA.
  - Information systems that support COOP functions must have an RTO that meets COOP requirements.
  - Information systems that do not support COOP functions do not *require* alternate sites as part of the ISCP recovery strategy, but may have an alternate site security control requirement.

Recovery Strategies

FIPS-199 availability impact level	Information system target priority and recovery	Backup/recovery strategy
Low	Low priority – any outage with little impact, damage, or disruption to the organization	*Backup*: Tape backup *Strategy*: Relocate or cold site
Moderate	Important or moderate priority – any system that, if disrupted, would cause a moderate problem to the organization and possibly other networks or systems	*Backup*: Optical backup. WAN/VLAN replication *Strategy*: Cold or warm site
High	Mission-critical or high priority – the damage or disruption to these systems would cause the most impact on the organization, mission, and other networks and systems	*Backup*: Mirrored systems and disc replication *Strategy*: Hot site

Site	Cost	Hardware equipment	Telecommunications	Setup time	Location
Cold site	Low	None	None	Long	Fixed
Warm site	Medium	Partial	Partial/full	Medium	Fixed
Hot site	Medium/high	Full	Full	Short	Fixed

As an assessor, the job here is to evaluate and assess whether the numbers identified above do three things:

1. Provide the appropriate level of recovery in relation to the security categorization of the system under review

2. Provide the level of recovery expected and documented in the BIA for the system under review
3. Provide the level of recovery expected by the end using organization and their financial commitment

The various recovery processes and procedures need to be verified and validated, which is typically done through the use of testing and exercises conducted in accordance with SP 800-82.

SP 800-82, Guide to Test, Training, and Exercise Programs for IT Plans and Capabilities

Organizations have IT plans in place, such as contingency and computer security IR plans, so that they can respond to and manage adverse situations involving IT. These plans should be maintained in a state of readiness, which should include having personnel trained to fulfill their roles and responsibilities within a plan, having plans exercised to validate their content, and having systems and system components tested to ensure their operability in an operational environment specified in a plan. These three types of events can be carried out efficiently and effectively through the development and implementation of a test, training, and exercise (TT&E) program. Organizations should consider having such a program in place because tests, training, and exercises are so closely related. For example, exercises and tests offer different ways of identifying deficiencies in IT plans, procedures, and training.[11]

TEST

Tests are evaluation tools that use quantifiable metrics to validate the operability of an IT system or system component in an operational environment specified in an IT plan. For example, an organization could test if call tree cascades can be executed within prescribed time limits; another test would be removing power from a system or system component. A test is conducted in as close to an operational environment as possible; if feasible, an actual test of the components or systems used to conduct daily operations for the organization should be used. The scope of testing can range from individual system components or systems to comprehensive tests of all systems and components that support an IT plan. Tests often focus on recovery and backup operations; however, testing varies depending on the goal of the test and its relation to a specific IT plan.

TRAINING

Training, in this recovery context, refers only to informing personnel of their roles and responsibilities within a particular IT plan and teaching them skills related to those roles and responsibilities, thereby preparing them for participation in exercises, tests, and actual emergency situations related to the IT plan. Training personnel on their roles and responsibilities before an exercise or test event is typically split between a presentation on their roles and responsibilities and activities that allow personnel to demonstrate their understanding of the subject matter.

EXERCISES

An exercise is a simulation of an emergency designed to validate the viability of one or more aspects of an IT plan. In an exercise, personnel with roles and responsibilities in a

---

[11]SP 800-82, p. ES-1.

particular IT plan meet to validate the content of a plan through discussion of their roles and their responses to emergency situations, execution of responses in a simulated operational environment, or other means of validating responses that does not involve using the actual operational environment. Exercises are scenario-driven, such as a power failure in one of the organization's data centers or a fire causing certain systems to be damaged, with additional situations often being presented during the course of an exercise. There are several types of exercises, and this publication focuses on the following two types that are widely used in TT&E programs by single organizations:

- *Tabletop*: Tabletop exercises are discussion-based exercises where personnel meet in a classroom setting or in breakout groups to discuss their roles during an emergency and their responses to a particular emergency situation. A facilitator presents a scenario and asks the exercise participants questions related to the scenario, which initiates a discussion among the participants of roles, responsibilities, coordination, and decision making. A tabletop exercise is discussion-based only and does not involve deploying equipment or other resources.
- *Functional*: Functional exercises allow personnel to validate their operational readiness for emergencies by performing their duties in a simulated operational environment. They are designed to exercise the roles and responsibilities of specific team members, procedures, and assets involved in one or more functional aspects of a plan (e.g., communications, emergency notifications, IT equipment setup). Functional exercises vary in complexity and scope, from validating specific aspects of a plan to full-scale exercises that address all plan elements. They allow staff to execute their roles and responsibilities as they would in an actual emergency situation, but in a simulated manner.

Contingency Plan Testing

Contingency plan testing always requires special attention for assessors as this is often the only way to fully check out the alternative operations and support efforts that the organization has placed into operations but only activates when they are required to do so. The following table reflects the areas of CP controls to evaluate and obtain evidence and proof of accomplishment for testing of the various parts of the system or organization's contingency plans and COOP preparations:

Control	Testing event	Sample event to document
CP-3	CP training	A seminar and/or briefing used to familiarize personnel with the overall CP purpose, phases, activities, and roles and responsibilities
CP-3	Instruction	Instruction of contingency personnel on their roles and responsibilities within the CP and includes refresher training and, for high-impact systems, simulated events
CP-4	CP testing/exercise	Test and/or exercise the CP to determine the effectiveness and the organization's readiness. This includes both planned and unplanned maintenance activities
CP-4	Tabletop exercise	Discussion-based simulation of an emergency-based situation in an informal stress-free environment; designed to elicit constructive scenario-based discussions for an examination of the existing CP and individual state of preparedness

Control	Testing event	Sample event to document
CP-4	Functional exercise	Simulation of a disruption with a system recovery component such as backup tape restoration or server recovery
CP-4	Full-scale functional exercise	Simulation prompting a full recovery and reconstitution of the information system to a known state and ensures that staff are familiar with the alternative facility
CP-4, CP-7	Alternate processing site recovery	Test and/or exercise the CP at the alternate processing site to familiarize contingency personnel with the facility and available resources and evaluate the site's capabilities to support contingency operations. Includes a full recovery and return to normal operations to a known secure state. If high-impact system, the alternate facility should be fully configured as defined in CP
CP-9	System backup	Test backup information to verify media reliability and information integrity. If high-impact system, use sample backup information to validate recovery process and ensure backup copies are maintained at alternate storage facility

Now, each of these areas of focus for assessment of the CP controls should be tied into and reflected in the system contingency plan and its design efforts as reflected in the following:

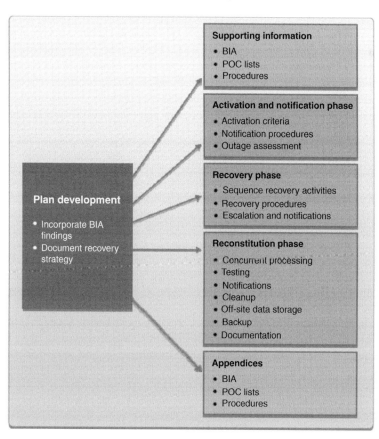

Incident Response

The current state of the security of systems across the enterprise often requires organizations to develop and conduct IR activities due to breaches, malware infections, "phishing" events, and outright external attacks. The state of the cybercrime and hacking communities has developed dramatically over the past few years and now includes "hack-in-a-box" and fully developed malicious software development efforts including formal version controls, automated delivery channels, testing against known antivirus signatures, and malware as a service (MAAS) cloud-based delivery mechanisms. The goals of any IR effort are as follows:

- Detect incidents quickly.
- Diagnose incidents accurately.
- Manage incidents properly.
- Contain and minimize damage.
- Restore affected services.
- Determine root causes.
- Implement improvements to prevent recurrence.
- Document and report.

The purpose of IR is to manage and respond to unexpected disruptive events with the objective of controlling impacts within acceptable levels. These events can be technical, such as attacks mounted on the network via viruses, denial of service, or system intrusion, or they can be the result of mistakes, accidents, or system or process failure. Disruptions can also be caused by a variety of physical events such as theft of proprietary information, social engineering, lost or stolen backup tapes or laptops, environmental conditions such as floods, fires, or earthquakes, and so forth. Any type of incident that can significantly affect the organization's ability to operate or that may cause damage must be considered by the information security manager and will normally be a part of incident management and response capabilities.

The US government has long recognized the need and requirements for computer IR and, as a result, has developed many documented resources and organizations for IR to include the US-Computer Emergency Response Team (CERT), various DOD CERT organizations, joint ventures between various governmental agencies, incident handling guides, procedures and techniques, and the NIST SP 800-61.

SP 800-61 – Computer Security Incident Handling Guide

As the introduction at the beginning of SP 800-61 says: "Computer security incident response has become an important component of information technology (IT) programs. Cybersecurity-related attacks have become not only more numerous and diverse but also more damaging and disruptive. New types of security-related incidents emerge frequently. Preventive activities based on the results of risk assessments can lower the number of incidents, but not all incidents can be prevented. An incident response capability is therefore necessary for rapidly detecting incidents, minimizing loss and destruction, mitigating the weaknesses that were exploited, and restoring IT services. To that end, this publication provides guidelines for incident handling, particularly for analyzing incident-related data and determining the appropriate response to each incident. The guidelines can be followed independently of particular hardware platforms, operating systems, protocols, or applications.

Because performing incident response effectively is a complex undertaking, establishing a successful incident response capability requires substantial planning and resources. Continually monitoring for attacks is essential. Establishing clear procedures for prioritizing the handling of incidents is critical, as is implementing effective methods of collecting, analyzing, and reporting data. It is also vital to build relationships and establish suitable means of communication with other internal groups (e.g., human resources, legal) and with external groups (e.g., other incident response teams, law enforcement)."[12]

Incident Handling

The incident response process has several phases. The initial phase involves establishing and training an incident response team, and acquiring the necessary tools and resources. During preparation, the organization also attempts to limit the number of incidents that will occur by selecting and implementing a set of controls based on the results of risk assessments. However, residual risk will inevitably persist after controls are implemented. Detection of security breaches is thus necessary to alert the organization whenever incidents occur. In keeping with the severity of the incident, the organization can mitigate the impact of the incident by containing it and ultimately recovering from it. During this phase, activity often cycles back to detection and analysis—for example, to see if additional hosts are infected by malware while eradicating a malware incident. After the incident is adequately handled, the organization issues a report that details the cause and cost of the incident and the steps the organization should take to prevent future incidents.[13]

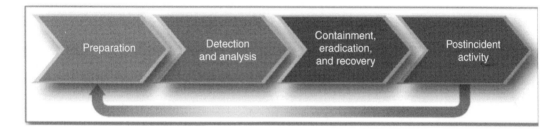

PREPARATION

IR methodologies typically emphasize preparation – not only establishing an IR capability so that the organization is ready to respond to incidents but also preventing incidents by ensuring that systems, networks, and applications are sufficiently secure. Although the IR team is not typically responsible for incident prevention, it is fundamental to the success of IR programs.

As an assessor of IR capacity and incident handling activities, it is important to understand the process itself is often chaotic and can appear haphazard when the response is active. One of the critical areas to focus on during the review is the documented and defined training for the responders, as well as the organizational policies and procedures for IR. Each of these areas helps determine the success or failure of the response team, their interactions with the rest of the organization, and ultimately the minimization of the impact of the incident on the organization, its people, and its mission.

[12]SP 800-61, rev. 2, p. 1.
[13]*Ibid.*, p. 21.

DETECTION AND ANALYSIS

For many organizations, the most challenging part of the incident response process is accurately detecting and assessing possible incidents—determining whether an incident has occurred and, if so, the type, extent, and magnitude of the problem. What makes this so challenging is a combination of three factors:

- Incidents may be detected through many different means, with varying levels of detail and fidelity. Automated detection capabilities include network-based and host-based IDPSs, antivirus software, and log analyzers. Incidents may also be detected through manual means, such as problems reported by users. Some incidents have overt signs that can be easily detected, whereas others are almost impossible to detect.
- The volume of potential signs of incidents is typically high—for example, it is not uncommon for an organization to receive thousands or even millions of intrusion detection sensor alerts per day.
- Deep, specialized technical knowledge and extensive experience are necessary for proper and efficient analysis of incident-related data.

Signs of an incident fall into one of two categories: precursors and indicators. A *precursor* is a sign that an incident may occur in the future. An *indicator* is a sign that an incident may have occurred or may be occurring now.

Incident detection and analysis would be easy if every precursor or indicator were guaranteed to be accurate; unfortunately, this is not the case. For example, user-provided indicators such as a complaint of a server being unavailable are often incorrect. Intrusion detection systems may produce false positives—incorrect indicators. These examples demonstrate what makes incident detection and analysis so difficult: each indicator ideally should be evaluated to determine if it is legitimate. Making matters worse, the total number of indicators may be thousands or millions a day. Finding the real security incidents that occurred out of all the indicators can be a daunting task.

Even if an indicator is accurate, it does not necessarily mean that an incident has occurred. Some indicators, such as a server crash or modification of critical files, could happen for several reasons other than a security incident, including human error. Given the occurrence of indicators, however, it is reasonable to suspect that an incident might be occurring and to act accordingly. Determining whether a particular event is actually an incident is sometimes a matter of judgment. It may be necessary to collaborate with other technical and information security personnel to make a decision. In many instances, a situation should be handled the same way regardless of whether it is security related. For example, if an organization is losing Internet connectivity every 12 hours and no one knows the cause, the staff would want to resolve the problem just as quickly and would use the same resources to diagnose the problem, regardless of its cause.[14]

CONTAINMENT, ERADICATION, AND RECOVERY

Containment is important before an incident overwhelms resources or increases damage. Most incidents require containment, so that is an important consideration early in the course of handling each incident. Containment provides time for developing a tailored remediation strategy. An essential part of containment is decision making (e.g., shut down a system, disconnect it from a network, or disable certain functions). Such decisions are much easier to make if there are predetermined strategies and procedures for containing the incident. Organizations should define acceptable risks in dealing with incidents and develop strategies accordingly.

Containment strategies vary based on the type of incident. For example, the strategy for containing an email-borne malware infection is quite different from that for a network-based DDoS attack. Organizations should create separate containment strategies for each major incident type, with criteria documented clearly to facilitate decision making.[15]

---

[14]SP 800-61, rev. 2, p. 25, 28.

[15]SP 800-61, rev. 2, p. 35.

After an incident has been contained, eradication may be necessary to eliminate components of the incident, such as deleting malware and disabling breached user accounts, as well as identifying and mitigating all vulnerabilities that were exploited. During eradication, it is important to identify all affected hosts within the organization so that they can be remediated. For some incidents, eradication is either not necessary or is performed during recovery.

In recovery, administrators restore systems to normal operation, confirm that the systems are functioning normally, and (if applicable) remediate vulnerabilities to prevent similar incidents. Recovery may involve such actions as restoring systems from clean backups, rebuilding systems from scratch, replacing compromised files with clean versions, installing patches, changing passwords, and tightening network perimeter security (e.g., firewall rulesets, boundary router access control lists). Higher levels of system logging or network monitoring are often part of the recovery process. Once a resource is successfully attacked, it is often attacked again, or other resources within the organization are attacked in a similar manner.

Eradication and recovery should be done in a phased approach so that remediation steps are prioritized. For large-scale incidents, recovery may take months; the intent of the early phases should be to increase the overall security with relatively quick (days to weeks) high value changes to prevent future incidents. The later phases should focus on longer-term changes (e.g., infrastructure changes) and ongoing work to keep the enterprise as secure as possible.[16]

POSTINCIDENT ACTIVITY

One of the most important parts of incident response is also the most often omitted: learning and improving. Each incident response team should evolve to reflect new threats, improved technology, and lessons learned. Holding a "lessons learned" meeting with all involved parties after a major incident, and optionally periodically after lesser incidents as resources permit, can be extremely helpful in improving security measures and the incident handling process itself. Multiple incidents can be covered in a single lessons learned meeting. This meeting provides a chance to achieve closure with respect to an incident by reviewing what occurred, what was done to intervene, and how well intervention worked.

Small incidents need limited post-incident analysis, with the exception of incidents performed through new attack methods that are of widespread concern and interest. After serious attacks have occurred, it is usually worthwhile to hold post-mortem meetings that cross team and organizational boundaries to provide a mechanism for information sharing. The primary consideration in holding such meetings is ensuring that the right people are involved. Not only is it important to invite people who have been involved in the incident that is being analyzed, but also it is wise to consider who should be invited for the purpose of facilitating future cooperation.[17]

As an IR assessor and evaluator, you will be looking for the required training and exercise documentation for each responder on the team. The policies for IR, handling, notification, and board review all need to be identified, reviewed, and assessed. The supporting procedures for handling and response efforts all need review and correlation to the policies, the security controls for IR from SP 800-53 and the actual IR plan for each system as it is reviewed and assessed.

Federal Agency Incident Categories

To clearly communicate incidents and events (any observable occurrence in a network or system) throughout the Federal Government and supported organizations, it is necessary for the government incident response teams to adopt a common set of terms and relationships between those terms. All elements of the Federal Government should use a common taxonomy.

Below please find a high level set of concepts and descriptions to enable improved communications among and between agencies. The taxonomy below does not replace discipline (technical, operational, intelligence) that needs to occur to defend federal agency computers/networks, but provides a common platform to execute the US-CERT mission. US-CERT and the federal civilian agencies are to utilize the following incident and event categories and reporting timeframe criteria as the federal agency reporting taxonomy.

[16]SP 800-61, rev. 2, p. 37.
[17]SP 800-61, rev. 2, p. 38–39.

Federal Agency Incident Categories

Category	Name	Description	Reporting Timeframe
CAT 0	Exercise/Network Defense Testing	This category is used during state, federal, national, international exercises and approved activity testing of internal/external network defenses or responses.	Not Applicable; this category is for each agency's internal use during exercises.
CAT 1	Unauthorized Access	In this category an individual gains logical or physical access without permission to a federal agency network, system, application, data, or other resources	Within one (1) hour of discovery/detection
CAT 2	Denial of Service (DoS)	An attack that *successfully* prevents or impairs the normal authorized functionality of networks, systems or applications by exhausting resources. This activity includes being the victim or participating in the DoS.	Within two (2) hours of discovery/detection if the successful attack is still ongoing and the agency is unable to successfully mitigate activity.
CAT 3	Malicious Code	*Successful* installation of malicious software (e.g., virus, worm. Trojan horse, or other code-based malicious entity) that infects an operating system or application. Agencies are NOT required to report malicious logic that has been *successfully quarantined* by antivirus (AV) software	Daily. Note: Within one (1) hour of discovery/detection if widespread across agency.
CAT 4	Improper Usage	A person violates acceptable computing use policies.	Weekly
CAT 5	Scans/Probes/Attempted Access	This category includes any activity that seeks to access or identify a federal agency computer, open ports, protocols, service, or any combination for later exploit. This activity does not directly result in a compromise or denial of service.	Monthly. Note: If system is classified, report within one (1) hour of discovery.
CAT 6	Investigation	*Unconfirmed* incidents that are potentially malicious or anomalous activity deemed by the reporting entity to warrant further review.	Not Applicable; this category is for each agency's use to categorize a potential incident that is currently being investigated.

- CAT 0 - Exercise/Network Defense Testing
- CAT 1 - *Unauthorized Access
- CAT 2 - *Denial of Service (DoS)
- CAT 3 - *Malicious Code
- CAT 4 - *Inappropriate Usage
- CAT 5 - Scans/Probes/Attempted Access
- CAT 6 – Investigation

*Any incident that involves compromised PII must be reported to US-CERT within 1 hour of detection regardless of the incident category reporting timeframe.[18]

Now, as of October 1, 2014 US-CERT posted a new taxonomy and methodology for reporting of incidents. US-CERT posted the following information and table for the new requirements, which are required to be used after September 1, 2015:

> Please use the table below to identify the impact of the incident. Incidents may affect multiple types of data; therefore, D/As may select multiple options when identifying the information impact. The security categorization of federal information and information systems must be determined in accordance with Federal Information Processing Standards (FIPS) Publication 199. Specific thresholds for loss of service availability (i.e., all, subset, loss of efficiency) must be defined by the reporting organization.[19]

Impact Classifications	Impact Description
Functional Impact	**HIGH** - Organization has lost the ability to provide all critical services to all system users.
	MEDIUM - Organization has lost the ability to provide a critical service to a subset of system users.
	LOW - Organization has experienced a loss of efficiency, but can still provide all critical services to all users with minimal effect on performance.
	NONE - Organization has experienced no loss in ability to provide all services to all users.
Information Impact	**CLASSIFIED** - The confidentiality of classified information [5] was compromised.
	PROPRIETARY [6] - The confidentiality of unclassified proprietary information, such as protected critical infrastructure information (PCII), intellectual property, or trade secrets was compromised.
	PRIVACY - The confidentiality of personally identifiable information [7] (PII) of personal health information (PHI) was compromised.
	INTEGRITY - The necessary integrity of information was modified without authorization.
	NONE - No information was exfiltrated. modified, deleted, or otherwise compromised.
Recoverability	**REGULAR** - Time to recovery is predictable with existing resources.
	SUPPLEMENTED - Time to recovery is predictable with additional resources.
	EXTENDED - Time to recovery is unpredictable; additional resources and outside help are needed.
	NOT RECOVERABLE - Recovery from the incident is not possible (e.g., sensitive data exfiltrated and posted publicly).
	NOT APPLICABLE - Incident does not require recovery.

To minimize damage from security incidents and to recover and to learn from such incidents, a formal IR capability should be established. The organization and management of an IR capability should be coordinated or centralized with the establishment of key roles and responsibilities. In establishing this process, employees and contractors are made aware of procedures for reporting the different types of incidents that might have an impact on the security of organizational assets. Incidents occur because vulnerabilities are not addressed

---

[18]https://www.us-cert.gov/government-users/reporting-requirements, retrieved 2/1/2015.

[19]https://www.us-cert.gov/incident-notification-guidelines, retrieved 2/1/2015.

properly. Ideally, an organizational computer security incident response team (CSIRT) or CERT should be formulated with clear lines of reporting, and responsibilities for standby support should be established. An assessor should ensure that the CSIRT is actively involved with users to assist them in the mitigation of risks arising from security failures and also to prevent security incidents.

The assessor needs to check for, evaluate, and assess the following areas of IR:

A. **Organizations must create, provision, and operate a formal incident response capability. Federal law requires Federal agencies to report incidents to the United States Computer Emergency Readiness Team (US-CERT) office within the Department of Homeland Security (DHS).**
   The Federal Information Security Management Act (FISMA) requires Federal agencies to establish incident response capabilities. Each Federal civilian agency must designate a primary and secondary point of contact (POC) with US-CERT and report all incidents consistent with the agency's incident response policy. Each agency is responsible for determining how to fulfill these requirements. Establishing an incident response capability should include the following actions:

1. Creating an incident response policy and plan
2. Developing procedures for performing incident handling and reporting
3. Setting guidelines for communicating with outside parties regarding incidents
4. Selecting a team structure and staffing model
5. Establishing relationships and lines of communication between the incident response team and other groups, both internal (e.g., legal department) and external (e.g., law enforcement agencies)
6. Determining what services the incident response team should provide
7. Staffing and training the incident response team.

B. **Organizations should reduce the frequency of incidents by effectively securing networks, systems, and applications.**
   Preventing problems is often less costly and more effective than reacting to them after they occur. Thus, incident prevention is an important complement to an incident response capability. If security controls are insufficient, high volumes of incidents may occur. This could overwhelm the resources and capacity for response, which would result in delayed or incomplete recovery and possibly more extensive damage and longer periods of service and data unavailability. Incident handling can be performed more effectively if organizations complement their incident response capability with adequate resources to actively maintain the security of networks, systems, and applications. This includes training IT staff on complying with the organization's security standards and making users aware of policies and procedures regarding appropriate use of networks, systems, and applications.

C. **Organizations should document their guidelines for interactions with other organizations regarding incidents.**
   During incident handling, the organization will need to communicate with outside parties, such as other incident response teams, law enforcement, the media, vendors, and victim organizations. Because these communications often need to occur quickly, organizations should predetermine communication guidelines so that only the appropriate information is shared with the right parties.

D. **Organizations should be generally prepared to handle any incident but should focus on being prepared to handle incidents that use common attack vectors.**
   Incidents can occur in countless ways, so it is infeasible to develop step-by-step instructions for handling every incident. This publication defines several types of incidents, based on common attack vectors; these categories are not intended to provide definitive classification for incidents, but rather to be used as a basis for defining more specific handling procedures. Different types of incidents merit different response strategies. The attack vectors are:

- **External/Removable Media:** An attack executed from removable media (e.g., flash drive, CD) or a peripheral device.
- **Attrition:** An attack that employs brute force methods to compromise, degrade, or destroy systems, networks, or services.

- **Web:** An attack executed from a website or web-based application.
- **Email:** An attack executed via an email message or attachment.
- **Improper Usage:** Any incident resulting from violation of an organization's acceptable usage policies by an authorized user, excluding the above categories.
- **Loss or Theft of Equipment:** The loss or theft of a computing device or media used by the organization, such as a laptop or smartphone.
- **Other:** An attack that does not fit into any of the other categories.

E. **Organizations should emphasize the importance of incident detection and analysis throughout the organization.**

   In an organization, millions of possible signs of incidents may occur each day, recorded mainly by logging and computer security software. Automation is needed to perform an initial analysis of the data and select events of interest for human review. Event correlation software can be of great value in automating the analysis process. However, the effectiveness of the process depends on the quality of the data that goes into it. Organizations should establish logging standards and procedures to ensure that adequate information is collected by logs and security software and that the data is reviewed regularly.

F. **Organizations should create written guidelines for prioritizing incidents.**

   Prioritizing the handling of individual incidents is a critical decision point in the incident response process. Effective information sharing can help an organization identify situations that are of greater severity and demand immediate attention. Incidents should be prioritized based on the relevant factors, such as the functional impact of the incident (e.g., current and likely future negative impact to business functions), the information impact of the incident (e.g., effect on the confidentiality, integrity, and availability of the organization's information), and the recoverability from the incident (e.g., the time and types of resources that must be spent on recovering from the incident).

G. **Organizations should use the lessons learned process to gain value from incidents.**

   After a major incident has been handled, the organization should hold a "lessons learned" meeting to review the effectiveness of the incident handling process and identify necessary improvements to existing security controls and practices. Lessons learned meetings can also be held periodically for lesser incidents as time and resources permit. The information accumulated from all lessons learned meetings should be used to identify and correct systemic weaknesses and deficiencies in policies and procedures. Follow-up reports generated for each resolved incident can be important not only for evidentiary purposes but also for reference in handling future incidents and in training new team members.[20]

System Maintenance

As an assessor of federal information systems, what do you need to know about operations and maintenance (O&M) of information systems?

In the maintenance area for systems, focus on the policies and procedures for the maintenance activities of the assigned personnel first. Then look at the maintenance records, logs, and reports of the maintenance staff. Check these records against the requests and help desk tickets to ensure the maintenance is requested legitimately, performed appropriately, and completed successfully.

Areas for review include the following parts of the Maintenance and Support program of the agency:

- Nonlocal maintenance = remote access/maintenance:
  - FIPS-201-1 Common Identification – Personal Identity Verification (PIV; IA)
  - SP 800-63 e-authentication (IA)
  - FIPS-197 Advance Encryption Standard (systems and communications protection (SC))
  - FIPS-140-2 Cryptography Standard
  - SP 80-88 Media Sanitization (MP)

---

[20]SP 800-61, rev. 2, p. 2–3.

- Planning for failure of equipment:
  - Mean time between failures (MTBF)
  - Mean time to repair (MTTR)

Encryption Standards for Use and Review in Federal Systems

FIPS-140-1 was developed by a government and industry working group composed of both operators and vendors. The working group identified requirements for four security levels for cryptographic modules to provide for a wide spectrum of data sensitivity (e.g., low-value administrative data, million dollar funds transfers, and life-protecting data) and a diversity of application environments (e.g., a guarded facility, an office, and a completely unprotected location). Four security levels are specified for each of 11 requirement areas. Each security level offers an increase in security over the preceding level. These four increasing levels of security allow cost-effective solutions that are appropriate for different degrees of data sensitivity and different application environments. FIPS-140-2 incorporates changes in applicable standards and technology since the development of FIPS-140-1 as well as changes that are based on comments received from the vendor, laboratory, and user communities. The basic level guidance from the FIPS is provided as follows:

1. *Security Level 1*: Security Level 1 provides the lowest level of security. Basic security requirements are specified for a cryptographic module (e.g., at least one approved algorithm or approved security function shall be used). No specific physical security mechanisms are required in a Security Level 1 cryptographic module beyond the basic requirement for production-grade components. An example of a Security Level 1 cryptographic module is a personal computer (PC) encryption board.

   Security Level 1 allows the software and firmware components of a cryptographic module to be executed on a general-purpose computing system using an unevaluated operating system. Such implementations may be appropriate for some low-level security applications when other controls, such as physical security, network security, and administrative procedures, are limited or nonexistent. The implementation of cryptographic software may be more cost-effective than corresponding hardware-based mechanisms, enabling organizations to select from alternative cryptographic solutions to meet lower-level security requirements.

2. *Security Level 2*: Security Level 2 enhances the physical security mechanisms of a Security Level 1 cryptographic module by adding the requirement for tamper-evidence, which includes the use of tamper-evident coatings or seals or for pick-resistant locks on removable covers or doors of the module. Tamper-evident coatings or seals are placed on a cryptographic module so that the coating or seal must be broken to attain physical access to the plaintext cryptographic keys and critical security parameters (CSPs) within the module. Tamper-evident seals or pick-resistant locks are placed on covers or doors to protect against unauthorized physical access.

   Security Level 2 requires, at a minimum, role-based authentication in which a cryptographic module authenticates the authorization of an operator to assume a specific role and perform a corresponding set of services.

   Security Level 2 allows the software and firmware components of a cryptographic module to be executed on a general-purpose computing system using an operating system that:

a. Meets the functional requirements specified in the Common Criteria (CC) Protection Profiles (PPs)

b. Is evaluated at the CC evaluation assurance level EAL2 (or higher)

An equivalent evaluated trusted operating system may be used. A trusted operating system provides a level of trust so that cryptographic modules executing on general-purpose computing platforms are comparable to cryptographic modules implemented using dedicated hardware systems.

3. *Security Level 3*: In addition to the tamper-evident physical security mechanisms required at Security Level 2, Security Level 3 attempts to prevent the intruder from gaining access to CSPs held within the cryptographic module. Physical security mechanisms required at Security Level 3 are intended to have a high probability of detecting and responding to attempts at physical access, use, or modification of the cryptographic module. The physical security mechanisms may include the use of strong enclosures and tamper detection/response circuitry that zeroizes all plaintext CSPs when the removable covers/doors of the cryptographic module are opened.

Security Level 3 requires identity-based authentication mechanisms, enhancing the security provided by the role-based authentication mechanisms specified for Security Level 2. A cryptographic module authenticates the identity of an operator and verifies that the identified operator is authorized to assume a specific role and perform a corresponding set of services.

Security Level 3 requires the entry or output of plaintext CSPs (including the entry or output of plaintext CSPs using split knowledge procedures) be performed using ports that are physically separated from other ports, or interfaces that are logically separated using a trusted path from other interfaces. Plaintext CSPs may be entered into or output from the cryptographic module in encrypted form (in which case they may travel through enclosing or intervening systems).

Security Level 3 allows the software and firmware components of a cryptographic module to be executed on a general-purpose computing system using an operating system that:

a. Meets the functional requirements specified in the PPs listed in Annex B with the additional functional requirement of a trusted path (FTP_TRP.1)

b. Is evaluated at the CC evaluation assurance level EAL3 (or higher) with the additional assurance requirement of an informal Target of Evaluation (TOE) Security Policy Model (ADV_SPM.1)

An equivalent evaluated trusted operating system may be used. The implementation of a trusted path protects plaintext CSPs and the software and firmware components of the cryptographic module from other untrusted software or firmware that may be executing on the system.

4. *Security Level 4*: Security Level 4 provides the highest level of security defined in this standard. At this security level, the physical security mechanisms provide a complete envelope of protection around the cryptographic module with the intent of detecting and responding to all unauthorized attempts at physical access. Penetration of the cryptographic module enclosure from any direction has a very high probability of being detected, resulting in the immediate zeroization of all plaintext CSPs. Security Level 4 cryptographic modules are useful for operation in physically unprotected environments.

Security Level 4 also protects a cryptographic module against a security compromise due to environmental conditions or fluctuations outside of the module's normal operating ranges for voltage and temperature. Intentional excursions beyond the normal operating ranges may be used by an attacker to thwart a cryptographic module's defenses. A cryptographic module is required either to include special environmental protection features designed to detect fluctuations and zeroize CSPs or to undergo rigorous environmental failure testing to provide a reasonable assurance that the module will not be affected by fluctuations outside of the normal operating range in a manner that can compromise the security of the module.

Security Level 4 allows the software and firmware components of a cryptographic module to be executed on a general-purpose computing system using an operating system that:

a. Meets the functional requirements specified for Security Level 3

b. Is evaluated at the CC evaluation assurance level EAL4 (or higher)

An equivalent evaluated trusted operating system may be used.

5. *Advanced Encryption Standard*: FIPS-197, Advanced Encryption Standard (AES), specifies the Rijndael algorithm, a symmetric block cipher that can process data blocks of 128 bits, using cipher keys with lengths of 128, 192, and 256 bits.

The algorithm may be used with the three different key lengths indicated above, and therefore these different "flavors" may be referred to as "AES-128," "AES-192," and "AES-256."

Media Protection

- SP 800-88 – sanitization
- SP 800-111 – storage encryption

Media Sanitation

The information security concern regarding information disposal and media sanitization resides not in the media but in the recorded information. The issue of media disposal and sanitization is driven by the information placed intentionally or unintentionally on the media.

Information systems capture, process, and store information using a wide variety of media. This information is located not only on the intended storage media but also on devices used to create, process, or transmit this information. These media may require special disposition in order to mitigate the risk of unauthorized disclosure of information and to ensure its confidentiality. Efficient and effective management of information that is created, processed, and stored by an IT system throughout its life, from inception to disposition, is a primary concern of an information system owner and the custodian of the data.

With the use of increasingly sophisticated encryption, an attacker wishing to gain access to an organization's sensitive information is forced to look outside the system itself for that information. One avenue of attack is the recovery of supposedly deleted data from media. These residual data may allow unauthorized individuals to reconstruct data and thereby gain access to sensitive information. Sanitization can be used to thwart this attack by ensuring that deleted data cannot be easily recovered.

When storage media are transferred, become obsolete, or are no longer usable or required by an information system, it is important to ensure that residual magnetic, optical, electrical, or other representation of data that has been deleted is not easily recoverable. Sanitization refers to the general process of removing data from storage media, such that there is reasonable assurance that the data may not be easily retrieved and reconstructed.

Information disposition and sanitization decisions occur throughout the system life cycle. Critical factors affecting information disposition and media sanitization are decided at the start of a system's development. The initial system requirements should include hardware and software specifications as well as interconnections and data flow documents that will assist the system owner in identifying the types of media used in the system.

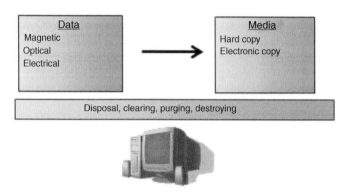

Types of Media

1. *Hard copy*: Hard copy media is physical representations of information. Paper printouts, printer, and facsimile ribbons, drums, and platens are all examples of hard copy media. These types of media are often the most uncontrolled. Information tossed into the recycle bins and trash containers exposes a significant vulnerability to "dumpster divers," and overcurious employees, risking accidental disclosures.
2. *Electronic (or soft copy)*: Electronic media are the bits and bytes contained in hard drives, random access memory (RAM), read-only memory (ROM), disks, memory devices, phones, mobile computing devices, networking equipment, and many other types.

There are different types of sanitization for each type of media. Media sanitization is divided into four categories in NIST SP 800-88: disposal, clearing, purging, and destroying.

1. *Disposal* is the act of discarding media with no other sanitization considerations. This is most often done by paper recycling containing nonconfidential information but may also include other media.
2. *Clearing* information is a level of media sanitization that would protect the confidentiality of information against a robust keyboard attack. Simple deletion of items would not suffice for clearing. Clearing must not allow information to be retrieved by data, disk, or file recovery utilities. It must be resistant to keystroke recovery attempts executed from standard input devices and from data scavenging tools. For example, overwriting is an acceptable method for clearing media.
3. *Purging* information is a media sanitization process that protects the confidentiality of information against a laboratory attack. For some media, clearing media would not suffice for purging. However, for Advanced Technology Attachment (ATA) disk drives manufactured after 2001 (over 15 GB) the terms clearing and purging have converged.

4. *Destruction* of media is the ultimate form of sanitization. After media are destroyed, they cannot be reused as originally intended. Physical destruction can be accomplished using a variety of methods, including disintegration, incineration, pulverizing, shredding, and melting.

Sanitization and Disposition Decision Flow

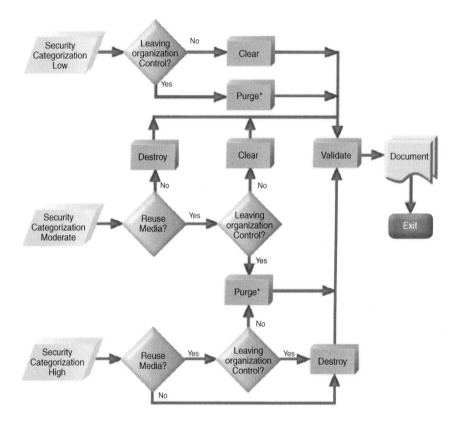

Organizations make sanitization decisions that are commensurate with the security categorization of the confidentiality of information contained on their media. The decision process is based on the confidentiality of the information, not the type of media. Once organizations decide what type of sanitization is best for their individual case, the media type will influence the technique used to achieve this sanitization goal.

Storage Encryption Technologies

SP 800-111 provides a high-level overview of the most commonly used options for encrypting stored information: full disk encryption (FDE), volume and virtual disk encryption, and file/folder encryption. It briefly defines each option and explains at a high level how it works.

1. *FDE*, also known as whole disk encryption, is the process of encrypting all the data on the hard drive used to boot a computer, including the computer's OS, and permitting access to the data only after successful authentication to the FDE product. Most FDE products are software-based.

   FDE software works by redirecting a computer's master boot record (MBR), which is a reserved sector on bootable media that determines which software (e.g., OS, utility) will be executed when the computer boots from the media. Before FDE software is installed onto a computer, the MBR usually points to the computer's primary OS. When FDE software is being used, the computer's MBR is redirected to a special preboot environment (PBE) that controls access to the computer.

   FDE software is most commonly used on desktop and laptop computers. The requirement for preboot authentication means that users have to be able to authenticate using the most fundamental components of a device, such as a standard keyboard – because the OS is not loaded, OS-level drivers are unavailable. For example, a personal digital assistant (PDA) or smart phone could not display a keyboard on the screen for entering a password because that is an OS-level capability.

2. *Virtual disk encryption* is the process of encrypting a file called a container, which can hold many files and folders, and permitting access to the data within the container only after proper authentication is provided, at which point the container is typically mounted as a virtual disk. Virtual disk encryption is used on all types of end user device storage. The container is a single file that resides within a logical volume. Examples of volumes are boot, system, and data volumes on a PC, and a Universal Serial Bus (USB) flash drive formatted with a single file system.

Characteristic	Full disk encryption	Volume encryption	Virtual disk encryption	File/folder encryption
Typical platforms supported	Desktop and laptop computers	Desktop and laptop computers, volume-based removable media (e.g., USB flash drives)	All types of end user devices	All types of end user devices
Data protected by encryption	All data on the media (data files, system files, residual data, and metadata)	All data in the volume (data files, system files, residual data, and metadata)	All data in the container (data files, residual data, and metadata, but not system files)	Individual files/folders (data files only)
Mitigates threats involving loss or theft of devices?	Yes	Yes	Yes	Yes
Mitigates OS and application layer threats (such as malware and insider threats)?	No	If the data volume is being protected, it sometimes mitigates such threats. If the data volume is not being protected, then there is no mitigation of these threats	It sometimes mitigates such threats	It sometimes mitigates such threats

(Continued)

Characteristic	Full disk encryption	Volume encryption	Virtual disk encryption	File/folder encryption
Potential impact to devices in case of solution failure	Loss of all data and device functionality	Loss of all data in volume; can cause loss of device functionality, depending on which volume is being protected	Loss of all data in container	Loss of all protected files/folders
Portability of encrypted information	Not portable	Not portable	Portable	Often portable

3. *Volume encryption* is the process of encrypting an entire logical volume and permitting access to the data on the volume only after proper authentication is provided. It is most often performed on hard drive data volumes and volume-based removable media, such as USB flash drives and external hard drives.

   The key difference between volume and virtual disk encryption is that containers are portable and volumes are not – a container can be copied from one medium to another, with encryption intact. This allows containers to be burned to CDs and DVDs and to be used on other media that are not volume-based. Virtual disk encryption also makes it trivial to back up sensitive data; the container is simply copied to the backup server or media. Another advantage of virtual disk encryption over volume encryption is that virtual disk encryption can be used in situations where volume-based removable media needs to have both protected and unprotected storage; the volume can be left unprotected and a container placed onto the volume for the sensitive information.

4. *File encryption* is the process of encrypting individual files on a storage medium and permitting access to the encrypted data only after proper authentication is provided. Folder encryption is very similar to file encryption, only it addresses individual folders instead of files. Some OSs offer built-in file and/or folder encryption capabilities and many third-party programs are also available. Although folder encryption and virtual disk encryption sound similar – both a folder and a container are intended to contain and protect multiple files – there is a difference. A container is a single opaque file, meaning that no one can see what files or folders are inside the container until the container is decrypted. File/folder encryption is transparent, meaning that anyone with access to the file system can view the names and possibly other metadata for the encrypted files and folders, including files and folders within encrypted folders, if they are not protected through OS AC features. File/folder encryption is used on all types of storage for end user devices.

PHYSICAL SECURITY

As an assessor, physical security reviews are usually conducted via "security walk-throughs" which are inspections of the facilities and their various components. These "walk-throughs" are just that, walking through the facility looking at the various equipment, configurations, electrical panels, HVAC systems, generators, fire suppression systems, and physical access on doors and rooms. The primary areas for physical ACs to review and inspect include:

- Badges
- Memory cards
- Guards
- Keys
- True-floor-to-true-ceiling wall construction, especially in data centers and controlled access rooms
- Fences
- Locks

The primary areas to review during inspections for fire safety and suppression systems include:

- Building operation
- Building occupancy
- Fire detection equipment such as the various kinds of sensors
- Fire extinguishment, including fire extinguishers and delivery mechanisms for rooms

Reviewing the physical security of the facilities also includes the supporting utilities and their delivery. This includes:

- Air-conditioning system
- Electric power distribution
- Heating plants
- Water
- Sewage
- Alternative power and its delivery to the facility

Some of the more critical areas to focus on include looking at the positive flow for both air and water such that the flow is out of the room, rather than into the room, and the point of delivery of the utilities to the facility – is it secure from tampering or inadvertent accidents?

PERSONNEL SECURITY

The PS component is often overlooked and not reviewed in detail by assessors. This area has critical issues in today's world with insider threats, lack of reviews for new or transferring employees, as well as dealing with the US government's requirements for PIV credentials necessary for all users on government systems. Some of the documents and regulations which cover this area include:

- 800-73
- 800-76
- 800-78
- 5 CFR 731.106, Designation of Public Trust Positions and Investigative Requirements
- ICD 704, Personnel Security Standards Sensitive Compartmented Information (SCI)

Proper information security practices should be in place to ensure that employees, contractors, and third-party users understand their responsibilities, and are suitable for the roles they are considered for, and to reduce the risk of theft, fraud, or misuse of facilities, specifically:

- Security responsibilities should be addressed prior to employment in adequate job descriptions and in terms and conditions of employment.
- All candidates for employment, contractors, and third-party users should be adequately screened, especially for sensitive jobs.
- Employees, contractors, and third-party users of information processing facilities should sign an agreement on their security roles and responsibilities.
- Security roles and responsibilities of employees, contractors, and third-party users should be defined and documented in accordance with the organization's information security policy.

The basic staffing process is shown below and the assessor should ensure the processes, procedures, and organizational policies provide the necessary guidance to the HR staff to accomplish these steps in a professional and secure manner throughout the recruitment, hiring, and employee life cycle for each and every employee and contractor involved in the governmental support efforts for their agency.

Staffing

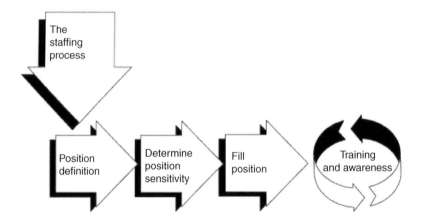

Areas for coverage of personnel which the assessor should review include areas in user administration such as:

- User account management
- Audit and management reviews
- Detecting unauthorized/illegal activities
- Temporary assignments and in-house transfers
- Termination
  - Friendly termination
  - Unfriendly termination

Throughout the personnel process which is under review, the assessor should check on all of the user activities.

SYSTEM INTEGRITY

Integrity reviews often require an assessor to test a system capability either via automated tool employment or through the use of manual scripting efforts. These activities will require the assessor to have knowledge and skills in scripting languages and manual test development. Automated tool use will need the assessor to have experience in the use of the tool and the results expected from the tool. One of the principal ways of automated tool use is through employing vulnerability scanners which often can review the system and determine if there are configuration errors or misaligned areas of code within the application or the operating system. This includes patches for systems as well as code issues.

Patching and flaw remediation are areas of system integrity and system maintenance which the assessor should focus on first when testing and evaluating system integrity. Other areas are found in the following Special Publications:

- 800-40 – Patching (RA family of controls)
- 800-45 – Email
- 800-83 – Malware
- 800-92 – Logs (audit and accounting (AU) family of controls)

Malware Incident Prevention and Handling

SP 800-83, *Guide to Malware Incident Prevention and Handling*, provides recommendations for improving an organization's malware incident prevention measures. It also gives extensive recommendations for enhancing an organization's existing IR capability so that it is better prepared to handle malware incidents, particularly widespread ones. The recommendations address several major forms of malware, including viruses, worms, Trojan horses, malicious mobile code, blended attacks, spyware tracking cookies, and attacker tools such as backdoors and rootkits. The recommendations encompass various transmission mechanisms, including network services (e.g., email, web browsing, file sharing) and removable media.

The basic structure of SP 800-83 addresses focal points of interest for the assessor, such as:

- Malware categories
- Malware incident prevention:
  - Policy
  - Awareness
  - Vulnerability mitigation
  - Threat mitigation
- Malware IR

Malware Categories

- Viruses:
  - Compiled viruses

- • Interpreted viruses
- • Virus obfuscation techniques
- Worms
- Trojan horses
- Malicious mobile code
- Blended attacks
- Tracking cookies
- Attacker tools:
  - • Backdoors
  - • Keystroke loggers
  - • Rootkits
  - • Web browser plug-ins
  - • Email generators
  - • Attacker toolkits
- Non-malware threats:
  - • Phishing
  - • Virus hoaxes

This area of security should always be closely looked at and examined by the assessor as it is often used by attackers as one major area for exploitation of systems through many areas. Often I have found organizations only partially address flaws and remediation efforts and leave potential large and major exposures available for attacks to work against successfully.

Email Security – Spam

As the Special Publication, SP 800-45, states in the Executive Summary: "Electronic mail (email) is perhaps the most popularly used system for exchanging business information over the Internet (or any other computer network). At the most basic level, the email process can be divided into two principal components: (1) mail servers, which are hosts that deliver, forward, and store email; and (2) mail clients, which interface with users and allow users to read, compose, send, and store email. This document addresses the security issues of mail servers and mail clients, including Web-based access to mail.

Mail servers and user workstations running mail clients are frequently targeted by attackers. Because the computing and networking technologies that underlie email are ubiquitous and well-understood by many, attackers are able to develop attack methods to exploit security weaknesses. Mail servers are also targeted because they (and public Web servers) must communicate to some degree with untrusted third parties. Additionally, mail clients have been targeted as an effective means of inserting malware into machines and of propagating this code to other machines. As a result, mail servers, mail clients, and the network infrastructure that supports them must be protected."[21]

Understanding the email system within the organization requires understanding of the various potential attack and exposure areas such as:

---

[21]SP 800-45, p. ES-1.

- To exchange email with the outside world, a requirement for most organizations, it is allowed through organizations' network perimeter defenses. At a basic level, viruses and other types of malware may be distributed throughout an organization via email. Increasingly, however, attackers are getting more sophisticated and using email to deliver targeted zero-day attacks in an attempt to compromise users' workstations within the organization's internal network.
- Given email's nature of human to human communication, it can be used as a social engineering vehicle. Email can allow an attacker to exploit an organization's users to gather information or get the users to perform actions that further an attack.
- Flaws in the mail server application may be used as the means of compromising the underlying server and hence the attached network. Examples of this unauthorized access include gaining access to files or folders that were not meant to be publicly accessible, and being able to execute commands and/or install software on the mail server.
- Denial of service (DoS) attacks may be directed to the mail server or its support network infrastructure, denying or hindering valid users from using the mail server.
- Sensitive information on the mail server may be read by unauthorized individuals or changed in an unauthorized manner.
- Sensitive information transmitted unencrypted between mail server and client may be intercepted. All popular email communication standards default to sending usernames, passwords, and email messages unencrypted.
- Information within email messages may be altered at some point between the sender and recipient.
- Malicious entities may gain unauthorized access to resources elsewhere in the organization's network via a successful attack on the mail server. For example, once the mail server is compromised, an attacker could retrieve users' passwords, which may grant the attacker access to other hosts on the organization's network.
- Malicious entities may attack external organizations from a successful attack on a mail server host.
- Misconfiguration may allow malicious entities to use the organization's mail server to send email-based advertisements (i.e., spam).
- Users may send inappropriate, proprietary, or other sensitive information via email. This could expose the organization to legal action.[22]

The areas for the assessor to review should, therefore, include the following configuration items:

- Ensuring that spam cannot be sent from the mail servers they control
- Implementing spam filtering for inbound messages
- Blocking messages from known spam-sending servers

The assessor should examine the mail servers, clients, and organization's security architecture for the focal points as follows to ensure proper security for email systems:

1. Email message signing and encryption standards
2. Planning and management of mail servers
3. Securing the operating system underlying a mail server
4. Mail server application security
5. Email content filtering
6. Email-specific considerations in the deployment and configuration of network protection mechanisms, such as firewalls, routers, switches, and intrusion detection and intrusion prevention systems
7. Securing mail clients
8. Administering the mail server in a secure manner, including backups, security testing, and log reviews

[22]SP 800-45, p. ES1–ES2.

Each area should be tested for configuration, compliance, and actual security actions when dealing with this very sensitive organizational support area of email.

TECHNICAL AREAS OF CONSIDERATION

The common way for validating and verifying the technical controls is to employ automated testing tools and techniques as found in the NIST SP 800-115 testing guide. There are many tools which can be utilized to evaluate the various technical components, equipment, and configuration used by the IT staff, network support staff, and the agency. The basic four areas of technical controls are as follows:

1. AC
2. AU
3. IA
4. SC

We will examine each area and the parts of each with technical focus from an assessment perspective as we review the technical components that make up these controls.

ACCESS CONTROL

There are many NIST Special Publications for the various AC methodologies and implementations. Each one has a specific area of AC that it covers. Here are just some of the SPs available for review and reference as the controls are identified, implemented, and evaluated:

- 800-46 (Telework)
- 800-77 (Internet Protocol Security (IPSec))
- 800-113 (SSL)
- 800-114 (External Devices)
- 800-121 (Bluetooth)
- 800-48 (Legacy Wireless)
- 800-97 (802.11i Wireless)
- 800-124 (Cell Phones/PDA)
- OMB M 06-16 (Remote Access)

Logical Access Controls

Logical ACs are the primary means of managing and protecting resources to reduce risks to a level acceptable to an organization. They are tools used for identification, authentication, authorization, and accountability. They are software components that enforce AC measures for systems, programs, processes, and information. The logical ACs can be embedded within operating systems, applications, add-on security packages, or database and telecommunication management systems. In applying management-designed policies and procedures for protecting information assets, logical ACs are the primary means of managing and protecting these resources to reduce risks to a level acceptable to an organization. For example, the concept of AC relates to managing and controlling access to an organization's information resources residing on host- and network-based computer systems. Assessors need to understand the relationship of logical ACs to management policies and procedures for information security. In doing so, assessors should be able to analyze and evaluate a logical AC's effectiveness in accomplishing information security objectives.

Inadequate logical ACs increase an organization's potential for losses resulting from exposures. These exposures can result in minor inconveniences up to a total shutdown of computer functions. Exposures that exist from accidental or intentional exploitation of logical AC weaknesses include technical exposures and computer crime.

For assessors to effectively assess logical ACs within the system under review, they first need to gain a technical and organizational understanding of the organization's IT environment. The purpose of this is to determine which areas from a risk standpoint warrant special attention in planning current and future work. This includes reviewing all security layers associated with the organization's IT information system architecture.

These layers are as follows:

- Network layer
- Operating system platform layer
- Database layer
- Application layer

Paths of Logical Access

Access or points of entry to an organization's information system infrastructure can be gained through several avenues. Each avenue is subject to appropriate levels of access security. For example, paths of logical access often relate to different levels occurring from either a back-end or a front-end interconnected network of systems for internally or externally based users. Front-end systems are network-based systems connecting an organization to outside untrusted networks, such as corporate websites, where a customer can access the website externally in initiating transactions that connect to a proxy server application which in turn connects, for example, to a back-end database system in updating a customer database. Front-end systems can also be internally based in automating business, paper-less processes that tie into back-end systems in a similar manner.

General Points of Entry

- General points of entry to either front-end or back-end systems relate to an organization's networking or telecommunications infrastructure in controlling access into their information resources (e.g., applications, databases, facilities, networks). The approach followed is based on a client–server model where, for example, a large organization can literally have thousands of interconnected network servers. Connectivity in this environment needs to be controlled through a smaller set of primary domain controlling servers, which enable a user to obtain access to specific secondary points of entry (e.g., application servers, databases).

General modes of access into this infrastructure occur through the following:

- Network connectivity
- Remote access
- Operator console
- Online workstations or terminals

Logical Access Control Software

IT has made it possible for computer systems to store and contain large quantities of sensitive data, increase the capability of sharing resources from one system to another, and permit many users to access the system through internet/intranet technologies. All of these factors have made organizations' information system resources more accessible and available anytime and anywhere.

To protect an organization's information resources, AC software has become even more critical in assuring the confidentiality, integrity, and availability of information resources. The purpose of AC software is *to prevent unauthorized access and modification to an organization's sensitive data and use of system critical functions*.

To achieve this level of control, it is necessary to apply ACs across all layers of an organization's information system architecture. This includes networks, platforms or operating system, databases, and application systems. Attributes across each commonly include some form of IA, access authorization, checking to specific information resources, and logging and reporting of user activities.

The greatest degree of protection in applying AC software is at the network and platform/operating system levels. These layers provide the greatest degree of protection of information resources from internal and external users' unauthorized access. These systems are also referred to as general support systems, and they make up the primary infrastructure on which applications and database systems will reside.

Operating system AC software interfaces with other system software AC programs, such as network layer devices (e.g., routers, firewalls), that manage and control external access to organizations' networks. Additionally, operating system AC software interfaces with database and/or application system ACs to protect system libraries and user datasets.

Logical Access Control Software Functionality

1. *General operating system AC functions include*:
    a. Apply user IA mechanisms.
    b. Restrict log-on IDs to specific terminals/workstations and specific times.
    c. Establish rules for access to specific information resources (e.g., system-level application resources and data).
    d. Create individual accountability and auditability.
    e. Create or change user profiles.
    f. Log events.
    g. Log user activities.
    h. Report capabilities.

2. *Database and/or application-level AC functions include:*
   a. Create or change data files and database profiles.
   b. Verify user authorization at the application and transaction levels.
   c. Verify user authorization within the application.
   d. Verify user authorization at the field level for changes within a database.
   e. Verify subsystem authorization for the user at the file level.
   f. Log database/data communications access activities for monitoring access violations.

Assessing ACs and AC systems:

- Start with obtaining a general understanding of the security risks facing information processing, through a review of relevant documentation, inquiry, observation, and risk assessment and evaluation techniques.
- Document and evaluate controls over potential access paths into the system to assess their adequacy, efficiency, and effectiveness by reviewing appropriate hardware and software security features and identifying any deficiencies or redundancies.
- Test controls over access paths to determine whether they are functioning and effective by applying appropriate testing techniques.
- Evaluate the AC environment to determine if the control requirements are achieved by analyzing test results and other evidence.
- Evaluate the security environment to assess its adequacy by reviewing written policies, and observing practices and procedures, and comparing them with appropriate security standards or practices and procedures used by other organizations.
- Familiarization with the IT environment:

  - This is the first step of the evaluation and involves obtaining a clear understanding of the technical, managerial, and security environment of the information system processing facility. This typically includes interviews, physical walk-throughs, review of documents, and risk assessments, as mentioned above in the physical security control area.

- Documenting the access paths:

  - The access path is the logical route an end user takes to access computerized information. This starts with a terminal/workstation and typically ends with the data being accessed. Along the way, numerous hardware and software components are encountered. The assessor should evaluate each component for proper implementation and proper physical and logical access security.

- Interviewing systems personnel:

  - To control and maintain the various components of the access path, as well as the operating system and computer mainframe, technical experts often are required. These people can be a valuable source of information to the assessor when gaining an understanding of security. To determine who these people are, the assessor should interview with the IS manager and review organizational charts and job descriptions. Key people include the security administrator, network control manager, and systems software manager.

- Reviewing reports from AC software:
  - The reporting features of AC software provide the security administrator with the opportunity to monitor adherence to security policies. By reviewing a sample of security reports, the assessor can determine if enough information is provided to support an investigation and if the security administrator is performing an effective review of the report.

- Reviewing Application Systems Operations Manual:
  - An Application Systems Manual should contain documentation on the programs that generally are used throughout a data processing installation to support the development, implementation, operations, and use of application systems. This manual should include information about which platform the application can run on, database management systems, compilers, interpreters, telecommunications monitors, and other applications that can run with the application.

- Log-on IDs and passwords:
  - To test confidentiality, the assessor could attempt to guess the password of a sample of employees' log-on IDs (though this is not necessarily a test). This should be done discreetly to avoid upsetting employees. The assessor should tour end user and programmer work areas looking for passwords taped to the side of terminals or the inside of desk drawers, or located in card files. Another source of confidential information is the wastebasket. The assessor might consider going through the office wastebasket looking for confidential information and passwords. Users could be asked to give their password to the assessor. However, unless specifically authorized for a particular situation and supported by the security policy, no user should ever disclose his/her password.

- Controls over production resources:
  - Computer ACs should extend beyond application data and transactions. There are numerous high-level utilities, macro or job control libraries, control libraries, and system software parameters for which AC should be particularly strong. Access to these libraries would provide the ability to bypass other ACs. The assessor should work with the system software analyst and operations manager to determine if access is on a need-to-know basis for all sensitive production resources. Working with the security administrator, the assessor should determine who can access these resources and what can be done with this access.

- Logging and reporting of computer access violations:
  - To test the reporting of access violations, the assessor should attempt to access computer transactions or data for which access is not authorized. The attempts should be unsuccessful and identified on security reports. This test should be coordinated with the data owner and security administrator to avoid violation of security regulations.

- Follow up access violations:
  - To test the effectiveness and timeliness of the security administrator's and data owner's response to reported violation attempts, the assessor should select a sample

of security reports and look for evidence of follow-up and investigation of access violations. If such evidence cannot be found, the assessor should conduct further interviews to determine why this situation exists.

- Identification of methods for bypassing security and compensating controls:

  - This is a technical area of review. As a result, the assessor should work with the system software analyst, network manager, operations manager, and security administrator to determine ways to bypass security. This typically includes bypass label processing (BLP), special system maintenance log-on IDs, operating system exits, installation utilities, and I/O devices. Working with the security administrator, the assessor should determine who can access these resources and what can be done with this access. The assessor should determine if access is on a need-to-know/have basis or if compensating detective controls exist.

- Review ACs and password administration:

  - Ensure password control is active for all accounts and users. Ensure password complexity and renewal requirements are enforced for all users and accounts. Ensure password criteria for elevated privilege accounts are more complex and longer than for standard user accounts as part of Separation of Duties review.

- Restricting and monitoring access:

  - There should be restrictions and procedures of monitoring access to computer features that bypass security. Generally, only system software programmers should have access to these features:

    - *BLP*: BLP bypasses the computer reading of the file label. Since most AC rules are based on file names (labels), this can bypass access security.
    - *System exits*: This system software feature permits the user to perform complex system maintenance, which may be tailored to a specific environment or company. They often exist outside of the computer security system and, thus, are not restricted or reported in their use.
    - *Special system log-on IDs*: These log-on IDs often are provided with the computer by the vendor. The names can be determined easily because they are the same for all similar computer systems. Passwords should be changed immediately, on installation, to secure the systems.

- Auditing remote access:

  - Remote use of information resources dramatically improves business productivity, but generates control issues and security concerns. In this regard, IS auditors should determine that all remote access capabilities used by an organization provide for effective security of the organization's information resources. Remote access security controls should be documented and implemented for authorized users operating outside of the trusted network environment. In reviewing existing remote access architectures, IS auditors should assess remote access points (APs) of entry in addressing how many (known/unknown) exist and whether greater centralized control of remote APs is needed. IS auditors should also review APs for appropriate controls, such as in the use of virtual private networks (VPNs), authentication mechanisms, encryption, firewalls, and IDS.

IDENTIFICATION AND AUTHENTICATION

IA is the process of proving one's identity. It is the process by which the system obtains from a user his/her claimed identity and the credentials needed to authenticate this identity, and validates both pieces of information.

LOG-ON IDS AND PASSWORDS

Features of passwords:

- A password should be easy for the user to remember but difficult for a perpetrator to guess.
- Initial passwords may be allocated by the security administrator or generated by the system itself. When the user logs on for the first time, the system should force a password change to improve confidentiality.
- If the wrong password is entered a predefined number of times, typically three, the log-on ID should be automatically and permanently deactivated (or at least for a significant period of time).

Token Devices, One-Time Passwords

A two-factor authentication technique, such as a microprocessor-controlled smart card, generates one-time passwords that are good for only one log-on session. Users enter this password along with a password they have memorized to gain access to the system. This technique involves something you have (a device subject to theft) and something you know (a personal identification number). Such devices gain their one-time password status because of a unique session characteristic (e.g., ID or time) appended to the password.

Biometrics

Biometric ACs are the best means of authenticating a user's identity based on a unique, measurable attribute or trait for verifying the identity of a human being. This control restricts computer access, based on a physical (something you are) or behavioral (something you do) characteristic of the user.

Management of Biometrics

Management of biometrics should address effective security for the collection, distribution, and processing of biometric data.

Management should develop and approve biometric information management and security (BIMS) policy. The auditor should use the BIMS policy to gain a better understanding of the biometric systems in use.

Single Sign-On (SSO)

Users normally require access to a number of resources during the course of their daily routine. For example, users would first log into an operating system and thereafter into various applications. For each operating system application or other resource in use, the user is required to provide a separate set of credentials to gain access; this results in a situation wherein the user's ability to remember passwords is significantly reduced. This situation also increases the chance that a user will write them down on or near their workstation or area of work, and thereby increase the risks that a security breach within the organization may occur.

To address this situation, the concept of SSO was developed. SSO can generally be defined as the process for consolidating all organization platform-based administration, authentication, and authorization functions into a single centralized administrative function. This function would provide the appropriate interfaces to the organization's information resources, which may include:

- Client–server and distributed systems
- Mainframe systems
- Network security including remote access mechanisms

The SSO process begins with the first instance where the user credentials are introduced into the organization's IT computing environment. The information resource or SSO server handling this function is referred to as the primary domain. Every other information resource, application, or platform that uses those credentials is called a secondary domain.

The authorization process of AC often requires that the system be able to identify and differentiate among users. For example, AC is often based on least privilege, which refers to the granting to users of only those accesses required to perform their duties.

Access rules (authorization) specify who can access what. Access should be on a documented need-to-know and need-to-do basis by type of access.

Having computer access does not always mean unrestricted access. Computer access can be set to many differing levels. When IS auditors review computer accessibility, they need to know what can be done with the access and what is restricted. For example, access restrictions at the file level generally include the following:

- Read, inquiry, or copy only
- Write, create, update, or delete only
- Execute only
- A combination of the above

Authentication of an individual's identity is a fundamental component of physical and logical AC processes. When an individual attempts to access security-sensitive buildings, computer systems, or data, an AC decision must be made. An accurate determination of identity is needed to make sound AC decisions.

A wide range of mechanisms is employed to authenticate identity, utilizing various classes of identity credentials. For physical access, individual identity has traditionally been authenticated by use of paper or other nonautomated, hand-carried credentials, such as driver's licenses and badges. Access authorization to computers and data has traditionally been authenticated through user-selected passwords. More recently, cryptographic mechanisms and biometric techniques have been used in physical and logical security applications, replacing or supplementing the traditional credentials.

The strength of the authentication that is achieved varies, depending on the type of credential, the process used to issue the credential, and the authentication mechanism used to validate the credential. This document establishes a standard for a PIV system based on secure and reliable forms of identification credentials issued by the federal government to its employees and contractors. These credentials are intended to authenticate individuals who require access to federally controlled facilities, information systems, and applications.

SYSTEMS AND COMMUNICATIONS PROTECTION

Network Layer Security

There are multiple methods and techniques employed by organizations for deploying and enhancing network security. All methods provide differing levels of confidentiality, integrity, and availability depending on their technology, location on the network, and method of installation. We will highlight several of these methods to properly review, examine, and evaluate each to ensure the use of and actions conducted by these methods are functional, operational, and secure. We will start with VPNs, and then discuss wireless networking, IDS, encryption, and firewalls.

VPN

A VPN is a virtual network, built on top of existing physical networks, which can provide a secure communications mechanism for data and other information transmitted between networks. Because a VPN can be used over existing networks, such as the internet, it can facilitate the secure transfer of sensitive data across public networks. This is often less expensive than alternatives such as dedicated private telecommunications lines between organizations or branch offices. We will examine the two most common types of VPNs utilized in today's networks in order to properly assess them: IPSec and SSL-based VPNs. "IPsec has emerged as the most commonly used network layer security control for protecting communications, while SSL is the most commonly used transport layer security control. Depending on how IPsec and SSL are implemented and configured, both can provide any combination of the following types of protection:

- **Confidentiality.** IPsec and SSL can ensure that data cannot be read by unauthorized parties. This is accomplished by encrypting data using a cryptographic algorithm and a secret key—a value known only to the two parties exchanging data. The data can only be decrypted by someone who has the secret key.
- **Integrity.** IPsec and SSL can determine if data has been changed (intentionally or unintentionally) during transit. The integrity of data can be assured by generating a message authentication code (MAC) value, which is a keyed cryptographic checksum of the data. If the data is altered and the MAC is recalculated, the old and new MACs will differ.

- **Peer Authentication.** Each IPsec endpoint confirms the identity of the other IPsec endpoint with which it wishes to communicate, ensuring that the network traffic and data is being sent from the expected host. SSL authentication is typically performed one-way, authenticating the server to the client; however, SSL VPNs require authentication for both endpoints.
- **Replay Protection.** The same data is not delivered multiple times, and data is not delivered grossly out of order.
- **Traffic Analysis Protection.** A person monitoring network traffic cannot determine the contents of the network traffic or how much data is being exchanged. IPsec can also conceal which parties are communicating, whereas SSL leaves this information exposed. Frequency of communication may also be protected depending on implementation. Nevertheless, the number of packets being exchanged can be counted.
- **Access Control.** IPsec and SSL endpoints can perform filtering to ensure that only authorized users can access particular network resources. IPsec and SSL endpoints can also allow or block certain types of network traffic, such as allowing Web server access but denying file sharing."[23]

So we start with IPSec VPNs, and then we will discuss SSL/Transport Layer Security (TLS) VPNs.

IPSec VPN – SP 800-77

IPSec is a framework of open standards for ensuring private communications over public networks. It has become one of the most common network layer security controls, typically used to create a VPN.

There are three primary models for VPN architectures, as follows:

1. *Gateway-to-gateway*: This model protects communications between two specific networks, such as an organization's main office network and a branch office network, or two business partners' networks.

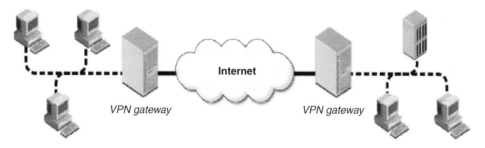

2. *Host-to-gateway*: This model protects communications between one or more individual hosts and a specific network belonging to an organization. The host-to-gateway model is most often used to allow hosts on unsecured networks, such as traveling employees and telecommuters, to gain access to internal organizational services, such as the organization's email and web servers.

---

[23]SP 800-113, p. 2-3, 2-4.

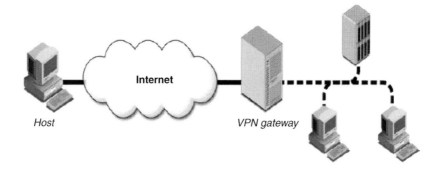

3. *Host-to-host*: A host-to-host architecture protects communication between two specific computers. It is most often used when a small number of users need to use or administer a remote system that requires the use of inherently insecure protocols.

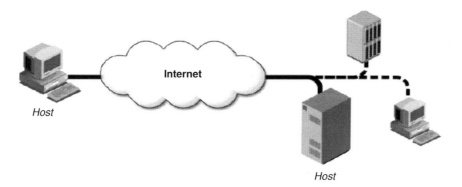

VPN Model Comparison

Feature	Gateway-to-gateway	Host-to-gateway	Host-to-host
Provides protection between client and local gateway	No	N/A (client is VPN end point)	N/A (client is VPN end point)
Provides protection between VPN end points	Yes	Yes	Yes
Provides protection between remote gateway and remote server (behind gateway)	No	No	N/A (server is VPN end point)
Transparent to users	Yes	No	No
Transparent to users' systems	Yes	No	No
Transparent to servers	Yes	Yes	No

IPSec is a collection of protocols that assist in protecting communications over IP networks. IPSec protocols work together in various combinations to provide protection for communications.

- IPsec fundamentals:

  - *Authentication Header (AH)*: AH, one of the IPSec security protocols, provides integrity protection for packet headers and data, as well as user authentication. It can optionally provide replay protection and access protection. AH cannot encrypt any portion of packets.
  - *AH modes*: AH has two modes – *transport* and *tunnel*. In tunnel mode, AH creates a new IP header for each packet; in transport mode, AH does not create a new IP header. In IPSec architectures that use a gateway, the true source or destination IP address for packets must be altered to be the gateway's IP address. Because transport mode cannot alter the original IP header or create a new IP header, transport mode is generally used in host-to-host architectures.
  - *Encapsulating Security Payload (ESP)*: ESP is the second core IPSec security protocol. In the initial version of IPSec, ESP provided only encryption for packet payload data. Integrity protection was provided by the AH protocol if needed. In the second version of IPSec, ESP became more flexible. It can perform authentication to provide integrity protection, although not for the outermost IP header. Also, ESP's encryption can be disabled through the Null ESP Encryption Algorithm. Therefore, in all but the oldest IPSec implementations, ESP can be used to provide only encryption, encryption and integrity protection, or only integrity protection.

    ESP has two modes: *transport* and *tunnel*. In tunnel mode, ESP creates a new IP header for each packet. The new IP header lists the end points of the ESP tunnel (such as two IPSec gateways) as the source and destination of the packet. Because of this, tunnel mode can be used with all three VPN architecture models.
  - *Internet Key Exchange (IKE)*: The purpose of the IKE protocol is to negotiate, create, and manage security associations (SAs). *SA* is a generic term for a set of values that define the IPSec features and protections applied to a connection. SAs can also be manually created, using values agreed upon in advance by both parties, but these SAs cannot be updated; this method does not scale for real-life large-scale VPNs. IKE uses five different types of exchanges to create SAs, transfer status and error information, and define new Diffie–Hellman groups. In IPSec, IKE is used to provide a secure mechanism for establishing IPsec-protected connections.
  - *IP Payload Compression Protocol (IPComp)*: In communications, it is often desirable to perform lossless compression on data – to repackage information in a smaller format without losing any of its meaning. The IPComp is often used with IPSec. By applying IPComp to a payload first, and then encrypting the packet through ESP, effective compression can be achieved.

    IPComp can be configured to provide compression for IPSec traffic going in one direction only (e.g., compress packets from end point A to end point B, but not from end point B to end point A) or in both directions. Also, IPComp allows administrators to choose from multiple compression algorithms, including DEFLATE and LZS.49. IPComp provides a simple yet flexible solution for compressing IPSec payloads.

IPComp can provide lossless compression for IPSec payloads. Because applying compression algorithms to certain types of payloads may actually make them larger, IPComp compresses the payload only if it will actually make the packet smaller. IPSec uses IKE to create SAs, which are sets of values that define the security of IPsec-protected connections. IKE phase 1 creates an IKE SA; IKE phase 2 creates an IPSec SA through a channel protected by the IKE SA. IKE phase 1 has two modes: main mode and aggressive mode. Main mode negotiates the establishment of the bidirectional IKE SA through three pairs of messages, while aggressive mode uses only three messages. Although aggressive mode is faster, it is also less flexible and secure. IKE phase 2 has one mode: quick mode. Quick mode uses three messages to establish a pair of unidirectional IPSec SAs. Quick mode communications are encrypted by the method specified in the IKE SA created by phase 1.

SSL VPNs – SP 800-113

An SSL VPN consists of one or more VPN devices to which users connect using their web browsers. The traffic between the web browser and the SSL VPN device is encrypted with the SSL protocol or its successor, the TLS protocol. This type of VPN may be referred to as either an SSL VPN or a TLS VPN.

> Secure Sockets Layer (SSL) virtual private networks (VPN) provide secure remote access to an organization's resources. An SSL VPN consists of one or more VPN devices to which users connect using their Web browsers. The traffic between the Web browser and the SSL VPN device is encrypted with the SSL protocol or its successor, the Transport Layer Security (TLS) protocol. This type of VPN may be referred to as either an SSL VPN or a TLS VPN. This guide uses the term SSL VPN. SSL VPNs provide remote users with access to Web applications and client/server applications, and connectivity to internal networks. Despite the popularity of SSL VPNs, they are not intended to replace Internet Protocol Security (IPsec) VPNs.1 The two VPN technologies are complementary and address separate network architectures and business needs. SSL VPNs offer versatility and ease of use because they use the SSL protocol, which is included with all standard Web browsers, so the client usually does not require configuration by the user. SSL VPNs offer granular control for a range of users on a variety of computers, accessing resources from many locations.[24]

SSL PORTAL VPNS

An SSL portal VPN allows a user to use a single standard SSL connection to a website to securely access multiple network services. The site accessed is typically called a portal because it has a single page that leads to many other resources. SSL portal VPNs act as transport-layer VPNs that work over a single network port, namely the TCP port for SSL-protected HTTP (443).

SSL TUNNEL VPNS

An SSL tunnel VPN allows a user to use a typical web browser to securely access multiple network services through a tunnel that is running under SSL. SSL tunnel VPNs require that the web browser be able to handle specific types of active content (e.g., Java, JavaScript, Flash, or ActiveX) and that the user be able to run them. (Most browsers that handle such applications and plug-ins also allow the user or administrator to block them from being executed.)

[24]SP 800-113, p. ES-1.

ADMINISTERING SSL VPN

The administration of both SSL portal VPNs and SSL tunnel VPNs is similar. The gateway administrator needs to specify local policy in at least two broad areas:

- **Access**. All SSL VPNs allow the administrator to specify which users have access to the VPN services. User authentication might be done with a simple password through a Web form, or through more sophisticated authentication mechanisms.
- **Capabilities**. The administrator can specify the services to which each authorized user has access. For example, some users might have access to only certain Web pages, while others might have access to those Web pages plus other services.

Different SSL VPNs have very different administrative interfaces and very different capabilities for allowing access and specifying allowed actions for users. For example, many but not all SSL VPNs allow validation of users through the Remote Authentication Dial-In User Server (RADIUS) protocol. As another example, some SSL VPNs allow the administrator to create groups of users who have the same access methods and capabilities; this makes adding new users to the system easier than gateways that require the administrator to specify both of these for each new user.[25]

SSL VPN ARCHITECTURE

The five phases of the recommended approach are as follows:

1. **Identify Requirements.** Identify the requirements for remote access and determine how they can best be met.
2. **Design the Solution.** Make design decisions in five areas: access control, endpoint security, authentication methods, architecture, and cryptography policy.
3. **Implement and Test a Prototype.** Test a prototype of the designed solution in a laboratory, test, or production environment to identify any potential issues.
4. **Deploy the Solution.** Gradually deploy the SSL VPN solution throughout the enterprise, beginning with a pilot program.
5. **Manage the Solution.** Maintain the SSL VPN components and resolve operational issues. Repeat the planning and implementation process when significant changes need to be incorporated into the solution.[26]

Note: Many of the cryptographic algorithms used in some SSL cipher suites are not FIPS-approved, and therefore are not allowed for use in SSL VPNs that are to be used in applications that must conform to FIPS-140-2.

SSL VPN ARCHITECTURE

Typical SSL VPN users include people in remote offices, mobile users, business partners, and customers. Hardware clients include various types of devices, such as public kiosks, home personal computers (PC), PDAs, or smart phones, which may or may not be controlled or managed by the organization. The SSL VPN may also be accessed from any location including an airport, a coffee shop, or a hotel room, as long as the location has connectivity to the Internet and the user has a Web client that is capable of using the particular SSL VPN. All traffic is encrypted as it traverses public networks such as the Internet. The SSL VPN gateway is

[25]SP 800-113, p. 2-5, 2-6.
[26]SP 800-113, p. ES-3.

the end point for the secure connection and provides various services and features (most SSL VPN products are standalone hardware appliances, although there are some software-based solutions that are installed on user-supplied servers).[27]

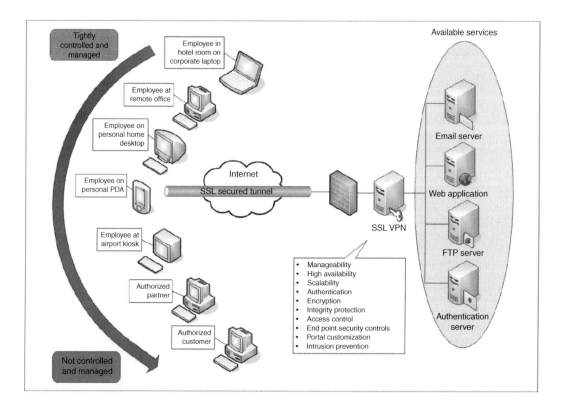

SSL PROTOCOL BASICS

The security of the data sent over an SSL VPN relies on the security of the SSL protocol. The SSL protocol allows a client (such as a web browser) and a server (such as an SSL VPN) to negotiate the type of security to be used during an SSL session. Thus, it is critical to make sure that the security agreed to by the remote user and the SSL gateway meets the security requirements of the organization using the SSL VPN.

There are three types of security that the client and the server can negotiate: the version of SSL, the type of cryptography, and the authentication method.

- *Versions of SSL and TLS*: The terms SSL and TLS are often used together to describe the same protocol. In fact, SSL refers to all versions of the SSL protocol as defined by the Internet Engineering Task Force (IETF), while TLS refers only to versions 3.1 and later of the SSL protocol. Two versions of TLS have been standardized: TLS 1.0 and TLS 1.1.

[27]*Ibid.*, p. 3-1.

TLS 1.0 is the same as SSL 3.1; there are no versions of SSL after 3.1. As of the writing of this guide, work is being done on TLS version 1.2.

TLS is approved for use in the protection of federal information; SSL versions other than 3.1 are not.

- *Cryptography used in SSL sessions*: There are many types of cryptographic functions that are used in security protocols. The most widely known cryptographic features are confidentiality (secrecy of data), integrity (the ability to detect even minute changes in the data), and signature (the ability to trace the origin of the data). The combination of these features is an important aspect of the overall security of a communications stream. SSL uses four significant types of features: confidentiality, integrity, signature, and key establishment (the way that a key is agreed to by the two parties).

  SSL uses cipher suites to define the set of cryptographic functions that a client and a server use when communicating. This is unlike protocols such as IPSec and Secure/Multipurpose Internet Mail Extensions (S/MIME) where the two parties agree to individual cryptographic functions. That is, SSL exchanges say in effect, "Here is a set of functions to be used together, and here is another set I am willing to use." IPSec and S/MIME (and many other protocols) instead say, "Here are the confidentiality functions I am willing to use, here are the integrity functions I am willing to use, and here are the signature algorithms I am willing to use," and the other side creates a set from those choices.

  Just as the SSL client and server need to be able to use the same version of SSL, they also need to be able to use the same cipher suite; otherwise, the two sides cannot communicate. The organization running the SSL VPN chooses which cipher suites meet its security goals and configures the SSL VPN gateway to use only those cipher suites.

- *Authentication used for identifying SSL servers*: When a web browser connects to an SSL server such as an SSL VPN gateway, the browser user needs some way to know that the browser is talking to a server the user trusts. SSL uses certificates that are signed by trusted entities to authenticate the server to the web user. (SSL can also use certificates to authenticate users to servers, but this is rarely done.)

  The server authentication occurs very early in the SSL process, immediately after the user sends its first message to the SSL server. In that first message, the web browser specifies which type of certificate algorithms it can handle; the two common choices are RSA and DSS. In the second message, the SSL server responds with a certificate of one of the types that the browser said it understands. After receiving the certificate, the web browser verifies that the identity in the certificate (i e., the domain name listed in the certificate) matches the domain name to which the web browser attempted to connect.

  Some SSL VPNs use certificates issued by the vendor of the SSL VPN, and those certificates do not link through a chain of trust to a root certificate that is normally trusted by most users. If that is the case, the user should add the SSL VPN's own certificate to the user's list of directly trusted certificates. It is important to note that users should not add the root certificate of the SSL VPN's manufacturer to the list of certification authorities that the user trusts, since the manufacturer's security policies and controls may differ from those of the organization. Other SSL VPNs produce self-signed certificates that do not chain to any trusted root certificate; as before, the user should add the SSL VPN's own certificate to the user's list of directly trusted certificates.

Transport Layer Security

The Netscape Corporation designed a protocol known as the SSL to meet security needs of client browsers and server applications. Version 1 of SSL was never released. Version 2 (SSL 2.0) was released in 1994 but had well-known security vulnerabilities. Version 3 (SSL 3.0) was released in 1995 to address these vulnerabilities.

During this timeframe, Microsoft Corporation released a protocol known as Private Communications Technology (PCT), and later released a higher performance protocol known as the Secure Transport Layer Protocol (STLP). PCT and STLP never commanded the market share that SSL 2.0 and SSL 3.0 commanded. The IETF (a technical working group responsible for developing internet standards to ensure communications compatibility across different implementations) attempted to resolve, as best it could, security engineering and protocol incompatibility issues between the protocols. The IETF standards track Transport Layer Security Protocol Version 1.0 (TLS 1.0) emerged and was codified by the IETF as [RFC2246].

While TLS 1.0 is based on SSL 3.0, and the differences between them are not dramatic, they are significant enough that TLS 1.0 and SSL 3.0 do not interoperate. However, TLS 1.0 does incorporate a mechanism by which a TLS 1.0 implementation can negotiate to use SSL 3.0 with requesting entities as if TLS were never proposed. However, because SSL 3.0 is not approved for use in the protection of federal information (Section 7.1 of [FIPS140-2l]), TLS must be properly configured to ensure that the negotiation and use of SSL 3.0 never occurs when federal information is to be protected.

The NIST guidelines (SP 800-52, SP 800-77, and SP 800-113) attempt to make clear the impact of selecting and using secure web transport protocols for use in protecting sensitive but unclassified US government information.

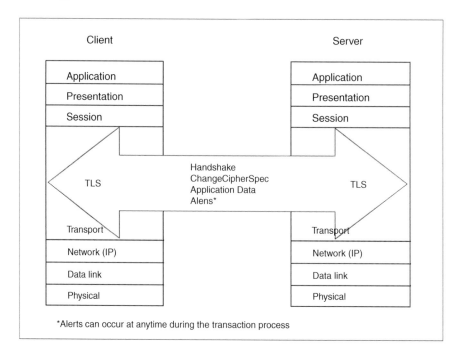

*Alerts can occur at anytime during the transaction process

Both the TLS 1.0 and the SSL 3.0 protocol specifications use cryptographic mechanisms to implement the security services that establish and maintain a secure TCP/IP connection. The secure connection prevents eavesdropping, tampering, or message forgery. Implementing data confidentiality with cryptography (encryption) prevents eavesdropping, generating a message authentication code (MAC) with a secure hash function prevents undetected tampering, and authenticating clients and servers with public key cryptography-based digital signatures prevents message forgery. In each case – preventing eavesdropping, tampering, and forgery – a key or shared secret is required by the cryptographic mechanism. A pseudo-random number generator and a key establishment algorithm provide for the generation and sharing of these secrets.

The rows in the following table identify the key establishment, confidentiality, digital signature, and hash mechanisms currently in use today in TLS 1.0 and SSL 3.0. The columns identify which key establishment, confidentiality, and signature algorithms and which hash functions are FIPS.

Mechanism	SSL (3.0)	TLS 1.0	FIPS reference
Key establishment	RSA	RSA	
	DH-RSA	DH-RSA	
	DH-DSS	DH-DSS	
	DHE-RSA	DHE-RSA	
	DHE-DSS	DHE-DSS	
	DH-Anon	DH-Anon	
	Fortezza-KEA		
Confidentiality	IDEA-CBC	IDEA-CBC	FIPS46-3.FIPS81
	RC4-128	RC4-128	
	3DES-EDE-CBC	3DES-EDE-CBC	
	Fortezza-CBC		
		Kerberos	
		AES	FIPS-197
Signature	RSA	RSA	FIPS-186-2
	DSA	DSA	FIPS-186-2
		EC	FIPS-186-2
Hash	MD5	MD5	
	SHA-1	SHA-1	FIPS-180-2, FIPS-198

WIRELESS NETWORKING

In today's networks, there are often many methods for communications used and deployed. Some of these methods take advantage of nonwired connectivity by utilizing wireless technology. There are several types of wireless-based networking methods currently used all based on radio-frequency (RF) methods of communications for the transmission and reception of the signals carrying the digital data across and external to the network. Examples of wireless networks include cell phone networks, Wi-Fi local networks, and terrestrial microwave networks.

Every wireless LAN network consists of an AP, such as a wireless router, and one or more wireless adapters. As shown in the standard two deployment modes below, there are many security controls from SP 800-53 which are applicable and necessary to secure wireless LANs and Wi-Fi networks. The assessor needs to focus on the technology deployed, review all design and implementation documents, and test the actual APs (aka hotspots) and the client adapters used to prove the encryption and communications used during the wireless activities remain active and constant during all phases of transmission of the data over the airwaves via the RF signals used.

A *wireless AP* is a device that allows wireless devices to connect to a wired network using Wi-Fi, or related standards. The AP usually connects to a router (via a wired network) as a stand-alone device, but it can also be an integral component of the router itself. An AP is differentiated from a hotspot, which is the physical space where the wireless service is provided. A hotspot is a common public application of APs, where wireless clients can connect to the internet without regard for the particular networks to which they have attached for the moment.

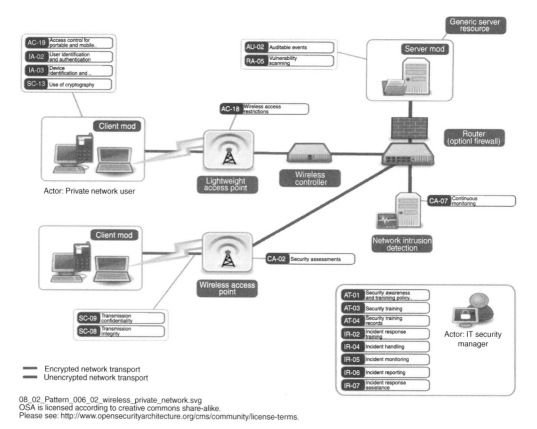

08_02_Pattern_006_02_wireless_private_network.svg
OSA is licensed according to creative commons share-alike.
Please see: http://www.opensecurityarchitecture.org/cms/community/license-terms.

Private wireless network

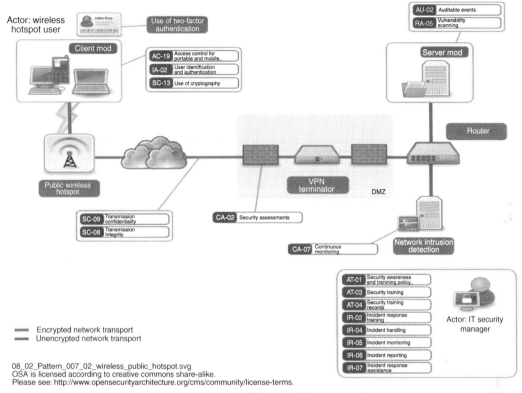

Actor: wireless hotspot user

Use of two-factor authentication

Client mod

AC-19 Access control for portable and mobile..
IA-02 User identification and authentication
SC-13 Use of cryptography

AU-02 Auditable events
RA-05 Vulnerability scanning

Server mod

Router

Public wireless hotspot

VPN terminator

DMZ

SC-09 Transmission confidentiality
SC-08 Transmission Integrity

CA-02 Security assessments

CA-07 Continuous monitoring

Network intrusion detection

AT-01 Security awareness and tranining policy..
AT-03 Security training
AT-04 Security training records
IR-02 Incident response training
IR-04 Incident handling
IR-05 Incident monitoring
IR-06 Incident reporting
IR-07 Incident response assistance

Actor: IT security manager

▦ Encrypted network transport
▬ Unencrypted network transport

08_02_Pattern_007_02_wireless_public_hotspot.svg
OSA is licensed according to creative commons share-alike.
Please see: http://www.opensecurityarchitecture.org/cms/community/license-terms.

Private wireless network

Wireless security is the prevention of unauthorized access or damage to computers using wireless networks by utilizing different methods of encoding and encryption, based on the parameters of the RF carrier and bandwidth used by the particular type of Wi-Fi being employed. The most common types of wireless security are Wired Equivalent Privacy (WEP) and Wi-Fi Protected Access (WPA). WEP is a notoriously weak security standard. The password it uses can often be cracked in a few minutes with a basic laptop computer and widely available software tools. WEP is an old IEEE 802.11 standard from 1999 which was outdated in 2003 by WPA or WPA. WPA was a quick alternative to improve security over WEP. The current standard is WPA2 which uses an encryption mechanism which encrypts the network with a 256-bit key; the longer key length improves security over WEP.

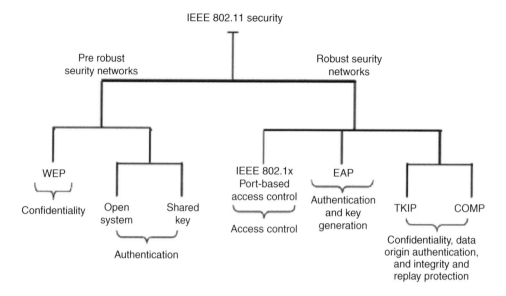

The major terms and security areas of focus include the following:

WPA: Initial WPA version, to supply enhanced security over the older WEP protocol. Typically uses the Temporal Key Integrity Protocol (TKIP) encryption protocol.

WPA2: Also known as IEEE 802.11i-2004. Successor of WPA, and replaces the TKIP encryption protocol with Counter Cipher Mode with Block Chaining Message Authentication Protocol (CCMP) to provide additional security.

TKIP: A 128-bit per-packet key is used, meaning that it dynamically generates a new key for each packet. This is part of the IEEE 802.11i standard. TKIP implements per-packet key mixing with a rekeying system and also provides a message integrity check. These avoid the problems of WEP.

CCMP: An AES-based encryption mechanism that is stronger than TKIP; sometimes referred to as AES instead of CCMP.

EAP: Extensible Authentication Protocol. EAP is an authentication framework providing for the transport and usage of keying material and parameters generated by EAP methods since EAP uses a central authentication server.

WPA-Personal: Also referred to as WPA-preshared key (PSK) mode. Is designed for home and small office networks and does not require an authentication server. Each wireless network device authenticates with the AP using the same 256-bit key.

WPA-Enterprise: Also referred to as WPA-802.1X mode, and sometimes just WPA (as opposed to WPA-PSK). Is designed for enterprise networks, and requires a Remote Authentication Dial-In User Server (RADIUS) authentication server.

This requires a more complicated setup, but provides additional security (e.g., protection against dictionary attacks). An EAP is used for authentication, which comes in different flavors (e.g., EAP-TLS, EAP-Tunneled Transport Layer Security (TTLS), EAP-security information management (SIM)).

Bluetooth is a proprietary open wireless technology standard for exchanging data over short distances.

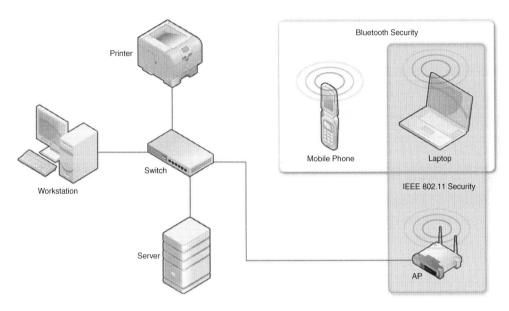

Bluetooth wireless

Cumulatively, the various versions of Bluetooth specifications define four security modes. Each version of Bluetooth supports some, but not all, of the four modes. Each Bluetooth device must operate in one of the four modes, which are described below.

Security Mode 1 is nonsecure. Security functionality (authentication and encryption) is bypassed, leaving the device and connections susceptible to attackers. In effect, Bluetooth devices in this mode are "promiscuous" and do not employ any mechanisms to prevent other Bluetooth-enabled devices from establishing connections. Security Mode 1 is supported only in v2.0 + enhanced data rate (EDR) (and earlier) devices.

In *Security Mode 2*, a service level-enforced security mode, security procedures are initiated after Link Management Protocol (LMP) link establishment but before Logical Link Control and Adaptation (L2CAP) channel establishment. L2CAP resides in the data link layer and provides connection-oriented and connectionless data services to upper layers. For this security mode, a security manager (as specified in the Bluetooth architecture) controls access to specific services and devices.

The centralized security manager maintains policies for AC and interfaces with other protocols and device users. Varying security policies and trust levels to restrict access may be defined for applications with different security requirements operating in parallel. It is possible to grant access to some services without providing access to other services. In this mode, the notion of authorization – the process of deciding if a specific device is allowed to have access to a specific service – is introduced.

In *Security Mode 3*, the link level-enforced security mode, a Bluetooth device initiates security procedures before the physical link is fully established. Bluetooth devices operating in Security Mode 3 mandate authentication and encryption for all connections to and from the device. This mode supports authentication (unidirectional or mutual) and encryption.

Similar to Security Mode 2, *Security Mode 4* (introduced in Bluetooth v2.1 + EDR) is a service level-enforced security mode in which security procedures are initiated after link setup. Security requirements for services protected by Security Mode 4 must be classified as one of the following: authenticated link key required, unauthenticated link key required, or no security required. Whether or not a link key is authenticated depends on the Secure Simple Pairing association model used.

Cryptography

Three types of encryption as currently used in security controls:

1. *Symmetric*: One method of cryptography is *symmetric cryptography* (also known as *secret key cryptography* or *private key cryptography*). Symmetric cryptography is best suited for bulk encryption because it is much faster than asymmetric cryptography. With symmetric cryptography:

   a. Both parties share the *same* key (which is kept secret). Before communications begin, both parties must exchange the shared secret key. Each pair of communicating entities requires a unique shared key. The key is not shared with other communication partners.

   Note: Other names – secret key, conventional key, session key, file encryption key, etc.

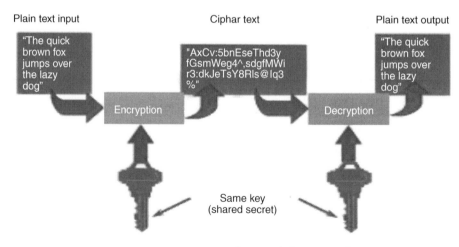

Symmetric key encryption

Pros:

a. Speed/file size:

- Symmetric-key algorithms are generally much less computationally intensive which provides a smaller file size that allows for faster transmissions and less storage space.

Cons:

a. Key management:

- One disadvantage of symmetric-key algorithms is the requirement of a *shared secret key*, with one copy at each end. See drawing below.
- In order to ensure secure communications between everyone in a population of n people a total of $n(n-1)/2$ keys are needed. Example: key for 10 individuals, $10(10-1)/2 = 45$ keys.
- The process of selecting, distributing, and storing keys is known as key management; it is difficult to achieve reliably and securely.

Symmetric

Symmetric cryptography has an equation of $n \times (n-1)/2$ for the number of keys needed. In a situation with 1000 users, that would mean *499,500 keys*.

Asymmetric

Asymmetric cryptography, using key pairs for each of its users, has n as the number of key pairs needed. In a situation with 1000 users, that would mean *1000 key pairs*.

Symmetric algorithms:

Methods	Characteristics
Data Encryption Standard (DES)	• Created in 1972 and recertified in 1993 • Uses a 64-bit block size and a 56-bit key • Can be easily broken
Triple DES (3DES)	• Applies DES three times. Uses a 168-bit key • Replaced with AES

(Continued)

Methods	Characteristics
Advanced Encryption Standard (AES)	• Uses the Rijndael block cipher (rhine-doll) which is resistant to all known attacks • Uses a variable-length block and key length (128-, 192-, or 256-bit keys)
Blowfish	• Variable block size, variable key size (up to 448 bits)
Twofish	• Uses 128-bit blocks and variable key lengths (128-, 192-, or 256 bits)
Carlisle Adams Stafford Tavares (CAST)	• Two implementations: 64-bit block size with 128-bit key, 128-bit block size with 256-bit key. Used by Pretty Good Privacy (PGP) email encryption
International Data Encryption Algorithm (IDEA)	• Two implementations: 64-bit block size with 128-bit key, 128-bit block size with 256-bit key. Used by PGP email encryption

Rivest	• Includes various implementations:
	  • RC2 with 64-bit blocks and a variable key length (any size)
	  • RC4 with 40- and 128-bit keys
	  • RC5 with variable blocks and keys (any size)
	  • RC6 an improvement on RC5

2. *Asymmetric*: *Asymmetric* cryptography is a second form of cryptography. It is scalable for use in very large and ever expanding environments where data is frequently exchanged between different communication partners. With asymmetric cryptography:

a. Each user has two keys: a *public* key and a *private* key.
b. Both keys are mathematically related (both keys together are called the *key pair*).
c. The public key is made available to anyone. The private key is kept secret.
d. Both keys are required to perform an operation. For example, data encrypted with the private key is unencrypted with the *public* key. Data encrypted with the public key is unencrypted with the *private* key.
e. Encrypting data with the private key creates a digital *signature*. This ensures the message has come from the stated sender (because only the sender had access to the private key to be able to create the signature).
f. A digital envelope is signing a message with a recipient's public key. A digital *envelope*, which serves as a means of AC by ensuring that only the intended recipient can open the message (because only the receiver will have the private key necessary to unlock the envelope; this is also known as *receiver authentication*).
g. If the private key is ever discovered, a new key pair must be generated.

Asymmetric cryptography is often used to exchange the secret key to prepare for using symmetric cryptography to encrypt data. In the case of a key exchange, one party creates the secret key and encrypts it with the public key of the recipient. The recipient would then decrypt it with their private key. The remaining communication would be done with the secret key being the encryption key. Asymmetric encryption is used in key exchange, email security, web security, and other encryption systems that require key exchange over the public network.

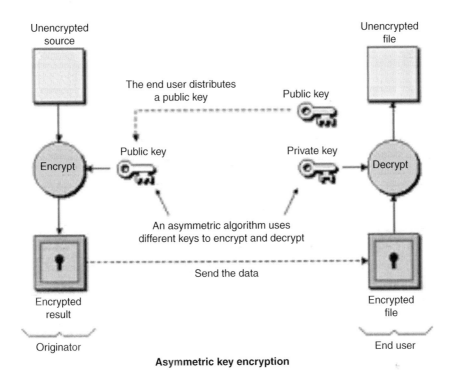

Asymmetric key encryption

Pros:

a. Key management:
- Two keys (public and private), private key cannot be derived for the public so the public key can be freely distributed without confidentially being compromised
- Offers digital signatures, integrity checks, and nonrepudiation

Cons:

a. Speed/file size:
- Because symmetric-key algorithms are generally much less computationally intensive than asymmetric-key algorithms.
- In practice, asymmetric-key algorithm are typically hundreds to thousands times slower than a symmetric-key algorithm.

Asymmetric algorithms:

Method	Characteristics
Rivest–Shamir–Adleman (RSA)	• Uses a specific one-way function based on the difficulty of factoring N, a product of 2 large prime numbers (200 digits)

Diffie–Hellman key exchange	• Known as a *key exchange algorithm*
	 • Uses two system parameters (p and g)
	  • p is a prime number
	  • g is an integer smaller than p generated by both parties

(Continued)

Method	Characteristics
ElGamal Elliptic curve (EC)	• Extends Diffie–Hellman for use in encryption and digital signatures • Used in conjunction with other methods to reduce the key size • An EC key of 160 bits is equivalent to 1024-bit RSA key, which means less computational power and memory requirements • Suitable for hardware applications (e.g., smart cards and wireless devices)
Digital Signature Algorithm (DSA)	• Used to digital sign documents • Performs integrity check by use of SHA hashing

3. *Hashing*: A *hash* is a function that takes a variable-length string (message), and compresses and transforms it into a fixed-length value.
   a. The hashing algorithm (formula or method) is public.
   b. Hashing uses a secret value to protect the method.
   c. Hashing is used to create checksums or message digests (e.g., an investigator can create a checksum to secure a removable media device that is to be used as evidence).
   d. The hash ensures data integrity (i.e., the data have not been altered). The receiving device computes a checksum and compares it to the checksum included with the file. If they do not match, the data has been altered.
   e. Examples include message digest (MD2, MD4, MD5) and Secure Hashing Algorithm (SHA).
   f. SHA, Race Integrity Primitives Evaluation Message Digest (RIPEMD), and Hash of Variable Length (HAVAL).

Name	Class	Hash length
MD5	*512-Bit blocks*	*Digest size(s)*: 128 bits *Rounds*: 4
SHA-1	*512-Bit blocks*	*Digest size(s)*: 160 bits *Rounds*: 80
SHA-2 SHA-224/256	*512-Bit blocks*	*Digest size(s)*: 256 bits *Rounds*: 64
SHA-2 SHA-384/512	1024-Bit blocks	*Digest size(s)*: 512 bits *Rounds*: 80
RIPEMD-160		*Digest size(s)*: 128,160, 256, and 320 bits
HAVAL		*Digest size(s)*: 128, 160, 192, 224, and 256 bits *Rounds*: 3, 4, or 5

Secure Hash

The secure hash function takes a stream of data and reduces it to a fixed size through a one-way mathematical function. The result is called a message digest and can be thought of as a fingerprint of the data. The message digest can be reproduced by any party with the same stream of data, but it is virtually impossible to create a different stream of data that produces the same message digest.

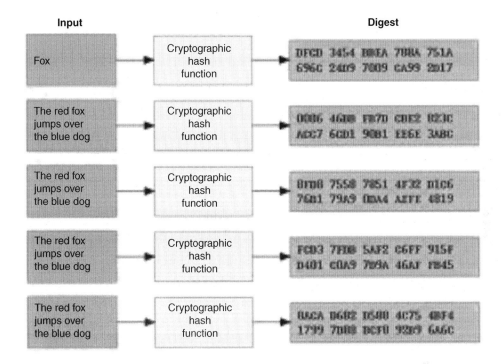

Input		Digest

Secure Hash Standard

The Secure Hash Standard specifies five SHAs: SHA-1, SHA-224, SHA-256, SHA-384, and SHA-512. All five of the algorithms are iterative, one-way hash functions that can process a message to produce a condensed representation called a *message digest*. These algorithms enable the determination of a message's integrity: any change to the message will, with a very high probability, result in a different message digest. This property is useful in the generation and verification of digital signatures and MACs, and in the generation of random numbers or bits.

The five algorithms differ most significantly in the security strengths that are provided for the data being hashed. The security strengths of these five hash functions and the system as a whole when each of them is used with other cryptographic algorithms, such as Digital Signature Algorithms (DSAs) and keyed-hash MACs, can be found in SP 800-57 and SP 800-107.

Additionally, the five algorithms differ in terms of the size of the blocks and words of data that are used during hashing.

HMAC

Providing a way to check the integrity of information transmitted over or stored in an unreliable medium is a prime necessity in the world of open computing and communications. Mechanisms that provide such integrity checks based on a secret key are usually called MACs. Typically, MACs are used between two parties that share a secret key in order to authenticate information transmitted between these parties. This standard defines a MAC that uses a cryptographic hash function in conjunction with a secret key. This mechanism is called Hash-Based Message Authentication Code (HMAC). HMAC shall use an approved cryptographic hash function [FIPS-180-3]. It uses the secret key for the calculation and verification of the MACs.

So, in review, the table below covers the three types of encryption and their particular uses:

- Encryption provides confidentiality.
- Hashing provides integrity (like a checksum).
- Digital signatures provide authentication and integrity.
- Digitally signed encryption provides confidentiality, authentication, and integrity.

Mechanism		Data integrity	Confidentiality	Identification and authentication	Nonrepudiation	Key distribution
Symmetric-key cryptography	Encryption	No	Yes	No	No	No
	Message authentication codes	Yes	No	Yes	No	No
	Key transport	No	No	No	No	Yes – requires out-of-band initialization step or a TTP
Secure hash functions	Message digest	Yes	No	No	No	No
	HMAC	Yes	No	Yes	No	No
Asymmetric cryptography	Digital signatures	Yes	No	Yes	Yes (with a TTP)	No
	Key transport	No	No	No	No	Yes
	Key agreement	No	No	Yes	No	Yes

Intrusion Detection Systems

Another element to securing networks complementing firewall implementations is an IDS. An IDS works in conjunction with routers and firewalls by monitoring network usage anomalies by being deployed in a demilitarized zone (DMZ) on the edge of the network or it is utilized as a network-based device inside the network to monitor for specific traffic patterns and alert when these patterns are identified so it protects a company's information system resources from external as well as internal misuse.

An IDS operates continuously on the system, running in the background and notifying administrators when it detects a perceived threat. For example, an IDS detects attack patterns and issues an alert. Broad categories of IDS include:

- *Network-based IDSs*: Identify attacks within the monitored network and issue a warning to the operator. If a network-based IDS is placed between the internet and the firewall, it will detect all the attack attempts, whether or not they enter the firewall. If the IDS is placed between a firewall and the corporate network, it will detect those attacks that enter the firewall (it will detect intruders). The IDS is not a substitute for a firewall, but it complements the function of a firewall.

- *Host-based IDSs*: Configured for a specific environment and will monitor various internal resources of the operating system to warn of a possible attack. They can detect the modification of executable programs, detect the deletion of files, and issue a warning when an attempt is made to use a privileged command.

Common Intrusion Detection Methodologies

- Signature-Based Detection
  A *signature* is a pattern that corresponds to a known threat. *Signature-based detection* is the process of comparing signatures against observed events to identify possible incidents. 5 Examples of signatures are as follows:
      A telnet attempt with a username of "root", which is a violation of an organization's security policy.
      An email with a subject of "Free pictures!" and an attachment filename of "freepics.exe", which are characteristics of a known form of malware.
      An operating system log entry with a status code value of 645, which indicates that the host's auditing has been disabled.
      Signature-based detection is very effective at detecting known threats but largely ineffective at detecting previously unknown threats, threats disguised by the use of evasion techniques, and many variants of known threats.
- Anomaly-Based Detection
  Anomaly-based detection is the process of comparing definitions of what activity is considered normal against observed events to identify significant deviations. An IDPS using anomaly-based detection has *profiles* that represent the normal behavior of such things as users, hosts, network connections, or applications. The profiles are developed by monitoring the characteristics of typical activity over a period of time. The major benefit of anomaly-based detection methods is that they can be very effective at detecting previously unknown threats.
- Stateful Protocol Analysis
  Stateful protocol analysis is the process of comparing predetermined profiles of generally accepted definitions of benign protocol activity for each protocol state against observed events to identify deviations. Unlike anomaly-based detection, which uses host or network-specific profiles, stateful protocol analysis relies on vendor-developed universal profiles that specify how particular protocols should and should not be used. The "stateful" in stateful protocol analysis means that the IDPS is capable of understanding and tracking the state of network, transport, and application protocols that have a notion of state.
      Stateful protocol analysis can identify unexpected sequences of commands, such as issuing the same command repeatedly or issuing a command without first issuing a command upon which it is dependent. Another state tracking feature of stateful protocol analysis is that for protocols that perform authentication, the IDPS can keep track of the authenticator used for each session, and record the authenticator used for suspicious activity. This is helpful when investigating an incident. Some IDPSs can also use the authenticator information to define acceptable activity differently for multiple classes of users or specific users.
      The "protocol analysis" performed by stateful protocol analysis methods usually includes reasonableness checks for individual commands, such as minimum and maximum lengths for arguments. If a command typically has a username argument, and usernames have a maximum length of 20 characters, then an argument with a length of 1000 characters is suspicious. If the large argument contains binary data, then it is even more suspicious.[28]

Types of IDSs include:

- *Signature-based*: These IDS systems protect against detected intrusion patterns. The intrusive patterns they can identify are stored in the form of signatures.

---

[28]SP 800-94, p. 2-4 to 2-6.

- *Statistical-based*: These IDS systems need a comprehensive definition of the known and expected behavior of systems.
- *Neural networks*: An IDS with this feature monitors the general patterns of activity and traffic on the network and creates a database. This is similar to the statistical model but with added self-learning functionality.

Signature-based IDSs will not be able to detect all types of intrusions due to the limitations of the detection rules. On the other hand, statistical-based systems may report many events outside of defined normal activity but which are normal activities on the network. A combination of signature- and statistical-based models provides better protection.

Uses of IDPS Technologies

- Identifying possible incidents
- Identifying reconnaissance activity
- Identifying security policy problems
- Documenting existing threat to an organization
- Deterring individuals from violating security policies

The table below is a high-level comparison of the four primary IDPS technology types. The strengths listed in the table indicate the roles or situations in which each technology type is generally superior to the others. A particular technology type may have additional benefits over others, such as logging additional data that would be useful for validating alerts recorded by other IDPSs, or preventing intrusions that other IDPSs cannot because of technology capabilities or placement.[29]

IDPS Technology Type	Types of Malicious Activity Detected	Scope per Sensor or Agent	Strengths
Network-Based	Network, transport, and application TCP/IP layer activity	Multiple network subnets and groups of hosts	Able to analyze the widest range of application protocols; only IDPS that can thoroughly analyze many of them
Wireless	Wireless protocol activity; unauthorized wireless local area networks (WLAN) in use	Multiple WU\Ns and groups of wireless clients	Only IDPS that can monitor wireless protocol activity
NBA	Network, transport, and application TCP/IP layer activity that causes anomalous network flows	Multiple network subnets and groups of hosts	Typically more effective than the others at identifying reconnaissance scanning and DoS attacks, and at reconstructing major malware infections
Host-Based	Host application and operating system (OS) activity; network, transport, and application TCP/IP layer activity	Individual host	Only IDPS that can analyze activity that was transferred in end-to-end encrypted communications

[29]SP 800-94, p. 8-1.

Key areas which the assessor should focus on when reviewing and evaluating IDS deployments include:

- Recording information related to observed events
- Notifying security administrators of important observed events
- Producing reports
- Response techniques:
  - Stops attack
  - Changes security environment
  - Changes attack's content
- False-positive adjustments
- False-negative adjustments
- Tuning
- Evasion

FIREWALLS

Firewall Security Systems – SP 800-41

Every time a corporation connects its internal computer network to the internet it faces potential danger. Because of the internet's openness, every corporate network connected to it is vulnerable to attack. Hackers on the internet could theoretically break into the corporate network and do harm in a number of ways: steal or damage important data, damage individual computers or the entire network, use the corporate computer's resources, or use the corporate network and resources as a way of posing as a corporate employee. Companies should build firewalls as one means of perimeter security for their networks. Likewise, this same principle holds true for very sensitive or critical systems that need to be protected from untrusted users inside the corporate network (internal hackers). Firewalls are defined as a device installed at the point where network connections enter a site; they apply rules to control the type of networking traffic flowing in and out. Most commercial firewalls are built to handle the most commonly used internet protocols.

To be effective, firewalls should allow individuals on the corporate network to access the internet and, at the same time, stop hackers or others on the internet from gaining access to the corporate network to cause damage. Generally, most organizations will follow a deny-all philosophy, which means that access to a given resource will be denied unless a user can provide a specific business reason or need for access to the information resource. The converse of this access philosophy, not widely accepted, is the accept-all philosophy under which everyone is allowed access unless someone can provide a reason for denying access.

Firewall General Features

Firewalls are hardware and software combinations that are built using routers, servers, and a variety of software. They should control the most vulnerable point between a corporate network and the internet, and they can be as simple or complex as the corporate information security policy demands. There are many different types of firewalls, but most enable organizations to:

- Block access to particular sites on the internet
- Limit traffic on an organization's public services segment to relevant addresses and ports
- Prevent certain users from accessing certain servers or services
- Monitor communications between an internal and an external network
- Monitor and record all communications between an internal network and the outside world to investigate network penetrations or detect internal subversion
- Encrypt packets that are sent between different physical locations within an organization by creating a VPN over the internet (i.e., IPSec VPN tunnels)

Firewall Types

Generally, the types of firewalls available today fall into four categories which include:

- *Packet filtering*: *Packet filtering* is a security method of controlling what data can flow to and from a network. It takes place by using Access Control Lists (ACLs), which are developed and applied to a device. The ACL is just lines of text, called rules, which the device will apply to each packet that it receives. The lines of text give specific information pertaining to what packets can be accepted and what packets are denied. For instance, an ACL can have one line that states that any packets coming from the IP range 172.168.0.0 must be denied. Another line may indicate that no packets using the FTP service will be allowed to enter the network, and another line may indicate that no traffic is to be allowed through port 443. Then it can have a line indicating all traffic on port 80 is acceptable and should be routed to a specific IP address, which is the web server. Each time the device receives a packet, it compares the information in the packet's header to each line in the ACL. If the packet indicates it is using FTP or requests to make a connection to the 443 port, it is discarded. If the packet header information indicates that it wants to communicate through port 80 using HTTP over TCP, then the packet is accepted and redirected to the web server.

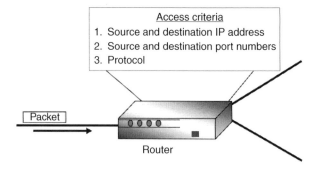

This filtering is based on network layer information, which means that the device cannot look too far into the packet itself. It can make decisions based on only header information, which is limited. Most routers use ACLs to act as a type of router and to carry out routing decisions, but they do not provide the level of protection that other types of firewalls, which look deeper into the packet, provide. Since packet filtering looks only at the header information, it is not application dependent like many proxy firewalls are. Packet filtering firewalls do not keep track of the state of a connection, which takes place in a stateful firewall.

Pros:

- Scalable
- Provides high performance
- Application independent

Cons:

- Does not look into the packet past the header information
- *Low security relative to other options*
- *Does not keep track of the state of a connection*

Note: Packet filtering cannot protect against mail bomb attacks because it cannot read the content of the packet.

- *Application firewall systems*: *Application-level firewalls* inspect the entire packet and make access decisions based on the actual content of the packet. They understand different services and protocols and the commands that are used within them. An application-level proxy can distinguish between an FTP GET command and an FTP PUT command and make access decisions based on this granular level of information, where packet filtering firewalls can only allow or deny FTP requests as a whole, not the commands used within the FTP protocol.

  An application-level firewall works for one service or protocol. A computer can have many different types of services and protocols (FTP, Network Time Protocol (NTP), Simple Mail Transfer Protocol (SMTP), Telnet, etc.); thus, there must be one application-level proxy per service. Providing application-level proxy services can be much trickier than it appears. The proxy must totally understand how specific protocols work and what commands within that protocol are legitimate. This is a lot to know and look at during the transmission of data. If the application-level proxy firewall does not understand a certain protocol or service, it cannot protect this type of communication. This is when a circuit-level proxy can come into play because it does not deal with such complex issues. An advantage of circuit-level proxies is that they can handle a wider variety of protocols and services than application-level proxies, but the downfall is that the circuit-level proxy cannot provide the degree of granular control that an application-level proxy can. Life is just full of compromises.

  So, an application-level firewall is dedicated to a particular protocol or service. There must be one proxy per protocol because one proxy could not properly interpret all the commands of all the protocols coming its way. A circuit-level proxy works at a lower layer of the Open Systems Interconnection (OSI) model and does not require one proxy per protocol because it is not looking at such detailed information.

- *Stateful inspection*: When regular packet filtering is used, a packet arrives at the router, and the router runs through its ACLs to see if this packet should be allowed or denied. If the packet is allowed, it is passed on to the destination host or another router, and the router forgets it ever received this packet. This is different from stateful filtering, which remembers what packets went where until that particular connection is closed. Stateful routers also make decisions on what packets to allow or disallow, but their logic goes a step farther. For example, a regular packet filtering device may deny any UDP packets requesting service on port 25, and a stateful filtering device may have the rule to allow UDP packets through only if they are responses to outgoing requests. Basically, the stateful firewall will want to allow only those packets in that its internal hosts requested.

  If User A sends a request to a computer on a different network, this request will be logged in the firewall's state table. The table will indicate that User A's computer made a request and there should be packets coming back to User A. When the computer on the internet responds to User A, these packets will be compared to data in the state table. Since the state table does have information about a previous request for these packets, the router will allow the packets to pass through. If, on the other hand, User A did not make any requests and packets were coming in from the internet to him, the firewall will see that there were no previous requests for this information and then look at its ACLs to see if these packets are allowed to come in.

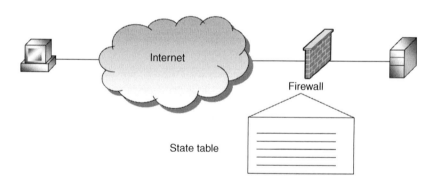

So, regular packet filtering compares incoming packets to rules defined in its ACLs. When stateful packet filtering receives a packet, it first looks in its state table to see if a connection has already been established and if this data was requested. If there is no previous connection and the state table holds no information about the packets, the packet is compared to the device's ACLs. If the ACL allows this type of traffic, the packet is allowed to access the network. If that type of traffic is not allowed, the packet is dropped. Although this provides an extra step of protection, it also adds more complexity because this device must now keep a dynamic state table and remember connections. This has opened the door to many types of denial-of-service attacks. There are several types of attacks that are aimed at flooding the state table with bogus information. The state table is a resource like a system's hard drive space, memory, and CPU. When the state table is stuffed full of bogus information, it can either freeze the device or cause it to reboot. Also, if this firewall has to be rebooted for some reason, it loses its information on all recent connections; thus, it will deny legitimate packets.

Note: Context AC pertains to a sequence of events proceeding the access request and specifics of the environment within a window of time. Content pertains to making an AC decision based on the data being protected.

- A stateful firewall is a context AC.
- Fourth-generation firewall = dynamic packet filter.
- Fifth-generation firewall = kernel proxies.

- *Circuit or application proxy*: A *proxy* is a middleman. If someone needed to give a box and a message to the President of the United States, this person could not just walk up to him and give him these items. The person would have to go through a middleman who would accept the box and message and thoroughly go through the box to ensure nothing dangerous was inside. This is what a proxy firewall does: it accepts messages either entering or leaving a network, inspects them for malicious information, and, when it decides things are okay, passes the data on to the destination computer.

  A proxy will stand between a trusted and untrusted network and will actually make the connection, each way, on behalf of the source. So if a user on the internet requests to send data to a computer on the internal, protected network, the proxy will get this request and look it over for suspicious information. The request does not automatically go to the destination computer; the proxy server acts like the destination computer. If the proxy decides the packet is safe, it sends it on to the destination computer. When the destination computer replies, the reply goes back to the proxy server, who repackages the packet to contain the source address of the proxy server, not the host system on the internal network. All external connections heading to the internal network are terminated at the proxy server. This type of firewall makes a copy of each accepted packet before transmitting it. It will repackage the packet to hide the packet's true origin.

  Just like the packet filtering firewalls, proxy firewalls also have a list of rules that are applied to packets. When the proxy firewall receives a packet, it runs through this list of rules to see if the packet should be allowed. If the packet is allowed, the proxy firewall repackages the packet and sends it on its way to the destination computer. When users go through a proxy, they do not usually know it. Users on the internet think they are talking directly to users on the internal network and vice versa. The proxy server is the only machine that talks to the outside world. This ensures that no computer has direct access to internal computers. This also means that the proxy server is the only computer that needs a valid IP address. The rest of the computers on the internal network can use private (nonroutable IP addresses on the internet) addresses, since no computers on the outside will see their addresses anyway.

  Many times, proxy servers are used when a company is using a *dual-homed firewall*. A dual-homed firewall has two interfaces: one facing the external network and the other facing the internal network. This is different than a computer that has forwarding enabled, which just lets packets pass through its interfaces with no AC enforced. A dual-homed firewall has two network interface cards (NICs) and should have packet forwarding and routing turned off. They are turned off for safety reasons. If forwarding were enabled, the computer would not apply the necessary ACL rules or other restrictions necessary of a firewall. Instead, a dual-homed firewall requires a higher level of intelligence to tell it what packets should go where and what types of packets are acceptable. This is where the proxy comes in. When a packet comes to the external NIC from the untrusted network on a dual-homed firewall, the computer does not know what to do with it, so it passes it up to the proxy software. The proxy software inspects the packet to make sure that it is legitimate. Then the proxy software makes a connection with the destination computer on the internal network and passes on the packet. When the internal computer replies, the packet goes to the internal interface on the dual-homed firewall, it passes up to the proxy software, the proxy inspects the packet and slaps on a different header, and the proxy passes the packet out the external NIC that is connected to the external network.

Pros:
- Looks at the information within a packet all the way up to the application layer
- Provides better security than packet filtering
- Breaks the connection between trusted and untrusted systems

Cons:
- Some proxy firewalls are limited to what applications they can support.
- Degrades traffic performance.
- Poor scalability for application-based proxy firewalls.

Note: Breaks client/server model – which is good for security, but at times bad for functionality.

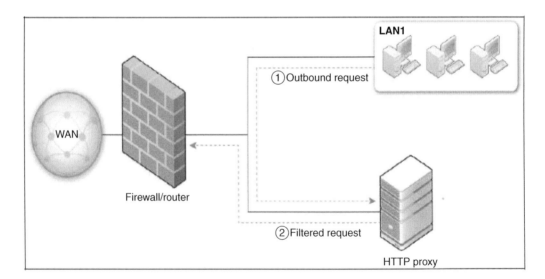

Firewall Utilization

- Most companies have firewalls to restrict access into their network from internet users. They may also have firewalls to restrict one internal network from accessing another internal network. An organizational security policy will give high-level instructions on acceptable and unacceptable actions as they pertain to security. The firewall will have a more defined and granular security policy that dictates what services are allowed to be accessed, what IP addresses and ranges are to be restricted, and what ports can be accessed. The firewall is described as a "choke point" in the network, since all communication should flow through it and this is where traffic is inspected and restricted. A firewall is actually a type of gateway that can be a router, server, authentication server, or specialized hardware device. It monitors packets coming into and out of the network it is protecting. It filters out the packets that do not meet the requirements of the security policy. It can discard these packets, repackage them, or redirect them depending on the firewall configuration and security policy. Packets are filtered based on their source and destination addresses and ports, by service, packet type, protocol type, header information, sequence bits, and much more. Each vendor has different functionality and different parameters they can use for identification and access restriction.

Examples of Firewall Implementations

Firewall implementations can take advantage of the functionality available in a variety of firewall designs to provide a robust layered approach in protecting an organization's information assets. Commonly used implementations available today include:

- *Screened-host firewall*: Utilizing a packet filtering router and a bastion host, this approach implements basic network layer security (packet filtering) and application server security (proxy services). An intruder in this configuration has to penetrate two separate systems before the security of the private network can be compromised. This firewall system is configured with the bastion host connected to the private network with a packet filtering router between the internet and the bastion host. Router filtering rules allow inbound traffic to access only the bastion host, which blocks access to internal systems. Since the inside hosts reside on the same network as the bastion host, the security policy of the organization determines whether inside systems are permitted direct access to the internet, or whether they are required to use the proxy services on the bastion host.
- *Dual-homed firewall*: A firewall system that has two or more network interfaces, each of which is connected to a different network. In a firewall configuration, a dual-homed firewall usually acts to block or filter some or all of the traffic trying to pass between the networks. A dual-homed firewall system is a more restrictive form of a screened-host firewall system, when a dual-homed bastion host is configured with one interface established for information servers and another for private network host computers.
- *DMZ or screened-subnet firewall*: Utilizing two packet filtering routers and a bastion host, this approach creates the most secure firewall system, since it supports both network and application-level security while defining a separate DMZ network. The DMZ functions as a small isolated network for an organization's public servers, bastion host information servers and modem pools. Typically, DMZs are configured to limit access from the internet and the organization's private network. Incoming traffic access is restricted into the DMZ network by the outside router and protects the organization against certain attacks by limiting the services available for use. Consequently, external systems can

access only the bastion host (and its proxy service capabilities to internal systems) and possibly information servers in the DMZ. The inside router provides a second line of defense, managing DMZ access to the private network, while accepting only traffic originating from the bastion host. For outbound traffic, the inside router manages private network access to the DMZ network. It permits internal systems to access only the bastion host and information servers in the DMZ. The filtering rules on the outside router require the use of proxy services by accepting only outbound traffic on the bastion host. The key benefits of this system are that an intruder must penetrate three separate devices, private network addresses are not disclosed to the internet, and internal systems do not have direct access to the internet.

Note: In UNIX systems, the product TCP Wrappers can be used as a personal firewall or host-based IDS.

The assessor should review and test the following areas when conducting a comprehensive evaluation of the firewall and its technology:

- Scanning firewall from the outside and inside
- Scanning with firewall down to see level of exposure if it went off-line
- Directional control
- Incoming packet with internal source address
- Outgoing packet with external source address
- FTP out but not in
- Making sure that access to the firewall is authorized
- How are employees and nonemployees given access
- Obtaining a list of users on the firewall
- Cross-checking with staff lists/organization chart
- Remote administration:
  - One-time passwords
  - Other secure methods
  - Encrypted link
- How is access changed or revoked
- How is access reviewed:
  - Mechanics of authentication
  - Frequency of review
  - Password reset/changing passwords
  - Root password control
- Need for firewall to enforce security policy (encryption, viruses, URL blocks, proxy/packet filter types of traffic):
  - The rule set obtained?
  - How are rule sets stored to maintained to ensure that they have not been tampered with?
  - Checksums regularly verified?
- Determining whether the effectiveness of firewall has been tested
- Reviewing processes running on firewall; are they appropriate:
  - Does the firewall provide adequate notice when an exploit is attempted?

AUDIT AND ACCOUNTING

Most, if not all, of the guidance for the audit and accountability family of controls can be found in the SP 800-92, *Guide to Log Management*.

Log Management

A log is a record of the events occurring within an organization's systems and networks. Logs are composed of log entries; each entry contains information related to a specific event that has occurred within a system or network. Many logs within an organization contain records related to computer security. These computer security logs are generated by many sources, including security software, such as antivirus software, firewalls, and intrusion detection and prevention systems; operating systems on servers, workstations, and networking equipment; and applications. Logs are emitted by network devices, operating systems, applications, and all manner of intelligent or programmable devices. A stream of messages in time sequence often comprises the entries in a log. Logs may be directed to files and stored on disk, or directed as a network stream to a log collector. Log messages must usually be interpreted with respect to the internal state of its source (e.g., application) and announce security-relevant or operations-relevant events (e.g., a user log-in, or a systems error).

A fundamental problem with log management that occurs in many organizations is effectively balancing a limited quantity of log management resources with a continuous supply of log data. Log generation and storage can be complicated by several factors, including a high number of log sources; inconsistent log content, formats, and timestamps among sources; and increasingly large volumes of log data. Log management also involves protecting the confidentiality, integrity, and availability of logs. Another problem with log management is ensuring that security, system, and network administrators regularly perform effective analysis of log data. This publication provides guidance for meeting these log management challenges.

Originally, logs were used primarily for troubleshooting problems, but logs now serve many functions within most organizations, such as optimizing system and network performance, recording the actions of users, and providing data useful for investigating malicious activity. Logs have evolved to contain information related to many different types of events occurring within networks and systems. Within an organization, many logs contain records related to computer security; common examples of these computer security logs are audit logs that track user authentication attempts and security device logs that record possible attacks.

The Special Publication 800-92 defines the criteria for logs, log management, and log maintenance in the following control areas:

- Auditable events
- Content of audit records
- Audit storage capacity
- Response to audit processing failures
- Audit review, analysis, and reporting
- Audit reduction and report generation
- Timestamps

- Audit record retention
- Audit generation

The SP defines the four parts of log management as follows:

1. Log management:
   a. Log sources.
   b. Analyze log data.
   c. Respond to identified events.
   d. Manage long-term log data storage.
2. Log sources:
   a. Log generation.
   b. Log storage and disposal.
   c. Log security.
3. Analyzing log data:
   a. Gain an understanding of logs.
   b. Prioritize log entries.
   c. Compare system-level and infrastructure-level analysis.
   d. Respond to identified events.
4. Manage long-term log data storage:
   a. Choose log format for data to be archived.
   b. Archive the log data.
   c. Verify integrity of transferred logs.
   d. Store media securely.

To address AU-10, nonrepudiation, the information system protects against an individual falsely denying having performed a particular action. Nonrepudiation protects individuals against later claims by an author of not having authored a particular document, a sender of not having transmitted a message, a receiver of not having received a message, or a signatory of not having signed a document. Nonrepudiation services are obtained by employing various techniques or mechanisms (e.g., digital signatures, digital message receipts).

The Digital Signature Standard defines methods for digital signature generation that can be used for the protection of binary data (commonly called a message), and for the verification and validation of those digital signatures.

There are three techniques which are approved for this process:

1. The DSA is specified in this standard. The specification includes criteria for the generation of domain parameters, for the generation of public and private key pairs, and for the generation and verification of digital signatures.
2. The RSA DSA is specified in American National Standard (ANS) X9.31 and Public Key Cryptography Standard (PKCS) #1. FIPS-186-3 approves the use of implementations of either or both of these standards, but specifies additional requirements.
3. The Elliptic Curve Digital Signature Algorithm (ECDSA) is specified in ANS X9.62. FIPS-186-3 approves the use of ECDSA, but specifies additional requirements.

When assessing logs look for the following areas:

- Connections should be logged and monitored.

- What events are logged?
  - Inbound services
  - Outbound services
  - Access attempts that violate policy
- How frequent are logs monitored?

  - Differentiate from automated and manual procedures.

- Alarming:
  - Security breach response
  - Are the responsible parties experienced?
- Monitoring of privileged accounts

SIEM

Security information and event management (SIEM) is a term for software products and services combining SIM and security event management (SEM). The segment of security management that deals with real-time monitoring, correlation of events, notifications, and console views is commonly known as SEM. The second area provides long-term storage, analysis, and reporting of log data and is known as SIM.

SIEM technology provides real-time analysis of security alerts generated by network hardware and applications. SIEM is sold as software, appliances, or managed services, and is also used to *log security data* and generate reports for compliance purposes. The term Security Information and Event Management (SIEM), coined by Mark Nicolett and Amrit Williams of Gartner in 2005, describes the product capabilities of gathering, analyzing, and presenting information from network and security devices; identity and access management applications; vulnerability management and policy compliance tools; operating system, database, and application logs; and external threat data. A key focus is to monitor and help manage user and service privileges, directory services, and other system configuration changes, as well as providing *log auditing and review* and IR.

CHAPTER

12

Evidence of Assessment

Evidence of the test, evaluation, and assessment activities is often critical to the authorizing official in making the risk-based decision concerning the operation of the system under review. As SP 800-53A states: "Building an effective assurance case for security and privacy control effectiveness is a process that involves:

(i) Compiling evidence from a variety of activities conducted during the system development life cycle that the controls employed in the information system are implemented correctly, operating as intended, and producing the desired outcome with respect to meeting the security and privacy requirements of the system and the organization; and

(ii) Presenting this evidence in a manner that decision makers are able to use effectively in making risk-based decisions about the operation or use of the system.

The evidence described above comes from the implementation of the security and privacy controls in the information system and inherited by the system (i.e., common controls) and from the assessments of that implementation. Ideally, the assessor is building on previously developed materials that started with the specification of the organization's information security and privacy needs and was further developed during the design, development, and implementation of the information system. These materials, developed while implementing security and privacy throughout the life cycle of the information system, provide the initial evidence for an assurance case.

Assessors obtain the required evidence during the assessment process to allow the appropriate organizational officials to make objective determinations about the effectiveness of the security and privacy controls and the overall security and privacy state of the information system. The assessment evidence needed to make such determinations can be obtained from a variety of sources including, for example, information technology product and system assessments and, in the case of privacy assessments, privacy compliance documentation such as Privacy Impact Assessments and Privacy Act System of Record Notices. Product assessments (also known as product testing, evaluation, and validation) are typically conducted by independent, third-party testing organizations. These assessments examine the security and privacy functions of products and established configuration settings. Assessments can be conducted to demonstrate compliance to industry, national, or international information security standards, privacy standards embodied in applicable laws and policies, and developer/vendor claims. Since many information technology products are assessed by commercial testing organizations and then subsequently deployed in millions of information systems, these types of assessments can be carried out at a greater level of depth and provide deeper insights into the security and privacy capabilities of the particular products."[1]

In order to properly gain all the necessary evidence of the proper functioning of the system along with its critical security objectives being met, the assessor often obtains artifacts and evidence from the product review cycle received during acquisition of the security component.

> Organizations obtain security assurance by the *actions* taken by information system developers, implementers, operators, maintainers, and assessors. Actions by individuals and/or groups during the development/operation of information systems produce *security evidence* that contributes to the assurance, or measures of confidence, in the security functionality needed to deliver the security capability. The depth and coverage of these actions (as described below) also contribute to the efficacy of the evidence and measures of confidence. The evidence produced by developers, implementers, operators, assessors, and maintainers during the system development life cycle (e.g., design/development artifacts, assessment results, warranties, and certificates of evaluation/validation) contributes to the understanding of the security controls implemented by organizations.
>
> The *strength* of security functionality (The *security strength* of an information system component (i.e., hardware, software, or firmware) is determined by the degree to which the security functionality implemented within that component is correct, complete, resistant to direct attacks (strength of mechanism), and resistant to bypass or tampering.) plays an important part in being able to achieve the needed security capability and subsequently satisfying the security requirements of organizations. Information system developers can increase the strength of security functionality by employing as part of the hardware/software/firmware development process:
>
> (i) Well-defined security policies and policy models;
> (ii) Structured/rigorous design and development techniques; and
> (iii) Sound system/security engineering principles.
>
> The artifacts generated by these development activities (e.g., functional specifications, high-level/low-level designs, implementation representations [source code and hardware schematics], the results from static/dynamic testing and code analysis) can provide important evidence that the information systems (including the components that compose those systems) will be more reliable and trustworthy. Security evidence can also be generated from security testing conducted by independent, accredited, third-party assessment organizations (e.g., Common Criteria Testing Laboratories, Cryptographic/Security Testing Laboratories, FedRAMP 3PAO's, and other assessment activities by government and private sector organizations).
>
> In addition to the evidence produced in the development environment, organizations can produce evidence from the operational environment that contributes to the assurance of functionality and ultimately, security capability. Operational evidence includes, for example, flaw reports, records of remediation actions, the results of security incident reporting, and the results of organizational continuous monitoring activities. Such evidence helps to determine the effectiveness of deployed security controls, changes to information systems and environments of operation, and compliance with federal legislation, policies, directives, regulations, and standards. Security evidence, whether obtained from development or operational activities, provides a better understanding of security controls implemented and used by organizations. Together, the actions taken during the system development life cycle by developers, implementers, operators, maintainers, and assessors and the evidence produced as part of those actions, help organizations to determine the extent to which the security functionality within their information systems is implemented correctly, operating as intended, and producing the desired outcome with respect to meeting stated security requirements and enforcing or mediating established security policies—thus providing greater confidence in the security capability.[2]
>
> With regard to the security evidence produced, the *depth* and *coverage* of such evidence can affect the level of assurance in the functionality implemented. Depth and coverage are attributes associated with assessment methods and the generation of security evidence. Assessment methods can be applied to developmental and

---

[1]SP 800-53A, rev. 4, IPD, p. 8.
[2]SP 800-53, rev. 4, p. 22–23.

operational assurance. For developmental assurance, depth is associated with the rigor, level of detail, and formality of the artifacts produced during the design and development of the hardware, software, and firmware components of information systems (e.g., functional specifications, high-level design, low-level design, source code). The level of detail available in development artifacts can affect the type of testing, evaluation, and analysis conducted during the system development life cycle (e.g., black-box testing, gray-box testing, white-box testing, static/dynamic analysis). For operational assurance, the depth attribute addresses the number and types of assurance-related security controls selected and implemented. In contrast, the coverage attribute is associated with the assessment methods employed during development and operations, addressing the scope and breadth of assessment objects included in the assessments (e.g., number/types of tests conducted on source code, number of software modules reviewed, number of network nodes/mobile devices scanned for vulnerabilities, number of individuals interviewed to check basic understanding of contingency responsibilities).[3]

TYPES OF EVIDENCE

It is recognized that organizations can specify, document, and configure their information systems in a variety of ways, and that the content and applicability of existing assessment evidence will vary. This may result in the need to apply a variety of assessment methods to various assessment objects to generate the assessment evidence needed to determine whether the security or privacy controls are effective in their application.[4]

Assessment, testing, and auditing evidence is the basis on which an auditor or assessor expresses their opinion on the security operations of the firm being assessed. Assessors obtain such evidence from tests that determine how well security controls work (called "compliance tests") and tests of confidentiality, integrity, and availability details such as completeness and disclosure of information (called "substantive tests").

The results of substantive testing would include existence, rights and obligations, occurrence, completeness, valuation, measurement, presentation, and disclosure of a particular transaction of security control in action. Therefore, there are many mechanisms by which the assessor gains the appropriate evidence for the evaluation. These include those given in the next subsections.

Physical Examination/Inspection

Inspection involves examining records or documents, whether internal or external, in paper form, electronic form, or other media, or physically examining an asset. Inspection of records and documents provides audit evidence of varying degrees of reliability, depending on their nature and source and, in the case of internal records and documents, on the effectiveness of the controls over their production. An example of inspection used as a test of controls is inspection of records for evidence of authorization.

- Inspection or count by the auditor of a tangible asset:
  - This involves verifying the existence of an asset and the condition of the asset. It is important to record the asset name or model, serial number, or product ID, and compare it to the asset register.
- Different from examining documentation is that the asset has inherent value.

---

[3]SP 800-53A, supplemental guidance.
[4]SP 800-53A, rev. 4, IPD, p. 18.

Inspection of records is often used because the reliability of the records depends on the source. Information obtained directly from the system is more reliable than information obtained from the system and then customized by the auditee. For example, most system administrators would rather purge backup status results every three months due to system capabilities. The intention is to free up server space. They usually record the backup results in a spreadsheet that they retain to show that the control has been operating throughout the year. An example of such a form is depicted in **figure 2**.

Figure 2—Example of a control operation form		
Month: February 2012		
Backup daily results		
Day	**Status**	**Comments**
1	Successful	None
2	Failure	The files that failed to back up were for user folders and, therefore, have no implication.
3	Successful	None
4	Successful	None
5	Successful	None
Tasked performed by: BK		
Task reviewed by: RS		

The information in **figure 2** is less reliable than if the system administrator had saved the results in PDF format in a folder and recorded the data only for monitoring purposes. Using **figure 2** would enable confirmation of the recordings. [1]

Confirmation

A confirmation response represents a particular form of audit evidence obtained by the auditor from a third party in accordance with Public Company Accounting Oversight Board (PCAOB) standards (used in financial and corporate environments). Confirmation is the receipt of a written or oral response from an independent third party. The assessor has an organizational request that the third party respond directly to the assessor.

Confirmation, by definition, is the receipt of a written or oral response from an independent third party verifying information requested by the assessor. Because of the independence of the third party, confirmations are a highly desirable, though costly, type of evidence. Some audit standards describe two types of confirmations.

A positive confirmation asks the respondent to provide an answer in all circumstances, while a negative confirmation asks for a response only if the information is incorrect. As you might predict, negative confirmations are not as competent as positive confirmations. Note that SAS 67, Audit Standard, requires confirmation of a sample of accounts receivable due to the materiality of receivables for most companies. Note the provision that confirmations must be under the control of the auditor for maximum reliability of the evidence.

Confirmation is often viewed as audit evidence that is from an external independent source and is more creditable than evidence from an internal source. Most financial auditors confirm balances (e.g., creditor's balances and debtor's balances) by sending out confirmation letters to external independent sources such as banks and vendors.

However, in the majority of IT audits, audit evidence is derived from the system configurations. Configurations obtained by an auditor through observation of the system or via a reliable audit software tool are more reliable than data received from the auditee.

Documentation

Documentation consists of the organization's business documents used to support security and accounting events. The strength of documentation is that it is prevalent and available at a low cost. Documents can be internal or externally generated. Internal documents provide less reliable evidence than external ones, particularly if the client's internal control is suspect. Documents that are external and have been prepared by qualified individuals such as attorneys or insurance brokers provide additional reliability. The use of documentation in support of a client's transactions is called vouching.

Documentation review criteria include three areas of focus:

1. *Review* is used for the "generalized" level of rigor, that is, a high-level examination looking for required content and for any obvious errors, omissions, or inconsistencies.
2. *Study* is used for the "focused" level of rigor, that is, an examination that includes the intent of "review" and adds a more in-depth examination for greater evidence to support a determination of whether the document has the required content and is free of errors, omissions, and inconsistencies.
3. *Analyze* is used for the "detailed" level of rigor, that is, an examination that includes the intent of both "review" and "study," adding a thorough and detailed analysis for significant grounds for confidence in the determination of whether required content is present and the document is correct, complete, and consistent.

Analytical Procedures

Analytical procedures consist of evaluations of financial information made by a study of plausible relationships among both financial and nonfinancial data. They also encompass the investigation of significant differences from expected amounts. Recalculation consists of checking the mathematical accuracy of documents or records. It may be performed manually or electronically.

Analytical procedures are comparisons of account balances and relationships as a check on reasonableness. They are required during the planning and completion phases of all audits and may be used for the following purposes:

1. To better understand the organizational business and mission objectives
2. To assess the organization's ability to continue as a going concern
3. To indicate the possibility of misstatements ("unusual fluctuations") in the organizational documented statements
4. To reduce the need for detailed assessment testing

One of the primary ways that assessors and testers verify large system functioning and activities is through the use of sampling.

Sampling

Sampling is an audit procedure that tests less than 100 percent of the population. There are different types of sampling methods that an IS auditor can apply to gather sufficient evidence to address the audit objectives and the rate of risk identified. Sampling methods can be statistical or nonstatistical. Statistical sampling involves deriving the sample quantitatively. The statistical methods commonly used are random sampling and systematic sampling. Nonstatistical sampling involves deriving the sample qualitatively. Commonly used nonstatistical methods are haphazard and judgmental sampling.

The sampling size applied depends on the type of control being tested, the frequency of the control and the effectiveness of the design and implementation of the control.

Type of Controls and Sample Size

The following are the two types of controls:

- **Automated controls**—Automated controls generally require one sample. It is assumed that if a program can execute a task—for example, successfully calculate a car allowance due based on a base percentage of an employee's salary—and the program coding has not been changed, the system should apply the same formula to the rest of the population. Therefore, testing one instance is sufficient for the rest of the population. The same is true for the reverse; if the system incorrectly calculates the allowance, the error is extrapolated to the rest of the population.
- **Manual controls**—Depending on which sampling method an IS auditor uses to calculate the sample size, the following factors should be taken into consideration to determine the sample size:

1. Reliance placed on the control
2. The risk associated with control
3. The frequency of the control occurrence

Examples of manual controls include review of audit log monitoring, review of user authorization access forms, and review of daily IT procedures, server monitoring procedure and help-desk functions. **Figure 3** provides examples of IT controls, the technique that can be used to gather evidence and the sampling method that can be used.

Figure 3—Examples of controls, evidence-gathering techniques, evidence collected and sampling method			
Control	Evidence-gathering technique	Evidence collected	Sampling method
Data owners authorize user access and user rights on the systems.	• Interview • Extraction of system parameters (automated/manual)	• User policy and procedure • User listing report with user creation dates • User access request form/emails showing management approval	Random selection
Users have unique IDs.	• Interviews of relevant IS personnel • Extraction of system parameters • Data interrogation	• User policy and procedure • User listing report from the system • ACL/IDEA report showing results obtained • Manual excel sheet showing results obtained	Random sampling or an IS auditor performing a 100 percent review of the population by finding duplicate user IDs using CAATs (ACL/IDEA)
Systems are protected through strong passwords.	• Interviews • Extraction of system parameters	• User policy and procedure • System configuration/screen prints for the password policy	No sampling, as this is an automated control (as noted previously, additional testing may be required on some systems.)
Privileged roles (administrator) have been granted to appropriate personnel.	Extraction of system parameters	• Policies and procedures • User listing/role reports • Job descriptions	• A 100 percent review of the population by extracting users with administrator rights using CAATs (ACL/IDEA) • Random sampling

Quality evidence collected during the audit process enhances the overall quality of the work performed and significantly reduces audit risk. Failure to collect quality evidence may result in the auditor or company facing litigation, loss of reputation and loss of clientele. It is important to ensure that the audit evidence obtained from the auditee is of high quality and supports the understanding of the IT control environment. [1]

Here are the types of evidence that are typically sampled:

- *Tangible assets*: If, for example, a business states that it owns 300 company cars. You do not hunt down all 300 cars; you just select a sample of the cars to track down to verify their existence.
- *Records or documents*: Records or documents are also known as source materials, and they are the materials on which the numbers in financial statements are based. For example, the amount of sales that a financial statement represents is derived from the data on customer invoices, which in this case is your sampling unit.
- *Reperformance*: This term refers to checking the sampling work the client has already done. For example, company policy dictates that no employee is paid unless he or she has turned in a timesheet. The client states that this rule is in use for 100% of all paychecks. You can test this client assertion by taking a sample of payroll checks and matching them to the timesheets.
- *Recalculation*: This term refers to checking the mathematical accuracy of figures and totals on a document. For example, a sample may have three columns: cost per item, items ordered, and total. You perform recalculation if you verify the figures on the invoice by multiplying cost per item times items ordered and making sure the figure equals the total.
- *Confirmation*: This term refers to getting account balance verification from unrelated third parties. A good example is sending letters to customers or vendors of the business to verify accounts receivable or accounts payable balances.

Interviews of the Users/Developers/Customers

Questions of users, key personnel, system owners, and other relevant personnel in the organization are often used as a starting point to determine the proper use of and implementation of controls. Interviews are the process of holding discussions with individuals or groups of individuals within an organization to, once again, facilitate assessor understanding, achieve clarification, or obtain evidence.

Typically, the interviews are conducted with agency heads, chief information officers, senior agency information security officers, authorizing officials, information owners, information system and mission owners, information system security officers, information system security managers, personnel officers, human resource managers, facilities managers, training officers, information system operators, network and system administrators, site managers, physical security officers, and users.

Often questionnaire are used to gather data by allowing the IS personnel to answer predetermined questions. This technique is usually used to collect data during the planning phase of the audit. Information gathered through this process has to be corroborated through additional testing. Inquiry alone is regarded as the least creditable audit evidence. This is especially true if the source of the information is from the auditee who performs or supervises the function about which one is inquiring. If inquiry is the only way to get the evidence, it is advisable to corroborate the inquiry with an independent source. If one is auditing proprietary software and the IT officer has no access to the source code and cannot demonstrate from the system configurations that there were no upgrades carried out in the year under review, one can corroborate the inquiry with the users of the applications. Although inquiry is the least creditable when carrying out control adequacy testing, it is deemed sufficient during the planning stage.

SP 800-53A does provide some guidance for the interview process and the detail of how in-depth the interviews should be conducted as follows:

> The *depth* attribute addresses the rigor of and level of detail in the interview process. There are three possible values for the depth attribute:
>
> (i)   *Basic;* Basic interview: Interview that consists of broad-based, high-level discussions with individuals or groups of individuals. This type of interview is conducted using a set of generalized, high-level questions. Basic interviews provide a level of understanding of the security and privacy controls necessary for determining whether the controls are implemented and free of obvious errors.
>
> (ii) *Focused;* and Focused interview: Interview that consists of broad-based, high-level discussions **and more in-depth discussions in specific areas** with individuals or groups of individuals. This type of interview is conducted using a set of generalized, high-level questions **and more in-depth questions in specific areas where responses indicate a need for more in-depth investigation**. **Focused** interviews provide a level of understanding of the security and privacy controls necessary for determining whether the controls are implemented and free of obvious errors **and whether there are increased grounds for confidence that the controls are implemented correctly and operating as intended**.
>
> (iii) *Comprehensive.* Comprehensive interview: Interview that consists of broad-based, high-level discussions and more in-depth, **probing** discussions in specific areas with individuals or groups of individuals. This type of interview is conducted using a set of generalized, high-level questions and more in-depth, **probing** questions in specific areas where responses indicate a need for more in-depth investigation. **Comprehensive** interviews provide a level of understanding of the security and privacy controls necessary for determining whether the controls are implemented and free of obvious errors and whether there are **further** increased grounds for confidence that the controls are implemented correctly and operating as intended **on an ongoing and consistent basis, and that there is support for continuous improvement in the effectiveness of the controls**.[5]

SP 800-53A does provide some guidance for the interview process and the detail of how much should be covered in the interviews as follows:

> The *coverage* attribute addresses the scope or breadth of the interview process and includes the types of individuals to be interviewed (by organizational role and associated responsibility), the number of individuals to be interviewed (by type), and specific individuals to be interviewed. The organization, considering a variety of factors (e.g., available resources, importance of the assessment, the organization's overall assessment goals and objectives), confers with assessors and provides direction on the type, number, and specific individuals to be interviewed for the particular attribute value described.
>
> There are three possible values for the coverage attribute:
>
> (i)   *Basic;* Basic interview: Interview that uses a representative sample of individuals in key organizational roles to provide a level of coverage necessary for determining whether the security and privacy controls are implemented and free of obvious errors.
>
> (ii) *Focused;* and Focused interview: Interview that uses a representative sample of individuals in key organizational roles **and other specific individuals deemed particularly important to achieving the**

---

[5]SP 800-53A, rev. 4, IPD, p. D-4, D-5.

assessment objective to provide a level of coverage necessary for determining whether the security and privacy controls are implemented and free of obvious errors **and whether there are increased grounds for confidence that the controls are implemented correctly and operating as intended**.

(iii) *Comprehensive.* Comprehensive interview: Interview that uses a **sufficiently large** sample of individuals in key organizational roles and other specific individuals deemed particularly important to achieving the assessment objective to provide a level of coverage necessary for determining whether the security and privacy controls are implemented and free of obvious errors and whether there are **further** increased grounds for confidence that the controls are implemented correctly and operating as intended **on an on-going and consistent basis, and that there is support for continuous improvement in the effectiveness of the controls**.[5]

Reuse of Previous Work

Reuse of assessment results from previously accepted or approved assessments is considered in the body of evidence for determining overall security or privacy control effectiveness. Previously accepted or approved assessments include:

(i) Those assessments of common controls that are managed by the organization and support multiple information systems; or

(ii) Assessments of security or privacy controls that are reviewed as part of the control implementation.

The acceptability of using previous assessment results in a security control assessment or privacy control assessment is coordinated with and approved by the users of the assessment results. It is essential that information system owners and common control providers collaborate with authorizing officials and other appropriate organizational officials in determining the acceptability of using previous assessment results. When considering the reuse of previous assessment results and the value of those results to the current assessment, assessors determine:

(i) The credibility of the assessment evidence;

(ii) The appropriateness of previous analysis; and

(iii) The applicability of the assessment evidence to current information system operating conditions.

If previous assessment results are reused, the date of the original assessment and type of assessment are documented in the security assessment plan or privacy assessment plan and security assessment report or privacy assessment report.

The following items are considered in validating previous assessment results for reuse:

- **Changing conditions associated with security controls and privacy controls over time.** Security and privacy controls that were deemed effective during previous assessments may have become ineffective due to changing conditions within the information system or its environment of operation. Assessment results that were found to be previously acceptable may no longer provide credible evidence for the determination of security or privacy control effectiveness, and therefore, a reassessment would be required. Applying previous assessment results to a current assessment necessitates the identification of any changes that have occurred since the previous assessment and the impact of these changes on the previous results.
- **Amount of time that has transpired since previous assessments.** In general, as the time period between current and previous assessments increases, the credibility and utility of the previous assessment results decrease. This is primarily due to the fact that the information system or the environment in which the information system operates is more likely to change with the passage of time, possibly invalidating the original conditions or assumptions on which the previous assessment was based.
- **Degree of independence of previous assessments.** Assessor independence can be a critical factor in certain types of assessments. The degree of independence required from assessment to assessment

should be consistent. For example, it is not appropriate to reuse results from a previous self-assessment where no assessor independence was required, in a current assessment requiring a greater degree of independence.[6]

Automatic Test Results

Scanners, integrity checkers, and automated test environments are all examples of these types of outputs which are used by the assessors. Scanning reviews typically involve searching for large or unusual items to detect error in the results from the scans. For example, if there is a maximum or minimum loan amount, one can scan through the loan book for amounts outside the stated range. Configuration compliance checkers perform a process of reviewing system configuration and user account details through the use of manual or utility tools/ scripts, which are available freely online, developed in-house, or obtained off the shelf on the market. The available software includes, but is not limited to, Microsoft Baseline Security Analyzer (free), DumpSec (free), IDEA examiner, ACL CaseWare, and in-house-developed scripts. Alternatively, the assessor can read system manuals for the system being audited for guidance on how to retrieve system configurations and user accounts manually. For example, to get administrator access on a Windows 2003 server, the IS auditor would follow the following procedure: start → administrative tools → active directory users and computers → built in → select administrator → right click → select properties → select member.

Recalculation consists of checking the mathematical accuracy of documents or records. It may be performed manually or electronically. Automated testing tools are computer programs that run in a Windows environment, which can be used to test evidence that is in a machine-readable format. Additionally, there is software available that can be used to manage the assessment documentation and network sharing of files among the assessment team.

A common technique used during assessments is called data interrogation; this is a process of analyzing data usually through the use of Computer-Aided Audit Tools (CAATs). Generalized audit software can be embedded within an application to review transactions as they are being processed, and exception reports showing variances or anomalies are produced and used for further audit investigations. The most commonly used CAAT method involves downloading data from an application and analyzing it with software such as ACL and IDEA. Some of the tests include journal testing, application input and output integrity checks (e.g., duplicate numbers), gaps on invoices/purchase orders, and summarization of vendors by amounts paid.

In other portions of this handbook, I go into great detail about automated testing so it is unnecessary to further expand this area.

Observation

Observation consists of looking at a process or procedure being performed by others, for example, the auditor's observation of inventory counting by the company's personnel or the performance of control activities. Observation can provide audit evidence about the performance of a process or procedure, but the evidence is limited to the point in time at which the observation takes place and also is limited by the fact that the act of being observed may affect how the process or procedure is performed.

[6]SP 800-53A, rev. 4, IPD, p. 19–21.

It is suggested that observation should be carried out by two assessors. This is to corroborate what the assessor observed and to avoid instances in which management refutes the findings of the observation. In addition, observation is key in establishing segregation of duties. When assessing, where possible, the assessor should spend some time with the organizational administrators. This will afford the assessor the opportunity to see exactly what is happening, not what should happen.

SP 800-53A defines three methods for conducting detailed observations while examining security controls as follows:

1. *Observe* is used for the "generalized" level of rigor, that is, watching the execution of an activity or process or looking directly at a mechanism (as opposed to reading documentation produced by someone other than the assessor about that mechanism) for the purpose of seeing whether the activity or mechanism appears to operate as intended (or in the case of a mechanism, perhaps is configured as intended) and whether there are any obvious errors, omissions, or inconsistencies in the operation or configuration.
2. *Inspect* is used for the "focused" level of rigor, that is, adding to the watching associated with "observe" an active investigation to gain further grounds for confidence in the determination of whether the activity or mechanism is operating as intended and is free of errors, omissions, or inconsistencies.
3. *Analyze*, while not currently used in the assessment cases for activities and mechanisms, is available for use for the "detailed" level of rigor, that is, adding to the watching and investigation of "observe" and "inspect" a thorough and detailed analysis of the information to develop significant grounds for confidence in the determination as to whether the activity or mechanism is operating as intended and is free of errors, omissions, or inconsistencies. Analysis achieves this both by leading to further observations and inspections and by a greater understanding of the information obtained from the examination.

DOCUMENTATION REQUIREMENTS

The process of documenting the assessment evidence is usually determined by the criteria needed to provide the support documentation to the authorizing official as they make their risk-based decisions concerning the system under review. Multiple types of evidence documentation are produced during the assessment process, as well as actual Assessment Artifact documents. Each of these pieces of documentation require the assessor to identify it, correlate it to the assessment plan step it is relevant to, and determine how it supports the findings and recommendations in the Security Assessment Report (SAR). The SAR is the primary document resulting from the assessment and we will discuss that specific document and its supporting artifacts in the next chapter.

Documentation is the principal record of testing and assessment procedures applied, evidence obtained, and conclusions reached by the assessor. Often evidence is documented in what are known as audit working papers. Audit working papers achieve following objectives:

- Aid in the planning, performance, and review of audit work
- Provide the principal support for audit report and conclusions

- Facilitate third-party/supervisory reviews

Using work papers, a common auditing methodology, provides the following advantages:

- Provides a basis for evaluating the internal audit activity's quality control program
- Documents whether engagement objectives were achieved
- Supports the accuracy and completeness of the work performed

There are two types of work papers used in today's processes. They are as follows:

1. *Permanent file*: Information that is relevant for multiple years on recurring engagements
2. *Current file*: Information relevant for a given assessment for a particular assessment period

Key characteristics of work papers are as follows:

1. *Complete*: Each work paper should be completely self-standing and self-explanatory. All questions must be answered; all points raised by the reviewer must be cleared and a logical, well-thought-out conclusion reached for each assessment segment.
2. *Concise*: Audit work papers and items included on each work paper should be relevant to meeting the applicable assessment objective. Work papers must be confined to those that serve a useful purpose.
3. *Accurate*: High-quality work papers include statements and computations that are accurate and technically correct.
4. *Organized*: Work papers should have a logical system of numbering and a reader-friendly layout so a technically competent person unfamiliar with the project could understand the purpose, procedures performed, and results.

Work papers should include the following key elements:

- Name of assessment area.
- *Source*: The name and title of the individual providing the documentation should be recorded to facilitate future follow-up questions or assessment.
- *Scope*: The nature, timing, and extent of procedures performed should be included on each work paper for completeness.
- *Reference*: A logical work paper number cross-referenced to assessment plan steps and issues should be included.
- *Sign-off*: The preparer's signature provides evidence of completion and accountability, which is an essential piece of third-party quality review.
- *Exceptions*: Assessment exceptions should be documented and explained clearly on each work paper using logical numbering that cross-reference to other work papers.

Trustworthiness

The purpose of the development and production of the assessor evidence is to build the trustworthiness for the authorizing official of the assessment results and conclusions provided by the security control assessor. Additionally, the trustworthiness is then built of the operating organization and the system owner in their operational status reporting and ongoing continuous monitoring activities which the authorizing official is participating in during normal operations of the system under review. As SP 800-53A shows us in the following diagram, the security evidence gathered during the assessment process provides the ultimate trustworthiness evaluation criteria for the system owner, authorizing official, and the operational managers to use to run and operate the system under review:

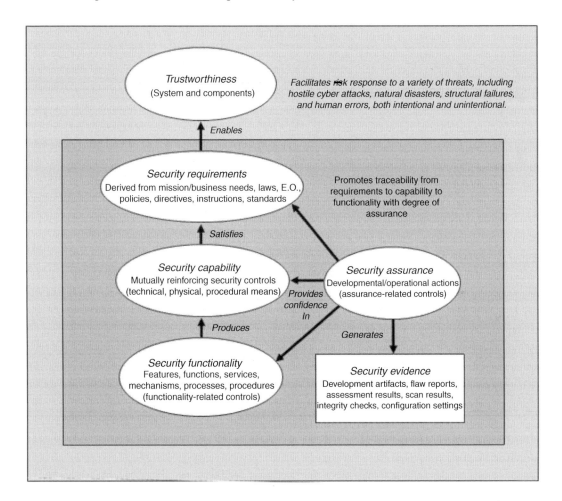

Reference

[1] Audit evidence refresher. ISACA J 2012;3:1–4.

13

Reporting

I often explain to interested people and my students that the number 1 job of any security professional is the secure the data and the number 2 job is to "report, report, and report again." We often have to spend a great deal of time and effort in gathering the data for and producing various different kinds of reports and documents to support our security efforts. The various reporting requirements often are externally provided to the assessor via compliance needs, external agency needs, or internal department needs. Each component needing the assessor report has a distinct and, I hope, clearly defined method for reporting along with the data and results necessary for the report to contain:

1. SAR
2. Rescue and Recovery (RAR)
3. Artifacts as reports
4. Public Inquiry and Response (PIAR)
5. Remediation actions
6. Plant Operation and Maintenance (PO&Ms)

The primary purpose of the *security* and *privacy assessment reports* is to convey the results of the security and privacy control assessments to appropriate organizational officials. The security assessment report is included in the security authorization package along with the security plan (including an updated risk assessment), and the plan of action and milestones to provide authorizing officials with the information necessary to make risk-based decisions on whether to place an information system into operation or continue its operation. Organizations may choose to include similar privacy-related artifacts in the authorization package to convey essential information to authorizing officials. All issues associated with compliance to privacy-related legislation, directives, regulations, or policies are coordinated with the Senior Agency Official for Privacy (SAOP)/ Chief Privacy Officer. As the assessment and authorization process becomes more dynamic in nature, relying to a greater degree on the continuous monitoring aspects of the process as an integrated and tightly coupled part of the system development life cycle, the ability to update the security and privacy assessment reports frequently becomes a critical aspect of information security and privacy programs.

It is important to emphasize the relationship, described in Special Publication 800-37, among the three key documents in the authorization package (i.e., the security plan, the security assessment report, and the plan of action and milestones). It is these documents that provide the most reliable indication of the overall security state of the information system and the ability of the system to protect to the degree necessary, the organization's operations and assets, individuals, other organizations, and the Nation. Updates to these key documents are provided on an ongoing basis in accordance with the continuous monitoring program established by the organization. Updates to similar privacy-related documents occur at a frequency and format determined by the SAOP in coordination with authorizing officials.

The security and privacy assessment reports provide a disciplined and structured approach for documenting the findings of the assessor and the recommendations for correcting any weaknesses or deficiencies in the security and privacy controls. This appendix provides a template for reporting the results from security and privacy control assessments. Organizations are not restricted to the specific template format; however, it is anticipated that the overall report of an assessment will include similar information to that detailed in the template for each security and privacy control assessed, preceded by a summary providing the list of all security and privacy controls assessed and the overall status of each control.[1]

KEY ELEMENTS FOR ASSESSMENT REPORTING

The following elements are included in security and privacy assessment reports:

- Information system name
- Security categorization
- Site(s) assessed and assessment date(s)
- Assessor's name/identification
- Previous assessment results (if reused)
- Security/privacy control or control enhancement designator
- Selected assessment methods and objects
- Depth and coverage attributes values
- Assessment finding summary (indicating satisfied or other than satisfied)
- Assessor comments (weaknesses or deficiencies noted)
- Assessor recommendations (priorities, remediation, corrective actions, or improvements)

THE ASSESSMENT FINDINGS

Each determination statement executed by an assessor results in one of the following findings:

1. Satisfied (S)
2. Other than satisfied (O)

During an actual security and privacy control assessment, the assessment findings, comments, and recommendations are documented on appropriate organization-defined reporting forms. Organizations are encouraged to develop standard templates for reporting that contain the key elements for assessment reporting described above. Whenever possible, automation is used to make assessment data collection and reporting cost-effective, timely, and efficient.

---

[1]SP 800-53A, rev. 4, p. G-1.

SECURITY ASSESSMENT REPORT

The results of the security control assessment, including recommendations for correcting any weaknesses or deficiencies in the controls, are documented in the *security assessment report*. The security assessment report is one of three key documents in the security authorization package developed for authorizing officials. The assessment report includes information from the assessor necessary to determine the effectiveness of the security controls employed within or inherited by the information system based upon the assessor's findings. The security assessment report is an important factor in an authorizing official's determination of risk to organizational operations and assets, individuals, other organizations, and the Nation. Security control assessment results are documented at a level of detail appropriate for the assessment in accordance with the reporting format prescribed by organizational and/or federal policies. The reporting format is also appropriate for the type of security control assessment conducted (e.g., developmental testing and evaluation, self-assessments, independent verification and validation, independent assessments supporting the security authorization process or subsequent reauthorizations, assessments during continuous monitoring, assessments subsequent to remediation actions, independent audits/evaluations).

Security control assessment results obtained during system development are brought forward in an interim report and included in the final security assessment report. This supports the concept that the security assessment report is an evolving document that includes assessment results from all relevant phases of the system development life cycle including the results generated during continuous monitoring. Organizations may choose to develop an *executive summary* from the detailed findings that are generated during a security control assessment. An executive summary provides an authorizing official with an abbreviated version of the assessment report focusing on the highlights of the assessment, synopsis of key findings, and/or recommendations for addressing weaknesses and deficiencies in the security controls.[2]

Here is a governmental-based SAR-formatted Table of Contents for use and suggestions:

EXECUTIVE SUMMARY

Introduction

Risk Summary

Conclusion

1 INTRODUCTION

1.1 Scope

1.2   Background

1.3   Assessment Methodology

    1.3.1   Likelihood Determination

    1.3.2   Impact Determination

    1.3.3   Risk Scale

    1.3.4   Mitigation Actions

1.4   Assumptions and Constraints

---

[2]SP 800-37, rev. 1, p. 32.

2 SYSTEM DESCRIPTION

3 THREAT STATEMENT

4 SECURITY ASSESSMENT RESULTS

4.1 Automated Scan Results

5 STATEMENT OF WEAKNESSES

5.1 Management Controls

5.2 Operational Controls

5.3 Technical Controls

5.4 Risk Based Decision Recommendation

6 SUMMARY AND SIGNATURES

Appendix A: Detailed Security Assessment Results

This SAR covers the full scope of the SCA activities defined in SP 800-37 and in this book, so the report should reflect all of the activities the SCA took during the assessment.

RISK ASSESSMENT REPORT

The essential elements of information in a risk assessment can be described in three sections of the risk assessment report (or whatever vehicle is chosen by organizations to convey the results of the assessment):

(i)　An executive summary;
(ii)　The main body containing detailed risk assessment results; and
(iii)　Supporting appendices.

A. Executive Summary

* List the date of the risk assessment.
* Summarize the purpose of the risk assessment.
* Describe the scope of the risk assessment.
  - For Tier 1 and Tier 2 risk assessments, identify: organizational governance structures or processes associated with the assessment (e.g., risk executive [function], budget process, acquisition process, systems engineering process, enterprise architecture, information security architecture, organizational missions/business functions, mission/business processes, information systems supporting the mission/business processes).
  - For Tier 3 risk assessments, identify: the information system name and location(s), security categorization, and information system (i.e., authorization) boundary.
* State whether this is an initial or subsequent risk assessment. If a subsequent risk assessment, state the circumstances that prompted the update and include a reference to the previous Risk Assessment Report.
* Describe the overall level of risk (e.g., Very Low, Low, Moderate, High, or Very High).
* List the number of risks identified for each level of risk (e.g., Very Low, Low, Moderate, High, or Very High).

B. Body of the Report

- Describe the purpose of the risk assessment, including questions to be answered by the assessment. For example:
  - How the use of a specific information technology would potentially change the risk to organizational missions/business functions if employed in information systems supporting those missions/business functions; or
  - How the risk assessment results are to be used in the context of the RMF (e.g., an initial risk assessment to be used in tailoring security control baselines and/or to guide and inform other decisions and serve as a starting point for subsequent risk assessments; subsequent risk assessment to incorporate results of security control assessments and inform authorization decisions; subsequent risk assessment to support the analysis of alternative courses of action for risk responses; subsequent risk assessment based on risk monitoring to identify new threats or vulnerabilities; subsequent risk assessments to incorporate knowledge gained from incidents or attacks).
- Identify assumptions and constraints.
- Describe risk tolerance inputs to the risk assessment (including the range of consequences to be considered).
- Identify and describe the risk model and analytic approach; provide a reference or include as an appendix, identifying risk factors, value scales, and algorithms for combining values.
- Provide a rationale for any risk-related decisions during the risk assessment process.
- Describe the uncertainties within the risk assessment process and how those uncertainties influence decisions.
- If the risk assessment includes organizational missions/business functions, describe the missions/functions (e.g., mission/business processes supporting the missions/functions, interconnections and dependencies among related missions/business functions, and information technology that supports the missions/business functions).
- If the risk assessment includes organizational information systems, describe the systems (e.g., missions/business functions the system is supporting, information flows to/from the systems, and dependencies on other systems, shared services, or common infrastructures).
- Summarize risk assessment results (e.g., using tables or graphs), in a form that enables decision makers to quickly understand the risk (e.g., number of threat events for different combinations of likelihood and impact, the relative proportion of threat events at different risk levels).
- Identify the time frame for which the risk assessment is valid (i.e., time frame for which the assessment is intended to support decisions).
- List the risks due to adversarial threats (see Table F-1).
- List the risks due to non-adversarial threats (see Table F-2).

C. Appendices

- List references and sources of information.
- List the team or individuals conducting the risk assessment including contact information.
- List risk assessment details and any supporting evidence (e.g., Tables D-7, D-8, F-5, F-3, F-6, H-4), as needed to understand and enable reuse of results (e.g., for reciprocity, for subsequent risk assessments, to serve as input to Tier 1 and Tier 2 risk assessments).[3]

With the redesign of SP 800-30, revision 1, the RAR is not always a deliverable item for RMF activities, but often is used to supplement ongoing remediation efforts and major change analysis efforts for system. Additionally, RAR process reports are used when threat environments or operational environments are changed with respect to the system under review.

---

[3]SP 800-30, rev. 1, p. K-1, K-2.

ARTIFACTS AS REPORTS

Often the development and production of assessment artifacts creates reports and deliverables of their own, and these documents become part of the supplemental and supporting information that goes with the authorization package to the Authorizing Official (AO) and Authorizing Official Designated Representative (AODR) for review and approval. Items such as Vulnerability Scan Reports, Configuration Change Request Installation Reports, and Contingency Plan Test Results all are used in both cases: as support for authorization package and as security report deliverables.

PRIVACY IMPACT ASSESSMENT REPORT

Privacy reporting usually entails two different kinds of reporting criteria. First type involves the actual reporting of the Personally Identifiable Information (PII) on the system under review. Types of data collected and retained and their security and privacy requirements are defined in these types of reports. The second type of report is the status reporting needed for governmental agencies to give external organizations, such as Congress, a view of PII and privacy in each agency.

The format and data requirements for Privacy Assessment Reports are agency and governance based and vary for each agency. If you have any questions, typically you should contact your agency Privacy Office, since federal law requires each agency to have such an office.

Remember, Appendix J of SP 800-53, rev. 4, has a listing of all the privacy controls and their requirements now mandated for all agencies by OMB.

REMEDIATION EFFORTS DURING AND SUBSEQUENT TO ASSESSMENT

The security assessment report provides visibility into specific weaknesses and deficiencies in the security controls employed within or inherited by the information system that could not reasonably be resolved during system development or that are discovered post-development. Such weaknesses and deficiencies are potential vulnerabilities if exploitable by a threat source. The findings generated during the security control assessment provide important information that facilitates a disciplined and structured approach to mitigating risks in accordance with organizational priorities. An updated assessment of risk (either formal or informal) based on the results of the findings produced during the security control assessment and any inputs from the risk executive (function), helps to determine the initial remediation actions and the prioritization of such actions. Information system owners and common control providers, in collaboration with selected organizational officials (e.g., information system security engineer, authorizing official designated representative, chief information officer, senior information security officer, information owner/steward), may decide, based on an initial or updated assessment of risk, that certain findings are inconsequential and present no significant risk to the organization. Alternatively, the organizational officials may decide that certain findings are in fact, significant, requiring immediate remediation actions. In all cases, organizations review assessor findings and determine the severity or seriousness of the findings (i.e., the potential adverse impact on organizational operations and assets, individuals, other organizations, or the Nation) and whether the findings are sufficiently significant to be worthy of further investigation or remediation. Senior leadership involvement in the mitigation process may be necessary in order to ensure that the organization's resources are effectively allocated in accordance with organizational priorities, providing resources first to the information systems that are supporting the most critical and sensitive missions and business functions for the organization or correcting the deficiencies that pose the greatest degree of risk. If weaknesses or deficiencies in security controls are corrected, the security control assessor reassesses the remediated controls for effectiveness. Security control reassessments determine the extent to which the remediated controls are implemented correctly, operating as intended, and producing the desired outcome with respect to meeting the security requirements for the information system. Exercising caution not to change the original assessment results, assessors update the security assessment report with the findings from the reassessment. The security plan is updated based on the findings of the security control assessment and any remediation actions taken. The updated security plan reflects the actual state of the security controls after the initial assessment and any modifications by the information system owner or common control provider in addressing recommendations for corrective actions. At the completion of the assessment, the security plan contains an accurate list and description of the security controls implemented (including compensating controls) and a list of residual vulnerabilities.[4]

POAMs

Once the Security Assessment Report is provided to the system owner and the AODR, the system owner develops the plans for remediation of the residual risk items identified by the SAR. These items are placed onto the Risk Register for the agency, known as the Plan of Action and Milestones (POAMs).

The *plan of action and milestones*, prepared for the authorizing official by the information system owner or the common control provider, is one of three key documents in the security authorization package and describes the specific tasks that are planned:

(i) To correct any weaknesses or deficiencies in the security controls noted during the assessment; and
(ii) To address the residual vulnerabilities in the information system.

The plan of action and milestones identifies:

(i) The tasks to be accomplished with a recommendation for completion either before or after information system implementation;
(ii) The resources required to accomplish the tasks;
(iii) Any milestones in meeting the tasks; and
(iv) The scheduled completion dates for the milestones.

The plan of action and milestones is used by the authorizing official to monitor progress in correcting weaknesses or deficiencies noted during the security control assessment. All security weaknesses and deficiencies identified during the security control assessment are documented in the security assessment report to maintain an effective audit trail. Organizations develop specific plans of action and milestones based on the results of the security control assessment and in accordance with applicable laws, Executive Orders, directives, policies, standards, guidance, or regulations. Plan of action and milestones entries are *not* required when weaknesses or deficiencies are remediated during the assessment or prior to the submission of the authorization package to the authorizing official.

---

[4]SP 800-37, rev. 1, p. 32–33.

Organizations define a strategy for developing plans of action and milestones that facilitates a prioritized approach to risk mitigation that is consistent across the organization. The strategy helps to ensure that organizational plans of action and milestones are based on:

(i)   The security categorization of the information system;
(ii) The specific weaknesses or deficiencies in the security controls;
(iii) The importance of the identified security control weaknesses or deficiencies (i.e., the direct or indirect effect the weaknesses or deficiencies may have on the overall security state of the information system, and hence on the risk exposure of the organization, or ability of the organization to perform its mission or business functions); and
(iv) The organization's proposed risk mitigation approach to address the identified weaknesses or deficiencies in the security controls (e.g., prioritization of risk mitigation actions, allocation of risk mitigation resources). A risk assessment guides the prioritization process for items included in the plan of action and milestones.[5]

POAM reporting is defined by OMB through its memoranda and currently is required for agency on a monthly basis. It had run on a quarterly basis for many years, but recent events have moved OMB to request these reports through CyberScope to be submitted on a monthly basis for budgetary and management purposes.

---

[5]SP 800-37, rev. 1, p. 34.

CHAPTER

14

Conclusion

At this point, we have developed a security test methodology and plan for evaluating the security of our system under test, conducted the test plan activities, produced the evidence to support the results of the testing, and then built reports for supporting the findings and conclusion as documented in the Security Assessment Report or other report to the supervisory and executive staff.

The evaluation and assessment of security and security controls involves much more than just looking at documents and running scan tools, although a lot of pundits would say that is all that is needed. Today's breaches, threats, and vulnerabilities all tell us that viewpoint is incorrect and doomed for failure and "front-page" news articles.

Understanding the variable nature of security control options as found in SP 800-53, the various ways and techniques to test and evaluate these controls as found in SP 800-53A, and the varied and diverse methods and tactics employed to breach our networks and our responses as found in SP 800-115 all give us an understanding and hope that we stay ahead of the adversary, understand his or her TTPs, and keep him or her at bay while conducting our business and achieving success in our mission.

Subject Index

Risk
  analysis, 499
  assessment, 8, 49, 546, 547
    component, 8
    frequency of, 8
    methodologies, 45
  based approach, 87
  based cost-effective security controls, 537
  based decisions, 5, 629
  based process, 24
  component, 8
  definition in SP 800-37, 5
Risk assessment family, 332, 546–548
  risk management, 546
    RA-5 vulnerability scanning, 548
    risk and vulnerability assessments, 547
    security categorization, 547
Risk executive (function)
  individual roles, 65–66
Risk management, 6
  activities, 7, 8, 533
  approach
    goal of, 6
  performance of, 7
  process, 7, 51
  review, 7
Risk management framework (RMF), 27, 35, 43–57, 79,
    542
  application of, 57
  approach, 503
  assessment, 50–52
  authorization, 52–54
    package, 55
  categorization, 44–46
  current systems, continuous monitoring for, 54–56
  implementation, 48–50
  monitoring, 54–56
  selection, 46–48
  step of, 43
Risk mitigation techniques, 78
RMF. *See* Risk management framework (RMF)
ROE. *See* Rules of engagement (ROE) document
Routine system development life cycle processes, 57
RPO. *See* Recovery point objective (RPO)
RSA DSA, 626
RTO. *See* Recovery time objective (RTO)
Rules of engagement (ROE) document, 105

S
Sampling, 634
Sandbox detection, 519
Sanitization, 576
  types of, 577
SAOP. *See* Senior Agency Official for Privacy (SAOP)

SAP. *See* Security assessment plan (SAP)
SAP developmental process, 105
SAR. *See* Security assessment report (SAR)
Sarbanes–Oxley Act (SOX), 18
SCA. *See* Stored Communications Act (SCA)
SCADA. *See* Supervisory control and data acquisition
    (SCADA) systems
Scanning, 512
  personal bluetooth devices, 522
SCAP-validated tools, 94, 96, 101
Schedule assessment, 105
SDLC. *See* System development life cycles (SDLC)
SEC. *See* Securities and Exchange Commission (SEC)
SecCM. *See* Security-focused configuration
    management (SecCM)
Secret key cryptography, 608
Secure hash function, 612
Secure hashing algorithm (SHA), 612
  SHA-1, 518
Secure Hash Standard (SHS), 22, 613
Secure/multipurpose internet mail extensions (S/
    MIME), 601
Secure sockets layer (SSL), 552
  servers
    identifying, authentication used for, 601
  sessions
    cryptography used in, 601
  virtual private networks (VPN), 598
    SP 800-113, 598–603
      administering SSL VPN, 599
      SSL portal VPN, 598
      SSL protocol basics, 600–602
      SSL tunnel VPN, 598
      SSL VPN architecture, 599
      transport layer security, 602–603
Secure Transport Layer Protocol (STLP), 602
Securities and Exchange Commission (SEC), 18
Security administrator, 511
Security and privacy assessment reports, 643
  primary purpose of, 643
Security and privacy controls, 644
Security architect
  individual roles, 62–63
Security architecture validation, 500
Security assessment, 84, 545
Security assessment and authorization, 545
Security assessment plan (SAP), 105
Security assessment policy, 105
Security assessment report (SAR), 93, 639, 649, 651
Security authorization, 60
  package, 47
  process, 49, 61, 64
Security awareness, 550
Security awareness and training (AT), 550

Printed in the United States
By Bookmasters